THE ILLUSTRATED DICTIONARY OF BRITISH HISTORY

THE ILLUSTRATED DICTIONARY OF BRITISH HISTORY

GENERAL EDITOR: ARTHUR MARWICK

Contributing Editors
Christopher Harvie, Charles Kightly, Keith Wrightson

with 372 illustrations

THAMES AND HUDSON

Publisher's note

Cross references from one entry to another are
identified by words printed in small capitals; they
have been used where they might reasonably guide
the reader to further information rather than
employed as an inflexible rule on every occasion.

Printed and bound in Great Britain by Jarrold and Sons, Norwich.

Introduction

History is an important subject; indeed, I would go as far as to say that it is an essential subject. It is impossible to understand the world, the society, the community in which we live, without knowing something of past developments in that world, society and community. Each is the creation of past events, and past decisions, and of the activities, deliberate and unconscious, of multitudes of human beings in the past. History is to the community as memory is to the individual. A society without a knowledge of its history is a society without memory and without identity. To him who asks: 'What is the use of history?', the best answer is: 'Imagine what it would be like to live in a society in which there was no knowledge of history.' We call upon history all the time in everyday conversation, as when we argue about events in Northern Ireland or discuss the decline in the influence of the family. To talk of such a decline implies a reference to a past time when the family had a different status.

History is not a given series of facts. The evidence upon which the historian builds up his account of events has to be ascertained from often difficult, complicated, and sometimes conflicting evidence. A second, more mundane justification for the study of history is that, being fundamentally concerned with the handling of all sorts of source material, it provides a specially valuable training in coping with the immense deluge of conflicting evidence presented in newspapers, on television, by 'experts' and by word of mouth, which assaults us all the time in everyday life.

Many, however, would reject utilitarian justifications for the study of history. That there is an enjoyment in the study of history, a poetic fascination with the past, is amply demonstrated by the success of local historical societies and by the sales of popular historical works. Much of the work of G. M. Trevelyan has now been superseded, but one can still agree with him that there is a sense of wonder over 'the quasi-miraculous fact that once, on this earth . . . walked other men and women, as actual as we are today, thinking their own thoughts, swayed by their own passions, but now all gone, one generation vanishing after another, gone as utterly as we ourselves shall shortly be gone like ghosts at cockcrow.' The meticulous medieval scholar May McKissack suggested that there exists in the human imagination an 'instinctive wish to break down the barriers of time and mortality and so to extend the limits of human consciousness beyond the span of a single life.' That instinct, it has been said, is akin to that aroused on those autumnal days when there is wood smoke in the air and a strange disordered nostalgia pervades the mind; or to the emotions inspired by distant church bells on a calm Sunday morning.

Do such poetic explanations of the appeal of history sound too remote from everyday experience? They should not, for history is above all a subject for everyman. History is all around us in buildings, place names, enduring traditions. History, though a complex art and a taxing science when practised by its leading figures, needs no baffling equations and conjures up no erudite jargon. History is important to everyone, and can be accessible to everyone.

Historical study is not about individual 'facts', but about the relationships between facts. However, there can be no study at all of the important relationships without a knowledge of the basic raw material, people, events, and a broad knowledge of the order in which these occurred or appeared. This dictionary sets out to provide, among many other things, some of this basic raw material. Historical works, even those consciously aimed at the general reader, necessarily take facts and persons and events for granted; after all, in history, there are an awful lot of them. Readers wishing to check up on names so carelessly thrown out may, we hope, find them, and some guidance upon them, here. The lay reader, since history is so important and so all-embracing, will constantly come up against references to historical events, in newspapers, perhaps, or in novels, or in conversation: we hope he will be able to check up on these events here. But the serious student, too, cannot carry all relevant facts and dates in his mind: he or she, too, will be able to use this dictionary for reference.

There are many topics which we, the editors, believe it would be good if you, the reader, knew something about. But this dictionary is not deliberately didactic in that sense. The entries, which come in straightforward alphabetical order, are intended to be the sort that the ordinary lay person would have occasion to want to look up. History is concerned with many other things than the organization and manipulation of power. It is concerned with social groups and social customs, as well as with great men. There has also been particular emphasis upon 'history-on-the-ground': if we visit an old castle, a medieval town or a Roman villa, we want to know more about it; this dictionary tries to help. Also, because history belongs to everyman, and because many people have an interest in trying to practise it, in however a modest and local way, entries have been included on some of the technical terms and sources of history: on 'blue books', for instance, and 'wills'. On the whole, artistic and scientific developments are left out. The importance of visual sources – paintings, etchings, photographs – is increasingly being recognized: the illustrations in this dictionary are largely designed to show some of the potentialities of such 'documents'.

History depends upon both *selection* and *interpretation*. It is no more possible in this dictionary than it is in any history of Britain or any history of any particular period or topic to put in everything of significance. History is also, in the end, the historian's own interpretation; there is never any God-given unchallengeable record. We try to present in our entries the accepted, uncontroversial facts. But still, even in the briefest entries, there must be some element of interpretation as well as selection. The longer the entry, the more scope there is for the legitimate interpretation of the individual contributor. But, of course, in a dictionary our aim must be to present what is widely accepted among the best authorities. Authorities, inevitably, disagree. This dictionary is no place for the provision of extended bibliographical information. But here and there, where we are citing an important interpretation which is particularly associated with one distinguished historian, we refer to that historian and give an example or two of his best-known work. More than that, a distinctive feature of this dictionary is the 22 'interpretative essays' which make possible the exploration of an important topic not possible in the more basic treatment of names and events. So that they do not get lost in the general alphabetical presentation, here at the outset is a list of them (note that Scotland and Ireland are not mentioned because they are dealt with in many separate entries):

Prehistoric Britain (Charles Kightly)
Roman Britain (Charles Kightly)
The church before the Reformation (Charles Kightly)
Feudalism (Charles Kightly)
Wales (Charles Kightly)
Monarchy (Charles Kightly and Keith Wrightson)
Law (Keith Wrightson)
Parliament (Keith Wrightson)
The Reformation (Keith Wrightson)
The civil wars (Keith Wrightson)
The Industrial Revolution (Keith Wrightson)
The family (Keith Wrightson)
The British empire (Christopher Harvie)
The navy (Christopher Harvie)
The army (Christopher Harvie)
Transport since 1830 (Christopher Harvie)
The women's movement (Christopher Harvie)
The Economy since 1870 (Christopher Harvie)
World War I (Christopher Harvie)
World War II (Christopher Harvie)
The welfare state (Christopher Harvie)
Class (Arthur Marwick)

The authorship of the shorter entries has not been identified. Broadly, those up to 1500 have been written by Charles Kightly, those from 1500 to 1820 by Keith Wrightson, and those since 1820 by Christopher Harvie. For what has been put in, these three contributing editors are largely responsible; for what has been cut out, I am solely responsible. The overall aim, within the limits set out above, has been *comprehensiveness*, but also *compression* within a dictionary of manageable size and tolerable price.

Lastly, I would like to thank my publishers who, against my initial reluctance, persuaded me to take on this enterprise and who provided the logistic support necessary for carrying it through.

Arthur Marwick

Abdication crisis After a popular career as prince of Wales, EDWARD VIII succeeded his father George V on 20 January 1936. But his romance with a divorced socialite, Wallis Simpson, drew opposition from the church and dominion governments, and Baldwin, the prime minister, forced him to choose between her and the throne. Despite much public support, orchestrated by Churchill and Beaverbrook, he chose love and abdicated (11 December), passing the rest of his life in expensive obscurity as duke of Windsor.

Aberdeen, George Gordon, earl of 1784–1860. A Conservative statesman, who followed Peel out of the party over FREE TRADE, and became leader of a Whig-Peelite ministry (1852). He fell from office in January 1855, when the house voted in favour of a select committee into mismanagement of the CRIMEAN WAR.

Abyssinia expedition 1864. Its aim was to punish the eccentric King Theodore, who had imprisoned some British citizens. The campaign was badly run, the captives were released and Theodore committed suicide.

Abyssinian war Italy invaded Abyssinia (3 October 1935). The LEAGUE OF NATIONS imposed sanctions, but Britain's initial firm pro-League line was vitiated by the compromise of the Hoare-Laval pact (1936) which suggested a partition of Abyssinia. The Italians won outright and stayed until expelled by the British (1941).

Acton, John Dalberg, lord 1834–1902. Catholic Liberal politician and historian, friend of NEWMAN, Acton challenged the growing power of the papacy and attempted to apply the rigour of German scholarship to British history writing, founding the *English Historical Review* (1885) and planning the *Cambridge Modern History* shortly before his death.

Addington, Henry *see* SIDMOUTH, HENRY ADDINGTON, 1ST VISCOUNT

Addled parliament 1614. The parliament sat for only 8 weeks and passed no legislation. The

commons attacked James VI and I's alleged management of the elections, challenged privy councillors' membership of the house and criticized customs 'impositions' introduced since BATE'S CASE (1606). Parliament was dissolved after refusing to vote taxes until impositions were removed.

Aden Annexed by the British in 1839, the coaling station of Aden and its hinterland was handed over to its inhabitants in November 1967, following a terrorist campaign. It became the republic of South Yemen. *See* BRITISH EMPIRE.

Admonitions to the parliament 1572. The 1st admonition was an appeal by the Puritans John Field and Thomas Wilcox for the introduction of Presbyterian institutions in the church of England. The ensuing pamphlet war provoked a 2nd admonition (possibly by CARTWRIGHT). Meanwhile a Presbyterian Bill was introduced and defeated in parliament.

Adrian IV pope (1154–9). Nicholas Breakspear, an Englishman, and so far the only British pope.

'Adullamites' The right-wing Liberals who, under LOWE, successfully opposed John Russell's 2nd REFORM BILL (1866). They were named after the 'cave of Adullam' (1 Samuel 22, 1–2), where 'everyone who was discontented' gathered to David.

Aedan mac Gabhran Chosen and supported by Columba, Aedan mac Gabhran became perhaps the greatest king of DALRIADA (*c.* 574–606), uniting all Irish settlers in Scotland under its control and establishing its independence from Ireland. He campaigned against the Picts and Bernicia, but was defeated by Aethelferth at DEGSASTAN (603/4).

Aelle The founder of SUSSEX (*c.* 457 or *c.* 477), Aelle was recognized (probably from personal prestige) as the 1st BRETWALDA, and may have led the Anglo-Saxon confederacy at BADON HILL (*c.* 495).

Aethelbert king of KENT (555–616). Aethelbert's conversion by AUGUSTINE (597) made him the 1st Christian Anglo-Saxon monarch. Though defeated by CEAWLIN (568), he was apparently recognized as BRETWALDA from *c.* 585 until his death.

Aethelferth king of BERNICIA (593–616). Aethelferth's victories over the armies of British Rheged, of Manau Gododdin (*c.* 598), of Dalriada (at DEGSASTAN in 603/4), and of north Wales (at

CHESTER *c.* 614) established the Angles as the dominant power in northern England. In 604 he annexed Deira and founded Northumbria, but was overthrown by Edwin and Raedwald, the southern BRETWALDA (616).

Aethelflaeda d. 918. The eldest daughter of Alfred, Aethelflaeda married his ally Aethelred of Mercia by 889, after whose death (910) she ruled as 'Lady of the Mercians'. This remarkable woman then built many burhs, personally planned and led expeditions against the Vikings, and materially assisted Edward the Elder in the conquest of the FIVE BOROUGHS.

Aethelred Unraed king of England (978–1016; b. *c.* 965). The 'No-counsel' (foolish) rather than 'the Unready', Aethelred was a son of Edgar's 2nd marriage. His implication in the murder of his half-brother Edward the Martyr (975–8) weakened his prestige from the beginning, and when Viking attacks resumed (980) and then worsened (991) neither his incompetent military efforts nor his payment of DANEGELD proved able to halt them. His massacre of Anglo-Danes (1002) exacerbated matters and, when Sweyn Forkbeard invaded (1013), English morale collapsed and Aethelred fled. Restored and briefly victorious on Sweyn's death (1014), he died hard-pressed by CNUT. *See* EDMUND IRONSIDE; EMMA.

Aethelstan king of Wessex and Mercia (924–39; b. *c.* 893). The eldest son of Edward the Elder, Aethelstan conquered Norse-Irish York (927), receiving then the submission of Alba, Northumbria and Strathclyde and subsequently of most of Wales (*see* HYWEL DDA). His kingship of all England and overlordship of Britain was confirmed at BRUNANBURH, but his empire collapsed at his death (*see* EDMUND). He maintained close relations with France, Germany and Scandinavia.

Afghan wars The 1st war (1839–42) culminated in a disastrous attack on Afghanistan in which a whole British force was annihilated while attempting to support a pro-British ruler. The British then withdrew until the 2nd war (1878–80), conducted by Roberts, which secured a pro-British rather than a pro-Russian regime in Kabul.

Agadir incident 1911. When France intervened in Moroccan politics, Germany dispatched the gunboat *Panther* to Agadir, a stratagem designed to prise Britain and France apart. Lloyd George, however, warned them off in his 'Mansion House' speech and

Aethelred Unraed portrayed on a contemporary Anglo-Saxon penny.

The execution of the Kotwal (chief magistrate) of Kabul, 26 October 1879, during the 2nd **Afghan war**. Unlike many pictures in the *Illustrated London News*, this one (3 January 1880) was actually sketched on the spot.

the ENTENTE CORDIALE came through the experience strengthened.

Agincourt, battle of 25 October 1415. The greatest English victory of the HUNDRED YEARS' WAR. Henry V's march from Harfleur to Calais was intercepted by a French army (led by the Constable d'Albret) outnumbering his force by perhaps 10 to 1, but he adopted the tactics of CRÉCY and routed them with catastrophic losses, mainly inflicted by archers.

Agricola, Gnaeus Julius governor of Roman Britain (78–85). Having consolidated the conquests of CERIALIS and JULIUS FRONTINUS, Agricola nearly doubled the size of the province, pushing its frontiers northwards with 6 successive campaigns in Scotland. In 84 he defeated the Caledonians at Mons Graupius (near Inverness) but he was then recalled, and soon afterwards the Romans withdrew to southern Scotland.

Agricultural depression This hit Britain after 1873, when grain could be cheaply imported from America and east Europe. Rents fell and small tenants were evicted, causing land agitation in Ireland and Scotland, although market gardening, stock-rearing and milk were less affected. The depression did not fully lift until World War II.

Agricultural Revolution Traditionally presented as a swift and dramatic process, associated with the names of such 18th-century 'improvers' as TULL, 'Turnip' TOWNSHEND and Robert Bakewell, the transformation of British agriculture is now seen as a very gradual process of change, encompassing much regional variation in both its nature and chronology.

The essential conditions of this long revolution were provided by the population rise, urban growth and price inflation of the period 1500–1650, which stimulated increased production, followed by the stabilization of prices (1650–1750) which encouraged cost-reducing innovations. Under these influences a complex of interconnected changes took place. By 1650 COPYHOLD land tenure had largely given way to LEASEHOLD, larger farms were being consolidated and ENCLOSURE was proceeding in many areas, while drainage and forest-clearance schemes expanded the cultivated area. The peasantry of the 16th century slowly polarized into large tenant farmers and proletarianized agricultural labourers. All these trends continued into the 18th century, enclosure in particular being accelerated. Meanwhile, productivity-enhancing tech-

The enclosure of land was an essential part of the **Agricultural Revolution**: surveyors at work on Henlow enclosure, Bedfordshire. Watercolour drawing, 1798.

niques such as convertible husbandry, the floating of water-meadows and the use of new grasses, turnips and carrots were introduced (often on the initiative of GENTRY landowners) and slowly spread out from eastern and central England, popularized both by example and the writings of agricultural improvers. Improved stock-breeding and implements completed the catalogue of innovations which by 1750 had so enhanced the output of grain, meat and dairy produce as to make England able not only to feed herself but also to meet renewed population expansion.

In Scotland the 18th century saw the appearance of a literature of agricultural improvement in imitation of that of England and the beginnings of a similar process of land reclamation and tenurial, organizational, social and technical change. By 1830 lowland farming had been brought up to the highest contemporary standards. Meanwhile the HIGHLAND CLEARANCES transformed the highlands.

The overall process of modernization up to 1800 had results of the greatest significance. Despite its social cost, it enabled Britain to support a much larger population, released rural labour for industrial employment, generated capital for other economic activities and reduced food prices sufficiently to release purchasing power for manufactured goods. The 'Agricultural Revolution' was therefore both a forerunner of and an essential part of the process of industrialization which gathered pace after 1750.

Aidan, St d. 651. Effectively the founder of the northern English church, Aidan headed the deputation of monks from Iona whom Oswald summoned to reconvert Northumbria after the overthrow of CADWALLAWN (633). Becoming bishop of Lindisfarne (634), he evangelized the kingdom on foot, and was much venerated for his humility. *See* CHURCH, PRE-REFORMATION.

Aircraft The 1st ascent of a human being in a hot-air balloon was made in France in 1783, and the Channel was crossed in 1785. Balloons were soon used for scientific research and military observation, and in 1894 the Royal Aeronautical Establishment was set up at Farnborough. Airships were experimented with in France from 1852, and adopted by the navy in 1909. Development continued with fair success until brought to an end by the R101 disaster (1930).

The 1st aeroplane flight in Britain was made in 1905, 2 years after the Wright brothers' Kittyhawk flight, and by 1918 the ROYAL AIR FORCE had multiple-engined aircraft capable of bombing Germany and in 1919 flying the Atlantic. Biplanes lasted until the early 1930s, when the fast multiple-gunned fighter and the heavy bomber (*see* BOMBING) were developed. (The fighter was to be the more significant, as the battle of Britain showed.) Sir Frank Whittle's jet engine was tested in flight in 1941 and the 1st jet fighter, the Gloster Meteor, took to the air in 1944. The 1st attempt to apply the jet engine to civil aviation, the Comet, was tragically delayed by 2 disasters, and the turbo-prop Viscount (1948) proved much more successful. But in the 1960s the decision to invest in the technologically superb – although commercially and environmentally unwanted – supersonic Concorde, finally consumed all the resources needed to modernize the industry, and brought its independent power to an end.

Air-raid precautions (ARP). Inaugurated by Sir John Anderson (1882–1958) in November 1938, the system involved the securing of hospital beds, the digging of trenches and shelters, and the evacuation of mothers, children under 5 and schoolchildren. A system of air-raid wardens was also created, and the national fire service organized out of the local brigades. Although 1½ million people left their homes during the main German 'blitz' (7 September – 2 November 1940) 60% of London families continued to sleep at home, under the security of the ARP system.

Aix-la-Chapelle, treaty of 1748. The treaty concluded the war of the AUSTRIAN SUCCESSION on the basis of a restoration of conquests by all belligerents save Prussia. Britain gained no ter-

ritory, but obliged France to recognize the Hanoverian succession and obtained a renewal of British participation in the Asiento (slave trade) with the Spanish colonies.

'Alabama' case 1862–72. An arbitration case in Geneva which assessed the responsibility of the British government during the American civil war for allowing the building and escape of the Southern commerce-raider *Alabama*, which subsequently did great damage to Northern shipping. Judgment went against Britain, and £3¼ million compensation had to be paid.

Aircraft: A British naval airship escorts a convoy during World War I.

A row of houses in Islington, London, is demolished by a flying bomb in 1944, but the **air-raid** shelters remain intact.

Alba The name (from the Irish word for Britain) used for the joint kingdom of Picts and Dalriadan Scots, established *c.* 850 by KENNETH MAC ALPIN, which after the 11th-century annexation of Lothian and Strathclyde became Scotland. Though its political centres, Scone and Stirling, were in Pictland, its language (perhaps because Pictish was apparently never written) was increasingly Dalriadan Gaelic. So were its church and (despite many attempts to maintain the Pictish matrilineal tradition) its patrilinear succession of monarchy.

Alban, St The earliest known British Christian martyr, Alban was executed (probably *c.* 208–9) outside VERULAMIUM at a place which by *c.* 400 had become his shrine. Round this developed the largest English Benedictine abbey and the town of St Albans.

The martyrdom of St **Alban**, from Matthew Paris's *Life* of the saint, *c.* 1240. The executioner catches his own eyes while Alban's soul, portrayed as a haloed dove, flies heavenward.

At the coronation of **Alexander III**, 1249, a highland bard relates the king's lineage and the great deeds of his ancestors, part of the ritual of Scottish coronations. From Fordun's *Scotichronicon*, 15th century.

Albany, John Stewart, 4th duke of *c.* 1484–1536. A French-educated cousin of James IV, Albany was chosen as governor of Scotland (1515) during James V's minority. He renewed the AULD ALLIANCE and sought a French bride for the king. After he visited France (1517), English diplomacy prevented him returning to Scotland save for brief visits (1521–2 and 1523–4).

Albany, Robert Stewart, 1st duke of *c.* 1340–1420. 2nd son of Robert II, Albany became regent during the captivity of JAMES I (1406–20). He was personally popular with the ordinary people, but his pragmatic and devious policy towards the magnates was less than successful in curtailing their lawlessness. He was succeeded as regent (1420–4) by his son Murdoch.

Albert, prince 1819–61. Prince of Saxe-Coburg Gotha, Albert married his cousin VICTORIA (1840) and replaced MELBOURNE as her chief adviser. Conscientious and progressive, he moderated the queen's prejudices and through enlightened and diplomatic patronage – notably his organization of the Great Exhibition (1851) – laid the foundation of the monarchy's later popularity.

Alcuin *c.* 735–804. The greatest of Anglo-Saxon teachers, Alcuin studied at the famous school in York (*see* BEDE), becoming master (767) and receiving many foreign scholars and pupils. From 782 he was the Emperor Charlemagne's doctrinal adviser and head of his palace school at Aachen, playing a major part in the renaissance of European learning.

Aldborough *see* BRIGANTES

Alderman *see* EALDORMAN

Alexander I king of Scotland (1107–24; b. 1078).

Alexander II king of Scotland (1214–49; b. 1198). The son of William the Lion. After supporting the English rebels against JOHN, Alexander established good relations with Henry III, and finally relinquished Scots claims to the border counties in return for English estates (1237). He began the attack on Norwegian suzerainty over the Western Isles, where he died on campaign.

Alexander III king of Scotland (1249–86; b. 1241). The son of Alexander II, he maintained good relations with England, and successfully concluded the struggle to end Norwegian rule of the Western Isles, ceded to Scotland (1266) after LARGS. A strong and popular king, his peaceful reign was remembered as a golden age long after his accidental death had led to the Scottish wars of independence.

Alexandra palace Built in 1867 as a north London exhibition and entertainment centre, it became the 1st television studio and transmitter (1936) and the broadcasting headquarters of the Open University (1970).

Alexandria, bombardment of 1882. The British fleet, in action for the only time between the Crimean war and 1914, bombarded the troops of Arabi Pasha, the insurgent Egyptian governor. This 'aggression' caused the resignation of BRIGHT from Gladstone's cabinet.

Alfred king of Wessex (871–99; b. 849). One of the most notable of all British rulers and certainly the greatest Anglo-Saxon king, Alfred was the youngest son of Aethelwulf (839–57) and grandson of Egbert. After visiting Rome in childhood, he served as second-in-command to his elder (and 3rd regnant) brother Aethelred, whose accession (865) coincided with the arrival of the great Viking army which by 869 had ravaged or extorted tribute from East Anglia, Mercia and Northumbria. In 870 this army invaded Wessex and, although defeated at Ashdown (where Alfred played the leading part), it could not be dislodged from its base at Reading. After a year-long campaign, including 9 indecisive battles, Alfred (who succeeded to the throne on Aethelred's death in April 871) was forced to buy its departure.

During the next 5 years all effective resistance to the invaders outside Wessex collapsed, and they began to settle the conquered lands. In 875 a Viking force renewed the assault on Wessex. Alfred managed to expel it by summer 877, but a surprise mid-winter attack (January 878) overran Wessex and drove Alfred to seek refuge on Athelney in Somerset. For a time all seemed lost, but Alfred rallied resistance and decisively defeated the Vikings at EDINGTON (May 878). Soon afterwards he constrained them to accept (for the 1st time) the baptism of their leaders, and they left to settle East Anglia.

The danger that the settlers would co-operate with new Viking raiders remained, and in 886 (aided by the ealdorman of the unconquered remnant of Mercia) Alfred occupied strategic London and fixed the boundary of the DANELAW by treaty. Now recognized as lord by all free

Alfred portrayed on a contemporary Anglo-Saxon penny.

Englishmen, he began to establish the 1st national defence system, reorganizing the FYRD to provide a more effective mobile army, raising fortified burhs as refuges against raiders, and eventually building a navy of large ships to fight the Vikings at sea.

These measures stood England in good stead when a new Viking army landed in 892. Although the rapid marches of the invaders and the assistance they received from the Danelaw settlers prevented a decisive engagement, their movements were continually shadowed by English and sometimes allied Welsh forces, and after Alfred's capture of their fleet on the Hertfordshire Lea (895) they finally dispersed (896). By Alfred's death, England was no longer in real danger of Scandinavian conquest, although she remained on the defensive until the subjugation of the Danelaw by his descendants Edward the Elder, Aethelflaeda and Aethelstan.

Alfred is also remembered for his services to learning. Always intellectually curious, he was determined to educate his people and reverse the decline in English culture and church life exacerbated by Viking attacks. To this end he learnt Latin, and pioneered the use of English prose for scholarship in his officially circulated, personal translations of important works on the duties of churchmen, theology, philosophy, history and geography. His biography was written by his friend and collaborator Bishop Asser (d. 909). *See* ANGLO-SAXON CHRONICLE.

All the talents, ministry of The name given to the Foxite WHIG ministry (1806–7), formed on the death of Pitt. Though successful in abolishing the slave trade, the 'Talents' failed to negotiate peace with Napoleon and resigned when defeated in an attempt to open high military appointments to Roman Catholics.

Field Marshal **Allenby** (centre) and the allies enter Jerusalem, December 1917. Pen and watercolour sketch by James McBey.

Allectus 'emperor' of Britain (293–6). *See* CONSTANTIUS.

'Alleluia victory' *see* GERMANUS, ST

Allen, William 1532–94. A selfless, austere and zealous Roman Catholic, Allen fled abroad in 1561 and founded the Douai seminary for English Catholics (1568). Made cardinal in 1587 and apostolic librarian in 1589, he was deeply involved in both the organization of the English mission and political plots against Elizabeth I.

Allenby, Edmund, viscount 1861–1936. The only cavalry commander to whom World War I gave an opportunity, Allenby pushed the Turks back from Egypt into Syria, liberating Jerusalem (December 1917). Subsequently he negotiated the armistice with the Turks and served as high commissioner in Egypt (1919–25).

Amboyna massacre 1623. The torture and execution of 10 servants of the English EAST INDIA COMPANY by the Dutch at Amboyna in the Moluccas. The event strained Anglo-Dutch relations and permanently weakened England's position in the spice islands, leading English merchants to concentrate on trade with the Indian mainland.

Ambrosius Aurelianus A Romano-British general, descended from Roman officials and perhaps an opponent of Vortigern, Aurelianus led successful British resistance to the Anglo-Saxons from *c*. 460. Apparently superseded *c*. 475 by Arthur, with whom he has (erroneously) been identified, he is the hero of many fabulous tales. His garrisions may be commemorated by place names like Ambrosden and Amesbury.

American civil war 1861–5. The Northern blockade of the confederacy shut off supplies of cotton, causing great distress in Lancashire. The government sympathized with the non-industrialized South, allowing armament supply (*see* ALABAMA CASE). Working-class organizations, however, supported the North, where victory helped reinforce their campaign for reform (though the notion of total working-class support for the North is a myth). *See* TRENT CASE.

American independence The American declaration of independence (4 July 1776) was the outcome of a growing divergence of interests between Britain and the 13 colonies which had become particularly marked after the removal of the threat of French Canada (1763). The fundamental problem was one of conflict between Britain's insistence upon parliament's right to legislate for the empire in accordance with British interests and the Americans' growing conviction that both their material interests and their accustomed liberties as British subjects were threatened by this situation.

From 1765 a series of controversial issues – American breaches of trade regulations, the question of trans-Appalachian expansion, the STAMP ACT and DECLARATORY ACT, Townshend's import duties, the BOSTON TEA PARTY and the subsequent COERCIVE (or 'Intolerable') ACTS – inflamed opinions on both sides of the Atlantic. Ministerial incompetence bedevilled Britain's responses, while in America specific conflicts slowly gave birth to statements of principle – no taxation without representation, rights of trial by jury and of colonial autonomy – for which farmers as well as traders and planters were prepared to fight. As John Adams later declared, 'the Revolution was effected before the war commenced. The Revolution was in the minds and hearts of the people.' While neither side was monolithic, opinion was increasingly polarized by 1775.

The slide into war was occasioned by the 1775 continental congress's condemnation of the 'Intolerable' Acts. General Gage's attempt to seize

Although responsibility for the Boston 'massacre' of 1770 remains uncertain, the incident was exploited for propaganda in the **American independence** struggle, as in this contemporary print, 'printed and sold by Paul Revere'.

arms at Concord, Mass., was resisted and BUNKER HILL followed. Hopes of peace were ended by the declaration of independence in which Jefferson metamorphosized colonial grievances into statements of fundamental constitutional principle. In the ensuing war the initial British strategy of driving a wedge between the colonies was defeated at SARATOGA (1777). Thereafter Britain attempted to take the south, successfully at first, but with increasing difficulty when French (1778), Spanish (1779) and Dutch (1780) intervention on the American side and the hostility of the armed neutrality of northern powers threatened British command of the sea. The disaster of YORKTOWN (1781) effectively ended the war.

By the treaty of Versailles (1783) the American colonies' independence was recognized and they were freed to devise their own constitutional future. At home, defeat was a profound shock, but not without positive results, for it was subtly to influence British attitudes in the handling of subsequent colonial aspirations towards self-government. *See* SAINTS, BATTLE OF THE.

American war 1812–15. War was declared by the United States ostensibly because of commercial grievances, but actually largely in the hope of conquering Canada. In addition to numerous naval duels, the war saw unsuccessful American attacks on Canada (1812–13), the burning of Washington (1814) and the battle of New Orleans (1815).

Amiens, battle of 1–8 August 1918. The final decisive battle of WORLD WAR I, in which Ludendorff's last offensive was turned back by the British (heavily armed by tanks) under Haig.

Amiens, peace of 1802. A short-lived peace settlement separating the Revolutionary and NAPOLEONIC WARS. Britain restored her colonial conquests (except Trinidad and Ceylon) to France, Spain and Holland, and Egypt to the Sultan. France undertook to evacuate south and central Italy and to compensate the house of Orange.

Amphitheatre In Roman Britain, an elliptical arena surrounded by tiers of seats on a raised bank. They have been found both near civilian towns such as Cirencester, where they were probably used for gladiatorial and wild-beast shows, and at fortresses such as Caerleon, where they were mainly employed for parades and weapon-training.

Amritsar massacre 13 April 1919. General Dyer ordered his troops to open fire on an unarmed crowd at Amritsar, killing 379 of them, for which he was congratulated by the right-wing press. This, the worst bloodshed since the Indian mutiny, triggered Gandhi's campaign of civil disobedience.

Roman **amphitheatre**, Caerleon, Wales.

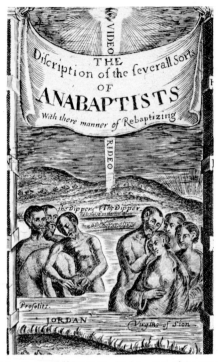

Adult baptism was the main heretical practice of **Anabaptists**, shown here on the title-page of Daniel Featley's *The Description of the Several Sorts of Anabaptists*, 1645.

Anabaptists Protestant sectaries who denied infant baptism and held a variety of other heretical and socially radical beliefs, Anabaptists first entered England from the Netherlands in the 1530s. By the 1540s several native congregations were established in the south-east. They were feared and persecuted by Anglican and Catholic churches alike.

Anarchists The Anarchist tradition was never strong in Britain after the early years of the 19th century, when it owed something to the pamphleteers William Thompson, John Gray and J.F. Bray. There was a brief emergency (1909) when a group of Russian Anarchists attacked a policeman and was besieged in London's east end at Sidney Street, but no major consequences resulted.

Anderson, Sir John *see* AIR-RAID PRECAUTIONS

Angel An English gold coin depicting the archangel Michael, worth 6s. 8d. (or 3 to a pound). Introduced at Edward IV's recoinage (1465), it was minted until early Stuart times.

Angevin empire *see* HENRY II

Angevins Name (derived from *Anjou*) used of the English kings descended from Geoffrey Plantagenet, count of Anjou, especially those from Henry II to Henry III. Their subsequent descendants, ending with Richard III, are usually called Plantagenets.

Angles Numerically the most important group of Anglo-Saxon settlers in Britain, where they peopled the kingdoms of East Anglia, Lindisse, Mercia and Northumbria. Their original homeland apparently centred on Angeln, near the borders of modern Denmark and Germany, whence their already well-established monarchy migrated to England in the late 5th century.

Anglo-Polish pact March 1939. Negotiated by Neville CHAMBERLAIN after the Germans broke the terms of the Munich agreement by occupying Prague, it offered an alliance to the Poles. With the German invasion of Poland (1 September 1939), adherence to it brought Britain into World War II.

Anglo-Saxon Chronicle The principal source for Anglo-Saxon history, and the earliest known, continuous vernacular history of any western nation. It was compiled *c.* 891 (perhaps at the instigation of Alfred, probably in south-west England) from earlier materials, whose chronology before *c.* 550 is suspect. Thereafter it was maintained at various centres of learning. Versions diverge widely after 915, one lasting until 1154. (*The Anglo-Saxon Chronicle*, trans. Garmonsway, 1972.)

Anglo-Saxons Name commonly (if somewhat misleadingly) used since the 18th century for the people from a closely related group of Germanic nations (ANGLES, FRISIANS, JUTES, SAXONS and perhaps others) who raided Roman Britain from the 3rd century, settling during the HEROIC AGE in modern England and substantially conquering it by *c.* 650. By this time their Christianization was far advanced (*see* CHURCH, PRE-REFORMATION) and the many originally separate groups of invaders had coalesced into the kingdoms of EAST ANGLIA, the EAST SAXONS, KENT, LINDISSE, MERCIA, NORTHUMBRIA, SUSSEX and WESSEX, each ruled by a dynasty claiming descent from pagan gods (*see* MONARCHY).

During the next 2 centuries these kingdoms moved gradually and fitfully towards unity, the greater tending to swallow up the lesser, and those south of the Humber normally falling under the authority of a single overlord or BRETWALDA. In the early 7th century the Northumbrian kings EDWIN, OSWALD and OSWIU even claimed the overlordship

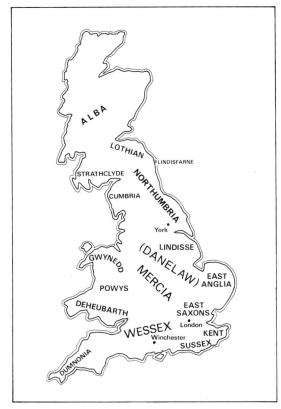

The best example of a surviving **Anglo-Saxon** church is at
Deerhurst, Glos. The fluting and entablature of these windows
are classically inspired; the triangular heads are an Anglo-Saxon
speciality.

The **Anglo-Saxon**
Strickland brooch: silver,
inlaid with gold plates
and niello, 9th century. It
is named after Sir
William Strickland, who
acquired it in the 19th
century.

Britain during the **Anglo-Saxon** period, showing the DANELAW,
the area settled by Vikings during Alfred's reign.

of the whole Anglo-Saxon people, but their
hegemony was ended by the growth of Mercia
under PENDA and Wulfhere (657–74), whose
descendants, Aethelbald (716–57) and the great
OFFA, came to dominate at least southern England
for much of the 8th century. Mercian ascendancy
was in turn ended when EGBERT of Wessex
temporarily conquered all England and permanently annexed Essex, Kent and Sussex (825–9).

Of the English kingdoms then remaining (East
Anglia, Mercia, Northumbria and Wessex) it was
Wessex alone which, under ALFRED, successfully
resisted the disastrous Viking attacks of the later 9th
century and survived them intact and strengthened.
Alfred's successors, notably EDWARD THE ELDER,
AETHELSTAN and EDMUND, then led the reconquest
first of Danish-occupied southern England and later
of Norwegian-held Northumbria, and by c. 975
EDGAR of Wessex could claim not only to be
undoubted ruler of a united and peaceful England
but also a personal overlord of Scotland, STRATH-
CLYDE and Wales.

The reign of Edgar's incompetent and unpopular

son AETHELRED UNRAED, however, coincided with
the renewal of serious Scandinavian attacks,
culminating in a full-scale invasion (1013) which –
despite the resistance of EDMUND IRONSIDE – led to
the expulsion of the English royal house and the
recognition of CNUT of Denmark as king (1016). For
the next 3 decades England formed part of a
Scandinavian empire and, although Cnut's strong
rule proved generally beneficent, the restoration of
Alfred's line with EDWARD THE CONFESSOR (1043)
found the Danish element in the state greatly
increased and the monarchy ultimately weakened
by the creation of semi-autonomous hereditary
earls. Godwin, the greatest of these, consistently
opposed Edward's Normanizing policies, and from
c. 1060 his son Harold Godwinson was the real
power in the land. On Edward's childless death
(1066) Harold became king (in defiance alike of the
claims of the Confessor's chosen heir, William the
Conqueror and of Cnut's self-styled heir, Harald
Hardrada) and the stage was set for the Norman
conquest. *See* CEORL; THEGN; WERGILD; WITAN.
(Frank Stenton, *Anglo-Saxon England*, 1971.)

Angus, Archibald Douglas, 6th earl of 1489–1557. A Scottish nobleman, Angus married James IV's widow (1514) but was driven from Scotland by ALBANY. Returning in 1517, he came to dominate Scotland (1525–7) before renewed exile in England (1528–43). Thereafter he first supported, then opposed, the treaties of GREENWICH (1543), fighting with distinction against the subsequent English invasions.

Anne queen of Great Britain (1702–14; b. 1665). 2nd daughter of James VII and II by his 1st marriage, Anne was a woman of firm loyalties but limited intelligence. A High Church TORY, she was principally interested in church affairs, instituting QUEEN ANNE'S BOUNTY (1704). Her reign is notable chiefly for the union with Scotland (1707) and Marlborough's wars.

Anselm, St archbishop of Canterbury (c. 1034–1109). Famous for his holiness and his theological treatises on the existence of God and the incarnation, Anselm reluctantly accepted the archiepiscopate from a reluctant William Rufus (1093), but after consistently denouncing his vices and exactions went into exile (1097). Recalled by Henry I, he won a long dispute over episcopal investitures (1107).

Anson, George, lord 1697–1762. First distinguished by his circumnavigation (1740–4), Anson served as 1st lord of the admiralty (1751–62) and was largely responsible for the improved training and organization which facilitated naval victory in the seven years' war (1756–63). An inspiring leader, he also fostered high naval morale.

Anti-corn-law league Formed in 1839 and largely run from Manchester, it was a group of northern business and publicists headed by BRIGHT and COBDEN, intent on repealing the CORN LAWS (1815) which, it alleged, increased the costs of industry. After a campaign waged in and out of parliament by newspaper, meetings and petitions, and aided by the new penny post, its success (1846) was a notable triumph for middle-class opinion.

Antonine wall A Roman turf wall on a stone foundation, it runs 37 miles (59 km) from Bridgeness on the Forth to Old Kilpatrick on the Clyde. The best-preserved stretch is around Rough Castle, near Bonnybridge, Central, one of the 18 forts along the wall. *See* ROMAN BRITAIN.

Apologetical declaration 1684. A manifesto composed by James Renwick declaring the COVENANTERS' intention to make war on all officials, soldiers, judges, conformist ministers and informers. The declaration heralded a murder campaign against such persons which provoked the repressive action of the KILLING TIMES.

Apology of the commons A declaration, drawn up at the close of the 1604 parliamentary session, expressing the commons' fear that their privileges were threatened and identifying financial and religious grievances as the cause of strained relations between crown and people. It remains uncertain how many of the commons the Apology actually represented.

Appanage Feudal estates, often hereditary, which were provided for the maintenance of a younger child of a landowner.

Appeal, court of *see* LAW

Appeals, Act in restraint of 1533. An Act forbidding appeals to foreign tribunals in testamentary, marital or spiritual revenue cases. Drafted by Thomas CROMWELL, it marked the official declaration of English independence from papal jurisdiction, its preamble being a notable statement of national autonomy. More specifically, it cleared the way for Henry VIII's divorce.

Appeasement A generic term which described attempts to preserve European peace by modifying the terms of the treaty of VERSAILLES (1919) in a spirit generous to Germany, both under the Weimar republic and under Hitler. It is particularly associated with Neville CHAMBERLAIN 's attempt to resolve Hitler's claims in the Sudetenland, which led to the Munich negotiations (September–October 1938). The subsequent total dismemberment of Czechoslovakia brought about the breakdown of the policy (March 1939).

Appellants Thomas of Woodstock, duke of Gloucester (and uncle of Richard II), Richard, earl of Arundel, and Thomas Beauchamp, earl of Warwick, lodged an 'appeal' of treason against a group of Richard II's friends (14 November 1387). Joined by Henry Bolingbroke (later Henry IV) and Thomas Mowbray, earl of Nottingham, they defeated a royalist force under Robert de Vere, earl of Oxford, at Radcot Bridge (19 December 1387) and triumphed at the MERCILESS PARLIAMENT. The king took his revenge (1397) by ordering the murder of Gloucester, the execution of Arundel and the exile of Warwick, and Bolingbroke and Nottingham were both banished (1398).

Apprenticeship The system whereby adolescents are bound by indenture to a master craftsman in order to learn a trade. Of medieval urban origin, it was extended to the countryside by the statute of ARTIFICERS (1563). Apprenticeship remained the only legal means of entering a trade until the 19th century.

Approvers In the medieval period, confessed criminals who endeavoured to gain pardon by informing on their accomplices or on other alleged law-breakers. Should their accusations be proved false (either in court or in trial by battle) the approver would be executed. The name was later applied to anyone who turned informer or 'state's evidence'.

Aquitaine *see* ELEANOR OF AQUITAINE; HUNDRED YEARS' WAR

Aragon, Catherine of 1484–1536. The daughter of Ferdinand and Isabella of Spain, Catherine came to England in 1501 as the bride of Prince Arthur (*d*. 1502). In 1509 she married Henry VIII, bearing him 6 children, only one of whom, MARY, survived infancy. Following the annulment of her marriage (1533) she lived in seclusion, never returning home.

Arbroath, declaration of 6 April 1320. An eloquently worded appeal for the recognition of Scottish independence, addressed by the Scottish magnates to the papacy. It expressed willingness to depose even Robert Bruce should he yield to England, 'for it is not for glory, riches nor honours that we fight, but for freedom alone, which no honest man gives up but with life itself'.

Arch, Joseph 1826–1919. A Warwickshire hedger and Methodist preacher, Arch founded the National Agricultural Labourers' Union (1872). This 'revolt of the field' was briefly successful in improving low wage rates, but was frustrated by the agricultural depression (1873). Despite Arch's later career as Liberal MP (1885–6 and 1892–1902), his union declined.

Archers A vital element of English armies from the late 13th to mid-16th centuries. They carried a 5- or 6-foot (1.5- or 1.8-metre) longbow of yew, ash or elm, capable of firing a yard-long (0.9-metre) arrow

English and Welsh **archers** in conflict with Genoese crossbowmen. This 15th-century stylized version of the battle of Crécy (1346), from Jean Froissart's chronicles, ignores the fact that the longbow was designed to fire a considerable distance.

from *c*. 350 yards (324 metres), but accurate only to *c*. 250 (*c*. 231 metres). They generally rode on campaign but fought dismounted.

Argyll, Archibald Campbell, 8th earl and 1st marquis of 1607–61. A leading supporter of the national COVENANT (1638), Argyll combined its defence with the extension of Campbell power in the highlands. He opposed the Scottish ENGAGEMENT (1647), but supported Charles II and crowned him in 1651. His later complicity with Oliver Cromwell's government resulted in his execution after the Restoration.

Argyll, Archibald Campbell, 9th earl of 1629–85. An active royalist, imprisoned 1657–60, Argyll became a privy councillor (1664) and was associated with persecution of the COVENANTERS. Convicted of treason (1681) for refusing the TEST ACT oath, he escaped abroad. Returning in 1685 to raise a rebellion in Monmouth's interest (*see* MONMOUTH'S REBELLION), he was taken and executed.

Argyll, John Campbell, 2nd duke of 1678–1743. A soldier of distinction and strong supporter of the UNION (1707), Argyll defended the Hanoverian succession in 1715, defeating the JACOBITES at SHERRIFMUIR. His followers, the 'Argathelians', subsequently dominated Scottish politics, supporting Walpole until the aftermath of the PORTEOUS RIOTS (1736) led Argyll to abandon Walpole in the 1741 election.

Aristocracy of labour *see* CLASS

Arkwright, Sir Richard 1732–92. Of humble Lancashire origins, Arkwright founded a great fortune upon his patenting of the 'water frame' (1769), a water-powered spinning machine. A ruthless, hard-fisted employer, he both made possible and pioneered the factory organization of cotton spinning (*see* INDUSTRIAL REVOLUTION), using London workhouse children in his Derbyshire mills.

Armada, Spanish 1588. The fleet of 130 ships intended to control the Channel while Spanish troops invaded England from the Netherlands. In a running battle (21–30 July) this was prevented. The Armada sailed round Britain and returned to Spain. Half its ships were lost, some in battle, more in storms off the Scottish and Irish coasts.

Armagnacs *see* BURGUNDIANS

Armed neutrality *see* AMERICAN INDEPENDENCE; NAPOLEONIC WARS

Arminians In reaction to the Calvinism of the Elizabethan church of England, the Arminians reasserted free grace against predestination and placed the sacraments rather than preaching at the centre of worship. Leading figures were Bishops Neale, Andrewes, LAUD, Montagu and Cosin. Their name derived from that of the Dutch theologian Arminius.

Army Before the civil wars the army establishment consisted only of the king's bodyguard and garrisons for his fortresses, forces raised for service abroad in particular emergencies, and the militia, usually 'embodied' only for local defence (*see* FEUDALISM). Many Englishmen, Scots and Irish had, however, participated in continental wars, and when the NEW MODEL ARMY was founded at Windsor (15 February 1645), it drew on a level of military expertise which was the equal of anything in Europe. However, the very existence of a standing army was contrary to the parliamentary ideology of the day, and the subsequent career of the army (and of Oliver CROMWELL, its leader), seemed to confirm that it could become an instrument for autocratic government. Charles II reduced it from 60,000–3,000 men at the Restoration (1660), although wars with the Dutch and colonial acquisitions caused this number to rise again, to 16,500 in 1685, the year of his death. Fears of a revival of the standing army threat led to the fall of James VII and II, who had expanded it to 20,000. On the accession of William of Orange parliamentary hostility to a standing army gave way, under pressure of French hostility and Irish rebellion, to qualified approval, signified by the MUTINY ACT (1689) which, renewed annually, permitted the crown autonomy in matters of military discipline, while transferring responsibility for financial support of the army to parliament.

This actually enabled army strength to climb back to Cromwellian levels, reaching 62,000 men in 1691. Throughout the 18th century the army's strength depended on the international situation, reaching around 70,000 men in time of war, and falling back to under 20,000 in time of peace, although its range of arms and theatres of operations steadily increased. Its cavalry acquired, under Marlborough, a European reputation, its artillery arm was developed, and its campaigns extended to India, where the East India Company subsequently built up armies in its 3 'presidencies' of Bombay, Madras and Bengal, and to America, where, after initial successes against the French, it suffered the setbacks of the American war of independence.

Army recruitment in the 18th century had changed little since the time of the hundred years' war. The crown contracted with a general or a local nobleman to raise a regiment, which he then recruited, selling the officers their commissions and settling details of their terms of enlistment with the rank and file. Service (until 1789) was nominally for life, mainly spent in camps or billets – barracks did not become commonplace until later in the 19th century. Tactics were still governed by the need to use the unwieldy smooth-bore musket effectively by predetermined patterns of fire, for which intensive drilling was necessary, reinforced by ferocious discipline and complemented – if circumstances warranted it – by the services of foreign MERCENARIES.

The NAPOLEONIC WARS introduced a much greater scale of military involvement throughout Europe. A new factor, the 'levée en masse' initiated by the revolutionary French, was later regularized as conscription. Although this was not introduced in Britain for over a century, and was as unpopular in the 19th century as a standing army had been in the 17th, over 7% of the male population may have served with the army in the course of the war.

The standard of **army** recruits was seldom high, as this cartoon of the late 18th century makes clear.

Even after the **army** reforms of the 19th century, wages and conditions for the ordinary soldier were still poor, the main point of this *Fun* cartoon, 'The Army of the Future', 1876.

Usually these men were selected for the local defence militia by ballot, and then persuaded one way or another into foreign service. During this period, the post of commander-in-chief was revived (1795) in the person of the king's brother, the duke of York, and the central administration and logistics of the army were much improved.

The ultimate success of the British campaigns against Napoleon, and the subsequent identification of WELLINGTON, as commander-in-chief, with anti-reforming conservatism, meant that the army marked time until the critical years of the 1850s, when the crises of the CRIMEAN WAR and the INDIAN MUTINY, coinciding with important technical innovations, provoked a period of reform. The publicity given, especially by *The Times*, to the disastrous mismanagement of the Crimean campaign – in which 22,200 died (mainly of wounds and disease – only 2,700 were killed) – meant that improvements had to be made to logistics, engineering and nursing services, and brought much criticism on the head of the traditional officer class; while in India the end of 'company rule' saw the creation of a European-officered force better fitted to police the subcontinent. In 1859 rumours of a French invasion caused the creation of a volunteer

army in which amateur soldiers, frequently from the middle class, began to take an increasing interest in military reform, epitomized by the furore which surrounded imaginary invasions such as Sir George Chesney's 'The Battle of Dorking' (1873). It was not, however, until Gladstone's 1st ministry (1868–74), under the secretaryship of CARDWELL, that many of the worst abuses were cleared up. Purchase of commissions was abolished, terms of service reduced, and regimental organization standardized on the 'linked battalion' system, whereby one battalion of each regiment served abroad (usually in India) for a period, replenished by the 'home battalion'. Nevertheless, in contrast to the popularity of the navy, public opinion still saw 'Tommy Atkins' as a ruffian who had lost caste by enlisting, and his officers as aristocratic ne'er do-wells, an impression borne out by the long career of the reactionary duke of Cambridge as commander-in-chief (1857–95).

Matters changed somewhat with the 'small wars' of the latter decades of the 19th century, which showed the small professional army (of less than 250,000 men), often to advantage, and were assiduously covered by the growing popular press which, since the Crimean war, the military

command had learned how to manage. The 2nd
BOER WAR, although scarcely more competently
organized than the Crimean campaign, was given
an adulatory coverage in the press, although British
isolationism and military unpreparedness were
commented on unfavourably elsewhere in the
world.

A period of major reform seemed overdue.
Some, such as ROBERTS, favoured the creation of a
conscript army on the continental pattern. Others
favoured a 'blue-water' approach, placing most
reliance on the navy, but making the professional
army cheaper, more efficient and capable of being
expanded in time of war. Under HALDANE, war
secretary (1905–12) in the Liberal government, the
latter group won out. A GENERAL STAFF was created,
and the regular army was supplemented by the
conversion of the militia into an organized reserve
and the volunteers into the 'Territorials'.

However, this centralization had the unfortunate
effect of exalting tactical ideas which reflected the
conservative predilections of the military caste, such
as their affection for cavalry. Furthermore, just
before the outbreak of WORLD WAR I, the CURRAGH
INCIDENT cast grave doubts on the loyalty that a
Liberal government could expect from a deeply
conservative officer class.

Confidence in that class was not enhanced by the
war. Right at the start, the new war minister,
KITCHENER, contemptuously rejected the Territorials in favour of directly recruiting his 'new
army'. He also devolved little responsibility to the

imperial general staff. However, the new army,
fresh but barely trained, had still to follow the tactics
laid down by the traditional military élite, which
resulted in the terrible casualties of the Somme
(July–November 1916), when straight lines of men
advanced, heavily burdened and incapable of
skirmishing manoeuvre, to be mown down by
German machine-guns. Even before this, in
January, volunteering for the new army had been
replaced by statutory conscription, which at last
made British military organization comparable
with that of the other European powers.

World War I was a turning-point in the
technologizing of war, most dramatically evidenced by the tank, the aircraft, high explosive
shells, barbed wire and the machine gun. Yet
military orthodoxy still saw the wearing down of
the enemy by infantry assaults on the western front
as the key to victory (although over a third of
Britain's troops were stationed elsewhere). The tank
had been proved technically feasible by May 1916
but only played a crucial role in a couple of battles,
although Major-General J. F. C. Fuller (1878–1966)
had drawn up plans for a mass tank assault in his
'Plan 1919' which foreshadowed the German
'Blitzkrieg' (1939). After the war, however,
conscription ended (until 1939) and the army was
reduced to 435,000 men. It was largely preoccupied
with imperial policing, and its finances were
restricted by the '10-year' rule, the assumption
being that there would be no war for at least that
long. Thus the conservative officer class was
preserved in control, and there was little development of the new technologies demonstrated in the
war until the very eve of the next outbreak.

This helped little in withstanding the German
tank assault on France (May 1940), after which 9 out
of 10 of the divisions of the British expeditionary
force made their escape from Dunkirk, removing,
from the beginning, the concentration on the
western front. The main British theatres of war
were then the Middle and Far East. The first became
a series of set-piece tank battles, fought out in an
atmosphere of almost medieval chivalry, the last
was an overwhelming disaster in which the British
were outfought by the Japanese and driven from
Hong Kong, Singapore and Burma. By late 1942
the British forces were fighting throughout the
world in close collaboration with the Americans, an
identity of interest secured by the careful organization of 'joint staffs' in north Africa and Italy, and
ultimately the invasion of France (June 1944). In
fact, in the crucial campaigns of the war the British
army assumed a subordinate position: the campaigns where it fought on its own – the desert and

Army conscription for possible war was announced in April
1939.

Burma – were never more than sideshows. During the war the technologizing of the army and its identification with a democratic society became complete, with the growth of wings such as the ordnance corps, the service corps, the electrical and mechanical engineers, and the education corps (the last of which was said to have played a notable part in the 1945 Labour victory). The officer élite did not so much change in social composition as in character and style: MONTGOMERY's motor caravans, in which he accompanied his troops and tanks, were a telling contrast with the chateaux, well behind the lines, which had accommodated the staffs in World War I. Montgomery, Alexander, Slim and WAVELL were approachable in a style foreign to the previous war, and in Lord Alanbrooke, chief of the imperial general staff, they had a political head subtle and astute enough to deal with Churchill.

After the war, conscription was retained, as were the global responsibilities of the British armed forces, although much of the raison d'être for this seemed to evaporate with the surrender of the Indian empire and its own army (1947). At the same time, Britain's finances were no longer extensive enough to make her capable of intervening directly when traditional interests were threatened, a point proved in 1947 when she handed over responsibility for coping with a Communist insurrection in Greece to the Americans. Not until the trauma of the SUEZ CRISIS (1956) did the changed situation fully dawn on the military and political leadership. But although the conscript army had been heavily included in 'emergencies' in Malaya, Kenya (*see* MAU MAU) and Cyprus, and in smaller flare-ups elsewhere, it avoided the bloodbaths which afflicted the French in Indo-China and Algeria, and the Americans in Vietnam. Conscription ended in 1960 and 3 years later a process of co-ordination and retrenchment was begun which swept away the old war and supply ministries, ended the career of many regiments and virtually wound up the Territorials. By the 1970s the army was reduced to the NATO forces in Germany, several token garrisons in the last imperial possessions and a growing force policing the intractable province of Ulster (*see* ULSTER EMERGENCY).

Arnold, Rev. Thomas 1795–1842. BROAD CHURCH-MAN, historian and reformer, Arnold became headmaster of Rugby school (1828), and the most noted reformer of public schools. Thomas Hughes, in *Tom Brown's Schooldays* (1857), made him legendary as a 'muscular Christian', but his influence was mainly moral, and made Rugby a seedbed of mid-Victorian liberals and reformers.

Thomas **Arnold** aimed for '1st, religious and moral principles: 2ndly, gentlemanly conduct: 3rdly, intellectual ability'. This portrait by A. Philips, 1839, caught the essence of Arnold's Victorian image.

Arran, James Hamilton, 2nd earl of, duc de Chatellerault 1516–75. As regent of Scotland (1543–54) Arran made and then repudiated the treaties of GREENWICH. Resigning power to MARY OF GUISE, he later rose against her with the lords of the CONGREGATION. A rebel against Mary Queen of Scots in 1565, he subsequently led the 'queen's party' (1569–73). He possessed little fixed purpose.

Arras, congress of 1435. A papal-sponsored peace conference designed to end the HUNDRED YEARS' WAR. Negotiations between England and France broke down, and the Burgundians transferred their support from the former to the latter, hastening England's eventual defeat.

Array, commissions of A system of raising troops, current from the 13th century, whereby commissioners (generally experienced soldiers) surveyed the able-bodied men of each shire, choosing the best as conscripts for the royal service. During and after the hundred years' war such troops were outnumbered by INDENTURED RETAINERS, but Charles I tried to revive the system during the civil wars.

Arthur One of the most famous figures in British legend, Arthur is now generally agreed to have been historical, a Romano-British general (*dux bellorum,* war-leader) who successfully contested Anglo-Saxon expansion at the turn of the 5th and 6th centuries (*see* HEROIC AGE). No directly contemporary record of him survives, but relatively early sources call him emperor, report his 12 great victories (apparently over Picts and Irish as well as Saxons) culminating in the historical BADON HILL (*c.* 495), and have him killed in battle, with or by Medraut (Mordred), at 'Camlann', perhaps *c.* 515. Claims have therefore been made, notably by John Morris's controversial but valuable *Age of Arthur* (1973), that he established a short-lived dominance over the whole of Britain. Certainly he is associated in legend with areas as far apart as Edinburgh, Wales and Dumnonia, though his main sphere of activity is usually held to have been south-west England. Other persistent traditions give his 'capital' as 'Camelot' (*see* CADBURY; COLCHESTER), maintain that he died at British hands and (less reliably) that he was buried at GLASTONBURY, though early Welsh tradition insists that his grave is unknown.

Whatever may be inferred from the preceding, it is clear that by the 7th century Arthur had become a well-known hero in the Celtic lands, and after the Norman conquest his story spread to England and Europe, acquiring all the trappings of chivalrous romance. William of Malmesbury, Geoffrey of Monmouth, Wace and Chretien de Troyes wrote of him in the 12th century; Layamon in the 13th; Sir Thomas Malory in the 15th; Spenser in the 16th; Dryden in the 17th; Tennyson and William Morris in the 19th; and T. H. White in the 20th. Though each saw Arthur through contemporary eyes and added features of his own, each retained the central and perhaps essentially historical element of the story, showing a strong and victorious ruler who protected his people from barbarism and oppression until eventually overthrown by treachery and disunion.

Arthur, Prince *see* ARAGON, CATHERINE OF; HENRY VII; HENRY VIII

Arthur of Brittany 1186–1203. The posthumous son of Richard I's elder brother Geoffrey, Arthur was acclaimed as Richard's heir by the barons of Anjou and supported by Philip Augustus. John captured him (1202) and allegedly murdered him in prison in a fit of drunken rage.

Articles, lords of the A committee to prepare business for the Scottish parliament, originating under James I. By James VI's reign it had virtually usurped the legislative powers of parliament, acting under the guidance of the privy council, which drafted legislation. Parliament, its initiative lost, enacted the recommended legislation. The committee was finally abolished in 1690.

Articles of Perth, the five 1618. Regulations governing religious observances in Scotland, pushed through the general assembly and Scottish parliament by James VI and abolished in 1638. The principal Christian festivals were re-established, baptism and communion were permitted in private, the need for confirmation was reasserted and kneeling to receive communion was ordered.

Artificers, statute of 1563. An Act seeking to codify and revise existing legislation governing wage levels, conditions of service and APPRENTICESHIP. Its more important provisions included the local assessment of wages by JUSTICES OF THE PEACE and the extension of the 7-year term of apprenticeship of urban GUILDS to the whole kingdom.

Arts Council Developed from the Council for the Encouragement of Music and the Arts, set up by Keynes and others (1941), its name was changed and it was given statutory authority to offer financial assistance in 1946.

Arundel, Thomas 1353–1414. Archbishop of Canterbury from 1396. Having supported the APPELLANTS, Arundel was banished by Richard II (1397). He returned 2 years later with Henry IV, becoming that king's most constant ally and serving him as chancellor (1407–10 and 1412–13). As a determined but humane opponent of the LOLLARDS, he was largely responsible for DE HERETICO COMBURENDO.

Ashanti wars The 1st war (1873–4) was fought between British forces under WOLSELEY and the Ashanti confederation in the area now known as Ghana, following a threat by the Ashanti tribes to invade the coastal area. Peace was made but hostilities broke out again (1896), following which Ashanti was annexed to the Gold Coast.

Ashdown, battle of *see* ALFRED

Ashingdon, battle of 18 October 1016. Edmund Ironside's English army was heavily defeated by Cnut's Danes near Southend, Essex, after the treacherous flight of part of the English force.

Asiento *see* AIX-LA-CHAPELLE, TREATY OF

Asquith, Herbert Henry, earl 1852–1928. A Yorkshireman, educated in London and Oxford, Asquith entered parliament (1886), rising rapidly to become home secretary in the Liberal government (1892–5). He later became chancellor of the exchequer (1905) and premier (1908), when he was preoccupied with the PEOPLE'S BUDGET, the Parliament Act and HOME RULE. The reorganization required by World War I proved beyond his failing powers: although he secured a coalition with the Conservatives (May 1915) he was driven from office (December 1916) by Lloyd George.

Asser, bishop *see* ALFRED

Assizes A system of visitations of the English provinces by royal justices, fully developed by the 14th century. Justices of assize 'rode' 6 circuits (reorganized into 8 for England and Wales in the 19th century), hearing both criminal and civil cases. Assizes were abolished in 1971.

Atlantic charter 14 August 1941. An 8-point declaration of 'war aims' issued by Churchill and Roosevelt while the USA was still theoretically at peace, it was incorporated in the declaration of the UNITED NATIONS (1 January 1942).

Atlantic triangle A term used to describe a triangular trading system of the 18th century involving the carriage of manufactured goods from Britain to west Africa, of slaves from Africa to the West Indian and American colonies and of colonial products back to Britain.

Atom bomb The basic research on nuclear fission had been carried out by Ernest Rutherford (1871–1937) and others between the wars. After 1940 British and American scientists collaborated on 'Project Manhattan' and the prototype was exploded in the New Mexico desert (17 July 1945). The bombing of Hiroshima (6 August) and Nagasaki (9 August) brought about the surrender of Japan (14 August). Britain tested the atomic bomb in 1952 and the hydrogen bomb in 1957.

Atrebates A British tribe of Belgic origin, who by *c.* 50 BC occupied central southern England. A century later Catuvellaunian pressure had reduced their territory to a coastal strip, disposing them to support the Roman conquest. Afterwards, their territory was divided into 3 CIVITATES, those of the Regni (roughly Surrey and Sussex), the Atrebates (roughly north Hampshire and Berkshire), and the

Belgae (south Hampshire, Wiltshire and north Somerset).

Attacotti A fierce and cannibalistic tribe, whose name means 'aborigines' and whose homeland may have been Ireland, the Western Isles, or northern Scotland. Having attacked Roman Britain in the BARBARIAN CONSPIRACY (367–9), some served as numeri (infantry) in the Roman army.

Attainder, Acts of Acts of parliament whereby accused persons were declared guilty of treason without proper trial. Attainder was commonly employed after rebellions and occasionally adopted as a means of judicial murder in politics. The 1st Act was passed in 1459, the last in 1798.

Atterbury plot *see* JACOBITES

Attlee, Clement, earl 1883–1967. Attlee went to Oxford and became a socialist at Toynbee Hall (*see* TOYNBEE, ARNOLD). After a gallant war record he became Labour mayor of Stepney (1919) and MP for Limehouse (1922). He survived the 1931 Labour collapse and became leader of the party in 1935. Having played an instrumental part in ousting Neville Chamberlain (May 1940) he became deputy prime

Clement **Attlee** speaking at an anti-Nazi rally in Hyde Park, London, October 1935. Next to him is Lady Reading, a leading Liberal.

minister with responsibility for domestic policy in Churchill's coalition cabinet, where his tact and administrative grasp complemented Churchill's imagination and eloquence. The 1945 election returned him with a mandate to nationalize key industries and create the national health service. His period of office (1945–51) also saw the granting of independence to India (1947) and, on a more sombre note, attempts to cope with a rundown economy and a worsening international situation. His 2nd government (February 1950–October 1951) joined the USA in the Korean war, but party divisions and the loss of Cripps and Bevin led to an election which he lost, and he was succeeded by Gaitskell (1955).

Attwood, Thomas 1783–1856. A Birmingham banker and currency reformer, Attwood's campaign for a flexible credit system led him to organize the political unions before 1832. He became Radical MP for Birmingham (1832), and (1838–9) a founder of 'moral force' CHARTISM.

Augustine, St d. 604–9. The founder of the English church (*see* CHURCH, PRE-REFORMATION), Augustine led Pope Gregory the Great's Roman mission to Kent (597), converted Aethelbert (already married to a Christian Frankish princess) and established a flourishing church at CANTERBURY. He was granted metropolitan power (601) but failed to reach agreement with the bishops of the Celtic church.

Augustinian canons The earliest and largest order of CANONS regular, the Black or Austin Canons were introduced to England in 1095 and to Scotland c. 1120. In England they had more native houses than any other religious order, though some were very small. Their offshoots included the Bonshommes (apparently peculiar to England), the PREMONSTRATENSIANS and the Victorines.

Augustinian friars Originating as Italian hermit communities, the Augustinians banded together as one order of FRIARS in 1243. Though also called Friars Hermits, they soon lost their eremitical tradition and, while maintaining specially close links with the papacy, specialized in preaching and theology. They were introduced to England in 1248, but were almost unknown in Scotland.

Auld alliance The traditional Scottish alliance with France against England – the 'auld enemy'. Originating in 1296 when John BALLIOL sought

French help against Edward I, it continued until the Scottish Reformation. Thereafter a common Protestantism and from 1603 the union of crowns led to friendly relations between Scotland and England.

Austrian succession, war of the 1740–8. Though fighting in Europe began in 1740, Britain was initially involved only in the subsidizing of Hanover. A French declaration of war (1744) brought official British entry in alliance with Austria. Battles included DETTINGEN, FONTENOY and Cape Finisterre. The war ended in the treaty of AIX-LA-CHAPELLE (1748).

Auxiliaries Recruited from native tribes within the Roman empire, non-citizens who were rewarded with citizenship on discharge, these troops formed much the largest proportion of the garrison of Roman Britain. *See* COMITATENSES; LEGION.

Avebury Wilts. One of the largest ceremonial sites in prehistoric Europe, Avebury is a HENGE MONUMENT covering $28\frac{1}{2}$ acres. The great circle of c. 100 stones and 2 smaller internal STONE CIRCLES were added during the Beaker period (c. 2000–1700 BC), as was an avenue of standing stones leading to the Sanctuary, another circle over a mile distant.

Avebury, Wilts.: part of the outer circle of stones.

Axe factories Sites in north and west Britain where, during the neolithic and succeeding period (*c*. 3500–1400 BC), suitable locally occurring volcanic rock was roughly shaped into axe-heads, which were then traded over long distances. Axes from Great Langdale, Cumbria, for instance, are found dispersed from Cornwall to Scotland. *See* FLINT MINES.

Aymer de Valence, earl of Pembroke d. 1324. Edward I's cousin and lieutenant in Scotland 1306–7 (*see* ROBERT BRUCE). Though a leading promoter of the ORDINANCES (1311), he was alienated from Thomas of Lancaster by the latter's murder of GAVESTON, and thereafter led a 'middle party' between the baronial extremists and Edward II's courtiers, supporting the king in the 1322 civil war.

Ayton, truce of *see* HENRY VII; JAMES IV

Babington plot 1586. A plot concocted by Anthony Babington and Father Ballard to murder Elizabeth I and, with Spanish help, place MARY QUEEN OF SCOTS on the throne. Mary's letters were intercepted by Walsingham from the outset and her approval of the plan was employed to overcome Elizabeth's resistance to her trial and execution.

Bacon, Sir Francis 1561–1626. Philosopher of science, essayist, historian and lawyer, Bacon possessed one of the most brilliant minds of his age. His political career, unsuccessful under Elizabeth I, took off under JAMES VI AND I and he rose to be lord chancellor (1618) only to face IMPEACHMENT for corruption and removal from office in 1621.

Badon Hill, battle of probably *c*. 495. A famous victory of the Britons over the Anglo-Saxons, which long halted their advance. The site of the 3-day 'siege' is uncertain, but was probably a hillfort near Bath. Arthur probably commanded the Britons against a confederation of the southern English, perhaps led by Aelle of Sussex and including Oisc of Kent.

Bagehot, Walter 1826–77. A Nonconformist, banker and editor of *The Economist*, Bagehot, in his book *The English Constitution* (1867), propounded the theory of 'CABINET government' in which the 'dignified' parts of the constitution, the crown and to a great extent the legislature, attracted the loyalty of the masses, while the 'efficient' part, the cabinet, governed them.

Bailiff From the Norman conquest, an officer appointed by the king or other overlord to administer a town, HUNDRED or other specific area. In Scotland a 'bailie' was the equivalent of a sheriff before the abolition of HERITABLE JURISDICTIONS (1747) and is now a municipal magistrate. Bailiffs were also manorial officials who collected rents and supervised husbandry.

Baillie, Robert 1602–62. A moderate Presbyterian in 1638, Baillie later served as a Scottish delegate to the WESTMINSTER ASSEMBLY OF DIVINES (1643–9). He remained in England until 1646, keeping a careful journal of events. In 1649 he was among those chosen to offer Charles II the Scottish crown and after 1660 became principal of Glasgow university.

Balaclava, battle of *see* CRIMEAN WAR

'I would live to study, and not study to live': Francis **Bacon** at his desk, a contemporary print by William Marshal.

Baldwin, Stanley, earl 1867–1947. A midlands ironfounder, educated at Harrow and Cambridge, and a Conservative MP from 1908, Baldwin served under Lloyd George (1916–22) but helped bring him down in 1922. He succeeded Bonar Law as prime minister (1923) but the election he called on his tariff reform policy resulted in MacDonald's 1st Labour government. He returned to office (1924–9), defeating the General Strike (1926). As deputy to MacDonald (1931–5), he effectively led the NATIONAL GOVERNMENT, becoming prime minister 1935–7. He was accused of being a political manipulator with no long-term views on foreign or domestic policy, but the National government's rearmament and military-scientific programme was begun under his leadership.

Balfour, Arthur James, earl 1848–1930. A Scots landowner, philosopher and nephew of Salisbury, Balfour entered politics as a Conservative (1874) and made his reputation as Irish secretary (1886–92) and leader of the commons 1895–1902 when he became premier. The TARIFF REFORM controversy split his cabinet and he lost power in 1905 and the Tory leadership in 1911. As foreign secretary (1916–19), he played an important part in the VERSAILLES settlement, and in the Balfour declaration (1917) promised Zionists a national home in PALESTINE.

Ball, John *see* PEASANTS' REVOLT

Balliol, Edward *c.* 1283–1364. The son of John Balliol and leader of the DISINHERITED, he was backed by Edward III as client-king of Scotland. Crowned after DUPPLIN (1332), he ceded southern Scotland to Edward, but was expelled in December 1332. Restored after HALIDON HILL, he was again expelled in 1334. *See* SCOTTISH WARS OF INDEPENDENCE.

Balliol, John king of Scotland (1292–6; b. *c.* 1250). The grandson of the eldest daughter of David (younger brother of William the Lion), Balliol was awarded the throne by Edward I, who thereafter made his position impossible by treating him as a subject and, after his eventual consequent defiance, ceremonially degraded and imprisoned him. Wallace fought in his name, and his son Edward revived his claim. *See* DISINHERITED; SCOTTISH WARS OF INDEPENDENCE.

Ballot Act 1872. Passed after a long campaign by radical groups, the Act was intended to protect the new working-class electorate from the coercion which accompanied 'open voting' on the HUSTINGS.

Balmoral castle Queen VICTORIA purchased the estate of Balmoral on Deeside in 1848. Prince Albert, with a local architect, William Smith, pulled down the old house and built the present 'Scots-baronial' building (1853–5). The royal family have, since then, passed the shooting season of August and September there. Accordingly, cabinet ministers have had to travel north for conferences with the monarch.

Banbury, battle of 26 July 1469. An army of northern rebels against EDWARD IV, encouraged by WARWICK THE KINGMAKER and led by his cousin Sir John Conyers (alias 'Robin of Redesdale'), defeated a force of Welsh loyalists under William Herbert, earl of Pembroke, at Edgecote near Banbury, Oxon. Warwick soon afterwards captured Edward but was unable to rule through him.

Bancroft, Richard 1544–1610. As chaplain to WHITGIFT, a leading member of HIGH COMMISSION, bishop of London (1597) and archbishop of Canterbury (1604), Bancroft was a militant opponent of Puritanism. Vigorous, combative and uncompromising by nature, he was restrained by James VI and I, but foreshadowed the Arminian church of LAUD.

Bank of England Established in 1694, the bank remained the only English joint-stock bank until 1826. Though technically a private institution, it was effectively the central bank and holder of English gold reserves. This was recognized by Peel, who attempted in his Bank Charter Act (1844) to impose on it some of the constraints of a central bank by separating its commercial from its note-issuing side and giving it an obligation to control the money supply (but *see* BANK OF SCOTLAND). Taken under government control by Bonar Law, Lloyd George's chancellor, in 1917, it nevertheless represented, between the wars, under its director Sir Montagu Norman, a temple of financial orthodoxy. It was nationalized by Attlee's government in 1946.

Bank of Scotland The 1st Scottish joint-stock bank, founded in 1695. It retains, like other Scottish banks, the right to issue its own notes, and was the first to issue £1 notes (1704).

Banneret During the later middle ages (especially the hundred years' war), bannerets were veteran knights who acted as commanders in battle or leaders of expeditions. Promotions were sometimes made on the battlefield by cutting off the tail of a knight's long pennon to make the characteristic square 'banneret' of the rank. *See* TITLES.

Bannockburn, battle of 23-4 June 1314. The most decisive battle of the SCOTTISH WARS OF INDEPENDENCE. Edward II's army of *c.* 20,000 men, moving to relieve Stirling castle, was attacked and routed in its badly chosen position by Robert Bruce's much smaller force of infantry SCHILTRONS, setting the seal on Bruce's recovery of Scotland.

Baptists A religious denomination practising adult baptism by total immersion. The 1st English congregation was founded by John Smyth in Holland (1608). Support grew during the interregnum (1649–60), but theological differences provoked a split between Particular and General Baptists, the latter eventually forming the New Connexion (1770). Reunification was completed in 1891. *See* DISSENTERS; NONCONFORMITY.

Barbarian conspiracy 367–9. A co-ordinated attack on Roman Britain by Picts, Attacotti and Irish raiders from the north and west, while seaborne Anglo-Saxons and Franks assaulted the east coast. The count of the SAXON SHORE was killed and much of the province overrun by plundering bands. Order was eventually restored by Theodosius, who afterwards reorganized Britain's defences.

Barebone's parliament 4 July–11 December 1653. An assembly of 140 members selected by Oliver CROMWELL's officers after the dissolution of the Rump. Though containing a group of religious radicals who urged legal and ecclesiastical reforms, it also had many conservative members who ultimately voted its dissolution. Its popular name derives from that of Praise-God Barebone, a London member.

Barlow report *see* ECONOMY, THE

Barnet, battle of 14 April 1471. EDWARD IV, having returned from exile and occupied London, sallied out to attack WARWICK THE KINGMAKER'S larger Lancastrian-Neville force at dawn on Easter Sunday. After a 3-hour fight in thick mist, 2 Lancastrian divisions mistakenly attacked each other and their army broke, Warwick being killed in flight.

Sometimes round **barrows** were used as foci for larger cemeteries in the early bronze age Wessex period, as at Lambourn Seven Barrows, Berks. Aerial view.

Baron *see* TITLES

Baron courts The private court of a Scottish laird at which tenants met to interpret agricultural custom and through which lairds enforced rent payment and services and punished minor offences. The baron courts survived the abolition of HERITABLE JURISDICTIONS (1747), but were generally moribund by 1800.

Baronet *see* TITLES

Barrows, long Communal burial mounds, generally trapezoidal or rectangular in shape, consisting of earth and chalk piled over a wooden 'mortuary house'. They appear mainly in the areas of south and east England occupied by the Windmill Hill people, and probably date from the early neolithic period (*c.* 3500–2500 BC).

Barrows, round Circular burial mounds, generally covering a single primary burial, sometimes with later additions. They were usually bowl-shaped, though those of the Wessex culture (*c.* 1700–1400 BC) may be bell-, disc- or saucer-shaped. The most numerous and widely distributed of British prehistoric monuments, they were mainly raised *c.* 2000–*c.* 1300 BC.

'Bastard feudalism' *see* FEUDALISM

Bate's case 1606. A test case in which the judges ruled that the king could impose customs duties for the purposes of regulating trade without parliament's consent. Bate, a member of the Levant Company, had refused to pay such a duty on imported currants. The decision opened the way to many new 'impositions'.

Bats, parliament of February 1426. Held at Leicester by Bedford to settle the differences of HUMPHREY and Cardinal BEAUFORT. Their retainers, on the verge of battle during 1425, were forbidden to carry arms, but appeared with 'bats' or clubs. A temporary and insincere reconciliation was effected, Beaufort resigning as chancellor.

Baugé, battle of 22 March 1421. Thomas, duke of Clarence, commanding in France during his brother Henry V's absence, impulsively attacked a Franco-Scottish army without waiting for his archers, and was defeated and killed. Though it broke a run of English victories, the reverse had little real effect on the HUNDRED YEARS' WAR.

Bawdy courts A popular name used in the 17th century for the courts of the Anglican church which had jurisdiction over moral, spiritual, marital and testamentary cases. Offenders were presented to the courts by their churchwardens, commonly for sexual misdemeanours. Regulation of this kind virtually disappeared after 1640, though the courts retained matrimonial and testamentary jurisdiction until 1857.

Baxter, Richard 1615–91. Baxter came to prominence as minister of Kidderminster (1641–60), chaplain in the parliamentary army (1642–7) and a prolific writer on religious and social affairs. Appointed royal chaplain (1660), he worked unsuccessfully for a moderate church settlement at

Detail from the **Bayeux tapestry**, stitched in England after the Norman conquest, showing William the Conqueror crossing to England with men and horses.

the SAVOY CONFERENCE and was deprived for Nonconformity in 1662.

Bayeux tapestry An embroidered hanging, over 230 feet (70 metres) long, illustrating in 'strip-cartoon' form the prelude and events of the NORMAN CONQUEST up to HASTINGS, from a Norman propagandist viewpoint. Probably commissioned by ODO OF BAYEUX and manufactured in England before 1070, it is uniquely important both historically and artistically. *See* ills. pp. 100, 208.

Beaker culture *see* AVEBURY; PREHISTORIC BRITAIN

Beaton, David 1494–1546. Made cardinal in 1538, Beaton succeeded his uncle as archbishop of St Andrews in 1539 and was appointed chancellor and papal legate in 1543. The effective ruler of Scotland during the regency of Arran, he vigorously championed Catholicism and the French alliance until his murder.

Beaufort, Cardinal Henry *c.*1377–1447. Bishop of Winchester from 1404. He acted periodically as chancellor under Henry IV (his half-brother), Henry V and Henry VI, when he opposed HUMPHREY's aggrandisement as 'protector' (*see* BATS, PARLIAMENT OF) and belligerent foreign policy, working instead for peace with France. Immensely rich, his influence was enhanced by huge loans to the government.

Beaufort family The descendants of John of Gaunt's liaison with Katharine Swynford, they were legitimized after the couple married (1396) but debarred by statute from the royal succession. *See* ROSES, WARS OF THE.

Beaverbrook, lord 1879–1964. A Canadian-born politician, press baron and owner of the *Daily Express. See* NEWSPAPERS.

Becket, St Thomas 1118–70. The son of a Norman merchant of London, Becket trained as an ecclesiastical lawyer and rose through the household of Archbishop Theobald of Canterbury to become successively the inseparable friend and chancellor (1154–62) and inveterate enemy and archbishop (1162–70) of Henry II. Martyred in his own cathedral at Canterbury (29 December 1170), and canonized (1173), he speedily became the most venerated saint in England, if not in western Europe. Although he was officially discredited at the Reformation, his complex character continues to fascinate authors and playwrights.

Bede, the Venerable 673–735. A MONK of Jarrow, Northumbria, Bede was famous in his lifetime for writings on scripture and science, but is best known as a historian, especially for his *Ecclesiastical History of the English People* (731). The renowned school at York, founded by his pupils, gave his work a European audience.

Bedford, John, duke of 1389–1435. Younger brother of Henry V, Bedford acted during the minority of Henry VI as regent and commander in France, where he pushed English conquests to their fullest extent. His influence also helped to maintain political stability at home, and its removal contributed greatly towards the decline of Lancastrian government. *See* BATS, PARLIAMENT OF; VERNEUIL, BATTLE OF.

Beeching report 1963. Lord Beeching's plan for the rationalization of the railways proposed closure of over a third of the system, cuts in stock and manpower, and extensive containerization. It gained Harold Macmillan's goverment hostility in Scotland and rural areas, while its proposals to attract more freight were only a limited success.

Beggars' Summons *see* REFORMATION

Belgae *see* PREHISTORIC BRITAIN

Benedictines Founded by St Benedict (480–550), the Black Monks are the oldest and largest Latin monastic order and, until the collective reforms of the Cluniacs, Carthusians and Cistercians, stood

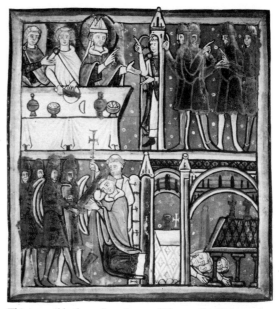

This is possibly the earliest picture of Thomas **Becket**'s murder (shown bottom left). The 12th-century manuscript from which it is taken then repeats the earliest account of the murder, by John of Salisbury.

The opening page of **Bede**'s *Ecclesiastical History*, describing the geography of Britain. The illuminated letters (left) convey the Latin for 'Britain, formerly known as Albion'.

alone. Brought to England by AUGUSTINE, they were strengthened under Theodore, revived by Dunstan and much reinforced at the Norman conquest, whereafter Margaret and her sons introduced them to Scotland.

Bentham, Jeremy 1748–1832. A wealthy legal reformer, Bentham attempted to systematize English law to meet his 'Benthamite' or Utilitarian principles (*see* UTILITARIANISM). He greatly influenced the MILLS, CHADWICK and Victorian middle-class economic and social reform.

Berlin, congress of June–July 1878. This revised the treaty of San Stefano (March), in which the Russians gained territory from the Turks as a result of intervention to protect Bulgarian and other Christian subjects (*see* BULGARIAN ATROCITIES). The alternative was war between Disraeli's government (the ally of the Turks) and the Russians, who had to concede some of their gains. Britain gained control over Cyprus, and Balkan politics were stabilized until the Balkan wars (1912–13). Although this was Disraeli's greatest success, Gladstone's agitation against his 'imperialism' paid off in his MIDLOTHIAN CAMPAIGN.

Bernicia An Anglian kingdom founded by Ida in 547 (perhaps from earlier FOEDERATI settlements) as a precarious coastal foothold around Bamburgh, Northumberland. After near extinction by British Rheged, from *c.* 593 it expanded rapidly (under Aethelferth) into Lothian, Cumbria and Yorkshire, annexing Deira (604) to form Northumbria.

Berwick, treaty of 1560. A treaty of mutual defence between Elizabeth I and the lords of the CONGREGATION directed against French intervention in Scotland. English ships and troops subsequently assisted in the siege of Leith and remained in Scotland until the treaty of EDINBURGH (1560).

Berwick-on-Tweed Originally Scottish, this important border port was taken by Edward I (1296), betrayed to Robert Bruce (1318), unsuccessfully besieged by Edward II (1319) and retaken by Edward III after HALIDON HILL (1333). Ceded to Scotland by Henry VI (1461), it was recovered in 1483 and, under Elizabeth I, was defended by bastioned artillery fortifications which still survive.

Bevan, Aneurin 1897–1960. A Welsh miner and left-wing Labour MP for Ebbw Vale from 1929, as minister of health (1945–51) Bevan established the

Aneurin **Bevan** (left) chats to a reporter in March 1955, during a period of intense conflict in the Labour party, after an attempt to expel him had failed.

national health service (1948) and carried the National Assistance Act which established much of the structure of the modern WELFARE STATE. In the 1950s he led a left-wing group, the 'Bevanites'.

Beveridge, Walter, viscount 1879–1963. Introduced to social problems through Toynbee Hall and the WEBBS, Beveridge joined the board of trade (1909–15), introducing labour exchanges, and was later involved with munitions and RATIONING (1916–18). Head of the London School of Economics (1918–36) he then returned to government (1940) and surveyed social security, reporting in December 1942. *See* ECONOMY, THE; WELFARE STATE.

Bevin, Ernest 1881–1951. Born in poverty in Somerset, Bevin rose to lead the dock-workers and create the great Transport and General Workers' Union (*see* TRADE UNIONISM). As leader of the reformist wing of the TUC (1930s), he favoured Keynesian economic remedies (*see* KEYNES, JOHN MAYNARD) and rearmament against Germany. Churchill made him minister of labour (1940–5), when he introduced civilian and female con-

Ernest **Bevin**'s message as minister of labour. After August 1940, while America remained neutral, exports continued to be important in the war effort.

scription and liaised closely with the unions. He was foreign secretary in Attlee's government (1945–51) and became a major protagonist of the western alliance.

Bible, English Though LOLLARD manuscripts circulated earlier, the 1st printed English scriptures were TYNDALE's New Testament (1526) and Pentateuch (1530). Tyndale deeply influenced subsequent translations, including those of COVERDALE (1535), the Matthew Bible (1537), the official Great Bible (1539), the Geneva or Breeches Bible (1560) and the Authorized Version (1611). Modern translations include the Revised Version (1881–5) and the New English Bible (1961–70).

Bill of Rights 1689. Bill enacting the DECLARATION OF RIGHTS. It maintained that James VII and II had abdicated, settled the succession on William III and Mary II, excluded Roman Catholics from the English throne and declared illegal various grievances, notably the exercise of the DISPENSING power and the keeping of a standing army in peacetime. *See* GLORIOUS REVOLUTION.

Birinus, St *see* CHURCH, PRE-REFORMATION

Bishop (Greek *episkopos*, overseer). An office of New Testament origin, known in Britain since the 4th century (*see* CHURCH, PRE-REFORMATION). Bishops rule DIOCESES, and have exclusive powers of confirmation and clerical ordination. Considered inimical to Puritanism, they were attacked during the 17th century, when abolished temporarily in the church of England and permanently in the church of Scotland.

Bishops' Book *see* REFORMATION

Bishops' registers Containing the principal acts of bishops (including ordinations, letters, deeds, trials of heretics and copies of wills), registers provide an invaluable source of social and political as well as ecclesiastical history. Many have been published, especially in England by the Canterbury and York Society.

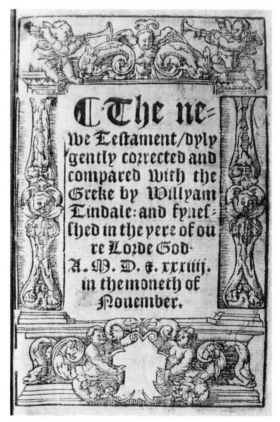

Tyndale's New Testament was the first English **bible** to be printed: the title-page of its first revision, 1534.

Charles I's religious innovations in Scotland provoked the National Covenant and **Bishops' wars**. Contemporary engraving by William Marshal.

Two **Black and Tans**, so called because of their uniform, half Royal Irish Constabulary black, half military khaki, apprehend a 'suspect', during the Irish 'troubles' of 1919–21.

Bishops' wars 1639–40. Campaigns of CHARLES I, intended to reimpose episcopacy and the prayer book in Scotland. The 1639 campaign was bloodless. Following the Short parliament, a 2nd campaign (1640) brought defeat at Newburn and the negotiation of the treaty of RIPON.

Black Acts 1584. In the aftermath of the raid of RUTHVEN, the Acts reasserted James VI's jurisdiction over the Scottish church, forbidding unauthorized church assemblies, discharging judgments of the church not approved by king and parliament, banning sermons in contempt of royal policy and laying down an episcopal form of church government.

Black and Tans A name given to emergency recruits to the Royal Irish Constabulary (1920), who wore army khaki breeches with black RIC tunics. They, and the 'auxiliary division', gained an unenviable reputation the next year for violence and brutality in their campaign against the Irish Republican Army. *See* IRISH CONSTITUTIONAL CRISIS.

Black Death A name coined in the 19th century for the pandemic of bubonic PLAGUE (spread by rat-fleas) and its directly infectious and almost invariably fatal pneumonic variant, which probably originated in central Asia and, after sweeping across Europe, invaded Britain in summer 1348. It reached its peak in England during 1349, affected Scotland (apparently less severely) in 1349–50, and had generally subsided by 1351. Modern estimates of its death-toll, based as they are on unreliable or patchily preserved records, range from 50% of the population down to 5%, but for England (where Lincolnshire, East Anglia, London, and towns in general were apparently the areas worst hit) a figure around 30% is widely accepted.

The immediate effect of this drop in population was a labour shortage, resulting in wage increases and increased labour mobility, while the price of foodstuffs fell from lack of demand and that of manufactured goods rose because of the mortality among skilled craftsmen. Government attempts to stabilize the situation culminated in the statute of LABOURERS. The long-term effects are harder to assess: the late medieval decline of feudalism, the growth of LEASEHOLD tenure and the general desertion of less fertile lands were all pre-existing tendencies lent impetus rather than initiated by the disaster. (P. Ziegler, *The Black Death*, 1969.)

Black Prince The nickname of Edward of Woodstock (1330–76), prince of Wales, eldest son of Edward III and hero of the hundred years' war. He led the vanguard at CRÉCY, but his greatest independent triumphs were his spectacular CHE-VAUCHÉES (1355–6) and his victory at POITIERS, Created prince of Aquitaine (1362), he gained another victory at NÁJERA, but antagonized his subjects by overtaxing them, and smirched his chivalric reputation by the sack of Limoges (1370).

Blackshirts The dress and name adopted by members of Oswald Mosley's British Union of FASCISTS (1932–6). After battles in London's east end, such uniforms were banned by the Public Order Act (1936).

Blackstone, Sir William *see* LAW

Blake, Robert 1599–1657. An officer in the parliamentary army and MP for Bridgewater, Blake was appointed 'general at sea' in 1649. In successful actions against royalist privateers (*see* PRIVATEERING), the Dutch, the Barbary corsairs and the Spanish, he did much to develop the pattern of future English naval tactics.

Blanketeers Radical Manchester HAND-LOOM WEAVERS who planned to march to London in 1817 (carrying their blankets) in order to petition against the repressive measures of SIDMOUTH. Alarmist rumours as to their intentions led to the arrest of some 200 blanketeers and the march was dispersed in Cheshire.

Blatchford, Robert 1851–1943. A Yorkshire socialist and journalist. His weekly *Clarion* (1891) and such pamphlets as *Merrie England* (1893) greatly encouraged grass-roots socialist agitation and organization. A strong anti-Liberal, his xenophobia carried him away from the Labour party after 1900.

Blenheim, battle of 13 August 1704. A battle of the war of the Spanish succession (*see* MARLBOROUGH'S WARS). British, Dutch and German troops under Marlborough marched from the Netherlands to Bavaria to join Prince Eugene's Austrians and inflicted a crushing defeat on French and Bavarian forces, thereby clearing southern Germany of the French and safeguarding Vienna from attack.

Blenheim palace A Baroque palace, presented by the nation to John Churchill, duke of Marlborough,

The **Black Prince**: gilt copper effigy in Canterbury cathedral, *c.* 1377–80.

Blenheim palace, by John Vanbrugh, from the south-east.

and built by Sir John Vanbrugh in 1705–22. Elaborate formal gardens of the early 18th century by Henry Wise partly survive. The landscaped park is by Capability Brown.

Bloody Assizes 1685. Following MONMOUTH'S REBELLION, Chief Justice Jeffreys rode the western ASSIZE circuit sentencing an estimated 150 rebels to death and some 800 more to transportation. Jeffreys's brutal conduct of the trials and the profits subsequently made by courtiers from the transportations further alienated the population from James VII and II's rule.

Police action on **Bloody Sunday** was presented as the 'Defence of Trafalgar Square' by the *Illustrated London News*, 19 November 1887.

The relief of Mafeking in the 2nd **Boer war** (17 May 1900) led to riotous celebrations. This contemporary illustration in the *Graphic* celebrates the defender of Mafeking, Col. Baden-Powell, in Piccadilly Circus, London. 'Mafficking' entered the language.

Bloody Sunday 13 November 1887. A riot in Trafalgar Square, London, which had started as a demonstration of the unemployed, and in which 1 demonstrator, Arthur Linnell, was killed. Morris, Burns and R.B. Cunninghame-Graham were among those involved. It may have had some part in stimulating research and action by BOOTH and others on working-class living conditions in London.

Blue Books A term for the accounts and reports to parliament from commissioners, public offices, royal commissions and select committees.

Boadicea *see* BOUDICA

Board of trade A board of 8 salaried members to formulate commercial and colonial policy was established by parliament (1696) to replace earlier advisory committees of the privy COUNCIL. Colonial affairs were separated off in 1768. Abolished by Burke in 1780, the board was re-established in 1784 and remained in being until the 1960s.

Boer wars The 1st war (1880–1) was provoked by Disraeli's annexation of the Boer republics of South Africa (the Transvaal and the Orange Free State) in 1877. In 1880, following the failure of attempts to repeal this, the Boers under Paul Kruger defeated the British and secured limited self-government.

After the discovery of gold and diamonds in the Transvaal, tension between the Dutch farmers and British 'uitlanders' mounted, aggravated by episodes such as the JAMESON RAID and the policy of MILNER, the British governor of the Cape. A Boer attack on Natal and Cape Colony (October 1899) started the 2nd war (1899–1902). British forces at Ladysmith, Mafeking and Kimberley were surrounded but counter-attacks (1900) by ROBERTS relieved them. From September 1900 until the peace of Vereeniging (May 1902) there was a prolonged guerilla war fought by Boer 'commandos', with the British putting civilians in 'concentration camps'. *See* PRO-BOERS.

Boleyn, Anne 1507–36. Anne was secretly married to Henry VIII in 1533, being already pregnant, and was crowned queen upon the annulment of Henry's 1st marriage. She bore ELIZABETH in 1533, but lost favour when she failed to produce a son and was beheaded on trumped-up charges of multiple adultery.

Bolingbroke, Henry *see* HENRY IV

Bolingbroke, Henry St John, viscount 1678–1751. A Tory minister under Anne, dismissed for JACOBITE sympathies (1714) and impeached (1715) for his part in the treaty of UTRECHT, Bolingbroke fled to France and became the Old Pretender's secretary. Returning in 1723, he adopted the role of Tory elder statesman and political theorist.

Bombing From 1917 bombing was the main raison d'être of the ROYAL AIR FORCE, which regarded it as a deadly and demoralizing weapon. In the 1930s, however, fighter performance radically improved, aided by RADAR. After 1937 policy was switched to fighter production, in time for the battle of Britain. However, Churchill's advisers, notably LINDE-MANN, assumed that bombing of German civilians would still produce greater breakdown. Bombing inaccuracy (barely a third of bombs hit within 5 miles of their target) suggested that only 'carpet' bombing was practicable. Although it was opposed both on moral and strategic grounds, the British persisted with it and 55,000 aircrew were lost.

Bond of association 1584. A pledge to revenge any attempt to assassinate Elizabeth I and place another person on the throne, directed against MARY QUEEN OF SCOTS. The bond was sealed by thousands of magistrates and gentlemen and formed the basis of the Act for the Queen's Surety (1584).

Bond servants 17th-century emigrants (also known as indentured servants) bound by indenture to work in the American colonies for a term of years in return for their passage, keep and a payment on gaining their freedom. This system provided labour for the plantation colonies before the widespread introduction of negro slaves.

Bonnie Prince Charlie *see* STUART, PRINCE CHARLES EDWARD

Bonshommes *see* AUGUSTINIAN CANONS

Book of Common Order Composed for the worship of the congregation of English exiles in Geneva (1550s), the book was brought to Scotland by KNOX and served as the liturgy of the church of Scotland from 1562 until the 1640s.

Book of Common Prayer The liturgy of the church of England. Prepared by CRANMER, the 1st prayer book (1549) was a masterpiece of doctrinal compromise. The second (1552) was more clearly Protestant in doctrine and ceremonies and was

The title-page of the **Book of Common Prayer**, 1549.

largely preserved in the Elizabethan book (1559). Further small modifications were made in 1604 and 1662.

Book of Sports Originally issued by James VI and I (1618) and later reissued by Charles I (1633), the book officially sanctioned traditional sports and festivities on Sundays after divine service. English Puritans were outraged by such sabbath-breaking and many ministers disobeyed Charles's order to read the book aloud to their congregations.

Books of Discipline The 1st book, drafted by KNOX (1560), provided for church government in Scotland by diocesan superintendents, ministers and elders and proposed schemes of education, poor relief and moral discipline. The second, by MELVILLE (1574), laid down a thoroughgoing Presbyterian system and asserted the kirk's independence of the crown. Neither book was wholly implemented.

Books of Homilies Volumes of officially approved sermons to be read aloud in Anglican churches in order to overcome the problems of extravagant, disaffected or inadequate preaching. The original book of 12 homilies by CRANMER, Harpsfield and Bonner was issued in 1547. An expanded version was issued by PARKER (1562).

Books of Orders 'Books' of emergency regulations were commonly issued to justices of the peace in years of dearth by Elizabethan and early Stuart governments. The most famous book, that of 1631, inaugurated a general tightening of local administration, with particular reference to the enforcement of the POOR LAWS.

Booth, Charles 1840–1916. From a well-connected Liverpool shipowning family (Beatrice Webb was his cousin), Booth pioneered statistical social investigation with his *Life and Labour of the People in London* (1891–1903) and, though politically right-wing, agitated for OLD AGE PENSIONS.

Booth, William *see* SALVATION ARMY

Booth's rising 1659. A royalist rising in Cheshire during the political turmoil preceding the Restoration, led by Sir George Booth. The rising was rapidly suppressed by Lambert at Winnington Bridge.

Boroughbridge, battle of 16–17 March 1322. Thomas of LANCASTER and his supporters, retreating from Edward II towards Scotland, were prevented from crossing the Ure by the Cumbrian levies under Sir Andrew Harclay. On the 17th a pursuing royalist force completed their encirclement and forced them to surrender, Lancaster being subsequently executed.

Boston tea party 16 December 1773. In protest against the EAST INDIA COMPANY's monopoly of tea exports to the American colonies, a group of colonists disguised as Mohawks boarded 3 tea ships and dumped their cargo in Boston harbour. The COERCIVE ACTS passed in reprisal provoked the meeting of the 1st continental congress.

Bosworth, battle of 22 August 1485. One of the most decisive of British battles. Henry Tudor's heterogeneous force of English, French and Welsh attacked Richard III's much larger army near Market Bosworth, Leics., with a force under Tudor's stepfather, Lord Stanley, equivocally looking on. One of Richard's divisions (under the Percies) refused to fight and, with the issue in doubt, he led a desperate charge at Tudor, whereupon the Stanleys intervened and killed him. The royalists fled, and Tudor was acclaimed as Henry VII on the battlefield (which is now open to the public).

Bothwell, James Hepburn, 4th earl of ?1535–78. A Scottish border magnate who, though a Protestant, supported MARY OF GUISE (1559–60). He later found favour with MARY QUEEN OF SCOTS, and married her (1567) after DARNLEY's murder, in which he was involved. Bothwell subsequently escaped to Scandinavia, but was imprisoned for life in Denmark.

Boudica Queen of the ICENI, Boudica's client kingdom was forcibly annexed to Roman Britain on the death of her husband (61), when she and her daughters were brutally treated. She then led her own tribe, with the Trinovantes and others, in a bloody revolt, ambushing Cerialis and part of the 9th legion and destroying Colchester, London and Verulamium with their 70,000 inhabitants. Her eventual defeat by Suetonius Paullinus (perhaps near Towcester, Northants.) was followed by a period of Roman repression.

Boulogne campaign 1544. An expedition under Henry VIII which enlarged the CALAIS bridgehead by capturing Boulogne. Though it was agreed by the treaty of Campe that the town would be restored to France in 1554, Henry spent vast sums on its refortification. It was eventually relinquished in 1550.

Bourgeoisie *see* CLASS

Bouvines, battle of *see* JOHN

Bovate (Lat. *bos*, an ox). In the feudal period, a measure of land, being the area that could be ploughed with a single ox in a year: hence one-eighth of a CARUCATE or 10–15 acres. It was also called an ox-gang. *See* VIRGATE.

Bow Street runners A force of constables established after 1748 by the Bow Street magistrates and brothers Henry and Sir John Fielding to check crime, in particular highway robbery, in and around the capital. Their activities were later extended over the whole country. They were superseded by the metropolitan POLICE (1829).

Boyd Orr, John, lord 1880–1971. A Scots-born agriculturalist, Boyd Orr's work on the nutritive value of foods added a new dimension to the study of poverty between the wars. After a brief spell as an Independent MP (1945) he became director of the United Nations' Food and Agriculture Organization (FAO).

The battle of the **Boyne** marked the defeat of James VII and II's cause in Ireland and the triumph of the Glorious Revolution. Contemporary oil painting by Jan Wyck.

Boyne, battle of the 11 July 1690. The victorious crossing of the Boyne by British, Dutch, Danish and Huguenot troops under William III against the resistance of James VII and II's Irish and French army. James retreated in good order to Dublin but, despairing too soon, fled to France, leaving William to consolidate the conquest of Ireland.

Bradlaugh, Charles 1833–91. After a short army career, Bradlaugh went into law and radical politics as a militant atheist. Elected Liberal MP for Northampton (1880), he refused to take the oath and was ejected. Subsequently elected and excluded twice until the law was changed, he was allowed to affirm and be admitted in 1886.

Brander, pass of, battle of the *see* ROBERT BRUCE

Breadalbane, John Campbell, 1st earl of 1635–1717. A singularly devious and untrustworthy politician, Breadalbane was responsible for bringing the highland chiefs to terms with William III's government (1691). Later suspected of JACOBITE sympathies, he maintained a very ambivalent stance during the rebellion of 1715.

Breda, declaration of 1660. Charles II's declaration on the eve of the RESTORATION, in which he undertook to grant a general pardon and liberty of conscience, subject to parliament's approval. He further promised to consent to parliament's determination of the land settlement and to the payment and future employment of Monck's army.

Brétigny, treaty of May 1360. This ended the 1st part of the HUNDRED YEARS' WAR. In return for renouncing his claim to the French crown, Edward III received full sovereignty over a much extended Aquitaine, Poitou and lands round Calais. It was never properly ratified by either party, and the resultant peace endured less than a decade.

Bretwalda The poetic title ('ruler of Britain') given by the Anglo-Saxon Chronicle to kings recognized as overlords of the English south of the Humber, chronologically AELLE of Sussex; CEAWLIN of Wessex; AETHELBERT of Kent; RAEDWALD of East Anglia; EDWIN, OSWALD and OSWIU of Northumbria; and EGBERT of Wessex. Wulfhere (657–74), Aethelbald (716–57) and OFFA of Mercia should properly be included.

Brigantes A large but loosely knit pastoral tribe, whose lands stretched from the Mersey-Humber line northward to southern Scotland. They were conquered by CERIALIS (71–4) and AGRICOLA (79), and their southern lands subsequently formed a CIVITAS centred on Isurium Brigantum (Aldborough, north Yorks.).

Bright, John 1811–89. A Radical carpet-manufacturer from Rochdale, Bright entered politics as a spokesman of the ANTI-CORN-LAW LEAGUE. A Quaker and leading orator, he became the most prominent advocate of democratic reform and the leading spokesman of the unenfranchised working class during the struggle for the 2nd REFORM BILL. His subsequent career was a failure.

A trades procession carrying a banner dedicated to John **Bright**, salutes him in the window of the local board offices, Birmingham, in 1883. Contemporary engraving.

Brighton royal pavilion The Brighton home of George IV when prince regent, rebuilt after 1811 to designs by John Nash as an Indian palace with onion domes, pavilion roofs, pinnacles and minarets and lavish interiors in the Chinese style. It ceased to be used by royalty in 1845, but was restored to its original condition after 1945.

Bristol riots 1831. The most destructive of a series of riots – also in Derby and Nottingham – in autumn 1831, following the rejection of the 1st REFORM BILL by the house of lords. The town hall and bishop's palace were burned down. This violence suggested that further opposition to reform might provoke revolution.

British empire The 1st shift in English foreign policy from European to overseas acquisitions came in the reign of Henry VII with the expeditions of the Genoese explorers, John and Sebastian Cabot (1497–8 and 1509), to find a western passage to the Far East. They failed in that, but did locate the Newfoundland cod fishery which provided a lucrative goal. But exploration remained dormant until revived by the war with Spain, the prime imperial power, in Elizabeth I's reign. Chartered trading companies were set up to trade with Turkey, Russia and the East Indies, the coast of North America was further explored and the 1st colonies ineffectually established (Newfoundland 1583, Virginia 1585). Despite Spanish opposition, this period also saw the beginnings of the slave trade between Africa and the West Indies (*see* SLAVERY), though this was overshadowed by the spectacular piratical expeditions of DRAKE and RALEIGH.

By 1607 a successful colony was established by a London company at Jamestown in Virginia; it was shortly followed by other more autonomous Puritan settlements further north, the exploitation of the Newfoundland fisheries and, nearer home, the start of the plantation of IRELAND. Again European rivalries with Spain, France and Holland were crucial and, as they developed, both under the Stuarts and Oliver Cromwell, the lineages of the mercantilist empire became apparent.

The goal of mercantilist policy, which held good until the early 19th century, was to secure privileged access to as much territory as possible, both as a source of raw material and, more importantly, as markets for home-produced or at least re-exported goods. This required restrictive legislation and a powerful navy. Initially the enemy was Holland, whose Dutch East India Company was the greatest trader of 17th-century Europe. Ascendancy over her had been established by 1674 (*see* DUTCH WARS),

Brighton royal pavilion: most bizarre of Regency buildings, designed by John Nash in the Indian style.

A reactionary is singed by popular protest in the **Bristol riots**. The real threat of these riots was even more serious than this cartoon of 1831 suggests.

and this was followed by an attempt to force access to the Spanish colonies, ultimately recognized as successful at the treaty of UTRECHT (1714). By this time Britain had acquired most of the seaboard coastline of North America, and the valuable Caribbean island of Jamaica, together with stations in west Africa, mainly for slaves, and 'factories' on the Indian coast.

From then on, most of her conflict was with Bourbon France, both in Canada and in India. By 1763 she had expelled the French from the St Lawrence basin and established dominance in India, although the EAST INDIA COMPANY still remained the agent of government. This was, however, soon to be followed by the eclipse of the 'Ist British empire' with the secession of the American colonists (1773–83), provoked into opposition by the requirement that they trade via Britain, and encouraged and sustained by the French (see AMERICAN INDEPENDENCE). The compensating discovery of Australasia by COOK and others (1768–79) was not then exploited.

Franco-British conflict reached its apotheosis in the Revolutionary and NAPOLEONIC WARS (1793–1815). Ultimately this placed France at a double disadvantage by destroying her coast-based industries and adding Dutch South Africa to Britain's overseas possessions. Henceforth Britain's major European opponent was to be Russia, whose expansion south and east threatened the growing British dominions in India.

Between 1786 and 1800 British administration in India was reformed by Charles Cornwallis (1738–1805) as governor-general. The monopolistic trade of 'John Company', although still powerful, was gradually being eclipsed by that of the government and the private traders. One result of this was a desire to modernize and anglicize Indian society – shared by many Indians themselves – which resulted in the suppression of such customs as were judged barbaric, the implementation of Utilitarian reforms (see UTILITARIANISM) in law and land, the construction of roads and waterways. This was also accompanied by the annexation of native states, the extension of British authority into neighbouring areas like Afghanistan and Burma, and an increasing preoccupation with communications between Britain and India.

The abandonment of the slave trade (1807) and the freeing of slaves within the empire (1833) removed one prop of the old mercantile empire. FREE TRADE, adopted in stages (1786–1846), removed the basis for the factories and the chartered companies, as well as abolishing the NAVIGATION ACTS. At the same time the progress of political reform in the settlements still under British rule was more rapid than in Britain itself, with the passage of the Canada Act (1791) giving elective self-government to Upper and Lower Canada, and setting up a precedent for such self-government in other colonies. This coincided with growing emigration, especially from Scotland and Ireland, and in due course the old colonial oligarchies, the practice of 'transporting' criminals and the policy of the colonial office in London were challenged by this influx, eager for land and democratic self-government, and impatient of native rights. The fate of the Red Indians, the Maoris and the Australian Bushmen at their hands was a sad one, despite the sympathetic involvement of the colonial office; the one threatened people that 'got away' were Boer farmers from the Cape, who trekked north to the Transvaal (1836–7).

For most of the 19th century there was no great governmental enthusiasm for territorial expansion. Even where politicians approved of the spread of the white race, they viewed with equanimity the self-governing colonies going their own way. Disraeli dismissed 'these damned colonies' as

An advertisement for Pears soap which suggests that the manufacturers are trying to cash in at home on imperial sentiment. *Illustrated London News*, 1887.

"NEW CROWNS FOR OLD ONES!"

(ALADDIN *adapted*.)

Disraeli's policy of imperialism came to a climax in 1876 when, on his advice, Queen Victoria assumed the title of empress of India. Tenniel's disapproving cartoon in *Punch*, 15 April 1876, portrays Disraeli as Aladdin's wicked uncle, Abanazar.

'millstones round our necks'. But, despite the fact that the ideology of free trade was similarly negative about colonies, expansion continued, with the acquisition of further trading concessions and posts which soon acquired additional importance as telegraph and coaling stations, such as ADEN (1839) and Hong Kong (*see* OPIUM WARS) in 1842. This 'imperialism of free trade' was further enhanced by philanthropic and strategic motives, such as the missionary efforts of the churches, accelerated by the Evangelical revival, and by traditional diplomatic obligations, such as keeping the Turkish empire intact.

From the middle of the century, however, a new spirit began to make itself felt. This was partly created by the INDIAN MUTINY (1857), itself provoked by the headlong modernization of the country, and it was accelerated by the new imperial policies of Disraeli in the 1870s. The new ideal of 'trusteeship' implied more toleration of native traditions and a more complex attitude to their development, partly founded on somewhat racialis-

tic generalizations from DARWIN's theory of evolution. This concept of imperialism as 'the white man's burden', in Kipling's famous phrase (1899), characterized the SCRAMBLE FOR AFRICA (1880s) and the imposition of European rule on China. It was soon challenged on the left by an economic explanation first advanced by J.A.Hobson (1858–1940) in *Imperialism* (1902), and later elaborated by Lenin. This argued that the low wages paid by industrial capitalism to its workers inhibited the growth of home markets and investment, and the profits of industry were thus more and more forced abroad into 'underdeveloped' territories which the new tariffs being imposed by European states were intended to convert into exclusive trading areas. From this worldwide spread of capitalist conflict, international tensions and the final breakdown of world war would spring. The theory scarcely met the facts of the case, as most European overseas investment went to areas such as the USA, which were not under colonial rule, but it proved a powerful reinforcement of the Russian Bolsheviks' case that their backward country had in 1914 been drawn into the vortex of the crisis of world capitalism.

The 2nd BOER WAR (1899–1902) was made the occasion of Hobson's attack, but the presence of contingents from Canada and Australia in South Africa showed the solidarity of the English-speaking dominions, as they became in 1907. However, this solidarity did not extend to the sharing of defence costs or to much support for ideas of TARIFF REFORM, as many of the white dominions had new industries which they wanted to shield from British competition. In fact, the 1st steps in the retreat from empire were already being taken as World War I broke out. Even in India a national congress had been established (1885) to agitate for responsible government, and the Liberal government's reforms (1909) had conceded a degree of indirectly elected authority. The wartime sale of investments and the cutting-off of British technology meant that many commercial links were loosened, while the struggle of the Irish to free themselves from British rule (*see* IRISH CONSTITUTIONAL CRISIS) and the Russian revolution provided models for the leaders of liberation movements in the Asian and African colonies. The Montagu-Chelmsford report (1918) advocated qualified self-government for India under a federal structure. After several non-violent campaigns by GANDHI, this was enacted in a modified form by the Government of India Act (1935). The statute of WESTMINSTER (1931) had prescribed the relationships between Britain and the self-governing dominions (Canada, Australia, New Zealand, South Africa and the Irish Free State) and introduced the concept of the 'Commonwealth of Nations'. In the following year the agreements at the OTTAWA CONFERENCE introduced a very limited degree of IMPERIAL PREFERENCE.

The post-World War I period saw the British empire at its fullest extent, as it gained, as 'trustee' under League of Nations mandate, former German and Turkish territories in Africa and the Middle East. In Africa the traditional trusteeship approach was upheld, with Africans given somewhat greater authority over local administration through the system of 'indirect rule'. Although Egypt in the north gained independence in 1922, the next year saw the sanctioning of white rule in Rhodesia (*see* RHODESIAN CRISIS). The mandate system also brought its problems in the Middle East, where the Balfour declaration (1917) had allowed Jewish immigration to Palestine, creating tension and violence between the Jewish incomers and the Palestinians, to whom the British were also pledged (*see* PALESTINE QUESTION).

During World War II the dominions came to the assistance of the UK with unanimity, except in India where Gandhi's pacifist programme had its effect. But the setbacks suffered, especially at the hands of the Japanese (*see* SINGAPORE, FALL OF), amounted to a notice to quit. Paradoxically, Hitler was keener to see the continuation of the empire (on racialist grounds) than was Roosevelt. While Hitler deprecated attempts to subvert the empire, the Americans were determined that the old order should not be restored, especially in the Far East. However, after the war, it was doubtful whether Britain had the resources to insist on anything else. As a result of a long-standing Labour pledge, India became independent (1947), although growing Hindu-Moslem tension led to the establishment of 2 states, India and the Moslem republic of Pakistan. Shortly afterwards Britain made an enforced withdrawal from Palestine, and was replaced by the United States as the main western presence in the Mediterranean.

Labour's colonial policy in Africa and the West Indies, however, was conservative, with economic development, achieved through agricultural improvement (*see* GROUND NUTS SCHEME), and regional federation given priority over self-government. Despite some armed 'liberation' campaigns in the early 1950s (*see* MAU MAU), only after the SUEZ CRISIS (1956) did the weakness of Britain's world position become apparent. Harold Macmillan's government instituted a policy of rapid decolonization. Less bloody than the contemporary French and Belgian

withdrawals from Africa, this left the new successor states to cope with the arbitrary boundaries and governing practices of colonial rule, which led frequently to a suspension of the model 'democratic' constitutions bequeathed by Britain, and to a savage civil war in Nigeria, the largest of the former British territories. The increasing power of the coloured peoples within the 'new commonwealth' led to the withdrawal of South Africa (1961), and her unsuccessful war with India caused Pakistan to leave (1972). Britain's entry into the European Economic Community (1973) caused her relations with Australia and New Zealand to weaken, while Canada was itself increasingly divided by the rise of French-Canadian separatism. Even in the new commonwealth, ideals of regionalism or Pan-African socialism were rapidly eroded by local disputes, the rise of despotic regimes (such as that of the horrendous 'Field-Marshal' Amin in Uganda), and the growing aggressiveness of Islam. By 1980, where any unity remained, it was cultural and educational rather than political.

British North America Act 1867. Passed by the Derby-Disraeli ministry, this set up Canada as a federation – initially of Quebec, Ontario, Nova Scotia and New Brunswick.

British schools Schools providing basic education in literacy and religious knowledge for the children of the poor. Founded after 1814 by the Nonconformist British and Foreign Bible Society, they employed the monitor system of Andrew Bell whereby older pupils taught the younger children.

Brittany *see* HENRY II; HUNDRED YEARS' WAR; LANCASTER, HENRY, DUKE OF

Broad Churchmen A term used to describe Anglicans who believe that the formulas of religious belief ought to be as flexible and comprehensive as possible, in order to justify the church as an establishment. They have been the dominant élite of the church of England since the 1870s.

Broadcasting An empire-wide system of wireless stations was set up before 1914 and by 1920 broadcasting for entertainment was possible. Despite this, the post office banned public broadcasting until January 1922, when Marconi was allowed to broadcast on 2LO. At the end of the year a private monopoly set up the British Broadcasting Company under Colonel John Reith (1889–1971). Both Reith and the government put high standards of performance and a high moral 'tone' before commercial success. In December 1926 the company, based since April 1923 at Savoy Hill, was nationalized as the British Broadcasting Corporation.

Reith, as director-general, was responsible to a board of governors (representing the political and religious establishment), nominated by the prime minister. His BBC was highly centralized in funding (by licence fees) and programme control. But it introduced new technologies, such as the powerful transmitters of its empire (later world) service (started 1937), pioneered public television transmission (November 1936), acted as a cultural patron and established its own orchestras and drama companies. Radio licences numbered 1·6 million in 1925, double that by 1930, and nearly 9 million in 1940.

During World War II, television was taken off the air and the regions suspended. But the BBC became a crucial alternative to scarce newsprint as a propaganda medium at home and abroad and – through its audience research department – as a means of consulting public opinion. The 'nationalization' of culture which took place also raised standards, and a 'quality' channel, the Third Programme (now Radio 3), was set up (1946) to supplement the undemanding fare of the 'Light Programme' (Radio 1 and 2) and the regional 'Home Service' (Radio 4).

Television transmissions resumed in London (June 1946), and spread to the midlands (1949), the north (1951), and Scotland (1952), being given a major boost by the coronation the following year. (TV licences numbered 344,00 in 1950 and 4 million in 1955.) But competition was on its way. A skilful

Public **broadcasting** by radio did not begin until 1922: this Pye Twin Triple Portable model of 1930 was probably one of the earliest to be mass-produced.

pressure-group campaign led to the setting up of commercial TV by Act of 1954, under the Independent Television Authority. A network was franchised 1955–8. Newspapers, cinema chains and electrical manufacturers were deeply involved. After a shaky start, most channels became prosperous and by 1960 the earthy approach of most contractors – greatly dependent on American imports – had captured 60% of the viewers. The BBC, however, fought back, aided by the granting of a 2nd channel, BBC2 (1964), and a young generation of producers and writers, reared in television, gained it a world reputation for quality of output. After 1970, it added to this a pioneering role as a vehicle for the broadcasts of the Open University.

When colour broadcasting started (1967), there were over 17 million TV licences, ensuring that transmissions reached 90% of households. But, despite this, radio underwent something of a revival: the BBC set up its own station, Radio 1, which was soon joined by local radio stations, based roughly on the same formula of pop music and news.

After 1970 the Conservatives added commercial local stations, under the ITA, now retitled the Independent Broadcasting Authority. After 1979 it was clear that the new 4th TV channel would be independent of government sponsorship.

Bronze age *see* PREHISTORIC BRITAIN

Brougham, Henry Peter, lord 1779–1868. Brilliant, eccentric and vain Whig politician of Scottish birth and education who, in a long career, promoted the abolition of slavery, repeal of income tax, Free Trade, legal and parliamentary reform and popular education. Though lord chancellor 1831–4, his unstable temperament excluded him from high office thereafter.

Brunanburh, battle of 937. Aethelstan, with the army of Wessex and Mercia, routed the invading forces of Olaf Guthfrithson (Norse-Irish Viking king of Dublin), King Constantine II of Alba and King Owen of Strathclyde. Fought on an unidentified site (perhaps in Mercia) it was commemorated by an Anglo-Saxon poem.

Brunel, Isambard Kingdom 1806–59. The son of an emigré French engineer, Brunel was an engineer of incredible originality and heroic quality, building the *Great Western*, the 1st Atlantic steamship (1836–8); the *Great Britain*, the 1st iron screw-driven liner (1841–5); meanwhile complet-

I. K. **Brunel** with the chain cable of the *Great Eastern* at Brown Lenox and Company's works, 1857. 'I asked Mr Lenox to stand with me,' he wrote on the back of the photograph, 'but he would not, so I alone am hung in chains.'

ing the Great Western Railway from London to Bristol, and the ill-fated giant *Great Eastern* (1852–8). *See* TRANSPORT.

Bryce, James, viscount 1838–1922. An Ulster-Scot historian, academic reformer and traveller, Bryce became a Liberal MP (1880), the party's main constitutional authority on home rule after 1886 and a leading pro-Boer. Unsuccessful as chief secretary for Ireland (1905–7), he was an outstanding ambassador to the USA (1907–13), subsequently doing much to bring America into World War I and to aid the foundation of the League of Nations.

Brycheiniog A principality in south-central Wales, traditionally founded in the 5th century by an Irish prince Brychan (*see* IRISH INVASIONS). Subsumed into DEHEUBARTH in the 10th century, it was overrun by Norman MARCHERS by 1100. At the Acts of Union (1536/42) it became a county (Brecknockshire), now forming part of Powys.

Buchanan report December 1963. A ministry of transport committee, under Colin Buchanan (later Sir), recommended the building of urban motorways on the pattern of that developed since the 1930s in Birmingham. This was carried out in Leeds, Newcastle and Glasgow, but within a decade the Buchanan formula had passed out of fashion.

Buckingham, Henry Stafford, duke of *c.* 1454–83. This enigmatic figure, an immensely wealthy but previously obscure magnate, was the principal supporter of Richard III's usurpation (June 1483). Only 3 months later, for reasons still unclear, he rebelled on behalf of Henry Tudor (later Henry VII) but, with his southern allies dispersed and his Welsh tenants unwilling to support him, was taken and executed.

Buckingham, George Villiers, 1st duke of (in the Villiers line) 1592–1628. A handsome and agreeable favourite of James VI and I and Charles I, by 1623 Buckingham exercised a near monopoly of royal favour and patronage. Corrupt and grossly incompetent in administration, diplomacy and war, he was loathed by parliament and was ultimately assassinated by an embittered soldier after the ILE DE RHÉ EXPEDITION.

Buckingham palace Originally built for the duke of Buckingham and Chandos, the palace was purchased in 1761 by George III, since when it has remained the London residence of the monarch. The Royal Mews, designed by John Nash for George IV, houses the state coaches used upon ceremonial occasions.

Building societies Like the Co-operatives, these became a feature of upper-working-class life in the long boom after 1848. The Building Societies' Association was founded (1869) and helped formulate the Act governing them (1874). Their real expansion, an essentially middle-class phenomenon, did not come until the 1930s.

George Villiers, duke of **Buckingham**: portrait of 1626.

Bulgarian atrocities 1875–6. Massacres of the Christian subjects of the Turks which were made the subject of a campaign by Nonconformists and High Churchmen – spearheaded by Gladstone – against Disraeli's foreign policy of supporting the Turkish empire.

Bunker Hill, battle of 17 June 1775. The 1st major action of the AMERICAN INDEPENDENCE struggle. British troops under General Howe stormed and took earthworks constructed by the rebel colonists outside Boston, but at the cost of massive casualties amounting to half Howe's force.

Bunyan, John 1628–88. The son of a Bedfordshire tinker, Bunyan was converted around 1649 and became a BAPTIST preacher in Bedford. Imprisoned (1660–72) for refusing to cease public preaching, he later served as pastor of the Bedford meeting. He is best known for his *Pilgrim's Progress* (1678), *Holy War* (1682) and *Grace Abounding* (1666).

Burghley house Northants. The superb mansion built (1552–87) for William Cecil, Lord Burghley. The house is square in design, built around a central courtyard, with rounded corner towers topped by turrets. The most notable early feature is the great hall, with its double hammerbeam roof.

Burgundians Supporters of the dukes of Burgundy, blood relations of the French crown whose lands lay in northern and central eastern France and modern Belgium. Their rivalry with the Armagnac faction, who murdered their Duke John the Fearless (1419), led to an alliance with England which profoundly affected the HUNDRED YEARS' WAR.

Burhs Communal fortresses established by Anglo-Saxon kings as defences against Viking attack, and later to consolidate Edward the Elder's conquest of the Danelaw. They included refurbished hillforts, Roman towns with repaired walls, and new earthwork fortifications. Some (hence the later name 'borough') were already thriving towns, and others became so with royal encouragement. The best surviving examples are Wallingford, Oxon.; Wareham, Dorset; and Witham, Essex.

Burke, Edmund 1729–97. A leading parliamentary opponent of North and Pitt, Burke was unsuccessful in practical politics. His greatness lay rather in his principled defence of the party system, championship of the American colonists and

assertion of concrete political rights over abstract natural rights theories, best expressed in his *Reflections on the Revolution in France* (1790).

Burmese wars The 1st war (1824–6) was fought to repel invasion of British territory. The 2nd war (1852) was undertaken to defend British merchants and ended with the annexation of Rangoon. The whole country was annexed in 1886.

Burnell, Robert d. 1292. A long-standing friend of EDWARD I, Burnell acted as chancellor and chief adviser 1274–92, the most successful years of the reign. Bishop of Bath and Wells from 1275, he had much to do with Edward's statutory legal reforms, and stabilized chancery at Westminster (1280).

Burnet, Gilbert 1643–1715. A brilliant Scottish minister and academic, Burnet was appointed a royal chaplain in 1675. Dismissed for his Whig sympathies (1684), he became a leading adviser of William of Orange. After 1688 he was made bishop of Salisbury, supported religious toleration and composed his *History Of My Own Time* (2 vols. 1724–34).

Burghley house, Northants.: courtyard and tower.

Burns, John 1858–1943. A violent SOCIAL DE-MOCRATIC FEDERATION agitator in the 1880s, 'Labour's lost leader' moved to the Liberals after he was elected MP (1892), becoming the 1st workman to enter the cabinet (1905) as president of the local government board. He resigned in protest against Britain's entry into World War I.

Bute, John Stewart, 3rd earl of 1713–92. A Scottish nobleman and parliamentary patron, Bute was greatly esteemed by the young George III. As secretary of state and 1st lord of the treasury (1761–3), he was violently abused for his handling of the peace of PARIS and extension of excise duties. He resigned in 1763, living privately thereafter.

Butler, Josephine 1828–1906. A pioneer of women's education in the 1860s, she subsequently dominated attempts to repeal the Contagious Diseases Acts (1864, 1866 and 1869) which had effectively legalized prostitution, succeeding in 1886.

Butt, Isaac 1813–79. A Protestant lawyer and editor, originally a Tory MP, who through his defence of the FENIAN prisoners became the founder and leader of the Irish home rulers (1871).

Cabal The name given to Charles II's ministers of 1667–73 – Clifford, Arlington, Buckingham, Ashley-Cooper and LAUDERDALE. The Cabal was ultimately broken by parliamentary hostility to its pro-French foreign policy and to the DECLARATION OF INDULGENCE (1672).

Cabinet British government is generally described as 'cabinet government', an explanation first put forward by BAGEHOT in *The English Constitution* (1867). More recent commentators, such as R.H.S. Crossman, have suggested that cabinet government is giving way to prime ministerial government. The political history of recent years has not wholly borne this out. *See* COUNCIL, THE.

Cadbury Originally a prehistoric HILLFORT near Wincanton, Somerset, it has been identified since at least the 16th century with ARTHUR's 'Camelot'. Excavations (1966–70) revealed that it had indeed been extensively refortified in the late 5th century, when it was apparently a specially important British military centre.

Cade's rising May–July 1450. SUFFOLK's murder triggered a revolt by the commons and lesser gentry of Kent (led by the mysterious Jack Cade) and riots elsewhere, directed at punishing the remainder of Henry VI's 'evil counsellors' and reinstating Richard of YORK. The rebels dispersed after lynching unpopular officials in London.

Cadwallawn king of Gwynedd (d. 633). The last British leader successfully to counter-attack the Anglo-Saxons, Cadwallawn allied with Penda of Mercia to overthrow Edwin near Doncaster (October 632), occupying and ravaging Northumbria until killed by Oswald near Hexham.

Caereni A northern Scottish tribe which inhabited western Sutherland at the time of Roman Britain.

Caerleon near Newport, Gwent (Roman 'Isca'). A LEGIONARY FORTRESS established for the 2nd legion Augusta (*c.* 75) by Julius Frontinus to control the Silures and south Wales. Rebuilt in stone during the 2nd century, and reconstructed during the early 3rd, it was disgarrisoned by *c.* 300. An excavated corner and an AMPHITHEATRE are now visible.

Caerwent *see* SILURES

Caister-by-Norwich *see* ICENI

Calais A French Channel port, invested by Edward III after CRÉCY and taken 11 months later on 4 August 1347, when it was depopulated and resettled with English colonists as a commercial entrepot, military base and reminder of the English claim to the French throne. Its loss (1558), a grave blow to England's prestige, was confirmed by the treaty of Cateau-Cambrésis (1559).

Calcutta, the Black Hole of 1756. The alleged suffocation of 123 British prisoners locked in a small room after the capture of Fort William, Calcutta, on the orders of Suraj-ud-Daulah. A further 23 prisoners were said to have survived the ordeal.

Caledonians A general name applied to the tribes inhabiting the lands between the Forth-Clyde line and the Great Glen. The Caledonii proper held the western part of the area. Though defeated by AGRICOLA (83–4), and by Severus (208–10), they remained a hostile element beyond the frontier of Roman Britain. They were known as PICTS after *c*. 300.

'Camelot' *see* ARTHUR; CADBURY; COLCHESTER

Cameron, Richard 1648–80. A covenanting field-preacher born in Falkland, Cameron founded the extremist Cameronian sect. After a brief preaching career he renounced the king's authority in the Sanquhar declaration (1680) and was hunted down by the privy council, defeated and killed at Airds Moss.

Campaign for democratic socialism The right-wing pressure-group within the Labour party, formed in 1960 to aid GAITSKELL against the unilateralists (*see* CAMPAIGN FOR NUCLEAR DISARMAMENT), in which it was successful in 1961.

Campaign for nuclear disarmament (CND) Formed in January 1958, its Easter marches from Aldermaston (1958, 1959 and 1960) attracted widespread support, and in 1960 the Labour party voted in favour of a unilateralist resolution, only to have GAITSKELL force it to reverse its stand a year later. Thereafter, Britain continued to possess nuclear weapons and, though her conventional forces shrank, CND waned faster.

Campbell-Bannerman, Sir Henry 1836–1908. The son of a wealthy Glasgow draper, Campbell-Bannerman became leader of the Liberal party following a feud between Rosebery and Harcourt (1899). He led the party to its greatest victory (1906), although a subsequent collapse in health meant he was never able to enjoy its fruits.

Camperdown, battle of *see* NAPOLEONIC WARS

Campion, Edmund 1540–81. A Londoner, educated at Oxford, Campion fled abroad (1571) and became a Jesuit. Accompanying PARSONS to England in 1580, he spent a year ministering to Roman Catholics before he was betrayed, tortured and executed. He was a gentle, attractive and genuinely non-political man.

Canada Act *see* BRITISH EMPIRE

Canals Prior to the railway age the extension of water TRANSPORT by cutting canals was the only means of significantly improving the transportation of bulky commodities. Piecemeal initiative by local companies (1750–1815) responding to the needs of the INDUSTRIAL REVOLUTION, led to the creation of a national network of canals. They were nationalized in 1947.

Canning, George 1770–1827. A brilliant disciple of Pitt, Canning early obtained office as under-secretary for foreign affairs (1796) and paymaster-general (1800). Though foreign secretary 1807–9, his later career was hampered by personal enmities. Following Castlereagh's death he regained the foreign secretaryship (1822–7) and became prime minister in 1827, shortly before his own death.

Cannon Probably first used in Britain at Berwick (1333), early cannon were weakly constructed (being forged rather than cast), unwieldy and (due to poor-quality gunpowder) inefficient. They scarcely influenced tactics until the 15th century (*see* CASTILLON, BATTLE OF; JAMES II), but in the 16th century the advent of cast guns on carriages revolutionized warfare.

George **Canning**: portrait by T. Lawrence and R. Evans.

Canon law The collection of ecclesiastically made rules governing the faith and discipline of the church. Canon law formerly also applied to the laity in matters such as sexual morality (*see* BAWDY COURTS), marriage, divorce and wills.

Canons Groups of priests working together for a specific common purpose who from the late 11th century fall into 2 classes. Secular canons served cathedrals, collegiate churches and minsters, owned personal property and neither took monastic vows nor necessarily lived communally. Regular canons followed a communal monastic rule in abbeys or priories, being in practice distinguishable from monks only by their invariable priesthood. *See* AUGUSTINIAN CANONS; GILBERTINES; PREMONSTRATENSIANS; TRINITARIANS.

Canterbury The ecclesiastical capital of England. Originally a Belgic settlement, it became successively (as Durovernum Cantiacorum) the centre of the CANTIACI and (as Cantwaraburh) the capital of Jutish KENT. Its ecclesiastical primacy, founded by AUGUSTINE, was confirmed by THEODORE and Lanfranc, and during the middle ages it was internationally famous as the shrine of BECKET.

Canterbury cathedral: the nave facing east.

The effect of **cannon** on siege warfare was considerable, for breaches in walls could be made and stormed without waiting for garrisons to be starved into surrender. A demonstration of the operation of cannon *c.* 1450, from a contemporary military handbook.

Canterbury cathedral One of the most beautiful English cathedrals. The chancel of the present church was built 1174–84, soon after BECKET's martyrdom, in the earliest style of Gothic architecture. The PERPENDICULAR nave was raised in the late 14th and 15th centuries and the central 'Bell Harry' tower in the early 16th century.

Cantiaci A group of Belgic tribes occupying Kent, described by Julius Caesar as 'the most civilized inhabitants of Britain, whose way of life differs little from that of the Gauls'. Their territory was annexed by Cunobelinus (*c.* 25). Soon after the Roman conquest they became a CIVITAS, with a capital at Durovernum Cantiacorum (Canterbury).

Cantref (Welsh 'hundred townships'). An ancient administrative unit in Wales, essentially the equivalent of a large HUNDRED, though they were not organized into SHIRES until the Acts of Union with England (1536/42). Each was generally divided into 2 commotes (with their own courts), whose lords originally exercised quasi-regal powers.

Canute *see* CNUT

Cape St Vincent, battle of *see* NAPOLEONIC WARS

Capital punishment The British penal code, theoretically the most draconian in Europe, was liberalized by Peel (1820s). In 1861 the grounds for capital punishment were diminished to murder, treason, piracy and arson in naval dockyards. The last public execution was carried out in 1868, and the numbers executed fell from 39 (1833) to 16 (1904). By the Criminal Justice Act (1956), the grounds were further diminished, and Harold Wilson's government abolished hanging in 1965.

Caratacus The joint king of the CATUVELLAUNI after Cunobelinus. With his brother Togodumnus, he led the opposition to the Roman invasion (43). Eventually defeated by Ostorius Scapula somewhere in mid-Wales (51), he escaped to the Brigantes, only to be betrayed by Queen Cartimandua and taken to Rome. *See* PREHISTORIC BRITAIN.

Carausius A low-born seaman from Gallia Belgica (modern Belgium) who rose to command the CLASSIS BRITANNICA. His successes made him popular in Roman Britain and Gaul where in 286 he declared himself emperor. In 288 he defeated and made peace with his Roman rival Maximian, but in 293 he was expelled from Gaul by CONSTANTIUS and murdered by his finance minister ALLECTUS.

Cardiff The site of a major late Roman fort and from *c.* 1095 of an important MARCHER castle. Cardiff's pre-eminence began with the growth of its coal-export trade after 1830. By 1913 it was the world's greatest coal-exporting port and the largest town in Wales, of which (despite north Welsh opposition) it became capital in 1954.

Cardwell, Edward, viscount 1813–86. As secretary for war (1868–74), Cardwell abolished the purchase of commissions and modernized ARMY organization.

Carham, battle of 1018. Malcolm II of Scotland and King Owen of Strathclyde heavily defeated Earl Uhtred of Northumbria on the Tweed, permanently securing Lothian to Scotland.

Carlyle, Thomas 1795–1881. Scottish historian and 'sage' whose assault on 19th-century materialism in *Sartor Resartus* (1829), *Chartism* (1839) and *Past and Present* (1843), fuelled much Victorian social criticism. Despite his own alternations of pessimism and trust in 'hero-figures' – which might be seen to prefigure fascism – his influence on Victorians as varied as ENGELS, RUSKIN, SMILES, MILL and HARDIE was enormous.

Carmarthen *see* DEMETAE

Carmelites Originating as hermit communities in Palestine, they fled the Saracens and were reconstituted as FRIARS with a special interest in education, principally by an Englishman, St Simon Stock (d. 1265). Also called White Friars, they were introduced to England (where they became numerous) in 1241 and to Scotland (1262).

Carnarvon, H. H. M. Herbert, earl of 1831–90. Colonial secretary in DISRAELI's 1874–80 government, his qualified sympathy for Irish home rule (1885) led to Parnell's backing of the Tories in the election.

Carnegie, Andrew 1835–1919. The son of a Chartist weaver in Dunfermline, Carnegie emigrated to the USA (1848), where his acumen and ruthlessness secured him a vast fortune made out of American railroads and steel (1850–80). He retired in 1899 and channelled his gains into educational, pacifist and radical causes.

Carnonacae A northern Scottish tribe which inhabited western Ross-shire at the time of Roman Britain.

Carr, Robert, 1st earl of Somerset ?1586–1645. A handsome Scottish favourite of James VI and I (1607–14), Carr was essentially a courtier. He had little influence on policy and was eventually disgraced, tried and imprisoned (1616–21) for his part in the murder of Sir Thomas Overbury during his wife's scandalous divorce from the earl of Essex (1613).

Carson, Sir Edward, lord 1854–1935. An Irish Protestant barrister and Conservative whose strong unionism (rather than Ulster nationalism) did much to intensify the IRISH CONSTITUTIONAL CRISIS (1911–14). He helped to bring down Asquith's coalition cabinet (1916). In Lloyd George's government (1916–21) he attempted to find solutions to the Irish problem.

Carteret, John Lord, Earl Granville 1690–1763. Long debarred from office by Walpole, Carteret became secretary of state in 1742, winning George II's approval with an ambitious, pro-Hanoverian foreign policy which brought Britain into the war of the Austrian succession. He was prime minister for 2 days in 1746 until inability to form a ministry forced his resignation.

Carthusians A strictly contemplative order of MONKS combining BENEDICTINE tradition with eremitical asceticism, they lived solitary lives within the monastery and met only for certain services. Introduced to England in 1175–6, they were unaffected by late medieval decline and remained greatly respected until the Reformation, 7 of the 10 English houses being founded 1343–1414 and the single Scottish house in 1429.

Cartulary A collection of copies of CHARTERS, often in 'ledger-book' form, recording the land title-deeds, privileges, etc. of a monastic foundation, institution, town, family or other landowner. They are especially valuable for topographical and genealogical research.

Cartwright, Thomas 1535–1603. Of Hertfordshire YEOMAN stock, Cartwright became Lady Margaret Professor of Divinity at Cambridge (1569) and as such advocated Presbyterian church government. Deprived in 1570 he went to Geneva, returning when appointed master of the hospital at Warwick (1585). Thereafter he divided his time between Warwick and extended visits abroad.

Carucate (Lat. *carrucata*, plough-land). After the Norman conquest, a measure of land, being the area (varying according to the soil) that could be tilled with an 8-ox plough in a year. Like the earlier HIDE, from which it differs only in conception, it averaged about 100 acres. *See* BOVATE; VIRGATE.

Casablanca conference January 1943. Roosevelt and Churchill met at Casablanca, set up the planning organization for the invasion of Sicily, and decided to adopt a policy of requiring 'unconditional surrender' from the Germans.

Casement, Sir Roger 1864–1916. An Irish Protestant, Casement was a British consul (1892–1911), who exposed exploitation in the Congo and Brazil. During World War I he gained German support for the Easter Rising (*see* IRISH CONSTITUTIONAL CRISIS). On its eve, he landed from a U-boat near Tralee but was captured, and hanged for

Roger **Casement** (left) photographed in the Congo in the 1890s.

high treason (August 1916). His 'black diaries', revealing his homosexuality, may have been used to discredit him.

Cassivellaunus *see* JULIUS CAESAR

Castile *see* HUNDRED YEARS' WAR; JOHN OF GAUNT; NÁJERA, BATTLE OF

Castillon, battle of 17 July 1453. The last battle of the HUNDRED YEARS' WAR. Talbot, attempting to relieve Castillon (near Bordeaux), ill-advisedly attacked Charles VII's French army (under Jean Bureau) in a fortified camp defended by cannon, but was beaten off and killed in the pursuit. The defeat entailed the final loss of English Aquitaine.

Castlereagh, Robert Stewart, viscount, 2nd marquis of Londonderry 1769–1822. As secretary of state for war (1805–7) and foreign minister (1812–22), Castlereagh contributed much to victory in the Napoleonic wars and the shaping of the European peace settlement at PARIS and VIENNA (1814–15). Diligent, firm and greatly respected for his diplomatic grasp, he committed suicide while mentally disturbed.

Castles A castle may be defined as a strongly fortified residence belonging to one lord, as opposed to the state-built and purely military forts of Roman Britain and the post-medieval period, or to communal defences such as hillforts, burhs and medieval walled towns. Remains of some 1,600 castles exist in England and Wales, with many more in Scotland. Origins are still in dispute, but castles in

Bodiam **castle**, Sussex. The quadrangular style, at the height of fashion when Bodiam was begun in 1385, conveniently combined an exterior of towered defences with an interior of comfortable rooms facing on to a pleasant courtyard.

the form of stone towers were certainly being built in France by *c.* 950. The 1st British castles, however, were the earthwork motte and bailey type introduced at the Norman conquest. These consisted of one or more fortified enclosures (baileys) dominated by a steep-sided earthen mound with a flattened top (the motte). Both were defended by ditches, banks and palisades or walls, and the motte was generally surmounted by a tower (or KEEP) built in timber or stone. The instrument and symbol of Norman domination, castles soon spread throughout England and followed the penetration of the MARCHERS into Wales, while the Norman allies of David I took them to Scotland. Hundreds more were thrown up by warring barons during the anarchic reign of Stephen.

A few very important castles (including the TOWER OF LONDON, and those at COLCHESTER and Chepstow) had always been equipped with massive stone keeps. Henry II, intent on strengthening the power of the crown through its fortresses, added considerably to their number, notably at Newcastle and DOVER. Such keeps were generally rectangular, with corners vulnerable to undermining and siege-engines. Towards the end of the 12th century efforts were made to obviate this problem by building polygonal (Orford) or cylindrical (e.g. Pembroke) keeps.

The castle's outer defences were also developing. Wooden palisades were replaced by stone curtain walls, and by Henry II's time these were being provided with strategically placed mural towers and strong gatehouses, whose fire could flank the whole length of the wall. The next step, first seen in western Europe at Dover, was to surround the keep with 2 concentric and mutually supporting rings of towered walls, often accompanied by a moat, so that attackers were faced with 3–4 successive lines of defence. The apogee of this style, and indeed of British castle-building in general, was attained in the concentric castles (including Beaumaris, Caernarvon, Conwy and Harlech) raised at the end of the 13th century by Edward I to consolidate his conquest of north Wales. Here the mural defences, often incorporating an immensely strong gatehouse capable of holding out independently, were so formidable as not to require a separate keep.

Keeps, nevertheless, continued to be important, especially in Scotland and the borders, where the disturbed conditions arising from the Scottish wars of independence produced a modified version, the TOWER HOUSE. These remained the standard type of gentry house in the area until the 17th century.

In 14th- and 15th-century England the desire for comfort and display progressively triumphed over the need for defence, and the distinction between castles and fortified manor houses became increasingly blurred. Yet strong castles continued to be built, often in the quadrangular style, with 4 ranges of buildings round a central courtyard (e.g. Bolton, Bodiam).

The development of cannon contributed comparatively little to the decline of the castle, a more important factor being the suppression of private feuds and the growth of a strong central government. They enjoyed a brief revival of importance during the civil wars, when many were seriously damaged. *See* ills. pp. 261, 297, 308.

'Cat and Mouse Act' 1913. Passed by the Liberals, this allowed the home secretary to release SUFFRAGETTE hunger-strikers when their health was in danger, and rearrest them when they recovered. *See* WOMEN'S MOVEMENT.

Cathedral The mother church of a DIOCESE, once containing the throne (Lat. *cathedra*) of its bishop, generally set behind the high altar. Although normally ruled by a dean and a chapter of secular canons, nearly half those in medieval England were manned by Benedictine monks, a phenomenon practically unknown elsewhere.

Catholic emancipation *see* ROMAN CATHOLICISM

Cato Street conspiracy 1820. A plot by some followers of SPENCE, led by Arthur Thistlewood, to assassinate the members of LIVERPOOL's cabinet and proclaim a republic. The plan was leaked by spies and the conspirators were arrested and some, including Thistlewood, subsequently hanged.

Catterick, battle of *see* MANAU GODODDIN

Catuvellauni A powerful Belgic tribe originally settled in the Hertfordshire area, it led the resistance to Julius Caesar (54 BC) and under CUNOBELINUS expanded to dominate south-east Britain. Conquered soon after the Roman invasion (*see* CARATACUS), it formed a CIVITAS centred on VERULAMIUM.

Caucus politics A name (derived from American practice) for the control of constituency politics by the local party association. First practised in Birmingham by Joseph Chamberlain and others after the 2nd Reform Bill (1867), it thereafter became widespread.

Causewayed camps Roughly circular enclosures surrounded by up to 4 concentric banks with external ditches, interrupted by many causeways. Probably built *c.* 3500–2500 BC by the neolithic Windmill Hill people (named after the largest example, covering 21 acres in Wiltshire) and used for periodic gatherings of scattered communities accompanied by rituals, feasting and trading. *See* HENGE MONUMENTS; PREHISTORIC BRITAIN.

Cavalier parliament 1661–79. So named because of its initial enthusiastic royalism (*see* CLARENDON CODE), it later proved willing to oppose royal policy, establishing the principle of appropriation of supply (1665) and the parliamentary committee of public accounts (1667) and passing the TEST ACT (1673). It was dissolved to save DANBY from impeachment.

Ceawlin king of Wessex (560–*c.* 591). Recognized as BRETWALDA, Ceawlin led the major southern Anglo-Saxon advance of the mid-6th century (*see* HEROIC AGE), campaigning in Wiltshire (556), winning at DYRHAM and perhaps penetrating to the Wye (584) before being overthrown by civil war.

Cecil, Robert, 1st earl of Salisbury 1563–1612. The younger son of William Cecil, Robert obtained the principal secretaryship in 1596 and emerged supreme after the fall of ESSEX. A skilful politician and administrator, he maintained his position under James VI and I and as lord treasurer attempted unsuccessfully to tackle the king's financial problems, notably with the GREAT CONTRACT.

William **Cecil**, Lord Burghley, presiding over a session of the court of wards and liveries. Anonymous painting, *c.* 1585.

Cecil, William, Lord Burghley 1520–98. After an administrative apprenticeship in Edward VI's reign, Cecil became principal secretary to Elizabeth I (1558). As secretary and subsequently lord treasurer (1572–98) his caution, moderation and administrative skill won him the queen's unfailing trust and favour and made him an indispensable partner in the achievements of her reign.

Cedd, St *see* CHURCH, PRE-REFORMATION

Cely papers *see* LETTERS, MEDIEVAL COLLECTIONS OF

Census Enumerations of the British POPULATION, first undertaken under the direction of John Rickman (1801) and repeated at 10-year intervals thereafter. Census reports are the responsibility of the registrar-general, the original returns remaining confidential and unavailable to other government departments or private individuals for 100 years.

Century *see* LEGION

Ceorl (churl; Old English 'man'). The free peasant who formed the basis of Anglo-Saxon society. Originally independent farmers holding on average a HIDE of land, they were liable to FYRD service and other obligations but subject only to the king. Their economic and social status generally declined (perhaps partly due to Viking devastation) and by the 11th century many outside the DANELAW had become semi-servile, a process accelerated by the Norman conquest.

Cerdic The traditional founder of WESSEX (*c.* 490) whose apparently British name has puzzled historians and led some to believe him a British prince employing Saxon mercenaries. The later kings of Wessex, of united Anglo-Saxon England and (through Matilda, wife of Henry I) the present royal family, all claim descent from him.

Cerialis, Quintus Petillius Governor of Roman Britain (71–4). In pursuit of Vespasian's policy of expanding the province, Cerialis invaded the Brigantes, defeated their king, Venutius, and established a fortress at York. He then overran most of their territory, but left the task of consolidation to Agricola. *See* BOUDICA.

Chadwick, Sir Edwin 1800–90. A Manchester-born lawyer, disciple and executor of BENTHAM, Chadwick was the main architect of the POOR LAW AMENDMENT ACT (1834), and his sanitary report (1842) led to the setting up of the general board of health (1848), with him in charge. His dismissal (1854) meant the end of centralization in sanitary reform and the premature end of his own career.

Chamber The financial department of the English ROYAL HOUSEHOLD and, under the early Norman kings, of the government as a whole. Replaced in the latter role by the EXCHEQUER by Henry I's reign, it retained its original purpose of providing monarchs with ready cash until superseded under Henry III by the WARDROBE. Revived under Edward II, it survived as an important household office until 1554.

Chamberlain, Sir Austen 1863–1937. The son of Joseph, Chamberlain was first elected Liberal Unionist MP in 1892. He was chancellor of the exchequer (1903–05) and in Lloyd George's coalition (1919–22), which he strongly supported. In Baldwin's 1924–9 government he was a conciliatory foreign secretary, concluding the LOCARNO PACTS (1925) which readmitted Germany into the international community and set up structures for international collaboration.

Chamberlain, Joseph 1836–1914. A Birmingham screw-manufacturer, Chamberlain started politics as a reforming mayor (1873–6) and Unitarian MP (1876–1910), encouraging public acquisition of land and utilities and GAS AND WATER SOCIALISM. He entered Gladstone's cabinet (1880), but despite his UNAUTHORIZED PROGRAMME (1885), he was outmanoeuvred on home rule by Gladstone, who forced him into an alliance with the

Austen **Chamberlain** at Geneva: drawing by David Low, 1926.

Joseph **Chamberlain**: hostile cartoon by F. Carruthers Gould.

Conservatives. As Unionist colonial secretary (1895), he increased imperial co-operation but became involved in the Boer war, and then split the party with his advocacy of TARIFF REFORM and helped ensure the Liberal landslide (1906).

Chamberlain, Neville 1869–1940. The son of Joseph, Chamberlain was mayor of Birmingham (1915–16) and unsuccessful director of national service (1916–17) before he became a Tory MP in 1918. He was a progressive minister of health (1923–9), carrying through housing and local government reforms. He succeeded Baldwin as premier (1937) and was the architect of APPEASE-MENT policies, as a man who believed he could

Neville **Chamberlain** reads out the promise of peace, signed by himself and Hitler, on his arrival at Heston airport, 1 September 1938.

negotiate with Hitler on equal terms. After the failure of this (March 1939), he allied with Poland (*see* ANGLO-POLISH PACT) and was thus drawn into war (September 1939). Chamberlain survived the PHONEY WAR but lost much Conservative support in the commons and was replaced by Churchill (May 1940).

Chanak crisis October 1922. It occurred when Turkish troops, pursuing a withdrawing Greek invasion force, threatened to clash with British troops outside Constantinople. Lloyd George and Churchill threatened Mustapha Kemal, the Turkish leader, with war. A settlement acceptable to the Turks was worked out, but disquiet at Lloyd George's bellicose attitude led to the Tories bringing down his coalition ministry.

Chancellor From late Anglo-Saxon times the head of CHANCERY and custodian of the GREAT SEAL, by the 13th century the chancellor had effectively become the king's chief minister and adviser. As the legal status of chancery grew, however, his position as the senior judge (still retained) overshadowed and eventually obliterated his other functions.

Chancellor of the exchequer *see* EXCHEQUER

Chancery Originally the office writing and issuing documents for the itinerant English royal household, it became static during the 13th century. While retaining for a time its administrative role, it developed by the mid-14th century into a popular court dealing with petitions and appeals, finally becoming a division of the high court (1873). *See* CHANCELLOR; LAW.

Chantries From the early 14th century until suppressed at the Reformation (1547), lands and rents were frequently granted for the endowment of a priest (who might also have educational and charitable duties) to say daily mass for the donor's soul, often in a specially built chapel attached to a parish church. Their dissolution, though justified by Protestant hostility to the doctrine of purgatory and the veneration of saints, was merely another stage in the seizure of church property in England.

Charity Organization Society Founded in 1869 largely by middle-class Liberals to encourage social and housing reform while requiring a rigid enforcement of the POOR LAW AMENDMENT ACT, it was unpopular with the working class and later with socialists such as Beatrice WEBB. Nevertheless, it pioneered social casework and some of its leaders, notably TOYNBEE, became noted critics of 19th-century society.

Charity schools Schools founded by the SOCIETY FOR THE PROMOTING OF CHRISTIAN KNOWLEDGE in the later 17th and 18th centuries and managed by local committees of subscribers. Though varying greatly in quality, they generally taught basic literacy, simple arithmetic and religious knowledge, with needlework for girls.

St Martin-in-the-Fields **charity school**, which issued this receipt, was opened in 1699. Supporting these schools was a favourite form of practical piety.

Charles I king of Great Britain (1625–49; b. 1600). Fastidious, dignified, pious and cultured, Charles's character was in marked contrast to that of his father James VI and I. He also lacked his father's political sense. At the crisis points of his reign he showed himself to be neither flexible nor honest, evasive in defeat and vindictive in victory. The best that even LAUD could say of him was that he was 'a mild and gracious prince who knew not how to be, or be made, great'. To his enemies he became 'Charles Stuart, that man of blood'.

As James's 2nd son, Charles became heir to the throne in 1612, on the death of his brother Henry, succeeding his father in 1625 and marrying in the same year the French princess HENRIETTA MARIA. Until 1628 his policy was shaped by the continuing dominance of his father's favourite BUCKINGHAM. The latter's military and administrative incompetence and the FORCED LOAN (1627) provoked a series of conflicts in parliament, culminating in the PETITION OF RIGHT (1628) and the dissolution of parliament (1629). Thereafter Charles embarked upon a 'personal rule' which increasingly alienated the POLITICAL NATION. The ecclesiastical policies of Laud aroused fears of 'popery', aggravated by Charles's uxorious relationship with his Catholic queen. Strafford's activities in the north and in Ireland threatened a new arbitrariness in government, summed up in the supposed policy of THOROUGH. The crown's financial expedients, DISTRAINT OF KNIGHTHOOD and forest-law fines, the sale of MONOPOLIES, extension of customs impositions and above all SHIP MONEY, posed a threat to property. Yet until 1638 the king appeared successful enough, presiding over a brilliant and cultured court and establishing himself as a great patron of the arts.

Charles's misguided Scottish policies proved his downfall. The national COVENANT (1638) and BISHOPS' WARS (1639–40) necessitated the calling of the SHORT and LONG PARLIAMENTS (1640) and England slid from constitutional revolution to CIVIL WAR. The war, made inevitable by the unwillingness of some MPs to push their opposition to Charles to extremes yet the inability of the opposition leaders to trust him, was in some ways the making of Charles the man. He proved capable of inspiring devotion in his followers and showed himself possessed of some military talent and strategic grasp. Yet in defeat his intransigence in the 1646–7 negotiations and his willingness to provoke renewed war by the Scottish ENGAGEMENT (1647) exhausted the patience and provoked the anger of the parliamentarian generals. Tried by a high court of justice set up by the RUMP PARLIAMENT (which

'The King cannot be tried by any superior jurisdiction on earth', exclaimed **Charles I** at the opening of his trial, 20 January 1649. Even Oliver Cromwell found it difficult to collect enough signatures for the death warrant. 17th-century engraving.

only managed to carry the Act by 26 votes to 20), he was condemned and executed on 30 January 1649.

Charles's execution occurred because there seemed no other way to break the political deadlock of 1648. Yet it horrified the nation, divided the parliamentarians and rendered a lasting settlement impossible. The Restoration did not come until 1660, but by his death, as he perhaps knew, Charles had saved the cause of a MONARCHY which his own folly had done so much to endanger.

Charles II king of Great Britain (1660–85; b. 1630). Eldest son of Charles I and Henrietta Maria, Charles's youth and early manhood were overshadowed by the events of the civil wars and interregnum. At 12 he was present at EDGEHILL. On parliament's victory he escaped abroad, but after his father's execution he was recognized in Scotland and landed there in 1650. Accepting the national COVENANT, he was crowned at Scone, but saw his hopes defeated at DUNBAR and WORCESTER. His dramatic escape after the latter battle was followed by 8 years of impecunious exile in France, Germany and the Netherlands until MONCK's march on London paved the way to the declaration of BREDA and the RESTORATION (1660).

The future **Charles II** in exile, dancing with his sister Mary, princess of Orange, at a ball in the Hague. Oil painting by Cornelius Johnson, 1650.

Charles entered his inheritance aged 30, an embodiment of relaxed and cynical reaction to the emotional exhaustion of the revolutionary years. Tall, athletic and handsome, vigorous in his pleasures (he had at least 14 bastard children by his many mistresses), witty and urbane, he was indeed a 'merry monarch'. In affairs of state he was indolent and unprincipled, but shrewd. He was content to accept the position of the MONARCHY as limited by the 1641 reforms embodied in the Restoration settlement. He was prepared to stand by no policy or servant in the face of concerted opposition, readily abandoning the tolerant aspirations of Breda, the DECLARATIONS OF INDULGENCE, CLAREN-DON, the CABAL and DANBY to their enemies. In foreign policy he preferred a subservience to France which Louis XIV rewarded with a pension, though he took no positive steps to further the interests of either France or Catholicism. The only principle which he was prepared to defend was his brother James's right to succeed him, and in the EXCLUSION CRISIS he defended it ably. Indeed, after the failure of exclusion (1681), the king enjoyed a position of considerable strength. Typically, he had neither the determination nor the temerity to try to exploit it to introduce the absolutism he admired.

Charles died of a stroke, leaving no legitimate child by his queen, Catherine of Braganza. On his deathbed he accepted the Catholicism of which he had professed himself convinced in the secret treaty of DOVER (1670). This belated act was one final example of the realism of a king who had his preferences, certainly, but held none of them so dear as to risk going once more upon his travels.

Charles, Thomas *see* WALES

Charter A legal document recording a grant of lands, privileges etc., usually in perpetuity. Generally sealed and witnessed, medieval charters may be in Latin, French or (during Anglo-Saxon times and the later middle ages) English. *See* CARTULARY; MAGNA CARTA.

Chartism In 1838 William Lovett (1800–77), a cabinet-maker, drafted on behalf of the London Working Men's Association a reform Bill which he called 'The Peoples' Charter'. This demanded (1) universal manhood suffrage, (2) annual elections, (3) the secret ballot, (4) equal electoral districts, (5) abolition of the property qualification for MPs, and (6) payment of MPs. For the next decade these '6 points' and the name Chartist were to be the sole unifying features of an otherwise highly disparate movement of working men and middle-class radicals.

Although originally a reversion to purely political agitation after the attempts at general union and co-operative versions of socialism in the early 1830s (*see* OWEN, ROBERT), Chartism was from the beginning bound up with far from consistent social and economic pressures. Apart from London, the main areas of 'moral force' Chartism, Birmingham and Scotland, combined the political demands with, respectively, currency reform and working-class self-improvement. In other areas it was associated with specific industrial tensions, and was correspondingly more militant when fuelled by the grievances of the impoverished HAND-LOOM WEAVERS of Lancashire or outworkers in the Yorkshire woollen industry. It was weak in the greatest of the industrial cities but strong in the medium-sized industrial towns; weak in 'new' industries such as railways, ironfounding and engineering, but strong among miners, rural cloth-workers and the traditional artisan trades.

Lovett, ATTWOOD and the 'moral force' Chartists, whose main effort to direct the movement, the People's Convention (February 1839), broke up in disorder, had looked for leadership to parliamentary radicals. Their failure left the initiative with

The final great demonstration of **Chartism**, on Kennington Common, 10 April 1848. This early photograph by W. E. Kilburn was lost for over a century and rediscovered in the royal archives.

radicals from northern England, deeply involved in the struggle against the 'bastilles' of the new poor law (*see* POOR LAW AMENDMENT ACT), and in the FACTORY MOVEMENT. These issues precluded much co-operation with the manufacturing interests, which supported the ANTI-CORN-LAW LEAGUE. This gained its success (1846) against strong Chartist opposition, mainly expressed through Feargus O'CONNOR and his newspaper the *Northern Star* (1832–52). The boom of the mid-1840s brought a temporary quiescence. Then there was a final flare-up (1848) when O'Connor mobilized the discontents of the immigrant Irish population and a new generation of London-based radicals, including George Julian Harney (1817–97) and Ernest Jones (1819–69), tried to emulate the events on the continent with a monster demonstration on Kennington Common (10 April), and the delivery to parliament of a petition with 2 million signatures in favour of the '6 points'. Although this took place in an atmosphere of extreme tension, it proved an anticlimax and a crop of bogus signatures allowed the petition to be laughed off. But many former Chartists were involved in the REFORM LEAGUE of the 1850s and some even survived to join the socialist organizations of the 1880s and 1890s.

Chaseabout raid 1565. The rebellion of MORAY against MARY QUEEN OF SCOTS, in resistance to the Darnley marriage and his own loss of influence. After a month-long chase across southern Scotland, Moray, who failed to muster adequate support, fled to England.

Chatham, William Pitt (the elder), 1st earl of 1708–78. As the favourite grandson of the tough East Indies merchant 'Diamond' Pitt, the young William was brought up to equate British greatness with the conquest of world trade. His public career was to be dedicated to that end. Entering parliament in 1735, he emerged after 1739 as an eloquent promoter of maritime and colonial warfare and opponent of continental campaigns to protect the 'despicable electorate' of Hanover. His hostility to Hanover earned him George II's hatred and it was not until 1746 that the king could be brought to accept him as paymaster-general. Though frustrated by the economies which followed peace in 1748, Pitt spent the succeeding years devising a strategy of empire, only to find himself dismissed (1755) on the eve of the SEVEN YEARS' WAR for opposing new German subsidies aimed at securing Hanover.

Pitt was an impossible colleague, but a wartime minister of genius. Haughty, incapable of delegation, condescending to colleagues, mentally unstable and at times megalomaniac, he was nonetheless a master of both strategy and logistic detail and an orator of inspirational power. 'I know that I can save this country', he declared, 'and that I alone can.' Many men believed him. Brought back as secretary of state in 1756, dismissed again and reinstated in 1757, he left domestic affairs to Newcastle and concentrated on the war. Supporting Prussia financially in Europe, while blockading the French fleet and directing campaigns in India, Canada, Africa and the Caribbean, he prepared the

George III's desire to rule personally caused the resignation of **Chatham** and the collapse of the Whig oligarchy. This cartoon of 1762 reflects both Chatham's popularity and the insecurity of his position.

way for the 'wonderful year' of victory (1759), which won even George II's admiration. But the triumph was brief. The accession of George III and the new king's hostility to the costly war led to Pitt's resignation (1761) and to the negotiation of the peace of PARIS (1763), despite his protest that 'we retain nothing although we have conquered everything'.

The remainder of Chatham's life was a bitter anticlimax. Increasingly isolated, prone to depression, tortured by gout and insomnia, his brief return to office (1766–8) and attempt to direct policy from the lords without party or cabinet support was a dismal failure. He retired deeply in debt and anguished by ministerial mishandling of colonial affairs. In 1778 he collapsed and died after a final speech on the American problem.

Chatham could sway parliament, but he could not, would not, exercise the arts of political management. He possessed vision but could not muster the firm support necessary for the implementation of his imperial conceptions. His advancement of national commercial aggrandisement in terms of patriotic principle was nonetheless prophetic of a will to empire which found a response in England's commercial classes and which would lead later generations to build upon the foundations he had laboured to establish.

Chatsworth house Derbys. The classical mansion built for the 1st duke of Devonshire by William Talman (1687–1707) and later extended by James Paine and Sir Jeffrey Wyatville. Chatsworth is particularly notable for its gardens and the landscaped park by Capability Brown.

Chester Originating as a LEGIONARY FORTRESS (c. 76–8), Chester's strategic position ensured its continued importance during the heroic age (see AETHELFERTH), under the Anglo-Saxons and (during the 10th century) as a stronghold of Norse Vikings. At the Norman conquest it became the seat of a COUNTY PALATINE, held from 1254 as part of the APPANAGE of the king's eldest son. It was besieged during the civil wars. Its Roman and medieval walls remain, as does its amphitheatre.

Chesterfield, Phillip Dormer Stanhope, 4th earl of 1694–1773. An opponent of Walpole and outspoken critic of Hanoverian interests in the war of the Austrian succession, Chesterfield was included in PELHAM's administration only after much opposition from George II. He was largely responsible for the calendar reform (1751) bringing Britain into line with continental practice.

Chatsworth house, Derbys.: the south front by William Talman, begun 1687.

Chevauchées Long-distance raids by mounted armies ('à cheval'), mainly English, during the hundred years' war. Designed, by plundering and devastating enemy territory, to weaken him materially and demoralize his civilian population, to demonstrate military might and challenge pitched battles (as at Crécy, Poitiers and Agincourt), and (not least) to enrich the participants.

Chevy Chase see OTTERBURN, BATTLE OF

Chichester see FISHBOURNE VILLA

Childers, Erskine 1870–1922. An Anglo-Irish writer, imperialist in sentiment, whose book *The Riddle of the Sands* (1903), about the threat of a German invasion, helped stimulate the demand for naval rearmament. Although he fought for the British (1914–18), he then became a SINN FEINER. After 1921, however, he took the republican side in the Irish civil war, until captured and shot.

Children see EDUCATION; FACTORY ACTS; FAMILY; INDUSTRIAL REVOLUTION

Chiltern Hundreds The ancient office of steward and bailiff of the Chiltern Hundreds of Buckinghamshire. Members of parliament, once elected, are forbidden to resign their seats. Instead they may 'take the Chiltern Hundreds' since, under 18th-century legislation against PLACEMEN, the holding of this office necessitates the vacating of a parliamentary seat.

Cholera epidemics Asiatic cholera hit Britain in 4 epidemics (1831–2, 1848, 1853 and 1866). A disease which induced violent vomiting and diarrhoea, rapidly bringing death to about 50% of those affected, it was only in 1853 that it was discovered to be disseminated by polluted drinking supplies. Thereafter its malignancy was curbed.

Christian Socialists Followers of F.D. Maurice (1805–72) and Charles Kingsley (1819–75) who attempted to mediate between what they considered the just demands of the CHARTISTS (1848) and the traditional institutions of the state. Their programme of co-operative workshops never got off the ground, but individual Christian Socialists did much for social reform.

Chronicles, monastic An invaluable (and at times virtually the only contemporary) source of history from the heroic age until the 15th century. The personal or corporate prejudices of the compiler, however, must always be taken into account.

Church, Pre-Reformation When Christianity first reached Britain is uncertain. ALBAN, the earliest known British martyr, apparently suffered *c.* 209, and soon afterwards Tertullian (writing in north Africa) could remark that Christ was worshipped even beyond the boundaries of the Roman province. By 314, when 3 British BISHOPS (of York, London and probably Lincoln) attended Constantine the Great's church council in Gaul, an ecclesiastical structure had been established, and archaeological evidence suggests that during the 4th century the British church became well-established and widespread. Its history is unrecorded, however, until the last years of Roman Britain, when it was influenced first by the monasticizing followers of St Martin of Tours (including NINIAN) and later by the heretical beliefs of PELAGIUS. Despite the efforts of GERMANUS, these last apparently persisted until the church in lowland Britain was destroyed, partially *c.* 450 and almost totally after 550, by the pagan Anglo-Saxons (*see* ARTHUR; HEROIC AGE). A strongly monastic church nevertheless survived in Wales (*see* DAVID, ST), Cornwall and the north-west, and flourished most vigorously in Ireland, where it had been established by Britons during the 5th and early 6th centuries. It was from there that the greatest missionary impulse now came, spreading monastic Christianity (notably through COLUMBA and his successors at IONA) first to pagan areas of Scotland and later to northern England.

The conversion of the Anglo-Saxons began, however, when AUGUSTINE introduced Christianity on the episcopal Roman pattern to Kent (597). Despite some setbacks it soon became firmly established there, but efforts to evangelize neighbouring kingdoms made little progress, and PAULINUS's initially successful Roman mission to Northumbria collapsed on the overthrow of his convert Edwin (632). Although during the 630s Sts Felix and Birinus, both upholders of Roman practice, established footholds respectively in East Anglia and Wessex, the main initiative in England now passed to Iona. Ionan MONKS under AIDAN founded LINDISFARNE (634) and began the reconversion of Northumbria. During the next 30 years they evangelized most of England north of the Thames, establishing flourishing outposts in Mercia and (under St Cedd) among the East Saxons. The inevitable clash between Rome and Iona was settled when the synod of WHITBY (664) decided for Rome, and the whole English church was thereafter united under the primacy of Canterbury by THEODORE. The last stronghold of paganism, Sussex, was Christianized in the 680s.

The 8th century saw the church in the forefront of a remarkable flowering of English learning and culture, resulting from a fusion of European and Irish traditions and best exemplified by the work of BEDE and ALCUIN. Both independent and BENEDICTINE monasteries abounded, and a new archbishopric was created at York (735). But the most notable organizational development was the beginning of the PARISH system, based initially on MINSTERS and later on smaller parish churches established by lay landowners. Culture and church organization alike suffered severely from the 9th-century Viking invasions, and, in the subsequent reconstruction, Alfred's efforts to revive learning and Edgar's sponsorship of DUNSTAN's 10th-century reforms emphasized the close links between the church and a sacerdotal monarchy. These survived the upheavals of the 11th century, both Cnut and Edward the Confessor being especial friends of the church, but in general the last years of the Anglo-Saxon state were a period of ecclesiastical decline.

Meanwhile the churches in Scotland (fully Christianized by *c.* 750) and Wales accepted Roman authority in the 8th century but retained many individualistic practices, notably a strong tradition of independent monasticism. In Scotland parochial minsters were paralleled by CULDEE foundations, but there too decline is observable in the 11th century.

All 3 British churches (English, Scottish and Welsh) were to be profoundly affected, and in many ways revitalized, by the Norman conquest. In England William the Conqueror used the eccles-

Above In Ireland the early church produced few monumental buildings. Monks inhabited separate stone beehive cells like this one, at Inishmurray, Co. Sligo, probably early 7th century.

Right Jedburgh abbey, Roxburghshire: the south aisle and nave. Founded by David I *c.* 1138 as a priory of Augustinian canons, it became an abbey in 1147. It was reduced to a ruin in 1545.

iastical authority inherited from his Anglo-Saxon predecessors to carry out sweeping reforms and establish the pattern of the medieval church settlement. Civil and CANON LAW were separated, ecclesiastical lands incorporated into the feudal system, rurally based DIOCESES transferred to large towns, and the primacy of Canterbury firmly upheld by LANFRANC. Monasticism made rapid progress, the foundation of alien PRIORIES being followed by the wholesale introduction of new, reformed RELIGIOUS ORDERS during the 12th century. This last also occurred in Scotland, becoming a special characteristic of the reform of the church on broadly Anglo-Norman lines by David I and his successors. In Wales the conquests of the Norman MARCHERS had by *c.* 1150 entailed the nominal submission of the native bishops to Canterbury, and the ancient semi-monastic *clasau* (independent communities of priests) were increasingly displaced by conventional Latin monasteries. Both processes were strongly opposed (efforts being made to erect an independent archbishopric of St David's) but were completed under Edward I. English attempts to control the Scottish church were less successful: it was placed under the direct protection of the papacy (1188), and after playing a leading role in the Scottish wars of independence it finally gained a metropolitan archbishop (of St Andrews) in 1472.

Since the medieval church affected almost every aspect of human activity from birth until death and beyond, its relationship with the state was always of paramount importance. The Norman conquest coincided with the growth of papal claims to temporal as well as spiritual power, and disputes between king and pope (generally but not invariably coinciding – *see* BECKET, ST THOMAS – with those between king and archbishop) all turned ultimately on who should have temporal control of the church. Their immediate causes were various. The earliest concerned bishops, now great feudal magnates and important royal servants. William the Conqueror (who, like his Anglo-Saxon predecessors, claimed supreme ecclesiastical authority) would therefore brook no papal interference in his episcopal appointments. But Henry I was eventually forced by ANSELM to compromise with papal claims, and thereafter appointments followed a bargain between king and pope. John's failure to conclude such a bargain (over LANGTON) resulted in the INTERDICT and the nominal surrender of all royal claims to ecclesiastical authority, and under Henry III foreign papal LEGATES (formerly virtually excluded) played an important and beneficial role in English politics.

The special papal relationship with England, however, allowed popes to appoint their own candidates (frequently absentee foreigners) not only

Salisbury cathedral: east walk of the cloister, looking north. The cloisters, never functional, were added *c.* 1270 possibly in imitation of the great Benedictine foundations.

Many changes in religious life occurred during the later middle ages. Regular monasticism (so long a vital element in the British church) had lost its impetus, and by the 14th century endowments, recruitment, and standards were all declining, new foundations being virtually confined to the still austere CARTHUSIANS. From the early 13th century monasteries also suffered competition from a new type of religious order, the mendicant and uncloistered FRIARS. These made a considerable impact both on education (*see* UNIVERSITIES) and, by their preaching and ministry, on parochial life in general. But their great initial popularity soon gave way to widespread criticism of their alleged peculation and excessive numbers. The church as a whole suffered from the Black Death and the Great SCHISM, and its preoccupation with political and other worldly affairs, strongest in the higher clergy, gave rise to anti-clericalism and even demand for the partial or total confiscation of ecclesiastical property. The doctrines of WYCLIFFE and the LOLLARDS, attacking not merely church institutions but the church itself, posed a potentially still greater threat, though their influence was limited after OLDCASTLE's rising (1414).

Despite all this, the majority of late medieval men continued enthusiastically to seek consolation within the church rather than outside it, and the decline of monasticism coincided with the development of institutions connected with a more participatory and personal style of religion. Large numbers of CHANTRIES, COLLEGIATE CHURCHES and medieval HOSPITALS were founded for the good of donors' souls, parish churches were everywhere rebuilt or refurbished, and urban guilds and religious fraternities flourished. SHRINES were thronged with pilgrims, and vernacular devotional treatises and MYSTERY PLAYS became increasingly popular. These essentially outward and secular forms nevertheless tended rather to conceal than to ameliorate the inward ills of the church, and all were to be swept away in the political and intellectual upheavals of the Reformation.

to bishoprics but also to cathedral canonries and even parish churches. The consequent export of English ecclesiastical revenues and damage to the rights of overriden English patrons made such 'papal provisions' bitterly resented. They were eventually technically forbidden by the statutes of Provisors (1351 and 1390) and PRAEMUNIRE (1353, 1365 and 1393), but continued thereafter in reduced numbers by tacit papal agreement with the crown. A compromise was also reached on the vexed question of clerical taxation (*see* PETER'S PENCE). Edward I gained the right to demand subsidies from the church without papal permission in an emergency, subsequently liberally interpreted. Despite pressure from parliament, the clergy nevertheless retained the right to tax itself independently through CONVOCATION, thus controlling the amount of the subsidy and the conditions upon which it was granted. Compromise between king, pope and clergy was, indeed, the basis on which the medieval ecclesiastical settlement rested, and the breakdown of this compromise over the question of Henry VIII's divorce was a crucial factor in the REFORMATION.

Church of England From the Elizabethan settlement of 1559 (*see* REFORMATION) until 1640 the hierarchy of the Anglican church faced the dual task of developing CRANMER's vision of the church as a distinctive Protestant middle way, while consolidating its position in the nation at large after the confusions of the Reformation. The historical and doctrinal claims of Anglicanism were advanced by FOXE and JEWEL against Catholicism, while WHITGIFT and BANCROFT struggled to contain PURITANISM within the church. Meanwhile there was a steady establishment of Protestantism in the country and improvement in the quality of the parish clergy, though the church's financial weakness meant the persistence of PLURALISM and NON-RESIDENCE.

The equilibrium achieved by the 1620s was upset by LAUD and the ARMINIANS whose alienation of the church's Puritan wing provoked the abolition of episcopacy and introduction of a Presbyterian system after the civil wars. Despite its failure and the upsurge of sectarian congregations during the interregnum, a degree of national organization was retained and the personnel and finances of the church were generally improved. At the RE-STORATION the church missed its opportunity for a comprehensive settlement at the SAVOY CONFERENCE (1661). Re-established and purged of DISSENTERS, it uneasily maintained its official monopoly until the TOLERATION ACT (1690). Thereafter it experienced a loss of vitality, weakened by continued clerical poverty and an increasingly inadequate parochial structure and unequal to the spiritual challenge presented by METHODISM in the 18th century.

In the early 19th century the church was both preoccupied with the impact of political reform and affected by changes in political control. First Catholic emancipation in 1829 (see ROMAN CATH-OLICISM) and then the REFORM BILL itself (1832) swelled the fear of the imminence of what NEWMAN called 'liberalism' or 'indifference' in doctrine and organization. The activist impulses which had hitherto fuelled Evangelicalism were attracted to the HIGH CHURCH revival of the OXFORD MOVEMENT. Although the EVANGELICALS remained dominant among the ranks of the clergy, the High Church-men claimed much support in the universities, despite the secession of many of their leaders to Rome (1845), while the small group of BROAD CHURCHMEN received government patronage (especially from the Whigs and Victoria) out of all proportion to their numbers. Hence the established church presented the confused spectacle of a conservative body led by liberals which was on the whole Catholic in its ideology. Such internal tensions were underlined by the findings of the religious census (1851), which showed that the church was reaching only c. 13–14% of the population (its strongest areas were Lancashire and the rural south), its position in Ireland and Wales being still more precarious.

Prescriptions for this situation differed within the establishment. Some High Churchmen believed that the link with the state was constricting and favoured 'disestablishment'. Gladstone was believed to agree with them. Some Evangelicals also favoured disestablishment because of their con-nections with NONCONFORMITY. But on the whole the main solution favoured was one of missions and church extensions both at home and abroad considerably aided by the move of industrial wealth from Nonconformity to the established church.

The weakness of Nonconformity after the 1850s also meant that as traditional Anglican preserves like the public schools and universities were 'national-ized', or freed from religious restrictions, they continued to preserve an unofficial Anglican dominance, while after the 1880s Anglican leaders spoke with greater authority partly because their grosser privileges had been abandoned. At the same time a real degree of authority was devolved from the bishops to the convocations of York and Canterbury (1852 and 1861) and in 1919 a representative body, the church assembly, was created, which 50 years later became the main legislative body of the church.

The 1919 Act effectively separated church and state, leaving to parliament only a veto power, last exercised during attempts to revise the prayer book (1927 and 1928). But the prestige of the church's leadership increased, probably reaching a peak during the archiepiscopate of TEMPLE (1941–4), who sought to identify it with the wartime spirit of radicalism and the welfare state. Since then its progress has been more hesitant – an intensification of Victorian trends – with the spread of unbelief among the educated classes and the decline of conventional morality and religious sanctions elsewhere in society.

Church of Scotland ('the kirk') Though the Scottish REFORMATION was essentially completed in 1572, a tension remained between the Congre-gational and Episcopalian elements in the con-stitution of the kirk, which was exacerbated by the dogmatic PRESBYTERIANISM of MELVILLE and was to persist until 1690. The uneasy equilibrium achieved by James VI and SPOTTISWOOD was upset by Charles I's innovations and, following the national COV-ENANT, episcopacy was abolished (1638). The Restoration brought its re-establishment (1662), the suppression of the GENERAL ASSEMBLY and open war between extreme COVENANTERS and the govern-ment. Only after the GLORIOUS REVOLUTION (1688) was the issue finally decided in favour of a fully Presbyterian system of church government (1690). But Presbyterian theocracy was averted by the firm subjection of the kirk to the Scottish parliament, the refusal to join civil penalties to excommunication which weakened the authority of KIRK SESSIONS, and the eventual repeal of the Act Concerning PATRONAGES (1712).

The 18th century saw a steady reduction in the severity of Presbyterian discipline and the triumph of moderation over Calvinist rigour in the kirk. At the same time, however, the kirk increasingly failed to contain the varieties of Scottish religious experience. Both Episcopalians and the extreme Presbyterian followers of CAMERON stood out against the 1690 settlement. In the mid-18th century the SECESSION CHURCHES, and in 1843 the formation of the Free Church (see DISRUPTION), added further to Scotland's religious pluralism. In 1900 the secession groups formed the United Free Church of Scotland which, with few exceptions, joined the church of Scotland in 1929. See BLACK ACTS; BOOKS OF DISCIPLINE.

Churchill, Lord Randolph 1849–94. The son of the duke of Marlborough, Churchill entered parliament as a Conservative (1874), becoming leader of the 'FOURTH PARTY'. As a TORY RADICAL and opponent of defence expenditure, he resigned as chancellor of the exchequer in Salisbury's government, believing he was indispensable (1886). But Goschen was appointed in his stead, and Churchill ended in the wilderness, a victim of a paralysing disease.

Randolph **Churchill**: drawing of the 1880s by the *Punch* cartoonist, H. Furniss.

Prime minister and war leader: Winston **Churchill** viewing the Alamein defensive position, 7 August 1942.

Churchill, Sir Winston 1874–1965. The son of Randolph, Churchill was educated at Harrow, without distinction. A war correspondent in the 2nd Boer war, he was elected Conservative MP for Oldham in 1900. He joined the Liberals (1904) because of his opposition to TARIFF REFORM, and was made president of the board of trade (1908), where he was closely identified with Lloyd George as an advocate of radical social reform. 1st lord of the admiralty from 1911 until the formation of the coalition (May 1915), he was then shunted into the duchy of Lancaster. He retired at the end of the year and went to serve as a colonel in the trenches: he had strongly supported the ill-fated DARDANELLES expedition, but had also initiated work on the 1st tanks. Lloyd George brought him back as minister of munitions (1917), and he served the coalition subsequently as secretary of state for war and air (1918–21) and as colonial secretary (1921–2). At the same time, however, his politics moved to the right. He reacted with great hostility to the Bolshevik revolution in Russia and was a champion of intervention on the side of the Whites. After rejoining the Tories (1924) – and serving (1924–9) as a highly orthodox and, in Keynes's view, disastrous chancellor of the exchequer – he drew the wrath of organized Labour (somewhat unfairly) for his bellicose role in the General Strike. By 1931 he seemed too far to the right even for his own party, chiefly because of his noisy opposition to Baldwin's Indian reforms. He took an increasingly strong anti-German line after the advent of Hitler in 1933.

On the outbreak of World War II he returned to the admiralty and was largely responsible for the disastrous Norwegian campaign (April 1940). However, on 10 May Chamberlain fell and, in default of Halifax (the candidate favoured by both

Labour and Conservative hierarchies), Churchill became prime minister and defence minister of the coalition government. Using broadcasting to carry the rhetoric of an earlier age, he made the rest of that year his – as well as the British people's – 'finest hour' and his personality and strong Anglo-American connections greatly aided the creation of the Atlantic alliance (1940–1). Of all British politicians, he clearly was best qualified for leadership in wartime, though as the war became extended his contribution inevitably diminished. Defeated in 1945, he had little to do with the reconstruction of his party, but benefited from it with a last period in office (1951–5), which included the coronation of Elizabeth II (1953), a ceremony not to be rivalled until his own funeral 12 years later.

Cinema From a music-hall turn, the cinema had established itself in most towns by 1914. The 3,000 of 1914 had swelled to a maximum of 4,800 by 1939, and 1946 was the peak year for admissions, with 1,635 million tickets sold. At first 90% of films were American, but the government made available subsidies to British film makers (1927–8), just in time for talkies. Britain's Hollywood – in the western suburbs of London – flourished for 2 decades, with spectacular productions by Sir Alexander Korda, much wartime patriotic fervour, both heroic and (at Ealing) quaint, and ultimately in the late 1950s a new social realism. But by then television had struck. By 1966 yearly admissions were down to 289 million.

Cinque ports A confederacy of south-eastern ports, named after the 5 'head ports' of Hastings, Romney, Hythe, Dover and Sandwich but also including up to 32 subsidiary ports or 'limbs'. From before the Norman conquest until the 16th century they provided ships and crews for royal service in return for certain privileges. *See* NAVY.

Circulating schools Welsh schools held by itinerant teachers, generally in the slack periods of the agricultural year. Established in the mid-18th century by Rev. Griffith Jones, they concentrated upon the teaching of basic literacy.

Cirencester Corinium Dobunnorum was the 2nd largest town in Roman Britain and among the most prosperous. It became the CIVITAS capital of the DOBUNNI *c.* 80. From *c.* 300 the capital of the province of Britannia Prima, it survived the heroic age in diminished form (*see* DYRHAM, BATTLE OF) to become a medieval wool town.

The harvest of toil: a **Cistercian** reaping, from a manuscript of *c.* 1111.

Cistercians Introduced to England in 1128 and Scotland in 1136, the White MONKS followed the austere reform of the BENEDICTINE rule originating at Cîteaux near Dijon. Stressing physical labour and seeking remote wastes for their houses, they became agricultural pioneers and sheep farmers on a massive scale, notably in Scotland, Wales and Yorkshire.

Civil list Funds voted by parliament from 1698 for the maintenance of the ROYAL HOUSEHOLD and (until 1831) the civil service and judiciary. The civil list could not be supplemented by drawing upon general revenues, which meant in effect that the monarch became the greatest salaried servant of the state.

Civil Service Direct employees of the government have traditionally been divided into the armed service (0·4 million 1970), their supporting civilians (0·13 million 1970), industrial (0·2 million 1970) and 'non-specialized' administrators (0·5 million 1970). Much the largest group of 'industrials' were the employees of the post office (0·25 million 1960) until its reorganization as a nationalized industry (1969). Among the 'non-specialized', recruitment was by patronage in the early period, but in principle has been organized by examination since the Northcote-Trevelyan report and the creation of the civil service commission (1854/5). This process was not completed until after World War I, although staff had risen to 0·18 million by 1914. The 'non-specialists' were divided into a 3-strata hierarchy, the administrative grade (recruited from the universities, with a bias to Oxford and Cambridge), executive and clerical grades. Both this, and the non-professional training attitudes of senior civil servants, were criticized by the Fulton report (1968).

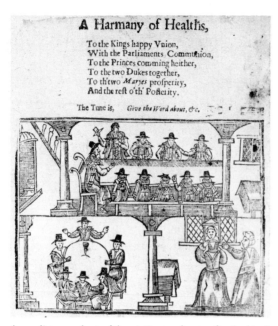

A royalist song-sheet of the **civil wars**, hoping for the king's return to London, and wishing death to 'the first Movers of this Distraction foule'.

Civil wars

Civil wars 1642–51. Though the preconditions of the civil wars can be traced back to the economic, social and religious changes of the 16th century, the origins of the political breakdown of 1642 lay more in the deterioration of relations between the crown and POLITICAL NATION during the reigns of JAMES VI AND I and CHARLES I, expressed in conflict between king and parliament. The financial and religious policies of Charles and LAUD (1630s) completed the alienation of the political nation in England and provoked rebellion in Scotland, the BISHOPS' WARS necessitating the summoning of the SHORT and LONG PARLIAMENTS (1640) and the initiation of constitutional reform in England. As the progress of reform slowed (1641), however, the solidarity of parliamentary opposition weakened and the IRISH REBELLION (1641) triggered a new crisis. Inability to trust the king led PYM to attempt to assert parliamentary control over the militia and the king's choice of councillors. After his unsuccessful attempt to seize the FIVE MEMBERS (January 1642), Charles abandoned the capital. A propaganda war ensued, culminating in Charles's rejection of the NINETEEN PROPOSITIONS and the raising of his standard at Nottingham (August 1642).

The basis of the formation of the royalist and parliamentarian sides in the ensuing war has been the subject of much debate. Parliament itself was split, a majority of the lords supporting the king and a majority of the commons supporting parliament. In the country a number of counties initially attempted to declare themselves neutral, but without success. Local rivalries among the gentry influenced the taking of sides, as did the question of which side succeeded in dominating a particular area in the early months of the war. Religion also played a major role, Puritans usually supporting parliament, and Roman Catholics and defenders of episcopacy rallying to the king. By 1643 Charles was broadly in control of the north and west, while parliament held the south-east and the city of London.

Despite its control of the wealth of London and the south-east, parliament's victory was neither inevitable nor initially sought for. Until 1644 parliament adopted a defensive strategy, in hope of a negotiated settlement on the basis of the position of 1642. The king, in contrast, aimed at the capture of Westminster and London. In 1642, after the 1st battle – at EDGEHILL – Charles almost succeeded in this, but RUPERT was halted at Turnham Green by the London train bands, and the king withdrew to Oxford. In 1643 there were royalist victories by NEWCASTLE in the north-east and HOPTON in the west and another drawn battle between the king's army and that of ESSEX at NEWBURY. Meanwhile Pym was actively organizing parliament's war finances with the excise and assessment system, while county committees governed the parliamentarian counties, which were grouped into military associations, the most famous being the Eastern Association. The SOLEMN LEAGUE AND COVENANT was also negotiated with the Scots. Scottish troops re-entered England (1644) and contributed to the victory of MARSTON MOOR. The advantage, however, was lost by Essex's surrender to the royalists at Lostwithiel and the distraction of the Scots by MONTROSE's highland campaigns. Following the indecisive 2nd battle of NEWBURY, disagreement in parliament between PRESBYTERIANS and INDEPENDENTS flared into a quarrel between Oliver CROMWELL and MANCHESTER over conduct of the war. This led to the SELF-DENYING ORDINANCE and the formation of the NEW MODEL ARMY under FAIRFAX. In 1645 the New Model defeated Charles at NASEBY and GORING at Langport, while in Scotland David Leslie defeated Montrose at Philliphaugh. In May 1646 Charles surrendered to the Scots at Newark, ending the 1st civil war.

Negotiations between parliament and the king began on the basis of the NEWCASTLE PROPOSITIONS (July 1646) and dragged on slowly. The situation was transformed early in 1647 by the resistance of the New Model to its disbandment and its seizure of the king at Holmby House. The army council now put forward the HEADS OF THE PROPOSALS to the king, negotiations continuing while the army occupied London in August. Charles attempted to play off the army against parliament, while Cromwell and IRETON struggled to control the LEVELLERS' influence at the PUTNEY DEBATES. In November 1647 the king fled to the Isle of Wight and renewed imprisonment at Carisbrooke Castle, where he received new delegates from parliament before concluding the ENGAGEMENT with Scottish commissioners. This triggered the 2nd civil war.

In 1648 there were revolts in Kent, Essex, Wales and the navy in anticipation of Scottish intervention on the king's behalf. The English risings were crushed by Fairfax at Maidstone and Colchester, and Cromwell took Pembroke before marching north to defeat the invading Scots at PRESTON. Meanwhile the renewal of parliamentary addresses to the king provoked the embittered army to reoccupy London and conduct PRIDE'S PURGE. On Cromwell's return, the RUMP PARLIAMENT proceeded with the trial and execution of the king, the abolition of MONARCHY and the establishment of the COMMONWEALTH.

The consolidation of the commonwealth and resistance to the Scottish championship of Charles II led to the final campaigns of the civil wars. Cromwell landed in Ireland (1649), took DROGHEDA and began a reconquest which was completed by Ireton (1651). Returning (1650), Cromwell defeated the Scots at DUNBAR and exactly a year later smashed Charles II's invading army at WORCESTER, while MONCK completed the conquest of Scotland. From 1651 the army maintained peace in England until Booth's Rising and the Restoration (1660).

The civil wars saw a development from defensive attempts to maintain the gains of 1641 to real revolution in 1649. They also witnessed the emergence, in the free atmosphere of wartime London and the New Model Army, of unprecedentedly radical demands for religious and political liberty. Though the Levellers, DIGGERS and FIFTH MONARCHY MEN were unsuccessful, the effective religious toleration which gave birth to such sects as the QUAKERS, RANTERS and MUGGLETONIANS was a result of the wars which Cromwell struggled to preserve in the 1650s. The Restoration meant the loss of much that had been fought for, but it preserved the principal reforms of 1641, while the legacy of the civil wars in thought, religious liberty and parliamentary government was to be taken up again after the Glorious Revolution (1688).

Thomas Fairfax presiding over the council of the army in 1647 when, disgusted by its treatment at the end of the **civil wars**, the army refused to obey the parliament that had created it. Woodcut from a contemporary pamphlet.

Civitates In Roman Britain, self-governing communities of non-citizens, generally coextensive with the territories of British tribes, though some artificial groupings were made. They were governed by a pair of magistrates and a council drawn from tribal notables and seated at the planned VICUS which constituted the civitas capital.

Claim of right 1689. A declaration by the Scottish estates accompanying their recognition of WILLIAM III and MARY II. It maintained the right of the estates to depose a king who had violated the laws, enumerated grievances against James VII and II, asserted the illegality of the lords of the ARTICLES and rejected episcopacy in the kirk.

Clans The traditional units of social organization of the Scottish highlands, based upon the real or imagined kinship between clansmen and their chief. The clansmen, who were commonly (though not always) tenants of their chief, supported him in war, accepted his authority and received his protection. The clan system was effectively broken in the aftermath of the JACOBITE '45' rebellion.

Clapham sect An Evangelical group of influential public figures, including WILBERFORCE, Henry

Thornton, Granville Sharp, Lord Teignmouth, Zachary Macaulay and James Stephen, centred on Rev. John Venn's church at Clapham and active 1790–1830. The 'sect' combined paternalistic philanthropy and support for moral reform with intense social conservatism.

de Clare, Richard *see* STRONGBOW

Clarence, George, duke of 1449–78. The younger brother of Edward IV, Clarence was suborned by the disaffected Warwick the Kingmaker, whose daughter he married (1469) and who possibly planned to make him king. After Warwick instead restored Henry VI, he rejoined his brother, but the breach was never fully healed and, after quarrelling with the Woodvilles, he was executed (probably by drowning in a barrel of wine) for treason.

Clarence, Thomas, duke of 1388–1421. The 2nd son of Henry IV. *See* BAUGÉ, BATTLE OF.

Clarendon, constitutions of *see* HENRY II

Clarendon, Edward Hyde, 1st earl of 1609–74. After initial support of the constitutionalist opposition, Hyde became royalist leader in the LONG PARLIAMENT and subsequently Charles I's principal civilian adviser. Pious, moral and economical, he was an unpopular chief minister to Charles II after 1660 and was dismissed in 1667. He died in exile after composing his *History of the Rebellion.*

Clarendon code The term used to describe the RESTORATION religious settlement enacted by the CAVALIER PARLIAMENT: the CORPORATION ACT (1661), Act of UNIFORMITY (1662), CONVENTICLE ACT (1664) and FIVE MILE ACT (1665). Though named after CLARENDON, it is likely that he would have preferred a more tolerant settlement.

Class Since the late 18th century the word 'class' has been used in many different ways by sociologists, political theorists, historians, and in ordinary speech. To many sociologists, 'class' is an abstract concept vital for the precise analysis of modern society, but given 'the complications of history' (as Professor Dahrendorf, in *Conflict after Class,* 1967, has put it) not corresponding directly with any exact social or historical reality. Disciples of the German sociologist Max Weber insist that distinctions should be made between a person's class (relating only to his economic position in society), his status (or social prestige) and his position in

regard to political power. Marxists have an overview of all historical development which envisages in the early modern period a bourgeois class struggling against a feudal class and, following the victory of the bourgeoisie (a word never admitted to any consistent or frequent usage in the ordinary English language but meaning, in its standard European sense, the town-based commercial groups who became increasingly influential from at least the 17th century onwards), a gathering struggle against it in the 19th and 20th centuries by the proletariat or working class. Most historians, however, prefer to try to use 'class' in the limited, though often complex, way in which real people in the past themselves used it. Classes, then, are inclusive groupings covering the whole of society, broadly recognized by members of that society themselves, and involving inequalities in such areas as power, authority, wealth, income, prestige, working conditions, life-styles and culture. It may well be, as Marxists contend, that a person's class is determined by his relationship to the means of production: certainly occupation would seem to be the single most important determinant of class. The problem, however, is that the nature and status of occupations change over time, that new occupations come into being, and that the same occupational label can conceal wide ranges in social status; a doctor ministering to an aristocrat, for instance, is almost certainly of higher status than one ministering to the members of a trade union medical scheme.

Class, in its limited historical usage, effectively comes into being under the impact of the social changes brought about by the INDUSTRIAL REVOLUTION. Professor Asa Briggs in his seminal article on 'The Language of Class' (in *Essays in Labour History,* 1965; ed. Briggs and Saville) has traced the earliest popular usage to 1818. Although the classes of modern industrial society were undoubtedly in formation over a much longer period of time (and although for analytical purposes the term 'class' may quite properly be used for earlier periods) it is in general best when referring to the pre-industrial period to speak of 'orders' or 'estates', as contemporaries did. The beginnings of the analytical study of class relationships (though the word itself was still not often used), indeed, is to be found among the 18th-century Scottish school of political economists and historians (such as William Robertson and Adam Ferguson). These early studies were taken immeasurably further by MARX who, drawing most of his evidence from mid-19th century Britain, argued that class conflict was the basic locomotive of historical change.

Meantime the labels 'working classes' and 'middle classes' were coming into widespread use (the plural form indicating that each 'class' contained a wide range of occupations and status and income groups). In the early decades of the 19th century the landed aristocracy and gentry (whose origins often lay in the former bourgeoisie) were still the most powerful political forces in the community, though reinforced, as they always had been, and now increasingly were, by more recent arrivals from commerce, industry and the professions. Nonetheless the old parliamentary system firmly excluded most of the 'middle classes'. However, the organized agitation associated with the passing of the REFORM BILL (1832) and perhaps still more the successes of the ANTI-CORN-LAW LEAGUE demonstrated their power and class consciousness. A few middle-class representatives sought the co-operation of members of the 'working classes', but the events of the 1830s and the 1840s, in particular the Owenite trade union movement (see OWEN, ROBERT) and CHARTISM, demonstrated that there was already a working-class consciousness hostile to the middle class. The distinguished Marxist historian E. P. Thompson has, in a famous book, written not inappropriately of *The Making of the English Working Class, 1780–1830* (1963).

The formation of the basic class structure of capitalist society in its heyday continued right on into the early 20th century. Industrialization did not proceed at an even pace. As well as mighty capitalists employing large numbers of industrial workers there were journeyman masters, and such examples of workers' co-operatives as the system of 'marras' or workers' companionships in the Durham coalfields. Beneath the industrial workers were what contemporaries called the 'sunken people', and what today social scientists call the 'under class'. There were many divisions within the working class and the gap between skilled and unskilled workers was especially wide. In 1867 a newspaper compositor could earn as much as 70 shillings a week, while a general labourer might be glad to get 12: contemporaries actually used the phrase 'aristocracy of labour' to describe the most prosperous and respectable workers. Differentials were still at least as great in 1914. Meantime a distinctive upper class took shape, an amalgam of the older aristocracy and new recruits from commerce, industry, government and the professions, with an ethos established by the half-dozen most prestigious PUBLIC SCHOOLS which took their definitive form in the 19th century. The middle classes had not as a class 'risen to power' (though

individuals had) but rather seemed happy to go on being ruled by this upper class. They did, however, enjoy a status and standard of living which meant that even the most prosperous members of the working class were sharply cut off from them, though the growing ranks of white-collar, lower-middle-class workers were clearly very conscious that it was culture and status rather than income that cut them off from the workers below.

Against the Marxist view of the inevitability of class conflict, many historians have presented a view of an essential harmony of interests in British society from mid-Victorian times onwards. In the 1850s the skilled workers began to form themselves into the new model unions (see TRADE UNIONISM), which seemed to be characterized by limited objectives and deference towards the middle class. In the 1880s there began the organization of the unskilled workers in the 'NEW UNIONISM', while unionization of skilled workers continued to expand rapidly. Clearly there was a development in working-class consciousness which could mean industrial militancy and even violence, yet evidence of widespread and consistent hostility to the capitalist system is harder to establish.

On-the-ground evidence of the class structure can be found in the elegant country and town mansions (the latter supplied with mews and individual stabling facilities) of the upper class, in the solid houses of the middle classes (a small flight of steps clearly indicating the provision for servants below stairs), and in the meaner terraces provided for the working classes near work places, or hard by railway lines and junctions.

Has the 20th century brought increasing polarization between an upper-class bourgeoisie and an increasingly class-conscious working class into which most of the middle classes are steadily thrust, as many Marxists argue, or has it brought a disintegration of the class structure as many contemporary sociologists argue? WORLD WARS I and II both helped to strengthen and consolidate the working class, intensifying the process of absorbing into it the old 'under class', and fostered a national spirit favourable to the diminution of class distinctions. The growth of the Labour party ensured that the special interests of the working class were advanced, and after 1945 the working class assumed a position in the community analogous to that occupied by the middle class after the 1832 Reform Bill.

Despite the growth of management divorced from ownership of capital, the persistence of the traditional upper class, which has absorbed into it the most successful managers, who in turn often possess themselves of considerable share capital, can be clearly seen. Threats, real or imagined, to middle-class income and status seem, however, to have resulted in more aggressive middle-class consciousness, rather than any identification with the working class. The fact is that historical trends seldom operate in a single direction: there has been both consolidation of classes (if not exactly polarization) and disintegration. There have been brief periods (in particular just before and just after World War I) of apparently bitter class antagonism, yet, as John Stevenson and Chris Cook have shown in *The Slump* (1977), even amid mass unemployment, class conflict was remarkably limited. In Britain perhaps more than most countries class distinctions remain sharp and create a kind of running cold war which, while probably conducive to political stability, may also be a factor in social and economic stagnation. Even so, class divides have since the late 1950s been steadily overlaid by the divides of race and nationalism and by the emergence of a new under class of outcastes.

Classes, Act of 1649. Act disqualifying from office in Scotland all former supporters of MONTROSE or of the Scottish ENGAGEMENT, persons who had not protested against the Engagement and persons of scandalous life. In addition lay patronage in the church was abolished. The Act led to a drastic purge of the church.

Classicianus, Julius Alpinus PROCURATOR of Roman Britain from 61, Classicianus opposed the excessively severe repression exercised by the governor Suetonius Paullinus after Boudica's rising, and was instrumental in his recall. His moderating and conciliating influence continued under succeeding governors. His tombstone remains in the British Museum.

Classis Britannica The Roman fleet based on Boulogne and Dover. From the 1st–3rd centuries it was used for transport and to supply the expeditions of Vespasian, Julius Frontinus, Agricola and Severus, but from *c.* 275 was employed defensively against Anglo-Saxon raiders, operating from the fortified harbours of the SAXON SHORE system.

Classis movement A movement of Puritan ministers of the CHURCH OF ENGLAND, organized by John Field in the 1580s. Ministers met voluntarily in regional *classes* after the Presbyterian manner (though without lay elders) to discuss matters of common concern. Attacked by Whitgift and Bancroft, the classes gradually ceased to meet.

Clergy, benefit of From the late 12th century, the right of persons successfully claiming clerical status, which was proved by a simple reading test, to escape the jurisdiction or full rigour of the secular courts. Increasingly restricted from the 16th century, it disappeared from English courts in the later 18th century.

Clergy, submission of the 1532. The acceptance by convocation of Henry VIII's demands that no ecclesiastical legislation be passed without the king's licence and that existing canons be approved by royal commissioners. The submission was subsequently incorporated in a statute (1534) placing ultimate authority in spiritual suits in lay hands.

Cleves, Anne of 1515–57. The sister of William duke of Cleves, Anne was chosen in 1539 as Henry VIII's 4th wife, largely for diplomatic reasons. Henry was disappointed with Anne who was shy and lacked courtly accomplishments. The unconsummated marriage was nullified in 1540 and Anne retired happily to estates provided by the King.

Clive, Robert 1725–74. Described by Chatham as 'a heaven-born general', Clive rose from a clerkship in the EAST INDIA COMPANY to command armies, defeating French rivalry in India and establishing British suzerainty over Bengal. Subsequently attacked for his unscrupulous methods, he successfully defended himself before parliament. He later committed suicide.

Clodius Albinus governor of Roman Britain (*c.* 191–7). Albinus declared himself emperor in 196 and (having fortified London and many other British towns) led much of the British garrison to Europe against his rival Severus, exposing the province to revolts and Caledonian invasions. He was defeated and killed near Lyons (197).

Close rolls Rolls of CHANCERY copies of English royal 'letters close' (letters of passing importance closed by the GREAT SEAL), surviving from 1204 until their discontinuance in 1903. They initially dealt with most types of government business but by the early 16th century their scope was confined to deeds. At present in course of publication.

Closed parishes A term used for closely regulated parishes of the 17th and 18th centuries in which the settlement of poor cottagers was discouraged by the landlords and principal inhabitants in order to keep down the poor rates. *See* OPEN PARISHES.

Anne of **Cleves**, 4th wife of Henry VIII: portrait by Holbein.

Robert **Clive** receiving from the Nawab of Bengal a grant to establish the fund for disabled officers and soldiers. Oil painting by Edward Penny, *c.* 1773.

Cloth trade From *c.* 1450 to *c.* 1700 the manufacture and export of woollen cloth was the backbone of English industry and trade. Undyed west country and Suffolk broadcloths exported to Antwerp dominated before 1550, joined thereafter by lighter finished cloths, the NEW DRAPERIES of East Anglia exported to both northern and Mediterranean markets. *See* COCKAYNE PROJECT.

Club, the A group of opponents of the Scottish administration early in the reign of WILLIAM III, including Sir Patrick Hume, FLETCHER of Saltoun, FORBES of Culloden, the duke of Argyll, Lord Ross and Sir James Montgomerie. They advocated a Presbyterian church settlement and a reassertion of the independence of the Scottish parliament.

Clubmen Associations of crudely armed countrymen, formed in the south-western counties of England (1645) for self-defence against plundering royalist and parliamentarian soldiers. Part popular movement and part gentry-led, the clubmen were dispersed by either force or persuasion as the New Model Army advanced.

Cluniacs Order of MONKS following the reformed BENEDICTINE rule established at the influential French abbey of Cluny (10th century). They concentrated on splendid worship and liturgy and were rigidly centralized, all houses being directly controlled by Cluny. English houses (founded from 1077) were thus technically alien PRIORIES, but obtained naturalization 1351–1407.

Cnut king of England, Denmark and Norway (1016–35; b. *c.* 994). Called 'the Great' and 'the Mighty', Cnut was the younger son of Sweyn Forkbeard, after whose death (1014) he was driven from England by Aethelred Unraed. In August 1015 he returned and reduced most of England, being widely recognized as king after Aethelred's death but not gaining full possession until the death of Edmund Ironside (1016). At first he ruled harshly, but having divided the land among earls, married EMMA and levied a huge DANEGELD to pay off his fleet, he agreed with the English nobility (1018) to observe the laws of EDGAR. He was thus secure enough to lead 4 expeditions to Scandinavia (1019–28), gaining control of Denmark and

King **Cnut** and Queen Emma place a cross on the altar of the new abbey at Winchester. Contemporary drawing from *Liber Vitae* of New Minster.

temporarily of Norway. He greatly increased the Danish element in Anglo-Saxon England (always the focus of his dominions) but was respected for his re-establishment of peace, his reinforcement of law (*see* TITHING) and his enthusiastic patronage of the church.

Cobbett, William 1762–1835. The self-educated son of a Surrey yeoman, Cobbett became a radical pamphleteer of great power. In the *Political Register* (founded 1802) and his *Rural Rides* he combined a deep sympathy for the rural poor with the castigation of corruption and greed. He was MP for Oldham 1832–5.

Cobden, Richard 1804–65. A cotton printer in Manchester, Cobden became a founder member and leader of the ANTI-CORN-LAW LEAGUE (1839). He negotiated the Cobden-Chevalier treaty with France (1860), the high-water mark of FREE TRADE, and between then and his death worked to ameliorate the strained relations between London and Washington caused by the American civil war.

Cockayne project 1614–16. Plan devised by Alderman Cockayne and adopted by the royal government to capture the finishing trade in broadcloth from the Netherlands. It failed due to insufficient investment, lack of skilled workers and the hostility of overseas markets and led to widespread depression in the English CLOTH TRADE.

Coercion A term applied to British attempts to suppress agrarian disorder in Ireland, chiefly under the Liberal chief secretary Forster (1880–2), and the Conservative Balfour (1886–92), mainly by dispensing with trial by jury and HABEUS CORPUS. *See* IRISH CONSTITUTIONAL CRISIS.

Coercive (or 'Intolerable') Acts 1774. Acts passed in retaliation for the BOSTON TEA PARTY, closing the port of Boston, quartering troops there, exerting greater control over the Massachusetts government and providing for the removal of officials accused of crimes in the colony for trial elsewhere. The Acts precipitated the AMERICAN INDEPENDENCE struggle.

Coffee houses Fashionable meeting places and centres of political, literary and commercial life, first established in the later 17th century and popular throughout the 18th. Some 3,000 coffee houses existed in London by 1708, among the most notable being Will's and Button's (patronized by literary men) and Lloyd's (a centre of marine insurance).

Cogidubnus Apparently an exiled ATREBATIC prince, who accompanied the Roman invasion (43), safeguarded its Sussex flank, and probably brought about the surrender of several British tribes. As a client-king he was a leading agent of Romanization, but the theory that he was rewarded with the title of imperial legate (based on the misreading of an inscription) has recently (1980) been disproved. *See* FISHBOURNE VILLA.

Cohort *see* LEGION

Coke, Sir Edward 1552–1634. A brilliant lawyer and author of the *Reports* (1600–15) and *Institutes of the Laws of England* (1628–44), Coke rose steadily after 1592 to become lord chief justice (1613). Dismissed in 1616 for attacking the ROYAL PREROGATIVE, he re-emerged as a leader of the parliamentary opposition (1621–8).

Colchester Camulodunum, the chief settlement of Cunobelinus, became the site of a Roman legionary fortress (43), replaced *c.* 49 by the Ist British COLONIA. Destroyed by Boudica (61), the rebuilt town survived (perhaps as Arthur's 'Camelot') to be occupied by Anglo-Saxons *c.* 600. A Viking stronghold reduced by Edward the Elder, and the site of an important Norman castle, Colchester was the scene of crucial civil war siege.

The **coffee house** in its heyday: engraving by W. Dickinson after H. Bunbury, 1781.

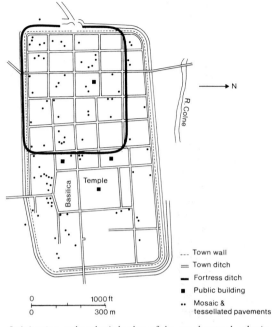

Town wall
Town ditch
Fortress ditch
Public building
Mosaic & tessellated pavements

0   1000 ft
0   300 m

Colchester: archaeologist's plan of the 1st chartered colonia, showing the site of the abandoned legionary fortress over which it was founded *c.* 49.

Cole, G. D. H. 1889–1959. An Oxford don, Cole became a left-wing Fabian (*see* FABIAN SOCIETY) of Syndicalist inclinations (*see* SYNDICALISM) and organizer of workers' education. He returned to Oxford (1925) but continued to advise the Labour party, to write labour history and to develop social policy until his retirement (1957). He was an important influence in moving a generation of university intellectuals such as Gaitskell towards moderate socialist politics.

Colet, John 1466–1519. A brilliant and austere Catholic reformer, friend of Erasmus and More, Colet did much as an Oxford lecturer, popular preacher, dean of St Paul's (1504–19) and founder of St Paul's School (1512), to introduce humanist scholarship (*see* HUMANISM) to England and to stimulate criticism of church abuses prior to the Reformation.

College of Justice *see* LAW

Collegiate churches Frequently large, these were served by a *collegium* (community) of secular CANONS. They might be MINSTERS or house a shrine, but in the later middle ages many were founded by magnates as multiple CHANTRIES, frequently connected with hospitals or almshouses or having an educational function.

Collins, Michael 1890–1922. A militant Irish nationalist and member of the Irish Republican Brotherhood, Collins was involved in the Easter Rising (1916) and imprisoned by the British. After his release he was elected to Dail Eireann (1918) and organized the Irish Republican Army's guerilla campaign (1919–21), but in June 1921, with the support of the IRB, he threw his weight behind the Free State compromise involved in the Anglo-Irish treaty. On GRIFFITH's death (January 1922) he became prime minister but in August he was killed in a republican ambush in his home county of Cork. *See* IRISH CONSTITUTIONAL CRISIS.

Coloniae The highest grade of town in Roman Britain, founded by official policy as settlements of time-expired legionaries, Roman citizens who were granted a plot of land in the town and another in its surrounding rural *territorium*. They were self-governing, with a senate and 2 consuls.

Columba, St *c.* 521–97. A prime mover in the Christianization of Scotland, Columba was an Ulster abbot of royal blood, expelled from Ireland (563) after involvement in dynastic warfare. He thereupon founded IONA and used it as a base for evangelization, strengthening Christian Dalriada and allegedly converting King Brudei of the northern Picts.

Combination Acts 1799. Acts ostensibly to prevent conspiracies in restraint of trade which effectively made trade unions criminal conspiracies. Their repeal in 1824 allowed unions legal existence though they remained vulnerable to prosecution for breach of contract or restraint of trade if they took strike action. *See* TRADE UNIONISM.

Comitatenses In the 4th century the Roman army (*see* AUXILIARIES; LEGION) was reorganized into comitatenses, who formed the mobile field forces normally commanded by a count, and limitanei, lower-paid garrison troops on frontier service.

Commendators *see* REFORMATION

Commissions of inquiry *see* INQUISITIONS

Committee of both kingdoms A committee of 21 members of the English parliament and 4 Scottish commissioners established following the

SOLEMN LEAGUE AND COVENANT (1643) to co-ordinate military operations in the civil wars. It was dissolved (1648) after the Scottish ENGAGEMENT.

Committee of estates A committee established by the Scottish parliament (1640–51, 1660–1 and 1688–9), which included non-members of parliament and had power to act on parliament's behalf, being in effect the executive government of Scotland in these years.

Committee of imperial defence The committee of the cabinet which attempted to co-ordinate and create policy for the service ministries. It existed in an *ad hoc* way from 1895 and was reorganized as the CID (1902–3). It included service chiefs and, before World War I, the leader of the opposition. It was revived (1919–39) with HANKEY as its secretary, and after 1945 its functions were split between the ministry of defence and a cabinet committee, now the Defence and Overseas Policy Committee.

Common law *see* LAW

Common Market It arose from various post-war, Europe-wide or regional agreements, of which the most important was the Coal and Steel Community (1951). Formally created by the treaty of Rome (1957), it operated from 1958. Harold Macmillan's government negotiated to join (1962–3), but was turned down by the personal veto of General de Gaulle. French intransigence also blocked an approach by Harold Wilson's government (1969) but Edward Heath's government was finally successful (1973), and Britain's adhesion was confirmed by a plebiscite in June 1975.

Britain's attempts to join the **Common Market** were twice blocked by the French. De Gaulle, the sentry, faces a Harold Wilson weighed down with commitments. *Die Zeit* cartoon, 'Thoughts are duty-free', January 1969.

Common Pleas, court of An English LAW court, originating in the 12th century, with jurisdiction over civil suits between subjects. Staffed by a chief justice and 5 judges, it sat at Westminster and was notoriously slow and expensive for litigants. In 1873 common pleas became a division of the high court of justice.

Common Wealth A radical party formed (1942) by Liberals and socialists to challenge the 'electoral truce' between the main parties during World War II. It was successful in 3 by-elections and, although as a political force it expired in 1945, it helped create the reforming atmosphere in which Labour won the 1945 election.

Commons, house of *see* PARLIAMENT

Commonwealth, the 1649–53. The English republic established after the execution of Charles I and ruled by the RUMP PARLIAMENT and a COUNCIL OF STATE. Despite its narrow basis of support, the regime established control over England, Ireland and Scotland. The commonwealth proper ended with the establishment of Oliver CROMWELL'S PROTECTORATE (1653).

Commote *see* CANTREF

Communist party of Great Britain Founded in 1920 by the merging of various leftist sects, largely breakaways from the SOCIAL DEMOCRATIC FEDERATION, it accepted from the beginning the leadership of the Soviet Union, through the 3rd INTERNATIONAL. Its membership was never large and was disproportionately Scottish and Welsh. It never had more than 4 MPs, but it secured much trade union influence, mainly among the miners and in the trades councils. It gained by the POPULAR FRONT policies of the 1930s, and lost by the Nazi-Soviet pact, but its membership reached an all-time peak through pro-Soviet enthusiasm in World War II. The Hungarian revolution (1956) caused a flight of members into NEW LEFT groups and, with the growth of other far left organizations (*see* TROTSKY-ITES), its decline has subsequently been a steady one, despite increasing independence of the Soviet line.

Company of Scotland *see* DARIEN SCHEME

Comyn, John, 'The Red' *see* ROBERT BRUCE

'Concert of Europe' A term for the settlement of disputes involving – directly or indirectly – the

19th-century 'great powers' by their concerted action. *See* SALISBURY, ROBERT CECIL.

Concordat of Leith *see* REFORMATION

Confession of faith *see* REFORMATION

Congregation, lords of the The group of Scottish nobles who in 1557 subscribed the First Band as the 'congregation of Christ' for the furthering of the REFORMATION in Scotland and subsequently (1559–60) fought against MARY OF GUISE in defence of Protestantism.

Congregationalists Originating with Elizabethan Puritan separatists believing in congregational independence and religious toleration, the Congregationalists grew in strength during the interregnum (1649–60) to become a major branch of English dissent. They achieved national unity in the congregational union (1832) and in 1972 joined English Presbyterians in the United Reformed church. *See* DISSENTERS; NONCONFORMITY.

Connolly, James 1870–1916. An Irish socialist theorist and organizer of unskilled labour in Belfast and Dublin with LARKIN. The failure of the DUBLIN TRAMWAYS STRIKE (1913) drove him into alliance with Pearse's militant nationalists and his citizen army into the Easter Rising (1916). Although wounded, he was executed after it. *See* IRISH CONSTITUTIONAL CRISIS.

Conscription *see* ARMY; WORLD WAR I; WORLD WAR II

James **Connolly** and some of his citizen army early in World War I, outside Liberty Hall, Dublin headquarters of his Transport and General Workers Union. The hall was shelled during the Easter Rising, 1916.

Conservative party The ideological origins of the modern Conservative party lie with BURKE's rejection of liberal dogma in his *Reflections on the Revolution in France* (1790). Politically its founder was the younger PITT and his political 'friends' who carried on the wartime government after his death. The ideal of a party pledged to conserve the existing political establishment while containing modern industrial and social development is, however, essentially associated with the hegemony of PEEL, whose Tamworth Manifesto (1834) accepted the REFORM BILL (1832) while pledging opposition to doctrinaire liberalism. In this it echoed the 'liberal toryism' of the 1820s, associated with men such as HUSKISSON and CANNING, but its attempt to turn this into a 'philosophy of government' after 1841 was vitiated by its continuing role as the 'country party' representing the agricultural interest, with its insistence on the maintenance of the CORN LAWS. Disraeli made it his business to transform this essentially myopic position into an anti-liberal stance with some TORY RADICAL pretensions, and orchestrated the resistance to Peel which forced him from the party after he had carried the repeal of the Corn Laws (1846). Apart from 3 ministries (1852, 1858–9 and 1866–8), the Conservatives were then doomed to a quarter of a century of opposition. Why then, after 1874, did they enjoy an equivalent dominance for over 30 years? Partly this was due to Liberal divisions, especially after 1886, when over 70 LIBERAL UNIONISTS united with them to oppose Gladstone's policy of Irish home rule. Partly, too, it reflected a broadening of electoral support as the city and the better-off suburbs deserted the Liberal party and campaigning among the working classes gained the Conservatives local dominance in such areas as Lancashire. It also owed greatly to Disraeli's ideal of the supremacy of the party, and the cohesion of its supporters. SALISBURY's party (1881–1902) rarely experienced the sectarianism and sectionalism that plagued its Liberal rivals, and when under BALFOUR (1902–11) it did split over ideology (1903–5), it was because of the ex-Liberal Joseph CHAMBERLAIN's policy of TARIFF REFORM.

From the consequences of this split, and the resulting Liberal landslide (1906), the Conservatives took time to recover. Before 1914, indeed, they flirted dangerously with extremism, especially over the Ulster issue, despite the fact that their leader Bonar LAW (1911–23) was privately reconciled to home rule for the rest of Ireland (*see* IRISH CONSTITUTIONAL CRISIS). It was the Liberal party's failure to cohere over the conduct of the war which brought the Conservatives into power, first as junior partners in the ASQUITH coalition (May 1915)

ELECTORS DONT TRY THE IMPOSSIBLE
SUPPORT THE MIDDLE COURSE OF JUSTICE TO ALL

TORN IN TWO

RICH RADICALISM   SOCIALISM

Mʳ ASQUITH –
"HOW I WISH I'D NEVER HAD ANYTHING TO DO WITH EITHER OF THEM"

BY VOTING FOR THE
UNIONIST CANDIDATE

This poster for the 2nd election of 1910 shows the **Conservatives** (known as Unionists in much of Britain) playing on Asquith's problem of reconciling his traditional business supporters with his party's dependence on Labour support.

and then as LLOYD GEORGE's predominant partners after December 1916. Their hold on power was consolidated by the COUPON ELECTION (1918) and that of 1922, which was fought after a rank-and-file revolt had brought down Lloyd George himself. By now they had taken over from the Liberals the representation of the business classes – symbolized by the adhesion of MOND (1926) – although their leader BALDWIN (1923–37) seemed to represent their inertia in the face of a worsening world depression, and the rise of the dictatorships. His 1924–9 government nevertheless extended and consolidated welfare legislation under Neville CHAMBERLAIN as minister of health, and its policy on India was conciliatory: both were at some remove from pre-World War I policy, and reflected the party's move to a centrist 'party of government' position. This was confirmed by its role in the NATIONAL GOVERNMENT (1931–40) which soon became a Conservative government in all but name.

The fall of Chamberlain (May 1940), demonstrating both the failure of his APPEASEMENT policies and his war leadership, badly damaged his

party. Winston CHURCHILL (1940–55) had little rank-and-file support and the success of the war effort tended to boost the reputation of Labour. The 1945 defeat was not, however, the occasion for another retreat into the ideological wilderness. Under WOOLTON and R. A. Butler the party's organization was modernized and its policies for a mixed economy made competitive with those of Labour. Although this achievement was masked by Churchill's persistence in office until 1955 and EDEN's (1955–7) responsibility for the Suez debacle, it had paid off by 1959, when Harold Macmillan (1957–63) trounced Labour and made inroads on its traditional vote, as well as taking over Labour's claim to be the party of planning and decolonization. Unfortunately, this ideological confluence was complicated for the Conservatives by a stagnating economy and a series of scandals of which the most pungent was the PROFUMO AFFAIR, a situation not aided by the less-than-democratic 'evolution' of Sir Alec Douglas-Home (1963–6) to the leadership after Macmillan's resignation. After the Labour victories (1964 and 1966) policy under Edward Heath (1966–75) shifted towards a greater degree of laissez-faire ('the Selsdon policy') and a strong commitment to devolution and to enter the COMMON MARKET (while it was also aided, unofficially, by the anti-immigrant propaganda of Enoch Powell), but the problems it was faced with in 1970–4 drove it back to centrist collectivist remedies. Following Heath's replacement by Margaret Thatcher (1975), the party's course seemed more nationalistic (anti-Europe, anti-immigrant, anti-devolution) and doctrinaire individualist than it had been for some time, an impression confirmed by its first actions in government after May 1979.

Constable (Old French 'count or officer of a stable'). Originally a household or military office (e.g. constable of England), constable came later to signify the peacekeeping officer of a HUNDRED or PARISH.

Constance, council of *see* SCHISM, GREAT

Constantine The 1st Christian Roman emperor (306–37).

Constantius As Caesar to the Emperor Maximian, he invaded a rebellious Roman Britain (296), overthrew Allectus, restored the country to imperial control and carried out various reforms. He returned as emperor (306) to mount a punitive expedition into Scotland and died at York.

Continental system *see* NAPOLEONIC WARS

Conventicle Act 1664. An Act prohibiting meetings of 5 or more persons not members of the same household 'under colour or pretence of any exercise of religion'. Aimed at Protestant DISSENTERS, the Act lapsed in 1668, was re-enacted in milder form (1670) and was repealed by the TOLERATION ACT (1689).

Convention of estates, Scottish *see* GLORIOUS REVOLUTION

Convention of royal burghs An assembly of representatives of the privileged royal burghs of Scotland which evolved from the 13th century and met annually in the 16th and 17th centuries to agree on economic and financial matters of mutual concern. It became the Convention of Scottish Local Authorities in 1975.

Convention parliament *see* DECLARATION OF RIGHTS; GLORIOUS REVOLUTION; RESTORATION

Convocation The assemblies of the clergy of the 2 provinces of the English church, summoned to decide matters of ecclesiastical law and government and grant taxes to the crown. They were reconstituted into the national assembly of the church of England – since 1970 the general synod.

Convoy system Groups of ships sailing together for protection were characteristic of the sailing navy. This tactic was revived in World War I, at first on a limited scale, then, after February 1917, as a protection against the U-boat campaign. Jellicoe fought against it, as it would deprive the grand fleet of escorts.

Cook, James 1728–79. The son of a Yorkshire labourer, Cook learned his seamanship in coastal colliers and cartography in the navy. He commanded 3 expeditions of Pacific exploration (1768–79), discovering and charting New Zealand, New South Wales and the Hawaiian islands. He was killed by natives in Hawaii.

Co-operative retail societies These existed in many industrial towns from the late 18th century. In 1832 OWEN attempted to organize them on a more systematic basis but failed. The 'ROCHDALE PIONEERS' society (1844) provided the prototype for widespread expansion in the 1850s and 1860s, the Co-operative Wholesale Society being set up in 1863 and the Co-operative Union in 1869.

Copenhagen, battle of 2 April 1801. Ignoring signals from Admiral Hyde Parker to return, NELSON entered Copenhagen harbour with 12 ships and destroyed the entire Danish fleet. The result was the dissolution of the league of northern powers sympathetic to Napoleon which had attempted to close the Baltic to British ships. *See* NAPOLEONIC WARS.

Copyhold A form of land tenure by 'copy' of the manorial court roll which emerged in the later middle ages as serfdom declined. Varying in its terms and in security of tenure, copyhold was largely displaced by LEASEHOLD in the 16th and 17th centuries, though not abolished until 1926.

Coritani A Belgic-influenced British tribe inhabiting Lincolnshire and the north-east midlands. It seems to have peaceably accepted Roman occupation (47), and by *c.* 80 had become a CIVITAS, with a capital at Ratae Coritanorum (Leicester).

Corn Laws Laws operative 1689–1846 encouraging the export and limiting the import of corn when prices were below a fixed point, in order to protect landowners. Modified by the introduction of a sliding scale of prices (1828), they were abolished after the militant agitation of the ANTI-CORN-LAW LEAGUE.

James **Cook**: portrait by Nathaniel Dance, 1776.

Cornavii A northern Scottish tribe which inhabited Caithness at the time of Roman Britain.

Cornovii A British tribe inhabiting the Shropshire-Cheshire area, apparently pro-Roman at the conquest. Its territory was occupied *c.* 50, and by *c.* 90 it had formed a CIVITAS centred on Wroxeter.

Cornwall, duchy of Estates and franchises, mainly in Cornwall and Devon, granted to the Black Prince (then created duke) as an APPANAGE (1337). It has since been held by the eldest son of the sovereign, or by the crown directly in default, and is now run as a private estate.

Cornwallis, Charles Cornwallis, marquess of *see* BRITISH EMPIRE; YORKTOWN, SURRENDER OF

Coronation The consecration of a monarch, in England including (since the 10th century) his anointment with holy oil, oath to rule justly, recognition by the people and crowning. Anointment, symbolizing the monarch's priestly role, was only included in Scottish ceremonies after the Scottish wars of independence. English coronations since the Norman conquest have generally occurred at Westminster abbey, Scottish (until 1651) usually at SCONE. *See* MONARCHY; ill. p. 12.

The **coronation** chair made for Edward I, containing the stone of SCONE on which Scottish kings used to be crowned.

Coroners *see* LAW

Corporal punishment Flogging in the navy was abolished in 1861, and in the army in 1881. It was maintained in civilian law and as a punishment in prisons until 1948. It remains widespread – and unique – in the British educational system.

Corporation Act 1661. An Act excluding from borough corporations persons who refused to take the Anglican communion or to subscribe to the oaths of allegiance and supremacy and declarations abjuring the SOLEMN LEAGUE AND COVENANT and declaring the unlawfulness of taking arms against the king. It was repealed in 1828.

Corunna, retreat to 1808–9. After advancing from Portugal to threaten the rear of Napoleon's invading army, 30,000 British troops under Sir John Moore retreated 250 miles through the mountains of northern Spain in the winter of 1808–9. Rallying his demoralized army at Corunna, Moore evacuated most of his force, but was himself killed in the final operation. *See* NAPOLEONIC WARS.

Council, the Though the monarchy always consulted councillors of its own choosing (*see* WITAN), in the early medieval period the king's 'great council' included not only ministers such as the chancellor but also the entire baronage (*see* TITLES) and bench of bishops. After this developed into PARLIAMENT during the 14th century, the importance of a small, informal and personally chosen 'privy council' increased, absorbing the advisory, administrative and judicial functions of the earlier council, to reach a peak under the early Tudors. Its political importance declined after 1660 with the emergence of a new inner group, the 'council in cabinet', and the growth of the party system in parliament. The evolution of the council has been described, with some over-simplification, as resembling the pulling out of the progressively smaller sections of a telescope: first the great council, then the privy council, then the council in cabinet, and then the CABINET.

Council in the marches of Wales A council for the government of WALES and the border shires, originating under Edward IV and restructured under the early Tudor kings. Its duties were principally judicial. The council, which was the only English court specifically authorized to use torture, was in abeyance 1641–60 and was abolished in 1689.

Council of state The executive body of the COMMONWEALTH (1649–53), consisting of 41 members chosen annually by parliament. The council, which was by 17th-century standards diligent, efficient and uncorrupt, transacted business through standing committees, notably those of the army, navy, Ireland and foreign affairs.

Council of the north The council, which originated under the Yorkist kings, became in 1537 a body of administrators and judges responsible for the government of the northern shires. Sitting at York, it exercised wide civil and criminal jurisdiction and did much to enforce royal policy. Its commission lapsed in 1641.

Count *see* COMITATENSES; SAXON SHORE

Country party A term used in the 17th and 18th centuries to describe opponents of the policies of the 'court' or royal government. Less an organized party than a state of mind, the 'country' was conservative, legalistic, fiercely Protestant and after 1688 generally opposed to political parties, PLACE-MEN, high taxes and the standing army.

County *see* SHIRE

The earliest form of **council**: a Saxon king and his WITAN. From Aelfric's paraphrase of the Old Testament, 11th century.

County court Almost omnicompetent in English local government during Anglo-Saxon and early medieval times, when it comprised all the free men of the SHIRE. It was presided over by the diocesan bishop and the king's deputy (initially the EALDOR-MAN, later the SHERIFF) and after the Norman conquest (when its ecclesiastical jurisdiction was removed) by the sheriff alone. From later medieval times its importance declined (though it still elected KNIGHTS OF THE SHIRE) until it was reconstituted as a local law court dealing mainly with debt (1846).

County Palatine Since the Norman conquest, a county where the lord, while remaining a subject of the king, enjoyed quasi-regal power and jurisdiction, e.g. at CHESTER, LANCASTER and DURHAM.

'Coupon election' The nickname for the general election of December 1918, so called because the mainly Conservative coalition government, headed by Lloyd George, endorsed or 'gave a coupon to' (borrowing from rationing) 1 candidate in each constituency. It secured a majority of 387 for the coalition over its Liberal and Labour opponents.

Court-baron *see* MANOR COURT

Court-leet *see* FRANKPLEDGE

Coutances, Walter of *see* RICHARD I

Covenant, the national 1638. The Scottish national protest against Charles I's ecclesiastical innovations, subscribed by nobles, ministers and burgesses in Greyfriars Kirk, Edinburgh. The covenant, initially neither anti-royalist nor anti-episcopalian, declared the signatories' intention to defend their religion against any change not approved by free assemblies and parliament.

Covenanters The supporters of the Scottish national COVENANT (1638) and their successors who opposed the reintroduction of episcopacy (1662). Excluded ministers, supported by small lairds and independent peasants, maintained an underground church in south-west Scotland, Fife and Easter Ross despite brutal repression (1678–85). *See* APOLOGETI-CAL DECLARATION.

Coverdale, Miles 1488–1570. A former friar, Coverdale joined Tyndale abroad (1529) and assisted in the translation of the Pentateuch. He subsequently published his own BIBLE (1535) and compiled the official Great Bible (1539). Bishop of

Exeter (1551–3), he spent the years 1553–8 in exile and helped produce the Geneva Bible (1560).

Cranfield, Lionel, 1st earl of Middlesex 1575–1645. A successful merchant and financier, Cranfield became surveyor-general of the customs (1613) and lord treasurer (1621) under James VI and I and attempted to bring economy and careful management to royal finance. He was impeached in 1624, ostensibly for corruption, but actually for opposing Buckingham's war policy, and lived thereafter in retirement.

Cranmer, Thomas 1489–1556. Appointed archbishop of Canterbury in 1533, Cranmer became the architect of the CHURCH OF ENGLAND. A moderate Protestant, he was in some danger in Henry VIII's conservative last years, but survived to accelerate the REFORMATION under Edward VI. On Mary I's accession he was deprived, recanted, withdrew his recantation and was burned.

Crécy, battle of 26 August 1346. Major English victory of the HUNDRED YEARS' WAR. Edward III and the Black Prince disposed their archers and dismounted men-at-arms in a defensive position and decimated a much larger pursuing force of undisciplined French cavalry and Genoese crossbowmen under Philip VI. *See* ill. p. 19.

Creones A northern Scottish tribe which inhabited western Inverness-shire at the time of Roman Britain.

Crichel Down case A case of bureaucratic arrogance, when land purchased by the air ministry (1937) was neither used nor sold by 1949, and passed to the ministry of agriculture, who refused to sell it to the heir of a previous owner. An inquiry (1954) condemned the ministry and brought about the resignation of the minister, Sir Thomas Dugdale.

Crimean war 1854–6. War started in March when Russian successes against the Turks appeared to threaten British interests in Turkey and routes to the East, and seemed to offer an opportunity to punish the Russians for their role in suppressing the 1848 revolutions. At first it was generally popular. An Anglo-French expeditionary force landed in the Crimea (September) to besiege Sevastopol, the Russians' main Black Sea naval base. Attempts by the Russians to break out resulted in the battles of Balaclava and Inkermann, but Sevastopol ultimately fell (September 1855). There was also a limited naval war in the Baltic. The war was fought

British war-wounded brought back to London from the **Crimean war**, 1855.

with incompetence by all concerned (so much so that the Aberdeen government fell on this issue in January 1855) and casualties from disease were much greater than from fighting (*see* ARMY). However, it did see the adoption of the rifle by the army and the conversion of the navy to steam power, as well as the improvements in nursing associated with Florence NIGHTINGALE.

Criminal appeal, court of *see* LAW

Cripps, Sir Stafford 1889–1952. An upper-class lawyer, Cripps became a leading left-winger (1930s). Churchill sent him as ambassador to Moscow (1940), and he served in the war cabinet with responsibility first for India, then for aircraft production (1942–5). Trade minister (1945–7), he then went to the exchequer as the executant of 'austerity' policies, until illness forced him to quit in 1950.

Crofters' party A group of Scottish radical MPs elected for highland constituencies (1885) after the 3rd REFORM BILL had given the vote to the Scottish crofters. Despite some connections with socialism, they reverted to Liberalism after the success of their campaign for highland land reform. *See* NAPIER COMMISSION.

Crofters' war Incidents (1882 and 1884) in which Scottish crofters resisted eviction by force until put down by police and marines. These publicized their case for land reform and led to the setting-up of the NAPIER COMMISSION.

Cromer, earl of 1841–1917. Born Evelyn Baring of the banking family, Cromer had a military education, largely in India. He then went to Egypt as British commissioner of the Khedive's debt (1876), virtually running the country 1883–1907, and instituting a thorough modernization of transport, agriculture and administration.

Crompton's 'mule' *see* INDUSTRIAL REVOLUTION

Cromwell, Oliver 1599–1658. Both the personality and career of Cromwell exhibited a remarkable mixture of the conventional and the extraordinary. Born to a family of Huntingdonshire gentry, his early life was typical of that of his class. Educated at Huntingdon, Cambridge and Lincoln's Inn, he lived from his modest estate, was active in local affairs and represented Huntingdon in the parliament of 1628 and Cambridge in the SHORT and LONG PARLIAMENTS. His social and political attitudes were largely conventional, while his Puritan religious devotion was shared by many of his contemporaries. Yet in him they became the mainsprings of an unexpected greatness.

Cromwell was 43 when the CIVIL WARS broke out. His subsequent career saw him oscillate between periods of sober state service and political interventions of increasing radicalism. Though altogether lacking military experience, he moulded a superb cavalry force, provided inspiring leadership and rose in 3 years from the rank of captain to that of lieutenant-general. Prior to 1645 he stood out as one of those parliamentarians determined to prosecute the war to victory. In 1647 his radicalism again emerged when he sided with the aggrieved army against parliament. After abortive negotiations with CHARLES I (1647) and renewed war, he became a prime mover in the trial and execution of the king. He replaced FAIRFAX as lord-general (1650), defended the COMMONWEALTH at DROGHEDA, DUNBAR and WORCESTER, and in 1653, after the expulsion of the RUMP PARLIAMENT and the experiment of BAREBONE'S PARLIAMENT, he became lord protector of the commonwealth.

Cromwell found himself in war and he was happiest when fighting for what he saw increasingly as God's cause. It was this conviction which made him both an inspired general and an explosive and unpredictable force in politics. Undoubtedly he was

Oliver **Cromwell** as defender of the English commonwealth: unfinished miniature by Samuel Cooper, *c.* 1650–3.

sincere, yet his role in defence of the godly certainly served his own ambition also, while his search for divine guidance legitimized an opportunism born of a remarkable sensitivity to shifts in political power. Otherwise he was unoriginal, borrowing his constructive ideas from IRETON, HARRISON and LAMBERT in turn. In his last years he searched for a settlement which would bring stability, while preserving the gains of the revolution, above all religious toleration. It evaded him. By 1658 he alone held things together and on his death only a restored monarchy seemed to offer hope of a lasting settlement. Perhaps he expected this. A man of agonies and exaltations, now sunk in melancholic self-doubt, now acting with self-righteous certainty, one of the most loved and most hated men of his age, he remains ultimately enigmatic. (Christopher Hill, *God's Englishman*, 1970).

Cromwell, Thomas 1485–1540. The principal minister of HENRY VIII (1532–40), and architect of the Henrician REFORMATION, the dissolution of the MONASTERIES and the 'TUDOR REVOLUTION IN GOVERNMENT'. Humbly born in Putney, Cromwell spent an adventurous youth as a soldier and merchant in Italy. He entered the service of Wolsey (1514) and on Wolsey's fall (1530), that of the king. As a statesman and administrator, Cromwell

The 3rd **crusade** aimed, but failed, to regain Jerusalem which had been captured by the Muslim leader Saladin in 1187. It was led by Richard the Lionheart who is unhorsing Saladin in this detail from the *Luttrell Psalter*, *c.* 1340.

The main avenue of **Crystal Palace** during the Great Exhibition, 1851. Contemporary engraving by H. Bibby.

After defeating the Jacobite cause at **Culloden**, the duke of Cumberland quickly earned the title 'butcher', forcefully portrayed in this caricature of 1746, by ordering wanton killing and devastation.

displayed subtlety, originality and determination, coupled on occasion with real ruthlessness. Traditionally seen as a cynical Machiavellian, the extent of his genuine commitment to administrative reform and religious reformation has been increasingly recognized in recent years. As a man, he had a lively intellect and warm personality. After Henry's dissatisfaction with his marriage to Anne of Cleves (1540) Cromwell fell rapidly from favour. His many enemies seized their opportunity and he was executed on trumped-up charges of treason and heresy.

Crossman, R.H.S. *see* CABINET

Crown A coin worth 5 shillings (or a quarter of a pound) minted in gold (1526–1685) and since then, infrequently, in silver. Now it is issued only to mark special occasions, most recently Elizabeth II's silver jubilee (1977).

Crown courts *see* LAW

Crusades Term applicable to any wars fought with ecclesiastical encouragement against infidels or (later) schismatics (*see* DESPENSER, HENRY), but more especially to the struggles to free the holy land from the Moslems (11–14th centuries). Britons were frequently involved, most notably under Robert Curthose during the 1st crusade (1096–1100) and Richard I during the 3rd (1190–2).

Crystal Palace Designed by Sir Joseph Paxton (1801–65) and measuring 1,600 × 384 feet (488 × 117 metres), it was erected from prefabricated metal and glass sections in Hyde Park, London, to house the Great Exhibition (1851). An outstanding success, morally and financially, it was re-erected at Sydenham, south London (1854), where it remained an important musical, exhibition and athletic centre until it burnt down in 1936.

Culdees (Gaelic *céle De*, servants of God). The name given to adherents of a reform movement in Irish monasticism, which spread to Scotland in the 9th century. During the 12th and 13th centuries most of them became canons regular.

Culloden, battle of 16 April 1746. Final battle of the JACOBITE '45' rebellion. Prince Charles Edward's highland army engaged Scots and English troops under the duke of Cumberland on Drummossie moor. The highlanders were slaughtered by artillery and musket fire and their rout was followed by savage repression, earning Cumberland the title 'butcher'.

Culross A splendidly preserved 17th-century Scottish burgh. Streets of 17th-century houses with pantiled roofs radiate from the market cross. Notable individual buildings include the Study, the town house, Bishop Leighton's house and Culross palace, one of the finest early domestic buildings in Scotland, built in 1597–1611 for Sir George Bruce.

Cunedda The founding father of Wales in the HEROIC AGE. Cunedda led the force of VOTADINI transferred there from MANAU GODODDIN (c. 430), probably by VORTIGERN. After expelling or containing Irish invasions, he founded the dynasty of GWYNEDD, and his descendants originated many other Welsh princely houses.

Cunobelinus c. 7–c. 40. King of the Belgic CATUVELLAUNI, Cunobelinus overran the neighbouring Trinovantes c. 10 and conquered Kent c. 25. By the end of his life he controlled most of southeast Britain, and the Roman historian Suetonius calls him 'king of the Britons'. He is the original of Shakespeare's Cymbeline. *See* COLCHESTER.

Curragh incident In March 1914, with the 3rd HOME RULE Bill about to become law, armed resistance was expected from the Ulster Unionists. Asquith's government intended to send the army into Ulster to suppress this, but officers at the Curragh camp near Dublin, many of whom were Irish Protestants, stated that they would refuse to accept those orders. The war minister, Colonel Seely, capitulated to them and resigned, thereby further complicating the pre-war crisis. *See* IRISH CONSTITUTIONAL CRISIS.

Cursuses Huge linear earthworks, about 300 feet (973 metres) wide and 1–6 miles (1·6–9·6 kilometres) long, formed by 2 roughly parallel banks and ditches. Built during the neolithic period (c. 3500–2000 BC), they are closely associated with barrows and henge monuments, may have been used for ritual processions and are apparently unique to Britain.

Curzon, George Nathaniel, marquess 1859–1925. A leading Conservative imperialist MP (1886–98), Curzon became a magnificent but ultimately unpopular viceroy of India (1898–1905). On his return he helped to persuade the house of lords to pass the PARLIAMENT Act (1911), joined the coalition government (1915) and later co-operated with Lloyd George, latterly as foreign minister (1919–22). This, and the fact that he was a peer, cost him the premiership (1923).

Cuthbert, St c. 634–87. The most revered of northern English saints, Cuthbert is famous for his ascetic life, miracles and evangelizing journeys in the Northumbrian hills. An Irish-tradition monk who bowed to Rome, he became bishop of LINDISFARNE (684), whence his relics were removed (875) and eventually taken to Durham cathedral (995).

Cymbeline *see* CUNOBELINUS

Cymry (British *combrogi*, fellow-countrymen). A word used by the post-Roman Britons to describe themselves. From it derive modern Cymru (i.e. Wales) and Cumbria, once part of Rheged.

Cynddylan d. c. 656. The last British prince to rule part of lowland England, the area round Wroxeter in Shropshire, Cynddylan was defeated and killed by the Anglo-Saxons. He is the subject of a Welsh lament.

Cyprus emergency Agitation for Enosis or union with Greece broke out in this colony (acquired 1878) in the early 1950s, and a full-scale terrorist campaign was waged (1955–7) by EOKA against the British and the Turkish minority, who wanted partition. After discussions between the Greek and Turkish leaders, Makarios and Denktash, a joint republic was formed (1960) under the former. Tension, however, continued, and following a right-wing coup against Makarios (1975), Turkey invaded, since when the island has been *de facto* partitioned.

D

Dalhousie, marquis of 1812–60. A Whig politician, on the board of trade (1845) and appointed governor-general of India (1847), Dalhousie annexed the Punjab and other Indian states, laid down railways and telegraphs and improved the economy, but alienated Indian opinion by the pace of change and created grounds for the INDIAN MUTINY.

Dalriada The kingdom of the SCOTTI, centred on Argyll and the Western Isles. Irish invasions of western Scotland, mainly from Ulster, had begun by the 4th century, and c. 500 Fergus mac Erc, king of Dalriada in Antrim, established a kingdom of the same name in Kintyre. Under his great-grandson AEDAN MAC GABHRAN this gained authority over all the Irish settlers, reaching the zenith of its power *c.* 640. *See* KENNETH MAC ALPIN.

Dalry, battle of *see* ROBERT BRUCE

Dame schools Small private schools of the 18th century kept by a single teacher, usually female, and teaching basic literacy to children of poor families.

Damnonii A British tribe, perhaps originally a branch of the DUMNONII, inhabiting the Clydesdale area. Occupied by AGRICOLA (82), it was apparently not unfriendly to Rome. After the BARBARIAN CONSPIRACY (367–9) the tribe became FOEDERATI, forming the core of the kingdom of STRATHCLYDE.

Danby, Thomas Osborne, 1st earl of 1632–1712. As Charles II's chief minister (1673–8) Danby stabilized royal finances and built up crown support in parliament. Impeached during the POPISH PLOT hysteria, he was imprisoned (1679–84) but re-emerged after 1688 as a supporter of William III and chief minister from 1690 until a 2nd impeachment for corruption (1694).

Danegeld A name loosely applied to money used to buy peace from Vikings, more properly to the national taxes on land levied for this purpose 991–1012 (*see* AETHELRED UNRAED). From 1012–51 (as 'heregeld') it was used to maintain HUSCARLES and a navy, and from the Norman conquest until 1162 was frequently levied for general purposes.

Danelaw A term used from AETHELRED UNRAED's reign (978–1016) for the part of England, south of the Tees and roughly north-east of a line from London to Liverpool, where Danish legal and social customs prevailed from the late 9th century until after the Norman conquest. It represents the area settled during Alfred's reign by VIKING armies centred on Yorkshire, the north-east midland FIVE BOROUGHS and East Anglia, the districts where Danish influence on place names and society is most observable. Conquered by Edward the Elder and Aethelstan, the Danelaw was granted legal autonomy by Edgar (957/9–75).

Danes *see* VIKINGS

Dardanelles Bombarded (February 1915) prior to landings at GALLIPOLI. *See* WORLD WAR I.

Henry Stewart, Lord **Darnley**, and his brother, Charles Stewart: portrait by H. Eworth, 1563.

Darien scheme 1698–9. An unsuccessful attempt by the Company of Scotland Trading to Africa and the Indies to establish a colony on the isthmus of Darien, in emulation of the colonial successes of England and Holland. The entire capital of the company was lost and many Scottish investors were ruined.

Darnley, Henry Stewart, lord 1545–67. The English-educated son of the 4th earl of Lennox, Darnley married MARY QUEEN OF SCOTS in 1565. Vicious, arrogant and resentful of his lack of authority, he became estranged from Mary, participated in Riccio's murder (1566) and was himself murdered at Kirk o' Field.

Dark ages *see* HEROIC AGE

Darwin, Charles 1809–82. Descended from one of the scientific and clerical families of the 'intellectual aristocracy', Darwin was educated at Cambridge and as a biologist on the *Beagle* expedition (1831–6). His poor health led him to study his findings in seclusion in Kent, and 20 years later he published his *Origin of Species* (1859) in which he argued that species evolve through 'natural selection' of the most fit in terms of environment and heredity. The book caused enormous controversy in a country beginning to notice the drift from religious faith. 'Evolution' had an equally profound effect on philosophizing about the social sciences.

David I king of Scotland (1124–53; b. 1084). 3rd regnant and most Normanized of the sons of Malcolm Canmore, David energetically prompted the spread of feudal tenure into Scotland, granting lands and offices to Anglo-Norman families such as the Bruces, Balliols and Stewarts. He also encouraged the reorganization of the church on regular diocesan and parochial lines, and personally founded many of the greatest Scottish abbeys. Supporting his niece MATILDA against STEPHEN, he lost the battle of the STANDARD, but annexed Northumberland and held Cumbria.

David II king of Scotland (1329–71; b. 1324). The son of Robert Bruce, David lived in exile in France 1334–41 (*see* SCOTTISH WARS OF INDEPENDENCE). His invasion of England (1346) resulted in his capture at NEVILLE'S CROSS and 11 years' subsequent confinement, during which he or his parliaments refused to make political concessions to Edward III, eventually agreeing instead on a ransom of 100,000 marks. Despite difficulties over paying this, on his return David ruled vigorously and intensively.

David, St *c.* 520–88. The English form of Dewi, best known of the many monastic saints of 6th-century Wales, of which he became patron. Active mainly in south-west Wales, he was nicknamed 'the water-drinker', and his followers were renowned for their rigid asceticism.

Davitt, Michael 1846–1906. An Irish immigrant, Davitt was involved with the FENIAN or Irish Republican Brotherhood conspiracy of the mid-1860s and spent 1870–7 and 1881–2 in jail. As organizer of the IRISH LAND LEAGUE (1879–81) and MP (1882–99), he was also closely associated with land nationalization and socialism, unlike Parnell, whose leadership he helped defeat (1890).

De heretico comburendo 1401. An Act which prohibited unlicensed preaching and allowed the burning of obdurate or relapsed heretics. Originally directed against LOLLARDS, it was repealed by Protector Somerset (1547), revived by Mary against Protestants, and finally abolished by Elizabeth (1559).

Charles **Darwin**: cartoon by 'Ape' in 'Men of the Day' series, *Vanity Fair*, 30 September 1871.

David II (left) with Edward III, from a 14th-century illuminated manuscript.

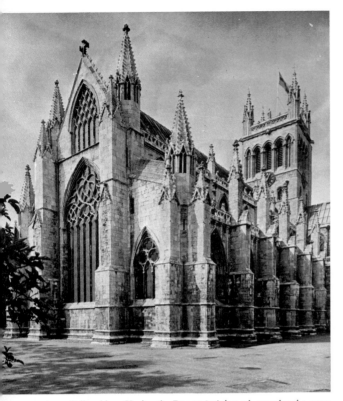

Selby abbey, Yorks.: the **Decorated** chancel, completed c. 1340. The great east window is a superb example of the flowing curvilinear manner of the Decorated style.

Death duties Taxation of inherited property was introduced by the Conservatives (1889), and increased by Harcourt (1894) and Lloyd George (1909). In 1975 it was incorporated into the Wilson government's capital transfer tax.

Decantae A northern Scottish tribe which inhabited Cromarty at the time of Roman Britain.

Declaration of Rights 1689. A document drawn up by the convention parliament declaring illegal those acts of James VII and II against which the GLORIOUS REVOLUTION had been directed. Presented to William and Mary for their acceptance before their proclamation as king and queen, it was subsequently embodied in law as the BILL OF RIGHTS (1689).

Declarations of Indulgence Royal declarations suspending penal legislation against religious nonconformity. Following an abortive attempt (1662), the 1672 declaration allowed Protestant DISSENTERS to worship in licensed meeting-houses and Roman Catholics to worship in private. Its cancellation was forced by parliament. The 1687–8 declarations provoked the SEVEN BISHOPS' CASE.

Declaratory Act 1766. Act passed after the repeal of the STAMP ACT, reasserting the right of parliament to legislate for the American colonies.

Decolonization Britain's cession of her colonial territories in the 1960s. *See* BRITISH EMPIRE.

Decorated architecture Less a single style than a phase of English Gothic lasting c. 1290–c. 1350. Its leading characteristics – complex ornamentation and an experimental approach – stemmed from St Stephen's chapel, Westminster Palace (begun 1292 and now mostly destroyed). An important feature is curvilinear window tracery based on S-curves or ogees (e.g. York minster, west front).

Dee, John 1527–1608. A Welsh mathematician, astrologer, alchemist and 'conjuror of spirits', Dee led a wandering life in search of the secret of the philosopher's stone and was favoured by Elizabeth I, the king of Poland and the Emperor Rudolf II. From 1595 he was warden of Manchester college.

Defence of the Realm Acts (DORA). A series of statutes passed during World War I which allowed the government to issue ORDERS IN COUNCIL subjecting industry and individuals to strict government control. They were used against the industrial unrest which followed the war.

Degeangli A British tribe inhabiting north-east Wales. Hostile to Rome, it was attacked in 48 and finally conquered c. 60. Its lead-rich territory thereafter remained under military government.

Degsastan, battle of 603 or 604. Aedan mac Gabhran of Dalriada, invading Lothian with mainland Irish allies, was decisively defeated by Aethelferth of Northumbria at a site usually identified with Dawston, Roxburghshire. Dalriada never again invaded Lothian.

Deheubarth (Lat. *dextralis pars Britanniae*, right-hand side of Wales, looking towards Rome). A name originally applied to all south Wales, later only to the principality formed under Hywel Dda (920) by the union of Ceredigion (subsequently Cardiganshire) and Ystrad Tywi (subsequently in Carmarthenshire) with ancient Dyfed. Brycheiniog was added in the 10th century. It resisted Marcher encroachment with varying success, reaching the height of its independent power under RHYS AP GRUFFYDD (1155–97). Declining thereafter, it was finally conquered under Edward I.

Deira Anglian kingdom occupying east and central Yorkshire, formed by *c.* 560 from 5th-century FOEDERATI settlements. It annexed British York (580), but was itself annexed to Bernicia by Aethelferth *c.* 604, and thenceforth (except 632–3 and 641–54) formed part of Northumbria.

Demesne Land kept by any lord for his own use and not granted to sub-tenants, e.g. the crown lands (royal demesne) or the home farm of a manor. *See* FEUDALISM.

Demetae A little-known tribe inhabiting southwest Wales. It apparently welcomed the Romans, and the only major fort in its lands was Moridunum (Carmarthen), which subsequently became its capital.

Demographic transition *see* POPULATION

Department of Scientific and Industrial Research A government-sponsored scientific research body, set up in mid-1915 to compensate for the withdrawal of German scientific imports, and subsequently extended.

Derby, Lord Stanley, earl of 1799–1869. A right-wing Whig nobleman, Derby joined the Tories (1835), serving Peel as secretary for war and colonies (1841–5), and then leading the party on Peel's defection over Free Trade. After heading 2 short unsuccessful ministries (1852 and 1858–9) he combined successfully with Disraeli (1867) to produce the 2nd REFORM BILL.

Despenser, Henry 1341/2–1406. Bishop of Norwich from 1370. More warrior than churchman, Despenser personally conducted the bloody suppression of the PEASANTS' REVOLT in East Anglia. His expedition to Flanders (1383), nominally a 'crusade' against the French 'schismatics' (*see* SCHISM, GREAT), became a discreditable plundering raid which achieved nothing, and he suffered impeachment by parliament. He was a persecutor of LOLLARDS.

Despensers, the Hugh Sr (1262–1326), a long-standing baronial supporter of Edward II, and his son Hugh Jr, had by 1320 gained control of royal government. Their land-grabbing from the MARCHERS caused their defeat and banishment (1321),

but after BOROUGHBRIDGE they became all-powerful and hated. They were both executed by ISABELLA and Mortimer.

Dettingen, battle of 27 June 1743. A victory by British, Austrian and Hanoverian troops commanded by GEORGE II over the French during the war of the AUSTRIAN SUCCESSION. It was the last occasion on which a reigning British monarch commanded troops in battle.

Deverel-Rimbury culture *see* PREHISTORIC BRITAIN

Devolution *see* CONSERVATIVE PARTY; HOME RULE; SCOTTISH NATIONAL PARTY; WELSH NATIONALISM

Dicey, Albert Venn 1835–1922. A leading academic and legal reformer who created much of the ideology of parliamentary sovereignty with his *Law and Working of the Constitution* (1885). Thereafter, he became a convinced opponent of home rule and of welfare legislation (*see* WELFARE STATE), even though his book, *Law and Public Opinion . . .* (1905), remained for many years the standard work on the latter.

Diggers Radical groups which established short-lived colonies on waste land at St George's Hill, Surrey and elsewhere (1649–50). The Surrey Diggers were led by Gerrard Winstanley, who advocated communal cultivation of common land and later, in *The Law of Freedom* (1652), put forward a blueprint for a communist commonwealth.

Dilke, Sir Charles 1843–1911. Traveller, imperialist (*Greater Britain*, 1868) and republican, by 1881 Dilke was, with Joseph Chamberlain, the leader of the Liberals' left wing. As local government minister he initiated an important enquiry into working-class housing and supported home rule and labour legislation, but was felled by a divorce scandal in 1886.

Diocese The ecclesiastical area ruled by a bishop. In the early church their number and boundaries fluctuated considerably, but from *c.* 1200 until the Reformation there were 17 in England, 12 in Scotland and 4 in Wales. More English dioceses were then created, and more again in the 19th and 20th centuries.

Directory of Worship The Presbyterian service book prepared by the WESTMINSTER ASSEMBLY OF DIVINES to replace the Book of Common Prayer and accepted by parliament in 1644. Though subsequently adopted by the church of Scotland its use was never enforced in England and it was displaced by the restored prayer book (1662).

Disarmament conference 1932–5. It took place under the chairmanship of HENDERSON in Geneva. Bedevilled by French insistence on a general security settlement, it broke up after the Nazis came to power.

Disinherited, the Name given (1) to the rebels against HENRY III disinherited by the statute of Winchester (1265), and (2) to the Scottish magnates and their descendants disinherited after BANNOCKBURN (1314) for their resistance to ROBERT BRUCE, and later led by Edward BALLIOL.

Dispensing and suspending powers The royal powers of suspending the operation of certain statutes or dispensing individuals from compliance with them, used by Charles II and James VII and II to evade the Act of UNIFORMITY (1662) and the TEST ACT (1673). Such practices were declared illegal by the BILL OF RIGHTS (1689).

Disraeli, Benjamin, earl of Beaconsfield 1804–81. Disraeli's father, Isaac, was a Jewish writer and editor who had been converted to Christianity, and attained modest wealth. His son approached politics, first as a radical, then as a Tory, but always as an opportunist. After a career, none too presentable, as a 'society' novelist and speculator, he entered parliament (1837) as MP for Maidstone, subsequently marrying the widow of his colleague and benefactor Wyndham Lewis. He allied himself with the TORY RADICALS, and harried that section of the party which, under Peel, appeared ready to compromise with the dominant ideology of the Liberals. From this period date his 'social novels' – romantic plotting with a leaven of pillaged BLUE BOOKS – *Coningsby* (1844) and *Sybil* (1845). In 1846 the Tory party split over the repeal of the CORN LAWS and Disraeli remained with its protectionist rump, as the lieutenant of Lord George Bentinck (1802–48). On Bentinck's death he succeeded him as leader in the commons with Derby in overall control, a partnership which lasted until 1868, although Tory ventures into government in the years of Whig-Peelite hegemony (1852 and 1858–9) were brief and undistinguished. The loss of talent in 1846 had been too great.

Disraeli's great political opportunity came with the 1866 REFORM BILL, on which the Liberal party, under John Russell, was split 3 ways. Disraeli was

Benjamin **Disraeli**: portrait by J. E. Millais, *c.* 1875.

determined to carry a Bill of his own, virtually regardless of what it conceded. Initially he allied with the ADULLAMITE rebels within the Liberal party to throw out Russell's Bill, whereupon Russell resigned and Derby and Disraeli formed a Tory ministry. He first attempted to conciliate the right wing of the party, under Viscount Cranborne (later marquess of Salisbury), but it rejected reform of any kind. So he introduced a much more drastic measure, offering household suffrage, though hedged with safeguards in the form of 'fancy franchises' and the demand that those enfranchised personally pay rates. In the course of the debates these qualifications were stripped away, by radicals who wished to go further than Gladstone was willing to do, and by Tories whom Disraeli instructed to get the Bill through at whatever price. Shortly afterwards (February 1868), Derby resigned, and Disraeli 'climbed to the top of the greasy pole', only to be defeated by Gladstone in the election held the same autumn.

The Liberal government had run out of reforming impetus by 1871 and it stumbled out of office early in 1874. Disraeli convincingly won the ensuing general election and embarked on a bold foreign policy, purchasing a controlling interest in the Suez Canal in 1875 (*see* SUEZ CANAL PURCHASE), and then protecting the Ottoman empire, and by implication India, against threats from Russia, especially after the latter's intervention in the Balkans following the BULGARIAN ATROCITIES (1876). The 2 countries came near to war (1877), and Disraeli substantially nullified Russia's military gains at the congress of BERLIN (1878), drawing from Bismarck the tribute 'the old Jew: that is the man!' His ministry had also introduced an important consolidated and extended Public Health Act (1875) – although Disraeli's desire to create a Conservative constituency among the working class through advanced social legislation has been exaggerated. His conferment of the title empress of India on Queen Victoria (1876) set the seal on a romantic relationship he had assiduously cultivated for decades, but the waywardness of his foreign policy gave valuable ammunition to Gladstone who, as a private politician, began the campaign which was to drive Beaconsfield from office (1880).

Disruption The split in the CHURCH OF SCOTLAND (1843) created the Free Church, which rejected lay patronage and destroyed much of the religious domination of Scottish economic and social life, while making religious issues an important political divide. The breach was not healed until 1929.

Dissenters A blanket term for PRESBYTERIANS, BAPTISTS, CONGREGATIONALISTS, QUAKERS and other Protestants dissenting from and failing to conform to the restored CHURCH OF ENGLAND in 1662. Persecuted under the CLARENDON CODE, they received toleration in 1689 but, like Methodists, remained subject to the TEST and CORPORATION ACTS until 1828.

Dissenting academies Schools established for the children of DISSENTERS excluded from English grammar schools and universities in the later 17th and 18th centuries. Notable for their advanced curricula, which included science, modern languages and history, they prepared ministers for the dissenting churches and provided the best secondary education available in 18th-century England.

Distraint of knighthood The requirement, originating in the 13th century, that men possessing lands of a particular value should accept knighthood, on pain of a fine. The crown's right to collect fines was revived and exploited by Charles I until its abolition by the Long parliament (1641).

District courts *see* LAW

Divine right of kings The theory that kings are ordained by God and that resistance to their authority is therefore unlawful. Though generally accepted in the 16th and 17th centuries, there was disagreement over whether the king was also subject to the law. The CIVIL WARS and GLORIOUS REVOLUTION demonstrated the limitations of the theory in practice, while its philosophical justification was demolished after 1688 by the political theory of John Locke. *See* MONARCHY.

Divorce Until 1857 a divorce in England was only obtainable by private Act of parliament (although it was relatively easy to get in Scotland) but in that year the divorce court made it generally available – to men on grounds of wives' adultery, to women on grounds of husbands' adultery plus cruelty – at a price. The 1968 Act greatly liberalized the law.

Dobunni A Belgic-influenced British tribe inhabiting the Cotswold-Mendip region. At the Roman conquest it was divided, the northern branch (perhaps in order to escape the domination of the Catuvellauni) quickly surrendering to the invaders. *See* CIRENCESTER.

Dock strike 1889. Rates of pay in London's east end docks were low and living conditions bad. When demonstrations on behalf of the socialist-led strike in Trafalgar Square revealed this, and the threat of a breakdown of law and order, the strike gained widespread middle-class support and was ultimately successful. It served to intensify social work and investigation in the east end.

Dock strike, 1889: a scene in East India Dock Road, London. Composed but atmospheric contemporary photograph.

Dogger Bank incident On 21 October 1904 the Russian Baltic fleet, steaming to the Russo-Japanese war theatre, fired on the Hull fishing fleet, thinking it was a Japanese torpedo-boat squadron. The crisis which followed nearly caused a Russo-British war but subsequent successful negotiations for compensation laid the foundations for an Anglo-Russian entente.

Doherty, John *see* GRAND NATIONAL CONSOLIDATED TRADE UNION

Domesday Book The name given since at least the 12th century to the great *descriptio* or survey of England made on the orders of WILLIAM THE CONQUEROR (1086). Its motivation remains controversial, but its inception at a time when William was desperately in need of funds and troops for defence makes it likely that his immediate object was to investigate the taxable value of his realm and to ascertain whether more could be exacted from it, as well as to see exactly what lands his barons held, and hence how many knights they were bound by feudal duty to supply him. Other important factors were probably a desire to underline his legitimate succession to EDWARD THE CONFESSOR, to register and legalize the great changes in landownership at and since the Norman conquest, and generally to discover (in the words of the Anglo-Saxon Chronicle) 'how [England] was peopled, and with what sort of men'.

Exactly how the survey was conducted is uncertain, but it seems that panels of commissioners headed by bishops were assigned to groups of counties (excluding the northern borders) where they made inquiries under oath of the sheriff, the barons and (apparently) of juries comprising the priest, REEVE and 6 men from each village. These were asked who held each manor, how many taxable HIDES it contained, how many ploughs, how much land in DEMESNE, how many VILLEINS, CEORLS, SERFS and freemen there were, how much pasture and how many mills and fisheries, whether it had increased or diminished in size, how much it was worth, and how much land each freeman held. Each detail was to be recorded thrice: as it was in Edward the Confessor's time (*tempore regis Edwardi*: TRE), when William granted the estate, and at the time of the survey. The results were checked by a 2nd set of commissioners, and the Anglo-Saxon chronicler complained that 'there was no single hide nor yard of land . . . left out'.

The final version (now in the public record office) was arranged on feudal lines within each SHIRE, the king's lands preceding those of ecclesiastics, monasteries, earls, other Norman lay tenants, SERGEANTRY tenants and Englishmen. What are apparently earlier drafts, containing subsequently omitted details of manorial livestock and under-tenants, survive for Cambridgeshire (*Inquisitio comitatus Cantabrigiensis*), the south-western counties (*Exeter Domesday*) and East Anglia (*Little Domesday*).

Incomplete and imprecise, difficult to interpret, and suffering from the fact that its compilers were describing an alien society in alien terms, Domesday Book is nevertheless an invaluable source for both pre- and post-conquest studies, and an administrative achievement without parallel in medieval European history.

An entry from **Domesday Book** relating to the property of Westminster abbey.

Dominicans Formally established in 1220, the FRIARS Preachers or Black Friars were founded by St Dominic to combat heresy and ignorance. While observing poverty and mendicancy, they were chiefly devoted to preaching, education and study. They reached England in 1221 and Scotland in 1230.

Don Pacifico A Portuguese moneylender based in Athens whose house was ransacked (1850) by an angry crowd, Don Pacifico claimed British citizenship on account of his birth in Gibraltar. Palmerston blockaded Greece on his behalf – a classic example of his chauvinist style in foreign policy.

Doodlebug An onomatopeic slang name for the German flying bombs with pulse-jet engines which fell on London 13 June–8 September 1944. Before effective means of dealing with them were found, they had killed 6,184 people.

A **doodlebug** falls silently from the sky, into a side street off Drury Lane, London, 1944.

Dorchester *see* DUROTRIGES; MUNICIPIA

Douglas, James *c.* 1286–1330. ROBERT BRUCE's earliest, staunchest and most ruthless supporter, Douglas led many raids into England (*see* MYTON, BATTLE OF), commanded a division at BANNOCK-BURN, was granted extensive lands and was killed in Spain bearing Bruce's heart against the Saracens. 'Good Sir James' to the Scots, he was called 'Black Douglas' in England.

Douglas family The 'Black Douglas' earls of Douglas, the descendants of Sir James, were the most powerful baronial family in southern Scotland from *c.* 1390 until their destruction by James II (1455). This position was then assumed (and held during the 16th century) by their relations, the 'Red Douglas' earls of ANGUS.

Dover Kent. Called 'the key of England', Dover was successively the site of a HILLFORT, a head-quarters of the CLASSIS BRITANNICA, and a Norman CASTLE massively rebuilt by Henry II (1180–90), where Hubert de Burgh held out for John and Henry III against Prince Louis (1216–17). It subsequently became an important naval base.

Dover, treaty of 1670. A treaty ostensibly allying France and England against Holland. Secret clauses pledged CHARLES II to declare his conversion to Catholicism when possible and promised French troops and money to support him. The secret was guessed at by parliament which met Charles's DECLARATION OF INDULGENCE (1672) with the TEST ACT (1673).

Dowding, lord 1882–1970. An artillery officer turned pilot who, after a distinguished career in World War I, helped build up fighter strength while on the air council (1930–6). As chief of fighter command, Dowding was the principal architect of victory in the battle of Britain, after which he was relieved of his command.

Downing Street, no. 10 The façade, built by speculator George Downing in 1684, conceals an elaborate reconstruction completed by William Kent in 1735. Offered then by George II to WALPOLE, the house has since been the PRIME MINISTER's official residence, though they have not all lived there.

Dowry The 'portion' of property traditionally provided by the family of the bride in the marriage contracts of the propertied classes, among whom the marital opportunities of daughters might depend heavily upon the dowry which they could provide.

Drake, Sir Francis 1540–96. The greatest of the Elizabethan 'sea dogs', Drake came to fame as a successful pirate on the Spanish Main (1570–3), confirming his stature with his circumnavigation (1577–80) and his daring exploits at Carthagena (1585–6) and Cadiz (1587). Less successful thereafter, he died in the Caribbean and was buried at sea.

Francis **Drake** soon after his circumnavigation of the world in the *Golden Hind*: miniature by Nicholas Hilliard, 1581.

Dreadnought An 'all-big-gun' battleship mounting ten 12-inch (0·30-metre) guns and using the new turbines to steam at 21 knots, laid down late in 1905 and commissioned in 1906. *See* NAVY.

Drogheda, massacre of 11 September 1649. The putting to the sword of the garrison of Drogheda after its storming by Oliver Cromwell's army. Having earlier called upon the town to surrender, Cromwell, in his severity, acted in accordance with the military rules of the day. However, it was also an example to cow future resistance in Ireland.

Druids The priests, seers, scholars and lawgivers who dominated the religion of later PREHISTORIC BRITAIN. Their orally transmitted beliefs apparently included the transmigration or reincarnation of souls and the sacredness of groves, springs and other natural features. According to the hostile accounts of the Romans, whom they strenuously resisted, they also practised human sacrifice.

Dublin tramways strike 1913. The climax of a movement to unionize low-paid Irish workers, North and South, led by the socialists LARKIN and CONNOLLY, the strike of tramway and dock workers dragged on for 6 months. Its failure drove Connolly towards extreme nationalism.

Duke *see* TITLES

Dumbarton Guarding the mouth of the Clyde, 'the stronghold of the Britons' (also called Alcluyt, 'the rock of Clyde') was the fortress-capital of STRATHCLYDE. Occupied and ravaged by Norse Vikings *c.* 870, it was an important Scottish royal fortress by the 13th century and permanently garrisoned until the Napoleonic wars.

Dumnonia The post-Roman kingdom of the DUMNONII, apparently extending in the 6th century as far as Somerset and Wiltshire (*see* WANSDYKE). From *c.* 600 it was under continuous pressure from English Wessex, which by *c.* 690 had reduced it to Cornwall. This, though attacked by Egbert and Athelstan, held out until *c.* 950.

Dumnonii The British tribal confederation inhabiting Devon and Cornwall. Isolated from Belgic influence, it had close trading and political connections with Brittany. The Romans occupied Devon and Cornwall (47 and *c.* 61), apparently without effective opposition, and *c.* 80 a Dumnonian CIVITAS was centred on the former legionary fortress of Isca Dumnoniorum (Exeter).

Oliver Cromwell's attack on **Drogheda**, notorious for its ruthlessness. Contemporary woodcut.

Dunbar, battle of 27 April 1296. Edward I's forces under John de Warenne, earl of Surrey, sent to take Dunbar, routed a relieving Scottish army and captured most of its leaders, thus opening the way for Edward's 1st conquest of Scotland in the SCOTTISH WARS OF INDEPENDENCE.

Dunbar, battle of 3 September 1650. A victory by English troops under Oliver CROMWELL over the Scots under David LESLIE. Trapped at Dunbar and about to evacuate his army, Cromwell surprised the over-confident Scots with a dawn attack and utterly routed them. Defeat gave rise to the conflict between REMONSTRANTS and RESOLUTIONERS in Scotland.

Duncan I king of Scotland (1034–40). The grandson and successor of Malcolm II. *See* MACBETH; MALCOLM CANMORE.

Dundas, Henry, 1st Viscount Melville 1742–1811. A Scottish lawyer, statesman and parliamentary patron, able to control the great majority of Scotland's parliamentary seats, Dundas was greatly valued by Pitt, who multiplied his offices after 1790. Hated by radicals as the personification of the traditional regime, he resigned in 1805 after being accused of malversation.

Dundee, James Graham of Claverhouse, 1st viscount (Bonnie Dundee) ?1649–89. An able soldier, Dundee came to prominence in the war against the COVENANTERS (1679–85). Harsh, but undeserving of his reputation for indiscriminate killing, he later raised the highlands for James VII and II and led his troops to victory at KILLIECRANKIE, where he met his death.

Dunkirk *see* WORLD WAR II

Duns and brochs The strongly defended home-steads of late iron age Scotland, duns occurred mainly in the west and brochs in the extreme north, Orkney and Shetland (*c.*150 BC–AD *c.* 100). Duns are essentially very small HILLFORTS, usually with solid walls but sometimes having inframural cells and galleries. Brochs are circular towers up to 50 feet (15·4 metres) high, with 3 or 4 superimposed mural galleries.

Dunstan, St *c.* 910–88. The inspiration of the BENEDICTINE revival of English monasticism after the Viking invasions, which he began as abbot of Glastonbury (940–55). He enjoyed the support of a succession of kings, notably Edgar, who made him archbishop of Canterbury (960). He was a scholar, artist, craftsman and organ-builder.

Dupplin, battle of 11 August 1332. Edward BALLIOL's small expeditionary force of DISINHERITED and English archers defeated with heavy casualties a much larger Scots army under Donald earl of Mar, guardian for David II. *See* SCOTTISH WARS OF INDEPENDENCE.

Durham cathedral It is among the most impressive of English cathedrals. The shrine of St CUTHBERT was established (995) on a defensible site above the river Wear. It was refounded as a BENEDICTINE priory (1083), and the present massive church was substantially built 1093–1133 (*see* NORMAN ARCHITECTURE). Monastic buildings, including the 14th-century great kitchen, also survive.

Durham, county palatine of Gifts of lands to St Cuthbert's relics had by the late 10th century made the bishops of Durham the rulers of a great lordship. Soon after the Norman conquest, this was created a COUNTY PALATINE as a bulwark against Scotland. Its 'prince-bishops' kept their special jurisdiction until 1836.

Right Henry **Dundas**, Lord Melville (left), and the Lord Advocate of Scotland. Etching, 1790.

Below St **Dunstan** at Christ's feet: detail of a 10th-century manuscript drawing, possibly made by Dunstan himself.

Durham cathedral, Co. Durham: the west façade towers above the steep banks of the Wear.

Durham, John George Lambton, earl of
1792–1840. A Whig reformer, Durham was sent to
Canada (as governor-general) by Melbourne to deal
with colonists' discontents (1838). His period was
short and unsuccessful, but the resulting Durham
Report advocated the granting of responsible self-
government to the colonies.

Durotriges A British tribal confederacy inhabiting
Dorset and adjacent parts of Wiltshire and
Somerset. They apparently maintained a rigid
independence of Belgic influences, and their fierce
opposition to the Roman conquest necessitated a
campaign by VESPASIAN (43–4) to reduce their many
hillforts (including MAIDEN CASTLE). They subsequently became a CIVITAS, whose capital was
Durnovaria (Dorchester).

Dutch wars A series of 3 inconclusive naval and
colonial wars against the Dutch republic (1652–4,
1665–7 and 1672–4) provoked by growing commercial rivalry. The principal outcome for England
was the capture of New Amsterdam (now New
York) in 1664, confirmed by the treaty of
Westminster (1674).

Dux Britanniarum The general commanding
HADRIAN'S WALL and the other northern frontier
defences of Roman Britain *c.* 300–*c.* 400, with a
headquarters at York. *See* MAGNUS MAXIMUS.

Dyrham, battle of 577. A major Anglo-Saxon
victory near Bath, where Cuthwine and CEAWLIN of
Wessex killed 3 British kings. It resulted in the
capture of Bath, Cirencester and Gloucester and the
lower Severn region, separating the Britons of
Dumnonia from those of Wales.

A contemporary Dutch propagandist broadsheet comments
satirically on the English republic's methods of raising money for
the 1st **Dutch war**.

Eadred *see* EDMUND

Ealdorman An Anglo-Saxon royal official, generally a nobleman, who governed a SHIRE or, during
the 10th century, a group of shires. Replaced by
EARLS under Cnut, their title (as 'aldermen')
survived for urban dignitaries, generally those
immediately subordinate to the mayor.

Earl (Old Norse *jarl*.) Title of non-royal commanders of Viking armies, applied in the 10th
century to Danelaw EALDORMEN and subsequently
to the governors of the provinces (East Anglia,
Mercia, Northumbria, Wessex) into which England
was divided from Cnut's time until the Norman
conquest. Much smaller earldoms were then
created, initially only on the coasts and borders (*see*
MARCHERS) but by the 12th century covering most
of England and becoming increasingly honorific
rather then administrative. *See* MORMAER; TITLES.

Early English architecture From *c.* 1160 English
church design was influenced by the Gothic style
invented around Paris *c.* 1140. But whereas the
French created effects of structural lightness by
systematically using pointed-arch rib vaults, the
English – most notably at LINCOLN (1190–1230) –
decorated walls of Norman massiveness with rich
mouldings, dark marble shafts and 'stiff-leaf'
carving.

East Anglia The kingdom of the East ANGLES,
occupying Norfolk, Suffolk and adjoining areas.
Established by the late 5th century, it achieved
power and prosperity under RAEDWALD and his
early 7th-century successors, but thereafter was
increasingly dominated by Mercia until 825, when
it allied with Wessex. It was extinguished by Viking
invasion after 865.

East India Company A JOINT-STOCK COMPANY,
founded 1600, having a trading monopoly with the
East Indies. The company early shifted its activities
to the Indian mainland and slowly built up, in wars
with the French and Indian princes, an empire
which was gradually transferred to the crown
(1773–1858). *See* BRITISH EMPIRE.

Lincoln cathedral was rebuilt from 1192 under the French-born St Hugh of Lincoln. The inventiveness of the **Early English** style is typified by this 'syncopated arcading' in St Hugh's choir.

Part of the list of subscriptions promised for the 1st voyage of the **East India Company**, dated 22 September 1599. At the top is the lord mayor of London, who subscribed £200.

East Saxons A small but distinct people whose kingdom, probably founded in the 6th century, was roughly coextensive with modern Essex. In the early 7th century it also included Middlesex and London, but by *c.* 750 these had been annexed by Mercia. Subsumed into Wessex in 825, Essex proper was overrun by Vikings in the 870s.

Easter Rising *see* IRISH CONSTITUTIONAL CRISIS

Eastern Association *see* CIVIL WARS; MANCHESTER, 2ND EARL OF

Eastern question The problem of settling the affairs of the moribund Turkish empire, involving the social and political rights of its minority subjects, and the ambitions of the great powers – Austria, France, Italy, Russia and Britain – in the Middle East. It caught fire at the time of the CRIMEAN WAR (1854–6), and in the run-up to the congress of BERLIN, 1874–8, before finally exploding in June–August 1914.

Eboracum *see* YORK

Ecclesiastical courts *see* BAWDY COURTS; HIGH COMMISSION; KIRK SESSIONS

Economy, the since 1870. The period 1873–95 has been described as 'the Great Depression', characterized by falling agricultural prices, falling returns on investment and a tendency to invest abroad. Domestically this was partially mitigated by rising real wages for workers, which permitted some expansion in consumer-goods industries. However, it also coincided with the full-scale exploitation of new technologies in steel, electricity and chemicals, and in each of these fields Britain was proving increasingly short-winded. In both coal and steel, for example, her output was being overtaken by Germany and America.

	Coal		Steel	
	Britain	Germany	Britain	Germany
	(in millions of metric tons)			
1850–54	50·2 m	9·2 m	—	—
1880–84	158·9 m	65·7 m	1·82 m	0·99 m
1910–14	275·4 m	247·5 m	6·93 m	16·24 m

Accelerated development was hampered by the technology, heavily capitalized yet antiquated, of the key industries of the 1st Industrial Revolution, such as the railways which had purchased and run down the canals, but were themselves using small and inadequate freight wagons. Yet, although the government controlled railway freight rates after 1888, economic orthodoxy was unwilling to sanction the scale of state intervention required for wholesale reconstruction of the transport system. Ideas of economic protection through tariffs were no more popular, as retaliation was feared. Although they gained some favour among agricultural Conservatives in the mid-1880s, an improvement in the economy in the early 1900s meant that Joseph Chamberlain's campaign for TARIFF REFORM (1903–5) split the Conservatives and aided the Free Trade Liberals, who still had much support in export-orientated districts such as cotton-producing Lancashire. The traditional industries went on to experience a dramatic export boom (1910–14), along with much factory construction.

Cotton Consumption 1865–1913
(in thousands of metric tons)

	Britain	France	Germany	Russia
1865–74	475·8	85·9	85·6	53·1
1885–94	691·8	127·0	208·2	158·3
1905–13	868·8	231·1	435·4	352·2

Similar upturns in coal exports and fisheries, however, showed a worrying concentration in low value-added industries. The immediate pre-war period was, moreover, also one of falling real wages. The trade unions, strengthened by Liberal government legislation, grew and seemed to posit an almost revolutionary challenge (1911–14), especially in the more antiquated industrial sectors such as the docks, mines and railways. This made the future control of such sectors (and the attitude of the state to them) critical.

World War I had two distinct economic impacts: one caused by the demands of the war itself, and the other by the long-term effects of the war on the world economy. The war stimulated agriculture, chemicals and electrical goods, turned many factories over to munitions work, and began to break up traditional working practices, while providing greater employment opportunities for women. And through submarine action it gravely diminished Britain's merchant marine. The post-war slump, after a brief 'reconstruction' boom (1919–21), showed the fundamental blows which the British economy had sustained. Diversion of resources to war production led both to over-capacity and to foreign, mainly American, penetration of traditional markets; large amounts of Britain's foreign investments were sold to subsidize her allies and meet war expenditure; investments in Russia were lost after the Bolshevik revolution; and the REPARATIONS burden placed on the defeated Germans in fact cheapened and thus stimulated their exports at the expense of Britain. At the same time the prices of primary products fell, lessening demand from the developing countries, traditional markets for Britain's exports.

The war period increased the role of the state, but although in its latter stages much attention was paid by LLOYD GEORGE to reconstruction along collectivist lines, this was brought to a halt by the

economic slump (1921) and the retrenchment programme (the 'GEDDES AXE'). Nevertheless, state power was greater in the interwar period than previously. In the 1920s the railways were reorganized, the BBC and the electricity grid set up, although, despite expert recommendations, the coal industry remained in private hands and the cause of considerable strife. Even here, however, NATIONALIZATION of mining royalties was eventually enacted (1938).

The weakness of the post-war economy was most dramatically demonstrated in those regions which were export-orientated: Scotland, Lancashire, south Wales and the north-east. Elsewhere in Britain, particularly in the midlands and the south-east, the increase in the real wages of the working and lower middle classes meant that new consumer-goods industries – motor cars, electrical goods and furniture – were developed, which had only been sketchily apparent before 1914.

Employing large numbers of immigrants from the 'depressed areas', and witnessing a remarkable building boom involving houses financed by building societies and 'consumer durables' made available by hire purchase, these areas contrasted starkly with the endemic unemployment of the older industrial regions. This unemployment rose to a peak after the 1929–31 crisis, exacerbated by 'rationalization' or the enforced closure of surplus capacity in the heavy industries, but provoked little reaction from the government or the labour movement. Even in the 1930s political extremism was very limited. Ameliorative legislation such as SPECIAL AREAS Act (1934), attempted to create light industries and industrial estates, and the prescriptions of KEYNES and Harold Macmillan suggested a 'middle way' of planned capitalism, but these were less effective, however, than the resumption of rearmament (1935).

Major Occupational Changes in Britain 1891–1971
(percentages of occupied population)

	1891	1921	1951	1971
Mining	5·0	6·1	3·0	1·7
Transport	7·8	8·0	7·8	6·3
Building	6·0	4·5	5·7	5·3
Metal manufacturing	8·0	12·5	12·0	16·8
White collar	4·0	7·5	12·0	20·5
Agriculture	10·7	7·0	5·0	1·5

World War II gave a much greater role to socialists in government than its predecessor had done; the presence in the treasury and elsewhere of Keynes and other intellectual advocates of a 'planned' mixed economy, meant that the dislocations that had succeeded World War I were avoided. The BEVERIDGE report (1942) had made full employment a target of government economic policy, while the Barlow and Uthwatt reports anticipated the direction of industry, public control of land and town-and-country planning. The Direction of Industry Act (1945) made permits necessary before factories could be built, and enabled the government to increase employment in problem regions. Such a policy accompanied the Attlee government's nationalization of coal, electricity, gas and the railways (1947–8). Yet major industrial change was limited, owing to a high demand for heavy industrial goods, following the destruction of enemy shipyards and workshops. This gave a respite of over a decade to the 'development areas', but after the 1958 slump their collapse was rapid, with the closure not only of mines, shipyards and heavy engineering works, but of many of the service and satellite industries connected with them.

By the time of the 1959 'affluent society' election, the dichotomy between the booming consumer-goods industries of the south and east and the declining heavy industries of the north and west was again apparent. To combat this, first Macmillan and then Wilson gave government policy a central role, not simply settling overall fiscal guidelines through taxation but attempting to direct regional policy both by financial incentives and through regional physical planning. This reached its climax in Labour's national plan (1965), in which regional development policy was to be centrally co-ordinated by the new department of economic affairs. But the slump of the following year resulted in a return to treasury policies of deflation and attempts to control wages.

The commitment to full employment predicated acceptance of an upward drift of wages and a steady growth of inflation. Attempts to constrain this by inhibiting the power of the trade unions, by both Labour and Conservative governments, were signal failures. The spiralling inflation of 1973 and after, however, could only be attributed to the increase of commodity and fuel prices and the decline of sterling. Thereafter the unions proved acquiescent in the face of Labour government policies which resulted in increased unemployment and statutory incomes control. Inflation in fuel prices did, however, make the exploitation of North Sea oil a commercial proposition. It was this good fortune (rather than any attempt at industrial recon-struction, capitalist or collectivist) that left Britain, at the end of the 1970s, superficially prosperous, but with most of her problems still not analysed, yet alone solved.

Edgar, king of England, portrayed on a contemporary Anglo-Saxon penny.

Eden, Sir Anthony, earl of Avon 1897–1977. Foreign secretary (1935–8), Eden resigned over his opposition to APPEASEMENT. He then served as Churchill's foreign secretary throughout the war and 1951–5. He was too long the heir apparent, and his own premiership, beginning with the triumph of the 1955 election, collapsed after the SUEZ CRISIS.

Edgar king of England (957/9–75; b. 943). Younger son of Edmund and father of Aethelred Unraed. His reign marks the zenith of the prestige of the West Saxon monarchy. The 1st king to rule all Anglo-Saxon England unopposed, he was also recognized without fighting as overlord of virtually all Britain. He granted DANELAW autonomy, worked closely with DUNSTAN for church reform, and set a pattern of internal order for future generations.

Edgar king of Scotland (1097–1107; b. 1074).

Edgar Atheling *c*. 1056–1125. Grandson of Edmund Ironside, Edgar was briefly the figurehead of English opposition to WILLIAM THE CONQUEROR after Hastings (1066). Thereafter he was in-termittently resident with his brother-in-law Malcolm Canmore, whose sons he established on the Scottish throne (1097).

Edgecote field *see* BANBURY, BATTLE OF

Edgehill, battle of 23 October 1642. The 1st battle of the English CIVIL WARS. Parliament's army under Essex attempted to halt Charles I's march on London. After an indecisive struggle, Charles resumed his march but was held by the London TRAIN BANDS at Turnham Green (13 November).

Edinburgh: the vennel, looking across the Grassmarket to the castle, where the Great Hall built by James IV is visible. To its left the turreted building is the Old Palace in which James VI was born.

Edinburgh 'Din Eidyn', Edinburgh rock, was the chief fortress of MANAU GODODDIN. It fell to Anglian Northumbrians (638) and remained in their hands until annexed by Scottish ALBA *c.* 955. Though increasingly favoured by Scottish kings from the time of Malcolm Canmore (1057–93), it was not firmly established as the national capital until the 15th century. Its immensely strong castle frequently played a leading part in Scottish history, notably during the Scottish wars of independence, the wars of Mary Queen of Scots and of the JACOBITES.

Edinburgh, treaty of 1560. A treaty between France and England whereby foreign forces were withdrawn from Scotland, and France recognized Elizabeth I as queen of England. The 'concessions' to the Scots settled the 1559–60 rebellion, but left the religious question undecided. However, the subsequent meeting of the Scottish estates declared Scotland Protestant.

Edinburgh-Northampton, treaty of 4 and 17 May 1328. ROBERT BRUCE's renewal of the Scottish wars of independence (1327) forced Roger MORTIMER's administration finally to recognize Scottish independence and territorial integrity. Sealed by the marriage of Edward III's sister Joan to the future David II, it made no provision for the DISINHERITED.

Edington, battle of May 878. ALFRED, emerging from hiding, gathered the FYRD of Somerset, Wiltshire and western Hampshire, and decisively defeated the Viking invaders of Wessex (under Guthrum) near Westbury, Wilts. The Danish leaders consented to Christian baptism 3 weeks later, and the Viking conquest of England was halted.

Edington, William Edward III's treasurer (1344–56), bishop of Winchester (1346–66), and chancellor (1356–63).

Edmund king of Wessex and Mercia (939–46; b. 922). The brother of Aethelstan, Edmund lost the FIVE BOROUGHS and York to the Norse-Irish Olaf Guthfrithson (940), but (in alliance with DANELAW settlers) reconquered both (942 and 944). His brother Eadred (946–55) finally annexed Northumbria after the death of Erik Bloodaxe (954).

Edmund Ironside d. 1016. The son of Aethelred Unraed, on whose death (23 April 1016) he was chosen king by the Londoners. He then rallied Wessex behind him and resolutely but inconclusively opposed Cnut until defeated at ASHINGDON, whereafter he conceded Cnut all England save Wessex. He died in November, leaving Cnut in full possession.

Education *see* BRITISH SCHOOLS; CHARITY SCHOOLS; CIRCULATING SCHOOLS; DAME SCHOOLS; DISSENTING ACADEMIES; GRAMMAR SCHOOLS; NATIONAL SCHOOLS; PETTY SCHOOLS; PUBLIC SCHOOLS; RAGGED SCHOOLS; SUNDAY SCHOOLS; UNIVERSITIES

Education since 1833. In contrast to Scotland, where Acts of 1616 and 1696 set up a public school in each parish, England had no state education until 1870. Until the 1830s there was a minimal provision by old endowed foundations (*see* PUBLIC SCHOOLS), charity and 'venture' schools, ranging from sophisticated DISSENTING ACADEMIES to primitive DAME SCHOOLS. In the early 1800s, however, population growth, industrial change and, in particular, sectarian rivalry, prompted nationwide

organization by the Anglican 'National Society'
(1811) and the dissenting British and Foreign School
Society (1814). This rivalry plagued educational
legislation for over a century.

By 1818 30% of children were receiving some
sort of education. This proportion was increased in
1833 by the FACTORY ACT and by the allocation of a
state grant of £20,000 to the 2 societies. This was
raised in 1839, subject to regular inspection by the
staff of the committee of the privy council on
education whose head, the vice-president, became
the effective minister of education (although that
title did not become official until 1944). KAY-
SHUTTLEWORTH, his secretary, overcame sectarianism sufficiently to phase out the monitor
system by 1846 in favour of teachers, properly
trained, in colleges.

The state grant steadily increased until by 1862
£6·7 million had been spent. This prompted the
education minister, LOWE, to set up the Newcastle
commission into elementary education, which led
to the introduction of 'payment by results', tieing
education firmly to the 'three Rs'. It was Lowe also
who observed after the 2nd REFORM BILL (which he
had opposed): 'We must compel our future masters
to learn their letters.' This was substantially the
motive behind the 1st 'state education' Act (1870),
carried by FORSTER, Gladstone's education minister
(or president of the board of education, as the title
now formally became). A Scottish Act (1872) made
school boards compulsory. These lasted until 1918.

Forster's Act led to the setting up of elected
school boards in areas where provision was
inadequate (effectively the larger towns) and
subsidized the national schools. The Nonconformists were infuriated, but as Anglican resources
were overstrained the ministry gained more
control. Education became compulsory in 1880 and
free in 1891. Some authorities also extended
secondary and technical education, aided (1892–5)
by the Liberal education minister A.H.D. Acland
(1847–1926), until restrained by court judgments
that they had exceeded their powers.

To remedy this, the Conservatives passed the
1902 Education Act, which abolished the school
boards in favour of county councils and county
boroughs. This did not alter the status of the church
schools (and so provoked Nonconformist anger),
but it did enable a comprehensive approach to be
made to secondary education. In 1918 FISHER, Lloyd
George's education minister, promoted an Act to
raise the school leaving age from 14–15, to separate
secondary from elementary education, and to
provide a system of part-time post-school education, but the GEDDES AXE ensured that much of it

Elementary **education** in the early years of the 20th century: a
nature study class in Albion Street school, London, 1908.

remained a dead letter. In the same year, Scottish
education was transferred to special local education
authorities, and in 1929 to county councils.

Meanwhile, there were considerable developments in educational ideology. The Hadow report
(1926) recommended the separation of elementary
and secondary education, and distinguished between academic and non-academic secondary
education, using assessments of average ability
based on highly structured examinations and
intelligence tests.

The 1944 Education Act, passed by the Churchill
coalition's education minister, R.A. Butler, recognized these trends, and resulted in the setting up
of a secondary system of grammar, secondary
modern and technical schools, into which entry was
governed by the 11-plus examination. Subsequently, there has been much debate over
whether this system should be superseded by
comprehensive schools or whether the independence of grammar schools should be preserved.

Edward the Elder king of Wessex (899–924). The
son of Alfred, Edward crushed a Northumbrian
Viking invasion at Tettenhall, Staffs. in 910.
Thereafter (assisted by AETHELFLAEDA and consolidating with burhs) he led the series of sustained
and well-organized campaigns which recovered all
the DANELAW south of the Humber by 918. The
rulers of Alba, Northumbria, Strathclyde and York
recognized him as overlord in 920.

Edward the Confessor is portrayed on the Bayeux tapestry as a regal, pious king, set apart from the turbulent warfare and politics of his time.

Edward the Confessor king of England (1042–66). The son of Aethelred Unraed by Emma, Edward was exiled in Normandy from 1016 until recalled as Harthacnut's heir (1041). His Norman blood, upbringing and sympathies made him inimical to the Anglo-Danish aristocracy established by Cnut, and he was soon at loggerheads with GODWIN, his father-in-law and mightiest subject. He drove Godwin into exile (1051), strengthening the Norman element in church and state and recognizing his cousin William the Conqueror as his successor, but in 1052 Godwin returned and expelled the Normans. Thereafter HAROLD GODWINSON became the dominant power in England, and the pious king interested himself mainly in good works and building Westminster abbey. Condemned by some historians for precipitating the NORMAN CONQUEST, he was viewed by many contemporaries as a saint, being eventually canonized (1161).

Edward I king of England (1272–1307; b. 1229). Edward is now remembered chiefly for his conquest of WALES and his part in the SCOTTISH WARS OF INDEPENDENCE, but the guiding principles of his reign were *legalitas* – the pursuit of legal rectitude – and his desire to lead a great crusade. Exceptionally tall and imposing, he was the eldest son of Henry III whom, apart from one lapse (1259–60), he served faithfully and effectively in England (*see* EVESHAM,

BATTLE OF) and Aquitaine, and whom he succeeded peacefully despite his absence on crusade. On his return (1274) he initiated, with the help of BURNELL and the co-operation of his subjects, a sweeping programme of statutory legal reforms designed both to redress longstanding grievances concerning land law and local government and to rectify usurpations of crown rights. These culminated in the statutes of QUIA EMPTORES and QUO WARRANTO in 1290. (*See* LAW.)

The pursuit of legal rights (to homage from Llywelyn ap Gruffydd) was also a principal motive for Edward's brilliantly planned invasion of Wales (1277), which confined Llywelyn to a reduced Gwynedd. After a rising by Llywelyn and his brother David (1282–3) the conquest was completed and consolidated by a system of great CASTLES and fortified towns, and a new Welsh revolt by Rhys ap Maredudd was easily crushed (1287).

In 1290, with England and Aquitaine quiet and his son's betrothal to Alexander III's heiress the 'Maid of Norway' affording him the prospect of effectively controlling Scotland, Edward stood at the zenith of success. His arrangements for a crusade, however, were now baulked by a series of misfortunes which began when both the Maid and his beloved wife Eleanor of Castile died, and continued when Philip IV of France attacked Aquitaine (1294). Madoc ap Llywelyn's dangerous Welsh rising prevented Edward from responding, and his insensitive pursuit of his legal rights as John BALLIOL's overlord (1295) precipitated a Franco-Scots alliance.

The military situation was improved by Edward's 1st conquest of Scotland (at DUNBAR) and the reinforcement of Aquitaine (1296), but by now both *legalitas* and Edward's relationship with his English subjects were breaking down under the financial strain of continual war. Archbishop Winchelsey, backed by the papal bull 'Clericis Laicos', refused to allow clerical taxation, and in summer 1297 a group of magnates brought the nation to the verge of civil war by refusing service in France and denouncing heavy financial exactions imposed without consultation.

The consequent failure of Edward's Flemish expedition (August 1297–March 1298) and the threat of WALLACE's Scots revolt forced the government to compromise, effectively agreeing to give parliament control of taxation. But protests continued until 1301, and it was not until 1303 that final peace with France enabled Edward to begin his 2nd conquest of Scotland, ostensibly completed by 1305. Edward therefore reacted to ROBERT BRUCE's coup (1306) with fury, and to his return from exile

(1307) by preparing yet another invasion, leading which he died near Carlisle (7 July). The 'Hammer of the Scots' and the 'English Justinian' though he undoubtedly was, Edward left his far less able son Edward II an unenviable legacy.

Edward II king of England (1307–27; b. 1284). The son of Edward I, who created him the 1st English prince of Wales (1301). Edward's reign was from the outset plagued by baronial opposition, engendered in his father's reign and exacerbated by English failures in the SCOTTISH WARS OF INDEPENDENCE, by famines and natural disasters and, above all, by Edward's own foolishness, extravagant expenditure and inordinate attachment to favourites such as GAVESTON. In 1311 he was forced to submit to the ORDINANCES and, although Gaveston's murder (1312) destroyed baronial unity, Edward's defeat at BANNOCKBURN made the opposition leader Thomas of LANCASTER the effective ruler of England until the emergence of a more sympathetic 'middle party' led by AYMER DE VALENCE (1316–17). But the rapacity of Edward's new favourites, the DESPENSERS, led to open civil war (1321–2). The king emerged triumphant after BOROUGHBRIDGE, but humiliating defeats by ROBERT BRUCE and in France, together with the Despensers' continuing unpopularity, soon fostered the growth of a new opposition round ISABELLA and Roger MORTIMER. In September 1326 they invaded England, gathered wide-ranging support, deposed Edward (January 1327) and had him brutally murdered (September). His disastrous reign, and the implications of his deposition, severely damaged the prestige of the MONARCHY and thus had far-reaching effects on late medieval English history.

Edward III king of England (1327–77; b. 1312). One of the greatest English warrior kings, Edward was the eldest son of Edward II by Isabella of Angoulême. He set out to restore the prestige of the monarchy, shattered by his father's disastrous reign. The death of Robert Bruce (1329) gave him the opportunity to reopen the SCOTTISH WARS OF INDEPENDENCE, first by covertly backing the DISINHERITED against the infant DAVID II and then openly, at HALIDON HILL and BERWICK (1333).

By 1337 he was ready to take on France, but the 1st phase of the HUNDRED YEARS' WAR was both inconclusive and expensive, and in 1340–1 he was faced with a governmental crisis which culminated in a quarrel with STRATFORD. Urgent financial need constrained Edward to make concessions to clergy, nobility and the growing power of the commons, and thereafter he adroitly associated the interests of

Edward III as a young man, on the Waterford charter roll granted by him. Mid-14th century,

all 3 estates with his war effort. In this he was assisted by a string of English victories (at CRÉCY, NEVILLE'S CROSS, CALAIS and POITIERS) with their spoils of war, and by his own flair for chivalric display (see GARTER, ORDER OF THE).

Edward's popularity reached its height with the treaty of BRÉTIGNY (1360). But when the hundred years' war reopened (1369) the treasury was empty and, with matters in France going from bad to worse, the heavily taxed lords and commons became increasingly restive. The ageing king became more and more content to leave both war and government to others. Following the GOOD PARLIAMENT's attack on royal authority (1377), Edward died amidst an atmosphere of demoralization and dissension at home and failure abroad.

Edward IV king of England (1461–70; 1471–83; b. 1442). The son of Richard of York by Cecily Neville, Edward was tall, handsome and affable, and a courageous and successful soldier. Acceding at the crisis of the wars of the ROSES, he immediately triumphed at TOWTON (1461). He then adopted a policy of conciliation, but his misalliance with Elizabeth WOODVILLE and his pursuit of a pro-BURGUNDIAN foreign policy alienated his would-be mentor Warwick the Kingmaker who, after several attempts to control him, drove him to exile in Burgundy (October 1470). After a brilliant 3-month campaign on his return (March 1471),

Edward IV: roughly contemporary portrait, now in the National Portrait Gallery.

Edward established himself more securely than before. His policies, though still pragmatic and highly personal, now became less conciliatory (*see* CLARENCE, GEORGE) and, if his invasion of France was scarcely glorious, he gave England much needed domestic peace. His failure to reconcile feuds at court – notably that between his brother Gloucester (later Richard III) and the Woodvilles – or to make proper arrangements for his succession, however, entailed the downfall of his house after his premature death.

Edward V *see* PRINCES IN THE TOWER

Edward VI king of England (1547–53; b. 1537). Although Edward never exercised power personally, as an ardent Protestant he supported the extension of the REFORMATION under SOMERSET and NORTHUMBERLAND. It is possible that Edward, dying of tuberculosis and anxious to frustrate the succession of the Catholic MARY I, initiated the plot to proclaim Jane GREY.

Edward VII king of Great Britain (1901–10; b. 1841). Eldest son of Queen Victoria, with whom his relations were strained. After Prince ALBERT's death (1861), Edward was quarantined from any political influence and his main achievement was to fall dangerously ill in 1871, frustrating republican agitation. A mild interest in foreign policy and

social reform was masked by indulgence in food, women, shooting and gambling, but (on the whole) personal affability went with greater judgment than his mother in politics.

Edward VIII king of Great Britain (January–December 1936; b. 1894; d. 1972). *See* ABDICATION CRISIS.

Edward prince of Wales (1453–71). The only son of Henry VI and Margaret of Anjou. *See* ROSES, WARS OF THE; TEWKESBURY, BATTLE OF.

Edwin king of Northumbria (616–32). The heir of DEIRA, Edwin was expelled by Aethelferth (604) but allied with Raedwald to overthrow him. His victorious campaigns against Gwynedd, Manau Gododdin and Wessex (626) made him BRETWALDA and the most powerful Anglo-Saxon king to date. Baptised by Paulinus (627), he was killed near Doncaster by the Anglo-Welsh alliance of Cadwallawn and Penda.

Egbert king of Wessex (802–39). BRETWALDA and founder of the West Saxon ascendancy over Anglo-Saxon England, Egbert defeated the Mercians at ELLENDUN (825) and in 829 occupied Mercia and received the submission of Northumbria. Mercian independence was soon regained, but Egbert repulsed several Viking raids and left Wessex much enlarged and strengthened.

Edward VII never had an easy relationship with his mother: cartoon by Max Beerbohm from his – violently hostile – *Edwardyssey*, 1903.

The **Eleanor cross** at Hardingstone, Northants. Only 3 of the original 12 crosses survive, each different in design and beautifully made.

El Alamein, battle of 23 October–4 November 1942. MONTGOMERY stopped Rommel's push towards Cairo, and started the process of expelling the Germans from north Africa. *See* WORLD WAR II.

Eleanor crosses These were erected by Edward I at each of the places where the body of his beloved wife Eleanor of Castile rested on its way from Harby, Notts., to Westminster abbey: Lincoln, Grantham, Stamford, Geddington, Hardingstone, Stony Stratford, Woburn, Dunstable, St Albans, Waltham, West Cheap and Charing (*chère reine*) Cross. Only those at Hardingstone, Geddington and Waltham survive.

Eleanor of Aquitaine 1122–1204. The beautiful and forceful heiress of Aquitaine, Eleanor married first Louis VII of France (1137) and then (8 weeks after Louis repudiated her in 1152) Henry II. Excluded from power, she conspired with her sons against her husband, who imprisoned her from 1173 until his death (1189), after which she strenuously supported her favourite son Richard I.

Eleven Years' Tyranny 1629–40. A term sometimes used to describe the period of CHARLES I's non-parliamentary rule.

Eliot, Sir John 1592–1632. A passionate, impetuous Cornish gentleman and a brilliant orator,

Eliot led the parliamentary opposition to BUCKINGHAM and CHARLES I (1626–9). Architect of the PETITION OF RIGHT (1628), he was several times imprisoned by the king, and died in the Tower of London.

Elizabeth I queen of England (1558–1603; b. 1533). The daughter of Henry VIII and Anne Boleyn, Elizabeth's conception precipitated the Henrician REFORMATION and her personality was formed in the shadow of the conflicts which that revolution unleashed. Her mother was executed by her father when she was 3. In her teens she was prey to the marital ambitions of Thomas Seymour. At 21 she was imprisoned in the Tower. At 25 she inherited from her half-sister Mary I a kingdom unstable politically, divided in religion and defeated in war.

From the outset Elizabeth showed that she had learned from her childhood. To a keen natural intelligence, splendidly schooled by the humanists Cheke and Ascham (*see* HUMANISM), she added political tact and shrewdness and a steely determination to pursue policies of moderation and stability. The religious settlement (1559) sought a protestant middle way from which she deviated little and which was sufficiently ambiguous to defer her excommunication by the pope until 1570. Her foreign policy sought to defend English security while avoiding war for as long as possible. Her hand in marriage was used as an effective diplomatic counter until it became clear with time that she had

The **Elizabeth** of legend: wearing a dress studded with jewels and under a canopy of cloth of silver, she is carried on high by bareheaded and adoring subjects, 1600. Oil painting attributed to Robert Peake, *c*. 1601.

determined never to marry – a decision both politically wise and personally attractive to her. In her choice of servants such as CECIL, LEICESTER, WALSINGHAM, PARKER, HATTON and HAWKINS, she showed both sound judgment and a care to avoid faction. Unoriginal perhaps, economical to the point of parsimony, certainly, infuriating to her more doctrinaire counsellors by her deliberate dilatoriness on issues of principle, she nonetheless wooed her people with her patriotism, her brilliant theatrical cult of regality and her personal charm. She also gave them peace and a new sense of confidence and identity.

The last 2 decades of her reign, though marked by brilliant cultural achievement, the conditions for which she had helped to create, saw a clouding of the political skies. War with Spain from 1585 brought few victories after the Spanish ARMADA's defeat (1588), yet was a constant drain of resources, the more so when complicated by TYRONE's rebellion in Ireland. As her great counsellors died away, faction at court revived more fiercely, culminating in the tragedy of the 2nd earl of ESSEX's rebellion. Parliamentary opposition became more vocal and the religious settlement came under sharp Puritan attack. Elizabeth was to leave severe problems unsolved to her successor. Yet while she lived her personal charisma retained its power; indeed, it survived her. Aged, toothless, bald and irascible, she was still *Gloriana* and could tell her last, difficult parliament: 'This I count the glory of my crown, that I have reigned with your loves.' It was no more than the truth.

Elizabeth II queen of Great Britain (1952– ; b. 1926). Her wedding to Philip Mountbatten and her coronation were high points in the swelling tide of popular feeling in support of the MONARCHY as one great British tradition which remained unimpaired, and her manifest dedication brought it further prestige. Scottish nationalists, however, objected to her styling herself the *second* Elizabeth of Great Britain.

Elizabeth of York queen of England *see* HENRY VII

Ellendun, battle of 825. EGBERT king of Wessex, defeated Beornwulf of Mercia near Wroughton, Wilts., ending the long Mercian ascendancy over Anglo-Saxon England. He then immediately annexed the Mercian tributary kingdoms of Kent, Sussex, Surrey and the East Saxons.

Ellis, Tom *see* WELSH NATIONALISM

Elmet A small post-Roman British kingdom occupying southern and western Yorkshire, it was annexed to English Northumbria by Edwin *c.* 619.

Emma d. 1052. The daughter of Duke Richard I of Normandy and great aunt of William the Conqueror. Her successive marriages to Aethelred Unraed (1002), by whom she had Edward the Confessor, and Cnut (1017), by whom she had Harthacnut, represented Norman alliances and gave her considerable power in England. She opposed Edward's accession.

Empingham, battle of *see* LOSE-COAT FIELD, BATTLE OF

Empire *see* BRITISH EMPIRE

Employment exchanges These were intended to enable workers to contact employers without the 'frictional' unemployment which resulted from job-seeking, and were the brainchild of BEVERIDGE, Churchill's adviser at the board of trade (1908–11). The first were opened in 1909.

Enclosure The hedging or fencing-in of formerly open-field or common pasture land. Much enclosure took place 1450–1700, sometimes with the agreement, sometimes against the opposition of tenants and commoners. From the 18th century planned enclosure by Act of parliament extended and completed the process in lowland England and Scotland. *See* ill. p. 10.

Aerial view showing the hedges of the **enclosure** movement cutting across the medieval ridge-and-furrow field system.

Enfeoffment An arrangement whereby landowners avoided ESCHEAT by making all or part of their lands over to groups of their associates or retainers (feoffees) who thus became the legal owners, though the feoffor generally retained the 'use' and profits of the estates for life. After his death the feoffees (in theory) obeyed his instructions regarding his debts, annuities and bequests, handing over the land when the heir was of age. It was common from the 14th century but its advantages were removed by the statute of Uses (1535).

Engagement, the Scottish 1647. An agreement between Charles I and Scottish commissioners whereby Scottish troops would fight to obtain better terms of settlement for the king in return for Charles's acceptance of a temporary Presbyterian church settlement in England. The engagement, which provoked the 2nd CIVIL WAR and divided Scottish opinion, led to James HAMILTON's invasion of England and defeat at PRESTON.

Engels, Frederick 1820–95. The son of a German textile merchant, Engels first came to Britain in 1842, as an agent in his father's Manchester office. His *The Condition of the Working Classes in England* was published in Germany in 1845, in which year he began his collaboration with MARX which culminated 3 years later in *The Communist Manifesto* (1848). After the revolutions of that year he returned to Manchester, supporting Marx in London and later editing the last 2 volumes of *Capital* (1885 and 1894).

Engrossing A term of disapproval, used in 16th- and 17th-century England to describe either the consolidation of 2 or more agricultural holdings into a single farm or the making of large-scale purchases of foodstuffs which left markets undersupplied for the poor.

Entente cordiale Britain and France came to an 'understanding' or 'entente' in 1904 – ostensibly on colonial questions – which was broadened to include Russia (France's ally since 1894) in 1908. Although this implied a defensive alliance with the first and a non-aggression pact with the second, it nevertheless stimulated German fears of 'encirclement'.

Epidii ('horse people'). A northern Scottish tribe which inhabited Kintyre at the time of Roman Britain.

Equity *see* LAW

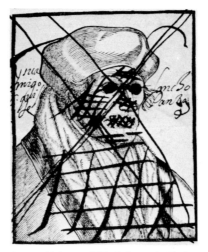

In 1537 the Inquisition prohibited the reading of **Erasmus**'s books in Spanish and ordered even the Latin editions to be expurgated: it was later responsible for this savaging of his portrait in Sebastian Munster's *Cosmographia* (Basle 1550 edn).

Erasmus, Desiderius 1466–1536. A Dutch humanist (*see* HUMANISM), Erasmus was editor of the Greek New Testament (1516) and author of biting satires on ecclesiastical corruption. A frequent visitor to England and friend of More, he also influenced the younger generation of English reformers. In 1548 his *Paraphrases* was ordered to be placed in every parish church.

Erik Bloodaxe d. 954. The last Scandinavian king of York. Driven from the Norwegian throne for excessive cruelty, he turned Viking, was accepted at York (947) but soon afterwards expelled. He returned (952) and reigned until overthrown and killed, probably by the Norse-Irish dynasty he had displaced. Northumbria was thereupon annexed to England.

Escheat A process whereby, on the death of a feudal landowner, his estates reverted to the overlord, to be held until a minor heir came of age or an adult paid a fine ('relief'). Royal rights in this regard were administered by an escheator. *See* ENFEOFFMENT.

Esquire A term used for the attendants of KNIGHTS (themselves usually aspirants to knighthood) as well as for other persons of the rank immediately below knighthood and for certain office-holders, e.g. esquires of the royal household. *See* TITLES.

Robert Devereux, 2nd earl of **Essex**: anonymous portrait, *c.* 1597.

Essex, Robert Devereux, 2nd earl of 1565–1601. The handsome stepson of Leicester, Essex was loved like a son by ELIZABETH I. Never supreme in her council, where he was checked by the Cecils, he eventually forfeited her favour by his arrogance and political and military ineptitude as lord-lieutenant of Ireland. He was executed after a desperate rising in 1601.

Essex, Robert Devereux, 3rd earl of 1591–1646. The son of Elizabeth I's favourite and an opponent of Charles I's government, Essex was appointed general of the parliamentarian army (1642) in the CIVIL WARS. A competent commander but lacking in initiative, he was forced to surrender at Lostwithiel (1644). He resigned before the passage of the SELF-DENYING ORDINANCE (1645).

Etaples, treaty of *see* HENRY VII; HUNDRED YEARS' WAR

Etcetera oath 1640. An oath of loyalty to church government by 'archbishops, bishops, archdeacons, deans etcetera' imposed by CONVOCATION as a means of detecting Presbyterian sympathizers during the BISHOPS' WARS (1639–40). The oath aroused great resentment among moderate Puritan clergymen by no means committed to a full Presbyterian system.

Ethel- *see* AETHEL-

European Economic Community *see* COMMON MARKET

Evangelicals The name given to an active group of deeply pious Anglican laymen of the late 18th and early 19th centuries, including the CLAPHAM SECT. Narrow in theology and socially conservative, but active in founding religious and philanthropic organizations, they were responsible for a revival of personal religion among the English ruling class.

Evesham, battle of 4 August 1265. Simon de Montfort's tired army, trapped in Evesham between Roger Mortimer and Prince Edward, was attacked by the latter. During a short, fierce and bloody fight Simon de Montfort and his leading supporters were slain, their defeat effectively breaking the back of the baronial opposition to HENRY III.

Evolution *see* DARWIN, CHARLES

Ex officio oath An oath administered in the church courts (especially high commission) binding persons to answer questions without any prior knowledge of the charge. It was much used to detect Puritanism among the clergy and was deeply resented both by them and by common lawyers. It was abolished by parliament (1641).

Exchequer So called from the chequered cloth on which coins were counted, the exchequer developed out of the CHAMBER of the ROYAL HOUSEHOLD to become by Henry I's reign the financial and auditing department of the English government as a whole. It remained so until gradually superseded by the treasury during the 16th and 17th centuries and abolished as a separate office in 1833. The importance of the treasury is recognized by the fact that prime ministers are also 1st lord of the treasury; nonetheless the government's chief finance minister is entitled chancellor of the exchequer.

Exchequer of pleas, court of An English LAW court, sitting at Westminster and presided over by the treasurer and barons of the EXCHEQUER. Originating in the 13th century to handle cases involving the royal revenues, the court gradually extended its competence from the 16th century. Its separate existence ended in 1873.

Excise A sales tax on beer, tobacco and other items, introduced by Pym (1643) as a wartime measure, but extended and continued thereafter. The excise was particularly unpopular in the later 17th and

18th centuries, as were its enforcement agents, the excisemen.

Excise crisis 1733. A crisis provoked by Walpole's scheme to reorganize the customs and EXCISE so as to prevent fraud and increase revenue. The opposition raised fears of a general excise prejudicial to liberty and property, Walpole's parliamentary majority slumped and he was forced to abandon his plans.

Exclusion crisis 1679–81. A political crisis produced by the attempts of WHIGS in the 3 'Exclusion parliaments' (1679–81) to pass Bills excluding the future James VII and II from the English throne as a Catholic and to replace him with Charles II's illegitimate son Monmouth. Charles repeatedly dissolved parliament and rode out the crisis.

Excommunication The formal exclusion of an individual from the communion of the church, used freely as a sanction by ecclesiastical courts up to the 17th century. Though it officially carried severe civil disabilities, excommunication became so commonplace that it held little terror for most people.

Exeter *see* DUMNONII

Eyre, Edward John 1815–1901. Eyre gained his reputation as an explorer in Australia, and his notoriety when, as governor of Jamaica, he put down with great ferocity a native rising (1865), arousing radical opinion in Britain. The 'Eyre case' was one of the first of many intellectual protests against colonial misgovernment.

Fabian Society A socialist research and propagandist group which evolved from 1884 to 1889, when *Fabian Essays*, written by, among others, George Bernard Shaw and Sidney WEBB appeared. They argued that the gradual expansion of public intervention nationally and locally would make

The court of **exchequer** collecting revenues and detaining those unable to pay. Gradually the exchange of parchment rolls was to supersede the use of cash. From an illuminated manuscript, *c.* 1460.

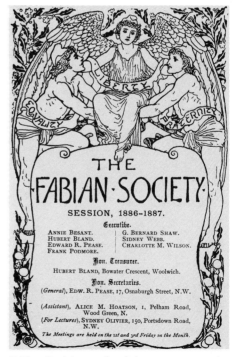

The **Fabian Society** was founded to reconstruct society 'in accordance with the highest moral possibilities'. This card of 1886 was designed by Walter Crane, a leading disciple of William MORRIS.

socialism inevitable. Although they helped found the INDEPENDENT LABOUR PARTY (1893), they still attempted to permeate the other parties, and not until 1918 did they become formally aligned with the Labour party.

Factories *see* FACTORY ACTS; FACTORY MOVEMENT; INDUSTRIAL REVOLUTION; NEW LANARK

Factory Acts Acts to regulate the work of children in factories were passed in 1802 and 1819, but their scope was narrow: the first dealt with parish apprentices, the second only with children in the cotton trade, and their enforcement, left to local JPs, was ineffective. After agitation by working-class groups, some employers, TORY RADICALS, SHAFTES-BURY and others, the Whig government set up a royal commission, managed by CHADWICK, which recommended (1833 Act) – for textiles only – a maximum of 12 hours daily labour for children aged 11–18, 8 for children from 9–11, and banned children under 9 from work, such regulations being enforced by a staff of 4 inspectors. Following further agitation, hours were limited to 10 for adults and children by the Ten Hours Act (1847). The Acts were made applicable to other industries (1867) and subsequently consolidated and extended.

Factory movement The agitation which secured the 1847 Ten Hours Act (*see* FACTORY ACTS). Largely led by TORY RADICALS, along with working men from Yorkshire and SHAFTESBURY, it was to some extent conceived of as retaliation for the success of the ANTI-CORN-LAW LEAGUE in the previous year.

Faculty of Advocates *see* LAW

Fairfax, Sir Thomas 1612–71. 'Black Tom' first distinguished himself as commander of the York-shire horse (1643–4) and subsequently led the NEW MODEL ARMY to victory in the CIVIL WARS. Sensitive, taciturn and merciful, he declined to take part in Charles I's trial and later resigned rather than attack Scotland, living privately thereafter.

Falkes de Breauté The principal captain of John's mercenaries, Falkes de Breauté helped set Henry III on the throne (*see* LINCOLN, BATTLE OF) but then fell foul of LANGTON and HUBERT DE BURGH. After un-successfully resisting the resumption of royal castles in his custody, he was driven into exile (1224).

Falkirk, battle of 22 July 1298. WALLACE's Scots army, fighting in defensive SCHILTRONS, was first broken by the fire of Edward I's Anglo-Welsh archers and then destroyed by his cavalry.

Falkland palace, Fife: the ruins of the magnificent hunting lodge of the Stewart kings of Scotland.

Falkland A picturesque burgh in the Fife hills, dominated by the impressive ruins of Falkland palace, the hunting lodge of the Stewart kings, completed in 1542 and much used by Mary Queen of Scots. The gardens have been restored to their 17th-century condition.

Family The family is an almost universal human institution, yet its history has only recently begun to be written. What follows relates principally to English evidence and involves findings which are frequently tentative.

Much is now known about the size and structure of the 'co-resident domestic group' (those persons resident within a single household) in England in the past, largely thanks to the work of Peter Laslett, *Household and Family in Past Time* (1972). Formerly it had been assumed that the processes of industrialization and urbanization after 1750 brought about a shift from large, complex or 'extended family' units to the simple 'nuclear family' structure of husband, wife and children. In fact, however, high mortality rates meant that the average pre-industrial family was small and 3-generation households very rare. Nevertheless, large and complex households did exist in the upper ranks of society. Indeed, from medieval times, the transfer of the children of poorer families into the households of wealthier persons as servants meant that a numerical majority of the population lived in the minority of larger households. SERVANTS IN HUSBANDRY had declined in numbers by 1850, though domestic service remained common for women until 1914. Meanwhile, industrial employment opportunities and educational change led to children staying at home longer, while urban conditions and longer life expectation in the 19th century saw an actual increase in the proportion of households containing grandparents and other relatives. The 20th-century family differs from its pre-industrial counterpart largely in the relative absence of great households and service, the postponement of children's departure from home and the more frequent presence of the elderly.

Several historians have advanced bold hypotheses about trends in family life since the 16th century. Most recently, Lawrence Stone in *The Family, Sex and Marriage in England, 1500–1800* (1977) has argued that the family has passed through 3 stages: the 'open lineage family' of the later middle ages, the 'restricted patriarchal nuclear family' (1550-1650) and the 'closed domesticated nuclear family' which developed after 1650, was the norm by 1800 and laid the foundations of modern family life, despite a brief Victorian reaction towards patriarchalism. Stone's arguments are confined largely to the middle and upper classes, which he sees as the leaders in changing family life. The process of development allegedly involved shifts from acceptance of the authority of the broader kin-group to the autonomy of the individual nuclear family; from arranged, unemotional marriages towards consensual and companionate marriages, and from the authoritarian rule of husbands and fathers and severe child-rearing towards strong affective ties and the granting of greater autonomy to both wives and children.

These hypotheses, though incorporating and developing some earlier conceptions of family history, are extremely controversial, and contradict other broader studies. Kinship, for example, does appear to have been of significance in the lives of propertied families conscious of their lineage and involved in political and business affairs on a scale which made kin support a matter of great practical importance. The special conditions of the Scottish highlands before 1750 and of the borderlands before 1600 also placed an emphasis on kinship (*see* CLANS). Lower in the social scale and in more secure societies, however, kinship ties outside those of the nuclear family seem never to have had overriding emotional or practical significance. Population

mobility, high since medieval times, has meant that more distant kin have rarely been close at hand. The conditions of 19th-century urban life may have given the kin-group a somewhat greater importance in mutual assistance, but the social services of the 20th century have eroded that temporary role.

The history of marriage also indicates strong elements of continuity over time. Age at 1st marriage in England has been rather high by world standards since at least the 16th century – women generally marrying in their mid- to late twenties and men an average of 2 years later. Outside the landed classes child marriage has been little known at any time and extremely rare even in the highest ranks by 1600. During the Industrial Revolution

The **family** at tea. 3 generations of a Victorian family gather for a child's birthday celebration: oil painting by W. P. Frith, 1856; in a prefab in 1944, the occasion is not such an expansive affair.

high earnings by young men allowed the average marriage age to drop in some areas, but this was a limited and temporary phenomenon. At all times marriage age appears to have been primarily determined by the fact that economic independence was necessary before a new nuclear family unit could be safely established. Parental influence in the choice of marriage partners could be very strong high in the social scale, where substantial property settlements were involved (*see* DOWRY). Among most of the population, however, young people commonly found their own partners and parental consent, though usually sought, was by no means obligatory. The ideal match appears to have long been considered one exhibiting a rough equality of wealth, age and reputation in the partners, together with emotional and physical compatibility. All this is recognizably similar to current realities, even the convention of romantic love being of long ancestry in popular culture.

The strength of the marriage bond itself has varied. In Saxon times espousal before witnesses was the customary form of marriage, and DIVORCE relatively easy. Ecclesiastical control of marriage, its sacramental status and consequent indissolubility appeared only in the middle ages. Indeed, espousals remained legally valid, if irregular, until the clarification of marital law by Hardwicke's MARRIAGE ACT (1753). Modern civil marriage appeared in 1836, while the divorce laws were reformed slowly after 1857. Before that date true divorce was possible only by private Act of parliament, though the labouring poor had their own extra-legal divorce ritual: the wife-sale. Desertion was also very common, while high death rates broke marriages and facilitated remarriage more commonly than divorce does today.

Within marriage women were, at least until very recent times, legally inferior, subject to a sexual double standard and expected to be subordinate to their spouses. Actual behaviour, however, must be distinguished from legal and moralistic pre-scriptions. Early diaries and letters indicate strong companionate elements in the marriages of people of middling rank, with couples sharing productive, decision-making and leisure activities. Peasant women and the wives of workers in domestic industry also shared fully in family production. Confinement to housekeeping was a later product of industries which offered no female employment and removed work from the household (though the Industrial Revolution gave many women factory work – *see* WOMEN'S MOVEMENT). It would be unwise to make too sharp a dichotomy between 'traditional patriarchal' and 'modern compan-ionate' marriage. Both situations have a long history as the poles of an enduring continuum in marital relations.

Similarly, social change can be shown to have altered the conditions of children's lives more than the nature of attitudes towards them. Before the 19th century children were expected to work and were employed at home or put into service at an early age. Nevertheless, this situation was not incompatible with parental recognition of the individuality and care for the welfare of their offspring. Child-rearing in the past, though not conforming to modern practices, was certainly less severe than is commonly alleged and there is substantial evidence that parent-child relations were warm and affectionate. The abolition of child labour (*see* FACTORY ACTS) and introduction of compulsory education have prolonged effective childhood, while economic and social change have afforded greater opportunities for the overt demonstration of parental care.

The history of the family thus contains a number of surprisingly enduring characteristics, together with variations in experience determined above all by the influence of economic advantages and constraints. Apparent change over time may owe more to changing socio-economic conditions and social-structural modifications than to fundamental shifts in familial values and aspirations. These, like the family itself, may be fundamental characteristics of a culture which has endured as well as developed over time.

Family allowances *see* WELFARE STATE

Faraday, Michael 1791–1867. An English scientist who discovered the principle of electro-magnetism, the basis of electrical energy (1831). He was also a pioneer of atomic theory.

Michael **Faraday** lecturing before Prince Albert (on the left) at the Royal Institution, London.

Farmtoun A traditional Scottish agricultural settlement, consisting of a hamlet centred on a notional farm and known in the highlands as a 'clachan'. The farm might be cultivated either by a single tenant employing labour or by a small group of joint tenants practising RUNRIG.

Fascism In imitation of Mussolini's Fascisti, various uniformed ultra-conservative and anti-semitic groups were set up, mainly by ex-officers and aristocrats, in the 1920s. None thrived. More serious was Oswald Mosley's British Union of Fascists (1932), formed from his New Party, whose 'blackshirt' parades through London's east end were banned by the Public Order Act (1936). After the war the banner of the racist right has been carried by the various groups which merged in 1967 to form the NATIONAL FRONT.

Fawcett, Henry 1833–84. Educated at Cambridge and blinded in a shooting accident (1858), Fawcett worked his way into academic and political life, as an ally of Mill, gaining a reputation as a 'laissez-faire' economist, radical MP (1865–84), critic of imperialism and advocate of women's rights. He became postmaster-general in Gladstone's 2nd government.

Fawcett, Millicent (*née* Garrett) 1847–1929. On the death of her husband, Henry Fawcett, Millicent pursued an independent political career as a LIBERAL UNIONIST organizer and, after 1896, president of the National Union of Woman Suffrage Societies, leading the non-militant campaign for the vote. She shrewdly exploited the opportunities offered by World War I which led to the winning of the vote (1918).

Fawkes, Guy 1570–1606. Born in York and early converted to Catholicism, Fawkes served in the Spanish army from 1590 and was involved in several plots for Spanish intervention in England before the GUNPOWDER PLOT. Arrested following the discovery of the plot, he was tortured and executed.

Felix, St *see* CHURCH, PRE-REFORMATION

Female labour Before the Industrial Revolution women frequently undertook hard manual work, but industrialization and the division of labour meant that this became on the whole lighter and more specialized. In the 19th century about a quarter of the female population over 15 worked, half of these in service. Otherwise textiles, at about

Female labour at an ironworks in south Wales, 1865.

An English view of the **Fenians**: 'The Knave and the Fool'. The knave is the American Irishman tempting to violence his brother back home, promising the cap of liberty but delivering a noose. Cartoon from the *Razor*, 1868.

5%, was the great employer. Work in the mines was banned in 1842; and by 1881 the numbers working on the land had dropped sharply. Office and shop occupations were beginning to grow by the end of the century, and the range of occupations was greatly extended by World War I, but it was not until after World War II that women finally moved out of domestic service. *See* WOMEN'S MOVEMENT.

Fenians An Irish nationalist movement founded in the USA in 1857, which gained support from discharged Irish soldiers after the end of the American civil war. In 1866–8 it was responsible for insurrections on the Canadian border, at Chester, and a bombing at Clerkenwell. It was dissolved in 1868 but the tradition was revived in the Irish Republican Brotherhood, which survived to co-ordinate Irish-American policy, and set up the Irish Republican Army (1918).

Feoffees *see* ENFEOFFMENT

Fergus mac Erc *see* DALRIADA

Festival of Britain 1951. Held on the South Bank of the Thames to celebrate the centenary of the Great Exhibition and the alleviating of 5 years of post-war 'austerity'. It was the last fling of the mildly left-wing writers, artist and planners who had thrived under the Labour government, but did much to encourage modern styles in painting and design.

Feudal aids Money payments leviable by the king or other lord on his feudal tenants at times of special need. At first undefined, these occasions were limited by MAGNA CARTA (1215) to the ransom of his body, the knighting of his eldest son and the 1st marriage of his eldest daughter.

Feudalism A term used (since the 17th century) for the organization of medieval society based on the holding of land in return for voluntary homage and specific services, normally military. Though 'feudal' elements existed in Anglo-Saxon society, there is little doubt that feudalism proper, originating in late Carolingian France, was introduced to Britain at the NORMAN CONQUEST, when sweeping changes in land-ownership allowed the establishment of a far more comprehensive and orderly system than had developed piecemeal in Europe.

Resting on the premise that all land must have an owner (*nulle terre sans seigneur*) but that it was held directly or indirectly of the crown rather than owned outright, English feudalism arose from William the Conqueror's need both to provide himself with an army of trained KNIGHTS and to reward his followers without detracting from his own power. He therefore granted FIEFS of land (often scattered through several shires and called HONOURS) to Norman lay magnates and (slightly later) to bishops and leading abbots. They in return were required to swear fealty to him, to do public homage by placing their hands between his and, most important, to perform 'knight service' by providing him on demand with an agreed number (not necessarily concomitant with the size of the fief) of knights. A minority of fiefs were held in return for other services, e.g. FRANKALMOIGN and SERGEANTY. All tenants-in-chief so created were also subject to 'feudal incidents', notably the king's right to levy FEUDAL AIDS, temporarily to repossess (ESCHEAT) the fief on a tenant's death, to exact a fine

or 'relief' from an adult successor and to control the WARDSHIP and marriage of under-age lay heirs.

At first tenants-in-chief fulfilled their military obligations by keeping households of landless stipendiary knights, but such measures were both costly and (especially for churchmen) inconvenient. Before Domesday Book, therefore, magnates had begun to maintain their supporters by granting them portions of land (of varying size) as 'knight's fees', exacting in return the same services and incidents as they themselves owed to the crown and thus establishing feudal states in miniature. This process of sub-infeudation, almost universal by *c.* 1150, was carried further when holders of one or more such knight's fees granted part of them, again for homage and service, to sub-tenants of their own, who might in turn grant part of their portion on similar terms to another, so that holdings of small portions of a knight's fee became common.

The feudal pyramid so formed made at first for a stable society, binding each landowner firmly to his immediate overlord, and ultimately to the crown. Its basic organizational unit was the MANOR, whose peasant inhabitants also held land by service to their lord, though such service (being neither voluntarily entered into nor military) was not strictly 'feudal'. For rent-paying freemen it included attendance at the MANOR COURT and occasional task work; but VILLEINS (much more numerous in most parts of England) were forced in return for their smallholdings to perform 2 or 3 days' labour service a week on the lord's DEMESNE, with extra 'boon work' at busy times, and were subject to onerous exactions such as HERIOT, MERCHET and arbitrary TALLAGE. Tied to the land, the poorer class of villeins (or SERFS) were their masters' chattels, but the better-off quickly began to commute their labour services for money payments or employ others to perform them.

Soon after the conquest, feudalism followed the Marchers into Wales, and in the 12th century it was introduced into southern Scotland with the Anglo-Norman allies of David I, spreading throughout the lowlands by the 13th century, but never effectively penetrating the highlands.

During the 12th and 13th centuries feudal law was almost constantly being redefined and reinterpreted, sometimes (under strong kings such as Henry II) in favour of the crown and sometimes (under weak or disadvantaged monarchs such as John) in favour of the tenants-in-chief (*see* MAGNA CARTA). The most significant developments, striking at the essentials of the system, were the increasing commutation of feudal services for money payments or rents and the decline of the feudal army. By 1100 scutage or shield tax (used for the employment of mercenaries) was accepted in England in lieu of knight service under certain circumstances, and by 1196 tenants-in-chief could purchase permanent exemption for a lump sum recouped by levying scutage on their sub-tenants. Scutage itself, made difficult to collect by multiple sub-infeudation, was by the late 13th century being replaced by taxes voted in parliament, and from the time of Edward I the unwieldy, inefficient and out-dated feudal army (last called out in 1327) was superseded by armies of INDENTURED RETAINERS serving by short-term contract for pay rather than land.

With its basic military objective lost, feudalism at all levels decayed rapidly during the 14th century, especially after the economic and population changes exacerbated by the BLACK DEATH. Estates changed hands exclusively for cash, demesnes were leased out and the increasing commutation of labour services for rents converted villeins to free smallholders. Though it remained formally intact, and many of its lucrative financial incidents (notably wardship) long continued to be enforced by kings and magnates, feudalism proper had by the time of Edward III (1327–77) been superseded as a social force by the institution somewhat mislead-ingly labelled 'bastard feudalism' by Victorian historians.

Unlike its predecessor, this had little to do with land tenure, its essence being that services were performed, under written contract, in return for an annual fee (LIVERY). It originated when great men began to maintain indentured retainers in peace as well as war, and often nominally for life. Such retainers (who might themselves be lords or knights retaining others in their turn) were expected to support their patron's interests and he theirs, saving allegiance to the crown. The king, however, was no longer the apex of a feudal pyramid of tenure and service, and while strong monarchs such as Henry V could control the system and use noble retinues or 'affinities' as the nucleus of efficient armies, under weak governments such as that of Henry VI it was undoubtedly conducive to disorder. Retinues were then used for the prosecution of the aristocratic feuds which escalated into the wars of the ROSES, and great men exercised a stranglehold over local government and law, supporting the illegal actions of their followers (see MAINTENANCE), retaining SHERIFFS and judges, and forcing lesser men to seek their 'good lordship'. When strong government returned under Edward IV and Henry VII, legislation attacked these abuses of 'bastard feu-dalism' rather than the institution itself, which lingered on into the Elizabethan period, being finally extinguished only by the advent of full state control of the army.

Fief An estate (in Britain always hereditary) held in return for homage and service to an overlord, who technically retained ownership. It might consist of a whole nation (see JOHN), wide lands or only half a manor. See FEUDALISM.

Field of Cloth of Gold 1520. The meeting near Calais of Henry VIII and Francis I of France, who hoped for English support against Emperor Charles V. The 'Field', with its temporary palace, pavilions, feastings, sports and tournaments, was a stupendous and costly spectacle. In terms of diplomacy, however, its results were negligible.

Fifteen rebellion see JACOBITES

Fifth Monarchy Men INTERREGNUM radicals, drawing their strongest support from among urban craftsmen, who expected the imminent 2nd coming and taking of political power by Christ. Their aims included legal and ecclesiastical reforms. After several plots during the protectorate, a rising was attempted in London (1661), following which the movement subsided.

Fire of London 2–7 September 1666. Starting in a bake-house in Pudding Lane, the fire rapidly got out of control and destroyed much of the city of London, including St Paul's cathedral and 89 churches.

The **Fire of London**, 1666: Old St Paul's is in the centre. Oil painting attributed to William van de Velde, c. 1667–70.

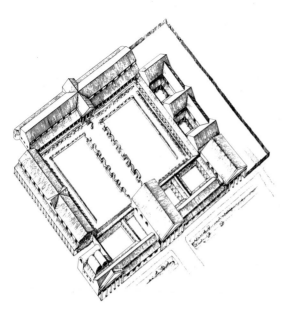

Fishbourne villa, Sussex: isometric drawing by David Neal.

First Band *see* CONGREGATION, LORDS OF THE; REFORMATION

Fishbourne villa Sussex. A palatial 10-acre VILLA, the largest and one of the earliest in Roman Britain, discovered in 1960 and now on view. A quadrangle arranged round a (restored) formal garden, it was begun *c.* 75, possibly as a reward for the loyalty of COGIDUBNUS, whose capital was nearby Chichester.

Fisher, Herbert A. L. 1865–1940. Oxford academic and Liberal historian who, after a spell as principal of Sheffield university, became president of the board of education in LLOYD GEORGE's coalition cabinet (1916–22) where he drafted and carried the 1918 Education Act. Thereafter he was warden of New College, Oxford.

Fisher, John ?1459–1535. Bishop of Rochester (1504), a theologian of distinction and supporter of humanist learning (*see* HUMANISM), Fisher opposed Henry VIII's divorce and resisted the Henrician REFORMATION both in CONVOCATION and by attempting to influence parliament. He was executed for refusing to subscribe to the Act of SUCCESSION (1534) and recognize the royal supremacy.

Fisher, John Arbuthnot, lord 1841–1920. One of the 1st generation of sailors to be raised in the 'steam navy', Fisher saw action at ALEXANDRIA (1882), and rose to become an innovating 1st sea lord. Obstreperous and charming, he pushed through the entire reconstruction of the fleet around the DREADNOUGHT battleship (1904–10). Returned to his post in 1914, he fell out with Winston Churchill over the DARDANELLES and resigned.

Fisher, Sir N. F. Warren 1879–1948. An Oxford-educated civil servant who rose by 1919 to become head of the civil service as permanent secretary to the treasury (1919–39), in which position he secured treasury domination over the other departments – to the detriment, as KEYNES believed, of intelligent economic policy. As regional commissioner for north-west England, he was sacked by the home secretary Morrison (1940).

Fitz Osbern, William d. 1071. The steward and most trusted friend of WILLIAM THE CONQUEROR, who granted him extensive lands in England (including the MARCHER earldom of Hereford) and made him joint regent there (with Odo of Bayeux) during his absence in Normandy (1067). He was a notable castle builder.

Fitzmaurice, James d. 1579. A nephew of the earl of Desmond, Fitzmaurice led a rebellion against Elizabeth I (1569–73). Forced to submit, he sought help abroad after 1575, returning to Ireland with papal backing (1579), only to be killed in a skirmish by his own cousin.

Five Boroughs, the Derby, Leicester, Lincoln, Nottingham and Stamford and the surrounding area were the bases of 5 Viking armies during Alfred's reign, and subsequently the most heavily Danish-settled part of the DANELAW. Conquered by Aethelflaeda and Edward the Elder (917–18), they were annexed by Norse-Irish York (940) but recovered by EDMUND (942).

Five Knights' case 1627–8. A test case brought by 5 of those imprisoned in 1627 for refusing to pay Charles I's FORCED LOAN. They sued a writ of HABEAS CORPUS in order to test the king's right to imprison them. The judges found for the king, though those imprisoned were soon released.

Five Members The 5 leaders of the commons in the LONG PARLIAMENT (PYM, HAMPDEN, Haselrig, Strode and Holles) whom Charles I attempted to arrest in the house (4 January 1642). They escaped to the city of London, while Charles withdrew from the capital. *See* CIVIL WARS.

Five Mile Act 1665. An Act prohibiting ministers ejected after the Act of UNIFORMITY (1662) from coming within 5 miles of the parishes where they had been incumbents or of any town or city. It was repealed by the TOLERATION ACT (1689).

Flambard, Ranulf d. 1128. The hated chief agent of William Rufus's financial exactions, notably the sale of ecclesiastical offices and the usurpation of episcopal revenues during forcibly prolonged vacancies. Made bishop of Durham (1099), but imprisoned on Henry I's accession (1100), he escaped to support Robert Curthose's invasion (1101), being reconciled to Henry after TENCHEBRAI (1106).

Flapper Vote An Act of 1928 enfranchised women aged 21–30, who voted for the 1st time in the 1929 election. *See* WOMEN'S MOVEMENT.

Fleetwood, Charles 1618–92. An officer in the NEW MODEL ARMY, Fleetwood became lord deputy of Ireland (1654), one of the MAJOR-GENERALS, and ultimately lord-general (1659). A competent soldier, but irresolute politician, he contributed to the fall of the protectorate, but failed to prevent the Restoration. After 1660 he lived in seclusion.

Fletcher, Andrew, of Saltoun 1653–1716. An East Lothian laird and opponent of LAUDERDALE in the Scottish parliament, Fletcher lived abroad 1681–8. Returning, he was a member of the CLUB, was involved in the DARIEN SCHEME, worked to promote Scotland's economic development and bitterly opposed the UNION (1707).

Flight of the Earls 1607. The flight into permanent exile of the earls of Tyrone and Tyrconnel, chiefs of the O'Neill and O'Donnell clans of Ulster. Though occasioned by summonses to attend James VI and I in London for the settlement of their rival claims, the motivation of their self-exile remains debatable.

Flint mines Dug during the neolithic period (*c.* 3500–2000 BC) to extract high-quality flint from underground seams for the production of axe-heads and other implements, which were then traded widely. They were the south-eastern counterpart of AXE FACTORIES. The best example is Grimes Graves, Norf., with its 30-foot (9·25-metre) shafts, and radiating galleries.

Flodden, battle of 9 September 1513. Victory by the English under the earl of Surrey over the invading army of JAMES IV, which was out-manoeuvred and then crushingly defeated at Flodden Edge. Among the dead were James himself, the archbishop of St Andrews, 2 abbots, 12 earls, 14 lairds and over 10,000 men.

Florin Named after a Florentine coin depicting a flower, an English gold florin worth 6 shillings was briefly current under Edward III. Reintroduced as a silver coin worth 2 shillings (or one-tenth of a pound) in 1849, florins continued to be minted until decimalization (1971), when they were replaced by 10-pence pieces.

Foederati In 4th- and 5th-century Roman Britain, foederati were barbarian tribes established under their own leaders on the coasts and frontiers of the province to defend these against other barbarians. The 1st Anglo-Saxon settlers were probably introduced in this role by Vortigern (*c.* 430). *See* MAGNUS MAXIMUS; THEODOSIUS, COUNT.

Fontenoy, battle of 11 May 1745. A battle of the war of the AUSTRIAN SUCCESSION. Despite the courage and discipline of the British infantry, allied troops under Cumberland were defeated by the French under Saxe. In consequence the Netherlands were overrun by the French.

Food-vessel culture *see* PREHISTORIC BRITAIN

Football The 'rules of the game' were drawn up in 1863 by a committee representing the 'Clarendon' PUBLIC SCHOOLS. The game was initially confined to these but grew popular in industrial districts, and the transition was symbolized by Blackburn Olympic winning the FA Cup (started 1871) in 1883. Professionals were recognized in 1885, and in 1888 the Football League was set up to organize regular inter-club matches. In 1886 a separate Scottish Football Association was formed. In 1871 a Rugby Union had been set up to codify the 'handling game' played at various public schools, which soon spread to the other countries of the British Isles and to other social classes, notably in Wales and in the north of England, although most of the clubs in the latter area, favouring professionals, broke away to form the Rugby League (1895). *See* GAELIC ATHLETIC ASSOCIATION.

Forbes, Duncan, of Culloden 1685–1747. A Scottish lawyer and statesman, as lord-advocate (1725–37), Forbes opposed government policy after the PORTEOUS RIOTS (1736) and as lord-president (1737) improved the efficiency of the court of SESSION. He helped keep the northern clans loyal (1745), but his attempts to mitigate Cumberland's savagery after CULLODEN were unsuccessful.

Forced loan Compulsory levies on wealthy subjects were occasionally resorted to by the Tudor and early Stuart monarchs in times of financial necessity. The most famous example was Charles I's forced loan (1627), occasioned by his failure to obtain parliamentary taxes, the resistance to which led to the FIVE KNIGHTS' CASE.

Foreign office Created along with the home office in 1782, it combined the 2 offices of northern and southern secretaries, becoming the chief agent of the crown in all foreign negotiations, treaties, and overseeing embassies and consulates. Until World War I it preserved an aristocratic, élitist tradition. Its influence has waned with Britain's decline as a world power, although in 1968 it took over the portfolios of the colonial and commonwealth offices.

Forests, royal Tracts of land (not necessarily wooded) where game was preserved for royal use. Instituted at the Norman conquest, and at their early 13th-century apogee covering nearly a third of England, they were subject to unpopular and rigorously applied forest laws. The 16th and 17th centuries saw much 'disafforestation' and sale, but the laws survived until the civil wars.

Forfeited estates, commissioners of Commissioners appointed to handle the listing, valuation, management or sale of estates forfeited by JACOBITES as a result of the rebellions of 1715 and 1745.

Forster, William Edward 1818–86. Bitterly attacked by Nonconformists for his EDUCATION Act (1870) which subsidized church schools from the rates, Forster as a result failed to become Liberal leader after Gladstone's resignation (1874). As chief secretary for Ireland (1880–2) he carried through a bold Land Act (*see* IRISH LAND ACTS) but resigned when Gladstone changed his policy and treated with Parnell. Shortly before his death, he became a strong opponent of home rule. *See* COERCION.

Forts, Henrician Built by Henry VIII (1539–47), these heavily fortified platforms for long-range cannon were the backbone of the 1st national system of coastal defence, stretching from Hull to Land's End. The best example is at Deal, Kent.

Forts, Roman The permanent bases of Roman auxiliary units. Normally playing-card shaped, these scaled-down LEGIONARY FORTRESSES were originally built in earth or turf and timber, but from *c.* 100 were constructed or reconstructed in stone.

Well-preserved examples are Hardknott (Cumbria) and Caernarfon (Gwynedd), while Baginton (Warwicks.) and Vindolanda (Northumberland) have been partially reconstructed. *See* ANTONINE WALL; HADRIAN'S WALL.

Forty-two Articles *see* REFORMATION

Forty-five rebellion *see* JACOBITES

'Fourth party' A group of young Tory activists (1880–5) – led by Balfour, Sir John Gorst and Randolph CHURCHILL – who applied Irish techniques of parliamentary obstruction to harass Gladstone's government and their own front bench, and demand more democratic organization in the Tory party.

Fox, Charles James 1749–1806. Fox entered parliament (1758) as a Whig and save for the years 1782–3 and 1806 spent his entire political career in opposition. Eloquent and charming, yet fundamentally irresponsible, he was eclipsed by Pitt after 1784. Though he maintained a substantial personal following, his positive political achievement was slight.

Fox, George 1624–90. The son of a Leicestershire weaver, Fox emerged after 1647 as one of the founders of the QUAKER movement. A charismatic preacher of the 'inner light', he travelled widely in Britain, the Netherlands and America and was largely responsible for the organization of the Society of Friends after 1660.

The largest of Henry VIII's coastal artillery **forts** was built at Deal, Kent, *c.* 1539–40, with 3 tiers of platforms for long-range cannon and handgun embrasures low down on each level.

A portrait of Charles James **Fox**, by K. A. Hickel, showing him as the lovable orator whom success eluded.

Foxe, John ?1516–87. A Protestant scholar and opponent of persecution. An exile in Switzerland during MARY I's reign (1553–8), Foxe composed his *Acts and Monuments* or 'Book or Martyres', a history of the English church. Published in English in 1563, the book was enormously influential and was ordered to be placed in every parish church.

Franciscans The original order of FRIARS, formally established by St Francis in 1209. Also called Greyfriars or Friars Minor, they reached England in 1224 and Scotland c. 1231. The strict 'Observants', a reaction to the order's decline from corporate poverty, reached Scotland c. 1462 and England in 1482. These strenuously opposed Henry VIII's divorce and were brutally suppressed (1534).

Frankalmoign (Norman-French 'free alms'). In the feudal period, a tenure whereby ecclesiastical institutions held land in return for perpetual prayers for the donor's soul. *See* FEUDALISM.

Franklin Originally a minor landowner of free but not gentle birth, by the 14th century the term was used of members of the county gentry who had not been knighted, but who were often wealthy and influential, frequently serving as KNIGHTS OF THE SHIRE and SHERIFFS.

Frankpledge A 12th-century development of the TITHING system, current in southern and midland England. The system was extended to include all persons free or unfree, excepting gentry, clergy and women, and was enforced by twice-yearly inspections, held either by the sheriff at the HUNDRED court or by the feudal lord at a court-leet (*see* MANOR COURT). Such 'views of frankpledge' also dealt with trivial offences against public order, and made preliminary investigations into more serious crimes.

Free Church *see* CHURCH OF SCOTLAND; DISRUPTION

Free Trade Those who followed the 'classical economics' of Adam SMITH in insisting that governments should not regulate foreign trade by bounties or tariffs were known as Free Traders. Their period of maximum influence began with the abolition of the CORN LAWS (1846) and culminated in the Cobden-Chevalier treaty (1860), although the defence of Free Trade against TARIFF REFORM helped the 1906 Liberal triumph. Only in 1932 did the British government desert the principle. *See* COBDEN, RICHARD.

Above The benefits of **Free Trade**: A *Punch* cartoon of 1846 predicts cheap food, drink and tobacco by 1850.

Right Brother William of St Albans, one of a family of artists and a **Franciscan**. Drawing by Matthew Paris in his *Chronica Majora*, mid-13th century.

French revolutionary war *see* NAPOLEONIC WARS

Friars (French *frères*, brothers). Members of the new religious orders which developed in the early 13th century from the inspiration of St Francis and the need for ministry to the poor and unlearned. They were uncloistered, mendicant and vowed to absolute personal and (initially) corporate poverty. Principal orders were the AUGUSTINIANS, CARMELITES, DOMINICANS and FRANCISCANS. Others known in Britain were the 'Crutched Friars' (Friars of the Holy Cross) and the short-lived Pied Friars and Friars of the Sack (both dissolved 1274).

Friendly Societies In practical terms, these were a form of mutual insurance by working people, with origins in the 17th century. But their rituals and class-basis meant that their boundaries from TRADE UNIONISM on one side and freemasonry on the other were difficult to define. In the 19th century government defined their insurance role more strictly by Acts of 1829, 1850 and 1875. By 1905 they had more than 13·9 million members, and in 1911 were associated with the Liberals' NATIONAL INSURANCE scheme.

Friends of the People, Society of A Scottish reform society, akin to the LONDON CORRESPONDING SOCIETY, founded in Edinburgh (1792) and supported by tradesmen and artisans throughout Scotland. There were 3 general conventions held (1792–3) before the society was broken by the trials and transportation of its leaders Thomas Muir and T. F. Palmer.

Frisians A Germanic race inhabiting the coasts and islands of northern Holland, whose language was closely related to early English and who apparently constituted an element in the Anglo-Saxon settlement of Britain, where they are recorded as AUXILIARIES and FOEDERATI from Roman times.

Frobisher, Sir Martin ?1535–94. An Elizabethan seaman, Frobisher led 3 expeditions in 1576–8 in search of the north-west passage and discovered the Frobisher strait, Hudson's strait and Hudson bay. He subsequently distinguished himself in the naval war with Spain and was killed in a combined operation in Brittany.

Fulford, battle of 20 September 1066. The forces of Mercia and Northumbria, under earls Edwin and Morcar, were heavily defeated outside York by HARALD HARDRADA's invaders. The losses suffered here by the northern English prevented them from participating at HASTINGS or effectively counter-attacking William the Conqueror.

Fyrd The peasant militia of Anglo-Saxon and early medieval England, in which all free men were bound to serve. It apparently did not usually serve beyond its shire of origin, but from the 9th century selective summons was employed to improve its quality, mobility and length of service. *See* ALFRED; ARRAY, COMMISSIONS OF.

Gaelic Athletic Association Created by Irish nationalists (1884), the GAA promoted the 'Irish' games of hurling and Gaelic FOOTBALL, and vetoed its members' participation in 'English' games such as association football. Many of its members subsequently played leading roles in militant republican politics.

Gaelic League Founded in Ireland (1893) to recover the country's Gaelic cultural heritage, it was less militant than the GAELIC ATHLETIC ASSOCIATION. However, PEARSE was for several years editor of its journal and its leader, the Protestant scholar Dr Douglas Hyde, became president of Ireland (1937–9).

Gaitskell, Hugh 1906–63. Oxford-educated economist and wartime civil servant, Gaitskell became a Labour MP (1945), a junior minister (1946) and then chancellor of the exchequer (1950–1). Succeeding Attlee as Labour leader (1955), he successfully fought off a challenge from the left and the CAMPAIGN FOR NUCLEAR DISARMAMENT (1960–1), although he failed to revise the socialist commitment of the Labour constitution.

Gallipoli A campaign (1915–16) in WORLD WAR I to land a force on the straits to the Black Sea, thereby cutting the Turks off from their German allies. Winston Churchill strongly supported this but was let down by timid commanders and incompetent logistics. Moreover, the force was confronted by the Turks under their most able general, Mustapha Kemal, later Ataturk. After being besieged for 6 months, the British withdrew, thus confirming the view of those who regarded the western front as all-important.

Game laws Laws intended to restrict the hunting of game to landowners by the placing of property qualifications on the right to hunt. The period between the substantial raising of the qualification (1671) and the overhaul of the laws (1831) was the classic age of conflict between country squires and poachers.

Gandhi, Mohandas 1869–1948. An Indian lawyer, trained in London and much influenced by Tolstoy and RUSKIN, who applied techniques of passive resistance to gain just treatment for Indians in South Africa (1907–14). After World War I he used the same tactics to frustrate British rule in India. He attended the 1931 conference but disapproved of the federal system it proposed. After 1942 he collaborated with Wavell and Mountbatten in securing independence, but his acceptance of partition led to his assassination by a Hindu fanatic. *See* AMRITSAR MASSACRE; BRITISH EMPIRE.

Gaol delivery In medieval times prisons were more often used to hold suspects awaiting trial than to punish convicted offenders. From the 13th century itinerant judges were periodically appointed to clear or 'deliver' them of prisoners by conducting trials, a function subsequently taken over by ASSIZES.

Garden cities In reaction to the unsanitary and congested state of the new industrial towns, Ebenezer Howard proposed (1898) the building of 'model' low density communities in which industry and dwellings would be segregated and ample open space planned. He was associated with pioneer ventures at Letchworth and Welwyn, and his ideas led directly to the succession of NEW TOWNS built after World War II, and to the town and country planning movement.

'Garden Suburb' The name given to Lloyd George's personal staff, when he was premier (1916–18), who were accommodated in temporary buildings in the garden of no. 10 DOWNING STREET.

Gardiner, Steven ?1483–1555. Bishop of Winchester (1531). Though supporting HENRY VIII's ecclesiastical supremacy, Gardiner detested Protestant doctrine. A clever and vindictive politician and enemy of Thomas Cromwell and Cranmer, he exercised much influence in Henry's last years. Deprived and imprisoned under Edward VI, he was restored by MARY I and helped initiate her religious persecutions.

Garter, order of the An order of chivalry, imitating Arthur's legendary Round Table, founded by Edward III (1348) for himself, the Black Prince and 24 other knights, mostly notables of the hundred years' war. It remains restricted to 26

Hugh **Gaitskell** (2nd left), at the 60th annual conference of the Labour party at Blackpool, October 1961, is somewhat grudgingly applauded by former opponents Harold Wilson and Richard Crossman.

The first **Garter** King-at-Arms, William Bruges, appointed by Henry V in 1415. His tabard is decorated with the fleurs-de-lis of France and the 3 lions of England. From Bruges's Garter Book, 15th century.

members, though distinguished foreign knights or monarchs are admitted in addition. *See* TITLES.

Gas and Water Socialism Utilities such as gas and water supplies were steadily taken over by municipalities from the 1860s on, followed by electricity and tramway undertakings. Some FABIANS (and their opponents) saw this as meaning the gradual achievement of a socialist society. *See* CHAMBERLAIN, JOSEPH; WELFARE STATE.

Gavelkind A system of inheritance, current in Kent from Anglo-Saxon times until the 18th century, whereby a person's estates were equally divided at his death between all his sons. By extension it was applied to similar systems of 'partible inheritance' customary in Ireland and (until the Acts of Union 1536/42) in Wales.

Gaveston, Piers A Gascon knight, Gaveston was the (probably homosexual) favourite of Edward II. Hated by the magnates for his influence over and lavish grants from Edward, he was banished in 1306–7, 1308–9 and (unsuccessfully) by the ORDINANCES. AYMER DE VALENCE captured him (May 1312) and promised to spare him, but he was seized and lynched (19 June) at the orders of Thomas of LANCASTER.

Geddes Axe The name for the economy cuts (1921–2) made by Sir Eric Geddes, Lloyd George's chancellor of the exchequer, which brought an end to hopes of post-war social reform.

General assembly of the church of Scotland The supreme body of the CHURCH OF SCOTLAND. The general assembly emerged as a gathering of lords, burgesses and clergy (1560), becoming a council of ministers and elders only after 1578. A century of struggle between Episcopalians and Presbyterians in the kirk followed until the general assembly achieved full authority in 1690.

General staff Such planning groups were standard in continental armies by the Franco-Prussian war (1870), but Britain's imperial general staff was not set up until 1904. *See* ARMY.

General Strike 1926. The strike was called by the trades union congress (4 May) in support of the miners, after the breakdown of wage negotiations. The Baldwin government was well-prepared: when the 'first line' industries – transport, building, mining and printing – struck it made effective use of road transport, the press (when it appeared) and

The **General Strike**, 1926: pickets prevent the entry of a van carrying fuel in East India Dock Road, London.

broadcasting, and the moderates on the TUC general council capitulated after 9 days. The miners stayed out on strike for the rest of the year. The government took its revenge by passing the Trades Disputes Act (1927), outlawing general strikes and making the political levy that trade unionists paid to the Labour party a case of 'contracting in' rather than 'contracting out'.

General warrants Warrants not directed to named persons, but ordering the arrest of all persons concerned in an offence. Their legality was challenged by WILKES in the case of the *North Briton* no. 45 (1763), and in 1765 parliament declared their illegality save in circumstances expressly permitted by statute.

Gentry A status term describing those English landowners placed between YEOMAN freeholders and the parliamentary peerage, and encompassing gentlemen, ESQUIRES, KNIGHTS and baronets. Varying in wealth, though increasingly homogeneous in culture, the gentry exercised great political and administrative power from the 16th to the 19th centuries. *See* TITLES.

George I king of Great Britain (1714–27; b. 1660). George succeeded to the British throne under the terms of the Act of SETTLEMENT (1701), the 1st monarch to be so bound. Unattractive but not unintelligent, he remained true to the Whigs in politics and to his electorate of Hanover in his affections (although his knowledge of English may not have been as limited as once thought).

George II king of Great Britain (1727–60; b. 1683). Unlike his father George I, whom he detested, George spoke English well and was prepared to exercise his will in ministerial appointments. Like his father he felt happier in Hanover than in Britain, was preoccupied with Hanoverian interests and had chronically bad relationships with his eldest son (Frederick, prince of Wales, d. 1751).

George III king of Great Britain (1760–1820; b. 1738). He inherited his grandfather George II's throne at 22 and was to occupy it for 60 years, longer than any British monarch save Victoria. By the time of his death, isolated, insane and long removed from power, he enjoyed a measure of affection among his people. In his youth, however, he had been regarded as a potential threat to the constitution.

The myth of the young George as a disciple of BOLINGBROKE, a 'patriot king' determined to reverse the erosion of royal power and guided in this by the sinister BUTE, was a creation of Whig propaganda. George sought no augmentation of royal authority. He simply wished to exercise the power which the monarchy undoubtedly still retained. Naïve, emotionally insecure, narrow-minded and obstinate, he had been brought up to believe that the political system of his grandfather's time was incorrigibly corrupt. George, who largely failed to understand the realities of political power, wished to cleanse politics, eliminating jobbery and faction. The result was a withdrawal of support from the Whig oligarchs, which produced a decade of political instability as the ministries of Bute, GRENVILLE, ROCKINGHAM, CHATHAM and Grafton sought in vain for stable parliamentary authority. After 1770, NORTH seemed to have restored stability, but his mishandling of the American situation, aggravated by the king's refusal to dispense with his services, introduced a new period of turmoil from which the country emerged only with the ministry of the younger PITT after 1784.

In Pitt, George at last had a minister in whom he could place his trust wholeheartedly, though he was to bring down Pitt in 1801 by his intransigence over Catholic emancipation. By then George was increasingly on the periphery of affairs, though never irrelevant. In his later years he was a pathetic figure, remote and withdrawn; the more so when, after 1811, his earlier mental instability became permanent derangement, and regency powers were given to his reprobate son. A reign which had seen American independence, the Industrial Revolution, the Napoleonic wars and the foundation of a 2nd empire, was for him a tragedy of disappointed hopes and perplexed ideals from which he took refuge in his farm in Windsor park and the delusions of his broken mind.

George II at the battle of DETTINGEN, the last occasion on which a reigning British monarch commanded troops in battle. Oil painting by David Morier.

George III reviewing volunteers for the French wars, 4 June 1799. Engraving by S. W. Reynolds after R. K. Porter, 1800.

Gent.   no Gent   & Re-gent !!

The degeneration of the future **George IV** from handsome 'Gent' to gouty 'Re-gent'. Cartoon by George Cruikshank, 1816.

George IV king of Great Britain (1820–30; b. 1762). Intelligent and cultured, but self-indulgent and extravagant, George led the fashionable world after 1783 and as prince regent (1812–20). Politically ineffective, he ultimately brought the monarchy into contempt, especially when the divorce Bill against Queen Caroline (1820) revealed the impropriety of his domestic life.

George V king of Great Britain (1910–36; b. 1865). 2nd son of Edward VII. George's reign was marked by a growing popular regard for the monarchy, culminating in his silver jubilee celebrations (1935).

George VI king of Great Britain (1936–52; b. 1895). Unexpectedly thrust into kingship by the ABDICATION of his brother Edward VIII, George impressed by the seriousness with which he approached his duties, and the courage with which he overcame a speech defect. Reactions to his decease indicated the continuing hold of monarchy in popular sentiment.

Germanus, St Bishop of Auxerre and a former general, Germanus was sent to Britain by the Gaullish church in 429 (when he won the spectacular 'Alleluia victory' against a force of Picts and Anglo-Saxons in Powys) and c. 447, but achieved only temporary success in countering the heresies of PELAGIUS.

Gibbeting The practice (abolished 1834) of hanging the corpses of certain executed felons in chains on gibbets, generally beside busy roads, as a public example. Gibbeting was most commonly

ordered in the cases of notorious highwaymen, smugglers, pirates and rioters.

Gibraltar Captured in 1704 by Sir George Rooke and ceded by Spain in the treaty of UTRECHT (1713), Gibraltar became a principal British naval base, withstanding Spanish sieges in 1727 and during the American independence war. It remains a crown colony with extensive self-government.

Gilbertines The only purely English religious order, founded by St Gilbert at Sempringham, Lincs., during the 1130s, initially for nuns with a CISTERCIAN-style rule. From 1148 canons regular were added to minister to them, and 11 of the 28 Gilbertine houses were double monasteries for separated men and women, the remainder being for canons only.

Gildas c. 495–c. 570. A British MONK, famous in his own time as a saint and monastic reformer, whose *De Excidio Britanniae*, a 'complaining book', against the monarchs and clergy of c. 540 is, though obscure, virtually the only contemporary source for the early HEROIC AGE. (*The Ruin of Britain*, ed. M. Winterbottom, 1978.)

Gillespie, Patrick 1617–75. Minister of Kirkcaldy (1642) and of the High Church, Glasgow (1648), Gillespie was an extreme COVENANTER. He opposed the Scottish ENGAGEMENT and sided with the REMONSTRANTS in 1650. Subsequently appointed principal of Glasgow university during the protectorate, he was deprived and imprisoned in 1660.

Gin age A name given to the orgy of gin-consumption among the poor of early 18th-century London, occasioned by the cheapness of London-distilled gin. Public outcry eventually produced effective legislation (1751 and 1753), which reduced sales from over 7 to under 2 million gallons a year.

Gladstone, William Ewart 1809–98. Gladstone's parents were both Scots. His father made a considerable fortune as a Liverpool merchant, and Gladstone was educated at Eton and Oxford, which university gained his most lasting loyalty. He entered parliament as MP for Grantham (1832) – 'the rising hope of the stern, unbending Tories' (as MACAULAY put it). But when Peel split the Tories over the repeal of the CORN LAWS (1846) Gladstone, who had been his president of the board of trade, followed him. He never rejoined the Conservatives and, from a 'Peelite' position, felled the Derby-Disraeli government (1852). He was chancellor in Aberdeen's government (1852–5) but his real

William Hogarth's *Gin Lane*, 1750/1, rendered with some satirical licence and perhaps a touch of sanctimony, made effective propaganda against the excesses of the **gin age**.

William Ewart **Gladstone** at Hawarden, Clywd, *c.* 1880. One of his favourite forms of exercise was chopping down trees – special trains were run to see him do it.

mastery as a government financier was not disclosed until 1859–66 when, as Palmerston's chancellor, he reduced government expenditure and extended FREE TRADE.

Although radicals still regarded him as suspect because of his High Church views and his ambivalence about democracy (he was a prominent supporter of the South in the American civil war), he became leader of the house of commons and deputy to John Russell on Palmerston's death, although he was badly outmanoeuvred by Disraeli over the 2nd REFORM BILL. He got his revenge in the 1868 general election, and his 1st ministry (1868–74) carried Irish disestablishment, the 1st IRISH LAND ACT, the abolition of UNIVERSITY tests and the EDUCATION Act (1870). However, the ministry was defeated over an attempt to reform the Irish university system and ran out of steam. After defeat by Disraeli's Conservatives, Gladstone retired from politics, but re-emerged (1876) at the head of the BULGARIAN ATROCITIES agitation, which he elaborated in his MIDLOTHIAN CAMPAIGN into an all-out assault on Disraeli's foreign policy.

This secured his return as Liberal prime minister (1880) – much to Queen Victoria's alarm. The next 5 years were marked by disorder in and out of the commons, chiefly on account of the IRISH CONSTITUTIONAL CRISIS. Nevertheless, the 2nd Irish Land Act and the 3rd Reform Bill were passed before mounting unpopularity, largely occasioned by the fall of Khartoum, brought the ministry down (June 1885).

Between then and the end of the year Gladstone moved towards HOME RULE as a definitive solution for Irish discontents – and as a means of securing Liberal party unity. He took office in February 1886 intent on carrying such a measure but although he secured widespread backing within the Liberal party he lost the support of Hartington's Whigs and Chamberlain's radical unionists. Possibly he intended this; certainly his greatest rivals were thus removed, and the centralized structure of the Liberal party confirmed. He won the 1892 election, but his leadership was now firmly tied to the Irish issue, and when the house of lords rejected his 2nd Home Rule Bill he resigned for the last time (May 1894). He lived to lead one more campaign (1896), against atrocities perpetrated by the Turks in Armenia, before he died at Hawarden (19 May 1898).

Glastonbury Somerset. Originally perhaps a prehistoric shrine and, according to legend, the site of Joseph of Arimathea's 1st-century church, the resting place of ARTHUR and the Holy Grail. Glastonbury's monastery seems in fact very early,

---

Glastonbury, Somerset: the abbots' kitchen seen from the ruined south transept of the abbey church.

The pass of **Glencoe**, Argyllshire: nature itself seems to echo Captain Campbell's orders, which were 'to fall upon the . . . MacDonalds of Glencoe and put all to the sword under seventy'.

being associated with St David and Gildas. Revived by DUNSTAN, it became one of the richest BENEDICTINE houses in England.

Glebe The portion of land held by a parish priest and in many areas personally farmed by him.

Glencoe, massacre of 13 February 1692. The slaughter of the chief and 37 of the Macdonalds of Glencoe, planned by the master of STAIR as an example and carried out by men of the Argyll regiment billeted in Glencoe. It did much to discredit William III's government and to confirm JACOBITE sympathies in the highlands.

Glendower, Owen c. 1354–1416. Lord of Glyndyfrdwy, Clwyd and heir of the princes of Powys and Deheubarth, Glendower turned a private feud with an English neighbour (1400) into a nationalist rising. He controlled most of Wales by 1404, when (as sovereign prince) he held a national parliament and concluded an alliance with France. But by 1406 he was losing ground to the English forces under the future Henry V. In 1415 he disappeared into hiding.

Glorious 1st of June, battle of the see NAPOLEONIC WARS

Glorious Revolution 1688. Responsibility for the 'Glorious Revolution' can be laid largely at the door of the deposed monarch JAMES VII AND II. Having inherited a very strong position from his brother Charles II (1685), James proceeded by his policy of Catholicization in the army and administration, his abuse of the DISPENSING POWER, his attempts to pack parliament and his DECLARATIONS OF INDULGENCE to alienate every important section of opinion in England. The birth of his son (June 1688) and the possibility of a Catholic succession finally provoked 7 leading statesmen to invite the intervention of James's son-in-law WILLIAM OF ORANGE. William landed at Torbay in November, issued a declaration promising to defend the liberties of England and the Protestant religion and to call a free parliament and marched unopposed on London. James's escape to France was then connived at, the king later being deemed to have abdicated by his flight abroad.

In February 1688 the English convention parliament met, denounced James in the DECLARATION OF RIGHTS and offered the throne to

William and Mary as joint sovereigns. Though presented as a conservative revolution, the subsequent passage of the BILL OF RIGHTS, the TRIENNIAL ACT and the Act of SETTLEMENT placed important legal limitations on the post-revolutionary MONARCHY, while the practical necessity of annual sessions of parliament after 1688 and the developing party system effectively restrained the exercise of the royal prerogative of appointing ministers and conducting foreign policy. The TOLERATION ACT made a measure of religious liberty a further plank of the revolutionary settlement in England. In Scotland the revolution was imported when the convention of estates recognized William and Mary (1689) and put forward the CLAIM OF RIGHT. Thereafter the abolition of episcopacy led to the victory of Presbyterianism in the kirk, while the abolition of the lords of the ARTICLES gave a novel freedom to the Scottish parliament.

The constitutional settlements took several years to work out. A more immediate consequence of the revolution, and that closest to William's heart, was England's involvement in the war of the LEAGUE OF AUGSBURG (1688–97). Resistance by Scottish JACOBITES was put down after DUNDEE's death at KILLIECRANKIE (1689), while Ireland was subdued after the BOYNE (1690). In 1690 the naval victory of La Hogue dispelled a French invasion threat and the war became centred in Flanders where British troops fought at STEINKIRK and Neerwinden. 'King William's war' introduced the policy of alliance with the Dutch and the empire against France which persisted until 1756, while the needs of war finance brought about the 'financial revolution' of the 1690s – the establishment of the land tax, the bank of England and the National Debt. Despite its limited aims, the *coup* of 1688 thus precipitated changes of momentous significance for the constitutional, political, diplomatic and economic development of Britain.

Godolphin, Sidney, baron 1645–1712. A Cornish gentleman, Godolphin served as a treasury commissioner under Charles II, James VII and II, and William III, and as lord treasurer under Anne before his dismissal in 1710. An able financier, he endeavoured unsuccessfully to dampen the influence of party allegiances in English politics.

Godwin, earl d. 1053. An Englishman of uncertain origin, Godwin became Cnut's earl of Wessex and chief adviser. His family's power increased under Edward the Confessor (who married his daughter) but his implication in the murder of Edward's brother (1036) and his opposition to Edward's

Normanizing made relations uneasy. Driven into exile in 1051, he returned in 1052 stronger than ever.

Gold standard A currency system under which, in Britain, sterling was fully convertible into gold from 1816 to 1914. Suspended during World War I, it was resumed in modified form by Churchill, as Baldwin's chancellor, in 1925. Keynes, and many others, argued that the return to gold made British goods overpriced and aggravated the depression. One of the 1st acts of the National government was to come off the gold standard (September 1931).

Good parliament April–July 1376. Led by Sir Peter de la Mare, the earliest identifiable SPEAKER, the commons refused to vote taxation until Edward III's corrupt favourites (including his mistress Alice Perrers, Lord Latimer and a group of financiers headed by Richard Lyons) were punished and replaced by counsellors selected by parliament.

Gordon, Charles George 1833–85. An engineer officer and CRIMEAN WAR hero, Gordon played an important part in suppressing the TAIPING REBELLION (1850–64) and subsequently explored central Africa. In 1884 he was sent to evacuate the Sudan, but was besieged at Khartoum by the forces of the Mahdi for 317 days and killed by them when it fell (26 January 1885). He became one of the great martyrs of the imperial age, and the Khartoum tragedy helped bring down Gladstone's 2nd government.

General **Gordon**, photographed as governor-general of the Sudan in 1880.

The Law Courts, London, by G. E. Street, 1874–82, built in the 19th-century **Gothic revival** style.

Gordon riots 2–9 June 1780. Sparked off by a procession organized by Lord George Gordon to petition parliament against the Catholic Relief Act (1778), the riots escalated from attacks on foreign chapels to the sacking of private houses and distilleries and the opening of London's prisons. Order was eventually restored by regular troops.

Gore, bishop *see* HIGH CHURCHMEN

Gorham judgment 1850. A privy council ruling which appeared to sanction unorthodox views on baptism in the church of England. It contributed to the revival of the convocation of Canterbury (1852) as an ecclesiastical court.

Goring, Lord George 1608–57. Courageous but unscrupulous and irresponsible, Goring had a history of double-dealing before declaring for the king in the CIVIL WARS (1642). As commander of royalist troops in the west (1645), he failed to join the king before NASEBY and was subsequently defeated at Langport. From 1650 he served in the Spanish army.

Goschen, George Joachim, viscount 1831–1907. In Gladstone's 1st government (1868–74), Goschen was in charge of the Poor Law (where he was a rigorous economist) and the

admiralty (where he spent heavily). He personified the right-wing 'financier' of the Liberal party, opposing home rule and and becoming Liberal-Unionist chancellor of the exchequer (1886–92) before returning to the admiralty (1895–1900), where he supported 'big fleet' policies.

Gothic architecture *see* DECORATED ARCHITECTURE; EARLY ENGLISH ARCHITECTURE; YORK MINSTER

Gothic revival The name associated with a revolution in architectural taste, away from the principles of classicism towards the style, and more important, the spirit, of the middle ages. Starting as a 'conceit' in the mid-18th century, with buildings such as Horace Walpole's 'Strawberry Hill', it attained its fullest development from the 1840s to 1880s with the Catholic revivalism of A.W.N. Pugin, the writings of RUSKIN, and the enormous output of commercial architects such as Sir George Gilbert Scott.

Grammar schools Endowed schools, sometimes of medieval origin, though commonly founded in the 16th and 17th centuries. Traditionally concerned with teaching classical languages, they fell behind the DISSENTING ACADEMIES in the 18th century. Revitalized thereafter, they were brought within the state system and have been gradually superseded by comprehensive schools since 1944 (*see* EDUCATION).

Grand National Consolidated Trade Union Although founded (early 1834) by OWEN, the union derived much of its strength from the organization of Lancashire cotton-spinners under John Doherty (1798–1854). It rapidly gained members, with its programme of a general strike, after which a co-operative commonwealth would be inaugurated. Following the government's prosecution of the TOLPUDDLE MARTYRS, it collapsed (October).

Grand Remonstrance 1641. A comprehensive indictment of Charles I's councillors, accusing them of having fostered a 'popish and malignant party' and of attempting to establish arbitrary government. After violent debates it passed the commons by only 11 votes and was ordered to be printed.

Great Contract, the 1610. A scheme of Robert Cecil whereby the crown would abandon certain ancient revenues (including WARDSHIPS and PURVEYANCE), in return for the granting by parliament of £600,000 for the payment of James VI and I's debts and an annual income of £200,000. Parliamentary suspicion of James's intentions ultimately undermined the negotiations.

Great council *see* COUNCIL, THE; PARLIAMENT

Great debasement A name given to debasements of the English coinage (1544–51). Undertaken to meet government war expenditure, they made profits of £1,300,000 for the state, but halved the value of sterling on the Antwerp exchanges and caused severe domestic inflation. The coinage was quickly restored after 1552.

Great Exhibition *see* CRYSTAL PALACE

Great rebuilding A term coined by W.G. Hoskins (in *Provincial England*, 1963) for the widespread remodelling of medieval open-hall houses and the spate of new house-building *c.* 1570–1640. Recent research has stressed the continuation of this process up to the early 18th century in some areas.

Great seal From late Anglo-Saxon times the indispensable authentication of all important government documents. Kept by the chancellor, it travelled with the monarch until the 13th century, whereafter it remained in CHANCERY at Westmister, its use authorized by PRIVY SEAL warrants. It depicts the reigning monarch, enthroned on one side and mounted on the other.

Greenwich, treaties of 1543. Treaties between England and Scotland, the first establishing peace, the second for a marriage between the future EDWARD VI and the infant MARY QUEEN OF SCOTS. Scottish revocation of the treaties (December 1543) provoked the ROUGH WOOING.

Grenville, George 1712–70. A competent administrator, though lacking in vision, Grenville succeeded Bute as 1st lord of the treasury. His ministry of 1763–5 was notable for the Wilkes affair (*see* GENERAL WARRANTS), and for the STAMP ACT, reduction of the forces and drift into diplomatic isolation which were to cost Britain dear in the American independence struggle.

Grenville, Sir Richard 1542–91. A Cornish gentleman, soldier and seaman, Grenville was active in colonizing ventures in Virginia (1585) and Ireland (1588–90). Tough, wild and somewhat unscrupulous, he is chiefly remembered for his heroic, but arguably unnecessary, death commanding the *Revenge* against overwhelming Spanish forces.

The **great seal** of King John, here attached to his charter providing for the annual election of a mayor of London, dated 9 May 1215.

Gresham's law The adage that 'bad money drives out good' is attributed to Sir Thomas Gresham (?1518–79), founder of the Royal Exchange (1564) and agent of the English crown at Antwerp (1551–74), whose shrewd handling of foreign loans did much to assist Elizabeth I early in her reign.

Grey, Charles, earl 1764–1845. Whig reformer who believed that the aristocracy should demonstrate its fitness to govern. Foreign secretary (1806–7), Grey was thereafter out of office because of his liberal views, until 1830, when William IV asked him to form the government which was to carry the 1st REFORM BILL. He retired in 1834.

Grey, Sir Edward, viscount 1862–1933. The foreign secretary who took Britain into World War I (shrewdly observing that 'the lamps are going out all over Europe'). A Liberal squire who before 1906 had never travelled outside Britain, Grey had reacted to German provocations in north Africa by strengthening the ENTENTE CORDIALE with France and extending it to Russia. His preparations for European conflict were realistic and his attempts at conciliation sincere.

Grey, Lady Jane 1537–54. The daughter of the marquess of Dorset, descendant of Henry VII and residual heir to the crown under Henry VIII's will,

Jane was designated successor in EDWARD VI's will in order to prevent the accession of the Catholic Mary I. Queen 10–19 July 1553, she was imprisoned on Mary's triumph and executed following WYATT'S REBELLION.

Griffith, Arthur 1872–1922. An Irish journalist, Griffith founded SINN FEIN (1905) on a programme (said to have Hungarian precedents) of establishing a parallel 'Dail' or parliament in Dublin, whether HOME RULE were conceded or not. When this happened in 1918 (*see* IRISH CONSTITUTIONAL CRISIS) he became Ireland's 1st prime minister.

Grindal, Edmund 1519–83. An exile under MARY I, Grindal returned on Elizabeth I's accession, becoming bishop of London and then archbishop of York. Appointed archbishop of Canterbury in 1576, he was suspended a year later for refusing to forbid PROPHESYINGS and remained so until he died.

'Groans of the Britons' *c*. 446. An unsuccessful appeal for aid against the Anglo-Saxons, addressed to Aetius, Roman commander in Gaul, apparently by Romano-British opponents of VORTIGERN: 'The barbarians push us to the sea, the sea pushes us back to the barbarians; between the two kinds of death we are either slain or drowned.' *See* HEROIC AGE.

Ground Nuts scheme A project by the government-aided Overseas Food Corporation to raise ground nuts in east Africa, which failed disastrously (1948), ruining much valuable equipment: hence the joke, 'give us the job and we'll finish the tools'. This was one of the Attlee government's most publicized setbacks.

Gruffydd ap Cynan 1054–1137. Of mixed Welsh and Norse-Irish blood, after a chequered career Gruffydd became king of GWYNEDD, successfully resisting MARCHER penetration. He is the subject of a notable medieval biography.

Gruffydd ap Llywelyn d. 1063. King of GWYNEDD and POWYS from 1039, by 1055 he ruled virtually all Wales. An inveterate and successful border raider, he burnt Hereford (1055), but after the death of his ally, the dissident Earl Aelfgar of Mercia, was defeated by Harold Godwinson and slain by his own men.

Guardians Persons appointed by the Scots parliament, either singly or in groups of up to six, as regents during the minority or incapacity of the monarch or (during the Scottish wars of independence) during an effective interregnum.

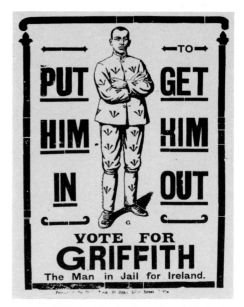

Arthur **Griffith**'s poster for the December 1918 elections: 36 elected Sinn Fein members of the first Dail Eireann were in jail.

Gruffydd ap Cynan escaping from the Tower of London. From a 13th-century illuminated manuscript of his biography.

Guild Socialism Much talked of before and during World War I by COLE among others, it drew upon the CO-OPERATIVE traditions of the British Labour movement and political theories of pluralism, to advocate a form of syndicalist organization of industry (*see* SYNDICALISM), but was effectively pre-empted by the COLLECTIVISM of the war years.

Guilds Fraternities with religious, social and (generally) commercial functions, which developed in the early middle ages. 'Guilds merchant' protected and monopolized trade within a town or in a commodity (*see* MERCHANT ADVENTURERS; STAPLE) while local craft guilds regulated manufacturing industries. They effectively lost their religious function at the Reformation, their regulating powers with the 19th-century decline of APPRENTICESHIP, and their monopolies with the development of capitalism.

Gunpowder plot 1605. A plot by the Catholics Robert Catesby, Thomas Tresham, Thomas Percy, Guy FAWKES and others to blow up JAMES VI AND I and parliament during the state opening on 5 November. A warning given to the Catholic Lord Mounteagle led to their discovery. Some conspirators were killed resisting arrest, others executed.

Gwynedd A principality comprising north-west Wales and Anglesey, essentially coextensive with the eponymous modern county but also claiming the Perfeddwlad or 'middle lands' between the Conwy and the Dee, now in Clwyd. Founded by CUNEDDA (5th century), it frequently dominated all Wales, reaching the height of its power under LLYWELYN THE GREAT (1173–1240) and LLYWELYN AP GRUFFYDD (d. 1282). It was finally conquered by Edward I (1282–4).

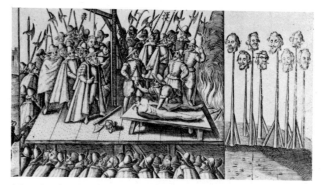

After the discovery of the **Gunpowder plot**, the surviving conspirators were 'hung, drawn and quartered', the ghastly punishment for traitors illustrated in this contemporary French engraving.

H

Habeas Corpus, writ of The medieval writ ordering the bringing of a prisoner before the courts, employed in the FIVE KNIGHTS' CASE (1627–8) to resist imprisonment without trial. The grant of the writ was made a right by the Habeas Corpus Amendment Act (1679) and remains a fundamental safeguard of personal liberty and the rule of law.

Hadrian's wall Certainly the most impressive monument of ROMAN BRITAIN, a frontier system running 80 miles (128 kilometres) across the Tyne-Solway isthmus from Wallsend, Northumberland, to Bowness, Cumbria. In its prime it comprised the wall itself, fortlets or 'milecastles', signal turrets, 16 FORTS, the vallum or ditch behind the wall, and a military road. Built by legionaries, it was gar-

The central section of **Hadrian's wall**, looking eastwards towards the fort at Housesteads, Northumberland.

risoned, at full strength, by *c.* 12,000 AUXILIARIES. *See* THEODOSIUS, COUNT.

Hague conferences 1899 and 1907. They were called to limit armaments. Although a permanent court of arbitration was set up at the Hague, this simply exposed the gulf between civilians and military men, and failed completely to stop the arms race.

Sir Douglas **Haig**, photographed in his headquarters train.

Haig, Sir Douglas, earl 1861–1928. A Scots-born cavalryman, Haig helped HALDANE implement his army reforms (1906–9), and in World War I became commander-in-chief on the western front (1915). He fought the war on strategies of attrition which led to enormous casualties. His counter-attack at AMIENS (August 1918) effectively broke the final German effort.

Hakluyt, Richard ?1552–1616. A leading Elizabethan geographer and propagandist of English maritime expansion. Hakluyt collected accounts of early voyages of exploration (often at first hand) and published them in his influential *Principal Navigations, Voyages and Discoveries of the English Nation* (1589 and 1598–1600).

Haldane, Richard Burdon, viscount 1856–1928. A leading Liberal advocate of imperialism and social reform, as war minister (1905–12) Haldane modernized the ARMY. He became lord chancellor (1912–15) but was forced out of office by anti-German hysteria. Subsequently he identified with the Labour party and was lord chancellor in MacDonald's 1st government (1924).

Halidon Hill, battle of 19 July 1333. EDWARD III and Edward BALLIOL, besieging Berwick, used archers to heavily defeat a Scots relieving force under Sir Archibald Douglas, guardian for David II. Berwick thereafter fell, David went into exile, and

the way apparently lay open for English reconquest of Scotland. *See* SCOTTISH WARS OF INDEPENDENCE.

Halifax, Charles Montagu, 1st earl of 1661–1715. A Whig statesman. As a treasury commissioner (1691–9) and chancellor of the exchequer (1694–9) Halifax was largely responsible for such far-reaching reforms as the establishment of the NATIONAL DEBT, the founding of the BANK OF ENGLAND (1694) and the 1696 recoinage. He was impeached in 1701, but acquitted.

Halifax, George Savile, 1st marquis of 1633–95. Urbane, brilliant and incorruptible, Halifax supported neither the Whigs nor the Tories, but pursued a middle way in the politics of Charles II's reign, an approach defended in his *Character of a Trimmer* (1688). Dismissed by James VII and II, he supported the Glorious Revolution and served briefly as lord privy seal (1689).

Halifax, Edward Wood, Viscount Irwin, earl of 1881–1959. A Conservative MP (1910–26) who was in the 1930s identified first with the granting of increased self-government to India (as viceroy 1926–31), then with Chamberlain's policy of APPEASEMENT, as foreign secretary (1938–40). Both Labour and Conservative front benches favoured him to succeed Chamberlain (May 1940), but he withdrew in favour of Churchill, who sent him as ambassador to Washington (1941–6), where he was very successful.

Hamilton, James, 3rd marquis and 1st duke of 1606–49. A Scottish nobleman, educated in England, Hamilton was Charles I's commissioner to the general assembly in 1639. Unsuccessful in promoting the king's interests, he was briefly imprisoned after his return (1644–6). He subsequently negotiated the Scottish ENGAGEMENT, led the invasion defeated at PRESTON and was executed by parliament.

Hamilton, William Douglas, 3rd duke of 1635–94. An opponent of LAUDERDALE in the Scottish parliament, Hamilton tried unsuccessfully to moderate government policy in Scotland and was excluded from the privy council. Restored in 1686, he became a prominent supporter of the Glorious Revolution (1688) and served as president of the Scottish convention of estates.

Hampden, John 1594–1643. A wealthy Buckinghamshire squire, Hampden came to prominence

John **Hampden**: oil painting attributed to Robert Walker.

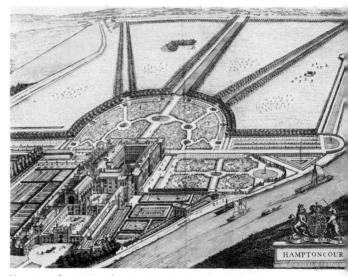

Hampton Court: line-drawing showing the formal gardens, from *Britannia Illustrata*, 1720.

when he was convicted for refusing to pay SHIP MONEY (1637–8). Courageous, honest and persuasive, he became a leader of the parliamentary opposition (1640–1) and was one of the FIVE MEMBERS. He was killed in a skirmish.

Hampden clubs Exclusive clubs of wealthy supporters of parliamentary reform, the first of which was founded by Sir Francis Burdett (1811). Each club remained autonomous in order to comply with the law, but their activities were coordinated by Major Cartwright. Their aim of extending the franchise to all taxpayers found little support.

Hampton Court The magnificent palace built round a series of courtyards for Wolsey (1514–26) and later Henry VIII, who added the Great Hall (1531–6). Improved and extended by Sir Christopher Wren, the palace remained a royal residence until 1760. The 18th-century gardens include a maze and vinery.

Hampton Court conference 1604. A conference of Anglican bishops and moderate Puritans called by JAMES VI AND I to discuss the MILLENNARY PETITION (1603). In generally amicable discussions a number of minor reforms were agreed and the BOOK OF COMMON PRAYER slightly modified. The decision was also made to undertake the Authorized translation of the bible.

Hand-loom weavers During the initial expansion of the textile industry (1770–1800) the failure to adapt weaving to power meant that there was a great demand for hand-weaving, and wages rose accordingly. But after 1800 an increasing labour force and the development of the power loom lowered wages, especially in the cotton industry, and eventually these dropped to starvation level. In 1842 the situation was so bad that there was a royal commission, but it was thereafter alleviated by diversifying employment opportunities. Hand weaving did not die out in the woollen industry of mainland Britain until the 20th century, and continues in the Harris Tweed industry in Scotland. *See* BLANKETEERS; INDUSTRIAL REVOLUTION.

Hankey, Sir Maurice, lord 1877–1963. Marine officer and protégé of Fisher, Hankey became secretary of the COMMITTEE OF IMPERIAL DEFENCE (1912), moving from there to Lloyd George's war cabinet (November 1916). Without him this supercentralized system would never have functioned. Until 1938 he was secretary to all the most important government committees and conferences, and thereafter a cabinet minister in the early years of World War II.

Hansard Luke Hansard (1752–1828) was printer to the house of commons and printed their journal; after 1803 his son published their debates, originally from newspaper reports. These were eventually made the official record and extended to the lords.

Hanseatic League The confederation of north German towns which from the 12th century dominated Baltic and North Sea trade. It enjoyed considerable privileges in England, including a 'steelyard' or sovereign headquarters in London, but the 'Easterlings' were much resented by native merchants, trading disputes causing their expulsion in 1463, 1555–7 and 1598. The league was dissolved after 1669.

Harald Hardrada king of Norway (d. 1066). The last great Viking leader, Harald 'Hard-Ruler' gained riches in Constantinople and Russia before succeeding in 1047. In pursuit of a claim to be Harthacnut's heir, he allied with Orkney Vikings and Harold Godwinson's dispossessed brother Tostig, and invaded England (1066), but though victorious at FULFORD he was defeated and killed at STAMFORD BRIDGE.

Harcourt, Sir William 1827–1904. A Whig politician who nevertheless accepted Gladstone's policy of Irish HOME RULE and led the Liberal party in the commons 1894–8.

Hardicanute see HARTHACNUT

Hardie, James Keir 1856–1915. Hardie was born illegitimate in Lanarkshire and went into the pits at the age of 10. Self-taught and profoundly religious in a non-doctrinaire way, he became a miners' union organizer and, as a marked man, had to support himself by journalism. Rebuffed for a Liberal candidacy, he founded the Scottish Labour party (1888), which became part of the INDE-PENDENT LABOUR PARTY (1893). Only then could Hardie properly be called a socialist. Hardie was MP for West Ham (1892–5) and for Merthyr (1900–15), championing the Boers, Indian independence and woman suffrage. He was only briefly leader of the parliamentary Labour party (1906–8) but, as a speaker and pamphleteer and chairman of the ILP, played an indispensable role in creating the party.

Harley, Robert, 1st earl of Oxford 1661–1724. Tory leader in the reigns of William III and Anne, Harley brought down the Whigs (1710) and was principal minister 1711–14. Impeached in 1714 for his part in the peace of UTRECHT, he was imprisoned for 2 years, though subsequently acquitted by the lords.

Harney, George Julian see CHARTISM

Harold Harefoot king of England (1037–40). Cnut's son by Aelfgifu of Northampton, Harold was popular in England, being recognized there as regent for the absent HARTHACNUT (1035) and as full king from 1037 until his death. Aelfgifu was probably the real ruler.

Harold Godwinson king of England (1066; b. c. 1022). Inheriting GODWIN's earldom of Wessex in 1053, Harold thereafter dominated England, successfully campaigning against GRUFFYDD AP LLYWELYN (1062–3). Though lacking royal blood, unloved in Mercia and Northumbria, and allegedly sworn to support William the Conqueror's claim, he was (to counter threats from Scandinavia and Normandy) unanimously elected king by the

James Keir **Hardie**: pencil sketch by Cosmo Rowe after a photograph.

Harold Harefoot portrayed on a contemporary Anglo-Saxon penny.

WITAN on Edward the Confessor's death. Victorious over Harald Hardrada at STAMFORD BRIDGE, he was defeated by William at HASTINGS.

Harris, Howel *see* WALES

Harrison, Thomas 1606–60. The son of a Staffordshire butcher, Harrison rose to the rank of major-general in the parliamentary army. A millennarian in religion, he was influential in the calling of BAREBONE'S PARLIAMENT (1653), but fell from power thereafter. Condemned as a regicide (1660), he died with notable courage and dignity.

Hart, Sir Basil Liddell 1895–1970. A former infantry officer who, with Major-General J. F. C. Fuller (1878–1966), was a strong advocate of tank warfare and the 'strategy of indirect approach' which he believed would avoid the attrition of the western front. The views of this school were more influential among German generals than in Britain until the disaster of May 1940.

Harthacnut king of England and Denmark (1040–2; b. *c.* 1018). Cnut's son by Emma and his chosen successor, Harthacnut was prevented by a threat to Denmark from displacing Harold Harefoot in England, but acceded on his death. Described by contemporaries as worthless, he died 'at his drink' after recognizing Edward the Confessor as his heir.

Hartington, marquess of, duke of Devonshire 1833–1908. Whig nobleman who succeeded Gladstone as Liberal leader (1875), but was replaced by him in 1880. He went to the India and then to the war office until he became leader of the LIBERAL UNIONIST PARTY, joining Salisbury's cabinet in 1895. His opposition to Joseph Chamberlain and TARIFF REFORM led to his withdrawal from the Balfour cabinet in 1903, and speeded the Unionist debacle of 1906.

Hastings, battle of 14 October 1066. The most decisive battle in English, if not in British history (*see* NORMAN CONQUEST). HAROLD GODWINSON, though weakened at Stamford Bridge, marched rapidly from Yorkshire and advanced on William the Conqueror without waiting for full reinforcement by the FYRD and THEGNS of the south. The English probably hoped to take William by surprise, but were themselves attacked at Battle, Sussex. After a day-long battle during which the Normans employed the tactic of feigned flight, Harold fell, and the defending English infantry broke before William's knights and bowmen.

Hatfield house, designed by Robert Lyminge: the hall, looking towards the gallery.

Hastings, Warren 1732–1818. Former governor of Bengal and the greatest 18th-century 'nabob', Hastings was impeached on the initiative of Burke and Charles Fox (1787). His long trial (1788–95) became a dramatic examination of the nature of British rule in India, though Hastings himself was ultimately acquitted of all charges.

Hatfield house The medieval Old Palace, completed in 1497 for the bishop of Ely, was the residence of Elizabeth I before her accession. The fine Elizabethan mansion designed by Robert Lyminge was built for Robert Cecil (1607–11) and remains the home of the Cecil family.

Hatton, Sir Christopher 1540–91. Though originally noticed by Elizabeth I for his skill at dancing, Hatton was no mere courtier. From 1577 he was the queen's principal spokesman in the commons and showed great skill as an orator and parliamentary manager. As lord chancellor (1587–91), he co-operated with Whitgift in opposing Puritanism.

Hawkins, Sir John 1532–95. A Devon seaman, Hawkins first emerged as a slave-trader to the Spanish colonies in America. From 1568 he was employed to build up the navy and his reduction of administrative corruption and championship of fast, manoeuvrable galleons went far to prepare England to meet the Spanish Armada.

Heads of the Proposals 1647. Proposals drawn up by IRETON as the basis of negotiations between Charles I and the officers of the NEW MODEL ARMY between the 2 CIVIL WARS. The terms included the redressing of the army's grievances, moderate parliamentary reforms and a tolerant religious settlement. Unfortunately, they failed to win Charles's approval.

Hearth tax A direct tax, periodically levied in the reign of Charles II and assessed upon the numbers of hearths in taxpayers' houses, the very poor being exempted. The tax was extremely unpopular and was abandoned after the Glorious Revolution (1688).

Henderson, Alexander 1583–1646. Minister of Leuchars (1612) and St Giles, Edinburgh (1639) and one of the framers of the national COVENANT. As moderator of the GENERAL ASSEMBLY OF THE CHURCH OF SCOTLAND, he presided over the abolition of episcopacy (1638) and later supported the SOLEMN LEAGUE AND COVENANT, travelling to London as a delegate to the WESTMINSTER ASSEMBLY OF DIVINES.

Henderson, Arthur 1863–1935. Secretary of the LABOUR PARTY (1911–34), Henderson served in Lloyd George's war cabinet (1916–17), and drafted, with Sidney WEBB, the constitution of the Labour party (1918). He was home secretary in MacDonald's 1st cabinet, and then foreign secretary (1929–31), continuing until 1935 as president of the doomed DISARMAMENT CONFERENCE in Geneva.

Henge monuments Circular ritual sites defined by a bank and a (generally internal) ditch, giving the effect of an amphitheatre. They appear from Cornwall to Orkney, with a concentration in Wessex. Unique to Britain, they probably developed from CAUSEWAYED CAMPS during the secondary neolithic period (c. 2500–2000 BC). A few contain later STONE CIRCLES, as at STONEHENGE.

Hengest Traditionally the 1st Anglo-Saxon leader to reach Britain, Hengest was probably a freebooting Jutish chieftain of very noble descent. Landing in Thanet c. 430, he took service with Vortigern against the Picts, but thereafter headed the Saxon attack on Britain and effectively founded Kent (440–60).

Henrietta Maria and Charles I departing for the hunt: oil painting by Daniel Mytens, c. 1630–2.

Henrietta Maria 1609–69. The youngest daughter of Henri IV of France, married to CHARLES I in 1625. Henrietta Maria exercised considerable influence over her husband, stiffening his intransigence in the face of parliamentary opposition and contributing by her Catholicism to fears for the king's religious reliability. From 1644 she lived mainly in France.

Henry I king of England (1100–35; b. 1068). The 4th son of William the Conqueror, the plenitude of whose power he sought to restore. Henry seized the throne on the death of William Rufus, promising a return to good government and wooing English support by emphasizing his native birth and marrying the half-English daughter of St Margaret. A baronial revolt backed by the invasion of Robert Curthose was neutralized when Henry and Robert came to terms (1101), but after defeating Robert de Bellême (1102) Henry turned to continue the conquest of Normandy, completed at TENCHEBRAI. He thereafter triumphed over French and Angevin opposition by a combination of war and diplomacy, but the WHITE SHIP disaster entailed a succession problem, unsatisfactorily solved by his nomination of MATILDA. Though oppressive, avaricious, and dissembling, the 'Lion of Justice' maintained a firm peace, remembered with nostalgia during the disorders of Stephen's reign. See ill. p. 208.

Henry II king of England (1154–89; b. 1133). Perhaps the most remarkable of medieval English kings, Henry was the son of Matilda by Geoffrey Plantagenet, count of Anjou. Though subject to ungovernable rages, and a notorious oath-breaker, he was gifted with boundless energy: the rapidity of his movements constantly startled contemporaries, and he was said never to sit save when eating or riding. This energy was devoted principally to identifying, recovering, maintaining and strengthening his rights to and within his vast dominions (sometimes called the 'Angevin empire'). By his accession these already included over half of France – Normandy (inherited from his mother), Anjou, Maine and Touraine (from his father) and Aquitaine (gained by his marriage to Eleanor of Aquitaine) – Brittany, Auvergne and Toulouse were added later.

England, providing Henry with a crown and much of his finance, became the most important of his territories. Here he set himself to restore order and royal prestige after the upheavals of Stephen's reign, re-establishing the strong central government of his grandfather Henry I by banishing mercenaries, demolishing unlicensed baronial castles, resuming alienated royal lands and fortresses and building great strongholds such as Dover, Orford and Newcastle.

His policy towards Wales and Scotland was at first belligerent and tactless. He failed to conquer the Welsh princes and, although he induced MALCOLM IV to return the border lands ceded to David I, he alienated Malcolm's successor WILLIAM THE LION. During the 1170s, however, he reached agreement with RHYS AP GRUFFYDD in Wales, and eventually restored good relations with Scotland. In 1171–2 he intervened in Ireland (*see* LAUDABILITER, BULL OF) to forestall Strongbow's foundation of an independent Norman state there, establishing instead a royal justiciar or viceroy, but subsequently failing to create an Irish kingdom as an APPANAGE for John.

Henry's relations with the church were dominated by his quarrel with BECKET, his close friend and chancellor since 1155, whom he appointed archbishop of Canterbury (1162), hoping thereby to regain the royal control over the church (formulated by the Constitutions of Clarendon, 1164) lost under Stephen. But Becket turned against him, vigorously upholding ecclesiastical rights, and a long and irreconcilable clash of personalities resulted in Becket's exile (1165–70) and martyrdom (29 December 1170). Despite the consequent upheaval, Henry gained most of his aims.

Concern about the succession caused Henry to crown his eldest son during his own lifetime (24 May 1170), but the feckless HENRY THE YOUNG KING

Henry II, portrayed enthroned, from a 13th-century manuscript.

rose in revolt (1173), supported by his mother and brothers and by Henry's inveterate enemies Louis VII of France and William the Lion of Scotland. While his justiciar Richard de Lucy held England, Henry defended Normandy (1173), and in 1174 the dangerous threat collapsed with the capture of William at Alnwick (13 June) and the surrender of Louis near Rouen (30 September), leaving Henry stronger than ever.

He now turned to schemes for turning his dominions into a federation of semi-autonomous states ruled by his sons (the Young King would hold England, Normandy and Anjou; Richard Aquitaine; Geoffrey Brittany and John Ireland) but was baulked by their rebellions and mutual animosities. Finally, in 1188, Richard (by then his heir) and his favourite John joined with Philip Augustus of France against him, hounding him to death at Chinon (6 July 1189), a broken and embittered man. (W. L. Warren, *Henry II*, 1973.) *See* LAW.

Henry the Young King 1155–83. The charming but feckless and treacherous eldest son of Henry II and Eleanor of Aquitaine, Henry was crowned in his father's lifetime (1170) but he was refused an APPANAGE, and became the figurehead of Henry's enemies 1173–4. Though defeated and forgiven, he remained disaffected, dying during a new revolt.

Henry III instructs his masons during the reconstruction of Westminster abbey. Drawing by Matthew Paris, 13th century.

Henry III king of England (1216–72; b. 1207). The son of John by Isabella of Angoulême, Henry succeeded (aged 9) at a time of crisis, with much of England in the hands of Prince Louis and the rebel barons. Henry's supporters, however (notably the papal legate, the regent William the Marshal, the JUSTICIAR Hubert de Burgh and Falkes de Breauté), won over many of the dissidents by issuing a modified version of Magna Carta, and their victories at LINCOLN and SANDWICH forced Louis to withdraw when the war ended with the treaty of Kingston-on-Thames (12 September 1217). After the Marshal's death (1219) England was ruled first by the Legate Pandulf and, from 1221, by Langton and Hubert de Burgh who (assisted by a majority of the magnates) gradually restored the royal and other castles and lands occupied during the war to their rightful owners.

Henry proclaimed his majority in 1227, but Hubert de Burgh remained influential until 1232, after which (and especially after his marriage to Eleanor of Provence in 1235) Henry was increasingly influenced by foreigners from Poitou, Provence and Savoy. The magnates resented these aliens, and pressed (especially in 1238 and 1244–5) for a direct share in government and in appointing royal councillors and ministers. Nothing, however, was achieved until Henry's difficulties in financing the SICILIAN BUSINESS forced him to accede to the demands of a united and determined baronage and accept the PROVISIONS OF OXFORD (1258).

But baronial unity was short-lived. By 1260 Henry (having concluded the treaty of PARIS) had recovered the initiative and prevented a nascent alliance between the baronial leader SIMON DE MONTFORT and his own son Edward. In 1261 he repudiated the Provisions and removed baronially appointed officials. However, the more determined reformers, joined by lesser gentry and south-eastern townsmen, rallied behind Montfort and the MARCHERS and forced a return to the Provisions (May–June 1263), but Edward (now reconciled with his father) soon afterwards won over the Marchers and prepared to oppose them. Louis IX was called on to arbitrate, and when he declared against the Provisions by the mise of Amiens (January 1264), civil war became inevitable.

At first Edward was successful, capturing many Montfortians at Northampton (7 April), but Montfort rallied his forces in the south-east and heavily defeated the royalists at LEWES (14 May). With both Henry and Edward in their power the reformers seemed secure, but in May 1265 Edward escaped from custody, rallied his Marchers, and defeated and killed Montfort at EVESHAM (4 August). The statute of Winchester (17 September 1265) embittered the remaining rebels (hereafter called the Disinherited) by confiscating their lands and distributing them among loyalists, and (despite the more conciliatory dictum of Kenilworth, 31 October 1266) the war dragged on until June 1267. The 'amelioration of the realm' was finally achieved by the statute of Marlborough (18 November 1267), which incorporated most of the legal reforms of the Provisions.

The remaining years of Henry's long reign were peaceful, and in 1269 he saw the completion of his lifelong ambition and greatest achievement, the rebuilding of Westminster abbey. An attractive character and a man of considerable intellect and taste, Henry's political misjudgments were generally redeemed by an ultimate readiness to compromise.

Henry IV king of England (1399–1413; b. 1366). Eldest son of John of Gaunt, Henry was one of the APPELLANTS against his cousin Richard II. Richard exiled him (1398), subsequently seizing his vast inheritance. But Henry deposed Richard after a virtually bloodless revolution and supplanted him on the throne (September 1399). Uncertainties about the legal basis of this action were a continual handicap to Henry, increasing the influence of parliament, and encouraging a succession of revolts by the PERCIES, SCROPE and GLENDOWER. In his later years his administration was dominated by ARUNDEL or his own eldest son, afterwards Henry V.

Henry V king of England (1413–22; b. 1387). The eldest son of Henry IV and Mary de Bohun. Created prince of Wales, after SHREWSBURY Henry increasingly took active command of operations against Glendower, and by 1408 had turned the tide of rebellion. Stories of the quarrels between father and son, like the tales of Henry's youthful wildness and dramatic conversion on his father's death, are perhaps exaggerated. Certainly he was well prepared to rule by education as well as experience: though fluent in Latin and French, he was the 1st king to use English in all correspondence, part of his policy of identifying himself with the interests of the nation as a whole.

After easily crushing OLDCASTLE'S LOLLARD rising, the new king turned his attention to France, with whom Richard II's long truce expired in 1414. Genuinely believing in his inherited claim to the French throne (*see* HUNDRED YEARS' WAR) and well aware of the dissension between BURGUNDIANS and Armagnacs, Henry set virtually impossible conditions on renewing the peace, meanwhile preparing an expeditionary force, which landed near Harfleur (13 August 1415), taking the town a month later. Heavy losses from dysentery prevented Henry from now advancing on Paris, and he decided instead on the provocative march to Calais which resulted in AGINCOURT.

Returning to England, he continued the war by diplomatic means (1416), concluding an alliance with the German Emperor Sigismund (who visited him as a mediator between England and France) and attempting another with the Burgundians. Bedford's naval victory off Harfleur (15 May 1416) meanwhile saved that town from blockade and capture, and there Henry returned (1 August 1417), intent on a policy of systematic conquest. Advancing steadily into Normandy, he took Caen (4 September 1418), Falaise (1 February 1418) and Rouen, the Norman capital (19 January 1419). This pushed the wavering Burgundians towards a united front with their Armagnac rivals, but the Armagnac murder of Duke John the Fearless (10 September 1419) brought them instead into firm alliance with Henry and paved the way for his triumph at TROYES (1420).

Henry felt secure enough to return to England with Queen Katharine of Valois on 1 February 1421. However, 6 months later the disaster of BAUGÉ recalled him to France, where he began reducing the surviving Dauphinist strongholds around Paris. Meaux, the most obstinate of these, fell on 2 May 1422, but during the 5-month siege Henry contracted the dysentery from which he died, aged 35 (31 August).

The poet Thomas Hoccleve presents his *Regement of Princes* to Prince Henry, the future **Henry V**, *c*. 1410.

Henry V, 'the mirror of all Christian kings', has always claimed a special place in English history and literature. Albeit an assiduous self-propagandist, and something of a self-righteous prig by modern standards, he seems indeed to have been an outstandingly able, efficient and just ruler, who by his personal leadership inspired quite remarkably unanimous respect and support from his people.

Henry VI king of England (1422–61; 1470–1; b. 1421). The only son of Henry V by Katharine of Valois, Henry succeeded to the thrones of England and France (*see* TROYES, TREATY OF) when less than a year old. During Henry's minority BEDFORD ruled efficiently in France, but HUMPHREY and Cardinal BEAUFORT quarrelled at home. He came of age in 1436 but (though devout and kindly) showed little inclination for ruling, being increasingly dominated by SUFFOLK and Queen Margaret of Anjou (*see* CADE'S RISING). His decline into intermittent insanity (1453) precipitated the wars of the ROSES, when he was merely a pawn of Margaret, the Beauforts and (during his restoration in 1470–1) of WARWICK. Taken at BARNET, he was murdered in the

Tower at Edward IV's orders. Perhaps the most unfortunate of medieval English kings, his only achievements were the foundations of Eton and King's College, Cambridge.

Henry VII king of England (1485–1509; b. 1457). Henry's father, Edmund Tudor earl of Richmond, was the son of Katharine of Valois, widow of Henry V, by her secret 2nd marriage to Owen Tudor, an obscure Welsh esquire who claimed descent from the princely house of Cadwallader. His claim to the throne, however, derived from his mother Margaret Beaufort, through whom, after the fatalities at TEWKESBURY (1471), he became the sole male heir of Lancaster. To avoid Henry's capture by EDWARD IV, his uncle Jasper Tudor then removed him to Brittany, where he remained an obscure exile until Richard III's usurpation (1483) alienated many Yorkists and prompted a conspiracy by his mother, MORTON and BUCKINGHAM to place him on the throne. The rising failed, but refugees from it joined him in Brittany, where they recognized him as king provided he would marry Edward IV's eldest daughter Elizabeth. In 1484 Richard III nearly succeeded in having him kidnapped, but he escaped to France, where he eventually obtained some assistance from King Charles VIII, and his small Anglo-French invasion force landed near Milford Haven on 1 August 1485. His march through Wales and the midlands was unopposed, and at BOSWORTH the timely intervention of his stepfather Stanley enabled him to defeat and kill Richard III.

Claiming the throne by conquest as well as descent, the new king was virtually a stranger in England, and chose his chief ministers from assured friends such as Morton. His position was strengthened by his marriage to Elizabeth and the birth of their 1st son Arthur (1486), but threatened by Yorkist pretenders (SIMNEL, WARBECK and the de la POLES) made more dangerous by foreign support. Henry's defensive but pacific foreign policy was thus at first directed at removing this support and gaining recognition for his dynasty, ends achieved by the treaty of Medina del Campo (1489) with Spain (which provided for a marriage between Prince Arthur and Catharine of Aragon, concluded in 1501), the treaty of Etaples (1492) with France (signed after Henry's token invasion), the commercial 'Intercursus Magnus' (1496) with Flanders, and the truce of Ayton (1497) with Scotland (leading to the marriage of James IV and Henry's daughter Margaret in 1503).

However, his overriding concern (no doubt influenced by his years of impecunious and insecure

Henry VII: portrait by Michael Sittow, 1505. He is holding a red and white rose, symbolizing the union of the families of Lancaster and York through his marriage to Elizabeth of YORK.

exile) was to make the monarchy rich and its subjects obedient. He gave assiduous personal attention to financial affairs, relentlessly exploiting the pecuniary rights of the crown, employing the legal system to collect debts and whenever possible preferring fines to other punishments (*see* STAR CHAMBER). Towards the end of his reign, after the deaths of all his sons save the future Henry VIII had made him again fear for the future of his dynasty, he secured the loyalty and good behaviour of nobility and gentry by sometimes extortionate financial bonds and RECOGNISANCES. But if he grew avaricious, he was far from niggardly, keeping a magnificent court and patronizing musicians, poets, architects and explorers.

Shrewd and prudent, Henry VII was no innovator, rather a man of great ability who built on the foundations of medieval monarchy. His great achievement was to give England (for the 1st time since the reign of Edward III) much needed stability under a strong and solvent monarchy.

Henry VIII king of England (1509–47; b. 1491). As the 2nd son of Henry VII, Henry became heir to the throne only after his brother Arthur's death (1501). He inherited his father's kingdom 8 years later and married his brother's widow Catherine of ARAGON.

The very image of a Renaissance prince, tall, handsome, active, cultured and intelligent, the young Henry was hailed by the humanist reformers of Europe (*see* HUMANISM) as a model virtuous ruler. Only gradually did his impetuous, wilful, vindictive and egotistical nature emerge from behind the mask of regal glamour. The judicial murders of Richard Empson and Edmund Dudley in 1509 and of the duke of Buckingham in 1522, the abandonment of servants such as WOLSEY, MORE and Thomas CROMWELL and his dealings with Queen Catherine and subsequent wives (Anne BOLEYN, Jane SEYMOUR, Anne of CLEVES, Catherine HOWARD and Catherine PARR) successively impressed upon his subjects the increasingly dangerous nature of the king's personality. At his death he was less loved by his subjects than respected and feared.

Henry came to the throne with no governmental experience whatsoever, nor had he much taste for the tedium of administration, which he entrusted in turn to Wolsey and Cromwell. Only in 1529–32 and 1540–7 did Henry rule in person, neither period being notable for its achievements. Prior to 1527, Henry was content to present himself to a hopefully admiring Europe as the exemplary courtier, scholar and soldier. His inconsequential French campaigns of 1513–14 and during the 1540s evidenced his desire to emulate his warlike ancestors and to rival his contemporaries Francis I of France and the Emperor Charles V. He failed in both. In 1521 his short book against Martin Luther won him the title 'Fidei Defensor', grudgingly accorded by the pope. Six years later, his pursuit of the annulment of his 1st marriage, essential if Henry was to beget a male heir, led him into conflict with the papacy and, under the guidance of Cromwell, into the English REFORMATION. After Cromwell's execution (1540) the king turned once more to war, while enforcing doctrinal conservatism on the infant church of England.

Though little involved in the detailed working out of policy, Henry never relinquished the final power in English government. His greatest servants well knew that they could stand only so long as they retained the trust and confidence of the king. That trust, lavishly bestowed in times of success, could never endure failure, as friends, wives and statesmen were to learn to their cost. From his golden youth to his gross decrepitude Henry remained king, awesome and magnificent. His regal personality impressed itself indelibly on both his contemporaries and posterity. As for his reign, in G. R. Elton's words, it 'owed its successes and virtues to better and greater men about him; most of its horrors and failures sprang more directly from himself' (*Reform and Reformation. England 1509–58*, 1977). *See* SUCCESSION, ACTS OF.

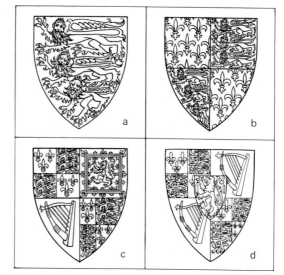

Heraldry: the earliest known representation of the arms of England (a) appears on Richard I's 2nd great seal, 1198; (b) in 1340 Edward III incorporated the French fleur-de-lis; (c) from 1603 to 1688 and 1702 to 1707 the arms of Scotland and Ireland filled the 2nd and 3rd quarters; (d) from 1688 to 1689 William and Mary's arms did not include Scotland. Modern line-drawings.

Heraldry Though the employment of personal or communal devices is almost immemorial, the systematic use of hereditary arms probably dates from the 12th century. A means of identification or propaganda and (especially during the 15th and 16th centuries) a symbol of family pride, heraldry remains a useful historical document.

Heregeld *see* DANEGELD

Heretics *see* DE HERETICO COMBURENDO; LOLLARDS; PELAGIUS; WYCLIFFE, JOHN

Hereward the Wake Famous in legend as the symbol of English resistance to William the Conqueror, Hereward 'the Watchful' was historically a Lincolnshire THEGN who (with Danish assistance) sacked the Norman-held abbey of Peterborough (June 1070), and afterwards held the Isle of Ely, attracting much support, until driven into hiding by William (summer 1071).

Heriot (Old English *here-geatwa*, army trappings). In Anglo-Saxon times, the term referred to military equipment restored to a lord on the death of his follower. In the feudal period, it applied to the best beast or piece of property belonging to a VILLEIN, seized by his lord as a death duty.

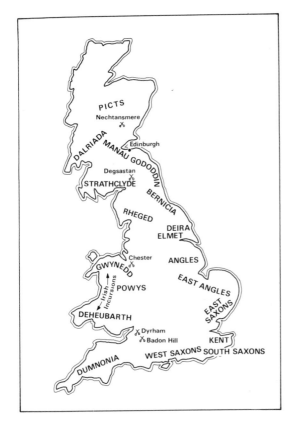

Britain in the **heroic age**.

St Ninian's Isle treasure: dating from the **heroic age** and probably a scabbard chape, this silver object is inscribed with the owner's name, 'Resad, son of Spussico'.

Heritable jurisdictions Hereditary legal powers held by the Scottish nobility. Though preserved at the union (1707), they were in decay in lowland Scotland in the 18th century. In the highlands, however, they remained an important part of the power of chiefs over their clansmen until their abolition in 1747.

Heroic age The centuries between the end of Roman Britain and the emergence of the recognizable forerunners of England, Scotland and Wales, form one of the most crucial periods of British history, yet one of the least studied or understood in its own right. Its history cannot be written in the conventional manner, but must be derived as much from archaeology, poetry and the study of place names as from the sparse and unreliable written records. This 'heroic' era, dominated by semi-legendary figures such as ARTHUR, has therefore generally been dismissed as an unfathomable and inconvenient 'dark age', and only very recently have efforts been made to render it intelligible.

Romano-British civilization survived for at least a generation after the removal of imperial control (410). VORTIGERN made himself supreme ruler in the south, employing CUNEDDA to contain Irish invasions and, from *c.* 430, introducing Anglo-Saxon FOEDERATI under HENGEST to defend the east coast against the PICTS and perhaps also to overawe his own British rivals. These Saxons, becoming increasingly numerous, rebelled *c.* 442, launching a series of far-ranging and devastating raids. The GROANS OF THE BRITONS produced no help from Gaul, British counter-attacks were nullified by further Saxon reinforcements from Europe, and *c.* 460 many Britons fled to Armorica, afterwards 'Brittany'.

From this time, however, British resistance (led at first by Ambrosius Aurelianus and later perhaps by Arthur) was increasingly successful, culminating in the great victory of BADON HILL (*c.* 495). Thereafter the Saxons were confined, apparently by treaty, to certain southern and eastern areas, and a long period of relative peace and security followed, enduring until the 540s (*see* GILDAS). The wars had nevertheless destroyed all but the vestiges of Roman government, and the British (or CYMRY) were by now divided into numerous independent monarchies ruled by 'TYRANNI'. These included, from south to north: DUMNONIA, DEMETIA, POWYS, GWYNEDD, YORK, ELMET, and RHEGED; and STRATHCLYDE and MANAU GODODDIN in modern Scotland. Anglo-Saxon states were meanwhile developing in KENT, SUSSEX, WESSEX, EAST ANGLIA, LINDISSE, DEIRA and BERNICIA.

In the 550s, after Britain had been struck by plague, a new Saxon attack began in Wiltshire, gathering momentum in the 570s with the capture of the British south midlands and, after Ceawlin's victory at DYRHAM, separating Dumnonia from Wales. In the north (previously little affected) Urien of Rheged temporarily contained Bernician expansion during the 580s, but British divisions and the conquests of AETHELFERTH made a unified English NORTHUMBRIA supreme by c. 610. Aethelferth's successor Edwin was recognized as high king (BRETWALDA) of all Saxon England, but was overthrown (632) by Cadwallawn of Gwynedd in the last major British counter-attack, itself soon decisively defeated by OSWALD. Oswald's own defeat by PENDA (641) began the dominance of Mercia over the southern English which (despite OSWIU's successes in 655–8) was to endure almost until the Viking invasions.

By the 660s the last British lowland kingdom (see CYNDDYLAN) had fallen, and the surviving independent Britons had become 'Welsh' (or 'foreigners'), permanently separated in Cornwall, Wales and Strathclyde, both from each other and from Anglo-Saxon England. They had lost their inheritance largely because they were unable to unite.

In the region beyond Hadrian's wall, the heroic age saw the PICTS of the centre and north and the Britons of Strathclyde and the south challenged, from the 6th century by the invading Scotti of DALRIADA and from the 7th by the Angles of Northumbria. Insofar as it is possible to summarize an overall pattern from the incessant wars and shifting alliances of these 4 peoples, it appears that Dalriadan expansion had been halted by c. 640 and Northumbrian colonization contained in Lothian by c. 690, leaving the Picts generally dominant (see DEGSASTAN, BATTLE OF; NECHTANSMERE, BATTLE OF; OENGUS MAC FERGUS). The 1st step towards unification was taken in the mid-9th century, when KENNETH MAC ALPIN, in the face of Viking attacks, united Picts and Scots in the kingdom of ALBA, which by the annexation of Lothian in 1018 (see CARHAM, BATTLE OF) and of Strathclyde by 1034 became substantially modern Scotland.

Hide In Anglo-Saxon times, the amount of arable land considered necessary to support a single household. Its size varied according to the soil, but was usually around 100 acres. Soon defined as a CARUCATE or ploughland in northern England, it was generally so classified after the Norman conquest. *See* HUNDRED; SHIRE.

High Churchmen Their origin lay in the OXFORD MOVEMENT. Later on in the 19th century, chiefly through the influence of Bishop Gore (1853–1932), 'Anglo-Catholicism' became identified with work among the poor and socialist ideas.

High commission Prerogative courts, exercising ecclesiastical jurisdiction under the royal supremacy in the provinces of Canterbury and York and the diocese of Durham. Much of the business of high commission courts was routine, but they became hated for their activities against Puritanism and were abolished in 1641.

High court of justice *see* LAW

Highland clearances The 'clearances' which transformed the Scottish highlands in the later 18th and early 19th centuries involved the mass eviction of small tenants by their landlords in order to create large sheep farms. A subject fraught with emotion both at the time and subsequently, it must be understood in the context of broader processes of change of which the clearances were only a part, though a tragic part.

In the late 18th century population in the highlands rose dramatically, partly as a result of declining mortality, partly in response to the economic opportunities provided by an unprecedented demand for the highland products of cattle, kelp, fish and wool. These developments, coupled with such agrarian changes as the abolition of RUNRIG and the consolidation and enclosure of farms, produced a congested and poverty-stricken society in which the majority of highlanders lived on tiny landholdings, sustained by potatoes and work in kelp-burning.

Emigration led by TACKSMEN displaced by agrarian reorganization began long before 1800, but it was initially opposed by landlords anxious to retain a large population to provide both labour for kelping and military recruits. After 1800 matters changed as the price of kelp and cattle fell. Large-scale sheep farming seemed the only profitable way to exploit highland estates and the clearances began. The most famous incidents occurred on the estate of the countess of Sutherland and Lord Stafford, who owned two-thirds of Sutherland. From 1807 to 1821 their factors executed the plans of their agent James Loch to clear the estate and remove the population to new fishing and industrial villages on the coast. Had these costly new settlements prospered, all might have been well. They failed and the dispossessed peasantry were faced either with existence in still more congested conditions or with emigration.

The Sutherland clearances were untypical in their systematic nature, in the fact that some efforts were made to provide a future for the highlanders and in the public attention focused on them by the trial of Patrick Sellar following his brutal clearance of Strathnaver (1814). Other evictions went on piecemeal and met little resistance from a people left leaderless by the departure of the tacksmen, betrayed by their chiefs and finding scant sympathy from their clergy. The final blow came when the potato blight (1840s) destroyed the highlanders' last prop and provoked mass emigration to lowland cities or the colonies.

Such emigration was perhaps ultimately inevitable. The clearances which preceded it were a mixture of failed good intentions and sheer callousness. The latter aspect has traditionally received the greater publicity. The former is a reminder that the true tragedy of the highlands lay in their inability to provide an adequate economic base for their people in a modern market economy.

Highland Host, the 1678. LAUDERDALE's attempt to cow the COVENANTERS of south-west Scotland by inviting highland chiefs to send clansmen to the area to live at 'free quarter'. Some 8,000 highlanders spent 2 months confiscating horses and arms and looting generally. They were withdrawn only after protests by William, duke of Hamilton.

Highwaymen Mounted robbers who haunted the lonelier roads from London in the later 17th and 18th centuries, specializing in the robbery of coaches. As a criminal élite they adopted genteel manners, and such figures as Claude Duval (1643–70) and Dick Turpin (1706–39) acquired a romantic reputation which they little deserved.

Hill, Rowland see PENNY POST

Hillforts Prehistoric enclosures defended by one or more earth and/or stone banks, generally accompanied by ditches. About 3,000 survive, those of maritime north and far west Britain being generally small and those further east often very large (see MAIDEN CASTLE). The earliest examples date from the late bronze age (c. 1000–650 BC). They usually had single timber-framed box-ramparts. By the 3rd century BC these were being replaced in southern Britain by earthen 'dump' or 'glacis' banks giving a continuous slope from ditch-bottom to rampart top. Multiple ramparts, perhaps related to the advent of sling-warfare, appear in the same area

c. 200 BC. In the Belgic-influenced south-east, hillforts were replaced by OPPIDA c. 100 BC, but elsewhere they continued in use until Roman times. *See* DUNS AND BROCHS; PREHISTORIC BRITAIN.

Hiring fairs Also known as 'statute sessions', 'stattis' and 'mops', the fairs were held for the hiring of SERVANTS IN HUSBANDRY, generally at Michaelmas, but at other seasons in some areas. Part labour exchanges and part lively social occasions, they declined in the 19th century as service in husbandry declined.

Hoare-Laval pact *see* ABYSSINIAN WAR

Hobson, J.A. *see* BRITISH EMPIRE; WELFARE STATE

Holkham Hall Norf. A Palladian mansion built by William Kent (1734–59) for Thomas Coke, particularly notable for its lavish interiors, with ceilings, furnishings and tapestries designed by Kent.

Home guard Inaugurated as the Local Defence Volunteers (1940), it had enrolled over a million men by that summer, and only then got any proper armament. Its maximum strength was 1·6 million (1942). Although rather more effective than its 'Dad's Army' image, it is probably as well that no one had to obey Churchill's injunction to 'take one with you'.

One of the earliest photographs of the Local Defence Volunteers, subsequently the **home guard**, stamped by the censor 'not to be published'.

Home office Created in 1782 under a secretary of state, it originally oversaw war (until 1794), Irish and colonial affairs (until 1801). Thereafter its main responsibilities have been police, justice and PRISONS.

Home rule The term, and the concept behind it – of 'devolved' rather than separate government – was coined by BUTT's Irish National party in the 1870s, and crystallized in GLADSTONE's 1st Bill (1886). This proposed to give Ireland a domestic legislature with limited powers. Originally there were to be no Irish MPs at Westminster, but this was withdrawn in Gladstone's 2nd Bill (1893). This Bill and that of 1912–14 would have created a quasi-federal constitution, especially if demands, consistently expressed by Scottish and Welsh Liberals, for home rule for their countries, were also acceded to. The possibility of this led to various schemes for 'home rule all round' being discussed – by Conservatives as well as Liberals – before World War I. After the troubles of 1919–21 (*see* IRISH CONSTITUTIONAL CRISIS) little more was heard of it until the nationalist agitation of the 1960s, but with the report of the Kilbrandon commission (1973), the devolution acts and referenda (1976–9), and the ULSTER EMERGENCY, it was a major if unresolved theme of 1970s politics. *See* SCOTTISH NATIONAL PARTY; WELSH NATIONALISM.

Homildon Hill, battle of 14 September 1402. The English under HOTSPUR cut off the retreat of a large Scots raiding force under Archibald Douglas 'the Tyneman' near Wooler, Northumberland. The Scots took up a defensive position, but were mown down by archers, and Douglas and the other Scots leaders were captured.

Hong Kong *see* BRITISH EMPIRE; OPIUM WARS

Honour A large FIEF forming the endowment of a great magnate, and commonly consisting of lands scattered over several SHIRES. It was generally named after the place which constituted its *caput* or administrative centre, e.g. the Honour of Wallingford. *See* FEUDALISM.

Hopton, Sir Ralph, 1st baron 1596–1652. Though a Puritan and opposition member in the LONG PARLIAMENT, Hopton felt bound to support the king in the CIVIL WARS. Raising troops in Cornwall, he defeated parliamentary forces at Braddock Down, Stratton and Lansdown and took Bristol (1643) only to be himself defeated at Cheriton (1644). He died in exile.

Hospitals *see* NATIONAL HEALTH SERVICE

Britannia, standing at the cross-roads, is offered conflicting advice. Is she to heed Gladstone the Liberal, holding the olive branch of **home rule**, or the Conservative Lord Salisbury, with nothing to offer but coercion? Cartoon by J. D. Reigh.

Hospitals, medieval Medieval hospitals were at first generally established by religious orders, but were later founded (on an increasingly elaborate scale) by magnates or GUILDS, often in connection with CHANTRIES or collegiate churches. Most frequently almshouses for the infirm or aged poor, though some (e.g. Bedlam, London) dealt with specific disorders.

Hospitallers, Knights The Knights of the Hospital of St John of Jerusalem were by the 12th century a military order with special responsibilities to pilgrims and the sick. Granted lands in England from *c.* 1100 and in Scotland from *c.* 1153, they were suppressed by Henry VIII (1540), their estates passing to the crown. *See* TEMPLARS, KNIGHTS.

Hotspur The nickname of Sir Henry Percy (1364–1403), a noted soldier and WARDEN OF THE MARCHES. He was captured at OTTERBURN. Having helped Henry IV to the throne and gained a victory for him at HOMILDON HILL (1402), he shortly afterwards rebelled, to be defeated and killed at SHREWSBURY.

Houses of correction Under the English POOR LAWS (1576 and 1597), houses of correction were to be established in every county and city for the correction of the idle poor and the punishment of rogues. By the mid-17th century they were well-established, functioning in effect as short-term prisons.

The **Houses of Parliament**, or New Palace of Westminster, by Charles Barry and A. W. N. Pugin, seen before the embankment of the Thames *c*. 1870.

Houses of Parliament The original palace of Westminster was built round Westminster Hall, which dates from the 11th century. The commons met in St Stephen's chapel from 1547, but in 1834 the palace, except for the hall, was burnt down. Its successor, by Sir Charles Barry and A.W.N. Pugin, was built in a revived Perpendicular style (1840–67) at a cost of £3 million.

Housing *see* WELFARE STATE

Howard, Catherine 1520–42. The lively, attractive and promiscuous niece of the duke of Norfolk, and the candidate of the conservative faction at court, Catherine became Henry VIII's 5th wife (1540). Henry, captivated by his young bride, was shattered by the discovery of her numerous adulteries. She was executed.

Howard, Charles, Baron Howard of Effingham and earl of Nottingham 1536–1624. After a career at court, Howard became lord admiral (1585) and commanded against the Spanish Armada (1588). Brave, judicious and conciliatory, he contributed much to the success of the war at sea, though peace brought a decline in naval efficiency which he did little to arrest.

Howard, Sir Ebenezer *see* GARDEN CITIES

Howell, George 1833–1910. A Somerset-born bricklayer, CHARTIST and trade unionist, Howell founded and became secretary of the REFORM LEAGUE (1863) and a member of the 'INTERNATIONAL' (1864). He was 1st secretary of the TUC's parliamentary committee and aided trade union legislation (1871 and 1876). As Liberal MP 1885–95, he had no sympathy with the socialist movement.

Hubert de Burgh d. 1243. Chamberlain to John, Hubert de Burgh became JUSTICIAR (1215), held Dover against Prince Louis, and strenuously supported the young Henry III, under whom he virtually ruled England 1221–32. Then his unpopularity with the baronage, the failure of his campaigns against Llywelyn the Great and the withdrawal of royal support encompassed his downfall.

Hudson, George 1800–71. A York draper and mayor, Hudson rose to enormous wealth and influence as chairman of the Midland Railway and other companies. By 1845 the 'Railway King' controlled a third of the British railway system and became a Tory MP. The collapse of RAILWAY MANIA and proof of fraud in his businesses led to his flight and after 1849 he lived mainly abroad.

Huguenots French Protestants fleeing from religious persecution, they settled in England in substantial numbers in the later 16th century and again after 1685, establishing communities in London, Canterbury, Norwich and Southampton. As skilled craftsmen, they introduced new and improved technologies, notably in the silk, linen and glass industries. *See* ILE DE RHÉ EXPEDITION.

Humanism The 'new learning' of the late 15th and early 16th centuries, espoused by ERASMUS, MORE, and COLET. Essentially a trend away from scholastic theology and philosophy and towards literary, historical and philological studies, humanism in northern Europe was particularly associated with scriptural scholarship and was critical and reformist in tone.

Humble Petition and Advice 1657. A petition of parliament, calling on Oliver CROMWELL to assume the crown and restore the ancient constitution. Though rejecting the crown, he accepted a modified version of the petition allowing him to choose his successor and establishing a nominated 'other house' in parliament. The system barely survived his death (1658).

Hume, Joseph *see* PLACE, FRANCIS

George **Hudson**, the 'Railway King': portrait attributed to Richard Doyle, 1845.

Humphrey, duke of Gloucester 1391–1447. The 4th son of Henry IV and 'protector' of England during the minority of his nephew Henry VI, Humphrey quarrelled with Cardinal BEAUFORT concerning his powers (*see* BATS, PARLIAMENT OF) and antagonized England's Burgundian allies. After ARRAS (1435) he urged determined prosecution of the hundred years' war, but was overruled by Suffolk and died under arrest. He was a leading patron of literature.

Hundred From Anglo-Saxon times until the 19th century, English SHIRES were subdivided into hundreds, each consisting in theory of 100 HIDES or households and each having its own court to deal with local affairs and apportion taxes. The number of hundreds per shire varied disproportionately, and in Kent and Sussex they were grouped into larger sub-units called 'lathes' and 'rapes' respectively. In the DANELAW counties of Yorkshire and the northeast midlands the equivalent units were wapentakes (from Old Norse *vapnatak*, the brandishing of weapons to show assent at a meeting). *See* CANTREF.

Hundred years' war 1337–1453. The name, first applied in the 19th century but understood as a concept by the 15th, for the Anglo-French conflict which began in 1337 and continued intermittently until 1453. Its origin was the ancient dispute over the status and boundaries of the large and prosperous duchy of Aquitaine (Gascony) held by the English crown (*see* ANGEVINS; HENRY II) as feudal

vassal of the kings of France. The death of the last Capetian king of France (1328) gave EDWARD III the opportunity to throw off this vassalage by claiming a better right to the French succession (albeit via the female line) than his overlord Philip VI. But it was not until Philip threatened to intervene on behalf of David II in Scotland and (on the pretext of Edward's own interference in the French sphere of Flanders) confiscated and invaded Gascony (May 1337), that the claim was pressed and open war began.

Its 1st phase was inconclusive, for though Edward destroyed the French fleet at Sluys (midsummer day 1340) he was unable to bring their army to battle in Flanders. In 1341, however, a civil war in Brittany enabled him to open a new front, and in 1346 his CHEVAUCHÉE in Normandy (designed to relieve French pressure on Henry of Lancaster in Aquitaine) ended triumphantly at CRÉCY, followed by further English successes at NEVILLE'S CROSS and CALAIS.

The Black Death and other factors inhibited further decisive action 1348–54. But then (Edward III having rejected terms which fell short of the French crown) the war continued with the BLACK PRINCE's successful chevauchées and his great victory at POITIERS (1356). With the capture of King Jean II, France seemed ready to collapse, but Edward's campaign of 1359–60 was inconclusive and he contented himself with the treaty of BRÉTIGNY.

But neither side was really satisfied. In 1369 (capitalizing on unrest in the Black Prince's

King John II of France (centre) surrenders to the Black Prince after the battle of Poitiers, 1356, in the **hundred years' war**. From *St Albans Chronicle*, 15th century.

Aquitaine) the capable Charles V reopened the conflict, refusing pitched battles and fighting a war of attrition which in a decade largely nullified previous English gains. Fighting then gradually petered out (*see* DESPENSER, HENRY) and a 28-year truce was sealed by Richard II's marriage to Isabella, daughter of Charles VI (1396).

The truce held until HENRY V renewed the claim to the French throne and launched the AGINCOURT campaign. In 1417 (assisted by divisions amongst the French nobility and after 1419 by a firm Anglo-BURGUNDIAN alliance) he began the systematic conquest of northern France, crowned by the treaty of TROYES (1420). Despite the setback of BAUGÉ, Anglo-Burgundian successes continued – after Henry's death (1422) under BEDFORD (*see* VERNEUIL, BATTLE OF) – until the victories inspired by JOAN OF ARC in 1429–30 (*see* ORLEANS) began to turn the tide, a process hastened by the Burgundian defection after ARRAS (1435).

Thereafter England, plagued by political dissension (*see* HENRY VI), lost the war in a generation despite the efforts of TALBOT and Richard of YORK. Charles VII reconquered Normandy by 1450 and Aquitaine (after the death of Talbot at CASTILLON) by 1453, leaving only Calais remaining of all the great Plantagenet dominions in France. Individual Englishmen, however, had been considerably enriched by SPOILS OF WAR. The conflict was not formally ended until the treaty of Etaples (1492) but the French expeditions of Edward IV (*see* PICQUIGNY, TREATY OF) and Henry VII were militarily insignificant postscripts.

Hunger marches A tactic devised by Wal Hannington, Communist organizer of the National Unemployed Workers' Movement (1921–39),

A **hunger march** approaching London, 1932. The banners show that the MEANS TEST was a particular grievance.

when bands of selected men from areas of mass unemployment marched to demonstrate in London. Frequently subject to police aggression, they nevertheless gained considerable middle-class sympathy. *See* JARROW CRUSADE.

Hunne affair 1515. The controversy surrounding the murder of Richard Hunne (1514), a London merchant imprisoned by the bishop of London, and the subsequent prevention of the trial of his murderers by the ecclesiastical authorities. It was a landmark in the development of anti-clericalism before the REFORMATION.

Huntly, George Gordon, 6th earl and 1st marquis of 1562–1636. Having assisted James VI's escape from the RUTHVEN raiders, Huntly became a privy councillor (1583). Later suspected of plotting a Catholic revival with Spanish aid, he was forfeited and exiled (1594–6). He entered the reformed church in 1597 and subsequently served as lieutenant and justiciar of the north.

Huntly, George Gordon, 2nd marquis of 1592–1649. A Scottish nobleman, brought up in England, Huntly supported Charles I and resisted the covenanting troops of MONTROSE (1638–9). Taking up arms again in 1644 he did little to assist his former enemy Montrose, and was himself defeated, imprisoned (1646–9) and executed by the COVENANTERS.

Husbandman An occupational and status term of the 16th and 17th centuries. Literally a person engaged in husbandry, or agriculture, the term was generally used to denote a small farmer whose wealth and status ranked below those of a YEOMAN.

Huscarles A highly disciplined company of professional soldiers, generally of Scandinavian origin, which formed the bodyguard of a king or nobleman and the nucleus of his army. Introduced by Cnut, they were maintained from DANEGELD until 1051 and thereafter granted estates, remaining available for instant war service. Equalling THEGNS in rank, they disappeared at the Norman conquest.

Huskisson, William 1770–1830. A Tory reformer, Huskisson was prejudiced against revolution by residence in France (1783–92). MP from 1796, he held various minor offices, then became president of the board of trade (1823–7), where he accelerated the move to FREE TRADE. He split with WELLINGTON soon after, and was killed by a train at the opening of the Liverpool and Manchester Railway.

'Hal being painted' is his wife's description of this picture of Thomas **Huxley** with a native, probably at Rockingham Bay, Queensland, Australia, while he was surgeon on the *Rattlesnake*, 1846–50, the voyage which established his scientific reputation.

Hustings Originally a Norse word for an assembly, it was later used to describe the platforms on which election candidates were nominated – until the BALLOT ACT (1872) – before becoming a synonym for elections.

Huxley, Thomas Henry 1825–95. 'DARWIN's bulldog'. Less original as a scientist, Huxley popularized and fought for Darwin's ideas and became the central figure of scientific politics in Victorian Britain, and the great developer of the scientific complex in South Kensington, London.

Hyde, Dr Douglas *see* GAELIC LEAGUE

Hyndman, Henry Mayers 1842–1921. A Tory Radical journalist educated at Cambridge, Hyndman became a convert to Marxist socialism (1880) and founded the SOCIAL DEMOCRATIC FEDERATION. He moved to the right in later years and became strongly bellicose in World War I.

Hywel Dda d. 950. One of the greatest of Welsh princes, this grandson of Rhodri Mawr became the 1st king of united DEHEUBARTH (920), annexing Gwynedd and Powys (942) and thus ruling all Wales save Morgannwg. He co-operated with Wessex, submitting to Edward the Elder and Aethelstan, and constructively imitated English civilization. Apparently the only Welsh ruler to mint coinage, Hywel the Good's greatest achievement was the collection, amendment and codification of Welsh laws.

Iceni A British tribal group occupying northern East Anglia. At the Roman conquest it became a pro-Roman client kingdom, but Roman annexation on the death of King Prasutagus (61) led to its revolt under BOUDICA. After this was suppressed it formed a CIVITAS whose capital was Venta Icenorum (Caistor-by-Norwich).

Ile de Rhé expedition 1627. An expedition commanded by BUCKINGHAM, involving the landing of 6,000 men on the Ile de Rhé off La Rochelle, in aid of HUGUENOT rebels against King Louis XIII of France. The operation was an unmitigated disaster, the English being forced to evacuate with heavy losses.

Immigration and race relations Migration within Britain as well as religious tolerance, made for the integration of substantial minorities after 1650. Dutch and Flemish merchants and artisans were commonplace, and after 1685 these were joined by HUGUENOT exiles from the persecution of Louis XIV. The union with Scotland (1707) brought increased immigration in its wake, and the Catholic Irish began to come over as seasonal labourers and soldiers. They could still be discriminated against as aliens, but from 1700 the naturalization laws were loosened, at least for aristocrats, and by the time the Naturalization Act was passed (1870), had become among the most liberal in Europe.

As Catholics, the Irish were condemned as immoral and treasonable and, as desperately poor immigrants, they aroused fear of job competition in the areas where their settlement was greatest, chiefly Lancashire (where a third of the Irish-born immigrants lived in 1871) and Scotland. Their absorption was not helped by their fidelity to the Italian papacy – foe to all Liberals – and the FENIAN terrorist campaign of the 1860s. But after 1886 they became absorbed into the British political system, as loyal clients of the Liberals, the HOME RULE party.

In the 1890s alien immigration grew, partly as a result of anti-Semitic pogroms in Russia, partly coming from Baltic countries to the mining areas. Large numbers of Jews (having been granted full emancipation in 1858) settled in London's east end,

Immigration has not only led to conflict: as well as the rioting at the Notting Hill carnival of 1978, different races enjoy the atmosphere in perfect amity.

and built up businesses in the SWEATED TRADES. In the 1880s and 1890s the Conservatives used concern about slums to demand a halt to alien immigration, and passed a stringent Aliens Act (1905). Since this emergency coincided with a revolution in Russia, figures probably would have fallen anyway.

In 1914 there were anti-German riots, whipped up by the sensationalist press, expulsions and internments. After the war only a third of the 52,000 Germans who had played music in the parks and run butchers' shops and restaurants, remained. Enthusiasm for the 119,000 refugees from 'plucky little Belgium' proved temporary.

Between the wars the main influxes were refugees from right-wing tyrannies on the continent – Germans, Austrians, Hungarians and (in lesser numbers, given the less vicious nature of the regime) Italians. Many were of Jewish descent: the number of Jews in Britain rose from 197,000 (1932) to 385,000 (1946), although for many more Britain was only a staging post for America. During the war itself many Poles fled to Britain and stayed, their numbers rising from 30,000 (1931) to 130,000 (1951). The expansion of the Italian population occurred from 1951–61 (20,000–66,000) as a result of immigration to work in factories and brickworks. There was also a large temporary migration from the Baltic states, mainly en route to the United States.

The demand for cheap labour in the 'boom years' of the 1950s and 1960s resulted in increased immigration from the 'new commonwealth'. Service industries such as the London Underground and the hospitals recruited directly from the West Indies, whose inflow by 1961 amounted to a peak of 66,300 per annum. Indian and Pakistani immigration, hitherto slower, rose considerably in 1961 (c. 7,000–50,000 per annum).

By then race had become a political issue, with white rioting against coloured immigrants at Notting Hill (1958) and increasingly strident reactions by Conservative MPs. The Conservatives passed a Commonwealth Immigrants Act (July 1962), cutting entry by nine-tenths, from 86,700 (January–July) to 8,290 (August–December). Labour pledged itself to repeal this, but the power of anti-immigrant politics at the 1964 general election made them change their policy to one of control and integration. They set up a race relations board (1965), and extended its powers in 1967. But a fresh crisis – the expulsion of Indian holders of British passports from east Africa – supervened. Labour passed further controls, such as the British Nationality Act (February 1968) – which restricted the rights of Kenyan Asians with British passports to enter Britain – accompanied by tougher antidiscrimination legislation. This was unpopular among the party's liberals, but the working classes responded to the lurid rhetoric of Enoch Powell prophesying 'rivers of blood' in a notorious speech (20 April 1968). Although this certainly aided the Conservatives in the 1970 election, Powell remained in the wilderness 1970–4, while Edward Heath's government maintained Labour's antidiscrimination legislation. Anti-immigrant politics became more the preserve of the extreme right, and the NATIONAL FRONT in particular. Powell retreated after 1974 to Ulster, where there certainly were rivers of blood; but the only black faces were those of British soldiers.

Impeachment A method of trial in parliament in which the commons acted as prosecutors and the lords as judges. Originating in the later middle ages, the procedure was revived in the early 17th century as a means of attacking ministers of the crown. It was last used in 1805.

Imperial federation A scheme for imperial unity popular among some Liberals, such as FORSTER and BRYCE, in the 1880s, which sought to give the 'white' empire territories representation in London, to reduce tariff barriers and to make the colonies responsible for a proportion of their defence costs. It foundered (1895) chiefly because of the reluctance of the colonies to contribute to the last item.

Imperial preference A scheme advocated by the National government at the Ottawa conference (1932), and more noisily by Beaverbrook (who called it Empire Free Trade), to create a trading group out of the imperial territories. It was never more than a qualified success, as most of the dominions still maintained tariffs against British goods.

Impositions *see* ADDLED PARLIAMENT; BATE'S CASE

Impropriations Parish TITHES appropriated for the upkeep of monastic houses, which passed into the hands of lay rectors after the dissolution of the monasteries (1536–9). The diversion of ecclesiastical revenues in this way left many parish clergymen severely impoverished.

Income tax Imposed first by Pitt (1793) as a war measure, it was abolished in 1815 and revived by Peel in 1842. A graduated, 'progressive' tax, it affected the incomes only of the middle and upper classes until World War I when, after 1915, it brought in the upper working class. Tax levels were lowered in the interwar years, but with Pay As You Earn (PAYE) in World War II, income tax became a phenomenon affecting all classes in society.

Indentured retainers During the later middle ages, persons bound by voluntary indentures or contracts, setting out terms of service and guaranteeing recompense, to the king or another lord (who might in turn be retained by the king or a greater lord). Such indentures were the most important means of raising troops during the hundred years' war and wars of the roses.

Independent Labour party Set up in 1893 at Bradford it included a number of socialist organizations, among them HARDIE's Scottish Labour party and various Labour unions. Only in 1900 did it link with the trade unions, when the Labour Representation Committee was formed; most of the 29 LRC MPs elected (1906) were members of the ILP. The ILP was split on World War I, taking a more critical and radical line than Labour. It was affiliated under the 1918 LABOUR PARTY constitution, and about half the Labour MPs were members. Relations with the Labour leadership deteriorated and in 1932 the ILP disaffiliated, lasting until the 1970s as a small sectarian group based largely on Clydeside but losing its last MPs in the 1940s.

Independents Originally a name for believers in congregational church government, the term was used in civil war politics to describe those parliamentarians who were sympathetic to religious toleration and to the grievances of the NEW MODEL ARMY, many of whom were not CONGREGATIONALISTS in religion.

Indian independence Granted by Attlee government (15 August 1947). *See* BRITISH EMPIRE.

Indian mutiny 1857–8. A rising of Indian forces against the British, triggered by traditionalist discontent at institutional reform, territorial expansion and annexation of native states. It began at Meerut, and was largely confined to the Ganges valley and the Bengal army. Much brutality was shown by the rebels, but by curbing what looked like being equally bloody reprisals, the governor-general, Earl Canning (1812–62), did much to stabilize British rule. The following year the East India Company was abolished.

Industrial depression Mainly used of 2 periods, after 1873, and 1921–39. *See* ECONOMY, THE.

Industrial estates These supplied subsidized accommodation, power and transport facilities for new, usually light industries, initially in southern England, but subsequently in areas of high unemployment, after the 2nd SPECIAL AREAS Act (1937). They were greatly extended by the Attlee government.

'Socialism the hope of the world': a souvenir membership card of the **Independent Labour party** at its coming of age in 1914, designed by Gordon M. Forsyth.

Industrial Revolution The industrialization of Britain in the later 18th and early 19th centuries has been described as the most important watershed in the economic history not only of Britain, but of the world. The 'Industrial Revolution' involved much more than technological innovation and economic expansion. Such phenomena had been known before. It involved a fundamental and irreversible change in the structure of the economy, a deployment of resources away from agriculture into manufacturing and distributive industries and sustained economic growth of an altogether new kind.

Britain's industrialization, unlike that of other countries, was spontaneous and unprecedented. It was also relatively slow, though revolutionary in its cumulative impact. Many factors were involved in the breakthrough of the later 18th century and their precise interrelationship remains a subject of debate. Nevertheless a broad consensus has emerged on the general course of change. Britain in the mid-18th century already possessed a complex society and economy. It was for the most part well-integrated politically, socially stable and relatively prosperous, with cultural values favourable to individual economic enterprise. The highly developed agriculture of the AGRICULTURAL REVOLUTION era and carefully protected trading strength, produced profits and investment capital little affected by taxation. Considerable natural resources, especially of coal and iron, were already being exploited, and a large manufacturing sector had been built up, notably in textiles and metal-working. A sophisticated marketing system with good water transport and developing TURNPIKE roads served the largest free trade area in Europe, while colonial possessions provided both further raw materials and exclusive markets. Advanced commercial and financial institutions existed to facilitate enterprise.

The initial impulse towards industrialization was provided by increased home demand acting within this socio-economic context. In the earlier 18th century a stable POPULATION and cheaper food led to rising real wages and a surplus of income over expenditure in the middle ranks of society. A new demand arose for cheap manufactured goods, aptly described as the 'decencies' of life, neither absolute necessities nor luxuries: soap, glass, metal-ware, domestic utensils and textiles. A slow expansion of manufacturing industry began to meet this market, which, after 1780, was further swelled by foreign demand for British products. By the 1760s, however, the pressure of demand meant that production had reached the ceiling possible within conventional technology. This fact, together with

the stimulus of a shortage of skilled labour, encouraged both the exploitation of existing but under-utilized innovations and new breakthroughs. In industry after industry, inventive men, usually narrowly concerned with particular problems, devised new techniques which were rapidly taken up by entrepreneurs possessed of a keen sense of economic opportunity and organizational talent. The result was the interrelated development of the coal, iron, textile and other industries.

Textiles, and in particular cotton, led the way. One innovation promoted another. After 1733, for example, the invention of Kay's 'flying shuttle' speeded up weaving and created a need for more efficient spinning to supply the looms. In the 1760s Hargreaves's 'spinning jenny', Crompton's 'mule' and ARKWRIGHT's 'water frame' revolutionized spinning. Water-powered machinery led to the factory organization of spinning. Steam power followed, while the new spinning capacity promoted the invention of the power looms which, after 1820, displaced the HAND-LOOM WEAVERS. Both the needs of machine-makers and independent demand for metal goods stimulated the coal and iron industries. Coal, earlier confined largely to domestic heating, was first used for smelting by Darby (1709), but the innovation was exploited largely after 1760. Then in 1784 Cort's 'puddling process' and the rolling mill began the transformation of iron and steel production. Both the coal and iron industries swiftly adopted Boulton and WATT's steam engines after 1775 and concentrated large-scale industry developed, while production soared. Meanwhile factory organization and its associated work-discipline was developed by such entrepreneurs as Arkwright, WEDGWOOD and OWEN to replace the PUTTING-OUT SYSTEM, while the needs of industry and commerce promoted further transport improvements, notably the CANALS.

By 1820 Britain's economic supremacy was well-established but the social cost of industrialization was increasingly apparent. Internal migration to the growing industrial towns created massive urban problems and appalling social conditions among the new industrial proletariat. Squalid living conditions, of course, were nothing new, but the industrial cities bred new horrors and focused attention on them as never before. Surviving pre-industrial practices such as the extensive use of child and FEMALE LABOUR also aroused protest when continued in the new conditions of the mills and mines. Undoubtedly the quality of life for the industrial masses deteriorated, though controversy still rages over trends in the 'standard of living'. During depression periods, such as the 1810s, 1830s

Mule-spinning in a textile factory, 1835. Engraving after a drawing by T. Allom.

The pit-head of a coal mine, with steam-powered winding gear (left) and an 'atmospheric' pumping engine (centre). In the midlands the former were known as 'whimseys'. Anonymous oil painting, c. 1820.

and 1841–3, there was terrible want. On the other hand, a rapidly increasing population was both supported and employed and real wages were often good, though varying much between industries and districts. The worst conditions and crudest exploitation derived above all from the unprecedented nature of the industrialization process and the slowness with which society adapted to change, either spontaneously – through the organization, for example, of FRIENDLY SOCIETIES and the development of TRADE UNIONISM – or through the public action of municipal reform and FACTORY ACTS regulating hours and labour conditions.

Such adaptation occurred mostly in the decades after 1830. By then cumulative innovation had led to the mechanization of more industries and the development of ever larger productive units, though some manufactures, notably the SWEATED TRADES, retained an essentially traditional organization. Distributive, service and TRANSPORT employment also expanded, especially after the advent of the railways facilitated by STEPHENSON's locomotives and the boom in railway building in the 1840s. The railways created a new industry, symptomatic of the trend towards the faster growth of heavy engineering after 1840 which gave heavy industry a more significant place in the national economy alongside the textile and consumer industries which had pioneered industrialization. By 1860 Britain stood pre-eminent as the world's 1st and leading industrial economy, sustaining the world's 1st industrial society, together with all the advantages and problems which these developments entailed.

Influenza epidemic The worst epidemic to date originated in the Near East (1918) and reached Britain in October, affecting three-quarters of the population and killing some 150,000.

Inkermann, battle of *see* CRIMEAN WAR

Innoculation After 1750, innoculation with infected material from smallpox victims became widespread and was of some significance in reducing smallpox mortality. It was superseded after 1798 by Jenner's system of vaccination, which was extremely effective in combating the disease.

Inns of court Institutions of legal education established in the later middle ages and comprising readers, barristers and students. In the 16th and 17th centuries attendance at one of the 4 inns was part of the education of most gentlemen, as well as of professional lawyers. They continue to flourish.

Inquisitions Processes whereby royal commissioners of inquiry, coroners, escheators and other officials obtained sworn information from a jury of local residents on subjects such as the lands and heirs of the deceased (inquisitions post mortem), the property of condemned rebels, the possible results of granting royal privileges, and dilapidations or damage to royal property.

Instrument of Government, the A system of government largely prepared by Lambert in 1653, vesting executive power in Oliver CROMWELL as lord protector and providing for triennial parliaments elected under a reformed system of representation. The Instrument, which owed much to Ireton's HEADS OF THE PROPOSALS, was superseded by the HUMBLE PETITION AND ADVICE (1657).

Interdict A papal decree ordering the clergy to suspend all services (including mass, marriage and burial) save baptism and deathbed confession. England was placed under interdict by Innocent III in 1208, and remained so until 1214, when John accepted LANGTON as archbishop and restored confiscated church property.

'International' The 1st International Working Men's Association was founded by a combination of English trade unionists and continental revolutionaries under MARX (1864). It lasted until 1876, but was effectively moribund in 1872 following a clash between Marx and the ANARCHIST wing led by Michael Bakunin (1814–76). The 2nd 'International' (1889), to which the INDEPENDENT LABOUR PARTY was affiliated, perished in 1914, and the 3rd 'COMMUNIST International' (Comintern) lasted from 1920–43. A 'Socialist International', which includes the LABOUR PARTY, still survives. For the 4th 'International' *see* TROTSKYITES.

Interregnum 1649–60. A term used to describe the period between the execution of Charles I (1649) and the RESTORATION (1660), embracing the various governments of the COMMONWEALTH and PROTECTORATE. *See* CIVIL WARS.

Inverurie, battle of *see* ROBERT BRUCE

Iona A monastery founded *c.* 565 by COLUMBA on an island off Mull, it swiftly became the powerhouse of northern British Christianity (*see* AIDAN, ST; LINDISFARNE). Its wider influence declined after the synod of WHITBY (663), but (despite Viking attacks) it remained the spiritual centre and royal burial place of Scotland until the 11th century.

Ireland, Cromwellian settlement of Following the Cromwellian reconquest (*see* CIVIL WARS), the Act for the Settlement of Ireland (1652) confiscated the estates of landowners of suspect loyalty (who were ordered to remove to Connaught and Clare) and transferred them to the state's creditors. In addition, Catholics were excluded from Irish cities and legislative union with England was established (until 1660).

Ireland, plantation of Following abortive attempts at the settlement of English colonists in Leinster and Munster in the 1570s and 1580s, lands confiscated in Ulster after the FLIGHT OF THE EARLS were systematically colonized from 1608. Land was divided into parishes and granted to 'undertakers' who introduced settlers, partly from England, but principally from Scotland, Presbyterians in search of religious freedom being particularly prominent among them.

Ireton, Henry 1611–51. The commissary-general of the NEW MODEL ARMY in the CIVIL WARS, an able politician and a constructive statesman, Ireton greatly influenced his father-in-law Oliver CROMWELL. After the failure of the HEADS OF THE PROPOSALS, he played a leading role in events preceding Charles I's execution and later succeeded Cromwell as lord deputy of Ireland.

Irish constitutional crisis 1886–1923. Agricultural depression, leading to evictions and the rise of the IRISH LAND LEAGUE and the spirited leadership of Irish MPs by PARNELL, resulted in an increasing preoccupation of parliament with Irish affairs (1880–5). GLADSTONE attempted to settle this and the future of the Liberal party by his HOME RULE policy, but the Liberal split and the period of Conservative dominance (1886–1905), meant that hopes of constitutional change had to be deferred.

Although the Conservative policy of 'killing home rule with kindness' greatly ameliorated Irish social conditions, enhanced peasant land-ownership and improved transport, political nationalism at Westminster persisted. After Parnell's fall and death (1890–1) Catholic nationalism became more idealistic and historicist, with the foundation of the GAELIC LEAGUE, GAELIC ATHLETIC ASSOCIATION and SINN FEIN. Home rule had little chance after the Liberal victory (1906), which made Campbell-Bannerman independent of Irish support. But after the 1910 elections – which were followed by the end of the house of lords' veto – Liberal dependence on the Irish MP's made a 3rd Home Rule Bill inevitable. Introduced in 1912, it became law in 1914. There was furious Conservative and Ulster Unionist opposition, led by Bonar Law and Carson, which by then had gone to the length of the importing of arms and the open drilling of the Ulster Volunteers. There was similar mobilization in the South. Attempts to get the army to intervene in Ulster led to the CURRAGH INCIDENT (March 1914) and by July a civil war in Ireland looked inevitable.

When the European war broke out, both parties in Ireland offered aid to Britain, but only that of Ulster was accepted. Home rule was 'frozen'. Southern volunteers continued to drill, reinforced

The aftermath of the Easter Rising, the climax of the **Irish constitutional crisis**: O'Connell Street, Dublin, 1916, with the ruins of the burnt-out post office which had been the headquarters of the Irish Nationalists.

by CONNOLLY's left-wing citizen army, and at Easter 1916 these rose in revolt in Dublin, expecting assistance from Germany. There was little public support for the Easter Rising, but the execution of the leaders won the Sinn Fein cause considerable sympathy, and the British conceded an Irish Convention (1917). This was abortive, and the British decision to proceed with conscription in the South unified Catholic church and people behind Sinn Fein, which had an overwhelming success in the 'COUPON ELECTION' (1918). The new MPs refused to sit at Westminster, and shortly the apparatus of British rule started to collapse.

The Irish Republican Army, set up in January 1919 under COLLINS and financed by Irish exiles in America, attacked the British administration and the Royal Irish Constabulary. Although it never consisted of more than 3,000 on active service, it killed over 700 police and soldiers, and provoked brutal reprisals by, among others, the BLACK AND TANS. In 1921, faced both with an intensification of the British campaign and increasing weariness within Britain, its leaders negotiated a truce (June) and a treaty setting up the Irish Free State (December). This gave the 26 southern counties dominion status, a constitution which protected Protestant rights and a boundary with the North to be determined by a commission. A large section of Sinn Fein and the IRA under DE VALERA rebelled against this, and there followed a brutal civil war (May 1922–May 1923) in which over 3,000 were killed. Subsequently, however, de Valera accepted

the constitution and, on forming a government (1932), suppressed the IRA. Although his new constitution (1937) was more republican and Catholic in tone, it was in fact the Free State party which led Ireland out of the British commonwealth (1949).

Irish famine *see* POTATO FAMINE

Irish Free State *see* IRISH CONSTITUTIONAL CRISIS; DE VALERA, EAMON

Irish invasions The Irish (or SCOTTI) were raiding Roman Britain by *c*. 260, and by the late 4th century had begun to settle western Scotland, north-west and south-west Wales and perhaps Cornwall. The threat receded with the Christianization of Ireland, and Welsh settlers were contained by Cunedda, but DALRIADA eventually became a dominant power in Scotland. *See* HEROIC AGE.

Irish Land Acts The first, passed by Gladstone (1870), allowed evicted tenants compensation for improvements but gave no protection from increased rents and eviction. Gladstone's 2nd Act (1881) granted 'dual ownership' – fixity of tenure, fair rents (determined by a land court) and free sale. Gladstone accompanied his Home Rule Bill (1886) with a proposal to buy out the Irish landlords, which was rejected. But the Conservative Wyndham Act (1903) made grants of up to £180 million to enable this to be done.

The plight of evicted Irish tenants, barricaded out of their house by their landlord, was brought home by the work of the photographer in the 1880s. The **Irish Land Acts** aimed at resolving the problem.

Irish Land League A militant organization set up by DAVITT (1879) to resist evictions, which linked the anti-landlordism cause with Irish nationalism. Banned by Gladstone's government (1881), it gave way to Parnell's National League.

Irish National party *see* BUTT, ISAAC; PARNELL, CHARLES STEWART

Irish rebellion 1641. Part nationalist and part religious in motivation and directed specifically against the plantation of IRELAND, the rebellion provoked political crisis in England and helped trigger the civil wars. Tales of Irish atrocities in 1641 also account for much of the savagery of the eventual Cromwellian reconquest of Ireland.

Irish Republican Army *see* IRISH CONSTITUTIONAL CRISIS; ULSTER EMERGENCY

Irish Republican Brotherhood *see* COLLINS, MICHAEL; DAVITT, MICHAEL; FENIANS

Iron age *see* PREHISTORIC BRITAIN

Isabella 1298–1358. The daughter of Philip IV of France and wife of Edward II, Isabella played a pacific role in English politics until finally alienated by the DESPENSERS after 1322. In 1325 she retired to France and gathered support, returning with her lover MORTIMER (1326) to depose her husband and rule through Edward III until 1330.

J

Bonnie Prince Charlie, now 'entirely master of the kingdom of Scotland', enters Edinburgh after the **Jacobite** victory at Prestonpans, September 1745. Engraving by Frederick Bacon after Thomas Duncan.

Jacobites The supporters of the claim to the British throne of the deposed JAMES VII AND II and his son James, the 'Old Pretender' (1688–1766). Following the conquest of Ireland (1691), Scotland became the centre of serious Jacobitism. In England many leading politicians kept secretly in touch with the exiled court at St Germain, but this was merely political insurance. Only a minority of diehard TORIES were prepared to promote a Jacobite restoration. There was likewise little true Jacobite support in Presbyterian lowland Scotland, given the Catholicism of the 'king over the water'. But,

among the Episcopalian lairds of the north-east lowlands and the highland chiefs, matters were different. The highlanders in particular remembered their support of James VII at KILLIE-CRANKIE and the treachery of William III's government at GLENCOE.

Numerous Jacobite plots, real and alleged, were uncovered in the 60 years after 1688, the most notable being that of Francis Atterbury, bishop of Rochester (1722), which was exaggerated and exploited by Walpole to smear his political opponents. Only 2 serious risings took place: the '15' and the '45'.

The rebellion of 1715 was aimed at overthrowing the recent Hanoverian succession. The main rising in Scotland, led by MAR and supported by Episcopalians and highlanders, was halted at SHERRIFMUIR in November by ARGYLL. Meanwhile a rising in Northumberland led by Thomas Forster MP and the earl of Derwentwater resulted only in a march to Lancashire and surrender at Preston (November). The Old Pretender landed in Scotland only in December and was forced to withdraw in February 1716. A handful of executions and much forfeiture of estates followed the suppression of the rebellion.

The '45' was a much more dangerous affair. In 1743 the Jacobite highland chiefs agreed to rise on condition that Prince Charles Edward STUART landed in Scotland with 10,000 French troops. Just such an expedition sailed in 1744 under Marshall Saxe, but failed to land. A year later 'Bonnie Prince

Charlie' decided to go it alone, landing on Eriskay in July and subsequently raising his standard at Glenfinnan. Charles Edward's support came mainly from the west and central highlands and the northern lowlands, the island CLANS refusing to join and the northern clans opposing the rebellion. Nevertheless, the prince succeeded in taking Perth and Edinburgh, defeated Cope at PRESTONPANS and entered England, turning back only at Derby in December 1745. Much of Scotland had meanwhile been retaken by the government and despite a victory at Falkirk the prince's army was forced to retreat north to be slaughtered at CULLODEN.

Jacobitism scarcely survived the '45' and the crushing of the clans which followed defeat. The French, whose support had been vital, abandoned the Pretender at the treaty of AIX-LA-CHAPELLE (1748). On his father's death Charles Edward went unrecognized and the Jacobite cause effectively died.

James I king of Scotland (1406–37; b. 1394). Sent abroad by his father Robert III (1406) to save him from the designs of Albany, James was taken at sea by the English. Whilst in captivity he had an opportunity to compare intensively governed England with the lawless state of his own nation. When he finally returned to Scotland (1424) he embarked on social and economic legislation on a massive scale. The totalitarian aspects of his rule, combined with increasing personal acquisitiveness, eventually made him unpopular, and his assassins maintained they had killed a tyrant.

James II king of Scotland (1437–60; b. 1430). The son of James I, he entered politics in 1449 and continued his father's policy of strengthening the monarchy. He thus quarrelled with the powerful DOUGLAS faction, personally assassinating its head (1452) and using heavy cannon to defeat it (1455). Intervening for Henry VI in the wars of the ROSES, he was killed by a misfiring gun at Roxburgh.

James III king of Scotland (1460–88; b. 1452). The son of James II, his marriage to Margaret of Norway (1469) gained Scotland control over the Orkneys and Shetlands. Evidence for his complex reign is sparse, but he seems to have been a cultured man whose currency reform, alleged acquisitiveness and patronage of low-born favourites (including poets, scholars and musicians) became the pretext for his overthrow by an aristocratic faction. Defeated at Sauchieburn (11 June 1488), he was mysteriously murdered.

James II as a young man, showing the birthmark which gave him the nickname 'James of the Fiery Face'. Illumination by Jörg von Ehingen.

James IV king of Scotland (1488–1513; b. 1473). Much the most successful of late medieval Scottish kings, James came to power as the figurehead of the faction which overthrew his father James III, and at first it seemed that he might remain their tool. He soon made it clear, however, that he meant to follow the lead of James I and James II in developing a strong, even an absolutist, 'new monarchy', and by 1492 had firmly established royal supremacy in the lowlands. He then abolished the semi-autonomous lordship of the isles hereditary to the MacDonald chiefs (1493) in an attempt to subject the highlands and islands to the same laws as the rest of the nation. Naval expeditions equipped with cannon put down the resultant unrest by 1506, but royal resources were ultimately inadequate to maintain direct rule in the north and west, and James fell back on establishing 2 powerful clans, the Gordons and the Campbells, as royal lieutenants there.

James's attitude towards England was at first belligerent, and in 1495–7 he actively supported WARBECK. After the repulse of his 'raid of Norham', however, he signed the truce of Ayton (30 September 1497) with Henry VII, which ultimately led to a treaty of 'perpetual peace' sealed by James's

'**James IV** married King Henry VII's daughter' is the inscription under this portrait of James and Margaret Tudor, from a 16th-century armorial.

marriage to Henry's daughter Margaret Tudor (1503). Under Henry VIII, however, Anglo-Scottish relations declined, and in 1512 James (moved by promises of French support for his projected crusade against the Turks) renewed Scotland's traditional alliance with France. When Henry VIII invaded the latter in 1513 (*see* SPURS, BATTLE OF THE), James was persuaded to launch a diversionary attack on England, but was out-manoeuvred by the earl of Surrey and (largely due to his own courageous foolhardiness) defeated and slain at FLODDEN.

James's enthusiasms were multiple, the foremost being law and education: his 'Education Act' (1496) ruled that the heirs of all substantial landowners must be taught Latin and afterwards study law or arts at a university, and his foundation at Aberdeen was the 1st British university with a separate faculty of medicine, another of James's personal interests. He patronized poets, masons, alchemists and craftsmen lavishly, and sponsored the introduction of PRINTING into Scotland (1507), while his determination to make Scotland a force in European politics led him to develop a native gun-founding industry and a navy headed by the *Michael*, the largest ship of her day. An immensely energetic man, James's frequent tours of Scotland, his charities, and his ability to speak Gaelic made him well-known and beloved by most of his subjects, and his reign has been seen as a 'golden age'. (R. L. Mackie, *King James IV of Scotland*, 1958.)

James V king of Scotland (1513–42; b. 1512). After a turbulent minority, James's personal rule was marked by energetic action against disorderly magnates, his search for wealthy foreign brides and the extortion of ecclesiastical revenues. He died broken in spirit by the death of his sons and defeat at SOLWAY MOSS.

James VI and I (b. 1566), king of Scotland (1567–1625), of Great Britain (1603–25). Only child of Mary Queen of Scots and Darnley, the infant James embodied both his parents' claims to the English throne and inherited his mother's Scottish crown upon her forced abdication (1567). As a child he was subject to a strict Protestant education and to the political tutelage of the regents Moray, the earl of Lennox, Mar and Morton. A brief attempt to assert himself in 1580–2 under the influence of Esmé Stewart, duke of LENNOX, was crushed by the raid of RUTHVEN (1582), which was followed by further aristocratic coups d'état up to 1585 when a more stable royal government emerged guided by MAITLAND of Thirlstane.

From 1585 James's policy was guided by Maitland's advice 'neither to cast out with the kirk nor with England' and by his determination to preserve a balance between the ultra-Protestant lords and the conservative earls of north-east

James VI and I: oil painting by Daniel Mytens, 1621.

Scotland. By shrewd and flexible diplomacy and a judicious blend of patronage and firmness, James succeeded in these aims and laid the foundations for the political stability, firm law-enforcement and gradual taming of the kirk which were the hallmarks of his later reign in Scotland. Meanwhile in 1603 he came into his English inheritance.

James's undoubted stature as a great king of Scotland contrasts strangely with his English reputation. His personality as he aged did nothing to endear him to the English: learned but pedantic, shrewd but idle, undignified, foul in language and in person, drunken, cowardly and showing distinct homosexual inclinations in his relationships with his favourites CARR and BUCKINGHAM. All this rendered the court odious, but need not have had more serious consequences had not James's financial irresponsibility, pro-Spanish foreign policy and impolitic assertions of his ROYAL PREROGATIVE led to deteriorating relations with parliament, an institution which he could neither manage nor ignore. The fault lay partly in unresolved problems inherited from Elizabeth I, but still more in James's inexperience of and failure to learn to understand either the peculiar institutions or the prejudices of his new subjects. Yet too much should not be made of this. Many of the difficulties of James's reign gain their resonance only from our knowledge of the later developments of his son Charles I's reign. James did much for Scotland, and if his English reign witnessed some political turbulence, it also saw a peaceful dynastic transition, a union of the British crowns of great consequence and an interval of relative calm under a monarch who was canny enough, if never heroic. *See* ill. p. 191.

James VII and II king of Great Britain (1685–8; b. 1633, d. 1701). James was a soldier and seaman of ability, but an inept politician. The personification of the 'popish threat' after his conversion to Catholicism, he nonetheless survived the EXCLUSION CRISIS and succeeded Charles II, only to be deposed when his efforts to recatholicize England provoked the GLORIOUS REVOLUTION. He died in France.

Jameson raid December 1895. Dr Leander Starr Jameson (1853–1917) of the British South Africa Company, staged an attack on the Transvaal to co-ordinate with a rising by 'uitlanders' – British diamond workers. But the rising did not materialize and Jameson was captured by the Boers. RHODES resigned because of complicity, although Joseph Chamberlain was exonerated. It increased the tensions which led to the 2nd Boer war.

Marchers on the **Jarrow crusade**, playing harmonicas to keep up their spirits. Between Bedford and Luton, 28 October 1936.

Jarrow crusade National Shipbuilders Security, 'rationalizing' the shipbuilding industry, closed down Palmer's yard at Jarrow on Tyneside (1935), throwing two-thirds of the town's workforce on the dole. The town sent a picked squad to march to London (1936) to dramatize the plight of 'the town that was murdered'. The campaign was in fact non-party but, largely through the efforts of the town's MP 'Red Ellen' Wilkinson, Labour took much of the credit for it.

Jeffreys, chief justice *see* BLOODY ASSIZES

Jellicoe, Sir John Rushworth, earl 1859–1935. A gunnery expert who commanded the grand fleet (1914–16), fighting the battle of JUTLAND. As 1st sea lord (1916–18), he became a reluctant convert to the CONVOY SYSTEM.

Jenkins' ear, war of 1739–48. An Anglo-Spanish naval war, occasioned by Spanish harassment of illicit trade with the Spanish colonies and merged eventually with the war of the AUSTRIAN SUCCESSION. Captain Robert Jenkins helped to excite war fever in 1738 by showing parliament his pickled ear – cut off by a Spanish coastguard in 1731.

Jesuits *see* CAMPION, EDMUND; PARSONS, ROBERT; ROMAN CATHOLICISM

The tomb of **John** in Worcester cathedral, made of Purbeck marble, 1225–30.

Jewel, John 1522–71. An exile during the reign of MARY I, Jewel returned on Elizabeth I's accession and was appointed bishop of Salisbury. He defended the Elizabethan religious settlement in his *Apology of the Church of England* (1562) and *Defence of the Apology* (1567). The latter was ordered to be placed in every parish church.

Joan of Arc d. 1431. A French peasant girl, Joan was directed by visions of saints to drive the English from France. She inspired the triumphant ORLEANS campaign and crowned Charles VII at Rheims (18 July 1429) but failed to take Paris. Captured by Burgundians (24 May 1430), she was sold to the English and burnt for witchcraft (20 May 1431).

John king of England (1199–1216; b. 1167). The 4th son of Henry II by Eleanor of Aquitaine, John's reputation as a black-hearted monster (based on the works of unreliable, hostile and non-contemporary chroniclers such as Roger of Wendover) has undergone considerable modification during the present century. Though he undoubtedly had a cruel and petty streak, and combined almost paranoid suspicion of his friends with a ruthless refusal to compromise with opposition, it is now recognized that (along with his father's energy, concern for government and justice and de-termination to uphold royal authority) he inherited the long stored-up resentment of the baronage against the intensive government and financial exactions of his immediate predecessors.

He had also to cope with the implacable hostility of PHILIP AUGUSTUS, who at John's accession supported his rival ARTHUR OF BRITTANY, and who in the 1202–4 war took advantage of the treachery and war-weariness of the Norman barons and of John's own poor leadership to annexe Normandy (1204), which the English magnates proved unwilling to help John recover.

His quarrel with the pope concerning LANGTON led to the INTERDICT (1208) and John's excommunication (1209). But he grew rich with the spoils of the church and remained defiant, only submitting (under threat of papal deposition and French invasion) in 1213, when he bought unqualified papal support by making England a FIEF of Rome. Meanwhile he mounted highly successful expeditions to Scotland (1209), Ireland (1210) and Wales (1211) and used his newly founded navy to destroy the French invasion fleet off Damme (30 May 1213). Attempts to follow up this victory by recovering Normandy, however, were frustrated by the defeat of his German and Flemish allies at Bouvines (27 July 1214) and early in 1215 English baronial unrest came to a head.

Civil war, at first averted by John's signature of MAGNA CARTA, broke out in September 1215. Using his unpopular mercenaries, and supported by William the Marshal, John had virtually defeated the rebels when Philip's son Prince Louis landed to support them (May 1216). Only the resistance of a few royal castles then saved the situation, but in September 1216 John again took the offensive, to die of dysentery at Newark in October, in the words of the Barnwell chronicler, 'a great prince but scarcely a fortunate one'. (W. L. Warren, *King John*, 1978.)

John of Gaunt 1340–99. The 3rd son of Edward III, John succeeded his father-in-law Henry as duke of Lancaster. His achievements in the hundred years' war were unspectacular, and his direction of home government during the last years of Edward III made him unpopular. But his influence on Richard II's policies was always for moderation.

Johnston, Archibald, of Warriston 1611–63. An Edinburgh advocate of extreme religiosity and one of the framers of the national COVENANT. He opposed both the Scottish ENGAGEMENT and recognition of Charles II and subsequently served the Cromwellian regime. Fleeing in 1660, he was captured in France, brought home and hanged.

Johnston, Thomas 1881–1965. Scots socialist journalist and politician whose period as secretary of state for Scotland (1941–5) saw the creation of much of its modern administrative system.

Joint-stock banks Banks in which the public were shareholders had always been allowed in Scotland but were banned in England until 1826, when the 1st ones were set up.

Joint-stock companies Chartered trading and colonizing companies, frequently enjoying MONO-POLIES and particularly active in the later 16th and early 17th centuries. Unlike REGULATED COMPANIES, they were associations of capital, open to any investor, and as such were able to spread the risks of establishing new trades or colonies.

Jointure Property guaranteed by the bridegroom's family in a marriage contract for the maintenance of the bride in her widowhood. The jointure provided a formal alternative to the customary 'dower right' or 'widow's thirds' which gave widows the right to one-third of their deceased husbands' estates.

Jones, Ernest *see* CHARTISM

Jones, Griffith *see* WALES

Jones, Thomas 1870–1955. Welsh socialist, educationalist and economist who became deputy secretary of the cabinet (1916–30), and an important reconciling figure in interwar politics. He was also associated with APPEASEMENT (1930s) and later with the foundation of the ARTS COUNCIL.

Jowett, Benjamin 1817–93. Oxford BROAD CHURCHMAN, classicist and university politician (as tutor and, 1870–93, master of Balliol college) who married the reform of the universities to that of the civil service and greatly influenced the recruitment of new élites to parliament and administration.

Joyce, William *see* LORD HAW-HAW

Judges Royal officers appointed solely to administer the law. The name is specifically applied, by usage, to full-time professional lawyers presiding over higher courts rather than to justices of the peace or ex-officio justices such as sheriffs.

Judicature Acts 1823 and 1824. Measures which conferred limited representative government in the Australian colonies. *See* BRITISH EMPIRE.

Julius Caesar ?102–44 BC. Caesar carried out raids on Britain, partly to discourage British aid for revolts in Roman-occupied Gaul and partly for political prestige. The first (55 BC) was a reconnaissance in force which scarcely gained a foothold before retiring. However, Caesar returned with about 25,000 legionaries and 2,000 cavalry (July 54 BC), and fought his way from Kent to storm the Hertfordshire OPPIDUM of Cassivellaunus, king of the Catuvellauni and leader of the British forces. Then, realizing the strength of the opposition and fearing a rebellion in Gaul, he made a treaty and withdrew, having 'revealed rather than bequeathed Britain to Rome' (Tacitus).

Julius Frontinus Governor of Roman Britain 74–8. In pursuit of Vespasian's forward policy, he achieved the final conquest of Wales (leaving only Anglesey to be taken by Agricola) and established LEGIONARY FORTRESSES at Caerleon and Chester to control it.

Benjamin **Jowett**: caricature by 'Spy', 1876.

Junta (Spanish 'council'). The leaders of skilled trade unionism in London in the 1860s, who led the campaign for repeal of the MASTER AND SERVANT LAWS, and helped to create the trades union congress (1868).

Junto A popular and pejorative name that was given to the group of lords (Orford, Somers, Wharton, Halifax and Sunderland) who led the WHIGS in the reigns of William III and Anne. The junto disintegrated after 1714, leaving a power vacuum in the divided Whig party which was ultimately filled by Walpole.

Jury (Lat. *jurati*, sworn men). An institution of Scandinavian rather than Anglo-Saxon origin, juries were first regularly employed in English law after the Norman conquest. Used first to provide sworn evidence to INQUISITIONS (e.g. for DOMESDAY BOOK) they came to try criminal charges only after the abolition of trial by ordeal (1215). *See* LAW.

Justices of the peace Local landowners, appointed after 1361 to keep the peace and try offenders in the English counties. Their duties were greatly expanded from the 16th century and they became the mainstay of LOCAL GOVERNMENT until the late 19th century. The system was introduced into Scotland by James VI but with very limited success.

Justiciar Under the Norman and Angevin kings, the royal official who headed the legal and financial administration while the monarch was at home, ruling as his viceroy while he was abroad. The office was discontinuously held, and lapsed in England after 1265, surviving longer in Ireland.

Justiciary, high court of The court of the justice-general of Scotland, sitting in Edinburgh. From the 1620s itinerant justices of the court were appointed and in 1672 the court was reorganized under 7 judges, 6 of whom rode 3 circuits annually to determine cases (*see* ASSIZES).

Jutes An Anglo-Saxon race which settled Kent, the Isle of Wight and parts of Hampshire. Their origins are highly controversial: their 1st homeland may have been Jutland in modern Denmark, but the strongly Frankish character of the legal, social and agricultural system of early Kent makes it likely that they came to England from the Rhine delta.

Jutland, battle of 31 May–1 June 1916. The only clash of battle-fleets in WORLD WAR I. Fought off the Danish coast, the battle resulted in severe British casualties, but in the long term it proved decisive, as the German surface fleet never again challenged British superiority in the North Sea.

Katharine of Valois *see* HENRY V; HENRY VII; TROYES, TREATY OF

Kay-Shuttleworth, Sir James 1804–77. A Lancashire man of farming stock, Kay-Shuttleworth studied medicine at Edinburgh, and practised in Manchester, where he fought the 1832 cholera epidemic and exposed the miseries of the cotton-workers. He was permanent secretary to the committee of council on EDUCATION (1839–49), and a pioneer of teacher training, founding his own training college.

Keep The strongest part of a CASTLE, containing the living quarters of its owner. Usually built in the form of a tower, some early keeps stood on mottes, but the largest were always founded at ground level. They are also called donjons or great towers.

Kenilworth, dictum of *see* HENRY III

Kenneth mac Alpin d. *c.* 860. Generally regarded as the founder of Scotland, Kenneth was a descendant of Aedan mac Gabhran. He became king of DALRIADA *c.* 841 (probably succeeding his father) and king of PICTS by *c.* 850 (perhaps through matrilinear descent and certainly after civil war). He then united the two in the kingdom of ALBA.

Kent The earliest and most civilized Anglo-Saxon kingdom, established *c.* 470 by HENGEST's lieutenant Oisc. Mainly populated by JUTES, it had strong connections with the Frankish Rhineland. Under Aethelbert, its 1st Christian king, it dominated southern England, but from *c.* 750 it became tributary to Mercia and in 825 was annexed to Wessex, though retaining distinctive customs.

Kenyan emergency *see* MAU MAU

Kett's rebellion 1549. A rising of the peasantry of Norfolk, caused by widespread agrarian grievances and led by Robert Kett. After besieging and taking Norwich, the rebels were bloodily suppressed at Dussindale by foreign mercenary troops, and Kett was executed. This was the last major peasant rebellion in English history.

Keynes, John Maynard, lord 1883–1946. A Cambridge economist and Bloomsbury group intellectual whose dissent from the punitive terms of the treaty of VERSAILLES (1919) won him notoriety. Between the wars he was the chief theorist of a planned, mixed economy, with his *General Theory of Employment, Interest and Money* (1936). His promotion to the treasury (June 1940) instituted a revolution in government control of the economy. Before his early death, he also played a critical role in setting up the world bank.

Khaki election 1900. The election was won by Salisbury's Conservative government on the patriotic tide unleashed by the 2nd Boer war in which the army fought in khaki uniforms.

Khartoum, fall of *see* GORDON, CHARLES GEORGE

Killiecrankie, battle of 27 July 1689. The rout of government troops in the pass of Killiecrankie by an army of highland JACOBITES led by 'Bonnie DUNDEE'. Dundee was killed in the battle and the highland army was subsequently held at Dunkeld by the Cameronian regiment.

Killing Times, the 1684–5. A period of severe repression of the COVENANTERS during which some 78 persons were summarily executed for refusing to abjure the bloodthirsty APOLOGETICAL DECLARATION. Other Covenanters were also executed after trial.

King, Gregory 1648–1712. King was an early pioneer of the collection of social and economic statistics, his most famous work being his *Natural and Political Observations upon the State and Condition of England*, which was unpublished in his lifetime.

King's bench, court of *see* LAW

King's Book *see* REFORMATION

Kingsley, Charles *see* CHRISTIAN SOCIALISTS

Kinsale, siege of 1601–2. Following the landing of over 4,000 Spanish troops at Kinsale (September 1601), the town was besieged by the English under MOUNTJOY. His defeat of a relieving force of Irish

rebels led by TYRONE (24 December) obliged the Spaniards to surrender in January 1602.

Kinship *see* CLANS; FAMILY

Kipling, Rudyard 1865–1936. The 'Laureate of Empire' was born in India and came to England and almost instant success as a satirical poet and short-story writer. He became a strong supporter both of imperial expansion and of Anglo-American co-operation (1890s), and later of the ENTENTE CORDIALE with France, although his hatred of liberalism made him a partisan figure in politics, both in the Boer war and the Ulster crisis.

Kirk o' Field *see* DARNLEY, LORD

Kirk sessions Parish committees of the CHURCH OF SCOTLAND, consisting of minister, elders and deacons, which exercised moral discipline over the laity. First established in the 1560s, they were strongest in the later 16th and the 17th centuries, before being weakened by the withdrawal of state-backing for excommunication (1690). Until 1845 they were responsible for poor relief, and until 1872 for education.

Rudyard **Kipling** as a war correspondent: an important agent of allied propaganda, especially to America, he is here photographed on a visit to the front line in August 1915. A few days later, his only son, aged 18, was killed.

'Your country needs you': **Kitchener**'s message on a World War I recruiting poster, by Alfred Leete, 1914.

Kitchener, Horatio Herbert, earl 1850–1916. A hero of the Sudan (*see* OMDURMAN, BATTLE OF) in 1896–8, and the 2nd Boer war (1899–1902), Kitchener was summoned in August 1914 as 'nonparty' war secretary. He was little more than 'a magnificent poster' (Arnold Bennett) and his death at sea (June 1916) was more of a relief than a loss to the government. *See* ARMY; WORLD WAR I.

Knights (Old English *cniht*, a retainer). In the feudal period, technically those holding land in return for personally serving in war as armoured and mounted soldiers. Knighthood soon became a distinct rank, to which men (generally of gentle birth) were admitted with elaborate ceremonial after serving an apprenticeship. After the Restoration (1660) the title became purely honorific. *See* DISTRAINT OF KNIGHTHOOD; ESQUIRE; TITLES.

Knights hospitallers *see* HOSPITALLERS, KNIGHTS

Knights of the shire From 1254, and regularly from *c.* 1325, each English SHIRE save the counties palatine of Chester and Durham sent 2 representatives to PARLIAMENT. Nominally chosen by the county court, these were not always KNIGHTS proper, but were generally substantial men with administrative experience. In the 15th century they were frequently also royal or aristocratic retainers. They had no medieval Scottish equivalent.

Knights templars *see* TEMPLARS, KNIGHTS

Knox, John ?1512–72. A fiery preacher, captured after the siege of St Andrews castle (1547), Knox spent 2 years in French galleys. He then preached in England before exile in Frankfurt and Geneva during MARY I's reign. Returning to Scotland (1559) he greatly influenced the Scottish REFORMATION despite renewed exile in 1565–8.

Kruger, Stephanus Johannes Paulus *see* BOER WARS

Knights in combat: miniatures from a military roll, *Sir Thomas Holme's Book, c.* 1443.

John **Knox** and Christopher Goodman blowing trumpets against 'the monstrous regiment of women'. Underneath are the words, 'No queene in her kingdome can or ought to sit fast.' From *An Oration against the unlawfull Insurrections . . .* , Peter Frarinus, Antwerp, 1566.

Labour aristocracy

A term used to describe workers in the skilled trades *c.* 1850–1900 – engineers, carpenters, printers – who restricted entry through APPRENTICESHIP and employed 'new model' TRADE UNIONISM to secure their position at the top of the working class.

Labour party

By resolution of the 1899 trades union congress the Labour Representation Committee was formed, linking together unions, the INDEPENDENT LABOUR PARTY and the socialist societies in a body whose one fundamental objective was to get labour men into parliament. In 1901, 3 LRC MPs were elected. Ramsay MACDONALD, secretary of the LRC, in 1903 negotiated a secret pact with the Liberal whips to give the LRC's candidates a straight run against the Tories. As a result 29 candidates were elected in 1906, and in parliament decided to call themselves the Labour party. One other trade union MP (elected as a Liberal) joined them, bringing the 1st parliamentary Labour party total to 30.

In 1909 the party was strengthened by the adherence of the Miners' Federation of Great Britain, hitherto a stronghold of 'Lib-Lab' politics; but it made no further electoral progress until after World War I. The extended franchise of 1918, growing trade union membership, the greater wartime role of the state, and the involvement of Labour politicians in government, prepared Labour to take advantage of the wartime decline of the Liberals, and in 1918 Sidney WEBB and HENDERSON created a new constitution which provided for individual membership but retained the ILP, as an autonomous party, within a federal Labour structure. Although Labour gained only 57 seats in 1918, it increased this to 142 in 1922, while the Liberals remained divided. MacDonald, its leader since 1922, was permitted by the other parties to form a minority government after the 1923 election. Although unremarkable save for John Wheatley's Housing Act and some conciliatory gestures in foreign policy, it proved decisive in making Labour the natural alternative to the Conservatives. However, the immaturity of its political ideology – a combination of orthodox Liberal attitudes in finance and foreign affairs with a moralistic

The formation of the first **Labour** government, 1923: Ramsay MacDonald and Arthur Henderson in the 'lum hats' against which some supporters protested, J. H. Thomas more self-consciously proletarian in his bowler, outside Buckingham palace.

commitment to a vague 'socialism' – proved disastrous when a further minority Labour government (1929–31) had to cope with the onset of world depression. Divided in its attitude to cuts in welfare benefits, it lost its most important leaders – MacDonald, SNOWDEN and J. H. Thomas (1874–1949) – to the NATIONAL GOVERNMENT, and was crushed in the election, its MPs falling in number from 288 to 52, of whom five disaffiliated with the ILP in 1932.

Recovery at the 1935 election was only partial, to 154 seats, and under its new leader, ATTLEE, the party was much more subject to union control. But its participation in the wartime coalition, its espousal of wartime reconstruction and welfare programmes (such as the BEVERIDGE report), and the support given by sympathetic economists, civil servants and publicists – coupled with the discredit of mainstream Conservatism and the rather isolated role in the Conservative party of Winston Churchill himself – helped build up the momentum for victory in 1945, when it gained 394 seats against the Conservatives' 213. The Attlee government of 1945–51 set up the national health service, nationalized railways, coal and steel, aviation, gas, electricity and the bank of England, but was handicapped by continuing shortages of food and raw materials, and the austerity consequent on diverting resources to the export drive. Nevertheless, in 1951, although losing the election, Labour gained its highest ever vote (13·9 million).

After another electoral defeat in 1955, Attlee was succeeded by GAITSKELL, who proved no more successful in 1959. He tried to move Labour to a more pragmatic, reformist position and caused a major split with the party's more ideological left, first grouped around BEVAN, then around the CAMPAIGN FOR NUCLEAR DISARMAMENT. By the time of Gaitskell's death in 1963 this split had been healed. His successor Harold Wilson, harnessing the party to a somewhat apolitical platform of technological development and economic planning, narrowly won the 1964 election, and was confirmed in power by the 1966 election with a majority of 96. However, this government was frustrated by an adverse economic situation which prompted a return to orthodox finance, and marked by failure in foreign affairs, over the COMMON MARKET, RHODESIA and the absence of any dissent from America's policy in Vietnam. It may well be most remembered for its liberalizing legislation in such spheres as equal rights and censorship.

The Conservatives under Edward Heath returned to power in 1970, but the election held in February 1974 enabled Labour to regain a precarious hold on office, confirmed in the 2nd 1974 election (October). In 1976 James Callaghan replaced Wilson as prime minister. Of the 15 years 1964–79 (when the Conservatives under Margaret Thatcher were returned) Labour ruled for almost 12. Despite an unimpressive record and increasingly adverse economic circumstances, it appeared to have established itself as a natural governing party. Yet after 1979 there was new evidence of a deterioration in membership and funds and of disagreement on future strategy.

Labourers, statute of 1351. Passed to stabilize the economic situation after the Black Death, this earliest English attempt at wage- and price-fixing legislation froze the wages of labourers and the price of manufactured goods at pre-plague levels, and severely restricted the movement of labour. A contributory cause of the peasant's revolt (1381), it was ultimately a failure.

Lambert, John 1619–84. The ablest of Oliver Cromwell's generals, Lambert achieved political prominence as author of the INSTRUMENT OF GOVERNMENT. Dismissed in 1657, he regained his commands at the fall of the protectorate (1658) and attempted unsuccessfully to oppose the Restoration. Condemned to death in 1662, he was imprisoned for life.

Lamberton, William d. 1328. Foremost (with WISHART) of the many ecclesiastics who supported the patriotic cause during the SCOTTISH WARS OF INDEPENDENCE, Lamberton was appointed bishop of St Andrews by WALLACE (1297), acted as chief

guardian (1299–1300) and supported Robert Bruce's coup d'état (1306).

Lancaster, duchy of A group of estates, including the COUNTY PALATINE of Lancaster, founded on the APPANAGE assembled by Henry III for his younger son Edmund, created earl of Lancaster in 1267. By the time the last duke ascended the throne, as Henry IV, the duchy had property in almost every English county as well as extensive lands in south Wales. Much reduced during the 17th century, the duchy lands remain the personal property of the crown and are separately administered as such. Today, the chancellor of the duchy of Lancaster is, in effect, a minister without portfolio.

Lancaster, Henry, duke of 1310–61. Henry of Grosmont, one of the greatest captains of the early HUNDRED YEARS' WAR, served his cousin Edward III successively as lieutenant in Aquitaine (1344–50), Flanders (1348), Poitou (1349–50) and Brittany (1355–8). Created duke of Lancaster in 1351, he wrote the unusual devotional treatise, *Le Livre des Seyntz Medicines*.

Lancaster, house of see ROSES, WARS OF THE

Lancaster, Thomas, earl of c. 1277–1322. The cousin and most powerful opponent of Edward II, whose undying hatred he incurred by murdering GAVESTON. A rigid upholder of the ORDINANCES, Lancaster virtually ruled England 1314–16, but thereafter (though still formidable) became increasingly isolated. He allied with the MARCHERS against Edward and the DESPENSERS (1321–2), but was defeated at BOROUGHBRIDGE and executed.

Land tax The principal direct tax of the 18th century. It generally stood at 4 shillings in the pound on rental income (valued in 1693) during wartime, less in time of peace, though inaccurate and outdated assessment reduced its real weight.

Lanfranc c. 1005–89. Prior of the famous Norman abbey of Bec (1045–66), this lawyer, famous scholar and devout monk became in 1070 probably the most influential English archbishop between Augustine and Cranmer. He worked closely with William the Conqueror for the post-Norman conquest reorganization of the English church.

Langton, Stephen d. 1228. A scholar and cardinal appointed archbishop of Canterbury (1206) by Pope Innocent III after a disputed election, his rejection by John led to the INTERDICT. Accepted in 1213, he headed the moderate party which produced MAGNA CARTA, and after 1216 used his immense influence in support of HENRY III.

Lansbury, George 1859–1940. A pacifist Labour MP, Lansbury resigned (1912) to fight, and lose, as a SUFFRAGETTE supporter. Imprisoned as the leader of POPLARISM (1921), he was a minister in the government of 1929–31 and survived the Labour collapse (1931) to become leader of the party, until ousted by the trade unions in favour of Attlee (1935). As an Irish MP said, Lansbury 'let his bleeding heart run away with his bloody head'.

Largs, battle of 2 October 1263. ALEXANDER III's army, in a confused seashore battle, drove off a landing party from King Haakon's Norwegian invasion fleet, which then withdrew to Orkney, where Haakon died. In July 1266 his successor Magnus IV ceded the Western Isles to Scotland in return for a modest annual subsidy.

Larkin, Jim 1876–1947. An Irish labour leader, Larkin was the founder, with CONNOLLY, of the Irish Transport and General Workers Union, and its leader in the DUBLIN TRAMWAYS STRIKE (1913). He shared Connolly's nationalism, but not his martyrdom, as he spent World War I in America.

Laski, Professor Harold 1893–1950. A Manchester-born Jewish political scientist, Laski lectured in the USA (1914–20), becoming noted as a left-wing liberal. After his return to the London School of Economics he moved to a Marxist position. In the 1930s he became a dominant figure in the LEFT BOOK CLUB and the Labour party, and after the 1945 election a bogey-man both to the Conservatives and to the Attlee government.

Lathes *see* HUNDRED

Latimer, Hugh ?1485–1555. Converted to Lutheranism in 1524, Latimer became England's leading Protestant preacher. Bishop of Worcester in 1535–9, he resigned and kept silent during Henry VIII's last years, but under Edward VI returned to the passionate preaching of Christian social morality. Arrested on MARY I's accession, he was burned in Oxford.

Latitudinarians A term used to describe the tolerant and undogmatic ecclesiastics of the church of England in the reigns of William III and Anne, exemplified by BURNET, bishop of Salisbury.

Laud, William 1573–1645. After an early career hampered by his extreme ARMINIAN opinions, Laud achieved power in church and state under CHARLES I. His policy of High Church uniformity and support for arbitrary measures did much to discredit Charles's government. Impeached and imprisoned by the Long parliament, he was later tried and executed.

Lanfranc, successively prior of Bec, abbot of Caen, and archbishop of Canterbury, from his *Book of the Body and Blood of Christ*.

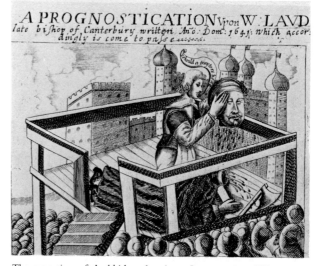

The execution of Archbishop **Laud**, 10 January 1645. This engraving from a broadsheet of 1645 is accompanied by hostile and prophetic verses, written in 1641, that conclude: 'Like a blest martyre you will dye / for churches good she riseth high / when such as you fall down.'

Laudabiliter, bull of *c.* 1155. Granted by the English pope Adrian IV (and probably promoted by Archbishop Theobald of Canterbury), this PAPAL BULL encouraged Henry II to conquer Ireland, reform the irregular practices of the church there and subject it to Canterbury. Henry's Irish intervention (1171), however, was prompted by STRONGBOW's activities and few reforms occurred.

Lauderdale, John Maitland, 2nd earl and 1st duke of 1616–82. Formerly a leading COVENANTER, Lauderdale became a loyal supporter of Charles II after 1649 and was imprisoned 1651–60. As secretary of state for Scotland (1661–80), he was responsible for severe repression of the covenanters and for the management of the Scottish parliament by corruption. In 1680 he retired to England.

Law The United Kingdom embraces 2 major systems of law, that of England, which obtains also in Wales and Northern Ireland, and that of Scotland. The Channel Islands and the Isle of Man retain distinct local legal systems.

English law developed from a fusion of Saxon and Norman legal customs and the innovations of the Plantagenet kings. The law codes of the early Saxon kings were essentially compilations of custom and of WERGILD payments. Attempts by later Saxon monarchs to restrain self-help and the blood feud and to establish the king's peace led in the 10th and 11th centuries to the emergence of royal SHIRE courts (*see* COUNTY COURTS), held by SHERIFFS acting on royal writs, and borough courts, alongside the customary courts of the HUNDREDS. The introduction of the TITHING system further placed responsibility for peace-keeping on local communities. All this was inherited by the Norman kings, who added the system of sworn jury INQUISITIONS, TRIAL BY BATTLE and feudal courts baron, while carefully confirming the existing laws of England.

Henry II greatly extended the judicial system. He expanded the sphere of royal justice and established regular provincial visitations by royal justices – the basis of the later ASSIZES. Grand juries of present-ment provided a public method of criminal prosecution to supplement private 'appeals'. Views of FRANKPLEDGE, held by sheriffs, or by feudal lords under franchise, consolidated and improved the petty policing functions of the tithing. Coroners were introduced to investigate sudden deaths, while the appointment of sergeants as peace officers for the hundreds initiated the office of chief constable. The expansion of the number of writs available for purchase by freemen provided a wider range of legal remedies in civil cases, which were increasingly tried by JURY rather than by combat.

The work of Henry and his successors established the supremacy of royal justice and the 'common law' (i.e. royal law common to the whole kingdom and based upon writs and judicial precedent). 13th-century developments consolidated this achievement. In 1215 trial by jury was established in criminal cases by the abolition of TRIAL BY ORDEAL. Courts settled in Westminster emerged from the peripatetic royal court. Judges devised new writs and a legal profession of pleaders and attorneys emerged, the most notable figure being Henry of Bracton, whose *On the Laws and Customs of England* (1250–6; pub. 1569) marked the 1st attempt to systematize the common law.

Further innovation came in the reign of EDWARD I, the 'English Justinian'. By now COMMON PLEAS, king's bench and EXCHEQUER OF PLEAS had emerged as distinct courts with increasingly specialized jurisdictions. Under Edward, yearbooks began to appear as works of reference and legal education. More fundamentally, Edward's numerous statutes both complemented and regulated the common law, arresting the growth of unenacted law and initiating the process whereby it became established that the law might be changed only with the consent of PARLIAMENT.

From the 14th to the 17th centuries common law became increasingly rigidified. Jurisdictions and procedures were well-established. The legal pro-fession acquired an educational system in the INNS OF COURT. Judge-made law was slowly swamped by statute law, increasingly so after 1530. JUSTICES OF THE PEACE were appointed to improve the policing and administration of the shires, their courts of QUARTER SESSIONS and PETTY SESSIONS gradually superseding the view of frankpledge. The major development of this period, however, was the emergence of courts of equity to supplement the common law with the dictates of natural justice in cases where it provided no remedy. Equity originated in judicial decisions of the royal council, with the equity courts of CHANCERY, STAR CHAMBER and REQUESTS only slowly acquiring their separate identities and special written procedure.

The early 17th century saw the common law employed by its champion COKE and other lawyers as legitimating ideology in the resistance of parliament to the policies of the early Stuart kings. Parliament's victory in 1641 brought the demise of Star Chamber and Requests, together with the ecclesiastical court of HIGH COMMISSION. In the course of the interregnum, however, demands for radical reform of the common law itself multiplied, though they achieved little success. The essentially medieval system survived intact into the 18th century and beyond. The complacency of the law in this period was enshrined in Sir William Blackstone's *Commentaries on the Laws of England* (1765) and, though the 18th century saw the gradual adjustment of the law to the needs of commerce, the adoption of English as the language of the courts (1731), developments in trial procedure and the encroachment of precedent upon conscience as the guiding principle of equity, there was no fundamental change in judicial administration.

By 1800 the demand for adaptation of the law to the needs of a modern industrial society was reaching a crescendo, the proponents of change including BENTHAM, BROUGHAM, MILL and James Fitzjames Stephen. Piecemeal change was achieved after 1832 by judicial decision, commissions of inquiry and statute. The creation of POLICE forces, reform of procedure and of punishments, removal of probate and matrimonial suits from the jurisdiction of the ECCLESIASTICAL COURTS, introduction of authoritative law reporting and rationalization of legal administration, prepared the way for the Judicature Act (1873). By this measure a supreme court of judicature was erected, divided into the high court of justice and the court of appeal. The high court fused common law and equity and was internally divided into the 3 divisions of queen's bench, chancery and the division of probate, divorce and admiralty. This fundamental recasting of the court system remains the basis of the modern judicial system, further modified by the abolition of assizes (1971) and the erection of crown courts.

Scottish law prior to the wars of independence followed a course of development similar to and partly influenced by that of England. Royal courts were held by sheriffs, burgh courts served the towns and BARON COURTS were held by feudal lords, while procedure in the royal courts was initiated by writ or 'brieve'. From the 14th century, however, Scots law was increasingly influenced by Roman law, with its characteristic deduction of law from abstract principles of justice, as distinct from the evolution of law from precedent which characterized English common law. As a result law and equity were never distinguishable in Scotland. The 'brieve' and jury system was gradually restricted to local courts in Scotland, while the central courts of royal justiciars, the lords auditors of causes and complaints and the lords of council and session developed a law in which remedies were deduced from rights rather than the reverse as in England. In 1532 the lords of council and session were reorganized as a college of justice with wide civil

'Term Time, or the Lawyers all alive in Westminster Hall': this cartoon of 1797 quotes Macklin's view that 'the **Law** is a sort of hocus-pocus service, that smiles in your face while it picks your pocket'.

jurisdiction, its 15 senators presiding over the court of SESSION. As the Faculty of Advocates and Society of Writers to the Signet evolved they were granted membership of the college, with exclusive rights to act as pleaders and solicitors. Criminal justice was further advanced by James VI's appointment of justices of the peace, though their activities were restricted until the later 18th century by the competition of other local courts. James also initiated the changes which led ultimately to the establishment of the high court of JUSTICIARY (1672) with its itinerant justices.

By the later 17th century the Scottish legal system had fully emerged and the task of systematizing Scots law into a coherent system was successfully undertaken by Viscount STAIR, an achievement consolidated by such 18th-century jurists as John Erskine, George Bell and Hume. Meanwhile the abolition of HERITABLE JURISDICTIONS (1747) and the decline of baron courts confirmed the pre-eminence of the SHERIFF COURTS in local judicial administration, supplemented by the courts of justices of the peace and burghs until their work was taken over by district courts in 1975. In the years 1808–30 a thorough reform of the court of session gave this institution its modern form, while the 20th century has added the court of criminal appeal (1926) to the Scottish legal system. Scots law retains some of its distinctive traits, though in the last century judicial precedent has become stronger in influence. As in England and Wales the place of statute law has also been vastly expanded.

In the 20th century the tide of legal reform in Britain has receded. Among recent changes the most notable are perhaps the introduction of legal aid (1949) and the abolition of CAPITAL PUNISHMENT (1965). Despite its peculiarities and anachronisms, the law remains fundamental to the defence of the liberties of the subject in Britain. Contemporary criticisms of its innate conservatism, its expense, of the deficiencies of the jury system and of the judiciary itself, derive largely from concern to improve the law's effectiveness in that role.

Law, Andrew Bonar 1858–1923. As a result of tied support for the 2 other candidates, Walter Long and Austen Chamberlain, Bonar Law became leader of the Conservative party in 1911. A bitter and extreme opponent of Asquith's government, his support of the Ulster Unionists aggravated the IRISH CONSTITUTIONAL CRISIS to near civil war in 1914, but in the following year he became a member of the Asquith and Lloyd George coalition governments. He became prime minister after the fall of Lloyd George (1922), but cancer forced him to resign in mid-1923, and he died shortly afterwards.

Law, John 1671–1729. A brilliant and dissipated Scottish gambler and pamphleteer on economic questions, Law succeeded in 1716 in persuading the regent of France to establish a bank of France and to back his 'Mississippi scheme' of trade and colonization. He fled when his system collapsed in 1720.

Lawrence, T. E. 1888–1935. The organizer of the Arab revolt against the Turks after December 1916, Lawrence destroyed enemy lines of communication, particularly the Hedjaz railway, and captured Damascus (October 1918). Thereafter he considered that the Arabs had been betrayed by the peace treaties and attempted to lose his identity as 'Lawrence of Arabia' by enlisting as an aircraftman in the RAF. He was killed in a motor-cycle accident in Dorset.

League of Augsburg, war of the 1688–97. A war between France and the allied powers of the league of Augsburg (1686), provoked by Louis XIV's declaration of war on Holland and invasion of the Palatinate and ended by the inconclusive peace of

Ryswick. Britain became involved in 1689 when the GLORIOUS REVOLUTION became linked to the European conflict. *See* STEINKIRK, BATTLE OF.

League of Nations Set up in 1920 in terms of the treaty of VERSAILLES (1919) to replace 'secret diplomacy' with 'open covenants openly arrived at', it was weakened from the start by America's failure to ratify the treaty, and was largely dominated by Britain and France, who were granted 'mandates' over former German imperial territories. The League was at its strongest during Germany's adhesion (1926–33), did useful work on frontiers and refugees, and set up the International Labour Organization. But it lacked the power to maintain its own armed forces and its 'sanctions' were ineffective against Japan in Manchuria and Italy in ABYSSINIA. Dissolved in 1946, it was replaced by the UNITED NATIONS.

Leasehold Though known since medieval times, leasehold became the predominant form of land tenure in England only in the later 16th and the 17th centuries when it replaced COPYHOLD. Initially involving leases for a stated number of lives, the lease for a period of years was the norm by 1650.

T. E. **Lawrence** (right) and Nesib el Bakri, a companion on his expedition, photographed in Akaba in 1918·by the journalist Lowell Thomas. It was Thomas who began the popularization of Lawrence in London with a series of lectures, illustrated with pictures such as this.

Ledger book *see* CARTULARY

Left Book Club Set up in 1935 by the publisher Victor Gollancz, LASKI and the Marxist theoretician John Strachey, the club offered cheap editions of left-wing tracts on contemporary affairs to a membership of 50,000 by 1937. These were mainly written from a COMMUNIST PARTY standpoint and, although an aspect of POPULAR FRONT activity in the 1930s, were highly propagandist in tone. Independent left-wingers such as Orwell had little encouragement.

Legate *see* LEGION

Legate, papal The personal representative and plenipotentiary of the pope, either a native prelate with special powers or a cardinal sent from Rome.

Legionary fortresses Permanent bases of Roman LEGIONS, covering *c*. 50 acres and containing barracks, officers' houses, headquarters, baths, hospitals and usually an amphitheatre. The 1st-century fortresses of COLCHESTER, LINCOLN, WROXETER, Gloucester and Inchtuthil, near Perth, were built in earth and timber, but CAERLEON, CHESTER and YORK, occupied longer, were subsequently reconstructed in stone. *See* FORTS, ROMAN.

Legions The senior units of the Roman army, consisting of *c*. 5000 heavy infantry commanded by a legate, assisted by 6 tribunes. They were divided into 10 cohorts, the first made up of 5 double centuries (160 men each) and the remainder of 6 ordinary centuries (*c*. 80 men each). *See* AUXILIARIES.

Leicester *see* CORITANI; MUNICIPIA

Leicester, Robert Dudley, earl of 1533–88. The handsome son of the duke of NORTHUMBERLAND, Leicester early captured the heart of Elizabeth I. Though her political prudence made their marriage impossible, he remained a leading (though never dominant) councillor, and despite his vanity, arrogance and incompetence as commander in the Netherlands (1585–7), retained her devotion, as she did his.

Leighton, Robert 1611–84. An opponent of extreme Presbyterianism and supporter of the Scottish ENGAGEMENT, Leighton became principal of Edinburgh university (1653). In 1661 he reluctantly accepted the bishopric of Dunblane and worked unsuccessfully to promote understanding between Episcopalians and COVENANTERS. He resigned in 1674 and retired to England.

Lennox, Esmé Stewart, 1st duke of 1542–83. A close kinsman of JAMES VI, brought up in France, Lennox returned to Scotland in 1579 and rapidly achieved great influence over the young king. Disliked and suspected by the kirk and rival nobles, he lost power after the raid of RUTHVEN and returned to France (1582).

Lennox, Matthew Stewart, 4th earl of 1516–71. An unsuccessful rival of ARRAN for the governorship of Scotland, Lennox was an exile in England (1546–64). There he married the daughter of Angus and Queen Margaret Tudor and fathered Darnley. He later held the regency of James VI briefly before his death in a skirmish at Stirling.

Leslie, Alexander, 1st earl of Leven ?1580–1661. The illegitimate son of the captain of Blair Atholl, Leslie served with distinction in the Dutch and Swedish armies. He led the Scottish invasion of England in the BISHOPS' WARS and subsequently commanded the Scottish contingent at MARSTON MOOR in the CIVIL WARS. Though opposed to the Scottish ENGAGEMENT, he supported Charles II in 1650–1.

The inscribed funerary stele of Favonius Facilis, centurion of the XXth **Legion**, from Colchester. He holds the vine staff marking his rank. 2nd century.

Leslie, David d. 1682. Of noble Scottish family, Leslie served in the Swedish army before returning to command the convenanting army in the CIVIL WARS and against MONTROSE. Opposed to the Scottish ENGAGEMENT, he later fought against Oliver Cromwell at DUNBAR and WORCESTER. Imprisoned 1651–9, he was created Lord Newark at the Restoration.

Letters, medieval collections of Though earlier manuals of letter-writing are known, comparatively few British personal letters (as opposed to official correspondence) survive from before the early 15th century, by which time most were being written in English. After that date several collections of family correspondence survive to throw valuable light on social, domestic and political affairs. Among them are the Paston letters (1422–1509), relating to a rising Norfolk family much plagued by neighbouring magnates; the Stonor letters (mostly late 15th century), to an Oxfordshire gentry family concerned with the wool trade; the Cely papers (1475–88), to merchants of the STAPLE of Calais with land in Essex; and the Plumpton correspondence (mainly late 15th-early 16th century), to a Yorkshire gentry family of Percy retainers.

Levellers INTERREGNUM radicals, led by LILBURNE, William Walwyn and Richard Overton, who opposed arbitrary government and advocated a broader franchise, legal reforms, religious toleration and the abolition of TITHES. They found strong support in the army (1647–9), notably at the PUTNEY DEBATES, but their influence faded thereafter.

Levellers' rising 1724. A protest movement in Dumfriesshire and Galloway against the eviction of small tenants and the enclosure of fields and commons for pasture. Organized bands of countrymen levelled enclosure dykes and maimed cattle. The movement was partly successful in slowing the pace of agrarian change in Galloway.

Lewes, battle of 14 May 1264. HENRY III and his son Edward attacked Simon de Montfort's smaller force of reformist barons and Londoners positioned on the downs above Lewes. Though Edward routed the Londoners, the royalists were utterly defeated, the king, Edward and most of the loyal magnates being taken.

Libelle of English Polycye c. 1436–7. An anonymous and chauvinistic 'little book' (libellus) composed after the congress of ARRAS. It advocated the establishment of a strong navy for the blockade of Flanders, the protection and expansion of trade and the absolute control of the Channel. Henry VI's council, to whom it was addressed, failed to act on its advice.

Liberal imperialism Liberals such as Rosebery, Asquith and Haldane approved of social reform and imperial expansion in the 1890s, and of the Boer war. They formed the Liberal League (1902), but threats of a split ended with the unifying of the party in opposition to TARIFF REFORM.

Liberal party Although individual MPs had called themselves Liberals before, the title 'Liberal party' replaced WHIG and 'Radical' in the years 1859–68. Local associations were formed, newspapers were set up and, at the centre, the leadership – especially GLADSTONE, RUSSELL, BRIGHT and the party's ideologue MILL – began to think in party rather than sectional terms. This leadership effectively chose the issue – disestablishment of the church of Ireland – on which the 1868 election was fought and won.

The Gladstone ministry (1868–74) lost its impetus after 1870, and the Nonconformist interest felt itself betrayed by Forster's EDUCATION Act (1870). Joseph CHAMBERLAIN organized this interest initially as the National Education League, and after Gladstone fell and temporarily retired from politics (1875), transformed this into the National Liberal Federation, which united the local associations or caucuses (see CAUCUS POLITICS). In 1877 Gladstone (still not leader) recognized the NLF but was averse to putting forward the sort of 'party programme' it wanted, believing that any programme, especially one cooked up by Nonconformists, cou^ld prove fatally divisive, and that 'great moral issues' were more likely to unite the party and give the leadership freedom of manoeuvre.

In 1885–6, Gladstone (prime minister again since 1880) was challenged by Chamberlain, who wooed the new working-class electorate with his UN-AUTHORIZED PROGRAMME. The Whigs, already disadvantaged by the BALLOT ACT (1872) and by the 3rd REFORM BILL (1884), moved towards alliance with the Conservatives. In the event, they took Chamberlain with them as Gladstone used Irish home rule to isolate Chamberlain and re-establish his own authority. The 1886 election, badly managed by the party, produced an anti-Gladstonian majority larger than it need have been, and confirmed the withdrawal of the Whigs and the city. The party actually recovered rapidly up to 1892, but the leadership crisis that followed

OBSCURING THE ISSUE

MR CHAMBERLAIN PROPOSES TO TAX YOUR FOOD.

BALFOUR & CHAMBERLAIN ARE LINKED TOGETHER AGAINST FREE TRADE.

TEN YEARS OF TORY RULE WHAT IT HAS COST US!

ARTHUR: "We must cover up these horrid Liberal bills, or we are lost!"

DON'T BE DECEIVED BY TORY TRICKS BUT VOTE LIBERAL

Free Trade was one of the main and most successful planks of the **Liberal party**'s 1906 election platform. 'Arthur' is A. J. Balfour, the Conservative leader.

Gladstone's departure, and the failure of ROSEBERY to liaise with his deputy HARCOURT in the commons cost it office (1895).

Thereafter policy and leadership were confused. Some of the followers of Rosebery, such as HALDANE, supported measures of social and educational reform, and were prepared to co-operate with Conservatives on grounds of promoting 'national efficiency'. The radical wing of the party varied from devoted adherents of laissez-faire to socialists. However, after the trough of the KHAKI ELECTION (1900), there were signs of regional revival, of policies more suited to a working-class electorate, and of the influence of middle-class theorists sympathetic to the Labour movement and state intervention. Debate among historians still continues as to whether it was this NEW LIBERALISM, or the old rallying-cry of FREE TRADE, that was the more influential in bringing about the 1906 landslide victory, although there is evidence that after that date the support for Liberalism was changing. Hitherto it had largely been regional and sectarian – dependent on Nonconformists and on Wales, Scotland and the east of England – but from 1906–10 it became much more class-based, partly as

a result of the trade union and social reform legislation of the ASQUITH government.

The party rapidly went into eclipse after 1914 largely because of its failure to sustain unity during the war, especially after LLOYD GEORGE's capture of the premiership (December 1916). After the COUPON ELECTION (1918), its parliamentary representation dropped from 272 (December 1910) to 161 (1918) and 40 (1924). After that there was some recovery, with Lloyd George's programme of Keynesian economic reform and public works (1929), before a final collapse (1931), after which the Liberals had only 33 MPs, split into 3 small groups. By the time party unity was secured (1945), there were only 12.

Until 1956 the Liberals remained a small, rather right-wing party, holding some of its seats by arrangement with the Conservatives, but during the leadership of Jo Grimond (b. 1913) it moved to the left of centre and in 1958 began the first of several revivals, in March 1962 gaining the Conservative stronghold of Orpington. Subsequently it did well in opinion polls, but neither under Grimond nor under his successors Jeremy Thorpe (b. 1929) and David Steel (b. 1938) was it able to convert this into seats. Ironically much of this support was forfeited by its support of the pact (1976–8) which sustained the Labour government of James Callaghan in office.

Liberal Unionist party Formed by those Liberals who opposed the 1st HOME RULE Bill (1886), it consisted mainly of WHIGS led by HARTINGTON, but with a radical wing led by Joseph CHAMBERLAIN. At first the party formed a loose coalition with Salisbury's Conservatives, but after 1891 Chamberlain moved it closer to Conservative policy. It was bitterly split by TARIFF REFORM after 1903.

Liberation Society Set up in 1852, mainly by CONGREGATIONALISTS, this Nonconformist body pressed for the repeal of disabilities such as the TEST ACT and the disestablishment of the church of England.

Licensing Acts An Act was passed by the Balfour government (1904) to limit the number of pubs, and offended Nonconformists by compensating landlords whose licences were not renewed by the new licensing courts. A more stringent law, which allowed 'veto' polls or local prohibition, was passed in 1913 for Scotland and Sunday closing was enforced in Wales after 1881. Restricted opening times were introduced during World War I. In the 1970s many of these restrictions were relaxed.

Sentenced in Star Chamber for helping to distribute seditious pamphlets against the bishops, John **Lilburne** was tied to a cart and whipped through the streets in 1638. From a Dutch propagandist attack on Archbishop Laud, published 1645.

Lilburne, John 1615–57. A Durham man, apprenticed in London, Lilburne was imprisoned (1638) for smuggling Puritan books. Released by the Long parliament, he served in the CIVIL WARS before emerging as a leader of the LEVELLERS. A passionate writer against all arbitrary government, 'Freeborn John' was twice acquitted of treason and frequently imprisoned.

Limerick, treaty of 1691. The treaty ending resistance to the GLORIOUS REVOLUTION in Ireland. James VII and II's Irish troops were allowed to withdraw to France. Roman Catholics were guaranteed their privileges as in Charles II's reign, subject to parliamentary confirmation, but this implied promise of religious toleration was betrayed by the subsequent passage of the PENAL CODE.

Limitanei *see* COMITATENSES

Limited Liability Acts 1855 and 1862. These Acts made shareholders liable for the debts of their companies only to the limit of their shareholding, which proved a vital stimulus to the widening of share-ownership and the accumulation of capital.

Lincoln Established *c.* 90 as a COLONIA at an abandoned LEGIONARY FORTRESS (occupied *c.* 61–*c.* 77), 'Lindum' became capital of Constantius's province of Flavia Caesariensis. Successively thereafter capital of Anglian LINDISSE and one of the Danish FIVE BOROUGHS, under the Normans it

became the site of an important castle and (*c.* 1086) the seat of a huge DIOCESE. *See* ill. p. 95.

Lincoln, battle of 2 February 1141. STEPHEN, besieging Lincoln castle, was defeated and captured by a relief force of MATILDA's supporters under Robert of Gloucester and Ranulf, earl of Chester. Matilda's autocratic behaviour, however, destroyed her chances of being crowned in Stephen's stead.

Lincoln, rout of 20 May 1217. The baronial rebels and part of Prince LOUIS's forces, besieging the castle held for HENRY III, were caught in the cathedral square between a sally by the garrison (under Falkes de Breauté) and a relieving army under William the Marshal, and completely routed.

Lindemann, Frederick A., Lord Cherwell 1886–1957. A German-born scientist who became professor of chemistry at Oxford. A member of Winston Churchill's entourage, Lindemann pressed for more scientific defence research in the early 1930s but was not a success as a member of TIZARD's committee. On Churchill's rise to power he replaced Tizard as chief scientific adviser and had a major role in the adoption of the policy of 'saturation bombing'.

Lindisfarne A tidal island off Northumbria, where a monastery and bishopric were established (634) by AIDAN's monks from IONA as a centre for the re-evangelization of northern England. Its prestige was

Lindisfarne: the 12th-century priory church, with Holy Island in the distance.

enhanced by CUTHBERT, but it was sacked by Vikings (793) and abandoned from 875 until refounded by BENEDICTINES (1082).

Lindisse The kingdom of the ANGLES occupying north Lincolnshire and south Humberside, it was possibly settled with British agreement in the late 5th century. Subsequently disputed between Northumbria and Mercia, it was finally annexed to the latter in 678. It was colonized by Danish Vikings in the late 9th century.

Little Englanders A term for those politicians, usually radicals of the MANCHESTER SCHOOL such as BRIGHT, who rejected foreign intervention and imperial expansion.

Liverpool, Robert Banks Jenkinson, 2nd earl of 1770–1828. A sensitive and nervous man of deeply conservative views, Liverpool became prime minister in 1812 and held office until 1827. His administration was marred by the depression and reactionary policies of the years immediately after the Napoleonic wars, but made tentative moves towards reform in the 1820s.

Livery The 'liberatio' or annual fee, often accompanied by a coat of distinctive colour and a badge, granted by a patron to his INDENTURED RETAINERS. Their indiscriminate grant was (with MAINTENANCE) a principal abuse of 'bastard FEUDALISM' and kings from Richard II to Henry VII attempted to restrict the classes who could give or receive them.

Livingstone, David 1813–73. A Scots factory boy who worked his way through medical school to become an African missionary. In a series of journeys, Livingstone both opened up central Africa to colonial rule and helped to suppress the slave trade. In 1865 he disappeared for 5 years and his rediscovery by Henry Morton Stanley (1871) was a major journalistic coup.

Lloyd George, David, earl 1863–1945. Brought up in north Wales, Lloyd George had his early politics moulded by the hatred a Welsh-speaking Nonconformist peasantry felt for its English and Anglican landlords. Elected MP for Carnarvon Boroughs (1890), he took his seat as a Welsh nationalist and radical, although on the Liberal benches. From there he championed the Boers and led the opposition to the EDUCATION Act (1902), urging that it be disobeyed in Wales. But by 1905 these earlier nationalistic enthusiasms were beginning to evaporate.

David **Lloyd George**: oil painting by W. Orpen, 1927.

President of the board of trade under Campbell-Bannerman (1905), Lloyd George then became chancellor of the exchequer in succession to Asquith (1908). His ingrained antipathy to the house of lords culminated after their rejection of his PEOPLE'S BUDGET (1909). But although extreme in public, he was anxious to gain constitutional agreements, even at the price of coalition. His warning to Germany at the time of the AGADIR INCIDENT (1911) established him as more a man of the centre, although he was weakened by his involvement in the MARCONI SCANDAL (1913).

When war broke out, he headed a 'peace party' in the cabinet until Germany invaded Belgium. Thereafter he took increasing responsibility for war material and, following the MUNITIONS CRISIS (1915), was appointed minister of munitions in Asquith's coalition. He used successive DEFENCE OF THE REALM ACTS to create an apparatus of state control which ranged from factories through housing, welfare facilities and liquor licensing. Under him munitions output (in tons of shells consumed on the front) climbed from 7,000 a quarter (1914) to 327,700 in the 3rd quarter of 1916 (the battle of the Somme). He succeeded Kitchener as war minister (although Ireland after the 1916 Easter Rising took up much of his time) but his dissatisfaction with Asquith increased and, with the backing of Bonar Law and Beaverbrook (December 1916), he demanded a 5-man war cabinet from which Asquith would be excluded. Having secured Asquith's resignation, he became prime minister. Asquith and his followers did not form an opposition but their detestation of Lloyd George was indelible.

Lloyd George's war cabinet consisted of himself, Bonar Law, Milner, Curzon and Henderson. Each could switch responsibilities as emergencies arose. Lloyd George had always distrusted the generals' concentration on the western front, and had backed 'sideshows' such as GALLIPOLI. He was forced to back Haig's 1917 offensives (see WORLD WAR I), but compelled JELLICOE to accept the convoying of merchantmen (February 1917). Later that year he succeeded, with the other allied leaders, Georges Clemenceau (1841–1929) and Woodrow Wilson (1856–1924), in creating, under Marshal Foch, a unified allied command.

Tentative negotiations for peace ended after March 1918, when Russia's removal from the allied side led to Germany's last offensive (March–July 1918). After the armistice Lloyd George shifted towards stricter terms, campaigning (in the COUPON ELECTION) on a platform of 'squeezing Germany till the pips squeak', to pay for post-war reconstruction. At VERSAILLES he proved much more conciliatory, although he had to compromise with Clemenceau's hard line and with Wilson, patently out of his depth in European politics.

He then had to tackle the Irish problem, which successive chief secretaries had exacerbated by reprisals and the use of the BLACK AND TANS. Early in 1921 he managed to get the Irish Republican Army to the conference table and in June secured the compromise which set up the Free State (see IRISH CONSTITUTIONAL CRISIS).

However, Lloyd George's deviousness, his 'betrayal' of the Liberal party, his selling of honours and his complicated private life combined to decrease confidence in him among his by now largely Conservative followers, and following the CHANAK CRISIS (1922) he was dumped.

The rest of his life was anticlimax. Innovative economic policies, culled mainly from his old opponent KEYNES, gave a reunited Liberal party new strength (1929), but illness prevented him intervening in the 1931 crisis, his party broke up again, and his talents went unused until his death.

Llywelyn ap Gruffydd d. 1282. The grandson of Llywelyn the Great, he became ruler of GWYNEDD in 1255, and soon recovered the lands lost to the English since his grandfather's death, declaring himself prince of all Wales in 1258. He then exploited the civil wars of Henry III and Simon de Montfort to expand still further, gaining English recognition of his title and conquests by the treaty of Montgomery (1267) and thus attaining greater

power than any Welsh prince since the Norman conquest. His policy of national centralization nevertheless offended the minor native rulers and, when his antagonization of Edward I (notably by his refusal to do homage and his betrothal to Montfort's daughter) resulted in a major English invasion (1277), his hegemony swiftly collapsed, leaving him only a reduced Gwynedd. Unwillingly drawn into a new war by his brother David (1282), 'Llywelyn the Last' was killed in a skirmish, and the final and complete English conquest of Wales followed.

Llywelyn the Great 1173–1240. The grandson of Owain Gwynedd, Llywelyn ap Iorwerth became ruler of all north Wales c. 1200. Initially friendly with John, whose illegitimate daughter he married (1205), he later sided with the barons and Prince Louis, taking advantage of the English civil wars to annex land from the MARCHERS and dominate all Wales by 1216. His conquests were recognized by the treaty of Worcester (1218) with Henry III, and subsequent English campaigns against him were largely failures. A considerable power in British politics, he strove against native opposition to establish a united Welsh principality on feudal lines and to secure dynastic monarchy by introducing PRIMOGENITURE, policies continued by Llywelyn ap Gruffydd.

Local government In the middle ages local government was essentially 'self-government at the king's command'. The officers of the SHIRES, HUNDREDS and boroughs (see MAYOR), and lords of the MANOR enjoyed considerable delegated powers, while individuals were granted 'franchises' which ranged from semi-regal powers to the right to hold views of FRANKPLEDGE in MANOR COURTS. The situation was more extreme in Scotland, where territorial magnates, although more obedient under James VI, enjoyed massive powers which they retained until the abolition of HERITABLE JURISDICTIONS (1747).

The 16th century saw the extension of more direct royal control in England and Wales. The COUNCIL OF THE NORTH and COUNCIL IN THE MARCHES OF WALES were established, Wales was divided into shires and territorial franchises were absorbed. The office of SHERIFF, much abused in the 15th century, declined in significance, and LORDS-LIEUTENANT were appointed. Above all, the responsibilities of the JUSTICES OF THE PEACE were multiplied and numerous statutes augmented the administrative role of the PARISH. By 1603 QUARTER SESSIONS had emerged as the fulcrum of local government, run by the JPs who were steadily harried by the privy COUNCIL into efficient performance of their duties. As trade prospered certain chartered towns had corporations and then, with industrial growth, a 4th form of local government emerged in the *ad hoc* urban commissioners for police, paving or water.

The great reforms of the 1830s (*see* REFORM BILLS) tried to deal with this patchy, often corrupt, mixture. In Scotland, where the self-elected, debt-ridden burgh councils were simply machinery to elect government MPs, reform came early, in 1833. The 1835 Municipal Reform Act for England officially extended the vote to all ratepayers. (The Irish reform of 1840 reflected English attitudes by winding up 58 corporations, transferring their powers to the 'reliable' county grand juries, and gravely restricting the powers of those corporations which still retained a representative element.)

In England *ad hoc* bodies were still often regarded as quite adequate and the POOR LAW AMENDMENT ACT (1834) had set up a potential rival in the unions of parishes set up to run the new workhouses. CHADWICK hoped to make these the basic units of future local government organization, but when local boards of health were set up under the Public Health Act (1848) their powers in urban areas were usually vested in the corporations. By 1858 anti-centralists had got rid of Chadwick's general board of health, but virtually all of the great towns had started taking over the *ad hoc* bodies and begun the schemes which were to be christened 'GAS AND WATER SOCIALISM' and were often to provide precedents for parliamentary 'permissive' legislation. In 1868 the municipal franchise was extended, and local politics shifted away from keeping the rates down to programmes such as those of Joseph CHAMBERLAIN. His use of municipal socialism and CAUCUS POLITICS captured a leading position for Birmingham, although other councils, such as Glasgow with its 'improvement trust' (1865), were even more advanced.

After 1870 powers were to be concentrated in fewer and fewer bodies. This process was first undertaken in the central supervisory area by GOSCHEN, in Gladstone's 1868–74 government. He amalgamated the POOR LAW board, the local government section of the home office, and Sir John SIMON's medical office of the privy council, to form the local government board in 1871 (amalgamated into the ministry of health in 1919). Disraeli's government consolidated local government Acts in 1875, but Goschen's associated plans, for representative county government, were not finally carried until 1888.

The County Councils Act (1888) created 50 county authorities in the rural areas, and 61 county boroughs (finally bringing to an end the political role of the JPs). By an Act of 1894, urban and rural district councils and the old parish vestries were reorganized as parish councils, but devolution to provincial or regional councils, suggested by Chamberlain in his UNAUTHORIZED PROGRAMME (1885), was shelved.

The balance of power of the various authorities subsequently changed. The county authorities gained education by the 1902 Act, but the Poor Law boards of guardians lasted until the BEVERIDGE reforms after World War II. Much of their power in fact passed to central government, as did local authority hospitals and gas and electric undertakings. In Scotland the school boards survived until 1918, and parish councils (introduced in 1894) were in 1929 replaced by the 31 county councils (1889), 4 counties of cities and 20 large burghs. Ireland gained a comprehensive settlement of elective county and district councils, with 6 county and 5 corporate boroughs. This arrangement lasted until 1971 in Ulster, and still continues today in Eire.

After World War II attempts at systematic organization were few. Labour attempted to sort out authorities with a boundary commission (1947–9) but failed utterly. Four more commissions set up in the 1950s succeeded only in imposing a new structure on London. But Harold Wilson's government (1964–70) appointed a commission to revise local authority organization and created a new central authority, the department of the environment. The Maud commission recommended (1969) a 3-tier system of regional councils, metropolitan and county authorities and local councils, but the 1972 Act of Edward Heath's ministry restored an intermediate tier of district councils, with housing, recreational and limited planning powers. What remained of local responsibility for health and police was transferred to nominated regional authorities. Transport in certain of the conurbations was handled by joint passenger transport authorities. In Scotland another Conservative Act (1973) created 9 large regions, 51 districts, and general purpose authorities for the Orkneys, Shetlands and Western Isles.

Public interest in local politics did not, however, recover, and national party fortunes influenced local politics unduly. Above all, the regional issue remained unsettled, after the report of the Crowther (later Kilbrandon) commission in November 1973, recommending devolution to national assemblies in Scotland and Wales, and frustration of this policy in 1979. *See* LONDON.

London's riverside: (above) looking from Southwark across to the north bank with London bridge on the right, from a 17th-century view by Visscher; (below) the National theatre (1967–76) by Denys Lasdun, on the south bank.

Locarno pacts 1925. A series of treaties negotiated and guaranteed by Britain which readmitted Germany as a European nation, guaranteeing the inviolability of her frontiers and extending international arbitration. They lapsed with Hitler's reoccupation of the Rhineland (March 1936).

Lollards (Dutch 'mumblers'). A name applied to heretics loosely basing their beliefs on WYCLIFFE's teaching but lacking a common corpus of opinion. Though most denied transubstantiation, they were generally more concerned with the temporal corruption of the church than with theological questions. Initial support from sections of the gentry and urban middle class was withdrawn after OLDCASTLE's rising (1414) had inextricably linked religious dissent with treason, and Lollardy was thereafter a lost cause, though scattered groups survived until the Reformation.

London London has always owed its importance and prosperity to trade. Originating as a Roman stores depot during the invasion of 43, it was ideally placed for continental traffic and soon developed into a thriving port, already the seat of the PROCURATOR when Boudica destroyed it (61). By c. 100 rebuilt 'Londinium' was both the provincial capital and much the largest city of ROMAN BRITAIN. Its immediate post-Roman history is obscure, but by c. 600 it was a populous Saxon trading town, and long before the Norman conquest it was again clearly pre-eminent, with a complex system of self-government administered by aldermen.

During the middle ages Londoners frequently played a crucial role in national politics, and monarchs wooed them, Henry I granting them the choice of SHERIFF and John the election of their MAYOR. The 13th century saw the rise of craft GUILDS, and in the 14th century there were repeated efforts by the lesser citizens to broaden the base of civic government, eventually defeated by the aldermanic oligarchy of rich merchants. Edward III's stabilization of royal administration at Westminster made London a true capital. Recruiting its population from all over the country, it was the only British medieval town comparable to the great European cities.

London's history 1500–1800 is one of massive growth and steady consolidation of its medieval pre-eminence. The population of the city and suburbs grew from around 40,000 in 1500 to 300,000 in 1700 and 900,000 in 1800, despite a death rate so high that constant immigration was necessary merely to sustain numbers. As the metropolis expanded it became increasingly polarized between the poor and overcrowded eastern parishes with their acute social problems and attendant disorders, and the elegant suburbs of the west, inhabited by merchants and professional people and the GENTRY who kept town houses for the season. By 1750 a tenth of the national population lived in London, while a still greater proportion had experience of life there, either as temporary inhabitants or as visitors for political, legal, business or social purposes.

London's domination was economic and cultural as well as demographic. From the 16th century the largest part of England's trade was directed from and passed through London. Feeding the growing population also required a steady extension of the London food market which helped to integrate the regional economies of England. London was also, as it has remained to the present, the centre of political, religious, literary and educational life, disseminating news (see NEWSPAPERS), fashions and ideas to the nation at large.

The special problems of governing so large a city (3·3 million in 1881) was recognized in the establishment of the London county council (1889). By 1960 London's population was 8·1 million, and in 1965 the LCC was superseded by the Greater London Council.

London, treaty of 1839. Negotiated by PALMER-STON, the treaty guaranteed the neutrality of Belgium, independent from Holland since 1830. It was Germany's violation of this (August 1914)) that gave Britain her *casus belli*, and so precipitated WORLD WAR I.

London clubs These originated as COFFEE HOUSES for politicians, officers and lawyers in the Westminster area in the late 18th century. After about 1815 they were systematically developed to provide lodgings, newsrooms and dining facilities, mainly for gentry unable or unwilling to keep up a town house. Built in Italianate styles, they tended to perpetuate 'in town' the relationships of occupation, university and party.

London Corresponding Society A radical society of independent craftsmen, similar to the Society of FRIENDS OF THE PEOPLE, it was founded to support parliamentary and social reform (1792). Books and pamphlets were lent to members and correspondence was established with provincial societies. The secretary, Thomas Hardy, was tried for treason (1794) and acquitted. The society was suppressed in 1799.

The lord mayor beginning the extension of the inner circle of the **London Underground**: *Illustrated London News*, 17 September 1881.

London Underground The 1st 'underground' railway in London was the sub-surface, steam-operated, Metropolitan line between Paddington and Kings Cross, opened in 1867. Other such lines were built, and electrified in the 1900s. In 1890 the first 'tube' electric line was opened between Monument and Stockwell. Extended systems of both types remained in private hands until nationalized (along with buses and trams) by the 2nd Labour government as the London passenger transport board (1933). Thereafter the LPTB established a remarkable record for efficiency, profitability and good design.

Long parliament 1640–60. The parliament which won constitutional reforms (including the 1st TRIENNIAL ACT) from CHARLES I and subsequently defended them in the CIVIL WARS. Reduced to the Rump at PRIDE'S PURGE, it was recalled in 1660, only to dissolve itself after ordering the issue of writs for the election of a free parliament.

Longchamp, William *see* RICHARD I

Lord Haw-Haw William Joyce (1906–46), an American-born fascist who emigrated to Germany (1939), was executed (through the technicality of having illegally taken out a British passport in 1938) for having acted as the 'star' of German propaganda broadcasts to Britain – although his most famous exploits were largely mythical.

Lords, house of *see* PARLIAMENT

Lords auditors of causes and complaints *see* LAW

Lords of council and session *see* LAW

Lords-lieutenant Local magnates commissioned to administer and command the militia of specified English districts. Occasionally used under Henry VIII, the system of appointing lords-lieutenant became regularized after 1550 and subsequently they and their county deputies accumulated additional tasks of LOCAL GOVERNMENT. The lord-lieutenant remains a leading county dignitary.

Lose-coat field, battle of 12 March 1470. Failing to control Edward IV after BANBURY (1469), WARWICK THE KINGMAKER and George, duke of CLARENCE, exploited a Lincolnshire feud to foment a rising. Led by Sir Robert Welles, the rebels were marching to join Warwick when Edward intercepted them at Empingham, Leics., routing them so quickly that they discarded their coats in flight.

Lothian A name which was originally applied to all the lands between the Tweed and the Forth. Occupied by the Votadini in Roman times, it subsequently formed part of Manau Gododdin, and was overrun by Anglian Northumbria in the 7th century. Edgar ceded it (*c.* 970) to Scotland, which permanently secured its possession at CARHAM (1081).

Loudoun, John Campbell, 1st earl of 1598–1663. A leading promoter and defender of the national COVENANT (1638–40), Loudoun was lord chancellor of Scotland 1641–50. After negotiating with Charles I (1646–7), he opposed the Scottish ENGAGEMENT, but later supported Charles II and withdrew to the highlands after DUNBAR. At the Restoration he was nonetheless fined and deprived of office.

Loudoun Hill, battle of *see* ROBERT BRUCE

Louis, Prince The son of Philip Augustus, Louis was offered the English crown by the rebels against JOHN, landed in May 1216, and was initially successful. Failing to take Dover, however, he was defeated at LINCOLN and SANDWICH, and by the treaty of Kingston-on-Thames (12 September 1217) abandoned his claim. He subsequently became Louis VIII of France (1223–6).

Lovett, William *see* CHARTISM

Lowe, Robert, Viscount Sherbrooke 1811–92. A radical Utilitarian administrator (*see* UTILITARIANISM) in Australia and Britain, where he was responsible for EDUCATION (1859–64), setting up royal commissions on elementary and secondary education and public schools, and introducing payment by results. After brief fame as leader of the ADULLAMITES, the Liberal opponents of the 2nd Reform Bill (1866–7), Lowe became chancellor of the exchequer in Gladstone's government (1868–74).

Luddites Bands of workers who resisted the mechanization of the depressed Nottinghamshire knitting industry in 1811 by smashing machinery, supposedly under the leadership of 'General Ludd'. Further outbreaks in Lancashire and Yorkshire (1812) were directed against power looms and shearing machines. 'Luddism' was suppressed after severe emergency legislation and several executions.

Ludlow, rout of 12–13 October 1459. Threatened by MARGARET OF ANJOU, YORK and WARWICK THE KINGMAKER mustered their supporters at Ludlow, where they were joined by a NEVILLE force which had fought off a Lancastrian attack at Blore Heath (23 September). When the main Lancastrian army appeared, however, their men deserted, and York fled to Ireland, Warwick to Calais.

Lugi A northern Scottish tribe which inhabited eastern Sutherland at the time of Roman Britain.

Macaulay, Thomas Babington, lord 1800–59. From an Evangelical background, Macaulay was a Whig MP from 1830. Although from 1834–8 engaged in Indian reform, his main work was his *History of England* (1848–55), the greatest of 'Whig histories'.

Macbeth king of Scotland (1040–57). MORMAER of Moray and grandson of Malcolm II, the historical Macbeth killed his cousin Duncan I in battle, made a pilgrimage to Rome, and was eventually defeated and killed by Malcolm Canmore, not at Dunsinane but near Lumphanan, Aberdeenshire.

MacDonald, Alexander 1821–81. A Lanarkshire miner, MacDonald worked his way through Glasgow university to become a lawyer and miners' trade union leader and the 1st working man to sit in parliament, as Liberal MP for Stafford (1874).

MacDonald, James Ramsay 1866–1937. From its foundation in 1900 MacDonald was secretary of the Labour Representation Committee and then the LABOUR PARTY (as the LRC became in 1906) until 1911 and, in effect, party leader until 1914. He opposed the war and lost his seat (1918). First ever Labour premier (1924) and again in 1929–31, his formation of the NATIONAL GOVERNMENT (August 1931) was traumatic for Labour, but scarcely 'treachery'.

Macleod, Ian 1913–70. Conservative minister of health (1952–5) and minister of labour (1955–9), Macleod became colonial secretary (1959–61) and, with Harold Macmillan's backing, accelerated decolonization (*see* BRITISH EMPIRE). He resigned rather than serve under Sir Alec Douglas-Home, but became Edward Heath's chancellor of the exchequer in 1970. He died only a month later.

Maes Howe near Kirkwall, Orkney. The finest MEGALITHIC CHAMBERED TOMB in Britain, it dates from *c.* 2000 BC and consists of a beehive-shaped burial chamber and entrance passage, expertly

Maes Howe, Orkney: the central burial chamber with the entrance passage in the background.

constructed from huge dry-stone slabs and covered by a ditched mound over 30 metres (100 feet) in diameter.

Magna Carta The 'great charter of liberties' signed by John at Runnymede near Windsor (15 June 1215). Citing the precedent of an unconfirmed charter of liberties issued by Henry I at his coronation, the extremist baronial opposition, by 1215 threatening civil war, demanded written concessions from John. Their demands were modified and generalized by Langton's moderate party, and the charter finally agreed upon was essentially a codification of the feudal and legal relationship between crown and barons, intended to secure practical reforms and protect the upper class (expanded by Langton to include 'any freeman') from despotic monarchs.

The charter first guarantees the freedom and rights of the church. A quarter of the 61 clauses into which the charter has been divided by modern editors deal with ESCHEATS, FEUDAL AIDS, WARD-SHIPS, WILLS and other matters concerning inheritance and tenure; 9 others limit royal financial exactions; 8 curtail the powers of royal officials; while others guarantee the expulsion of royal mercenaries and make concessions to baronial allies such as Alexander II, Llywelyn the Great and London.

The most notable clauses, however, and the ones which give Magna Carta its symbolic importance as a statement of the superiority of law over arbitrary rule, are those which declare: 'No freeman shall be arrested or imprisoned or disseised or outlawed or exiled . . . except by the lawful judgment of his peers and by the law of the land', and 'To none will we sell, to none will we refuse or delay right or justice.'

Guaranteed by a codicil subjecting John to a baronial committee, the charter was soon repudiated both by John and his more extreme opponents, to be reissued in various modified forms under HENRY III. Many times subsequently confirmed as the criterion of good government, the charter was much cited (though misinterpreted) during the constitutional struggles of the 17th century. (J. C. Holt, *Magna Carta*, 1965.)

Magnus Maximus A Roman general, probably a DUX BRITANNIARUM, Magnus Maximus removed troops from Roman Britain to make himself emperor (383) but was defeated in 388. To replace them he created native FOEDERATI kingdoms in Wales (where 'Macsen Wledig' is remembered in legend and as the founder of several princely houses) and Scotland (*see* NOVANTAE).

Maiden Castle, Dorset: aerial view of the hillfort.

Maiden Castle Dorset. One of the most spectacular British HILLFORTS, Maiden Castle illustrates the continuity of use of many prehistoric sites, having been successively the location of a CAUSEWAYED CAMP, a long BARROW and a single- and multi-ramparted stronghold of the Durotriges. It was stormed by Vespasian (43).

Mainprise A medieval form of bail, whereby a person accused of an offence could remain at liberty by finding others, known as mainpernors, to guarantee his appearance in court when summoned. If he failed to appear the mainpernors would forfeit their money pledges or, in some cases, suffer imprisonment themselves.

Maintenance The perversion of law whereby lords upheld the court actions of their INDENTURED RETAINERS, or suppressed actions against them, by extra-legal and sometimes violent means. The most serious abuse of 'bastard FEUDALISM', it was frequently legislated against, though with little effect, from the 14th to the early 16th century, but survived in remoter parts of England until the civil wars.

Maitland, Sir John, of Thirlstane 1543–95. The younger brother of William Maitland. Having supported Mary Queen of Scots until 1573, Maitland became a lord of session, secretary and finally chancellor (1587) under James VI. He successfully pursued administrative efficiency, judicial reforms and the careful maintenance of good relations with the kirk, England and the rival noble factions of Scotland.

Maitland, William, of Lethington 1525–73. Though secretary of state to Mary of Guise, Maitland supported the rebellion of 1559–60. After seeking an accommodation between Elizabeth I and MARY QUEEN OF SCOTS, he was a party to Darnley's murder, later backing first MORAY, then the queen. He died in Edinburgh castle, possibly by his own hand.

Major-generals, the 1655–6. Military governors of the English provinces, appointed after PENRUDDOCK'S RISING to improve security and promote moral and religious reform. Each maintained a troop of horse financed by a tax on former royalists. Loathed by the county gentry, the major-generals were voted down by the parliament of 1656–7.

Malcolm I king of Scotland (934–54).

Malcolm II king of Scotland (1005–34). *See* DUNCAN I; MACBETH.

Malcolm III Canmore king of Scotland (1057–93; b. *c.* 1031). Generally considered the father of medieval Scotland, Malcolm 'Great Head', son of Duncan I, succeeded after defeating Macbeth with English assistance. He married first Ingibjorg of Orkney (*c.* 1060) and then (1069) the Anglicizing St Margaret, sister of Edgar Atheling. He supported Edgar's claims to England with a series of invasions, but was forced to submit by WILLIAM THE CONQUEROR (1072) and WILLIAM RUFUS (1091) and was killed at Alnwick.

Malcolm IV king of Scotland (1153–65; b. 1141). The grandson of David I, Malcolm was called 'the Maiden' because of his chastity and 'angelic' appearance. Sickly but courageous, he defeated highland separatist risings and lowland revolts against Normanization, but was subservient to Henry II, to whom he restored the English border counties (1157).

Maldon, battle of August 991. Ealdorman Byrhtnoth of Essex, with the local FYRD, was defeated by Viking raiders on the Blackwater estuary (afterwards Aethelred Unraed began paying DANEGELD). Byrhtnoth's THEGNS fought to the last man round their leader's body, their heroism being commemorated in the greatest of all Anglo-Saxon battle-poems.

Malplaquet, battle of *see* MARLBOROUGH'S WARS

Malthus, Thomas 1766–1834. A Lincolnshire parson and fellow of St John's college, Cambridge, Malthus won fame with his *Essay on the Principle of Population* (1798), a work of demographic theory of abiding insight and relevance. From 1804 he was professor of history and political economy at the East India Company's college at Haileybury.

Manau Gododdin The late- and post-Roman kingdom of the northern Votadini, stretching from the Tweed to the Stirling area and centred on Edinburgh. Soon after the defeat of its army at Catterick by Aethelferth (*c.* 598) – the subject of *Y Gododdin*, the earliest surviving British epic – it was overrun by English Northumbria.

Manchester, Edward Montagu, Viscount Mandeville and 2nd earl of 1602–71. One of the leaders of the parliamentary opposition to Charles I (1640–1), Manchester commanded the army of the Eastern Association (1643–4). His cautious campaigning in the CIVIL WARS was vehemently opposed by Oliver Cromwell. Displaced by the SELF-DENYING ORDINANCE and politically inactive after 1648, he welcomed the Restoration (1660).

Manchester School A name applied in the 1840s to the defenders of FREE TRADE, such as COBDEN and BRIGHT, largely because of the identification of the cotton capital with their ANTI-CORN-LAW LEAGUE.

Mann, Tom 1856–1941. A socialist activist, Mann was responsible for creating the Amalgamated Engineering Union, and was a founder of the COMMUNIST PARTY OF GREAT BRITAIN.

Manning, Henry Edward 1808–92. A HIGH CHURCH rector who quit the church of England over the GORHAM JUDGMENT (1850) – which seemed to him to sanction heretical views on baptism – and joined the ROMAN CATHOLIC church. He rose rapidly to become archbishop of Westminster (1865) and cardinal (1875), where he did much to make Catholicism socially respectable and politically oriented towards liberalism and social reform.

Manor The basic unit of English medieval territorial organization, essentially the residence of a landowner with the estate belonging to it. The concept appeared in Anglo-Saxon times and was incorporated into feudalism. Though they generally included both DEMESNE and land occupied by free tenants and VILLEINS, their size, structure and the 'customs' which governed their administration varied widely.

Manor court A court held (generally fortnightly) by the lord of a MANOR or his representative, with the compulsory attendance of his free tenants. Also called a court-baron or hallmote, it dealt with trespasses, failure to perform labour services and other internal matters, and in many places also acted twice yearly as a court-leet to take views of FRANKPLEDGE.

Mansfield judgment 1772. The ruling by Lord Chief Justice Mansfield, in the case of the runaway negro slave James Somerset, that SLAVERY was neither allowed nor approved of by English law. This judgment effectively abolished slavery within England and Wales.

Mar, John Erskine, 11th earl of 1672–1732. Nicknamed 'Bobbing John' for his political inconsistency, Mar was no JACOBITE prior to his loss of influence on George I's accession. In 1715 he raised the highlands for the Old Pretender, but was defeated at SHERIFFMUIR and subsequently escaped into exile.

Marchers (borderers). Norman adventurers, originally based in William the Conqueror's Welsh border earldoms of Chester, Shrewsbury and Hereford, they conquered land in WALES by private enterprise from 1066, establishing independent lordships wherein they exercised quasi-regal power and jurisdiction. Though occasionally checked or expelled by Welsh resistance (notably in 1136–54 and 1215–67), they expanded to Ireland under Henry II, gained more land after Edward I's Welsh conquests and played a leading role in every crisis of English politics until the reign of Edward II. By the late 15th century much of 'the March' had passed to the crown by confiscation or inheritance, and its independent status was abolished by the Acts of Union (1536/42).

Marching camps Earthwork defences constructed by Roman armies for overnight or short-term protection while campaigning in hostile territory. The best-preserved examples are Rey Cross, near Bowes, north Yorks. (dating from Cerialis's campaigns); Raedykes, near Stonehaven, Grampian (Severus's expeditions); and Y Pigwn, Trecastle, Powys (*c.* 47–78).

Marconi, Guglielmo *see* BROADCASTING; WIRELESS

Marconi scandal 1912–13. Several Liberal ministers, including Lloyd George, were found to be speculating in the shares of the Marconi Wireless

Company, at the same time as the company was granted the contract for an empire-wide radio system. Allegations of corruption were made by Conservatives and anti-Semitic journalists but, although the ministers' purchases were unwise (and in fact unprofitable), no connection with the contract existed.

de la Mare, Sir Peter *see* GOOD PARLIAMENT; SPEAKER

Margaret, 'maid of Norway' *see* EDWARD I; SCOTTISH WARS OF INDEPENDENCE

Margaret, St *c.* 1046–93. The sister of Edgar Atheling. Margaret fled with him to Scotland after the Norman conquest, marrying Malcolm Canmore in 1069. Famous for her charity, she laboured to reconcile the Celtic church of Scotland to Roman orthodoxy, patronized both BENEDICTINES and CULDEES, and introduced English and Anglo-Norman customs, courtiers and traders.

Margaret of Anjou 1430–82. Having married Henry VI (1445) and borne his only son Edward (1453), this 'great and strong-laboured' French-woman became the mainspring of the Lancastrian party during the wars of the ROSES. Driven into exile in 1463, she allied herself with Warwick the Kingmaker (1470), returning in 1471 to final defeat at TEWKESBURY. She died in exile.

St **Margaret**: miniature from an illuminated manuscript made at Bourges in France for a Scottish lady, 15th century.

Mark A unit of account rather than a coin, it originated in the DANELAW where it represented 128 pennies (10*s*. 8*d*.). It was revalued at 13*s*. 4*d*. (or two-thirds of a pound) during the medieval period, when it was current all over Britain.

Marlborough, John Churchill, 1st duke of *see* BLENHEIM PALACE; MARLBOROUGH'S WARS

Marlborough, statute of *see* HENRY III

Marlborough's wars 1702–13. The war of the Spanish succession, popularly known as Marlborough's wars, was the last and bloodiest of the wars fought against Louis XIV of France. It was provoked in 1700 by Louis's acceptance of the bequest of the Spanish empire to his grandson Philip of Anjou in defiance of the PARTITION TREATIES, and his subsequent prohibition of English imports and recognition of the Old Pretender. England prepared for war by forming a grand alliance with Holland, the Empire, Hanover and Prussia against France, Spain, Bavaria and Savoy. On the death of William III (1702) leadership passed to John Churchill, earl of Marlborough (1650–1722), a soldier and administrator of long experience and proven ability, though also of unstable loyalty and consuming ambition.

As commander of the English and Dutch land forces and ambassador to the Dutch republic, Marlborough had direction of the war in the Netherlands, while his political position at home was secured by his wife Sarah's pre-eminence in the favour of Queen Anne. Initial success in the Netherlands (1703) was threatened by French victories in Bavaria, but Marlborough saved Austria by his march across Germany and brilliant victory at BLENHEIM (1704). Thereafter he attempted a more mobile war in the Netherlands, winning victories at Ramillies (1706), Oudenarde (1708) and Malplaquet (1709), but failing to secure allied support for a thrust at Paris. Meanwhile the imperialists under Eugene cleared Italy of the French, while the Austrian Archduke Charles, with British support, campaigned in Spain. GIBRALTAR (1704), Barcelona (1705) and Madrid (1706) were taken, but defeat at Almanza in 1707 checked allied success and by 1710 only Catalonia remained to Charles.

By then dissatisfaction with the long and costly war was growing in Britain. Marlborough's political position was eroded by his wife's fall from favour, and a Tory election victory (1710) finally destroyed his influence. A year later, accused of corruption, he was stripped of his offices. The

The duke and duchess of **Marlborough** with their 5 children: contemporary oil painting by Closterman.

The battle of Malplaquet, 11 September 1709: the terrible losses of the allies (24,000 out of less than 100,000 troops) made it impossible to exploit this hard-won victory during **Marlborough's wars**.

unexpected accession of the Archduke Charles as emperor (1711) sapped British enthusiasm for his claim to Spain and peace negotiations were commenced without consulting Britain's allies. By 1712 Britain had effectively withdrawn from the war, the new commander Ormonde being ordered to risk no battle or siege, and in 1713 the treaty of UTRECHT was concluded. Marlborough, who had withdrawn abroad from 1712 until Anne's death (1714), returned to the dukedom and the estate and palace of Blenheim with which he had earlier been rewarded. Restored to his offices under George I, he enjoyed some influence, while dabbling cautiously in Jacobite intrigues, until incapacitated by a stroke (1716). His campaigns had done much to raise Britain into the position of a leading European power.

Marprelate tracts 1588–9. A series of 7 satirical pamphlets attacking episcopacy, probably written by Job Throckmorton and John Penry under the pseudonym Martin Marprelate. Elizabeth I's government was greatly alarmed and vigorously pursued the secret Marprelate press. Moderate Puritans repudiated the tracts for their extremism and scurrility.

Marras see CLASS

Marriage see DOWRY; FAMILY; JOINTURE; MARRIAGE ACT; POPULATION

Marriage Act, Lord Hardwicke's 1753. Framed by Lord Chancellor Hardwicke to prevent clandestine marriages, the Act demanded the consent of parents and guardians to the marriages of minors and specified that, with certain exceptions, marriages must take place in Anglican churches. The Act, which clarified English marriage law, was amended to permit civil and non-Anglican ceremonies in 1836.

Marrowmen Supporters, in the 1720 general assembly, of the tenets of Edward Fisher's *Marrow of Modern Divinity*. This work, republished in 1718, sought to mitigate the full rigour of the Calvinist doctrine of justification.

Marston Moor, battle of 2 July 1644. The defeat of 17,000 royalists under Rupert and Newcastle by 27,000 parliamentarians and Scots under Manchester, David Leslie, Fairfax and Oliver Cromwell. Though arguably saving parliament from losing the CIVIL WARS, the victory, which was not followed up, did not decisively turn the tide in its favour.

Martello towers Squat, massively built towers mounting a traversable cannon on their roof, inspired by the Torre di Mortella, Corsica. From 1805–12, 103 were built to guard the vulnerable coastlines from Aldeburgh, Suffolk, to Clacton, Essex, and from Folkestone, Kent, to Seaford, Sussex, against Napoleonic attack. The example at Dymchurch, Kent, has been restored.

Marx, Karl 1818–83. From a German Jewish family at Trier, Marx went to the universities of Bonn and Berlin, where he imbibed the 'dialectical' system of G.W.F. Hegel (1770–1831), and then turned to radicalism. He was first introduced to British industrialization by ENGELS (1846), with whom he collaborated on *The Communist Manifesto* (1848). After the failure of the revolutions of 1848–9 he spent the rest of his life in London, as a scholar of economics and history, journalist, radical agitator and organizer of the INTERNATIONAL. The 1st volume of his greatest work, *Capital*, appeared in 1867, but the rest (still incomplete) did not appear until the 1890s.

Mary I ('Bloody Mary') queen of England (1553–8; b. 1516). Soured by her experiences after the divorce of her mother, Catherine of Aragon, from Henry VIII, Mary came to the throne determined to restore Catholicism to England. Her marriage to Philip II of Spain was a political and personal disaster exceeded only by her policy of persecution, which saw almost 300 burnings and earned her the epithet 'bloody'.

Mary I portrayed as the fanatic and persecutor who earned the epithet 'bloody': print by Delaram.

William III and **Mary II**: the globe under William's left hand indicates that Scotland and England are now 'free', and that France and Ireland are 'to be freed', from Catholicism. Contemporary engraving by de Hooghe.

Mary II queen of Great Britain (1689–94; b. 1662). Eldest daughter of James VII and II, Mary was brought up a Protestant and in 1677 married WILLIAM OF ORANGE. Despite her devotion to her father, she sincerely supported the GLORIOUS REVOLUTION and insisted on William's assumption of full royal power, taking no significant political role herself.

Mary Queen of Scots 1542–67; b. 1542, d. 1587. The daughter of James V and Mary of Guise, Mary inherited the Scottish crown when 6 days old. Shipped to France at the age of 6, to escape English attempts to enforce her marriage to Edward VI, she married the dauphin Francis in 1558, became queen of France in 1559 and was widowed in 1560. A year later she returned to Scotland.

Tall, attractive and vivacious, the young queen marked the early years of her personal rule by remarkable success in overcoming the factionalism which had rent the kingdom under her mother's regency. Advised by MORAY and MAITLAND of Lethington, she wooed the nobility, placated the reformed church (while remaining a Catholic herself) and sought recognition from ELIZABETH I of her claim to the English succession. The delicate balance achieved by 1565 was, however, upset by her disastrous marriage in that year to the worthless DARNLEY which, though it provided an heir, touched off the turmoil of the CHASEABOUT RAID, the

The arrangements made for the execution of **Mary Queen of Scots**, depicting 3 stages of the procedure: the entry of the queen from the left, her preparation and her execution. Ink sketch preserved among the papers of Robert Beale, clerk to the council of Elizabeth I.

slaughter of Mary's favourite Riccio, and then Darnley's murder at Kirk o' Field (1567). Whether or not Mary was directly involved in the last of these events remains doubtful, but certainly she was by this time BOTHWELL's mistress. In May 1567 she became his wife, an act of utter folly which precipitated rebellion, forced abdication in favour of her infant son James (see JAMES VI AND I) and imprisonment in Lochleven castle (July 1567). Escaping in 1568, she was defeated at Langside and fled to England where, after an inconclusive trial before Elizabeth's commissioners, she began the period of imprisonment which ended only with her execution at Fotheringay.

Years of incarceration and death on the block were to lend Mary an aura of romance and a martyr's glamour which she little deserved. She lost her crown not for her Catholicism, nor as an innocent pawn in power politics, but for scandalous behaviour which was condemned by the papacy, France and Spain as well as by her subjects. The opportunism and lack of moral or even political sense of her last years in Scotland was to be further evidenced in her willing acquiescence as the focus of Catholic plots in England, which by 1587 made her too dangerous to Elizabeth in a time of war to be allowed to live. Like her grandson Charles I, she redeemed herself in the eyes of posterity by dying well. She would have served herself and her country better had she lived more wisely.

Mary of Guise 1515–60. The daughter of the duc de Guise and 2nd wife of JAMES V of Scotland (1538). Following James's death she supported a strongly pro-French policy, sending her daughter to France. As regent (1554–60) she contained Protestantism until the rebellion of the lords of the CONGREGATION, dying shortly before their victory.

Master and Servant laws Medieval laws had made breach of contract by a master a civil offence, while breach of contract by a workman was a criminal offence. They were liberalized in 1867 and abolished in 1875. See JUNTA.

Matilda 1102–67. Married first to the holy Roman emperor (and hence called 'the empress') and afterwards to Geoffrey of Anjou, Matilda was the only surviving legitimate child (see WHITE SHIP) and chosen heir of Henry I. Haughty and unpopular, she was rejected in favour of STEPHEN, but after a long civil war (with battles at LINCOLN and WINCHESTER) saw her son crowned as Henry II.

Mau Mau Following attacks on Europeans by Mau Mau, an organization of Kikuyu militants, a state of emergency was proclaimed in Kenya (1952). It lasted until 1956, during which time 100 Europeans, 2,000 African loyalists and 11,000 rebels were killed. 20,000 Kikuyu were also detained for 're-education'.

Mau Mau suspects are rounded up for questioning by men of the King's African Rifles regiment, near Fort Hall, Kenya, January 1953.

Simon Eyre, draper and lord **mayor** of London, in 1445. He was responsible for building Leadenhall and left endowments for a chapel and school. Contemporary manuscript drawing.

Maurice, F. D. *see* CHRISTIAN SOCIALISTS

Maynooth grant 1844. A proposal to increase the endowment of the Irish Roman Catholic seminary near Dublin, which provoked much Nonconformist opposition and a revolt within the Tory party.

Mayor The head of the corporation of a town or borough. During the medieval period the existence of an official so named indicated that the municipality enjoyed internal self-government. He is called lord mayor in towns with county status.

Means test Instituted in 1931 by the National government to investigate family incomes of those claiming unemployment benefit, the means test was seen by the Labour movement as class legislation.

Medina del Campo, treaty of *see* HENRY VII

Megalithic chambered tombs Neolithic communal tombs, derived either from Mediterranean prototypes or from long BARROWS, and differing from the latter mainly in that their burial chambers are constructed of great stones (Greek *mega lithos*), enabling them to be used over several centuries. They appear principally in Ireland and north and west Britain, notably in the Cotswold-Severn region and the Orkneys (*see* MAES HOWE).

Melbourne, William Lamb, 2nd viscount 1779–1848. He entered the commons as a Whig follower of Fox (1806). After a period as a supporter of Canning he reverted to Whiggism, and was Earl Grey's home secretary (1830–4), when he suppressed the SWING RIOTS with great severity. As prime minister (1834 and 1835–41) he gained an ascendancy over the young Queen Victoria, whose resulting Whiggism was only to succumb to Disraeli.

Melville, Andrew 1545–1622. Returning from a university post in Geneva, Melville became principal of Glasgow university (1574) and of St Mary's college, St Andrews (1580). He revitalized the Scottish universities and struggled to promote strict Presbyterianism in the kirk. Austere and tactless, he was disliked by James VI, who contrived to keep him out of Scotland after 1606.

Mercantilism The term used to describe government economic regulation of a nationalist and protectionist character, as practised in the 17th and 18th centuries. The supposed underlying principles of mercantilism were first analysed (critically) by SMITH, though in reality there was never a coherent mercantilist economic doctrine.

Mercenaries Foreign troops serving entirely for gain have frequently been employed in Britain, most notably by the Romans (*see* FOEDERATI), by JOHN, by Somerset in the 1540s, by William III and (for the last time) against the Jacobites (1745–6).

Merchant adventurers GUILDS of merchants formed from the 14th century to 'adventure' overseas, principally trading English cloth for a wide variety of commodities, often in the face of foreign opposition. The London Company (1407) became a national organization, successfully rivalling the HANSEATIC LEAGUE during the 16th century.

Merchants of the Staple *see* STAPLE

Merchet A fine exacted by the lord whenever a VILLEIN gave a daughter in marriage. Its payment was, with labour service, a legal test of servile status in the feudal period.

Mercia The Anglian kingdom of the 'march (boundary) people', originally occupying the Trent valley frontier with the Britons and centred on Tamworth. During the 7th century the prestige of PENDA's dynasty, claiming descent from the rulers of all the ancestral Angles, helped it to subsume the Middle Angles, Lindisse and the lesser midland peoples, thus expanding to cover the whole area between Thames, Severn, Humber and East Anglia. The dominant Anglo-Saxon kingdom during the 8th century (*see* OFFA), its ascendancy was broken at ELLENDUN (825). Its eastern section was settled by Danish Vikings from 877, the remainder being effectively dependent on Wessex thereafter.

Merciless parliament February–June 1388. Steered by the APPELLANTS, this parliament (by proceedings of dubious legality) executed a number of Richard II's supporters for treason (including Chief Justice Tresilian and the king's tutor Sir Simon Burley) and imprisoned others, also establishing controls on the king's prerogative and his royal household.

Merthyr riots *see* WALES

Mesolithic *see* PREHISTORIC BRITAIN

Mesopotamian campaign A disastrous and prolonged campaign against the Turks in WORLD WAR I. An Anglo-Indian force penetrated as far as Kut (1915), but after a 3-month siege surrendered (April 1916). A campaign in January–February 1917 was more successful and Baghdad was captured.

Methodism The name 'methodists' was first applied scornfully to the members of an Oxford 'holy club' founded in 1729 by John Wesley (1703–91) and his brother Charles. The spiritual pilgrimage of the Wesleys was to continue until 1738 when, after coming under the influence of Moravian Christians, John felt his heart 'strangely warmed' and found assurance of his own salvation. This experience was to sustain an extraordinary mission of 53 years.

Taking the world as his parish, Wesley became a tireless evangelist, stressing the redeeming love of Christ and the necessity of personal faith and preaching in the open air, often in defiance of official disapproval and mob violence. In 1739 he broke with his fellow preacher George Whitefield over the issue of predestination and went on to build up a massive following, especially among the labouring poor of industrial areas feebly served by the established church. In the 1740s the foundations

John Wesley preaching at Nottingham to a segregated **Methodist** audience. Engraving from *Wesley, his own biographer*, 1891.

of Methodist organization were laid. Local 'bands' met for prayer and moral criticism; smaller 'classes' whose members paid regular subscriptions were established under carefully selected leaders, usually of middling social rank. An annual conference met from 1742. Simple new chapels were erected by subscription (356 by 1784) and a growing body of itinerant lay preachers ministered to their congregations in services marked by fervent prayer and hymn-singing.

Until John Wesley's death Methodism remained, however uncomfortably, within the CHURCH OF ENGLAND. In 1795, however, the need for episcopal ordination was rejected and a new denomination emerged. The removal of 'Pope' John's autocratic control facilitated internal fissions: the New Connexion (1797), Independent Methodists (1805), Primitive Methodists (1810), Bible Christians (1815), Wesleyan Methodist Association (1835) and Wesleyan Reformers (1849) broke away in turn from the original Wesleyan Methodist church. Subsequent Methodist history is largely the story of the independent flourishing and subsequent contraction and merger of these churches, which in

1932 became the united Methodist church of Great Britain (*see* NONCONFORMITY).

The most controversial aspect of Methodist history is that of its social role in the 19th century, in particular whether it inhibited or fostered working-class movements. Certainly early Methodism was 'not a religion of the poor, but for the poor' in J. H. Plumb's words (*England in the 18th Century*, 1950). Wesley wished to save the souls of the poor, but was politically and socially conservative, as were later Wesleyan leaders who defended child labour and opposed the teaching of writing in SUNDAY SCHOOLS. The New Connexion were, however, more radical, while Primitive Methodists were emphatically democratic in organization and working-class in membership and sympathies. But however problematic its direct influence, Methodism clearly had an indirect role in trade union and radical political activity. It nursed and educated working-class leaders, providing them with self-respect and organizational experience and infusing them with moral courage. That was no small contribution.

Methuen treaty 1703. A trading treaty with Portugal whereby she was opened to English textiles and her wines were imported to England at a very favourable duty. The popularity of port in England dates from this agreement.

Methven, battle of *see* ROBERT BRUCE

Metropolitan police *see* PEEL, SIR ROBERT; POLICE

Midlands rising 1607. A widespread outbreak of rioting in Leicestershire, Northamptonshire and Warwickshire, directed against the ENCLOSURE of common fields. The rising, led by John Reynolds, alias 'Captain Pouch', involved little violence, but was repressed with severity by an alarmed government.

Midlothian campaign 1879–80. GLADSTONE's campaign to win the Tory seat, in which he and his lieutenant, Rosebery, combined American election techniques with appeals to the 'high seriousness' of the Victorian electorate over the issue of DISRAELI's foreign policy (*see* BULGARIAN ATROCITIES).

Military conversations Authorized by the ENTENTE CORDIALE (1904), these contacts between the British and French general staffs were put into operation, without the knowledge of the Campbell-Bannerman cabinet, in 1905. They affected the disposition of forces in 1914, making Britain's involvement in WORLD WAR I inevitable.

Mill, John Stuart 1806–73. A Liberal philosopher, reared from an early age in the utilitarian principles (*see* UTILITARIANISM) of his father James Mill and Jeremy Bentham, Mill stressed the need for the redistribution of wealth, public education and the preservation of individual rights, notably of minorities and of women. Although for most of his life a senior civil servant at the India office, he sat in parliament as Radical MP for Westminster (1865–8).

Millennary petition 1603. A Puritan petition presented to James VI and I on his arrival in England and ostensibly representing the views of 1,000 ministers. James arranged for the studiously moderate requests of the petitioners, concerning clerical standards, church government and liturgy, to be discussed at the HAMPTON COURT CONFERENCE.

Milner, Alfred 1854–1925. Journalist and administrator, Milner's inflexibility was credited with accelerating the 2nd Boer war, but he became a leading exponent of 'enlightened' imperial administration, with a 'kindergarten' of devoted followers and publicists. Lloyd George brought him, after a period of somewhat extreme conservative activity, into the war cabinet (1916) where he took a leading role in setting up RATIONING, organizing the CONVOY SYSTEM and establishing the ministry of health (1919). As colonial secretary (1919–21) he negotiated the semi-independence of Egypt.

Ministry of health *see* MILNER, ALFRED; MORANT, SIR ROBERT; WELFARE STATE

Ministry of transport *see* ROAD FUND; TRANSPORT

Minster (Lat. *monasterium*). Strictly the mother church of a large primitive parish (i.e. of a sizeable division of a DIOCESE made in Anglo-Saxon times and much subdivided later). Though sometimes literally monastic in origin, minsters were often served by a group of secular CANONS.

Missionary societies The 1st British missionary society was the Society for the Propagation of the Gospel (1701), founded to work in the British colonies. The Evangelical revival subsequently stimulated new foundations, including the Baptist (1792), London (1795), Church (1799) and Wesleyan (1813) societies and the British and Foreign Bible Society (1814).

Model parliament *see* PROVISIONS OF OXFORD

Monarchy As the undivided rule of a state by a single person, monarchy certainly existed in prehistoric Britain. Archaeological evidence suggests that the rule of warrior aristocracies, if not of individual chieftains, was replacing theocracy by *c.* 1500 BC, and by the late iron age hereditary dynasties, sometimes dominated by over-kings such as CUNOBELINUS, were ruling at least the southern tribes. Some prehistoric monarchies were matrilinear (*see* BOUDICA), this system prevailing among the PICTS until the 9th century. Roman Britain was administered by imperial governors, but from the 4th century Roman-appointed dynasties ruled the frontier FOEDERATI (*see* MAGNUS MAXIMUS) and after the removal of imperial control (410) the province itself split up into several kingdoms as generals and aristocrats seized power (*see* HEROIC AGE).

The ANGLO-SAXON kings who ultimately replaced them based their claims on ancient descent from pagan gods and heroes but not on strict PRIMOGENITURE, kingship being theoretically elective within the royal family. The consolidation of royal power was not, however, hampered (as in Wales) by the custom of GAVELKIND, and by the 10th century the Wessex dynasty ruled all England. Almost from the conversion Saxon kings dominated church as well as state (*see* WHITBY, SYNOD OF), reigning by the grace of God and being regarded as Christ's vicar among their people. From the 8th century the priestly nature of their office was emphasized by religious elements in the CORONATION ceremony (notably the anointment with holy oil and vesting with eucharistic robes) which have endured until the present. However, by the 11th century, the monarchy's control over the church was being resisted by an increasingly powerful papacy (*see* CHURCH, PRE-REFORMATION).

The NORMAN CONQUEST greatly strengthened the hitherto declining English monarchy by making it the apex of the feudal pyramid, and throughout the medieval period government and monarchy were virtually synonymous. Royal power and prestige nevertheless fluctuated with the personal capability of individual kings: suffering a disastrous blow under STEPHEN, they recovered under HENRY II, to decline again under JOHN. The troubles of HENRY III's reign firmly established the necessity of royal co-operation with the aristocracy, and this policy lay behind the achievements of EDWARD I, under whom medieval royal government attained the height of its success.

By the end of his reign, however, the principal weaknesses of English late medieval monarchy – its inability to control its greatest subjects and the inadequacy of its financial resources in the face of

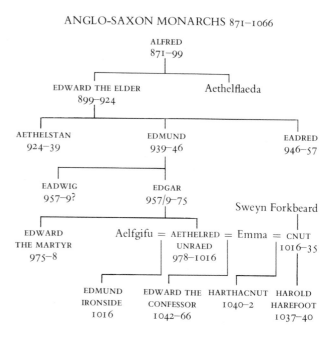

ANGLO-SAXON MONARCHS 871–1066

ALFRED
871–99

EDWARD THE ELDER
899–924

Aethelflaeda

AETHELSTAN
924–39

EDMUND
939–46

EADRED
946–57

EADWIG
957–9?

EDGAR
957/9–75

Sweyn Forkbeard

EDWARD
THE MARTYR
975–8

Aelfgifu = AETHELRED = Emma = CNUT
UNRAED   1016–35
978–1016

EDMUND
IRONSIDE
1016

EDWARD THE
CONFESSOR
1042–66

HARTHACNUT
1040–2

HAROLD
HAREFOOT
1037–40

continuous foreign wars – were already becoming apparent. These combined with EDWARD II's personal deficiencies to compass his deposition, a setback to royal prestige which EDWARD III triumphantly overcame, but only by linking effective monarchy more closely to martial success and curtailing its powers by sweeping concessions to PARLIAMENT and aristocracy. RICHARD II, unwarlike but autocratic, endeavoured to reverse this trend and enhance the mystique of kingship, but his attempt at royal absolutism resulted in his deposition, and HENRY IV's replacement of an ancient dynasty by one with an insecure title further lowered the monarchy's stock, rendering it more dependent than ever on the goodwill of magnates and commons. The victorious HENRY V, perhaps more than any other medieval king, achieved this goodwill, and his success illumined his son's minority. But when HENRY VI's incapacity became clear the monarchy's prestige plummeted, and during the wars of the ROSES the crown was virtually the pawn of aristocratic factions. Under the capable and popular Yorkist EDWARD IV (1461–70 and 1471–83), the monarchy, freed from the financial strain of foreign war and enriched by new land revenues, regained considerable respect and power.

The reigns of the Tudor monarchs (1485–1603) saw the pinnacle of royal power in England. Despite the weakness of his title to the throne, HENRY VII successfully eliminated rival claimants and initiated

MONARCHS OF ENGLAND 1066–1603

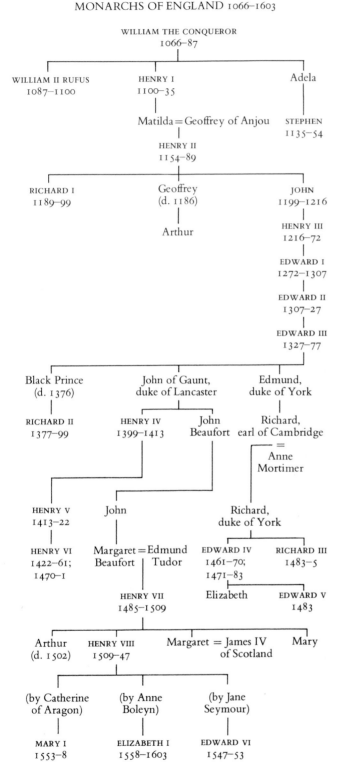

a reassertion of the crown's latent power which was consolidated and developed by HENRY VIII (see TUDOR REVOLUTION IN GOVERNMENT). Obedience to the king was stressed in theory and improved in practice. The military strength of the crown became unrivalled. The retaining of personal followers by great nobles was regulated. Liberties where the king's writ did not run were absorbed. The REFORMATION brought supremacy in the church as well as in the state and an extension of the TREASON laws to defend that position. Finally, the dignity and majesty of the crown were stressed by the splendid theatre of court life.

The Tudors were strong, but not absolute monarchs. Whatever emphasis they laid on their ROYAL PREROGATIVE, they remained under the law. Sovereignty was that of the king in parliament, not of the king alone, and though the Tudors successfully wooed and influenced parliament, it was never subservient to them. The financial and legislative needs of government ensured parliament's continued influence, while the maintenance of a careful dialogue with the POLITICAL NATION, supplemented with a judicious distribution of favour and patronage, was the true foundation of the Tudor monarchy.

In Scotland monarchy developed somewhat differently. Patrilinear primogenitive succession was established by the sons of MALCOLM CANMORE (1057–93), and before their dynasty ended abruptly with ALEXANDER III the Scottish kings had, despite the geographical diversity of their realm, created a relatively harmonious political atmosphere. But their independence remained doubtful, and not until after the crisis of the SCOTTISH WARS OF INDEPENDENCE did the new line of ROBERT BRUCE achieve recognition of full sovereign status by England and the papacy, which in 1331 conceded DAVID II the right of coronation and anointment. Under the earliest Stewart kings, ROBERT II and ROBERT III, kingship declined, but during the 15th century JAMES I, JAMES II and especially JAMES IV made considerable progress in establishing intensive royal government and a strong, almost absolutist, 'New Monarchy'. Its development was, however, interrupted by the minority of JAMES V and religious and political upheavals under MARY QUEEN OF SCOTS, not being resumed until JAMES VI's assumption of power in 1585.

As king of Scotland James successfully extended royal authority over a nobility possessing immense territorial powers and as prone to fight over the control of the powers, privileges and patronage of the crown as to obey their monarch. In 1603 James inherited the English throne as James I, thus uniting

James VI and I, upholder of the divine right of the **monarchy**, in parliament. Contemporary engraving by Renold Elstrack.

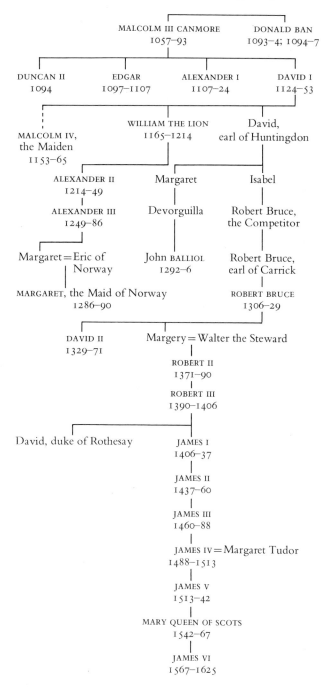

the crowns of the 2 countries. In England his reign saw increasing conflict between the crown and the political nation, while his Scottish achievement was to be shaken in his son's reign. Fundamental to the situation was the deteriorating financial position of the monarchy, aggravated by unpopular religious and foreign policies, impolitic assertions of theories of the DIVINE RIGHT OF KINGS and prerogative power and a failure properly to manage royal patronage, which fell increasingly under the control of Buckingham. Opposition became the norm in parliaments convinced that the 'ancient constitution' was under attack, a conviction strengthened by CHARLES I's rule after 1629. The events of 1638–42, however, with rebellion in Scotland and the constitutional reforms of the Long parliament in England, showed the weakness of the king's position in the face of concerted opposition, though the fact that Charles could raise a following in the subsequent CIVIL WARS demonstrated the power of loyalty to the throne when events reached their climax.

In neither England nor Scotland were the civil wars an attack upon monarchy in itself. It was the impossibility of reaching a peace settlement with Charles which led to his execution in 1649 and the abolition of the monarchy in England. These actions horrified most Englishmen and were repudiated in Scotland, where CHARLES II was crowned. Only military defeat ensured the revolution's triumph in Scotland. Thereafter the INTERREGNUM saw a steady drift back to traditional forms of government in the semi-monarchical PROTECTORATE. Oliver Cromwell refused the crown, but the stage was set for the almost universally popular RESTORATION (1660).

MONARCHS OF GREAT BRITAIN 1603–1980*

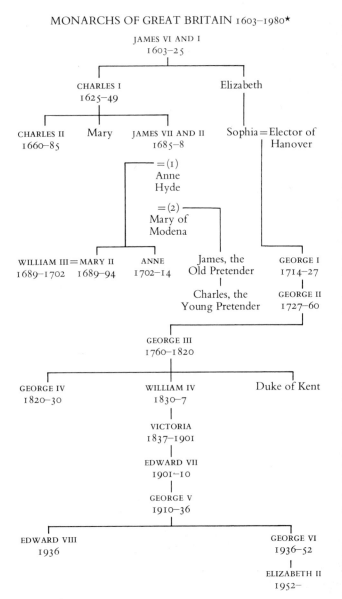

```
                    JAMES VI AND I
                       1603–25
        ┌──────────────────────┴──────────────┐
     CHARLES I                             Elizabeth
     1625–49
   ┌─────┬────────────┐              ┌─────────┴────────┐
CHARLES II   Mary   JAMES VII AND II   Sophia = Elector of
1660–85               1685–8                     Hanover
                        ┌── =(1) ──┐
                           Anne
                           Hyde
                        ┌── =(2) ──┐
                         Mary of
                         Modena
 ┌──────────┬──────────┬──────────┐         ┌──────────┐
WILLIAM III = MARY II   ANNE    James, the      GEORGE I
1689–1702   1689–94   1702–14  Old Pretender    1714–27
                                                     │
                              Charles, the      GEORGE II
                              Young Pretender    1727–60
                    ┌──────────────┴──────────────┐
                            GEORGE III
                            1760–1820
   ┌──────────────┬──────────────────┐
 GEORGE IV      WILLIAM IV        Duke of Kent
 1820–30         1830–7
                     │
                  VICTORIA
                  1837–1901
                     │
                 EDWARD VII
                  1901–10
                     │
                  GEORGE V
                  1910–36
   ┌─────────────────┴──────────────┐
 EDWARD VIII                     GEORGE VI
   1936                           1936–52
                                      │
                                 ELIZABETH II
                                    1952–
```

The restored monarchy was based upon the constitutional situation of 1641. The king retained control of the administration and of policy formation, though his financial weakness meant that he was unable to sustain either ministers or policies without parliamentary support. Charles II's victory in the EXCLUSION CRISIS demonstrated the nation's continued devotion to hereditary monarchy, but the position established by Charles was destroyed by JAMES VII AND II's abuses of the

*Although England and Scotland were not formally united until 1707, for convenience the title of monarch of Great Britain has been adopted from 1603.

prerogative and the threat of Catholic absolutism which provoked the GLORIOUS REVOLUTION. Under WILLIAM III and MARY II and then ANNE, the long struggle between prerogative and parliamentary rule was settled in favour of the latter, and explicit limitations on the crown were laid down in the BILL OF RIGHTS, CLAIM OF RIGHT, TRIENNIAL ACT and Act of SETTLEMENT.

The 18th century saw the working out of a new equilibrium in the constitution. The king retained a voice in policy and his power to choose ministers, though his choice was effectively limited to those who could maintain a parliamentary majority. GEORGE I and GEORGE II chose to take little initiative in government, though GEORGE III proved more assertive until he was incapacitated by insanity. As the forms of constitutional monarchy were elaborated, however, the estimation of the monarchs fell, especially under the despised GEORGE IV.

Revival of respect for the throne was a product of VICTORIA's long reign. No mere cipher, the queen was prepared to intervene in government and to express her marked political prejudices, but the growth of political parties and the advent of democracy eroded her effective weight. The position of the monarch in the reigns of EDWARD VII and GEORGE V came to approximate closely to BAGEHOT's formulation. The monarch stands above party as a symbolic representation of sovereign authority and national unity and as a personal link between the nations of the empire and latterly of the British commonwealth. No longer an independent political force, the crown retains 3 rights: to be consulted, to encourage and to warn, with a residual duty to intervene in the interests of the public good should political crisis demand such action.

The coronation of Elizabeth II, Westminster abbey, June 1953, one of the great symbolic occasions of contemporary **monarchy**. The queen is wearing St Edward's crown, and holding the rod with dove (of equity and mercy) in her left hand and the sceptre with cross (of kingly power) in her right.

Fountains abbey, Yorks.: built by Cistercians, it was reduced to ruins after the dissolution of the **monasteries**.

George **Monck**, both a steadfast follower of Oliver Cromwell and architect of the Restoration. Contemporary engraving, attributed to Robert Gaywood.

Monasteries, dissolution of the Motivated by the financial needs of the English crown and excused on the grounds of the alleged decadence of the monastic orders, the dissolution proceeded in 2 stages, smaller houses being dissolved in 1536 and the greater houses in 1539. Their landed wealth was rapidly dispersed by sales and grants. *See* PILGRIMAGE OF GRACE.

Monck, George, 1st duke of Albemarle 1608–70. Monck was a professional soldier who served in turn Charles I, the commonwealth and the protectorate (*see* CIVIL WARS), achieving distinction as both a general and an admiral. Governor of Scotland from 1654, his march south in 1660 paved the way to the RESTORATION.

Mond, Sir Alfred, Lord Melchett 1868–1930. A Jewish chemical magnate and MP (1906–28), Mond inherited a major role in the firm of Brunner Mond (founded 1881) and consolidated it into Imperial Chemical Industries (1926). Although he moved from Liberalism to Conservatism (1926) he was associated with enlightened employment, and the 1927 Mond-Turner talks on industrial harmony (with Ben Turner, head of the TUC) did something to mitigate the animosities which had erupted in the 1926 General Strike (*see* TRADE UNIONISM).

Monday club Founded in 1960, a right-wing pressure group in the Conservative party analogous to, but less disciplined than, Labour's TRIBUNE GROUP.

Monitor system *see* BRITISH SCHOOLS; EDUCATION; NATIONAL SCHOOLS

Monks Men (at first rarely priests) of a religious community, living an enclosed life of poverty, chastity and obedience, monks were the chief teachers and civilizing agents of Europe during the dark and early middle ages. In Britain the Celtic or Irish tradition of monasticism (*see* CHURCH, PRE-REFORMATION) was succeeded by the Roman (*see* BENEDICTINES, CARTHUSIANS, CISTERCIANS, CLUNIACS).

Monmouth's rebellion 1685. The rebellion against JAMES VII AND II of James Scott, duke of Monmouth (b. 1649), the illegitimate son of Charles II (*see* EXCLUSION CRISIS). Landing at Lyme Regis, Monmouth collected a small army of west-countrymen but his poorly armed troops were crushed at SEDGEMOOR, defeat being followed by Monmouth's execution and the BLOODY ASSIZES.

Monopolies Grants to private individuals of the sole right to sell specified commodities, greatly exploited by Elizabeth I, James VI and I and Charles I as a means of raising revenue. Attempts by parliament to restrict this abuse of the royal prerogative to regulate trade culminated in the abolition of monopolies of this kind in 1641.

Monroe doctrine 1823. Promulgated in Washington by President James Monroe (1758–1831), with the acquiescence of Canning's British government, this excluded the European powers from South America but effectively (through her commercial links) maintained a privileged status for the British.

Montagu-Chelmsford report 1918. This recommended partially responsible government for India. *See* BRITISH EMPIRE.

Negotiating surrender: Viscount **Montgomery** (centre) and General Admiral von Freideberg meet prior to the German surrender at Luneberg, May 1945. Montgomery, in characteristic contrast to Eisenhower, insisted on receiving the Germans personally.

Montgomery, Bernard, viscount 1887–1976. An Anglo-Irish soldier, Montgomery entered the army (1908) and survived the trenches. An unsurpassed field commander, in WORLD WAR II he took over command of the 8th army in north Africa (1942), defeated Rommel at EL ALAMEIN and then drove the Germans out, following them to Italy. He commanded the British forces in the invasion of Europe (1944) and accepted the German surrender at Luneberg.

Montgomery, treaty of *see* LLYWELYN AP GRUFFYDD

Montrose, James Graham, 5th earl and 1st marquis of 1612–50. An active covenanter (1638–40), Montrose later rallied to Charles I's cause in the CIVIL WARS and led highland and Irish troops in a series of spectacular victories (1644–5) before being defeated by David Leslie at Philliphaugh. After exile (1645–50) he returned to Scotland, but was defeated, betrayed and summarily executed.

Morant, Sir Robert 1863–1920. As head of the EDUCATION department Morant was architect of the Education Act (1902). A ruthless and untiring autocrat, he went on to become chairman of the national health insurance commissioners (1911) and 1st secretary of the new ministry of health (1919).

Moray, Andrew *see* SCOTTISH WARS OF INDEPENDENCE

Moray, Sir Andrew 1298–1338. The son of Andrew Moray, brother-in-law of Robert Bruce and guardian for David II, Moray led the successful resistance to Edward III's occupation of Scotland (1335–8), adopting Bruce's guerilla tactics and systematically attacking and demolishing English-held fortresses. *See* SCOTTISH WARS OF INDEPENDENCE.

Moray, James Stewart, earl of 1531–70. An illegitimate son of James V, intended for the church, Moray joined the rebellion of 1559–60 and subsequently directed the policy of MARY QUEEN OF SCOTS. After resistance to the Darnley marriage in 1565 (*see* CHASEABOUT RAID), he fled to England, but on Mary's deposition returned as regent (1568) until his murder by rival noblemen.

More, Sir Thomas 1479–1535. A lawyer and scholar, internationally known for his *Utopia* (1516), More entered Henry VIII's service in 1517. Thereafter he championed Catholic orthodoxy and as lord chancellor (1529–32) pursued heretics and opposed Henry's divorce. In 1532 he resigned, but his tacit refusal to recognize the Henrician REFORMATION led to his arrest, trial and execution.

Morgan, Sir Henry 1635–86. Of Welsh origin, Morgan emerged as 'admiral' of the Caribbean buccaneers (1668) and for 4 years led buccaneer fleets in exploits of great ingenuity, courage and savagery. Sent home under arrest (1672), he won Charles II's favour and was appointed deputy governor of Jamaica (1674).

Morgannwg A principality in south-east Wales, comprising modern Glamorgan, Gwent (formerly Monmouthshire) and part of western Hereford and Worcester. Civilized and prosperous, it generally remained aloof from the dynastic wars between other Welsh principalities, but by 1095 had been completely conquered by the MARCHERS.

Morley, John, viscount 1838–1923. Having become a Radical MP (1883), Morley rose rapidly to the post of Irish secretary (1886 and 1892–5). Home rule appealed to him as a way of unifying the Liberal party on a 'great moral issue' and of avoiding commitments to social reforms which, as COBDEN's and GLADSTONE's biographer, he distrusted. He spent the 1890s intriguing among the divided Liberal leadership, and then became a rather conservative Indian secretary (1906–10), and lord president 1910–14, when he resigned over the war.

Mormaer The 'great steward' or head of a province of ALBA, in 12th-century Scotland the title became equated with EARL.

Thomas **More**: portrait after Holbein.

Morris, William 1834–96. From a Pre-Raphaelite background, Morris, a noted poet and designer, went into politics via the BULGARIAN ATROCITIES agitation. Moving further to the left, he joined the SOCIAL DEMOCRATIC FEDERATION (1883), withdrew a year later to found the Socialist League, and in 1890 formed the Hammersmith Socialist League. He attempted, in his utopian novel *News from Nowhere* (1891), to fuse the Marxist forecast of class struggle with his own artistic views, substantially derived from RUSKIN.

Morrison, Herbert, lord 1885–1965. A London Labour politician, Morrison's creation of the London passenger transport board (1933) as a member of MacDonald's 2nd Labour government, was the model for later nationalized industries. He became leader when Labour won the London county council (1935). Winston Churchill made him home secretary (with great success) in his wartime coalition, and he continued thus under Attlee, although he was briefly foreign secretary (1951).

Mortimer, Roger 1287–1330. A leading MARCHER opponent of the DESPENSERS, Mortimer was sentenced to life imprisonment by Edward II (1322), but escaped from the Tower of London to France (1323), becoming by 1326 the ally and lover of ISABELLA. After their deposition of Edward he virtually ruled England through her, but his avarice made him unpopular and he achieved little save the humiliating treaty of EDINBURGH-NORTHAMPTON. He was kidnapped and executed by Edward III in 1330.

Mortimer family A powerful MARCHER family with hereditary interests in Ireland. The marriage of Edmund, 3rd earl of March (1351–81), to the grand-daughter of Edward III made them technically the heirs (albeit in the female line) of Richard II, a claim revived by Richard, duke of YORK, whose mother was the last of the Mortimer line. *See* ROSES, WARS OF THE.

Mortimer's Cross, battle of 2 or 3 February 1461. A Yorkist victory in the wars of the ROSES. The earls of Pembroke and Wiltshire, leading an army of Welsh Lancastrians and French mercenaries to join MARGARET OF ANJOU's advance on London (*see* ST ALBANS, 2ND BATTLE OF), were intercepted and beaten near Wigmore, Herefs. and Worcs., by Edward of March (soon afterwards crowned Edward IV).

Morton, James Douglas, 4th earl of 1516–81. Morton took part in the rebellion of 1559–60 and became chancellor of Scotland (1563). A leading actor in Riccio's murder and in the deposition of MARY QUEEN OF SCOTS, he became regent (1572–80), favouring Protestantism and the English alliance. Disliked by James VI, and denounced as one of Darnley's murderers, he was executed.

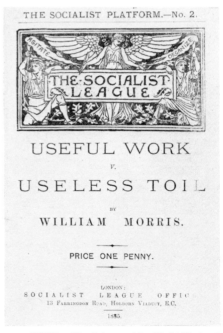

The cover of William **Morris**'s pamphlet, *Useful Work v. Useless Toil*, 1885, in which he predicted that the machine would reduce man's work to 4 hours a day.

Morton, John *c.* 1420–1500. A veteran Lancastrian, as bishop of Ely Morton was prime mover of Henry Stafford, duke of BUCKINGHAM's rising (1483), and warned Henry VII of Richard III's plot to kidnap him (1484). Soon after Henry's accession he became archbishop of Canterbury and chancellor, remaining the king's most trusted adviser until his own death.

Motor industry In 1914, 16,320 cars were built in Britain, and 12,556 imported, mainly from France. Production was restricted during World War I, but real expansion began 1922–39: Austin's Longbridge factory was by 1937 producing 78,000 cars a year, drawing, like other plants, on the small-parts industry of the west midlands. Morris and Austin merged as the British Motor Corporation (1952) and the only major works outside the west midlands

Above The beginnings of the **motor industry**: a ten-horsepower, two-cylinder Rolls Royce, 1905.

Left Earl **Mountbatten** photographed in Singapore at the time of the Japanese surrender, September 1945.

were those owned by American firms, Vauxhall (General Motors since 1925) at Luton and Fords since 1931 at Dagenham. In the early 1960s new factories were opened in Scotland and Merseyside, but these were plagued by transport costs, mounting labour troubles and, after 1973, foreign imports, which by 1980 had increased from under 30% to over 60% of sales. In 1975 British Leyland (formed in 1968 out of a merger between Leyland and BMC) had to be taken over by the state and Chrysler heavily subsidized, although by the end of the decade the economic situation of the industry had still not improved.

Motoring organizations The (Royal) Automobile Club was set up in 1897 to fight harsh treatment of motorists by magistrates, and a more militant breakaway, the Automobile Association, started functioning in 1905. By 1970 the RAC had 1·5 and the AA 4 million members, who took no part in the running of the organizations nor in the formation of their pro-private transport policies.

Motorways Limited-access highways for fast motor transport were pioneered in America and by the totalitarian regimes of Germany and Italy before World War II, but pressure for such construction was contained in Britain until 1955, when the London-Yorkshire motorway (M1) was authorized. The 1st section of it was opened in 1959, and by 1973 over 1,000 miles had been built, although by then enthusiasm for them as a panacea for economic and traffic problems was on the wane.

Motte and bailey *see* CASTLES

Mountbatten of Burma, Louis, 1st earl 1900–79. Of royal blood but progressive views, Mountbatten entered the navy (1913) and began WORLD WAR II as an impressive destroyer commander, rising rapidly to become chief of combined operations (1942–3), and supreme allied commander, south-east Asia (1943–6). He was the last viceroy and 1st governor-general of India (1947–8), tactfully easing the subcontinent through the last stages of British rule, before retiring to become eventually chief of the defence staff (1959). He was killed (August 1979) when his boat was blown up by the Irish Republican Army, off Mullaghmore, Co. Sligo.

Mountjoy, Charles Blount, 8th lord 1563–1606. An Elizabethan courtier, scholar and soldier who, despite his poor health, succeeded the 2nd earl of Essex as lord-lieutenant of Ireland (1600). A fine strategist, cautious, yet capable of bold action,

Mountjoy rapidly subdued Ulster and Connaught and defeated the Spaniards and TYRONE at KINSALE (1601–2).

Muggletonians An INTERREGNUM sect founded by Ludowick Muggleton. In addition to his other unorthodox beliefs, Muggleton claimed to be one of the messengers prophesied in Revelations, and to have been granted the power of deciding who should be damned and who saved.

Munich crisis *see* APPEASEMENT

Municipia In Roman Britain, towns technically inferior to COLONIAE in that their inhabitants were not essentially Roman citizens, but otherwise self-governing in much the same way. Verulamium was certainly granted this status during the 1st century, and Cirencester, Leicester, Dorchester, Canterbury and London were probably promoted to it.

Munitions crisis 1915. In the spring a series of 3 bloody but inconclusive battles on the western front were explained away by the generals in terms of shell shortages. By the end of the year traditional armaments factories had been replaced by a ministry of munitions under Lloyd George, after a campaign headed by Northcliffe's newspapers.

Murage From the early 13th until the late 15th centuries, successive kings granted many towns the right (for limited periods) to levy a duty on certain goods entering the town for sale, the proceeds of this murage being devoted to the construction or repair of the town walls and defences.

Murdoch, duke of Albany *see* ALBANY, ROBERT, DUKE OF

Mutiny Acts Acts of parliament passed annually (1689–1879) granting the right to enforce military discipline in peacetime and thereby legalizing the standing ARMY. The Acts are sometimes said to have necessitated annual sessions of parliament after 1689, though in fact no Mutiny Act was passed from 1697–1701.

Mystery plays Cycles of mystery plays survive from York, Wakefield ('Towneley'), Chester and East Anglia ('N-Town') as well as fragmentary records from elsewhere. These metrical vernacular dramatizations of the bible were apparently performed on Corpus Christi day. Each episode was enacted by a GUILD (i.e. 'mystery') on its wagon at certain 'stations' along a traditional route.

Myton, battle of 20 September 1319. James Douglas and Randolph, sent by ROBERT BRUCE into England to divert Edward II from besieging Berwick, easily scattered Archbishop Melton of York's motley army of peasants and clerics at Myton-on-Swale, Yorks., so many priests being killed that the rout was nicknamed 'the Chapter of Myton'.

Nájera, battle of 3 April 1367. The BLACK PRINCE, supporting King Pedro the Cruel of Castile against his half-brother, Henry of Trastamara, led an Anglo-Gascon-Spanish army (including English archers) to rout a force of French mercenaries near Pamplona. Two years later Pedro was murdered, and Trastamaran Castile fell under French influence.

Napier commission 1884. Formed to inquire into land in the Scottish highlands after the CROFTERS' WAR, the commission recommended land reform based on common ownership of rural townships. This was not followed up, but Scottish crofters were granted rent control and security of tenure administered by a Crofters' commission.

Napoleonic wars 1803–15. These were essentially an extension of the French revolutionary wars (1793–1802), which by 1796 had become dominated by the personality of Napoleon Bonaparte.

Having overrun the Austrian Netherlands and opened the Scheldt, the revolutionary French government declared war on a reluctant Britain in February 1793. Allied with Austria, Holland, Prussia and Sardinia in the 1st coalition, Britain attempted initially to avoid heavy continental commitments. A landing at Toulon in support of French monarchists was defeated in 1793. In 1794 British troops under the duke of York were forced into ignominious retreat from the Netherlands and eventual evacuation from Bremen (1795) while Holland fell to the French. Meanwhile (1794–6) West Indian operations of mixed success cost 40,000 British troops, most of them fever victims, while Britain occupied former Dutch colonies in Africa and the East Indies. Only Howe's defeat of a French

The battle of Waterloo, 1815, which ended the **Napoleonic wars**. Oil painting by John W. Cook, 1819.

fleet on the 'Glorious 1st of June' 1794 relieved the general gloom.

In 1796 Napoleon's defeat of the Austrians in Italy left Britain without allies and threatened by the SPITHEAD AND NORE MUTINIES (1797). Invasion was pre-empted by Duncan's naval victory at Camperdown, while Jervis and NELSON defeated France's Spanish allies at Cape St Vincent (14 February 1797). A year later Napoleon's Egyptian expedition and the rebellion of the UNITED IRISHMEN presented new threats. Nelson's annihilation of the French fleet at the NILE, however, stranded Napoleon's army in the east while a 2nd coalition was formed and Russian troops recaptured north Italy. Napoleon's return alone in 1799 turned the tables. Austrian defeat and Russian withdrawal left Britain alone again and hampered by the armed neutrality of northern sea-powers which necessitated Nelson's destruction of the Danish fleet at COPENHAGEN. In 1802 the peace of AMIENS provided a temporary respite.

War was renewed in 1803 over Britain's refusal to surrender Malta. Once more allied to Austria, Prussia and Russia, Britain prepared to meet an invasion by Napoleon, now emperor of France. TRAFALGAR ended any invasion threat, but Napoleon's sweeping victories over Austria, Prussia and Russia (1805–6) destroyed the 3rd coalition. For 2 years Britain fought alone, dispatching expeditions to Naples, Buenos Aires and Copenhagen, but weakened by Napoleon's efforts to strangle British trade with Europe by his Continental

System. The French attempt to coerce Spain in 1808, however, led to revolt and the PENINSULAR WAR (1809–13) in which victory slowly swung to WELLINGTON's army. As the tide turned in Spain, Napoleon's disastrous Moscow campaign (1812) led to the forming of the 4th coalition and the continental allies' defeat of Napoleon at Leipzig (1813). Paris fell and Napoleon abdicated in 1814. His escape in 1815 led to his utter defeat at WATERLOO, the final peace settlement being established by the congress of VIENNA and treaties of PARIS. Despite the strain of a generation of warfare Britain emerged economically supreme and indisputably the world's greatest power. *See* NAVY.

Naseby, battle of 14 June 1645. A battle of the CIVIL WARS. In a hard-fought engagement, the New Model Army defeated a smaller royalist force under Charles I. Charles withdrew with 4,000 horse and the battle's decisiveness became apparent only with the defeat of Goring's army at Langport a month later.

National debt Originating in borrowing to meet war expenditure after the Glorious Revolution and secured against the revenue, the national debt stabilized government finance by providing a secure investment for lenders. It has grown steadily ever since, despite several unsuccessful attempts to systematically redeem the debt by means of 'sinking funds', notably those established by Walpole (1717) and Pitt (1786).

National fire service *see* AIR-RAID PRECAUTIONS

National Front A far-right party formed (1967) by a merger between the neo-Nazi John Tyndall's British Movement and A.K. Chesterton's League of Empire Loyalists. In the mid-1970s it gained some electoral success on an anti-immigrant ticket mainly in London and the midlands, and held marches through immigrant areas on the pattern of Oswald Mosley's through London's east end in 1935. *See* FASCISM.

National government 1931–40. Set up in August by Ramsay MACDONALD and 3 of his senior colleagues in the Labour cabinet, it was a predominantly Conservative coalition, which won an overwhelming victory (October) and continued under MacDonald (-1935) BALDWIN (1935–7) and Neville CHAMBERLAIN until May 1940.

National health service *see* ATTLEE, CLEMENT; BEVAN, ANEURIN; WELFARE STATE

National insurance Enacted by Lloyd George in 1911, there were 2 schemes (taking effect 1913), one for sickness and one, limited to a few industries prone to seasonal lay-offs, for unemployment. The scope of the latter scheme was greatly extended after World War I, while the health scheme now lagged behind. By the National Insurance Act (1946), a central item in the WELFARE STATE, state insurance was extended to every citizen, rich or poor.

National plan *see* ECONOMY, THE

National schools Primary schools founded after 1811 by the National Society for the Education of the Poor in the Principles of the Established Church. The schools, which employed the monitor system of teaching and rivalled the Nonconformist BRITISH SCHOOLS before 1870, came under local authority control in 1902.

Nationalization The state had always owned arsenals and dockyards and in Ireland and Scotland had built canals, roads and harbours and established industries and fisheries. The new industrialist supporters of FREE TRADE were strongly against state control, but from the 1850s some radicals urged the takeover of 'natural monopolies', such as certain types of communications and land needed for urban development. The TELEGRAPH system was bought over (1869) but most action came from local authorities (*see* GAS AND WATER SOCIALISM) until electricity transmission (1926), London Transport (1932) and British Overseas Airways (1939) were nationalized. The Labour party was pledged to nationalization by clause IV of its 1918 constitution: the Attlee government took over the bank of England, coalmining, telecommunications and civil aviation (1946), railways, some road transport and electricity (1947), gas (1948), and iron and steel (1949–51). The Conservatives denationalized road transport and steel (1951–3), only to have Labour take the latter back (1966), and to find themselves nationalizing Rolls Royce (1971). Labour took over the British Aerospace Company, shipbuilding and British Leyland (1975), set up the British National Oil Corporation, and established the National Enterprise Board to take holdings in the private sector.

Navigation Acts 1651, 1660 and 1663. Intended to foster English trade by cutting out Dutch competition, the Acts reserved colonial trade to English ports and shipping, while requiring that imports from Europe must be carried in English ships or ships of their country of origin. Liberalized by the Tories before 1832, the Acts were abolished in 1849.

Navy Until 1638 the royal navy was specifically the possession of the monarch, who appointed its lord high admiral or a commission to direct the fleet (both of the monarch's own ships and of ships drafted when needed from the main ports) through a range of 'navy offices' dotted throughout London. The expansion of commerce in the early 17th century meant that royal revenue – mainly customs – was no longer sufficient, but Charles I's attempt to make parliament pay (*see* SHIP MONEY) proved one of the crucial issues in the descent to civil war (1641). The navy benefited the king little, for the lord high admiral, the earl of Northumberland, handed it (42 vessels of 22,411 tons) over to parliament. It was used effectively to cut off supplies to the king and then, under Admiral BLAKE, to undertake profitable attacks on the Portuguese, Dutch, various Mediterranean powers and the Spaniards. By the Restoration (1660) the fleet stood at 154 ships of 51,463 tons.

Its responsibilities had also increased: the NAVIGATION ACTS closed the British empire to foreign shipping, and the expanded British merchant marine had to be protected, chiefly from the Dutch, who were most disadvantaged by this. Two hard fought and expensive wars (1665–7 and 1672–4) saw the ultimate eclipse of the smaller nation. Throughout this period the matériel and administration of the navy was reorganized under Charles II's brother, the duke of York (later James VII and II), and Pepys as secretary to the admiralty. When parliament formally took over responsibility for it (1688), the fleet stood at 173 ships of 101,892 tons.

The next 130 years were marked by a recurrent struggle with France for European supremacy, but

The *Ark Royal*, Lord Effingham's ARMADA flagship, was a four-master of 800 tons and carried 425 men. Anonymous woodcut, late 16th century.

the maritime issue was virtually settled in favour of England after the war of the Spanish succession (*see* MARLBOROUGH'S WARS) of 1702–13 had proved France unable to sever England's sea communication, and gained England monopoly trading rights in the Spanish colonies. The war of the AUSTRIAN SUCCESSION (1740–8) was less decisive, but England in the SEVEN YEARS' WAR (1756–63) owed its North American and Indian successes to the annihilation of the French fleet at QUIBERON BAY (1759). The subsequent loss of the American colonies in the 1775–83 war was partly due to a fleet too overstretched and inadequate to relieve Charles Cornwallis at YORKTOWN (1781). Partly as a result of this success, the French navy which confronted Britain in 1793 was at its most powerful. On the other hand, the discontinuity of the revolution had proved too much for its staffing and morale.

The French revolutionary wars also proved almost too much for the royal navy, as the SPITHEAD AND NORE MUTINIES (1797) bore witness. These reflected living conditions for seamen (more than half of them 'pressed' – *see* PRESS GANGS) which were frequently appalling, and discipline which was brutally enforced.

In the NAPOLEONIC WARS the fleet was mainly occupied in blockade, which virtually destroyed the vital industrial economy of the French coastal towns. The lead that English trade then gained over France was never lost. Moreover, in the major battles – Cape St Vincent (1797), the NILE (1798) and TRAFALGAR (1805) – British commanders, trusting to the superiority of their crews, broke with the traditional line-ahead formation and employed the annihilation tactics of the close-quarter mêlée, in which they were brilliantly successful. After 1807 the French no longer challenged the English at sea. Towards the end of the war America had become the main maritime enemy, and it was in New York harbour (1815) that Robert Fulton tried out the *Demologos*, the 1st steam-powered warship.

Although steam was already technically feasible, it was 40 years before the navy converted its main battle-fleet, and only after overt opposition. Some was justified: until BRUNEL had successfully demonstrated the screw propeller (1845), the paddle-wheel gravely lessened the broadside and presented a huge target. Wooden walls were being built as late as 1848. But at Sinope (1853) Turkish wooden walls proved terrifyingly vulnerable to explosive shell; and the British sailing fleet bombarding Sevastopol (1854) in the CRIMEAN WAR was badly shelled as it tried to manoeuvre. Thereafter development was rapid. In 1858 the French laid down their armoured cruiser, the *Gloire*; Britain then built her 1st armour-clad iron battleship, the *Warrior* (commissioned 1861). The American civil war, with the use of heavy turret-guns and the total abandonment of masts and sails on Ericsson's *Monitor* (1862), soon showed how essential such developments were. The admirals, however, wished to retain sail as it allowed ships to maintain station for long periods. But the sinking of Captain Cole's experimental turret sail/steamship HMS *Captain* (1870) showed the difficulty of doing this, and by 1871 the navy's latest warship, the *Devastation*, was effectively the 1st modern 'mastless' battleship.

Calibre of guns and thickness of iron armour escalated, until the 'mastless' *Inflexible* (1876) had four 16-in. (40·6-cm) guns and 24 in. (61 cm) of armour. Thereafter steel armour and special armour-piercing shells somewhat reduced dimensions. In response to a further French challenge in the mid-1880s the Spencer programme introduced a new generation of battleships, equipped with lighter guns to tackle the new menace of small high-speed torpedo boats, first seen in action in the Russo-Turkish war (1876–8).

This technology lasted until the DREADNOUGHT revolution (1905–6), but was overshadowed by an enormous growth of interest in naval affairs, encouraged by the publication of propagandist works by the American Admiral Mahan, notably *The Influence of Sea Power Upon History* (1890). These identified sea power as a crucial factor in past wars and insisted on its importance in any future ones. His lessons were taken to heart by Alfred von Tirpitz (minister of marine) in Germany; and the expansion of the German fleet after 1897, challenging the 'TWO-POWER' STANDARD, was based on the assumption that a powerful German navy could challenge the royal navy on the North Sea, as much of its strength would be dissipated in distant waters. The *Dreadnought* and the ENTENTE CORDIALE changed this. Although the need to re-equip the whole British fleet seemed to put the British at a disadvantage, Germany now had to face a navy relieved of its Mediterranean commitments and armed with ships of unprecedented power. By 1914 Germany's naval strategy was in ruins.

At the same time, however, the appearance of new weapons and equipment – submarines, mines, aircraft and radio – meant that the whole game could be changed. After the outbreak of WORLD WAR I Tirpitz was quick to see this. The German fleet proved a liability, unable even to take advantage of its tactical victory at JUTLAND, but the U-boat proved a deadly threat to British supplies, even when curbed for all of 1916 by German adherence – on American pressure – to a law of the

The 14-inch guns of the battleship *Duke of York*: its sinking of the German *Scharnhorst* in 1943 was the last action between battleships in European waters. Photographed December 1943.

sea substantially drawn up by the British in their own interests. The appalling sinkings of early 1917 produced a near-paralysis on the part of JELLICOE and the naval leadership, only broken by direct political intervention to institute a CONVOY SYSTEM.

Towards the end of World War I the navy commissioned its 1st aircraft carriers and successfully experimented with precision bombing and torpedo attacks, only to be frustrated from developing this new arm by the switching of naval aviation to the new ROYAL AIR FORCE in 1919. The Japanese drew heavily on British experience, and were later to put this to good effect. Between the wars naval (and army) policy existed in a limbo created by international agreements – the WASHINGTON CONFERENCE (1921–2) – and conservatism. When a rearmament programme was begun (1935), it contained only 2 aircraft carriers to 4 large battleships. A weakness in escorts remained while aircraft, given back to the navy in 1937, were almost totally obsolete.

Not surprisingly, surface ships fared badly in WORLD WAR II: the outfighting of the pocket battleship *Graf Spee* in the River Plate (October 1939) was to be more than outweighed by the sinking of the *Royal Oak* at Scapa Flow, the expensive destruction (1941) of the *Bismarck* (in which HMS *Hood* blew up), the sinking by the Japanese of the *Prince of Wales* and *Repulse* later that year and the channel escape of the *Scharnhorst* and *Gneiseau* (1942). Only in the Mediterranean did Admiral Cunningham use a surface fleet to establish command of the sea.

On the other hand, after the fall of Norway and France (1940) German U-boats were much better placed to raid merchant shipping than they had been in World War I. Their technical capabilities were much greater and 'packs' of them were capable of taking on convoys. This menace was beaten back by a rapid concentration on commissioning escorts and light carriers and providing air cover, co-ordinated by effective combined operations work and the use of operational research methods to establish the best methods of destroying submarines. By mid-1942 the battle of the Atlantic was won – although had German mass-production techniques been used to produce U-boats before 1942 and had the development of some of their deadly experimental boats been accelerated, the result might have been different.

The great surface warships had their taste of action bombarding the French coast before the NORMANDY LANDINGS (June 1944), though the navy still managed to commission its last battleship, HMS *Vanguard*, in 1946. By the time this was withdrawn (1955), the fleet was beginning the process of reduction which has continued to the late 1970s, with the Polaris nuclear submarine (1964) now the 'capital ship', the largest carriers now replaced by 'through-deck' cruisers, and cruisers themselves replaced by guided missile destroyers. The lords of the admiralty did not stay to the end: they left in 1963 when a unified ministry of defence was instituted.

Navy League Founded in 1895, in imitation of Alfred von Tirpitz's organization in Germany (*see* NAVY), to press for naval recruitment, it never represented more than naval enthusiasts, and had little impact on the DREADNOUGHT programme.

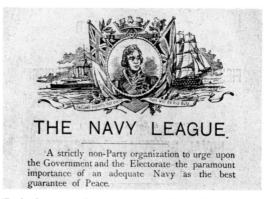

'England expects that every man will do his duty': an advertisement for the **Navy League**, March 1898.

James **Nayler** in 1656 was whipped, pilloried, had his 'tongue bored through with a hot Iron, and [was] Stigmatized in the Forehead with the Letter B'. Etching by Wenceslaus Hollar, 1656.

Nayler, James ?1617–60. After service in the New Model Army, Nayler took up itinerant preaching. The most politically and socially radical of the early QUAKER leaders, he was savagely punished for blasphemy by the 1656 parliament, despite Oliver Cromwell's intervention on his behalf.

Nechtansmere, battle of 20 May 685. Brudei, king of PICTS, decisively defeated an invasion force under King Egfrith of Northumbria at Dunnichen, near Forfar, permanently halting Northumbrian expansion beyond the Forth and ending the Anglian domination of northern Britain.

Nehru, Jawaharlal 1889–1964. Harrow- and Cambridge-educated Indian lawyer, Nehru joined GANDHI in the 1920s in the civil disobedience campaign, although he did not share his leader's absolute pacifism. After 9 years in prison he became the independent nation's 1st premier (1947), and the chief actor in the transformation of the BRITISH EMPIRE into a commonwealth largely composed of 'non-aligned' nations.

Nelson, Horatio, viscount 1758–1805. The son of a Norfolk parson, restless, brave and flamboyant, Nelson proved himself a naval commander of genius, winning decisive victories at the NILE, COPENHAGEN and TRAFALGAR in the NAPOLEONIC WARS. Though he was notorious for his insubordination and for his liaison with Lady Hamilton, his brilliance won the adulation of both his seamen and the public.

Neolithic *see* PREHISTORIC BRITAIN

Neville family Probably the most powerful baronial family in 15th-century England, the Nevilles owed much of their influence to their manifold marriage alliances. Their feud with their PERCY cousins helped spark off the wars of the ROSES, in which Richard, earl of Salisbury, and his son WARWICK THE KINGMAKER both played crucial roles.

Neville's Cross, battle of 17 October 1346. DAVID II of Scotland, responding to his French ally's call to distract EDWARD III from the siege of Calais by invading England, was defeated and captured near Durham by a force of levies (notably archers) led by the archbishop of York and the northern English barons.

'The hero of the Nile': caricature of Horatio **Nelson**, wearing his plume of triumph. Drawing by James Gillray, 1798.

Ralph **Neville**, 1st earl of Westmorland, and the 12 children of his 2nd marriage to Joan Beaufort, daughter of John of Gaunt. The family badge is on their collars. Miniature from a French manuscript, 15th century.

New draperies Woollen textiles, lighter, cheaper and more colourful than traditional English broadcloth. Initially introduced by Protestant refugees from the Netherlands, the new draperies were established by 1600 in the weaving districts of Essex, Devon and Somerset and found ready markets in Europe, thereby helping to revitalize the English CLOTH TRADE.

New England The group of autonomous American colonies established by Puritan emigrants in the 17th century, which included Plymouth Colony (1620), Massachusetts (1628), New Hampshire (1629), Connecticut (1633), Maine (1635), Rhode Island (1636) and New Haven (1638). The name was coined by Captain John Smith and later adopted by the council for New England and other bodies.

New Lanark Textile mills and model village, established in 1786 by David Dale and managed by OWEN (1800–25). New Lanark was noted for its good housing standards, tight social discipline, cleanliness and educational facilities for the workers' children. Working hours, though long, were shorter than was usual at the time.

New Left A name given to the realignment of left-wing intellectuals after the Russian invasion of Hungary (November 1956) produced a major split in the COMMUNIST PARTY OF GREAT BRITAIN, although it also included members of the LABOUR PARTY and independent radicals. It had relatively little political impact but helped bring British intellectual life into the European mainstream.

New Liberalism Collectivist-inclined changes in Liberal ideology which affected the LIBERAL PARTY 1900–14.

New Look Women's fashion incorporating loosely pleated dresses which appeared in 1947 to tantalize those trapped in the 'austerity' programme of the Attlee government.

New Model Army A parliamentarian army in the CIVIL WARS, established early in 1645 and initially commanded by FAIRFAX. Largely formed from existing parliamentarian armies, its distinctive characteristics of firm discipline, high morale, promotion by merit and religious and political radicalism developed later, largely as a result of its victorious record and the personal influence of Oliver CROMWELL.

New model unionism *see* CLASS; TRADE UNIONISM

New Towns Drawing on the experience of the GARDEN CITY movement and a rise of interest in physical and economic planning, 14 'purpose-built' New Towns run by appointed corporations were designated in 1947–50 by the Labour government. Additional ones, of larger size, were founded in the 1960s, culminating in the 250,000-population New City at Milton Keynes. Thereafter, however, with a slowing of population growth, emphasis moved back to the older urban areas.

New unionism A name applied to the unionization of unskilled workers – dockers, gas-workers and general labourers – in the 1880s, frequently by socialist organizers. *See* TRADE UNIONISM.

The uniform of a cavalry trooper in the **New Model Army**. Over the leather coat is an iron back- and breast-plate, crossed by the sword belt. The left (or bridle) arm is shielded by an iron gauntlet. The 'pot' helmet has a vizor above the distinctive grid in front.

One of the first generation of **New Towns**: East Kilbride, near Glasgow, planned in 1947. Aerial photograph *c.* 1960.

Newbury, battles of 1643 and 1644. Battles of the CIVIL WARS. On 20 September 1643 the royalist army under Charles I attempted to block the return of the 3rd earl of Essex from Gloucester to London. After an inconclusive engagement Charles withdrew. A 2nd drawn battle (27 October 1644) was fought between Charles's army and the parliamentarians under Essex, Manchester, and Waller.

Newcastle, Thomas Pelham-Holles, duke of 1693–1768. As secretary of state (1724–54), Newcastle presided over the greatest electoral empire of the period and acted as the agent of government patronage for both Walpole and his brother Pelham. A successful partnership with CHATHAM from 1757 was disrupted by George III's accession, and Newcastle resigned in 1762.

Newcastle, William Cavendish, marquis and 1st duke of 1592–1676. A Nottinghamshire nobleman and courtier, Newcastle led royalist armies in the CIVIL WARS to victory in Yorkshire (1643), but fled abroad after the parliamentarian victory at MARSTON MOOR. Thereafter he took no part in politics, living quietly after 1660 as a patron of the arts and expert on horsemanship.

Newcastle programme A programme imposed on the Liberal party by the National Liberal Federation at its Newcastle conference (1891). It was the high-point of the old Radicalism, calling for triennial parliaments, the abolition of plural voting, licensing and local government reform, disestablishment of the Welsh and Scottish churches, employers' liability for accidents at work and HOME RULE. Gladstone was not enthusiastic and largely forgot about it when he gained power (1892).

Newcastle propositions July 1646. The terms for a peace settlement put to Charles I by parliament during the CIVIL WARS. The propositions, which were wholly unacceptable to the king, would have established a Presbyterian church, given parliament control of the militia for 20 years and punished most of the king's most devoted supporters.

Newman, John Henry 1801–90. An Oxford fellow who left the OXFORD MOVEMENT for the Roman Catholic church (1845). He founded the Catholic university in Dublin (1851) and then the Birmingham oratory. Created a cardinal (1879), he made a liberal version of Catholicism attractive to a number of English intellectuals.

One of the earliest **newspapers**, which flourished during the civil wars, was *Mercurius Civicus*. Front page of no. 12, 11 August 1643, with major news headlines printed above the title.

Newspapers Hand-written news-sheets were regularly dispatched to subscribers from London offices in the 16th century. The 1st one regularly printed dates from 1622 and, helped by the collapse of effective government censorship (1640), the press expanded during the civil war and interregnum. Numbers subsequently fell, but by 1712 the government computed there to be 44,000 copies of newspapers printed weekly and began to levy a stamp tax. By 1760 newspapers, now including many provincial ones, were selling 11 million copies a year, and this was before the daily newspaper got under way. During the Napoleonic wars, the government increased the stamp tax to 7 pence and attempted to crush the growing working-class press, nurtured by COBBETT and others, but the stamp was soon reduced to 1 pence (1835) and then abolished (1855).

The Times (founded 1785) now rose to preeminence, with a circulation at 60,000, 6 times larger than its nearest rival. This was attained by superior technology (it was printed on steam-powered presses from 1814 and made great use of the TELEGRAPH), by the quality of its journalists, such as (Sir) William Howard Russell, and by its authoritative 'establishment' opinion. Its re-

A **newspaper** stall on the eve of World War II, 22 August 1939.

velations of incompetent handling of the Crimean war (1854) brought down the Aberdeen government. The mass-circulation weekly papers were either politically radical, such as Feargus O'CONNOR's *Northern Star*, or sensationalist Sunday papers, or combinations of both. Provincial weeklies took most of their news from London papers and then added large amounts of local material.

In the 1870s and 1880s the railway enabled London papers to penetrate the provinces, but some provincial papers, such as the *Manchester Guardian*, also gained a national reputation. Under men such as STEAD at the *Pall Mall Gazette*, investigative and campaigning journalism increased, while the evening 'betting papers' grew up to cater for an increasing interest in horse-racing and football. But it was NORTHCLIFFE who discovered the formula for the cheap daily – huge circulation and advertising revenue. Northcliffe's *Daily Mail* and the *Daily Express* did much to sensationalize international affairs before World War I, which in due course gave full play to the political intrigues of their owners despite the rigid censorship of actual news.

After 1918, despite cinema and broadcasting, the press tapped the working-class market (traditionally buying only Sunday papers), with tabloids using a large number of illustrations, such as the *Daily Mirror*, and with extravagant free gifts offered in the 'circulation war' of the early 1930s. In the late 1930s photo-journalism, imported from Germany along with refugees from Hitler, produced effective social and political propaganda material, such as *Picture Post* and *Illustrated* which, along with the *Daily Mirror*, helped move the country to the left during World War II.

After the war the number of papers was reduced and circulations fell, under competition from television. But successes were registered at both ends of the social scale, with an expansion of sensational tabloids, such as the *Sun*, and of quality dailies and Sundays. The market for illustrated magazines, notably for women, and for children's comics, also increased. But the adoption of new technologies caused enormous labour problems in Fleet Street, which had not been overcome by the 1980s. *See* PRINTING.

Nigeria *see* BRITISH EMPIRE

Nightingale, Florence 1820–1910. From an upper-class family and trained as a nurse in Paris and Prussia, Florence took over the military hospital at Scutari near Constantinople (October 1854) and greatly improved the care of the wounded from the CRIMEAN WAR. After her return (1856) she left nursing, but continued to counsel 'her' nurses and to intervene in public health affairs.

'Mis(s)-Management': the contrast between Florence **Nightingale** and this Gamp-like figure was used to criticize government incompetence in the Crimean war. Cartoon, *c.* 1854.

Nile, battle of the 1 August 1798. The destruction or capture by a British fleet under NELSON, of an entire French fleet anchored in Aboukir bay after transporting Napoleon's army to Egypt. This battle of the NAPOLEONIC WARS won complete control of the Mediterranean for Britain, leaving Napoleon isolated in Egypt.

1922 committee The name for the back-bench assembly of the parliamentary CONSERVATIVE PARTY, after the party's decision (19 October 1922) to leave the LLOYD GEORGE coalition.

Ninian, St (or Nynia). The earliest known Christian evangelist to Scotland. A British follower of St Martin, trained in Rome, Ninian is said by Bede to have converted the southern Picts and founded (perhaps in 398) a church called 'Candida Casa' (the White House) at Whithorn in Galloway.

Noble An English gold coin worth 6s. 8d. (or a third of a pound), introduced in 1344 and superseded by the ANGEL and ROYAL in 1465.

Nonconformists *see* DISSENTERS

An English **noble** of Edward III, 1360–9.

St **Ninian** vested as a bishop. The donor at his feet is pleading, 'Pray for us, St Ninian.' From *Hours of Ninian*, 15th-century Scottish manuscript.

Nonconformity since 1830. After the repeal of the Test Acts in 1828 (*see* ROMAN CATHOLICISM) Nonconformists played a larger political role (*see* ANTI-CORN-LAW LEAGUE) but until the 1860s they still tended to operate through sympathetic Whig politicians. The 1851 religious census showed them roughly level with the Anglicans among the 47–54% who went to church. About half were METHODISTS of one sort or another (strongest in Wales, Yorkshire, Cornwall and Norfolk). The other major groups were CONGREGATIONALISTS and BAPTISTS (eastern counties) and Presbyterians (*see* PRESBYTERIANISM) in Northumberland and Durham. However 1851 showed Nonconformity rather weak in areas such as Lancashire and London. This led Nonconformists to worry about the revival of the church of England, and to become more political, allying themselves with the Liberals. The Congregationalists had already taken the lead in founding the LIBERATION SOCIETY and pressing for disestablishment (1840s). But much of the energy of Nonconformist-radical campaigns came from smaller sects of prosperous entrepreneurs, such as the QUAKERS (*see* BRIGHT, JOHN; ROWNTREE, B. SEEBOHM) and the UNITARIANS (*see* CHAMBERLAIN, JOSEPH). Only in the 1860s did the Methodists join them and work together for the removal of remaining disabilities, including UNIVERSITY tests, tithes and Anglican control of cemeteries, and for Nonconformist causes such as TEMPERANCE, Sunday observance and the PEACE MOVEMENT. The social and ideological cohesion of Nonconformity, however, was beginning to break up as fundamentalism retreated before the challenge of rationalism, and the wealthy shifted back to Anglicanism. Nonconformist leaders were prepared to take orders from non-dissenters such as the radical dons who ran the anti-tests campaign, or from Anglicans such as GLADSTONE.

The EDUCATION Act (1870), which maintained Anglican privileges, drove Nonconformists into local LIBERAL PARTY organization, where they tried to incorporate their demands in the party platform. Gladstone showed great skill in winning them to his 'great moral issue' view of politics by securing rank and file backing for home rule (1886), though many dissenting leaders left the party over this issue.

During this period and despite the popularity of American-style revivalism after Moody and Sankey's Crusade (1873–5), the integration of Nonconformists into the traditional politics of the country became complete: their colleges moved to Oxford and Cambridge, their newspapers to London. LLOYD GEORGE was the 1st Nonconformist prime minister (1916), but this period of power coincided with the turn of the tide. From 1910–65 Baptist membership fell from 419,000–295,000, Congregationalist membership from 494,000–198,000 and Presbyterian membership from 87,000–70,000. The Methodists amalgamated with the Primitive Methodists (1932) to produce a membership of 823,000 but by 1965 this had fallen to 690,000.

The interwar depression hit the areas hard in which Nonconformity was strong, migration disrupted old allegiances, and secularization and new forms of entertainment took their toll. The decline of Liberalism meant that the political role of Nonconformity was no longer a critical one. Its radical line in international affairs owed much to the rapid growth of daughter churches in the new commonwealth and in the 1970s traditional Nonconformity found itself challenged by revivalist religion among black immigrants in Britain.

Non-intervention A policy adopted by Britain, France, Germany and Italy in the Spanish civil war (1936–9) and adhered to by the first two, despite gross violations by the others.

Non-jurors Anglican clergy supporting the doctrine of non-resistance, who scrupled to take the oath of allegiance to William III and Mary II following the GLORIOUS REVOLUTION. Originally

including Archbishop Sancroft, 5 bishops and some 400 others, they had split into 3 groups by 1720 and maintained their separation until the early 19th century.

Non-residence The practice of clergymen failing to reside in their benefices. From the middle ages until the 19th century when the custom was abolished, non-residents, who included many persons engaged in administrative and academic duties, formed a substantial proportion of the clergy of many districts.

Norham, raid of *see* JAMES IV

Norman architecture Practically all Anglo-Saxon churches were replaced after the Norman conquest by much larger buildings in the Norman strain of Romanesque, a style current in France from *c.* 1000. Major Norman churches have elongated, aisled ground-plans, semicircular east ends (apses), massive round arches and huge pillars. DURHAM CATHEDRAL (begun 1093) pioneered rib vaults which became the basis of Gothic. *See* EARLY ENGLISH ARCHITECTURE.

Boxgrove priory, Sussex: view of the south aisle with its heavy columns, typical of **Norman architecture**.

Above The beginning of the **Norman conquest**: this detail from the Bayeux tapestry shows Harold struck down by a mounted Norman knight at the battle of Hastings.

Left The 4 **Norman** kings: William the Conqueror, William Rufus, Henry I and Stephen. From a mid-13th-century manuscript.

Norman conquest The achievement of WILLIAM THE CONQUEROR has always been recognized as the great turning-point of English history, but its interpretation has varied with the current political prejudices of historians who, for instance, persistently associated the Anglo-Saxons with the 'good old cause' of liberalism, democracy and Protestantism. It is nearer the truth to see the English, or rather Anglo-Danish, state of 1066 as a long-established monarchy in decline (with a somewhat moribund church) linked to the backward-looking Scandinavian world. On the death of the childless Edward the Confessor it seemed that Cnut's heir Harald Hardrada might even strengthen this connection, but his defeat by Harold Godwinson at STAMFORD BRIDGE, and Godwinson's own defeat at HASTINGS by Edward's chosen successor William (*see* FULFORD, BATTLE OF), ensured instead that England would henceforth form part of the mainstream of Latin European culture, represented by newly emerged Normandy.

The greatest internal change wrought by the conquest was the destruction of the old English aristocracy by death in battle or (especially after the rebellions of 1067–70) by dispossession and exile, and its replacement by a Norman ruling class including appreciable Breton and Flemish elements. This clean sweep of landowners (by the time of DOMESDAY BOOK, 1086, Englishmen held only about 8% of English land) facilitated the establishment of the new aristocracy on a basis of contractual military tenure – FEUDALISM – which (despite recent controversy) seems to have been virtually unknown in pre-conquest England, and which automatically enhanced royal power. The redistribution of land also enabled William (who incidentally exploited to the full the traditions and institutions of his native predecessors) further to increase this power by retaining about 20% of England himself and granting roughly another 25%, notably on the vulnerable coasts and borders (*see* MARCHERS), to a small group of his relatives and close associates.

Broadly similar changes occurred in the English church, which William and Lanfranc worked closely together to reform and revitalize on the disciplinarian lines of the church of Normandy. English bishops and abbots were largely replaced by Normans, the majority of monastic and all episcopal lands being subjected to military feudal tenure. The conquest also initiated a revival of monasticism and of church-building in the new NORMAN ARCHITECTURE.

The lower ranks of society, however, were comparatively little affected (though Domesday Book records a marked tendency for SERFS to rise, and for CEORLS to sink, to the intermediate status of

VILLEINS). Continuity with the pre-conquest world is also observable in the law, which was augmented rather than changed by the Normans, and to a lesser extent in the institutions and officials of government.

The Norman conquest, most aptly characterized by CASTLES and knights, nonetheless transformed England, and was soon to affect the remainder of Britain: William's establishment of Marcher earldoms provided the springboard for the piecemeal Norman invasion of Wales and (under Henry II) of Ireland, while under David I and his 12th-century successors Anglo-Normans also came to dominate Scotland. (R. A. Brown, *The Normans and the Norman Conquest*, 1969.)

Normandy A province of northern France, held directly by William the Conqueror and after TENCHEBRAI (1106), by Henry I and his descendants, until its loss under JOHN (1204). Reconquered by HENRY V (1417–19) during the hundred years' war, it remained English until overrun by Charles VII (1450).

Normandy landings 6 June 1944. These began on D-day to liberate France and establish a second front. The extent of the preparations, which included the floating Mulberry harbours and the Pluto oil pipeline, surprised the Germans (who were expecting an attack on a major port) and materially shortened WORLD WAR II.

Norsemen *see* VIKINGS

North, Frederick, 8th lord 1733–92. An easygoing politician lacking long-term objectives, North did much as prime minister (1770–82) to re-establish political stability after the 1760s. The American independence struggle, however, gradually destroyed his popularity and led to his resignation. He returned to power with Charles James FOX (1783) but was shortly dismissed by George III.

North Atlantic Treaty Organization Set up in 1949 as an American-led military alliance in expectation of aggression from the Soviet Union, NATO included all the west European states except Spain, Sweden, Switzerland, Austria and Finland. Greece, Turkey and West Germany later joined, but France withdrew in 1966 and Greece in 1974.

North Sea floods 1953. The worst floods for centuries hit the English coast from the Humber to

The **Normandy landings:** allied troops assemble on the Normandy beaches, June 1944.

'The Political Rat-catcher': engraved satire on Lord **North**, 1772.

the Thames on 31 January–1 February 1953. As a result 307 people were drowned, over 32,000 made homeless, and the damage was estimated at £40–50 million.

Northampton, battle of 10 July 1460. A Yorkist victory in the wars of the ROSES. Returning from exile, WARWICK THE KINGMAKER defeated the Lancastrians under Humphrey Stafford, duke of Buckingham, in a half-hour battle, and captured Henry VI.

Northcliffe, Alfred Harmsworth, viscount 1865–1922. An Irish-born press baron, Northcliffe was made director of propaganda to enemy countries by Lloyd George (1918) and later minister of aviation, before his mind gave way (1920). *See* NEWSPAPERS.

Northern rebellion 1569–70. A rising of the earls of Westmorland and Northumberland against Elizabeth I. The half-hearted rising, ostensibly in defence of the Catholic faith, Mary Queen of Scots and the provincial authority of the earls, was a fiasco. The earls fled to Scotland, whence Northumberland was returned in 1572 for execution.

Northumberland, earls of (14th to 16th centuries) *see* PERCY FAMILY

Viscount **Northcliffe** (right) and Marquess Curzon on their way to attend the first meeting of the new air board at Carlton House Terrace, in 1918.

Northumberland, John Dudley, earl of Warwick and duke of 1504–53. Though traditionally regarded as an unprincipled adventurer, Northumberland remains enigmatic. After winning a military reputation under Henry VIII and Somerset, he dominated EDWARD VI's council following Somerset's fall (1550). His brief period of power saw important financial reforms and the acceleration of the REFORMATION. He was executed for opposing Mary I's accession. *See* PERCY FAMILY.

Northumbria The kingdom of the ANGLES north of the Humber, formed by Aethelferth's union of Bernicia and Deira (604). At its 7th-century zenith it extended from south of Trent to north of Forth, and under EDWIN, OSWALD and OSWIU dominated all Britain. Its English hegemony ended with the rise of Mercia and its northward expansion was curbed by the Picts' victory at NECHTANSMERE. Despite civil wars it was an important cultural centre (*see* ALCUIN; BEDE) during the 8th century, but thereafter came under heavy Viking attack, the Danes settling its southern part from 876 and the Norwegians later colonizing its northern part. Its lands beyond Tweed were ceded to Scotland *c.* 970, the remainder becoming an Anglo-Danish earldom in the early 11th century.

Norwegians *see* VIKINGS

Notitia Dignitatum A document of disputed date (probably *c.* 400), listing civil and military officials and troop dispositions in the Roman empire, and important in the study of the end of Roman Britain.

Notting Hill riots *see* IMMIGRATION

Novantae The British tribe inhabiting Dumfries and Galloway. Hostile to Rome, they were conquered by Agricola (82), but revolted with their neighbours the Brigantes and the Selgovae several times during the 2nd century. In the late 4th century, however, they became FOEDERATI under a dynasty established by Magnus Maximus.

Novel Disseisin, assizes of A process introduced by Henry II (1166) to help those who had suffered 'recent dispossession' of their land to recover it in law. The time-limit for actions, originally very short, was progressively and almost infinitely extended, and fictional assizes were later employed to establish doubtful titles.

Nuclear disarmament *see* CAMPAIGN FOR NUCLEAR DISARMAMENT

Nuns Communities of religious women are known in Britain almost from the earliest Christian times, particularly in Anglo-Saxon England. During the middle ages nearly every religious order (except the CARTHUSIANS) had its branch for women: these (saving the GILBERTINES) lived in independent and strictly enclosed houses, generally small.

Oates, Titus 1649–1705. After a scandalous career as Anglican clergyman, Catholic apostate and Jesuit novice, Oates concocted the tale of the POPISH PLOT (1678) and acted as leading informer in the ensuing hysteria. Discredited, he was imprisoned for perjury (1685) but was released and granted a pension after 1688.

Observants *see* FRANCISCANS

Occasional conformity The practice of attending Anglican communion once a year, adopted by DISSENTERS in order to evade the TEST ACT and qualify for public office. The Occasional Conformity Act (1711–19) prevented this, but from 1727 annual Indemnity Acts protected dissenters from prosecution.

O'Connell, Daniel 1775–1847. An Irish Catholic landowner and barrister, O'Connell fought against the Anglo-Irish UNION from its inception (1800) and against the continuing legal disabilities of Irish Catholics. His Catholic Association of 1823 could claim to be the 1st political mass movement. Its growth, and his election for County Clare (1828) were instrumental in securing from Peel the passage of the 1829 Roman Catholic Relief Act (*see* ROMAN CATHOLICISM), which allowed him to take his seat. In the 1830s he co-operated with DRUMMOND, the reforming Whig chief secretary for Ireland but, on the Whigs' fall, concentrated on creating a popular movement for repeal of the union. This failed, partly because of the appeal of YOUNG IRELAND, and partly because of the disastrous impact of the potato famine (1845–7).

O'Connor, Feargus 1794–1855. An Irish radical who, after a spell as an MP (1832–5), became a leading figure of 'physical force' CHARTISM. He owned and edited the successful Chartist newspaper, the *Northern Star*, and gained great support among northern textile workers, especially for his 'land plan' for rural resettlement. Elected MP for Nottingham (1847), he was active in the last and largely Irish, phase of Chartism and introduced the 1848 petition to the commons. He went insane in 1852.

Odo *c.* 1030–97. Bishop of Bayeux and a half-brother of William the Conqueror, who made him earl of Kent and the greatest landowner in England. Imprisoned (allegedly for aspiring to the papacy) from 1082 until the Conqueror's death, he then led an unsuccessful revolt against WILLIAM RUFUS on behalf of ROBERT CURTHOSE (1088) and was banished to Normandy. *See* BAYEUX TAPESTRY.

In 1685 Titus **Oates** was ordered to 'be placed in the pillories five times a year for life . . . and thereupon immediately returned to prison': so runs the description underneath this picture on the frontispiece of an Italian broadsheet, *Military Affairs*, 1685.

The achievement of Catholic emancipation made Daniel **O'Connell** one of the best-known personalities in Europe: 'King O'Connell at Tara', with a shillelagh for a sceptre and the British constitution for a footstool. This *Punch* cartoon of 1844 demonstrates its vicious racial stereotyping of the Irish.

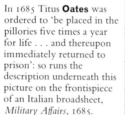

Offa portrayed on a contemporary Mercian penny.

One of the Dunloe **Ogham** stones at Coolmagort, Co. Kerry, Ireland. The Ogham characters use the nearside edge of the stone as a base line.

Oengus mac Fergus king of the Picts (729–61). The king under whom the Picts attained their greatest strength. Having united his own divided people, he campaigned against Northumbria (740) and, unsuccessfully, against Strathclyde (756), but his greatest achievement was the defeat and long-standing subjugation of Dalriada (741).

Offa king of Mercia (757–96). The greatest king of Mercia and one of the most notable of all Anglo-Saxon monarchs, Offa annexed Kent and Sussex and dominated East Anglia, Wessex and probably Northumbria, calling himself king of all England by 774 and defining the frontier with Wales by OFFA'S DYKE. The 1st English king to play an appreciable part in European politics, he corresponded on equal terms with Charlemagne, persuaded the pope to erect a short-lived Mercian archbishopric at Lichfield, encouraged continental trade, and introduced the standard silver PENNY, long the basis of English currency.

Offa's dyke The most impressive monument of the Anglo-Saxon period, an 80-mile (120-kilometre) long earthwork running discontinuously from the Irish Sea to the Bristol Channel. It was raised (probably between 784 and 796) by OFFA of Mercia as a boundary between England and Wales, and apparently represents a frontier negotiated by treaty.

Ogham An early Irish alphabet designed for carving, whose letters consisted of combinations of short straight lines crossing or joining a long base line at various angles. It has been found in Britain on numerous heroic age memorial stones in Cornwall, Scotland and, especially, western Wales. *See* IRISH INVASIONS.

Old age pensions These had been advocated since the 1890s, especially by BOOTH, as an alternative to the workhouse, which was the only provision the Poor Law Amendment Act (1834) had made. Lloyd George introduced them (1908) on a non-contributory basis at 5s. for a single person over 70, and 7s. 6d. for a couple. The qualifying age was reduced to 65 in 1928, and (for women) to 60 in 1940.

Old Pretender *see* JACOBITES; MAR, 11TH EARL OF; MARLBOROUGH'S WARS

Old Statistical Account A compilation of reports on the conditions of Scottish parishes in the 1790s supplied by ministers of the church of Scotland in response to a questionnaire prepared by Sir John Sinclair. It is an invaluable source for the social and economic history of the period.

Oldcastle, Sir John, Lord Cobham *c.* 1378–1417. An erstwhile friend of Henry V, he was imprisoned as a LOLLARD (1413), but escaped to co-ordinate a desperate national rising of his co-religionists. The few hundred rebels were easily rounded up outside Temple Bar, London, on the night of 9–10 January 1414, but Oldcastle escaped, to plot in hiding until captured and executed.

Omdurman, battle of 2 September 1898. The battle, fought near Khartoum, at which KITCHENER defeated the Dervishes and established British control over the Sudan.

O'Neill, Shane ?1530–67. An Ulster chieftain who, after recognition by Elizabeth I as captain of Tyrone (1562), rapidly extended his power. Raids on the PALE and treasonable negotiations with France and the papacy ultimately provoked a punitive expedition under Sir Henry Sidney (1567), following which O'Neill was defeated and then murdered by rival chieftains.

Open parishes In contrast to CLOSED PARISHES, open parishes failed to regulate the settlement of poor cottagers. They were frequently industrial parishes which needed an abundant supply of cheap labour and commonly had severe poverty problems.

Opinion polls Pioneered in the USA by George S. Gallup (b. 1901), these forecasting surveys of sociologically balanced public opinion were first used in 1939, and in a British election in 1945. Since then 3 further polls have come into existence: National Opinion Poll (1957), Opinion Research Centre (1965) and Louis Harris (1969).

Opium wars European penetration of the Chinese empire began with the Opium war of 1839–42, provoked by China's attempt to ban the import of opium from India. As a result, Britain gained Hong Kong (1842). In the Lorcha war (1856–8), Peking was captured and European trade and missionary stations established, being confirmed after another punitive expedition (1870), although challenged by the Boxer rising (1900).

Oppida Large settlement complexes, including farmland, in valley-side locations defended partly by massive earthwork ramparts and partly by rivers, marshes, woods and other natural obstacles. Introduced into south-eastern England by the Belgae during the 1st century BC, several (including Chichester and COLCHESTER) subsequently became the sites of Roman towns.

Orders in council Subordinate legislation usually of either a detailed or emergency kind, enacted by a committee of the privy COUNCIL under instruction from the CABINET. *See* DEFENCE OF THE REALM ACTS.

Ordinances, the 1311. The baronial demands assembled by a committee of 'ordainers' and forced on EDWARD II. They included the banishment of GAVESTON, baronial control of the appointment of principal government and royal household officials, financial retrenchment and annual parliaments. Effectively repudiated by Edward (1312), they were re-enforced (1314) and finally revoked after BOROUGHBRIDGE.

Ordovices A pastoral tribe inhabiting north-west and central Wales and Anglesey, they were hostile to Rome, and supported CARATACUS in 51. A Roman invasion of their territory (59–60) was curtailed by Boudica's revolt, and not until 77–8 were they finally conquered by Julius Frontinus and Agricola.

Orkneys An archipelago off northern Scotland, important in prehistoric times (*see* DUNS AND BROCHS; MAES HOWE; SKARA BRAE). Intensively settled by Norwegian Vikings from *c.* 800, they were annexed by King Harold Fairhair *c.* 900 to prevent piratical activity against Scandinavia, and thereafter formed a semi-autonomous Norwegian earldom. Ruled by Scottish earls from 1231, they were finally annexed to Scotland by James III.

Skara Brae, **Orkney**: the best-preserved of a group of late stone age houses. The interior, as excavated, shows a fireplace and a structure apparently used as a kind of dresser.

The siege of **Orleans**, 1429. The text below the picture explains that in the foreground are 'the earl of SALISBURY, Lord TALBOT, the earl of SUFFOLK and many other Englishmen'. From the *Chronique abrégée des Rois de France*, 15th century.

Orleans A French fortress town, besieged by the 4th earl of Salisbury from 12 October 1428 and after his death (with less success) by Suffolk and Talbot. It was relieved (3 May 1429) by an army inspired by JOAN OF ARC, which subsequently defeated English forces at Jargeau (12 June) and Patay (18 June). *See* HUNDRED YEARS' WAR.

Ormonde, James Butler, 12th earl and 1st duke of 1610–88. Of ancient lineage, proud, loyal and forthright, Ormonde championed Charles I's cause in Ireland first against Catholic rebels (1642–3) and subsequently parliamentarians. Defeated in 1649, he lived in exile from 1651–60, later serving as lord-lieutenant of Ireland (1661–9 and 1677–84). Thereafter he opposed James VII and II's Catholicizing policies but died before the Glorious Revolution.

Orwell, George 1903–50. The pseudonym of Eric Blair. Although educated at Eton, Orwell became a socialist journalist and novelist of a very distinctive sort, after a spell in the Burmese police. A patriotic radical in the style of COBBETT, he was alerted by the Spanish civil war to the totalitarian nature of Soviet Communism and his satires *Animal Farm* (1941) and

1984 (1948) became major propaganda works in the Cold War.

Osborne judgment *see* TRADE UNIONISM

Oswald king of Northumbria (633–41). The son of Aethelferth, Oswald reconquered Northumbria from Cadwallawn and Penda and sponsored its re-Christianization by AIDAN. His victorious campaigns (notably against Gwynedd and Strathclyde) gained him recognition as BRETWALDA and overlord of Picts, Scotti and Britons, but in 641 he was slain by Penda at Oswestry.

Oswestry, battle of *see* OSWALD; PENDA

Oswiu king of Northumbria (641–70). The brother of OSWALD, Oswiu ruled a reduced Northumbria until his victory over PENDA and his Anglo-Welsh allies at Winwaed near Leeds in 654 made him briefly BRETWALDA. But Mercia reasserted its independence in 657, and thereafter he campaigned only against Picts and Scotti. His decision at WHITBY aligned the English church with Rome.

Ottawa conference July–August 1932. A conference of the dominions which, by authorizing a limited degree of IMPERIAL PREFERENCE, ended the era of FREE TRADE. *See* BRITISH EMPIRE.

Otterburn, battle of 5 August 1388. A Scots raiding force under James, earl of Douglas (taking advantage of English distraction with the MERCILESS PARLIAMENT) was attacked by Hotspur at dusk. Though Douglas was killed, Hotspur was taken, and the Scots claimed a narrow victory in the hard-fought moonlight battle, also called 'Chevy Chase'.

Oudenarde, battle of *see* MARLBOROUGH'S WARS

Outcast London The phrase came from a book by Rev. Andrew Mearns, *The Bitter Cry of Outcast London* (1883), which awoke politicians and social reformers to the plight of those driven from London city-centre slums into the east end by railway building and redevelopment. This was the prelude to much investigation and organizational work by BOOTH, Toynbee Hall (*see* TOYNBEE, ARNOLD) and BEVERIDGE.

Outdoor relief *see* WELFARE STATE

Outlaws People placed outside the protection of the law, generally after repeatedly failing to appear when summoned to answer a criminal charge: their lands and goods were forfeit, and they could be pardoned only by the crown. A nominal form of outlawry was employed in debt cases from the 13th century.

Owain Gwynedd c. 1110–70. The son of Gruffydd ap Cynan, under whom he extended Gwynedd, becoming king in 1137. He then led the great Welsh counter-attack against the MARCHERS and, though he submitted to Henry II (1157), he subsequently co-operated with Rhys ap Gruffydd in further campaigns, conquering up to the Dee.

Owen, Robert 1771–1858. A philanthropist, social theorist and manager of NEW LANARK. In *A New View of Society* (1813), Owen argued that all social evils derived from a poor environment. He introduced improved conditions for his own workers, though remaining as authoritarian in his relations with them as any other contemporary industrialist. After 1830 he turned to CO-OPERATIVE RETAIL SOCIETIES and TRADE UNIONISM. He had enormous influence on a generation of working-class reformers.

Oxford group A well-heeled Evangelical pressure group founded by Frank Buchman c. 1925, which became identified with anti-communism during the post-war period and with Mary Whitehouse's crusade against 'filth in the media' in the later 1960s.

Oxford movement It originated with John Keble's Oxford sermon against 'national apostasy'

(1833) as an attempt to revitalize the HIGH CHURCH Anglican tradition. A series of *Tracts for the Times* were produced. In 1845 NEWMAN and others left for the Roman Catholic church, but the movement, which claimed GLADSTONE as a devoted adherent, still remained important in the established church.

Ox-gang *see* BOVATE

Oyer and terminer, commissions of From the 13th century onwards, judicial commissions (including both lawyers and county gentry) periodically appointed to 'hear and determine' the more serious criminal cases within each SHIRE.

Paine, Tom 1737–1809. Of Norfolk Quaker stock, Paine emigrated to America (1775) and wrote *Common Sense* (1776) in support of American independence. In 1791–2 he answered BURKE's *Reflections* with *The Rights of Man*. Elected to the French convention during the French revolution, he narrowly escaped execution during the Terror, and subsequently returned to America.

Outcast London: the kitchen of a common lodging-house in Spitalfields, London. Illustration from the *Graphic*, 24 April 1886.

'Tommy **Paine**, the little American Taylor, taking the measure of the Crown, for a new pair of Revolution-Breeches.' Hostile cartoon by James Gillray, 1791.

Palaeolithic *see* PREHISTORIC BRITAIN

Pale, the The area of late medieval Ireland which was under effective English rule. Of varying extent, the Pale stretched only 50 miles north of Dublin and 30 miles inland by 1500, though it was extended under Mary I. Beyond the Pale, royal authority existed in name only, effective power belonging to the great Irish chieftains.

Palestine question Britain acquired Palestine under LEAGUE OF NATIONS mandate (1920; in force 1923) after the BALFOUR declaration (1917) had sanctioned a Jewish national home there. Jewish immigration steadily increased but after World War II Britain attempted to check growing conflict with local Arabs by cutting down entry. A terrorist campaign ensued and Britain was forced to hand over her responsibility to the UNITED NATIONS (1947). British withdrawal (May 1948) was followed by an Arab-Israeli war in which the Israelis were victorious.

Palmerston, Henry John Temple, 3rd viscount 1784–1865. Temple inherited his Irish peerage in 1802. Still permitted to sit in the commons, he took his seat as MP for the pocket borough of Newport, Isle of Wight (1807), remaining until his death, and serving in every ministry save those of Peel and Derby. Until 1829 he was a Tory and follower of CANNING, and secretary at war (1809–28), responsible for the financing of the army.

He then joined the Whigs because of his desire for moderate reform and an active foreign policy, and served them as foreign secretary (1830–41), guaranteeing the neutrality of the new state of Belgium through the treaty of LONDON (1839) and supporting the Liberal-inclined queens of Spain and Portugal against absolutist pretenders. He had supported Greek independence, but now insisted on the integrity of Turkey and resisted any possible advance by the Russians on the Bosphorous and by the French on the Nile. When Turkey was threatened in the mid-1830s by the revolt of Mehemet Ali, governor of Egypt, he allied first with France, to prevent Turkey from capitulating to Russia, then with Russia against Mehemet Ali, whom France refused to coerce. By 1841 he was reckoned one of the most powerful figures in European diplomacy, but in that year the Whigs fell from power – probably fortunately as Palmerston had convinced himself that a war with France was inevitable and necessary.

He returned to office under John Russell (1846), only to find himself beaten by the French in

Viscount **Palmerston** speaking in the house of commons, 1860. Lord John Russell and W. E. Gladstone are behind him. Engraving after a painting by J. Philip.

promoting a candidate for the hand of the queen of Spain. In the 1848 revolutions he gave some assistance to Italian revolutionaries but otherwise maintained a non-intervention policy. His efforts to mediate between the Italians and Austrians were ill-considered, and Austria suppressed Hungarians and liberals with Russian assistance, before he could do anything about it. Thereafter his behaviour was high-handed and inconsistent: his patronage of the Hungarian patriot Kossuth insulted the Russians and Austrians, the DON PACIFICO affair irritated all the European powers, and his welcome for Louis Napoleon's seizure of power (1851) brought him down, as Queen Victoria's hatred of him coincided with popular resentment of French 'imperialism'.

He rejoined Aberdeen's government (1853) as home secretary, and when it fell, over mismanagement of the Crimean war, he became prime minister (February 1855) and reaped the credit for victory at the 1857 election. In 1858 there was a short, almost accidental, Conservative ministry, but the following year the Liberal party was reunited and Palmerston came back to office. He promoted FREE TRADE through the Cobden-Chevalier treaty with France (1860), but regarded Napoleon III with increasing suspicion and advocated rearmament against him. He remained neutral during the American civil war, although he personally sympathized with the South, but suffered a stinging defeat (1864) when Bismarck defeated Denmark in the Schleswig-Holstein war, despite his promises of help to the Danes. He had never been thought to regard domestic reform with much enthusiasm and his death (18 October 1865) began the campaign which, within 2 years, resulted in the 2nd REFORM BILL.

This may have been unfair. Under the bullying exterior he was a serious moderate reformer, and had proved an able home secretary. According to Professor John Vincent, in *The Formation of the British Liberal Party* (1966), he was 'not the masterly architect of a policy of supineness of the institutions and circumstances of the time'. His own somewhat baroque lifestyle, however, helped to crystallize the image. In 1863 he was expected to be cited as an adulterer. 'How do we know the affair has not been got up to dissolve on?', was Disraeli's comment.

Pankhurst, Emmeline, Christabel, Sylvia and Adela

Emmeline (1858–1928) founded the Women's Franchise League (1889) and, with her daughter Christabel (1880–1958), the militant Women's Social and Political Union (1903), initiating the violent SUFFRAGETTE campaign. The frequent arrests and imprisonments of mother and daughter did not, however, radicalize them socially. During World War I both became intensely bellicose and moved from the Independent Labour party to the Conservatives. Of her other daughters, Sylvia (1882–1960) remained true to her father's socialist views, organized women workers in

A suffragette procession of 1911, led by Mrs Emmeline **Pankhurst**.

London's east end, and then became a strong advocate of Abyssinia at the time of its invasion by Italy (1935); and Adela (1885–1961) became a leader of left-wing socialism in Australia. *See* WOMEN'S MOVEMENT.

Papal bull Formal papal promulgation authenticated by a seal (Lat. *bulla*) and generally named after its initial words or phrases, e.g. LAUDABILITER, Humanae Vitae, Clericis Laicos (*see* EDWARD I).

Pardons, medieval Except in a COUNTY PALATINE, the grant of pardons was the personal prerogative of the crown, though pardons for homicide in self-defence or by misadventure were issued automatically by CHANCERY. During the 15th century general pardons were periodically issued, and were purchased as a safeguard against prosecution.

Paris, peace of 10 February 1763. A separate peace signed by Britain, France, Spain and Portugal to conclude the SEVEN YEARS' WAR. Britain gained Canada, Florida and several West Indian islands from France and Spain. France regained a number of Caribbean islands and her Indian trading posts, and was guaranteed fishing rights off Newfoundland. (Austria and Prussia signed the peace of Hubertusburg 5 days later.)

Paris, treaties of 1814–15. Treaties settling Europe after the NAPOLEONIC WARS. France, reduced to the frontiers of 1792, was contained by the strengthened states of the United Netherlands, Hanover, Prussia and Piedmont. Britain gained the Cape of Good Hope, Guiana and Malta. Following WATERLOO, further territorial losses, an indemnity and temporary military occupation were imposed on France. *See* VIENNA, CONGRESS OF.

Paris, treaty of 4 December 1259. Signed by Henry III and Louis IX, the treaty finally recognized JOHN's loss of Normandy and Poitou to France, but confirmed the English crown's possession of Aquitaine, albeit as vassals of the kings of France – a situation which eventually gave rise to the hundred years' war.

Parish The area served by a church and a beneficed minister of the established church. The parochial structure emerged in England from the 8th century onwards and in Scotland from the 12th (*see* CHURCH, PRE-REFORMATION) and continues to develop. From the 16th to the 19th centuries parishes also played a major role in LOCAL GOVERNMENT, following their

adoption as the basic administrative units of the
POOR LAWS. *See* CLOSED PARISHES; OPEN PARISHES.

Parish registers Register books recording baptisms, marriages and burials performed in parish
churches. The keeping of such registers in English
and Welsh parishes dates from 1538 and in Scottish
parishes from 1552 (baptisms and marriages) and
1565 (burials).

Parish vestry The governing body of an English
PARISH for LOCAL GOVERNMENT purposes. Vestries
were commonly oligarchical in structure ('close' or
'select' vestries), though on occasion they were
broader assemblies of ratepayers. All ratepayers
were given a vote in vestry affairs in 1832 and in
1894 parish councils superseded vestries.

Parisi A British tribe which originated in northern
France and settled in east Yorkshire in the 5th or 4th
century BC, bringing with it the custom of cart-
burial. Occupied *c.* 70 as a prelude to the Roman
conquest of the Brigantes, it later became a CIVITAS,
with a capital at Petuaria (location uncertain).

Parker, Matthew 1504–75. The chaplain of Anne
Boleyn, tutor of ELIZABETH I and Master of Corpus
Christi, Cambridge, Parker was a moderate
Protestant and a scholar of distinction. As archbishop of Canterbury (1559–75) he presided over
the initial enforcement of the Elizabethan religious
settlement (*see* REFORMATION).

Parliament The evolution of parliament from a
medieval assembly of barons and prelates to its
position as the central institution of a system of
representative democracy is the most fundamental
theme of British constitutional history. That
development, however, was neither smooth nor
inevitable. Only after 1688 was parliament's
permanent place in the constitution assured, while
the process of adjustment to a changing society
thereafter has sometimes been turbulent.

Parliament (French *parlement*, a discussion)
originated in formalized meetings of the 'great
COUNCIL' of king, barons and leading prelates,
summoned in the early 13th century to give counsel
on major issues. The extension of its social
composition began in the baronial reform struggle
of the mid-13th century, as Henry III and Simon de
Montfort sought broader bases of support in the
kingdom. KNIGHTS OF THE SHIRE were first summoned by Henry III in 1254, while Montfort
summoned 2 burgesses from selected boroughs in
1265. By the reign of Edward III the summoning of

knights and burgesses was an established characteristic of parliament, and in 1429 the 40-shilling
freehold county franchise was introduced, borough
franchises remaining extremely varied. A further
15th-century development was the emergence of an
hereditary parliamentary peerage, both the names
and numbers of the peers summoned having varied
in earlier times. Parliament also met frequently
from the later 13th century, short annual sessions
being normal by the mid-14th century. Parliament
had become an institution rather than an occasion.

The 14th and 15th centuries saw further
institutional consolidation. By 1340 the commons
were conferring as a single house, acquiring a clerk
in 1363 and a SPEAKER in 1376. Meanwhile
parliament's legislative role had emerged. As the
highest court of justice, parliament had always
received petitions, but by 1300 the commons had
begun presenting petitions of grievances for redress.
Under EDWARD I, however, parliament was still less
a legislature than a convenient forum for the
promulgation of royal legislation. By 1350 parliamentary statute had gradually acquired its special
status as law and soon Bills were being presented in
the form of the required statute. In the same period
parliamentary control over taxation was established, the commons being conceded the initiative
in introducing taxation Bills by 1407. This power
was the basis of a growing assertiveness on their
part, aided by the development of the privileges of
free speech and freedom from arrest and by the
emergence of a core of experienced regular
members. Attempts were made to capture appropр-
riation of supply in the 14th century and (1401 and
1407) to withold supply until grievances were
redressed. IMPEACHMENT was introduced in 1376 as a
further means of checking misgovernment.

The later 15th and early 16th centuries saw a
severe decline in the frequency with which
parliaments were summoned by kings less reliant
than their predecessors upon grants of taxation. The
possibility of parliament declining in influence, like
the estates of many continental kingdoms, however,
receded after the meeting of the 'REFORMATION
parliament' in 1529. The legislation of the
Reformation era re-emphasized the composite
sovereignty of the king in parliament (*see* TUDOR
REVOLUTION IN GOVERNMENT), while later Tudor
parliaments, despite their relative infrequency, saw
a revival of initiative in the commons. A regular
legislative procedure was perfected and the
committee system emerged, while parliamentary
privileges were consolidated and extended. Representation was extended to Wales and to a larger
number of boroughs. The commons also developed

a more experienced and better-educated membership, willing to assert its views on such issues as religion, the royal succession and MONOPOLIES.

Under ELIZABETH I these developments were contained by the queen's tact, successful crown efforts to influence elections and the leadership of the commons by members of the privy council. Under the early Stuarts, however, crown leadership and management failed, while the commons increasingly claimed the right to debate matters reserved to the ROYAL PREROGATIVE. The parliaments of 1604–29 saw bitter disputes over finance, foreign policy and religion, and deteriorating crown-commons relationships were marked by the APOLOGY OF THE COMMONS, the revival of impeachment and the PETITION OF RIGHT. CHARLES I ruled without parliament (1629–40) in such a manner that the Short and Long parliaments mounted a massive attack on the royal government (1640–1), the latter body passing the 1st TRIENNIAL ACT and securing the right to consent to its own dissolution. Its subsequent attempt to assert control over the militia and royal appointments precipitated the CIVIL WARS.

Parliamentary administration during and after the civil wars provided Britain's 1st experience of government by parliamentary committees. It also stimulated the LEVELLERS' unsuccessful proposals for franchise reform. In 1649 the abolition of the MONARCHY and house of lords gave sovereignty to the commons until Oliver Cromwell's dissolution of the RUMP PARLIAMENT led, after BAREBONE'S PARLIAMENT, to the establishment of the protectorate. Cromwell's parliaments redistributed representation in favour of the counties and included Scottish and Irish members, but at the Restoration (1660) the traditional system was fully restored. This was of vital importance, since future success in the management of parliament by the executive was to depend above all on a predominance of borough members whose seats were subject to electoral influence.

Management of the commons was the crucial issue after 1660, since ministries could no longer be sustained without a majority in the commons. Nevertheless, full parliamentary ascendancy in government was achieved only after the GLORIOUS REVOLUTION, with the 3rd Triennial Act, BILL OF RIGHTS and Act of SETTLEMENT, the experience of annual sessions of parliament and the emergence of political parties. In 1707 these developments were supplemented by the legislative UNION with Scotland.

The Scottish parliament which accepted union and its own demise had had a considerably different development from its English counterpart. Parlia-

The lower house of **parliament**, 'which consists of knights, gentlemen and burgesses', as it was c. 1640. Contemporary engraving.

ments of barons, clerics and burgesses had met to promulgate laws since the 14th century, but burgh representation remained weak and sporadic until the 17th century, and the shires were represented only after 1587. Furthermore, the crown was able to exercise effective control over both the composition and the proceedings of the unicameral Scottish parliament. The 3 estates of the Scottish parliament broke free during the civil wars, gaining control of the executive, abolishing clerical representation and the lords of the ARTICLES and passing a Triennial Act, but union with England was enforced under Cromwell (1653–60) and was followed by the restoration of the traditional system. Though sessions of parliament became longer and opposition more vocal, it was only from 1688–1707 that the Scottish parliament enjoyed real independence again.

The ascendancy of the WHIGS after 1714 saw the consolidation under WALPOLE and Newcastle of a stable system of government through parliament. The SEPTENNIAL ACT made elections less frequent, while declining party strife made them less bitter. Electoral patronage and firm leadership in the commons rendered parliament generally, though never wholly, manageable so long as the crown chose ministers able to sustain a majority. In 1800 legislative UNION with Ireland was enacted. By 1784, however, demands for parliamentary reform had begun to be voiced. Muffled during the Napoleonic wars, these revived after 1815 and reached a crescendo in the agitation which preceded the 1st REFORM BILL (1832). This began the

Nancy Astor, the first woman to take her seat as a member of **parliament**, arguing with a spectator in the general election of November 1923, at Plymouth.

Charles Stewart **Parnell** at the special commission of inquiry of 1889, which refuted the allegations by *The Times* linking him with Irish terrorism.

dismantling of the old parliamentary regime by abolishing or drastically reducing the influence of ROTTEN and POCKET BOROUGHS and extending the franchise. The construction of a modern parliamentary democracy proceeded by slow stages thereafter. The Reform Bills of 1867 and 1884 further extended the franchise and redistributed seats. The BALLOT ACT (1872) introduced the secret ballot. The Parliament Act (1911) curtailed the power of the lords and initiated quinquennial elections, while the Franchise Acts of the 20th century brought full adult suffrage. In 1958 life peerages were introduced and in 1969 the voting age was reduced to 18. Meanwhile the crown had effectively relinquished the right to choose ministers, while the commons saw the evolution of standing committees, the elaboration of procedural standing orders, the abolition of property qualifications for membership (1858), the introduction of salaries for members (1912) and the development of unprecedentedly disciplined political parties. The creation of the Irish Free State (1921) reduced Irish representation to 12 members from Northern Ireland, while that province was given its own bicameral parliament, meeting in Stormont castle. *See* HANSARD.

Parnell, Charles Stewart 1846–91. An Anglo-Irish Protestant landowner, Parnell became leader of the Irish home rulers after BUTT was deposed (1877). A cold aloof man, he nevertheless managed to fuse the causes of HOME RULE and Irish land reform (*see* IRISH LAND LEAGUE). Although imprisoned by Forster as part of his policy of COERCION he was released by Gladstone and subsequently secured a powerful national consensus in Catholic Ireland which swept the country after the 3rd REFORM BILL (1884). In 1885 Gladstone was converted to home rule but his failure to carry it was followed by Parnell's expulsion from the Irish party (1890) after being cited in the O'Shea divorce case. His attempt to recapture control brought about his death in the following year.

Parr, Catherine 1512–48. An accomplished and intelligent widow, Catherine was chosen as Henry VIII's 6th wife (1543), despite her own wish to marry Thomas Seymour. She brought tranquillity to the lives of the royal children, whose education she supervised. On Henry's death she married Seymour, but died in childbed a year later.

Parsons, Sir Charles 1854–1931. The inventor of the steam turbine, which revolutionized shipping and naval warfare, and then power generation. He was also a valued government adviser.

Parsons, Robert 1546–1610. An Oxford scholar, Parsons became a Jesuit while in Italy (1575). Appointed superior of the English Jesuits, he returned to England (1580) to establish the Jesuit mission. Thereafter he remained abroad, directing the mission and engaging in papal and Spanish intrigues against Elizabeth I.

Partition treaties 1698 and 1700. Agreements between France, Holland and England, determining the division of the Spanish empire on the death of Charles II of Spain. The treaties were broken when Louis XIV accepted Charles's bequest of the entire empire to Philip of Anjou (1700). MARLBOROUGH'S WARS followed.

Paston letters *see* LETTERS, MEDIEVAL COLLECTIONS OF

Patent rolls Rolls of CHANCERY copies of English royal 'letters patent' (open letters of more than passing importance) surviving from 1201–2 until the present. Initially dealing with general government business, by the later middle ages they most notably record appointments of and orders to royal officials and commissioners. At present they are in course of publication.

Patronages, Act concerning 1690. An Act transferring the right of presenting ministers to vacant charges to the heritors and elders of parishes, on payment of a compensatory sum to the former patrons. Deeply resented by the Scottish nobility, the Act was superseded (1712) by a measure effectively restoring the patrons' powers.

Paulinus, St d. 644. A member of AUGUSTINE's mission, Paulinus accompanied the Christian Kentish princess who married Edwin of Northumbria in 625. His baptism of Edwin at York (627) was followed by the rapid but superficial conversion of Northumbria, his work being destroyed when Cadwallawn overran the kingdom in 632.

Peace movement In the 19th century the pacifist movement (distinguished from the anti-war movement) was mainly associated with the QUAKERS and other Nonconformist sects who established the Peace Society (1850). This held regular conferences and claimed much support from radical Liberal MPs. World War I was a major setback but resulted in a range of groups opposing conscription and favouring the LEAGUE OF NATIONS. *See* CAMPAIGN FOR NUCLEAR DISARMAMENT; PEACE PLEDGE UNION.

Peace Pledge Union Set up by Canon Dick Sheppard (1936). Its members signed a pledge renouncing any activity in war, but when faced with German aggression (1939) its support largely evaporated.

Pearse, Patrick 1879–1916. An Irish language enthusiast who served for many years as an official of the GAELIC LEAGUE but became associated with violent resistance to British rule (1914), believing that a blood sacrifice was necessary to secure an independent Ireland. This martyrdom he secured for himself after the 1916 Easter Rising (*see* IRISH CONSTITUTIONAL CRISIS).

Peasants' revolt May–July 1381. A loosely connected series of risings, sparked off by excessive POLL TAXES, misgovernment and reverses in the hundred years' war, but soon directed against villeinage (*see* VILLEIN) in general and divers local grievances in particular. It began in Essex and Kent, whose rebels, led by Wat Tyler, Jak Strawe and the egalitarian preacher John Ball, entered London on 13 June. There they lynched Sudbury the chancellor, the treasurer and many others before meeting Richard II at Smithfield on the 15th and (after Tyler's death) dispersing on promise of pardon (later revoked). By now the rising had spread to St Albans, East Anglia (where it was crushed by Bishop Despenser) and elsewhere in southern England, but by August it had been completely suppressed.

Wat Tyler, the leader of the **Peasants' revolt**, tries to draw his sword on Richard II, but is cut down by the lord mayor of London (left). After Tyler's death Richard declares himself the peasants' leader (right). From Jean Froissart's *Chronicles*, 1456.

A memorial cartoon to Robert **Peel** in praise of his repeal of the Corn Laws. *Punch*, 1850.

Peel, Sir Robert 1788–1850. Son of one of the first great textile magnates, Peel entered parliament as a Tory (1809), rapidly becoming secretary for Ireland (1812–18) and then home secretary (1821–7). He rejoined Wellington's government (1828), carrying Catholic emancipation (*see* ROMAN CATHOLICISM) and setting up the metropolitan POLICE (1829). Although he opposed the REFORM BILL, he accepted it in the TAMWORTH MANIFESTO and, when premier (1841–6), tried to bring the Conservative party to terms with industrial society, ultimately accepting the arguments in favour of FREE TRADE and abolishing the CORN LAWS (1846). An internal rebellion, headed by Disraeli, shortly turned him out, and he died in a riding accident 4 years later.

Peel tower *see* TOWER HOUSE

Peerage *see* PARLIAMENT; TITLES

Peine forte et dure The practice of pressing to death persons who refused to plead in felony and 'petty treason' cases, thereby protecting their dependents from the forfeiture of goods which attended conviction. The procedure derived from a statute of 1275 and was abolished in 1772, when 'standing mute' was declared equivalent to conviction.

Pelagius fl. 380–418. A British-born monk active in Rome, Pelagius attacked the Augustinian doctrines of original sin and predestination (with their corollary of a rigidly hierarchical church and state) upholding instead free will and the unaided perfectibility of mankind. Though banned in Rome in 418, his beliefs long remained popular in the British church. *See* GERMANUS, ST.

Pelham, Henry 1696–1754. Pelham emerged as leader of the WHIGS after Walpole's resignation. A shrewd politician of great financial ability and unimpeachable integrity, he enjoyed both royal and parliamentary support after 1746, successfully concluded the war of the Austrian succession and subsequently followed a policy of retrenchment and mild reform.

Penal code, the A series of penal laws passed by the Irish parliament (1692–1727), severely limiting the political, social, educational, economic and religious rights of ROMAN CATHOLICS. Termed by Burke 'that unparalleled code of repression', the penal statutes were gradually repealed (1778–1829).

Penda A nobleman and later king of MERCIA (632–54), whose greatness he founded. He campaigned against Wessex and East Anglia and ended the hegemony of Northumbria, killing Edwin (632) and Oswald (641) and thereafter remaining the dominant Anglo-Saxon ruler until his defeat by Oswiu at Winwaed, near Leeds (654). Mercian expansion continued under his son Wulfhere (657–74).

Peninsular war 1808–13. The Portuguese and Spanish campaigns of the duke of WELLINGTON. Wintering in Portugal (in 1810 behind the defensive lines of TORRES VEDRAS) and campaigning in Spain from spring to autumn, Wellington eventually liberated Spain and advanced into France. Principal battles were VIMEIRO (1808), TALAVERA (1809), Albuera (1811), SALAMANCA (1812) and VITORIA (1813). *See* NAPOLEONIC WARS.

Penn, William 1644–1718. The son of an admiral, Penn became a Quaker (1667) and used his court influence for his co-religionists until 1688, when his support for JAMES VII AND II ensured his political eclipse. In 1681 he founded Pennsylvania, drawing up the constitution and acting as 1st governor of the colony.

Penny A name used in England since at least the early 8th century for the basic unit of British currency. Offa ordered that 240 be minted from a POUND of silver and, until the reign of Henry III, this standardized silver penny was the only English coin used. Scottish pennies were first struck in the mid-12th century, but from 1367 were of lower absolute value than their English counterparts. From 1797 pennies were minted in copper, and from 1860 in bronze. At decimalization in 1971 they were superseded by 'new pence' (100 to a pound).

Penny Post Before 1840 all letters were paid for by the receiver and charges varied with distance (e.g. London–Dublin was 2 shillings). Rowland Hill proposed a system of prepaid stamps, determined by weight, not distance, with a minimum letter rate of 1 pence. This (with the aid of the new railways) increased mail traffic tenfold in 25 years. *See* POST.

Penruddock's rising 1655. A royalist rising in Wiltshire against the PROTECTORATE, led by Colonel John Penruddock. The rising was easily suppressed, but alarmed the government and led to the establishment of the MAJOR-GENERALS.

Pensions *see* OLD AGE PENSIONS

Pentland rising 1666. A rising of the COVENANTERS of south-west Scotland against the government of Charles II. After a march on Edinburgh, the rebels were defeated at Rullion Green by General Dalyell, their defeat being followed by severe repression.

People's Budget 1909. Introduced by LLOYD GEORGE, who had to find cash to pay for OLD AGE PENSIONS and the DREADNOUGHT programme. He did so by increasing income tax and death duties, taxing luxuries and attempting to set up a road fund. But he also imposed new taxes on high incomes, on undeveloped land and on the unearned increment resulting from land sales. This enraged the Conservatives and the aristocracy, led to the house of lords throwing out the budget and precipitated the constitutional crisis.

Pepys, Samuel 1633–1703. The most accessible of 17th-century Englishmen by reason of his remarkable diary (1660–9), Pepys was also, as secretary to the admiralty, responsible for important reforms in naval administration (1673–88). He lost office in 1688 for his loyalty to James VII and II.

Perceval, Spencer 1762–1812. The only British prime minister to have died by assassination. An earnest Evangelical and supporter of Pitt, Perceval

served as solicitor-general (1801) and chancellor of the exchequer (1807–9) before becoming both prime minister and chancellor in 1809. On 12 May 1812 he was shot by a deranged bankrupt.

Percy family Great feudal magnates and hereditary WARDENS OF THE MARCHES, holding extensive lands in Northumberland, Cumbria, Yorkshire and Sussex. Its members played an important role in English politics in the 15th and 16th centuries, their shifting allegiances being generally dictated by rivalry with their cousins and neighbours the NEVILLES. Henry, 1st earl of Northumberland (1342–1408), helped Henry IV to the throne but rebelled against him in 1403, 1405 and 1408; his son

The **Penny Post** derived its name from the 'Penny Black', issued 6 May 1840, which was the world's first adhesive postage stamp.

The bibliophile Samuel **Pepys** may actually have invented the glazed bookcase: these come from his library, Buckingham Street, London, and are now in the Pepys Library, Cambridge.

was HOTSPUR; Henry, 2nd earl (1394–1455), was killed fighting for Henry VI at ST ALBANS; Henry, 3rd earl (1421–61), died for the same cause at TOWTON; and Henry, 4th earl (1446–89), turned Yorkist, but abandoned Richard III at BOSWORTH.

A crisis occurred in the fortunes of the family on the death of Henry, 6th earl (c. 1502–37), whose brothers had taken part in the PILGRIMAGE OF GRACE. The title was forfeited and granted by Edward VI to John Dudley, earl of Warwick (see NORTHUMBERLAND, DUKE OF), who was attainted in the following reign. The title was then restored to Thomas, 7th earl (1528–72), who was executed as a leader of the NORTHERN REBELLION.

Perfeddwlad *see* GWYNEDD

Perpendicular architecture The most long-lived type of English Gothic, lasting *c.* 1330–1530. Virtually unknown outside England, Perpendicular was invented (almost simultaneously at Gloucester cathedral and Old St Paul's, London) by London architects strongly influenced by recent French

King's college chapel, Cambridge: antechapel looking west. The fan-vaulting, the finest in the country and typical of **Perpendicular architecture**, was probably designed by John Wastell in 1508.

Gothic. Its main feature is repetitive grid-like tracery, sometimes extended overhead to form 'fan-vaulting', notably at King's college chapel, Cambridge.

Peterloo, massacre of 1819. The name given to the killing of 11 people and wounding of 400 more by cavalry attempting to arrest 'Orator' Hunt at a reform meeting at St Peter's Fields, Manchester. The meeting of over 50,000 people had been orderly until the troops' intervention, and the incident provoked great public outcry.

Peter's Pence An annual sum paid by England to the papacy, levied as a HEARTH TAX and probably originated by Alfred. Also called 'Romescot', from the 13th century it was fixed at £200, the surplus being retained by the collecting bishops as part of their emoluments. It was abolished in 1534.

Petition of right 1628. An attempt by parliament, inspired by COKE, to commit fundamental rights to the statute book, by declaring illegal arbitrary taxation and imprisonment, compulsory billeting and the issuing of commissions of martial law. Though Charles I accepted the petition, he later declared it non-binding upon the crown.

Petty schools Small schools for the education of young children in reading and writing. Sometimes endowed, but more often not, petty schools were generally held in the schoolmaster's home or in a church. Their numbers greatly increased in the 16th and early 17th centuries.

Petty sessions Meetings of 2 or more JUSTICES OF THE PEACE, held between QUARTER SESSIONS from the 1630s, to deal with minor offences and administrative business for sub-divisions of their counties.

Petuaria *see* PARISI

Philip Augustus king of France (1180–1223). A shrewd politician determined to destroy the 'Angevin empire', Philip exploited the quarrels between HENRY II and his sons, and between Richard I and John. In 1204 he seized Normandy from John, but his son Prince Louis failed to conquer England in 1216–17.

Philliphaugh, battle of *see* CIVIL WARS; MONTROSE, 5TH EARL OF

Phoenix Park murders 6 May 1882. The assassination by Irish terrorists of the new and conciliatory Liberal chief secretary, Lord Frederick Cavendish, and his undersecretary, which set back GLADSTONE's agreement with PARNELL to allay the Irish land crisis (the 'Kilmainham treaty', May 1882). It had a serious impact on subsequent English views of Irish nationalism and home rule.

Phoney war 1939–40. The period of WORLD WAR II between the invasion of Poland (September 1939), and the invasion of Norway (April 1940), when lack of German action lulled the allies into a sense of false security.

Picquigny, treaty of 29 August 1475. Edward IV, intending to punish King Louis XI's support for his Lancastrian enemies and to aid his own Burgundian allies, invaded France with a large and well-equipped army. Receiving no help from Burgundy, however, he agreed at Picquigny to withdraw in return for a large lump sum and a substantial annual pension.

Picts (probably from Lat. *picti*, painted people, but perhaps related to Irish *cruithne*, Britons). A name applied from the 4th century to the CALEDONIANS and northern Scottish tribes. Despite many distinctive and enigmatic features, notably the matrilineal succession of property and kingship and traces of an indecipherable but apparently ancient and non-Indo-European language perhaps used for religious purposes, their society seems generally to have resembled that of other Britons. Though challenged during the heroic age by the Scotti of Dalriada and the Angles of Northumbria (*see* NECHTANSMERE, BATTLE OF; OENGUS MAC FERGUS) they emerged in the mid-9th century as the politically dominant partners in ALBA.

Pilgrim Fathers The group of 35 radical Puritans, originally from Nottinghamshire, Lincolnshire and Norfolk who, after settling in Leyden (1609–20), sailed in the *Mayflower* (1620), together with 66 other settlers from London and Southampton, to found Plymouth Colony.

Pilgrimage of Grace 1536. Risings in Lincoln-shire, Yorkshire and the northern counties in defence of the monasteries (*see* MONASTERIES, DISSOLUTION OF) and the Catholic faith and seeking redress of fiscal, political and economic grievances. Though the rebels, led by Robert Aske, were persuaded to disperse peacefully, further disturbances in 1537 were used to justify harsh repression by Henry VIII's government.

One of a number of incised bulls, exceptional in that they appear alone on small slabs, found at Burghead, Moray, a principal centre of the **Picts**. Note how well the interior scrolls are used to articulate the muscles of the animal.

Pilgrims *see* SHRINES

Pill-boxes Concrete emplacements which, with their accompanying dragons' teeth, were built (1939–40) in anticipation of a German invasion.

Piltdown man A skull, jawbone and tooth discovered 1908–12 at Piltdown in Sussex apparently belonged to an early Palaeolithic man, much the oldest humanoid found in Britain (*see* PREHISTORIC BRITAIN). In the 1950s, however, scientific analysis proved Piltdown man to be a fake.

Pinkie, battle of 10 September 1547. The rout of a large but poorly equipped Scottish army by English troops under SOMERSET, who had invaded Scotland to enforce the marriage of Mary Queen of Scots and Edward VI. Despite their victory, the English withdrew, leaving garrisons in selected strong-points. Mary was promptly dispatched to France by her mother.

Pipe rolls Exchequer documents (originally sewn end to end into annual rolls resembling pipes) recording crown income from the sheriff of each shire, set against his expenditure on government affairs. Preserved uninterrupted from 1156 until their discontinuance in 1831, they are especially important sources for 12th- and 13th-century history.

Pitt, William (the elder) *see* CHATHAM, 1ST EARL OF

'The Giant Factotum amusing himself': a satire of William **Pitt**'s dominance over the house of commons. Dundas, in a kilt, supports his right foot, while his left crushes the opposition. Cartoon by James Gillray, 1797.

Pitt, William (the younger) 1759–1806. As distinguished a minister in peace as his father CHATHAM had been in war, Pitt became prime minister at 24 and retained the post, save for 3 years, for the remainder of his life. A brilliant scholar, he had entered parliament in 1780 and was appointed chancellor of the exchequer under Shelburne 2 years later. His rise to the highest office was a superb display of political tactics. Supported by the king and powerful trading, financial and Evangelical pressure groups, he slipped into office in December 1783 on the defeat of Charles James Fox's India Bill, held out for 4 months and then scored a triumphant victory in the 1784 election.

Once firmly established in power Pitt concentrated upon 'economical reform', turning a deficit into a surplus, establishing a sinking fund to reduce the NATIONAL DEBT and bolstering public credit, while overhauling the customs and furthering the cause of Free Trade. In other reforms he had scant interest, taking the minimum action necessary to placate public opinion and retain the reformers' parliamentary support. He accepted the defeat of modest parliamentary reform measures and anti-slavery bills with equanimity, while his India Act provided a degree of reform which little disturbed the East India Company's directors.

In 1789, having weathered the crisis of George III's temporary madness, Pitt seemed supreme and immensely successful. The remaining years of his life were paradoxically to bring failure and yet confirm his stature as a national leader. His conduct of the war with France from 1793 demonstrated strategic shortsightedness and a parsimony which was repaid with military humiliations alleviated only by Nelson's victories. At home, radicalism was harshly repressed, while Ireland was savagely coerced and then bribed into an ill-considered legislative UNION. Unable to achieve a basis for negotiated peace and frustrated by George III's refusal to countenance Catholic emancipation, Pitt resigned in 1801, leaving Addington to negotiate the peace of Amiens. In 1804, with war renewed, Pitt returned only to have the triumph of TRAFALGAR blotted out by crushing defeats for Britain's allies in Europe. Broken in spirit and physically exhausted, he died in despair.

Pitt's character remains enigmatic. Arrogant, detached and uncommunicative in public, he could be a brilliant companion with his friends. A great financial minister, his private finances were a shambles. Fastidious and controlled in public affairs, he was also a frequent drunkard. His one clear characteristic was the driving ambition and conviction of his own destiny which brought him to power so young and sustained him there long enough in a time of national peril to make his name synonymous with that of an age.

Place, Francis 1771–1854. An English Radical tailor whose views bridged those of the organized working class and the Utilitarians (*see* UTILITARIANISM). With the Radical MP Joseph Hume (1777–1855), Place secured the repeal of the COMBINATION LAWS (1824), organized political unions and helped draft the 1838 charter (*see* CHARTISM).

Placemen Members of the house of commons holding royal pensions or places in royal administration. Attacks upon placemen recurred from 1678 through into the 18th century. Had they succeeded, the development of CABINET government would certainly have been impeded.

Plague The most dreaded of epidemic diseases, plague was endemic in Britain between the BLACK DEATH and the later 17th century, though in its bubonic form rather than in the even more virulent pneumonic form. A disease of rodents, transmitted to humans by infected rat fleas, it was primarily an urban phenomenon by 1500, active only in warm weather and most deadly to children and young adults. The Great Plague of London, which raged from April 1665, peaking in September and returning briefly the following spring, killed some 100,000 people. This outbreak, however, owes its notoriety to the fact that it was England's last great outbreak. London had suffered even worse plagues in 1563, 1603 and 1625. Other cities in England and Scotland had a similar history of periodic outbreaks, the last Scottish epidemic being that of the late 1640s, which was made worse by the movements of armies which spread infection.

The disappearance of plague remains a mystery which cannot be satisfactorily accounted for by medical or social improvements. Plague could be combatted only by flight and the quarantining of infected areas. Most probably it vanished as a result of bacteriological changes which left no evidence to the medical historian. *See* POPULATION.

Plantagenets *see* ANGEVINS

Plassey, battle of 23 June 1757. A battle of the SEVEN YEARS' WAR. Sepoy and British troops under CLIVE defeated Subahdar Siraj-ud-Daulah of Bengal, several of whose commanders were bribed to desert him in battle. One of these, Mir Jafar, was installed as puppet ruler, and British domination of Bengal was confirmed.

Playhouses Specialized buildings for the performance of plays. The first in England was built at Shoreditch by James Burbage in 1576. Early playhouses were circular, galleried buildings with projecting open-air stages, modelled on inn courtyards. Indoor theatres with proscenium arches appeared in the early 17th century.

Plimsoll line The loading line on ships, adopted in 1876 as a result of an energetic campaign carried out by a Liberal MP, Samuel Plimsoll (1824–98), after a series of sinkings of ships he believed to be deliberately overloaded for insurance claims.

Plough-land *see* CARUCATE

Plumpton correspondence *see* LETTERS, MEDIEVAL COLLECTIONS OF

Pluralism The practice of holding more than one ecclesiastical benefice. Though sometimes justified by the need to accumulate livings in order to support a clerical scholar or administrator, the

practice commonly simply reflected the good connections of the pluralist and was frequently denounced by church reformers.

Pocket boroughs Boroughs represented in parliament before the 1832 REFORM BILL which were effectively 'in the pocket' of patrons who could give or sell the seat to favoured candidates. Sir Lewis Namier, in *The Structure of Politics at the Accession of George III* (2nd edn 1957), estimated that 111 patrons controlled some 205 English borough seats in the 1760s. *See* ROTTEN BOROUGHS.

Poitiers, battle of 19 September 1356. A superior French force intercepted an Anglo-Gascon CHEVAUCHÉE led by the Black Prince, but was destroyed by a repetition of the tactics of CRÉCY. The capture of King Jean II constituted the worst French reverse of the earlier HUNDRED YEARS' WAR, paving the way for the treaty of BRÉTIGNY.

Pole, Reginald 1500–58. A cousin of Henry VIII and humanist scholar (*see* HUMANISM), resident at Padua from 1521, Pole rejected the Henrician REFORMATION in 1534. Made a cardinal in 1538, he received England's submission to Rome in 1554 and subsequently, as archbishop of Canterbury (1555–8), supported the persecution of Protestants under MARY I.

Swan theatre, London, by Francis Langley: a contemporary copy of a (now lost) drawing of the interior by Johannes de Witt, *c.* 1596. De Witt thought it 'the largest and most distinguished' of the **playhouses** 'since it contains three thousand persons' and is 'supported by wooden columns in . . . exact imitation of marble'.

A policeman of 1860: the uniform of the metropolitan **police** was much more similar to civilian dress than it is now, but their numbers enabled any member of the public to identify them.

de la Pole family This remarkable late medieval family was founded by William, merchant of Hull, knighted for financial services to Edward III. His son Michael became a baron (1366), chancellor (1383–6) and, having married a Suffolk heiress, earl of Suffolk (1385). Michael, 2nd earl (1389–1415), acquired further East Anglian lands, but the greatest was William, 4th earl and 1st duke of SUFFOLK. John, 2nd duke (1450–91), married Edward IV's sister Elizabeth, and their son John, earl of Lincoln (1464–87), became Richard III's chosen heir, but died at STOKE. The last of the line, Richard ('the White Rose') maintained the Yorkist claim to the throne, being killed in exile at Pavia (1525).

Police Britain is unique in Europe in having no state police. The old system of parish constables was in decline by the mid-18th century, when the Fielding brothers founded the BOW STREET RUNNERS (or 'thief-takers') and patrols against highwaymen. Both later came under the home office, but only in 1829 was the metropolitan police force set up under Peel, who had set up an Irish police in 1814. The Municipal Corporations Act (1835) required boroughs to set up police forces, under 'watch committees', and in 1856 such compulsion was extended to the counties. The metropolitan force's criminal investigation department was set up in 1878, drawing on French precedents, and a small group of detectives set up in 1842. The special branch dates from the Irish terrorist campaign of the mid-1880s. Separate police forces exist in nationalized transport, the port of London and the services, but a mounting police involvement in traffic regulation was curbed by the institution of traffic wardens in the 1960s, and police concerns have now reverted to those of crime prevention and detection and public order.

Political and Economic Planning Founded in 1931 by economists and progressive businessmen, PEP sought to equate the welfare state and central and regional planning with Keynsian capitalism (*see* KEYNES, JOHN MAYNARD). It has been the most significant of the 'middle opinion' groups founded in the 1930s.

Political nation A term used by historians of 16th- and 17th-century England to denote the politically active and conscious members of the nation, including the aristocracy, GENTRY, higher clergy and urban magistracies and occasionally persons of lower rank active in local affairs and qualified to vote in parliamentary elections.

Political saints Persons executed or murdered for political reasons and (though never officially canonized) afterwards accounted saints by the opponents of those who had caused their deaths.

Poll tax An unpopular tax payable by every adult person ('poll', head). Levied periodically 1222–1698, generally on a sliding scale according to wealth but occasionally (like the tax of 1380–1 which sparked off the peasants' revolt) at a fixed rate. Collectors' returns are useful in demographic and economic studies.

Poor Law Amendment Act 1834. A drastic reform of the POOR LAW, the Act proposed the abolition of outdoor relief and the use of the quasi-prison regime of the WORKHOUSE as a deterrent. Administered by unions of parishes, under a central 3-man commission which determined policy, and inspectors who enforced it, it rapidly took effect in southern England, but the workhouse system was inadequate to cope with industrial unemployment crises. *See* WELFARE STATE.

Poor Laws (England) The series of Tudor statutes culminating in those of 1597 and 1601 which made PARISHES responsible for the relief of their impotent and able-bodied poor by means of compulsory rates administered by overseers, while further ordering the punishment of 'rogues and vagabonds'. The system, generally well-established by 1640, was reformed by the POOR LAW AMENDMENT ACT (1834). *See* HOUSES OF CORRECTION.

This attack on the **Poor Law Amendment Act** depicts the aim of the workhouse as 'the mode of punishment for the incorrigible' and life inside it as unbearable. Contemporary broadsheet.

Poor Laws (Scotland) Introduced in imitation of English legislation by a series of enactments after 1574, the Scottish Poor Laws differed in that compulsory parish rates were rarely established, and no relief was given to the able-bodied poor. This parsimonious system, which was held to discourage idleness, was reformed in 1845 (*see* WELFARE STATE).

Popish plot 1678. A supposed Catholic plot to murder Charles II and install his brother James (later James VII and II) on the throne, invented by OATES. His allegations triggered a period of public hysteria which saw the judicial murder of 24 Catholics and was exploited by the Whigs to provoke the EXCLUSION CRISIS.

Poplarism An attempt in 1921 by Poplar borough council, led by LANSBURY, to force the wealthier London boroughs to contribute to poor relief in London's east end by refusing to collect rates for the London county council and other bodies. After court action and the imprisonment of Labour councillors a pooled poor-relief fund was set up, but the government later prohibited the Poplar guardians from offering poor relief that was higher than normal.

Popular Front A name for organizations set up (largely as a result of a change in Soviet policy) to demand an alliance of 'democratic' forces – Communist, Labour, Liberal and even Conservative – against FASCISM in the 1930s. They largely collapsed after the Nazi-Soviet pact (August 1939).

Population Establishing the exact population of Britain at any date before regular CENSUS returns began in the 19th century is an impossible task. Historians are forced to fall back on estimates based on indirect evidence, some of which remain highly controversial. Nevertheless, painstaking research has succeeded in revealing the general dynamics of population change in England from the 11th and in Scotland from the 17th centuries. These were determined by the relationship between the primary factors of fertility and mortality rates, which in turn were influenced by secondary factors such as marriage rates, migration and general economic conditions.

In England population growth occurred in 3 great waves. Population grew slowly during the centuries of settlement and internal colonization, to reach a total of perhaps 2 million at the time of Domesday Book (1086), accelerating thereafter to a ceiling of *c*. 5 million early in the 14th century. Famine in the 1310s checked further expansion, while the BLACK DEATH (1348–9) wiped out perhaps 30–50% of the population. Initial recovery from this catastrophe was checked by further epidemics in the later 14th and 15th centuries and a period of population stagnation or decline ensued. In 1500 population stood at *c*. 2·5 million.

From the early 16th century decreased epidemic mortality, coupled with economic circumstances favourable to younger marriages and higher fertility allowed renewed growth which resulted by 1650 in a population of *c*. 5 million, pressing heavily on economic resources. This time, however, population stabilized without catastrophe as the result of a trend towards higher marriage ages, the practice of family limitation within marriage and the effects of higher mortality rates in the country in general and in the growing towns in particular. Improved agricultural output and more effective relief organization also meant that dearth rarely led to famine in England by the 17th century. This new equilibrium was maintained until the later 18th century when developing resistance to endemic killer diseases and the progress of industrialization, which facilitated younger marriages, led together to a sustained population growth which accelerated in the early 19th century.

In Scotland population stood at *c*. 1 million in 1700 after a century marked by severe mortality from epidemics and famine. Reduced crisis mortality of this kind allowed an increase of population by perhaps a third by 1800, while accelerated

Unrestricted fertility combined with lower infant mortality to produce rapid **population** growth and families as large as this one, in late Victorian Britain.

growth in the early 19th century saw Scotland's population reach 3 million in 1870, despite emigration.

By the later 19th century Britain had completed one stage of the 'demographic transition'. The generally high fertility, high mortality and slow growth of pre-industrial times had given way to a pattern of continued high fertility but lowered mortality and rapid growth. The greatly increased population (10·4 million in 1801; 20·8 million in 1851) was sustained by a growing industrial economy. Thereafter the more widespread use of efficient contraception reduced fertility sufficiently to establish a new equilbrium of low fertility, low mortality and slow growth in the early 20th century, by which period the population of Great Britain had reached 45 million. In 1971 the population of Great Britain was approximately 53·8 million (England 45·9 million; Scotland 5·2 million; Wales 2·7 million).

Porteous riots 1736. The lynching by an Edinburgh mob of Black Jock Porteous, captain of the city guard, who had been condemned for firing on the crowd during the execution of a smuggler. The government retaliated by deposing the provost and fining the city, actions which cost Walpole the political support of the 2nd duke of Argyll.

Portland, William Bentinck, 1st earl of 1649–1709. A Dutch nobleman and friend and adviser of William III, Bentinck was the architect of the peace of Ryswick and the PARTITION TREATIES. Unpopular in England because of his nationality and influence, he nevertheless remained there after William's death.

Positivists The name adopted by the mid-Victorian followers of the French sociologist Auguste Comte (1798–1857), who prescribed the reorganization of society by an élite trained in the social sciences and dedicated to a non-theistic 'religion of humanity'.

Post A network of royal postmasters emerged in the 16th century to serve government needs. Private letters were accepted thereafter but costs were high and delivery uncertain. Oliver Cromwell's Post Office Act (1657) was the 1st comprehensive attempt to regulate the postal service by statute, establishing a government monopoly and providing for the post of postmaster general. The modern postal system with uniform charges paid in advance originated with Rowland Hill's PENNY POST (1840). The post office opened the post office savings bank in 1861, and started issuing postal orders in 1881, as well as taking over TELEGRAPHS (1869) and the telephone service (1912). It ceased to be a department of state and became a nationalized industry in 1968.

Potato famine In Ireland the potato, which had about 3 times the nutritive value of grain per acre planted, had sustained a huge population increase achieved through subdivision of holdings. In 1845, 1846 and 1848 the crop was struck by fungus and failed utterly. About 21,000 died of actual starvation, while diseases such as typhus, dysentry and cholera, preying on people in their weakened state, killed over 1 million. All the time grain continued to be exported to England, to sell in the dearer market beloved of economists. The Irish, in particular the 2 million who shortly emigrated, neither forgot nor forgave.

The **potato famine** produced an enormous death toll: in this funeral at Skibereen there is no money for coffins and little strength left in the horse. Engraving from a sketch made by H. Smith in Cork, *Illustrated London News*, 30 January 1847.

Pound Originally the weight of silver from which 240 PENNIES were struck, the pound was exclusively a unit of account until the 1st English 'sovereigns' were minted in 1489. From 1914 these were superseded by banknotes. The 'pound Scots', at first of equivalent value, was progressively debased after 1367, and by 1600 had fallen to one-twelfth the value of its English counterpart.

Powell, Vavasor *see* WALES

Powys (Lat. *pagenses*, rural people). The principality of central Wales, stretching at its fullest extent from around Mold (now in Clwyd) southwards to Hay-on-Wye: the eponymous modern county anachronistically includes BRYCHEINIOG. Centred on the lands of the CORNOVII, it was traditionally founded by VORTIGERN. Frequently at war with Gwynedd and in alliance with England, after Edward I's conquest of Wales its core became a MARCHER lordship, Welsh-held until 1309.

Praemunire The practice of taking to foreign courts (specifically the papal curia) any matter cognizable in English law (specifically disputes concerning church patronage). It was forbidden by statutes of 1353, 1365 and 1393, which were directed against 'papal provisions' (*see* CHURCH, PRE-REFORMATION), but only sporadically enforced, until Henry VIII used them against the church at the REFORMATION.

Prehistoric Britain The earliest evidence of human life in Britain occurs during the palaeolithic or old stone age, a period lasting *c.* 500,000–*c.* 12,000 BC. During this era Britain, still joined to Europe in one land mass, was subject to four or more ice ages (when glaciers advanced as far south as the Thames valley) interspersed with warmer periods when the ice retreated. The oldest known British human remains (flint implements have been found that are older still) are parts of a skull from a gravel pit at Swanscombe, Kent: classified as lower palaeolithic, they are held to date from the 2nd interglacial period, *c.* 250,000–200,000 BC. The middle palaeolithic era, which coincides with the beginning of the final glaciation (*c.* 70,000–50,000 BC), produced the 1st British cave-dwellings, notably Kent's Cavern, Torquay, where artefacts mingled with the bones of mammoth, woolly rhinoceros and hyena suggest men of the neanderthal type, though no skeletal remains of this species have yet been identified in this country. Homo sapiens sapiens, the earliest modern man and relative of the cave painters of southern France (Cromagnon man), first appears here in the late palaeolithic period, just before and after the coldest part of the last ice age (*c.* 18,000–14,000 BC).

From about 12,000 BC onwards the ice finally retreated, and during the mesolithic or middle stone age both temperatures and sea levels rose, cutting Britain off from Europe by *c.* 5000 BC and replacing the palaeolithic tundra by thick forest, with consequent changes in fauna and in the human way of life. The classic site of this period is Star Carr, north Yorks. (*c.* 7500 BC), whose occupants, like their palaeolithic predecessors, were semi-nomadic hunter-gatherers.

The neolithic or new stone age, however, saw a revolution in human development: the introduction of agriculture. Crop-raising and animal husbandry, apparently originating in the Middle East around 7000 BC, spread slowly westward, and are thought to have reached Britain by about 4000 BC, carried by immigrants from western Europe. Some of these incomers, classified as the Windmill Hill people from a Wiltshire type-site, occupied the lowlands south and east of a line from the Severn to Yorkshire, their primary settlement areas being the light-soiled and easily cleared chalk downs, most notably Salisbury Plain. Others, following the Atlantic sea-routes from the Mediterranean and Spain, settled south-west England, Wales, Ireland and much of Scotland. By about 3500 BC the agriculturalists were sufficiently well-established to organize the construction of great communal monuments and ceremonial sites, CAUSEWAYED CAMPS, CURSUSES and earthen long BARROWS being characteristic of the Windmill Hill culture, and MEGALITHIC CHAMBERED TOMBS (e.g. MAES HOWE) appearing mainly in the highland north and west. Both cultures introduced and used simple hand-made pottery, and practised trade based to a large extent on AXE FACTORIES and FLINT MINES.

During the latter part of the neolithic period (*c.* 2500–2000 BC) other distinctive cultures appeared, the product either of the fusion of the incomers with the native mesolithic population or (as is now considered more likely) of new migrations from Europe. The most important of these 'secondary neolithic' groups was the widespread Rinyo-Clacton culture, whose characteristic 'grooved ware' is found at SKARA BRAE and in connection with the ritual HENGE MONUMENTS (including STONE-HENGE) which begin to appear at this time.

Whatever the origin of these secondary neolithic cultures, there is little doubt that the next major influence on prehistoric Britain was the 'Beaker culture', named after distinctive pottery drinking vessels. Originating in the Rhineland and the Low

Bronze age axe-heads from a round barrow on Coombe Hill, Jevington, Sussex. All but one are broken across, common amongst funerary objects found in **prehistoric** graves.

porary (c. 1700–1400 BC) 'food-vessel' culture of northern and western Britain was broadly similar in character, but contained a larger native element and apparently used fewer metal implements.

The middle bronze age (c. 1400–1000 BC) saw bronze in general use for a diversity of tools and weapons, now including sickles and 'rapiers' or thrusting swords. Cremation, occurring alongside inhumation during the previous period, now became the almost universal burial rite, the burnt remains being deposited in large urns under round barrows or (later on) in flat 'urnfield' cemeteries. Great ritual monuments ceased to be built, but more substantial settlements, both enclosed villages and isolated farms, are recognizable. Perhaps the most important developments, however, were the agricultural improvements associated with the southern Deverel-Rimbury people (c. 1200–800 BC) who ploughed rectangular 'Celtic fields' instead of hoeing irregular plots, and practised large-scale cattle ranching. Increased food production may have resulted in the growth of population which, together with a gradual moistening and cooling of the climate, appears to have given rise to a shortage of easily cultivated land during the late bronze age (c. 1000–650 BC). Certainly the latter part of this period was one of increasing unrest and warfare, evidenced by a massive growth in weapon production (including the introduction of heavy cut-and-thrust swords, bronze shields and horse trappings) and the appearance of the heavily defended settlements called HILLFORTS.

This tendency towards aggression and tribalization continued and intensified during the iron age, many of whose general aspects also display a continuity with the preceding period. Iron weapons and implements were being manufactured in Britain by c. 650 BC, though their use did not become widespread until 2 or 3 centuries later. The introduction of the new metal, along with other iron age developments such as the appearance of a religious system dominated by DRUIDS, the resurgence of inhumation burial, the proliferation of hillforts, the advent of chariots and the appearance of fine curvilinear decoration on metal-work and pottery, was until recently attributed to 'Celtic' invaders or infiltrators from Europe. Though some small groups of European adventurers (notably the PARISI of east Yorkshire) did undoubtedly establish themselves here in the 5th–4th centuries BC, it is now considered more likely that such developments were either entirely insular or else the result of trade contacts with the continent.

The pattern of iron age culture, settlement and economy was not, in any case, uniform throughout

Countries, this began to infiltrate the south and east coasts c. 2000 BC, and gradually became established as a dominant element in native society. At much the same time, existing henge monuments were adapted, sometimes by the addition of STONE CIRCLES (as at Stonehenge and AVEBURY) and new burial practices introduced, single inhumations in unchambered round BARROWS being substituted by collective burials in long barrows. The grave-goods suggest a comparatively advanced culture based on mixed farming, with increasing specialization of trades such as leather-working; and new types of flint arrowhead, combined with bone wrist-bracers, indicate the use of efficient bows. Most important of all, occasional finds of copper and bronze daggers show that the Beaker culture had mastered metal-working, and its appearance marks the transition between the stone and bronze ages.

The use of metal, however, was slow to spread. It was not until c. 1700 BC that the full early bronze age began, with cultures produced by the integration of 'Beaker' and native stock. Central southern England was inhabited by the powerful and prosperous Wessex people, who probably completed Stonehenge, and who buried their chieftains in distinctive round barrows accompanied by bronze daggers, axes and spearheads, and ornaments made from imported gold and amber. The contem-

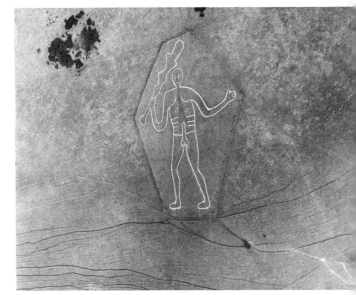

Smacam Down, Dorset: aerial view of Celtic fields, established in **prehistoric** England after *c.* 1200 BC. Rectangular in shape (unlike Saxon 'strip-fields') they may derive from a system dating back to the new stone age.

The Cerne Abbas giant, cut into the turf on a Dorset hillside in **prehistoric** times.

Britain, and by the 2nd century BC 4 distinctive regional variations are observable. The tribes of the maritime north and west practised a pastoral economy, living in small extended-family communities in strongly defended homesteads, such as the numerous small hillforts of the Cornish peninsula and west Wales and the DUNS AND BROCHS of northern and western Scotland. The scattered BRIGANTES of northern England and the borders were also mainly pastoral, but appear to have favoured homesteads that were enclosed rather than fortified, while in midland and eastern England a mixed farming economy based on villages and open settlements seems to have predominated. The most centralized and highly developed iron age society, however, flourished in southern England, the Welsh borderlands and the eastern lowlands of Scotland, where large and well-defended hillforts (*see* MAIDEN CASTLE) apparently acted as the foci of clearly defined tribal territories ruled by warrior aristocracies.

During the 200 years before the Roman conquest (43) the appearance of an attributable coinage, together with Roman literary sources, allows events in Britain to be traced for the 1st time by historical rather than archaeological methods. In the decades *c.* 100 BC the Belgae, a federation of warlike Celtic-Germanic tribes from the Seine-Marne-Rhine area,

began raiding and then colonizing the Channel coasts, bringing with them a money economy, the potter's wheel and improved methods of farming and textile production. Though opposed by the native tribes (a strengthening of whose hillforts is observable at this period) the Belgae soon extended their rule, or at least their influence, over much of south-eastern England, while maintaining close links with their kindred in Gaul. Their high king Diviciacus is known to have held sway on both sides of the Channel *c.* 80 BC, and British military assistance for anti-Roman rebellions in Gaul provided the principal motive for JULIUS CAESAR's punitive raids (55 and 54 BC).

The years after Caesar's departure saw the area of Belgic influence expanded into Wessex and the south midlands, accompanied by a process of proto-urbanization based on the replacement of hillforts by OPPIDA. In other parts of Britain, however, things continued much as before. Internecine warfare between Belgic tribes culminated *c.* 30–40 in the dominance of the CATUVELLAUNI under Cunobelinus over the whole south-east. Threatened native rulers looked to Rome, and an attack on the pro-Roman ATREBATES by Cunobelinus's sons Togodumnus and Caratacus was the pretext for the invasion of 43 and the establishment of Roman Britain.

Ruins of the **Premonstratensian** Dryburgh abbey, Berwick, Scotland, founded *c.* 1150.

An attack on the system of enforced conscription for army and navy by **press gang**: 'The Liberty of the Subject', cartoon by James Gillray, 1779.

The death of Captain Gardiner at **Prestonpans**, where government troops were put to flight by the Jacobites. Engraving after William Allan.

Premonstratensians Named after their mother-house of Prémontré in France, these CANONS regular followed a more austere version of the AUGUSTINIAN rule, and were influenced by the Cistercians. Also called White Canons, they were introduced to England in 1143 and to Scotland in 1150.

Presbyterianism The system of church government by presbyteries of ministers and elders. Triumphant in the CHURCH OF SCOTLAND (1690), Presbyterianism was also the strongest branch of English NONCONFORMITY before being weakened in the 18th century by conversions to UNITARIANISM. Reviving thereafter, the English and Welsh Presbyterian churches joined the CONGREGATIONALISTS in 1972 in the United Reformed church. *See* DISSENTERS.

'Presbyterians' A term applied to parliamentarian politicians in the CIVIL WARS who opposed religious toleration, were socially conservative, sympathetic to the Scots and prepared to support a moderate form of Presbyterianism in the CHURCH OF ENGLAND following the abolition of episcopacy.

Press gangs Naval or military detachments empowered to seize men for service. Employed by the army up to 1815 and by the navy until the 1830s, press gangs are particularly associated with the wars of the period 1688–1815.

Preston, battle of 17–19 August 1648. A battle of the CIVIL WARS. An invading army of Scots and English royalists under James HAMILTON was caught disunited at Preston by Oliver Cromwell and pursued south in a running fight. The Scottish infantry surrendered at Warrington on 19 August, the cavalry and Hamilton himself at Uttoxeter 6 days later.

Prestonpans, battle of 21 September 1745. A battle of the '45' rebellion. Bonnie Prince Charlie's highland army surprised and routed government troops under Sir John Cope advancing on Edinburgh. Cope fled to Berwick while Scotland fell completely into the hands of the JACOBITES.

Price rise, the A term used to describe the inflation of the 16th and early 17th centuries. Prices of foodstuffs rose sevenfold in England (1500–1640), while real wages were halved. Principal causes were population pressure on inelastic food resources, a general increase in money supply and debasements of the coinage (1544–51).

Pride's purge 6 December 1648. The arrest of 45 MPs and turning away of 96 more by troops under Colonel Thomas Pride, as a means of halting continued negotiations between parliament and Charles I. The surviving MPs, known as the Rump, proceeded to pass (28 December) an ordinance for the king's trial. *See* CIVIL WARS.

Prime minister WALPOLE is usually regarded as the 1st minister to 'impose harmony' on his cabinet, but the post was not officially recognized until 1905, when CAMPBELL-BANNERMAN was the 1st formal appointment. The World Wars seemed greatly to increase the power of the office, and led to it being regarded as akin to a president, but a succession of weak premiers in the 1960s and 1970s would seem to disprove that thesis.

Primogeniture A system of inheritance whereby a person's whole estate (and by extension the sole right to his rank or title) pass to his eldest son. In the feudal period, in the absence of sons the estates were divided between all the daughters.

Prince of Wales *see* WALES

Prince regent *see* GEORGE IV

Princes in the Tower The sons of Edward IV and Elizabeth Woodville, the nominal Edward V (aged 12) and Richard duke of York (aged 9), were imprisoned by RICHARD III in the Tower of London and probably murdered there on his orders between July and September 1483. Attempts have been made to shift the blame to BUCKINGHAM or (most implausibly) to HENRY VII, but the fact remains that Richard's deposition and illegitimation of the princes was tantamount to a death sentence.

Printing Printing was introduced to England by William Caxton (d. 1491) who, having learned the craft in Germany and the Netherlands, set up his press at Westminster in 1476. The works printed by Caxton were essentially traditional in nature, but the introduction of printing heralded a revolution. It allowed the production of more books, the stimulation of education, the speedy distribution of new thought, the provision of more accurate texts and the building up of individual libraries. Full realization of this potential, however, was slow. With only 4 presses in 1500 (at London, Cambridge, Oxford and St Albans) England lagged far behind Germany or Italy. Nevertheless, by the 1520s printing was making an impact which was soon to be strengthened by the stimulation of the Refor-

This page from Bartholomaeus Anglicus's *De Proprietatibus rerum*, printed in London *c.* 1495, with its exceptionally clear woodcut, shows the high quality that early **printing** could attain. Wynkyn de Worde, Caxton's foreman who took over his press after his death, was responsible.

mation. Though books remained generally large and relatively expensive and though the output of the presses was controlled by the government through the Stationers' Company (chartered in 1557), more presses were established and books were produced in ever larger numbers. By 1600 a ready market existed for legal and devotional works, classical literature, history and topography, poetry, ballads, news-sheets and broadsheets. In 1640 the collapse of effective government censorship saw an explosion of publication which continued throughout the civil war and interregnum. Thereafter the book trade grew in the provinces as reading became an established leisure activity. Larger editions, 'part-books' sold in instalments, NEWSPAPERS and periodicals testified to the existence by 1750 of a mass market to be satisfied by presses across the nation.

Scotland's 1st press was established in 1508 by Andrew Myllar and Walter Chapman, but for long Scottish book production was overshadowed by that of England, only some 380 titles having been published by 1600. The 1638 revolution helped swell the output of Scotland's presses, but greater expansion came in the 18th century when both Edinburgh and Glasgow became renowned for high-quality printing. By 1800 Edinburgh was the principal British centre of printing and publishing outside London.

The 19th century saw the continued expansion of the printing industry and the introduction of

A wooden **printing** press made in the early 18th century and used by Wyman and Sons, Great Queen Street, London.

significant innovations such as the steam press, stereotyping, rotary printing and mechanized composing. These advances were pioneered by the newspaper industry, which has remained at the centre of continued technological innovation in printing.

Priories The name given to houses of FRIARS and of some orders of CANONS regular, and also applied to lesser monastic houses technically or actually dependent on a parent abbey. After the Norman conquest many Anglo-Norman magnates granted English and Welsh lands to French monasteries, which established 'alien priories' upon them. From 1295 these lands were confiscated during Anglo-French wars, and from 1414 those which had not been granted naturalization were suppressed, their possessions generally going to endow chantries or educational foundations.

Prisons In the 1830s, transportation and small, local and ill-run lock-ups began to give way to a uniform system of incarceration in individual cells. From 1839–50, 55 new prisons on the model of Pentonville were built. Discipline was consolidated

by Act (1865) and prisons placed under control of the prison commissioners, responsible to the home office (1877), who rationalized the system. In 1899 a further Act humanized the system, and created new reformatories for young 1st offenders, named after the 1st institution at Borstal, Kent. Between the wars open prisons for non-violent offenders were pioneered, and the various grades of institution recognized by the Criminal Justice Act (1948). However, no balance has yet been achieved satisfactorily between retribution and re-education in the British prison system.

Privateering The practice of authorizing private vessels by 'letters of marque' to attack enemy shipping, thereby distinguishing them from mere pirates. Such captains as DRAKE and MORGAN sailed as privateers and the system was much used in the period 1550–1815, being abolished by international agreement only in the 19th century.

Privy council *see* COUNCIL

Privy seal The monarch's personal SEAL, important from the 13th century as authorization for the larger GREAT SEAL and in authenticating informal documents proceeding from the ROYAL HOUSEHOLD, especially the wardrobe. Superseded as personal seal by the SIGNET under Edward II, it became an instrument of government at large, particularly associated with the royal council during the 15th to 17th centuries.

In Pentonville **prison** in the mid-19th century even the chapel was run on the separate-cell system. Contemporary engraving.

Pro-Boers A name given to the radical Liberals headed by Lloyd George, who criticized British involvement in the 2nd BOER WAR (1899–1902).

Procurator The official in charge of the financial administration of Roman Britain. *See* CLASSICIANUS, JULIUS ALPINUS.

Profumo affair 1963. A sexual scandal involving the Conservative leader Harold Macmillan's minister of defence, John Profumo, who had misled the commons about his relationship with Christine Keeler, a demi-mondaine with connections in Soviet intelligence. That, and illness, were the factors which made Macmillan resign office in October.

Prophesyings Preaching exercises, organized by Puritan ministers of the church of England in the 1570s in order to raise clerical standards, and attended also by sympathetic laymen. Elizabeth I, who saw them as subversive, suspended GRINDAL for his defence of prophesyings (1577) and had them banned in the province of Canterbury.

Protectorate, the 1653–8. The government of Oliver CROMWELL under the INSTRUMENT OF GOVERNMENT and HUMBLE PETITION AND ADVICE. The protectorate succeeded only while Cromwell lived and collapsed after the succession of his incompetent son Richard.

Protestation oath 1642. An oath to 'maintain and defend the true Reformed Religion expressed in the Doctrine of the Church of England against all Poperie and Popish Innovation'. Parliament ordered that it be taken by every man over the age of 18. Original lists of subscribers occasionally survive in PARISH REGISTERS.

Provisions, papal *see* CHURCH, PRE-REFORMATION

Provisions of Oxford 1258. The programme for general reform devised and promulgated during the Oxford (or 'Model') parliament of June 1258 by a committee of 24, half chosen by Henry III and half by the baronage. It effectively established a limited monarchy controlled by a council of 15 advisers (appointed by the 24) who were to consult with the barons at triennial parliaments. This council was also to redress widespread grievances, and make sweeping local governmental, legal and administrative reforms (the 2 latter being codified by the provisions of Westminster in October 1259).

Provisors, statutes of *see* CHURCH, PRE-REFORMATION

Public Order Act *see* BLACKSHIRTS

Public schools The schools defined as such by the Clarendon commission in the 1860s were 7 boarding schools – Eton, Harrow, Westminster, Rugby, Winchester, Charterhouse and Shrewsbury – and (somewhat arbitrarily) 2 London day schools, St Paul's and Merchant Taylors'. But a further inquiry, the Taunton commission, covered all endowed secondary schools. The result of both was to redistribute endowments (often pre-Reformation in origin) and revise statutes in order to remedy low standards of teaching, discipline and organization. ARNOLD's Rugby tended to be adopted as a model for reforms which consisted of modernizing endowments and making scholarships competitive, providing a non-classical alternative ('the modern side'), establishing house and prefectorial systems, and stressing school spirit by the use of games.

In the 1850s and 1860s the disciples of Arnold were extremely liberal, such as Tom Hughes, who wrote *Tom Brown's Schooldays* (1857) and was a leading advocate of trade unions and reform in the 1860s. But Rugby also severed links with the local community and became socially exclusive. After the Taunton commission, which envisaged only 8% of male children getting any sort of secondary education, the residential, fee-paying ideal was

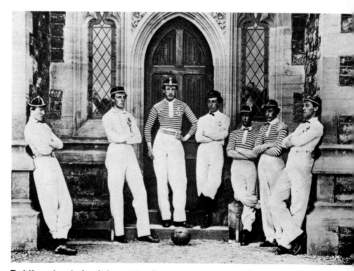

Public schools bred the spirit of easy superiority into future administrators and politicians: Clifton college caps, 1865.

consolidated, both in old foundations, such as Uppingham under Edward Thring (1821–87), and in new schools, such as those founded by Rev. Nathaniel Woodard (1811–91) which included Lancing and Hurstpierpoint.

Thereafter the emphasis on games increased and character and corporate identity were valued more highly than intellectual ability, creating an image which gained enormous popular appeal in literature ranging from H.A. Vachell's *The Hill* (1905) to the Frank Richards's *Gem* and *The Magnet* (c. 1907–39). In due course its values percolated down to the state system and, after the 1870s, across to the growing number of girls' public schools.

The public schools' dominance of entry into Oxford and Cambridge and so into the British political and administrative élite was rarely seriously challenged, nor did it significantly alter until the 1960s, despite some attempts to widen the intake in the 1940s (in anticipation of action from the Attlee government, which never came). Indeed, the expansion of the state caused the power of the administrative élite to grow, and frustrated attempts at intervention, such as the royal commission (1965–70) during Harold Wilson's government. The same government's phasing out of the direct-grant system, which linked many endowed day schools to the state system, caused an actual expansion in private education. *See* CLASS.

Puritanism Always easier to recognize than to define, Puritanism is best regarded less as an organized and ideologically consistent movement than as a broad trend within the late 16th- and early 17th-century CHURCH OF ENGLAND. The only common characteristics of Puritans were their militant, biblically based Protestantism and their desire for a more thorough purification of both the church and society, which would cast out 'popish' elements of ritual and doctrine and promote a thorough 'reformation' of life in accordance with God's word. From these roots grew the attacks upon the Anglican establishment, the advocacy of a disciplined godly life and the energetic evangelizing which are associated with Puritanism. Theologically most Puritans were, of course, Calvinists, but in this they differed little from the hierarchy of the Elizabethan and Jacobean church. Their differences lay in their conceptions of ecclesiastical organization and of the role the church should play.

Puritanism first emerged in the aftermath of the 1559 religious settlement (*see* REFORMATION), among Protestants anxious to move beyond the Elizabethan compromise to 'further reformation'. From the start it subsumed those who objected to tradi-

tional vestments in the VESTIARIAN CONTROVERSY and afterwards, those who demanded more preaching and better clerical standards and supported the PROPHESYING and CLASSIS MOVEMENTS and those who embraced the PRESBYTERIANISM of CARTWRIGHT. With the eventual defeat of their Presbyterian wing in parliament and the suppression of nonconforming ministers by WHITGIFT and BANCROFT after 1583, most Puritans confined their attention to moral reform, SABBATARIANISM and the promotion of personal and family piety. A minority moved into separation from the church and exile in the Netherlands and NEW ENGLAND. By the time of LAUD's ascendancy in the 1630s Puritanism had established solid support and a pattern of lay piety especially among the gentry, yeomen and urban 'middling sort' of southern and eastern England. Outrage at Laud's 'popish' policies further alienated them from the Anglican church and made possible the dismantling of the church of England during the CIVIL WARS when Puritanism gave an extra moral edge to the parliamentarian cause. After 1646, however, the centrifugal force of conscientious Puritan individualism was such that the erection of a national Presbyterian church proved impossible. By 1662, when the Anglican church was re-established, Puritanism had been metamorphosized into numerous denominations and sects of DISSENTERS.

Despite its failure within the church of England, Puritanism thus gave birth to numerous religious groups and ultimately to the ideal of religious toleration as a means of reconciling their diversity. The self-discipline, individualism, sense of personal calling and asceticism promoted by Puritan preachers also left their legacy, shorn of their former radicalism perhaps, but a powerful residual influence on attitudes and behaviour, especially among the emerging middle classes.

Purveyance The ancient right of the crown to purchase food for the needs of the royal household and armies at prices fixed by royal officials. Always unpopular, purveyance was particularly resented in the 16th and early 17th centuries.

Putney debates 1647. Debates in the army council between the officers of the NEW MODEL ARMY and the LEVELLERS on the constitutional settlement after the CIVIL WARS. Discussions, based on the Levellers' *Agreement of the People* (1647), were halted when Charles I escaped from captivity.

Putting-out system A decentralized system of industrial production, also known as 'domestic industry'. Raw materials were distributed by merchant entrepreneurs who later collected the finished goods. Well-suited to simple manufactures which could be conducted in the workers' cottages, the system was characteristic of British industries before the INDUSTRIAL REVOLUTION.

Pym, John 1583–1643. A Somerset squire, Pym entered parliament in 1621 and rapidly joined the opposition to the crown's policies. Tough and ruthless in politics, though essentially moderate in his aims, he led the commons in the constitutional revolution of 1640–1, thereafter organizing parliament's wartime finance and engineering the Scottish alliance. *See* CIVIL WARS.

John **Pym**, a champion of parliament and liberty against the 'tyranny' of Charles I: contemporary print by G. Glover.

Quadruple alliance 1718. The alliance of Britain, France, the Habsburg empire and the Netherlands, constructed by STANHOPE to guarantee the treaty of UTRECHT by settling the conflicting claims of Spain and the empire in Italy. A short war (1719–20) was undertaken to force Spanish compliance.

Quakers The popular name for the Society of Friends. The earliest Quakers, followers of George FOX and NAYLER, were notorious for their outspoken and unruly conduct and suffered much persecution as DISSENTERS. Subsequently organized by Fox, they developed a more sober piety and became notable for their tolerance and humanitarian concern. *See* NONCONFORMITY.

Quarter sessions Courts held by the JUSTICES OF THE PEACE of English counties and boroughs at the feasts of Michaelmas, Epiphany, Easter and S⁺ Thomas. The sessions lasted at least 3 days, during which time the justices tried minor crimes, following common law procedure, and dealt with administrative business. The fulcrum of LOCAL GOVERNMENT by 1603, they lasted until 1888.

Quebec, battle of 13 September 1759. A battle of the SEVEN YEARS' WAR. In a remarkable combined operation, British troops were landed beneath Quebec, scaled the Heights of Abraham and

Quakers, whose national organization was established by George Fox, gathered for an annual meeting in the time of Queen Anne. Contemporary print.

The death of General Wolfe at the climax of the battle of **Quebec**: oil painting by Benjamin West, 1770.

defeated the French under Montcalm, General Wolfe being killed in the moment of victory. The fall of Quebec signalled the end of French rule in Canada.

Queen Anne's bounty A fund for the augmentation of the livings of impoverished Anglican clergymen, established in 1704 by Queen Anne's grant of her revenues from the first-fruits and tenths of ecclesiastical benefices. Later augmented by parliamentary grants, it maintained a separate existence until 1948.

Queensberry, James Douglas, 2nd duke of 1662–1711. A Jacobite in 1689, Queensberry later served both William III and Queen Anne as royal commissioner to the Scottish parliament. He was a leading figure in the passing of the Act of UNION (1707) and was nicknamed the 'Union Duke'.

Quia Emptores, statute of July 1290 (Lat. 'since purchasers'). Passed by Edward I at the instance of his magnates, this attacked sub-infeudation by ruling that sub-tenants of lands (and not the tenants-in-chief from whom they held them) were directly responsible to the crown for the attached feudal services.

Quiberon bay, battle of 20 November 1759. A naval victory of the SEVEN YEARS' WAR in which Admiral Hawke trapped and defeated the French fleet in Quiberon bay. The victory removed a French invasion threat and effectively put the French navy out of action for the remainder of the war.

Quo Warranto, statute of 1290. The culmination of Edward I's searching inquiries into the usurpation or abuse of royal rights by landholders, and 'by what warrant' they exercised local rights and franchises, this statute established firmly that no baron could exercise judicial or local governmental authority except by royal grant.

R

Radar A directional range-finding device perfected by (Sir) Robert Watson-Watt in 1935 and rapidly deployed round the British coasts. Its use gave the ROYAL AIR FORCE a marked advantage in the battle of Britain.

Radicals As a generic term for the political left, its meaning shifted from identifying men of revolutionary inclinations (1789–1815), to signifying middle-class adherents of laissez-faire doctrines (*c.* 1830–60). Thereafter it had rather more socialistic, anti-clerical and pacifistic implications.

A helmet from the Sutton Hoo burial, probably commemorating **Raedwald**. It consists of an iron cap covered with impressed bronze sheets, and probably dates from the early 6th century.

240

Brook Street **ragged school**, London. *Illustrated London News*, 1853.

Radio *see* BROADCASTING

Raedwald king of East Anglia (d. *c.* 625). Most powerful of the kings of East Anglia, Raedwald was recognized as BRETWALDA on the death of Aethelbert (616), whereafter he overthrew Aethelferth of Northumbria. He is probably the person commemorated by the magnificent ship-burial discovered in 1939 at Sutton Hoo, Suffolk.

Ragged schools Intended to educate destitute children and save them from vagrancy, these were founded by John Pounds (1766–1839) and became the basis of the industrial-school method of coping with delinquent children.

Railway mania There were 2 periods during which an economic boom sent capital surging into railway investment: 1835–7, after which over 1,000 miles of track was built, and 1845–7 which created a further 5,000 miles. Huge fortunes were made by speculators and lawyers but many small investors lost heavily. Many more lines were promoted than were actually built. *See* HUDSON, GEORGE.

Raleigh, Sir Walter ?1552–1618. An accomplished courtier, soldier and navigator, Raleigh was nonetheless never entrusted with political power by Elizabeth I. He concerned himself instead with colonizing and exploratory ventures in the Americas. Condemned for treason by James VI and I, he was imprisoned (1603–16), released for an abortive expedition in search of El Dorado, then executed.

Ramillies, battle of *see* MARLBOROUGH'S WARS

Randolph, Thomas d. 1332. ROBERT BRUCE's nephew, from 1309 Randolph vied with James Douglas as his firmest supporter. Made earl of Moray in 1312, he seized Edinburgh castle (1314), commanded a wing at BANNOCKBURN and led raids into England (*see* MYTON, BATTLE OF). On Bruce's death he served efficiently as guardian for David II.

Ransoms *see* SPOILS OF WAR

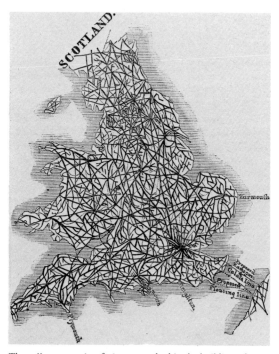

The **railway mania** of 1845–7 resulted in the building of 5,000 miles of track: this *Punch* cartoon of 1845 comments on the unchecked growth. 'Though England will never be in chains, she will pretty soon be in irons', was one *Punch* writer's comment.

Sir Walter **Raleigh**: miniature by Nicholas Hilliard, *c.* 1585.

A carefully set-up photograph, June 1945, designed to show the complications of dealing with **rationing** in a large family.

Men dressed as women attack a toll-gate during the **Rebecca riots** in Wales. *Illustrated London News*, August 1842.

Ranters Radical INTERREGNUM sectaries, who proclaimed their freedom from the moral law and were notorious for their verbal and sexual licence. Most active in 1649–51, they had no recognized leaders or organization, though prominent figures were Abiezer Coppe and Lawrence Clarkson. The name 'ranters' was later disparagingly applied to Primitive Methodists.

Rapes *see* HUNDRED

Rationing In World War I the most acute shortage was of sugar, largely imported from central Europe, which was put on ration in late 1917. Shortly afterwards, other commodities – meat, butter and lard – came in short supply and a local rationing scheme was devised for London. This was made national by a food-control system administered by BEVERIDGE (April–May 1918), but was never watertight or comprehensive, although sugar rationing lasted until late 1920.

In contrast, rationing preparations were made as early as 1938 for World War II and activated on 8 January 1940. The initial commodities rationed were butter, bacon and sugar; meat followed on 11 March. A general system of 'points' rationing, copied from Germany, was introduced for clothes in June 1942. At the end of the war, rationing was actually intensified, bread being rationed from July 1946–July 1948. Clothes rationing was abolished in March 1949; flour, eggs and soap were freed and the points system abolished in 1950. Sweets continued on ration until 1953, and petrol was briefly rationed after the SUEZ CRISIS (1956).

Rebecca riots 1839 and 1842–3. Agrarian discontent in south-west Wales, directed particularly at inefficient but extortionate TURNPIKE trusts, led tenant farmers dressed as women ('Rebecca and her daughters': Genesis XXIV, 60) to destroy toll-gates. They attracted public sympathy, and in 1844 Welsh trusts were replaced by county road boards.

Recognizance A document recognizing a previously established debt or undertaking (e.g. to keep the peace) and setting out the fine which would automatically be levied, either by the crown or with crown assistance, should the debt be unpaid or the undertaking not fulfilled. *See* HENRY VII.

Recusancy laws 1552, 1559, 1581 and 1587. Laws punishing failure to attend the service of the church of England with fines and confiscations of property. Aimed primarily at ROMAN CATHOLICS, who also suffered from other penal laws passed 1571–1610, the laws were rarely vigorously enforced.

Reeve (Old English *gerefa*). During Anglo-Saxon and medieval times, the agent, manager and representative of the king or other lord of a shire (*see* SHERIFF), hundred, town or manor. In the last case the reeve was often an elected VILLEIN.

Reform Bills The franchise was extended 3 times in the 19th century, by Acts (1832, 1867 and 1884) usually known as the 3 Reform *Bills*. This is significant, as it suggests that the process of passing the relevant Bill was as important as the final legislation itself. Moreover, franchise reform was carried on in the 20th century by further Acts (1918, 1928, 1948 and 1971).

The 1st, or Great Reform Bill, was the climax of over 50 years of agitation, from the time of Christoper Wyvill's YORKSHIRE ASSOCIATION (1782). Earl Grey, who finally carried it, had been associated with the cause for almost as long. Yet by the time it was passed it reflected a much more acute political contest. Reform had been deferred by the French revolution, which the doctrines of BURKE, as construed by Tories, interpreted as the 1st stroke of a Jacobin rampage. Since then, however, the great manufacturing towns had grown, unrepresented; questions of trade and domestic economic policy had come to the fore; and the working classes were reorganizing after 2 decades of repression. In France the Bourbons had gone down for the last time (1830). So, moderate though the Act was, it had the appearance of an expedient to forestall revolution. In the event it did not so much inaugurate as bring to a climax a period of political reform. Underprivileged groups, such as Catholics and trade unionists, made progress *before* not after it. Its effect was to standardize the urban franchise at £10 rental and end anomalies which had produced very democratic, as well as very corrupt, constituencies. In the shires it preserved Tory control by maintaining the old 40-shilling freeholders as well as enfranchising the more prosperous farmers and local merchants paying £10 for long leases and £50 for short leases. It removed 56 ROTTEN BOROUGHS entirely and took a member away from another 30. It gave 42 towns their 1st MPs and 62 more MPs to the counties. By raising the Scots electorate from under 5,000–65,000 it gave 'the greatest rotten borough' real representation for the 1st time. (A Scottish municipal reform Act had to follow in 1833, as the corrupt Scots burgh councils nominated their MPs. The English measure was not passed until 1835; *see* LOCAL GOVERNMENT.)

Some theorists and politicians – Bagehot, Lowe and Palmerston – believed that 1832 had settled the issue of reform and that any further action would imperil the rule of the educated classes. Agitations like CHARTISM confirmed their belief; but after its demise there was little enthusiasm for political innovation among a working class finding its economic feet. The Crimean war, and Palmerston's success in the 1857 election, further delayed reform.

BEFORE THE REFORM BILL.   JOHN BULL.   AFTER THE REFORM BILL.

Popular illusion as to what would be the results of the **Reform Bill** for John Bull, the ordinary Briton, is expressed in this cartoon of 1832.

But his death coincided with the 'triumph of democracy' in the American civil war, with enthusiasm for Garibaldi in Italy and the Polish uprising, with a growth in Liberal party organization and with a renewed interest in politics by trade unionists wanting legal rights, and UNIVERSITY intellectuals wanting the abolition of tests and eager to theorize about democracy.

Such forces organized to sustain reform when John Russell's Bill was defeated by the ADULLAMITE revolt (June 1866); they also provided a background for the parliamentary manoeuvering which accompanied DISRAELI's Bill of early 1867. In conferring household suffrage in towns and the £10 suffrage in the counties, this went further than most of the interested parties had anticipated, only Disraeli reckoning that the Conservatives could manage the extended electorate (it grew from 1,359,000–2,456,000). Unlike in 1832, there was no substantial redistribution of seats: many small boroughs were retained, and several cities were given 3-member seats, which (as voters had only 2 votes) gave a form of proportional representation. This, along with woman suffrage, was first pressed for during the debates on the Bill by Mill among others. An 'educational franchise' was also given limited recognition, with seats for Scottish, Irish and London universities. Another radical goal was conceded with the BALLOT ACT (1872).

To many Liberals the equalization of borough and county franchises now seemed inevitable, but this was not done until 1884, with little external agitation. Salisbury's quid pro quo for getting the lords to pass the Bill was to insist on a comprehensive redistribution Bill which threw the smaller boroughs in with the counties and so benefited the Conservatives. The single-member constituency now became normal throughout Britain.

The later Acts were less the result of agitation (but *see* WOMEN'S MOVEMENT) than recognitions of political and social change. That of 1918 granted suffrage to women over 30 and removed dis-qualifications which had diminished the male electorate by a quarter. That of 1928 (*see* FLAPPER VOTE) equalized male and female suffrage, and that of 1948 ended plural voting by abolishing the university seats and the business vote. Only in 1948 did 'one man one vote' become a fact, to be altered only when the age of majority was reduced to enfranchise the 18–21 year-olds (1971).

Reform League Founded by HOWELL and other London working-class radicals in 1863 to press for manhood suffrage, it soon had branches throughout the country. Its demonstration (23 July 1866) against the failure of the 2nd REFORM BILL resulted in riots in Hyde Park and helped pressure the new Derby-Disraeli ministry into adopting reform. It was used as an electoral organization by the Liberal party in the 1868 election, but expired shortly after.

Reformation Protestantism travelled to Britain along the trade routes from the Netherlands and north Germany and found fertile soil in the merchant communities of eastern England and Scotland and the universities of Cambridge and St Andrews. Only 3 years after Luther's initial protest of 1517 the 1st burning of smuggled Lutheran books took place in London and a Protestant cell was meeting at the White Horse tavern in Cambridge. Similar footholds were established in Scotland, the 1st Scottish martyr, Patrick Hamilton, being burned at St Andrews in 1528.

Though the response to the continental Reformation was swift, it was not widespread. Surviving pockets of LOLLARD heretics in England welcomed the new doctrine, but actual Protestants remained for long a tiny minority. More significant than the reformers' message was the prevailing climate of discontent with the Catholic church in both kingdoms. It would be wrong to see the church as totally moribund; areas of vital spirituality existed. Yet the church in England and Scotland was also disfigured by many abuses. Its wealth and privi-leged status aroused resentment. Its bishops were royal servants rather than spiritual leaders. The monasteries were frequently little more than property-owning corporations. The parish clergy were generally poor and often ignorant, if not immoral, while PLURALISM and NON-RESIDENCE

were widespread. Among humanist intellectuals (*see* HUMANISM) such as COLET and MORE these failings aroused sharp criticism. Among the general population they fostered a cynical anti-clericalism. Yet few people expected any better of the church and there was little spontaneous demand for change. The Reformation came from above, in response to political needs.

In England the crucial factor was HENRY VIII's need for an annullment of his 1st marriage (to Catherine of Aragon) and his inability to obtain it from a pope dominated by his wife's nephew, the Emperor Charles V. From 1529 the anti-clericalism of parliament was harnessed to bully the papacy into compliance. The English clergy were accused of PRAEMUNIRE in 1530. Then in 1532–4 Thomas CROMWELL put through a legislative programme which struck at the roots of papal authority. The submission of the clergy (1532) broke clerical resistance. Following CRANMER's consecration in 1533, the Act in restraint of APPEALS severed papal jurisdiction and facilitated Henry's annullment. In 1534 the submission of the clergy was embodied in legislation and the Act of SUPREMACY destroyed papal supremacy over the English church and transferred it to the crown.

The Henrician Reformation was legal and jurisdictional rather than doctrinal and met little opposition. The dissolution of the MONASTERIES which followed was likewise justified on non-doctrinal grounds, though it was resisted in the PILGRIMAGE OF GRACE. Cromwell and Cranmer made tentative moves towards real Protestant reform with the English BIBLE, Cromwell's in-junctions (1536 and 1538), the Ten Articles (1536) and the Bishops' Book (1538), but these were arrested by the Six Articles (1538) and the King's Book (1543), which reasserted the doctrinal orthodoxy favoured by Henry. Protestantism triumphed in England only after Henry's death, as Zwinglian and Calvinist ideas reached England and won qualified support from Cranmer. Under Edward VI the dissolution of the CHANTRIES (1547), the BOOKS OF COMMON PRAYER (1549 and 1552), Cranmer's Ordinal (1550) and the Forty-two Articles (1553) made the church Protestant in doctrine and ritual, though it remained traditional in organization. The WESTERN REBELLION challenged these innovations, but by 1553 Protestant support was well-established in south-east England. The reign of MARY I brought Catholic reaction and saw the flight abroad of many leading Protestants and the burning of Cranmer, RIDLEY, LATIMER and scores of humbler people. Ultimately, however, this damaged the Catholic cause by associating Catholicism with persecution and Spanish domination. The settlement on Elizabeth I's accession in 1558 restored a moderate Protestantism, enshrined in the Act of UNIFORMITY (authorizing the prayer book), the Act of SUPREMACY (1559) and the Thirty-nine Articles (1563), which codified the Anglican faith. The long process of Protestant consolidation in the CHURCH OF ENGLAND could now begin.

The Scottish Reformation, though certainly influenced by English events, followed a very different course. Under James V and the regents Arran and Mary of Guise Protestantism steadily gained support in the burghs and among the nobility, assisted after 1547 by its association with a policy of peace with England and hostility to French domination. In the 1550s the numerous Protestant congregations of the burghs were generally left in peace by Mary of Guise, who was anxious to maintain tranquillity until Mary Queen of Scots' marriage and the securing of the crown matrimonial for the French king. In 1557 the 'First Band' of Protestant lords was formed to seek recognition for the reformed church and in 1558 the 'Lords and Barons professing Jesus Christ' drew up proposals to that end. Events now came to a head. Elizabeth's accession in England encouraged Protestant militancy while Queen Mary's marriage freed Mary of Guise to turn against the reformers. On 11 May 1559, following the appearance on the doors of friaries of the Beggar's Summons calling upon the friar's to quit, and a fierce sermon by John Knox in Perth, there was iconoclastic rioting in several burghs. The regent mustered troops and the lords of the CONGREGATION rose to defend their faith. The arrival of French reinforcements tipped the scale in the regent's favour, but the treaty of BERWICK brought English intervention and a stalemate which was ended by the regent's death and the treaty of EDINBURGH. In August 1560 the Scottish parliament accepted a Calvinist confession of faith, abrogated papal authority and forbade the mass.

During the personal rule of Queen Mary (1561–7) an uneasy compromise was maintained. The old ecclesiastical structure persisted alongside the reformed organization initiated by the 1st BOOK OF DISCIPLINE. In the absence of a Protestant monarch, the GENERAL ASSEMBLY OF THE CHURCH OF SCOTLAND emerged to co-ordinate Protestant action, and in 1562 adopted the BOOK OF COMMON ORDER. The status quo was maintained over church lands, most of which were already held by noblemen, either by feu charter or as lay commendators of abbeys. From 1562 two-thirds of ecclesiastical revenues were guaranteed to the holders of benefices for life, the remaining third

Anti-Catholic propaganda was very effective in post-**Reformation** England: this print from Foxe's *Book of Martyrs*, 1563, shows how King John was supposed to have been poisoned by papal emissaries.

being divided between the crown and the reformed church. In 1567, however, Mary's deposition opened the way to further Protestant advance. In 1572 the concordat of Leith established a compromise between Episcopalian and Congregational elements in church government, while a year later all beneficed persons were required to subscribe to the confession of faith and the oath of supremacy, a measure which eliminated surviving Catholics from the church. The way was clear for further Protestant consolidation, though the return to Scotland of MELVILLE in 1574 was to awaken a tension between episcopacy and Presbyterianism in the CHURCH OF SCOTLAND which was not resolved until 1690.

For the mass of the populations of both kingdoms the political triumphs of Protestantism marked only the beginnings of a tide of religious change which reached its high-water mark only in the 17th century. By then Protestantism in its varied forms had become firmly established as a key element in their conceptions of national identity and as a powerful influence on their institutional' and cultural development. *See* WALES.

Reformation of Manners Societies Societies of earnest Low Church Anglicans and DISSENTERS active in London and provincial towns 1690–1738. They urged sterner action by magistrates in enforcing moral legislation and themselves undertook prosecutions for drunkenness, swearing, sabbath-breaking, whoring and suchlike offences.

Regional policy This originated in Britain in the 1930s as a means of coping with endemic unemployment in areas dominated by depressed heavy industry. The Special Areas Act (1934) made available grants for public works and, later, for factories and industrial estates, but only with the Distribution of Industry Act (1945) was this made part of a systematic process. Lying fallow under the Conservatives, regional policy was revived, after the 1957–8 depression, by Harold Macmillan's government (1961). Harold Wilson's government created a series of regional plans, co-ordinated by a national plan (1965), and sustained by financial incentives and high public spending on such things as roads. It was only partially successful and tended to give way in the 1970s to proposals for greater regional economic autonomy.

Regni *see* ATREBATES

Regulated companies Chartered companies for the control of particular branches of foreign trade. Boards of directors regulated trade and licensed entry to it but, unlike JOINT-STOCK COMPANIES, members traded individually. The great age for the foundation of such companies (e.g. the Eastland and Levant companies) was the late 16th century.

Reith, John, viscount *see* BROADCASTING

Reivers, border Members of the notoriously lawless 'surnames' of the Anglo-Scottish border country, also known as 'moss-troopers', who lived partly by pastoral agriculture and partly by cattle raiding and extortion. Though occasionally harried by punitive raids by the English or Scottish authorities, the borderers were pacified only slowly after 1603.

Relief *see* ESCHEAT; FEUDALISM

Religious orders Comprising all persons living a religious life according to a fixed rule, these may be divided into CANONS regular, FRIARS, MONKS, NUNS and military orders (*see* HOSPITALLERS, KNIGHTS; TEMPLARS, KNIGHTS).

Remonstrants Supporters of the Western Remonstrance which was put before the Scottish committee of estates in 1650 by extreme COVENANTERS calling for Charles II's removal from power and the enforcement of the Act of CLASSES. The Remonstrants were opposed by the majority of RESOLUTIONERS in the general assembly.

Reparations After World War I the allies attempted to make Germany pay their costs, of which the British share was computed as *c.* £2,000 million (1921). Rampant inflation checked German ability to pay, until the Dawes plan (1924) gave her loans, eventually amounting to rather more than the reparations themselves, which disappeared altogether in the SLUMP (1931).

Requests, court of A court of equity which developed from the royal council's role in redressing the wrongs of subjects too poor to use the common LAW courts. The competence of Requests, which had a continuous history from 1493, was increasingly questioned by common lawyers jealous of its rivalry to COMMON PLEAS. Requests lapsed in 1643.

Resolutioners Supporters of resolutions passed in the general assembly after DUNBAR, favouring co-operation with supporters of the Scottish ENGAGEMENT and the suspension of the Act of CLASSES. The Resolutioners adhered to Charles II in 1651 and were opposed to the REMONSTRANTS.

Restoration 1660. The restoration of the MONARCHY after the INTERREGNUM. Following MONCK's intervention, the election of a convention parliament and its acceptance of the declaration of BREDA, CHARLES II landed in May 1660. The constitutional settlement was based upon the 1641 reforms, while the religious settlement was embodied in the CLARENDON CODE.

Revocation, Act of 1625. The cancellation by Charles I of grants of crown property in Scotland made since 1540 and of temporal lordships created from ecclesiastical property. Church property was held thereafter on terms more favourable to the crown and the ministry. The Act was deeply resented by the Scottish nobility.

Rheged A post-Roman British kingdom occupying Lancashire and Cumbria (*see* CYMRY). Its most famous king, Urien, dominated north-west Britain *c.* 580 and defeated English Bernicia *c.* 590, but soon after his assassination by British neighbours Rheged was overrun by Aethelferth. Absorbed by Strathclyde in the 9th century, it finally became English only under William Rufus.

Rhodes, Cecil 1853–1902. An English clergyman's son, Rhodes founded De Beers (1880) and the British South African Company (1887) to develop what later became Rhodesia. Cape Colony

Cecil **Rhodes** (right) with Dr Jameson: part of a group photograph, October 1894.

premier from 1890, he resigned over complicity in the JAMESON RAID in 1896. He left over £6 million, much of it to create scholarships to weld together the Anglo-Saxon nations: the British empire, the USA and Germany.

Rhodesian crisis The territory administered by the British South African Company (*see* RHODES, CECIL) gained a constitution as Rhodesia (1923) in which powers were reserved to the white minority. It became a constituent of the Central African Federation (1953–63), but on its breakup interracial tensions and the failure to reach a constitutional settlement coincided with a move to the right among the white electorate, and on 11 November 1965 the government of Ian Smith (1965–79) made a Unilateral Declaration of Independence (UDI). Harold Wilson's government called for United Nations sanctions against Smith, but ruled out the use of force, and on 2 occasions (1966 and 1968) came close to an agreement with Smith which would effectively have legitimized the whites' privileged position. A similar settlement (1971) agreed between Smith and Edward Heath's government was only ruled out when the constitutional commission under Lord Pearce, sent to determine how acceptable it was to African opinion, was confronted with widespread opposition, orchestrated by a new black movement, Bishop Abel Muzorewa's African National Congress. In 1974–5, when the Portuguese withdrew from Angola and Mozambique, Smith became painfully conscious of his exposed position as a guerilla campaign against his regime began in earnest. In 1977 he announced himself willing to negotiate on the basis of 'one man one vote' and released the African leaders Ndabaningi Sithole and Joshua Nkomo who had been in detention since 1961. They refused, however, to negotiate and joined up with the guerillas. Smith reached an internal settlement with Muzorewa and Sithole (1978), but the guerilla campaign continued to threaten the new multi-racial government. In late 1979 the Conservative government was ultimately able to gain a settlement which was adhered to by all 3 parties. The country was put under colonial administration pending elections in 1980, which were won by the guerilla leader Robert Mugabe.

Rhodri Mawr d. 877. The 1st prince to unite most of Wales, Rhodri 'the Great' ruled Gwynedd from 844, obtaining Powys by marriage (855) and much of west Wales by inheritance (872). He successfully resisted Viking raiders, but was killed by the English. Though his confederacy died with him, it foreshadowed later Welsh unity.

Rhuddlan, statute of *see* WALES

Rhys ap Gruffydd 1132–97. Prince of DE-HEUBARTH from 1155, he played a leading role in the Welsh counter-attack on the MARCHERS, but in 1171–2 reached agreement with Henry II, who wished to counterbalance Marcher power. Recognized as effective ruler of south Wales, 'the Lord Rhys' thereafter supported Henry loyally through all crises, but died campaigning against Richard I. He was an enthusiastic patron of the monastic orders.

Riccio, David *see* DARNLEY, LORD; MARY QUEEN OF SCOTS

Richard I king of England (1189–99; b. 1157). The 3rd son and heir of Henry II by Eleanor of Aquitaine. Richard's reputation as a soldier and crusader has sometimes obscured his failings as king of England, where he spent only 6 months of his reign (August–December 1189 and March–May 1194). Despite his absence, his financial demands were heavy and continuous, first to pay for his CRUSADE (1190–2), then (having fallen into the hands of his enemy the German emperor in 1193) for his ransom, and finally for his successful war against Philip Augustus (1194–9). While he was abroad, power was exercised (until 1194 in the face of conspiracies by his brother John) by JUSTICIARS, principally the unpopular William Longchamp (1189–91), Walter of Coutances (1191–3) and Hubert Walter (1193–8).

Richard II commissioning his officials: decorated initial from a contemporary manuscript of instructions for a coronation.

Richard II king of England (1377–99; b. 1367). Succeeding his grandfather Edward III at a time of national crisis, Richard distinguished himself by his bravery during the PEASANTS' REVOLT (1381). In 1387 the APPELLANTS forced him to submit to the MERCILESS PARLIAMENT. Having regained power (1389), Richard (counselled by his uncle John of Gaunt) pursued a policy of moderation, obtaining credit for his 1st expedition to Ireland (1394–5), which achieved the submission of Art MacMurrough and other rebel Irish chieftains (in return for the concession of their full legal status under the English crown). But after 1397 he embarked on a period of 'tyranny', adding to his growing unpopularity by banishing Henry Bolingbroke (later Henry IV) and confiscating the Lancaster inheritance before ill-advisedly embarking on a 2nd Irish expedition (June–July 1399) when MacMurrough rebelled again. In his absence Henry's invasion met with scant opposition, and Richard was deposed (30 September) and imprisoned at Pontefract, where he was (probably) murdered before 17 February 1400.

Richard III king of England (1483–5; b. 1452). Richard served his brother Edward IV faithfully at BARNET and TEWKESBURY, and was declared protector of his young sons at Edward's death. He nevertheless seized control of the princes from their maternal Woodville relations (long Richard's enemies) and, with the support of

BUCKINGHAM, declared them illegitimate and imprisoned them, making himself king. But his usurpation and the suspicion that he had murdered the 'PRINCES IN THE TOWER' alienated the majority of his subjects, including the late king's friends. In October 1483 he put down Buckingham's southern rising, but in 1485 was defeated and killed at BOSWORTH.

Ridley, Nicholas ?1500–55. A Cambridge scholar of distinction and energetic Protestant reformer, Ridley did much as CRANMER's chaplain to influence the archbishop's doctrinal development and as bishop of London (1550) to advance the REFORMATION. Arrested on MARY I's accession, he was burned at Oxford with Latimer.

Ridolfi plot 1571. A plot masterminded by the Italian financier Roberto Ridolfi for a Catholic rising and Spanish invasion which would depose or assassinate Elizabeth I and place Mary Stewart on the throne. Rejected by Spain and discovered in England, the plot led only to the execution of the duke of Norfolk (1572).

Rinyo-Clacton culture *see* PREHISTORIC BRITAIN

Ripon, treaty of 1640. The treaty ending the BISHOPS' WARS. Under its terms the Scots occupied Northumberland and Durham, receiving £850 a day for their maintenance. This situation obliged Charles I to summon the Long parliament.

Rivers, Anthony, earl *see* WOODVILLE, QUEEN ELIZABETH

Road fund Set up by Lloyd George in his PEOPLE's BUDGET (1909) with the aim of using motor vehicle licence fees for road improvements. But the road board which was to oversee this never had the chance to operate properly and was superseded by the ministry of transport (1919), the fund going into general taxation.

Robert Bruce king of Scotland (1306–29; b. 1274). The hero of the SCOTTISH WARS OF INDEPENDENCE was descended from an Anglo-Norman family introduced to Scotland by DAVID I, and was grandson of Robert Bruce, Lord of Annandale (1210–95), whose collateral descent from WILLIAM THE LION made him John BALLIOL's chief rival for the throne in 1290–2. Robert, called earl of Carrick from 1292, was thus basically indisposed to support Scottish resistance carried out in Balliol's name: he supported EDWARD I (1296), submitted to him again after briefly joining WALLACE in 1297 and (after serving as joint guardian 1298–1300) once again in 1302.

His situation changed with the extinction of Balliol's cause by Edward's 2nd conquest of Scotland (1303–4) and by June 1304 he was planning (with the encouragement of LAMBERTON) to adopt the patriotic cause and seize the throne. Unable to persuade Balliol's powerful nephew John 'the Red Comyn' to support him, he murdered him at the high altar of Greyfriars Kirk, Dumfries (10 February 1306), thus incurring not only a blood feud with Comyn's kin but also excommunication for sacrilege. Despite the latter, he obtained the sanction of WISHART and Lamberton for his hurried coronation at Scone (25 March 1306) and attracted considerable lay support, but after a defeat by AYMER DE VALENCE at Methven (19 June), and another by Comyn's Gaelic kinsman John Mac-Dougall of Lorne at Dalry in July or August, he was forced into exile in Ireland or Orkney, leaving most of his family to be imprisoned or executed.

In February 1307 he nevertheless returned, holding out with a small force in the glens of Carrick and Galloway against English encirclement (and routing Valence at Loudoun Hill in May) until Edward I's death in July allowed him to take the initiative against his Scottish enemies. Moving north in November 1307, he defeated the Comyns at Inverurie (23 May 1308), and then turned against John of Lorne in Argyll, finally crushing him at the pass of Brander (autumn 1309).

Against the better-equipped English he had (with the aid of James DOUGLAS and later of RANDOLPH) already developed a policy of guerilla attacks, scorched-earth tactics and the piecemeal surprise and demolition of fortresses. He now employed this to frustrate Edward II's invasion (1310), clear the English garrisons north of Forth (1312–13) and by spring 1314 recover all Scotland save Berwick and Stirling castle.

Edward II's attempt to relieve the last resulted in his crushing defeat at BANNOCKBURN, but (despite his domestic troubles) he still refused to recognize Scottish independence, an attitude shared by the papacy (see ARBROATH, DECLARATION OF). Robert therefore launched devastating raids on northern England (1314–19), and then sponsored a 'second front' invasion of English-held Ireland by his brother Edward Bruce (1316–18). The failure of English attempts to recapture Berwick in 1319 (see MYTON, BATTLE OF) resulted in a short truce, and further English defeats in 1322 (when Edward II was nearly captured) in a longer one, but it was not until

he renewed the war on Edward's death (1327) that Robert was finally acknowledged as sovereign of an independent nation by the treaty of EDINBURGH-NORTHAMPTON. Shortly afterward the papacy followed suit and lifted his excommunication. He died in 1329 at the zenith of his achievements. (G. W. S. Barrow, *Robert Bruce and the Community of the Realm of Scotland*, 1965.)

Robert II king of Scotland (1371–90; b. 1316). The first of the royal Stewarts, Robert upheld the cause of his exiled uncle David II in the closing years of the SCOTTISH WARS OF INDEPENDENCE, and acted as lieutenant of Scotland during David's captivity after NEVILLE'S CROSS. By the time he succeeded he was comparatively aged, and his weak rule initiated a decline in the prestige of the Scottish monarchy.

Robert III king of Scotland (1390–1406; b. *c.* 1337). The son of Robert II, he was physically crippled, and left the business of government to his brother ALBANY. His reign saw 'discord, wrangles and strife betwixt magnates and nobles, because the king, . . . nowhere exercised rigour' (Bower's Chronicle).

Robert de Bellême, earl of Shrewsbury d. *c.* 1130. The most powerful of the Anglo-Norman opponents of Henry I, this exceptionally sadistic baron was expelled in 1102 after a major campaign, mounted with enthusiastic English support, had reduced his many castles.

Robert Curthose, duke of Normandy *c.* 1053–1134. The popular but inefficient eldest son of

Robert II, first of the Stewart kings, portrayed on a contemporary silver groat (fourpenny piece).

William the Conqueror, Robert Curthose was successively baulked of ruling England by WILLIAM RUFUS and HENRY I. Though he achieved fame during the 1st crusade (1096–1100), he finally lost Normandy to Henry at TENCHEBRAI, spending the remainder of his life in confinement.

Robert of Gloucester *see* LINCOLN, BATTLE OF; STEPHEN; WINCHESTER, BATTLE OF

Roberts, Frederick, lord 1832–1914. The hero of the Indian mutiny, Roberts was commander-in-chief during the 2nd BOER WAR and the last commander-in-chief before the general staff took over (1904). He advocated conscription.

Robin Hood The famous OUTLAW of medieval legend has been identified with various historical personages: whether he was essentially a peasant or a gentry hero is still disputed. Tales of him were current by the late 14th century and survive from the mid-15th. They initially had a roughly contemporary background, the alleged connection with Richard I appearing later. (M. H. Keen, *The Outlaws of Medieval Legend*, 2nd edn 1977.)

Robin of Redesdale *see* BANBURY, BATTLE OF

Rochdale Pioneers The name of the first of the new type of consumers' CO-OPERATIVE RETAIL SOCIETY, founded in Toad Lane, Rochdale (1844), offering a dividend but no credit. It started a pattern which was repeated throughout the country.

Rockingham, Charles Wentworth, 2nd marquis of 1730–82. Rockingham inherited Newcastle's place in Whig politics (1762) and in 1765 formed a brief ministry which repealed the STAMP ACT and declared GENERAL WARRANTS illegal. Thereafter he opposed North and the American independence war. He died shortly after returning to office with a programme of peace and economical reform.

Roman Britain The motives for the Roman decision to conquer Britain were various, foremost among them being the current drive towards imperial expansion, the desire of the new Emperor Claudius to emulate the military exploits of his predecessors, and the necessity of protecting British tribes allied to Rome against Catuvellaunian aggression (*see* CUNOBELINUS; PREHISTORIC BRITAIN). The prospect of mineral wealth and the hope of suppressing the anti-Roman Druids also played their part. In June or July 43 an invasion force of 4

LEGIONS and their AUXILIARIES (about 40,000 men in all) sailed from Boulogne under Aulus Plautius (governor 43–7). Exaggerated rumours of a Roman mutiny had misled the British forces under Togodumnus and CARATACUS, and Plautius landed unopposed at Richborough in Kent. Shortly afterwards, however, the Roman advance was disputed at the crossing of the river Medway near Rochester, and only after a desperate 2-day battle were they able to proceed. Several further skirmishes (in one of which Togodumnus was killed) occurred before they crossed the Thames and halted to await the arrival of Claudius to head a triumphal entry into the Catuvellaunian capital at COLCHESTER. Roman diplomacy, and the enmities caused by Catuvellaunian expansion, now brought about the surrender of several British tribes, and the western flank of Plautius's advance had been secured by the friendly Atrebates under Cogidubnus.

After Claudius's brief visit Plautius and his generals continued the conquest of lowland Britain. VESPASIAN, with the 2nd legion, struck towards the south-west and overran the Durotriges, while the 14th marched into the midlands and the 9th towards the north, the 20th remaining in reserve at Colchester. By 47 a defended frontier, marking the limit of intended Roman control, had been established along the line of the Fosse Way from Exeter in the south-west to the Humber in the north-east.

The hostility of the tribes beyond this geographically unsatisfactory frontier, however, made the Claudian policy of limited conquest impracticable. Plautius's successor Ostorius Scapula (47–51) found it necessary to advance to the line of the Severn, and penetrated Wales to defeat Caratacus. Didius Gallus (51–7) also campaigned against the Silures and intervened to support the pro-Roman Queen Cartimandua against her Brigantian subjects. The new province was proving more troublesome than anticipated, and Nero (54–68) is said to have contemplated complete withdrawal. But *c.* 57 he decided instead on a forward policy aimed at bringing the whole island under Roman control. Suetonius Paullinus (58–61) accordingly invaded Wales, but while he was attacking the Druidic stronghold of Anglesey Boudica's revolt broke out in his rear. The brutal suppression of the rising was followed by a period of recovery (*see* CLASSICIANUS, JULIUS ALPINUS) and by civil war in the empire, and it was not until after VESPASIAN became emperor (69) that the forward policy was resumed. The governorships of CERIALIS (71–4), JULIUS FRONTINUS (74–8) and AGRICOLA (78–84) saw continuous advance to the west and north, and at the end of this

Iron age and **Roman Britain**.

A carved stone slab from the Antonine wall, 2nd century, showing a **Roman** cavalryman riding down 4 Scottish tribesmen.

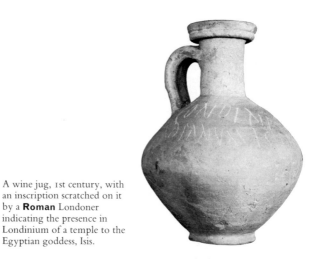

A wine jug, 1st century, with an inscription scratched on it by a **Roman** Londoner indicating the presence in Londinium of a temple to the Egyptian goddess, Isis.

period only the extreme north of Scotland remained unsubdued.

Meanwhile the province of Britain was being gradually Romanized. At the head of its administration stood the governor (*Legatus Augusti pro praetore*) directly appointed by and responsible to the emperor. Governors of Britain were invariably senators who had served as consuls, and often had considerable military experience. Their duties, indeed, were largely military, but they were also responsible for ROMAN ROADS, the supervision of CIVITATES, the supreme court of legal appeal (assisted by a Legatus Iuridicus) and all other aspects of government save finance. This last was, until the 4th century, the responsibility of an imperially appointed PROCURATOR based in London.

The initial agent of Romanization, and a continuing influence in the militarized border zones and around LEGIONARY FORTRESSES, was the Roman garrison. Numbering about 75,000 effectives at its peak under Agricola, its needs attracted trade, and its time-expired veterans frequently married and settled here, while the Britons it recruited served all over the empire. As the area behind the frontiers was pacified and demilitarized, however, civil government was established, based on a system of civitates which eventually covered almost the whole of Britain. Here Romanization was encouraged by the official establishment of towns, in order of status: COLONIAE, MUNICIPIA, civitas capitals and VICI.

Agricola's victories marked the high-water mark of Roman expansion in Britain. In 87 the transfer of 1 of the 4 British legions (the 2nd Adiutrix) to deal with trouble on the Danube frontier of the empire necessitated a retreat to southern Scotland, and *c.* 105 more troop transfers (accompanied by a rising of the Selgovae, Novantae and Brigantes) resulted in a further withdrawal to the Tyne-Solway line. The same tribes revolted again in 117–18, and in 122 the Emperor Hadrian visited Britain and ordered the construction of HADRIAN'S WALL to separate the Brigantes from their allies and (in pursuit of his policy of imperial consolidation) to act as a permanent frontier for the province. Early in the reign of Antoninus Pius, however, disturbances in southern Scotland (perhaps an attack on the pro-Roman Votadini) led to the abandonment of Hadrian's frontier and a new advance to the Forth-Clyde line, where the governor Lollius Urbicus (136–44) began the ANTONINE WALL c. 143. This new frontier was short-lived, being evacuated in 154–5 when the Brigantes and their allies rose behind it in a revolt serious enough to warrant reinforcements from Germany under the governor Julius Verus (c. 155–9). It was perhaps briefly regarrisoned c. 159, but c. 165 was finally abandoned in favour of a fully recommissioned Hadrian's wall.

This wall was itself broken by the southern Scottish tribes c. 180, but by c. 184 they had been heavily defeated by Ulpius Marcellus (180–5), who then bound them by treaty to act as buffer-states against the Caledonians. Their undertakings, however, did not prevent them from invading the province again when CLODIUS ALBINUS denuded Britain of troops (196–7). At this time, too, there were revolts by the Brigantes and in Wales, and it was not until c. 205 that peace was fully restored and Hadrian's wall repaired. After the Scottish punitive expeditions of SEVERUS and Caracalla (208–11), the frontier remained secure for almost a century.

From c. 213 to c. 270, indeed, Roman Britain as a whole enjoyed a period of peace. Now divided (to prevent a repetition of the Albinus affair) into the northern province of Britannia Inferior and the southern province of Britannia Superior, she was insulated by the Channel from most of the contemporary troubles of the Roman world (where at least 55 emperors were proclaimed 244–84), though she herself was attached to a Gallic separatist empire 259–74.

By 275, however, Anglo-Saxon and other sea-borne Germanic raiders were seriously threatening the south and east coasts. Many towns were fortified in stone, the SAXON SHORE fort system was established and the CLASSIS BRITANNICA strengthened. In 286 the latter's commander CARAUSIUS declared himself emperor, and Britain remained independent of Rome until 296. Then CONSTANTIUS re-established imperial control, restored the neglected northern defences (recently damaged by Picts and rebellious tribesmen) and appointed a DUX

BRITANNIARUM. He also reorganized Britain as a diocese of 4 provinces under the overall direction of a Vicarius seated at London, which was also the capital of the southern province, Maxima Caesariensis: others were Britannia Prima (Wales and western England, capital CIRENCESTER); Britannia Secunda (the north, capital YORK); and Flavia Caesariensis (eastern England, capital LINCOLN).

The Anglo-Saxon and Pictish threats receded 300–40, a period that has been described as the golden age of Roman Britain. Certainly her economic prosperity was at its height, for during her comparative isolation in the 3rd century she had become largely self-sufficient, with much of the wealth derived from her industries now in native hands. These industries included mining, especially for lead and silver (an imperial monopoly exploited through contractors since the conquest), iron-smelting, stone-quarrying, timber, pottery and, to a lesser extent, coal (from surface outcrops), salt, leather and oysters. Her balance of trade with the empire was also favourable, her principal export being high-quality woollens emanating from the numerous and prosperous VILLA farms of southern Britain. Corn was also exported as, on a minor scale, were jet, beer, hunting dogs and slaves taken in Scotland or Ireland.

New clouds appeared on the horizon in 342–3, when renewed attacks by Picts, Irish and Anglo-Saxons necessitated a visit to Britain by the Emperor Constans, who reorganized the northern frontier and strengthened the Saxon Shore system. From c. 360, nevertheless, there were further attacks, culminating in the BARBARIAN CONSPIRACY (367–9). The situation was restored by THEODOSIUS, and for a while Britain again enjoyed prosperity and security. But the barbarian threat was growing as the empire weakened, and the withdrawal of troops by MAGNUS MAXIMUS (despite his employment of FOEDERATI in their place) led to more Pictish raids and (in Wales) Irish invasions. The Emperor Honorius's general Stilicho led a successful expedition against the attackers (396–9), but barbarian pressure on Rome herself prevented him reinforcing the British garrison and c. 401 he withdrew more units to Europe. It was perhaps at this time that Hadrian's wall was finally abandoned, a small mobile army of COMITATENSES being established in compensation, only to be transferred to Europe in its turn by the British usurper Emperor Constantine III (407).

The end of Roman Britain proper came in 410, when the imperial government of Honorius refused a request by the British civitates for aid against an Anglo-Saxon attack. No longer able to intervene in Britain as it had done during previous crises, Rome thus finally lost control of the province, and during the ensuing HEROIC AGE the Romano-Britons were left both to defend and to rule themselves. (S.S. Frere, *Britannia*, rev. edn 1978.)

Roman Catholicism The separate history of Roman Catholicism in England and Wales dates from the excommunication of ELIZABETH I (1570) and the foundation of the English mission by ALLEN. Before 1570 adherents of the old faith (usually gentry families and their tenants, a tiny minority save in the north) commonly attended Anglican services and endeavoured to pass unnoticed. Thereafter missionary priests (many of whom were executed as traitors) stiffened their faith and demanded their separation from Anglicanism, the most vital role being played by the Jesuits following the mission of PARSONS and CAMPION (1580–1). As a result Catholics were increasingly regarded as politically unreliable and were harassed by RECUSANCY and penal laws (*see* PENAL CODE). Similarly in Scotland, missionary activity sustained a tenacious Catholic minority, with its greatest strength in Dumfriesshire and the central highlands.

For much of the 17th century Catholics were the object of popular fear and suspicion. Many supported Charles I in the CIVIL WARS, for which they suffered financial penalties. Later subjected to the TEST ACT (1673) and smeared by the POPISH PLOT (1678), they saw their last hope of the re-catholicization of Britain dashed by the GLORIOUS REVOLUTION (1688). Thereafter Catholicism accepted the position of a dissenting denomination. Though commonly branded as JACOBITES, Catholics enjoyed effective toleration in the 18th century, though the GORDON RIOTS showed how strong a prejudice remained. Their civil disabilities were eased by Saville's Act (1778) and by the Catholic Relief Act (1791) which also formally gave them freedom of worship, though full Catholic emancipation came only in 1829 with the Roman Catholic Relief Act, which was carried by Peel in response to the agitation brought to a head by O'CONNELL. This removed the 17th-century laws denying them civil rights, admitted them to all offices except those of regent, lord chancellor and lord-lieutenant of Ireland, and ended all restrictions on their ownership of property. UNIVERSITIES were fully opened to them in 1871.

The social nature of Roman Catholicism in mainland Britain was also undergoing great changes. Where it had survived the Reformation and the end of Jacobitism, Catholicism had in the main been aristocratic, the traditional belief of old gentry families in the north-west. Although this

An expression of friendship between the **Roman Catholic** and Anglican churches: Pope Paul VI and Donald Coggan, archbishop of Canterbury, in the Sistine chapel, Rome, April 1977.

core was strengthened by refugees from France after 1789, real change was provided by successive waves of Irish immigration. The Catholic percentage of the population of mainland Britain trebled during the 19th century to reach 5·9% (1901) and 9·2% (1966), mainly in central Scotland and Lancashire. Nevertheless, the 'old Catholics' remained substantially in control of the hierarchy, reinforced by converts from High Church Anglicanism (*see* OXFORD MOVEMENT). In 1850 the hierarchy was formally restored with an archbishop of Westminster and 12 dioceses. This 'papal aggression' caused the last widespread anti-Catholic agitation.

The 1st archbishop, Cardinal Nicholas Wiseman (1850–65), an Anglo-Irish scholar, moved the Catholic church in England closer in doctrine to Rome, supporting the dogma of the immaculate conception in 1854, and this ultramontane tendency was continued by his successor MANNING (1865–92). This accorded with the fundamentalist faith of the Irish immigrants, but tended to leave 'liberal Catholic' intellectuals such as NEWMAN isolated. Nevertheless, Manning greatly increased the church's social role and promoted its identification (virtually unique in Europe, where parties of the left tended to be anti-clerical) with the Liberal party and its policy of home rule for Ireland.

In the 20th century the certainty and rigour of Roman Catholic doctrines, allied to flexible and subtle political leadership from the hierarchy, sustained the church long after membership of the Anglican and Nonconformist churches had started to dip. In World War I, despite the Irish issue (*see* IRISH CONSTITUTIONAL CRISIS), it was conventionally patriotic; after the war it gained in Scotland a separate state-owned but Catholic-controlled educational system. With the decline of the Liberal party, Catholic support was systematically transferred to Labour, a shift that was crucial in bringing about Labour successes in areas such as Glasgow and Liverpool, although it was subsequently to have a retarding effect on educational and liberal reform policies.

In World War II the Catholic church, led until 1943 by Cardinal Hinsley, co-operated with Anglican reformers such as TEMPLE in agitation for a more equitable social order, but after the war it became more conservative, even when Rome was radicalized by the pontificate of John XXIII (1958–63). A formal end to the break with Rome was signalled by the visit of Elizabeth II to the Vatican (1961) and by the inauguration of ecumenical discussions with the church of England. In the 1970s the fidelity of Cardinal Heenan to John's more conservative successor, Paul VI, especially on matters of divorce and birth control, inhibited these discussions. But more conservative Catholics could still claim that where faith was strongest – as in Scotland and Ireland – dogma remained rigid.

Roman roads A vital element in the military and economic life of Roman Britain, and in communications ever since, these straight and well-built highways were originally constructed by legionaries. The most important were the Fosse Way (Exeter–Lincoln), Watling Street (Richborough–Canterbury–London–Wroxeter–Chester), Ermine Street (London–Lincoln–York) and the Portway (London – Silchester – the south-west). Well-preserved stretches remain at Wheeldale Moor, near Goathland, north Yorks., and Blackstone Edge, near Rochdale, Gtr Manchester.

Root and Branch petition 11 December 1640. A petition of 15,000 Londoners to the Long parliament demanding the abolition of episcopacy 'root and branch'. After violent debates and the introduction of a Bill in the commons, the issue was dropped by parliamentary leaders anxious to avoid a religious split in the opposition to Charles I.

Rose noble *see* ROYAL

Rosebery, Archibald Philip Primrose, 5th earl of 1847–1929. Foreign secretary (1885–6 and 1892–4), 1st chairman of the London county council (1888) and Liberal premier (March 1894–June 1895), Rosebery had little enthusiasm for

The **Roman road** at Blackstone Edge, showing the well-preserved sunken kerbstones and foundation of large stones on which the finished surface of gravel was laid.

The earl of **Rosebery**: his image as the gentlemanly amateur, apparently more devoted to his horses than to politics, is well-captured in this drawing by H. Furniss.

home rule and less for the NEW LIBERALISM, and although an active imperialist had no interest in social reform.

Roses, wars of the 1455–87. The intermittent civil wars of this period, during which the English crown changed hands 6 times. The name was first used in 1762, but reflects a contemporary conception. Tudor historians, anxious to emphasize HENRY VII's role as national saviour, viewed the conflict as a dreadful working out of divine retribution for the murder of Richard II, and until the 20th century it was widely believed to have decimated the nobility, killed hundreds of thousands and ruined the economy. More dispassionate modern study, however, has shown that the fighting (which occupied an aggregate of only 13 weeks) had little effect on England as a whole, that casualties were comparatively low and that the rate of extinction of noble families was actually below the medieval average. It has also tended to reject the

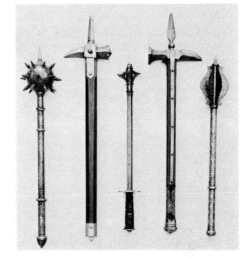

The battles of the wars of the **Roses** were mostly fought at close quarters: the maces and war-hammers shown here were useful weapons against the sophisticated armour of the period.

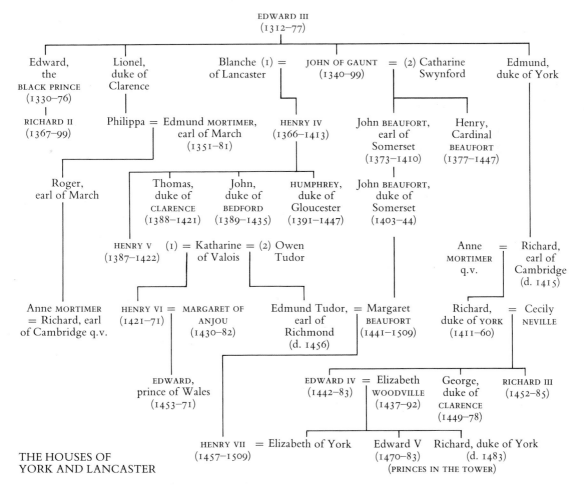

THE HOUSES OF
YORK AND LANCASTER

theories that the wars resulted from the growth of 'bastard FEUDALISM' (which, insofar as it existed, had developed by the early 14th century) or from the influx of unemployed soldiers from the hundred years' war (whose numbers were in fact negligible).

The most realistic view is that the wars were the outcome of an escalation of aristocratic feuds, unrestrained by the incompetent and unworldly HENRY VI and even exacerbated by the self-seeking courtiers (such as SUFFOLK) who surrounded him. Unable to trust a corrupt legal system to settle their disputes, lesser men increasingly relied on the MAINTENANCE of great magnates who, to further their own feuds, attached themselves either to the 'Lancastrian' court party (led by MARGARET OF ANJOU and the BEAUFORTS) or to the 'Yorkist' opposition (headed by Richard of YORK, the excluded heir-presumptive and ostensible champion of the popular reform movement).

Neither faction could rule without the nominal authority of Henry VI, upon whose control the

The marriage of the Lancastrian heir, Henry VII, to Elizabeth of York, eldest daughter of Edward IV, helped to unite the rival factions of the wars of the **Roses**. Elizabeth is holding the white rose of York in this anonymous portrait, late 16th century.

initial phase of the struggle turned. In 1455 York gained possession of him at the 1st battle of ST ALBANS, the 1st clash of the war but, during the uneasy peace that followed, the Lancastrians reassumed control, and in 1459 (at LUDLOW) drove York and his ally WARWICK THE KINGMAKER into exile. Then in 1460 Warwick returned to capture Henry at NORTHAMPTON, and soon afterwards York claimed the crown, though the magnates would recognize him only as heir. Queen Margaret, however, unwilling to accept the consequent disinheritance of her son Prince Edward, raised a northern army, slaying York at WAKEFIELD and repossessing Henry after a victory at the 2nd battle of ST ALBANS (February 1461).

MORTIMER'S CROSS and Margaret's failure to take London saved the Yorkists from complete disaster, and (having lost their puppet ruler) they now set up their own king, York's son EDWARD IV. He decisively defeated Margaret at TOWTON (March 1461), and swiftly made himself master of all England save the PERCY heartlands in the north-east, where the Lancastrians held out (with Scots and French support) until 1464.

The wars might now have ended, had not Warwick, baulked of his hopes of ruling through Edward, become increasingly disaffected. Allying himself with George, duke of CLARENCE, he fomented risings during 1469–70 (see BANBURY, BATTLE OF; LOSE-COAT FIELD, BATTLE OF) and finally defected to the Lancastrians, driving Edward into exile in October 1470 and restoring Henry VI. Edward returned 6 months later, however, and after killing Warwick at BARNET, defeating Margaret and killing Prince Edward at TEWKESBURY, and murdering Henry VI, established himself more firmly than ever.

Twelve years of domestic peace followed, and Edward's line seemed secure. But on his death (1483) the usurpation of RICHARD III alienated many Yorkists, paving the way for an invasion by the exiled Lancastrian heir Henry VII (1485). Having triumphed at BOSWORTH, Henry married Edward's daughter, Elizabeth of York, and claimed to have united the rival factions. His defence of his throne at STOKE (1487) was the last real battle of the war.

Rothes, John Leslie, 7th earl and 1st duke of 1630–81. A Scottish nobleman, Rothes supported Charles II in 1651 and was captured at WORCESTER and imprisoned until 1658. After 1660 he became head of the Scottish administration and followed a severely repressive policy against the COVENANTERS. Discredited after the PENTLAND RISING, he was replaced by Lauderdale.

Rotten boroughs Ancient boroughs which, despite their physical decay and decline in population, continued to return members to the house of commons prior to the 1832 REFORM BILL. The most famous example was Old Sarum. *See* POCKET BOROUGHS.

Rough Wooing 1545. The invasion of Scotland by English troops under the earl of Hertford, ordered by Henry VIII in revenge for Scotland's renunciation of the treaties of GREENWICH. Edinburgh, Leith and the towns and abbeys of the border country were burned.

Rowntree, B. Seebohm 1871–1954. Director of the confectionery firm and a Quaker, Rowntree was also a pioneer of social welfare policies. His *Poverty: A Study of Town Life* (1901), based on exhaustive research in his home town of York, indicated that almost a third of the urban population were living in poverty. Later surveys (1936 and 1950) showed considerable improvements in living standards.

Royal An English gold coin worth 10s., introduced at Edward IV's recoinage (1465) and revived under Henry VII. It was also called a rose noble from its reverse design. *See* NOBLE.

Royal air force The RAF, formed in 1918, was comprised of the royal flying corps, the special bomber force set up by TRENCHARD, and the royal naval air service (although it lost naval aviation in 1937). It then had 22,000 aircraft, almost wholly biplanes. For most of the interwar period it was committed to the idea of BOMBING offensives. Only in 1937 was priority given to the fighters, with which the battle of Britain was won. Its role in the bombing of Germany, especially after 1942, has proved controversial. After World War II it was responsible (1952–64), with its V-bomber force, for the delivery of Britain's nuclear deterrent, until this was taken over by the navy's Polaris submarines (1964).

Royal commissions Groups of the expert, the eminent or the representative, assembled by ministries to inquire into current social or administrative problems. They shifted during the 19th century from being intensely partisan (and often very effective), such as the Poor Law commission (1832–4), to being respectable, authoritative and ineffective, such as the housing commission (1884).

Royal forests *see* FORESTS, ROYAL

The **Royal air force** was one of the few areas of World War I where romance survived: poster published by the ministry of information.

Royal household (or Curia Regis). The English king's court and household was the source of all royal power in medieval and early Tudor times as well as catering for the monarch's domestic needs. Such departments as the CHANCERY and EXCHEQUER became elements of the government at large, to be replaced by new departments – the CHAMBER and WARDROBE – which in their turn passed into the public sphere. Staffed by men of the monarch's own choosing, and reflecting his personal character, the household was resolutely resistant to baronial or parliamentary control, and as such was frequently the target of attack, particularly under Henry III, Edward II, Richard II and Henry VI.

Royal prerogative The extensive but relatively undefined discretionary rights of the MONARCHY in administrative, economic, religious and foreign policy, which were the subject of dispute between crown and PARLIAMENT throughout the 17th century. The last vestige of the prerogative – the monarch's right to choose ministers – was relinquished in the 19th century.

Royal Society The society, which was incorporated under Charles II's patronage in 1662, grew out of informal meetings of eminent English

The frontispiece of Thomas Sprat's *History of the Royal Society*, 1667, designed by John Evelyn: the bust of the founder of the **Royal Society**, Charles II, is flanked by its first president, Lord Brouncker (left), and Francis Bacon.

'Be gone you Rogues, you have sate long enough': according to this contemporary Dutch satirical engraving, these are Oliver Cromwell's words as he dismisses the **Rump parliament**, 1653, while in the background Major-General Thomas Harrison lays hands on the Speaker.

scientists and thinkers during the interregnum. Fellowship of the society remains the greatest professional honour which can be conferred upon British scientists.

Royal Titles Act 1876. Disraeli succeeded, despite Liberal opposition, in granting Queen Victoria the title of empress of India. *See* ill. p. 42.

Rump parliament 1648–53 and 1659. The remnant of the Long parliament allowed to sit after PRIDE'S PURGE, which established the COMMONWEALTH by abolishing the monarchy and house of lords. Dismissed by Oliver Cromwell (who suspected it of intending to perpetuate its power indefinitely) in 1653, the Rump was recalled in 1659, only to be dissolved again.

Runes (Old English *run*, secret). An alphabet used by the Vikings and the pagan Anglo-Saxons. Its letters were formed of straight lines for easy carving. Traditionally invented by the god Odin and credited with magical properties, runes were much used for spells and memorial inscriptions.

Runrig A traditional form of agricultural organization in Scotland, whereby tenants farmed separate strips or 'rigs' within a FARMTOUN. Strips might be reallocated at intervals (periodic runrig) or permanently associated with particular holdings (fixed runrig). Fixed runrig evolved through the consolidation of strips (rundale) into the emergence of modern compact farms.

Rupert, prince 1619–82. Charles I's German nephew, Rupert was appointed general of horse in 1642. A superb cavalryman, but lacking discipline, he was dismissed in 1645 after surrendering Bristol. In 1649–52 he commanded privateers against the English republic and after 1660 served Charles II at sea. Essentially a fighting man, he never exercised political influence. *See* CIVIL WARS.

Ruskin, John 1819–1900. A wealthy Oxford-educated art critic, Ruskin originally emerged in *Modern Painters* (1833) as the champion of J. M. W. Turner, but then became a corrosive critic of the taste and social morality of mid-Victorian Britain. He had considerable influence not only on art and architecture but on the thought of the socialist movement.

Russell, Bertrand, earl 1872-1970. The greatest mathematical logician of his day, Russell was moved by World War I from liberalism to pacifist

A hostile view of Prince **Rupert** after his sacking of Birmingham on 3 April 1643. Woodcut from *The Bloody Prince, Or a Declaration of the most cruell Practices of Prince Rupert and the rest of the Cavaliers*, 22 April 1643.

Bertrand **Russell**, photographed at his home in Chelsea, London, *c.* 1960.

socialism. His libertarian influence – not unlike that of his 'godfather' Mill – lasted for the rest of a long life, in the campaign for nuclear disarmament, opposition to the Vietnam war and proposals for workers' control of industry.

Russell, Lord John, earl 1792–1878. Having aided Catholic emancipation (1829) and piloted the 1832 REFORM BILL through the commons, Russell became leader in the commons (1835–41). After being prime minister (1846–52), he served under Aberdeen and Palmerston (1852–5 and 1859–65). Premier again in 1865, he introduced a further Reform Bill. When it was defeated by the ADULLAMITE revolt in 1866, he resigned.

Rutherford, Ernest *see* ATOM BOMB

Ruthven, raid of 1582. The seizure at Perth of James VI by the earls of Mar and Gowrie, Lord Lindsay and Lord Boyd, who opposed the ascendancy of the duke of LENNOX. Their action was approved of by the general assembly. James was held for 10 months at Ruthven castle before escaping.

Rye house plot 1683. A plot to seize or kill CHARLES II near the Rye house at Hoddeston, Herts. Its discovery led to the suicide of the earl of Essex, the flight abroad of the duke of Monmouth and Lord Grey and the execution of Lord Russell and Algernon Sidney.

Ryswick, peace of *see* LEAGUE OF AUGSBURG, WAR OF THE; PORTLAND, 1ST EARL OF

S

Sabbatarianism The application to the Christian lord's day of the biblical restrictions of the Jewish sabbath. Sabbatarianism was an issue of controversy in the period 1580–1640. It was generally espoused by English Puritans and the stricter Scottish Presbyterians and became an enduring feature of English Nonconformity and Scottish Calvinism.

Sacheverell case 1710. The impeachment of Henry Sacheverell for preaching sermons which maintained that the church of England was in danger, reasserted the doctrine of non-resistance and challenged the Whig ministry's interpretation of the GLORIOUS REVOLUTION. The trial, accompanied by pamphleteering and riots, ended in Sacheverell's conviction, but gave him the moral victory.

Safety lamp Firedamp explosions in mines, caused by the use of naked flames, inhibited the opening up of deep seams, until a lamp was devised with a gauze shield which prevented the damp from penetrating to the flame. The principle was discovered almost simultaneously (1815–17) by Sir Humphrey Davy (1778–1829) and STEPHENSON.

St Albans *see* ALBAN, ST; VERULAMIUM

St Albans, 1st battle of 29 May 1455. The 1st battle of the wars of the ROSES and essentially an aristocratic faction fight. Richard of York (supported by Warwick the Kingmaker and the Nevilles) defeated and killed Somerset and Northumberland, the leaders of the Lancastrian court party, and gained short-lived control of Henry VI.

St Albans, 2nd battle of 17 February 1461. A Lancastrian victory in the wars of the ROSES. Warwick the Kingmaker attempted to block Margaret of Anjou's southward advance after WAKEFIELD, but his defensive position was surprised and out-flanked, and after a long and bloody fight the Yorkists fled. The victors captured Henry VI, but retired northward after failing to take London.

St Fagans, battle of *see* WALES

Saints, battle of the 12 April 1782. A naval victory in the AMERICAN INDEPENDENCE war by Admirals Hood and Rodney over the French fleet of De Grasse. The battle ended a French threat to the West Indies and regained British control of the Atlantic, the temporary loss of which had helped force Charles Cornwallis's surrender at YORKTOWN.

Salamanca, battle of 22 July 1812. A battle of the PENINSULAR WAR. British troops under WELLINGTON defeated Marmont's French army and subsequently took Madrid. A French revival and British failure to take Burgos, however, cost Wellington the advantage and obliged him to retreat into Portugal.

Salisbury, Richard Neville, earl of 1400–60. Neville derived his title from his marriage to the daughter of the 4th earl of SALISBURY, and was the father of Warwick the Kingmaker. *See* NEVILLE FAMILY.

Salisbury, Robert Cecil, marquess of 1830–1903. A cultivated, well-read reactionary with scientific interests, Salisbury opposed Disraeli over reform (1867), although he served him in the India and foreign offices (1874–8 and 1878–80). He secured the CONCERT OF EUROPE in the Mediterranean (1878), and kept the French from the Nile. He was foreign secretary as well as prime minister 1886–92 and 1895–1902.

Salisbury, Thomas Montacute, 4th earl of 1388–1428. A famous English captain of the hundred years' war, Salisbury served as Henry V's principal lieutenant in France. He was killed by a cannon ball at ORLEANS.

Salvation Army Formed in 1878 by an Evangelist from London's east end, William Booth (1829–1912), from his Christian Mission (originally the Christian Revival Association, 1865). It offered the underprivileged a mixture of fundamentalist religion, colourful services led by good brass bands, and sympathetic social welfare, a programme spelt out by Booth in his *In Darkest England and the Way Out* (1890). Its organization quickly became international.

Admiral Rodney breaks the line of French ships at the battle of the **Saints**, which enabled him then to isolate individual ships and prevent their escape. Engraving by J. Wells after Thomas Walker.

San Stefano, treaty of *see* BERLIN, CONGRESS OF

Sandwich, battle of 24 August 1217. A fleet carrying reinforcements for Prince LOUIS was defeated off Sandwich (partly by the use of wind-blown quicklime) by the ships of Henry III under William the Marshal, Hubert de Burgh and Philip Daubeny, leading directly to Louis's withdrawal.

Saratoga, surrender of 17 October 1777. The surrender by General Burgoyne of his entire army, which was trapped by American forces while attempting to cut off NEW ENGLAND from the southern colonies. This disaster altered the character of the AMERICAN INDEPENDENCE war, making it clear that no swift British victory was possible and encouraging French intervention.

Sauchieburn, battle of *see* JAMES III

Savoy conference 1661. A conference between leading Nonconformist ministers and Anglican bishops following the RESTORATION. Though agreeing on minor changes to the prayer book, the participants failed to devise a comprehensive religious settlement and remaining hopes of toleration were dashed by the subsequent passage of the CLARENDON CODE.

Saxon Shore A system of 9 or more forts (from Brancaster, Norfolk to Portchester, Hants.) defending the south-east coast of Roman Britain against Anglo-Saxon raiders. Each protected a harbour for the CLASSIS BRITANNICA and housed mobile troops to deal with landings. Established *c.* 275, it was augmented *c.* 342, when commanded by a count.

Saxons A term used generically for all ANGLO-SAXON or ancestral English peoples, and specifically for those who came from the north-west coast of Germany (between the Elbe and the Ems) to found the English kingdoms of Sussex, Wessex and the East Saxons.

The British surrender at **Saratoga**, 1777: General Burgoyne hands over his sword to the American victor, General Gates. Contemporary engraving.

The People's Mission hall, 188 Whitechapel Road, London, *c.* 1870, headquarters of William Booth's Christian Mission – which became known as the **Salvation Army** in 1878 – with a midday porch meeting in progress. Detail of wood engraving, *c.* 1870.

Portchester castle, Hants., the best surviving example of a **Saxon Shore** fort: the harbour it was built to protect lies in the background (right). The Roman walls also shelter a medieval castle and priory church.

Schiltrons The classic Scottish medieval battle formation, a solid square, circle or oval of infantry armed with long spears. Perhaps originated by WALLACE, it proved successful at STIRLING BRIDGE and BANNOCKBURN but disastrous at FALKIRK, FLODDEN and PINKIE.

Schism, Great 1378–1417/29. A division of the church originating in the rival elections of Urban VI (supported by England) and Clement VII (supported by Scotland and Glendower). The council of Pisa (1409) sought reunification but created a 3rd papal line. Martin V's election at the council of Constance (1414–18) achieved effective reunification, but outposts of schism lingered until 1429.

Schools, Act for Settling 1696. An Act requiring every Scottish parish to provide a school and schoolmaster paid for by landowners. Despite problems of enforcement, the Act laid the foundations of the Scottish educational system of the 18th century and made possible the achievement of high levels of popular literacy in the Scottish lowlands.

Scone, stone of The 'stone of destiny' on which early Scottish kings were seated for CORONATION. Though it is probably made of Perthshire sandstone, legend makes it Jacob's pillow, subsequently used by the Irish high kings at Tara and brought to Scotland by the DALRIADA. Carried off by Edward I (1296), it has since formed part of the coronation throne of English and British monarchs.

Scots (Lat. *Scotti*, allegedly derived from an Irish word for 'raider'). Originally applied to the Irish, including those who took part in the IRISH INVASIONS of Britain and founded DALRIADA or 'Scotland', from the 11th century the name was increasingly used for the whole of ALBA.

Scottish National party Founded as National Party of Scotland (1927), it amalgamated with the more right-wing Scottish party (founded 1933) in 1934. It achieved prominence in the late 1960s, when it won Hamilton and its membership rose from 2,000–100,000. Doing badly in the 1970 election, it nonetheless won 7 seats in February 1974 and increased these to 11 in October, but lost 9 of these in May 1979 after the failure of the referendum on the Scottish assembly.

Scottish wars of independence The long and bitter struggle to establish and maintain Scottish independence from English rule, which did much to weld the diverse racial elements of Scotland – Celts, Gaels, Angles and the Norman aristocracy introduced under David I and his successors – into one nation. It was precipitated by the premature death of Alexander III in 1286, followed in 1290 by that of his granddaughter and only direct heir, 'the Maid of Norway'. Threatened with civil war between the collateral descendants of earlier kings, of whom the foremost were John BALLIOL and the Bruces (*see* ROBERT BRUCE), the Scottish magnates called on the hitherto friendly EDWARD I for aid, but before he would arbitrate he induced all the 12 competitors for the throne to recognize the long-disputed and still undefined claims of English kings to be 'lords superior' of Scotland. In November 1292 a panel of auditors (mostly chosen by the principal contenders) declared for Balliol, who duly did homage to Edward after enthronement.

Edward's rigid and humiliating enforcement of his rights as overlord (and particularly his demands for Scottish help against France) soon provoked intense resentment, and in October 1295 Balliol was induced to conclude a French alliance and prepare to attack England. Edward replied by storming Berwick (30 March 1296) and defeating the Scots army at DUNBAR, and by October 1296 he had marched through Scotland, deposed Balliol and received the submission of a majority of Scots magnates, recorded on the 'Ragman roll'.

By May 1297, nevertheless, smouldering resistance to direct English rule and to the Anglicization of the Scottish church had flared into uprisings led by WALLACE in the south and Andrew Moray in the north. Their victory at STIRLING BRIDGE in September cleared Scotland of the invaders, and in November Wallace, now guardian, raided northern England. Edward returned from Flanders to defeat him at FALKIRK (July 1298), but despite further English campaigns in southern Scotland resistance continued under a succession of guardians until May 1303, when the conclusion of peace with France freed Edward for a full-scale invasion. Having reached and subdued the north in September 1303, Edward wintered at Dunfermline, and during spring 1304 received the surrender of most of the Scots leaders, who were thereafter allowed some share in the English-dominated government.

The coronation of Robert Bruce (1306) and Edward's death (1307), however, initiated the chain of events which by 1314 drove the English from Scotland (*see* BANNOCKBURN, BATTLE OF) and in 1328 forced them to recognize Scottish independence by the treaty of EDINBURGH–NORTHAMPTON.

In his determination to consolidate his conquest of Scotland during the **Scottish wars of independence**, Edward I compelled some 2,000 Scots magnates to seal the 'Ragman roll' in 1296. This shows a detail of the Norman-French oath of allegiance of Anneys de Bonkhill of Berwickshire.

In 1332 the weakness of Scotland after the death of Bruce and his principal lieutenants led Edward III to renew English claims to overlordship, first through Edward BALLIOL and the DISINHERITED (at DUPPLIN) and then in person (at HALIDON HILL). David II was driven into exile, but the resistance of Sir Andrew MORAY and others frustrated Edward's attempts at conquest during 1335–7 (after which he became preoccupied with the hundred years' war) and in 1341 David returned. Though Edward reoccupied southern Scotland after NEVILLE'S CROSS, and though Anglo-Scottish border warfare continued intermittently until the accession of James VI and I, Scottish independence was never again seriously threatened until the UNION (1707). (R. Nicholson, *Scotland: The Later Middle Ages*, 1974.)

Scramble for Africa A name for the competition between the European imperial powers to partition central Africa in the 1880s, culminating in the conference of Berlin (1884–5).

Scrope, Richard 1350–1405. Archbishop of York from 1398, in 1405 Scrope led a rebellion of Yorkshire clergy, gentry and citizens in support of the Percy family and against Henry IV. Tricked into disbanding his forces at Shipton Moor outside York, he was thereupon arrested and, after an irregular trial, executed in that city on 8 June. He subsequently became a POLITICAL SAINT.

Scutage *see* FEUDALISM

Seal A device, especially important before widespread literacy, for authenticating documents, produced by stamping warm wax with a matrix (generally of brass) bearing a device and legend or, in the case of double-sided pendant seals like the GREAT SEAL, by enclosing it in a press between 2 matrices. *See* PAPAL BULLS; PRIVY SEAL; SIGNET.

Secession churches Dissenting Presbyterian churches formed after secessions from the CHURCH OF SCOTLAND (1740 and 1752). They included the strangely named 'Old licht Burghers', 'Old licht Anti-burghers', 'New licht Burghers', 'New licht Anti-burghers' (the last two forming the United Secession church in 1820) and the Relief church.

Secretary of state for Scotland This office, set up in 1707, was abolished in 1746 but revived, as a result of agitation by ROSEBERY and others, in 1885. Restyled as secretary of state (1926), its powers over Scottish education, agriculture and social services were greatly expanded in 1941–5 by JOHNSTON and in 1964–70 by William Ross (b. 1911).

The **seal** of the city of Rochester, showing its Norman castle. 13th century.

Sedgemoor, battle of 6 July 1685. The battle ending MONMOUTH'S REBELLION. The rebels, trapped in Bridgewater by royal troops under Feversham and Churchill, attempted to break out by night and were routed on Sedgemoor.

Selden, John 1584–1654. Of Sussex yeoman stock, Selden made his name as a lawyer and antiquarian, proving in his *History of Tithes* (1617) that TITHES were not a divine institution. In the parliaments of the 1620s and the LONG PARLIAMENT, he supported the constitutionalist opposition to Charles I and commanded universal respect among parliamentarians.

Select committees Committees of members of either house of parliament formed to inquire into government expenditure and social or political problems.

Self-denying ordinance 1644–5. An ordinance by which members of parliament were discharged from offices and commands granted since November 1640. Intended to remove inadequate generals such as the 3rd earl of ESSEX and MANCHESTER, the ordinance allowed the reappointment of certain members, notably Oliver Cromwell. The establishment of the New Model Army followed rapidly. *See* CIVIL WARS.

Selgovae A British tribe inhabiting the central Scottish borders, with a hillfort capital at Eildon Hill (Borders). Consistently hostile to Rome, they were conquered by Agricola in 80–1, but several times rebelled during the 2nd century, often in conjunction with their neighbours the Brigantes and the Novantae.

Septennial Act 1716. Originally passed to postpone the 1718 general election necessitated by the TRIENNIAL ACT, the Act set the maximum duration of a parliament at 7 years and remained in force until the PARLIAMENT Act (1911).

Serf (Lat. *servus*, slave). Slavery flourished under the Romans and Anglo-Saxons, until by the Norman conquest some 10% of the population were serfs. Thereafter, absolute slavery declined rapidly, disappearing altogether in the 12th century in England, somewhat later in Scotland. Though serf became synonymous with VILLEIN, the latter had some personal rights and could not be arbitrarily killed or maimed by his master.

Sergeanty (Lat. *serviens*, servant). According to feudal custom, tenure of land on condition of performing some personal service, other than knight service, to the king. 'Grand sergeanties' included serving in the ROYAL HOUSEHOLD or providing foot soldiers, while 'petty sergeanty' might involve furnishing a pork dinner when the king hunted certain forests. It was soon commuted for rents.

Servants in husbandry Young, unmarried farmworkers of either sex, who lived in the households of their masters. Servants were hired annually at HIRING FAIRS. From the 16th to the 19th centuries most young people lived in service between their early teens and their mid-twenties, when they married and settled.

Session, court of The central Scottish court, sitting in Edinburgh. Founded in 1532, it was much used by James VI against the lawlessness and abuses of power of the Scottish nobility. A series of reforming statutes after 1808 divided the court into 2 jurisdictions and instituted trial by jury in civil cases.

Settlement, Act of 1701. An Act settling the royal succession on the descendants of Sophia of Hanover in the event of WILLIAM III and Queen ANNE dying without heirs, and placing restrictions on the future monarch in matters of religion, foreign affairs and judicial tenure. This disregarded 58 superior claims by descent, the claimants being Catholics.

Settlement laws 1662, 1691 and 1697. Acts intended to clarify rights of settlement for the purposes of POOR LAW administration in England by establishing national criteria of settlement. Contrary to legend, the Acts, which provided for the licensing of mobile labourers, did not have the effect of imprisoning the poor within their PARISHES.

Seven bishops' case 1688. The trial of Archbishop Sancroft and 6 bishops, charged with seditious libel for petitioning James VII and II to withdraw his order for the publication in churches of the DECLARATION OF INDULGENCE (1688) and challenging the royal DISPENSING POWER. The bishops were acquitted to general public rejoicing.

Seven years' war 1756–63. A war in which Britain allied with Frederick the Great of Prussia against France, Austria and Russia. British involvement was principally confined to naval and colonial campaigns against France (at QUEBEC and QUIBERON

The execution of Admiral Byng on board the *Monarque*, 1757, after he had been courtmartialled for failing to relieve Minorca during the **seven years' war**. Contemporary broadsheet.

The 'manner of the Barbarous murder' of James **Sharp**. Broadsheet, 1679.

BAY) and (from 1762) Spain, which established British supremacy in India and North America, confirmed by the peace of PARIS.

Severus, Septimius Roman emperor (193–211). Having defeated CLODIUS ALBINUS in 197, Severus dispatched successive governors to restore order in Roman Britain, and in 208 came in person to lead punitive expeditions against the Caledonians with his son Caracalla (211–17), who succeeded when he died at York in 211. One or other of them divided Britain into 2 provinces.

Seymour, Jane 1511–37. The 3rd wife of Henry VIII. The rather plain and colourless daughter of a Somerset squire, Jane married Henry 12 days after the execution of Anne Boleyn. She died in childbirth after bearing the king his much desired son, the future Edward VI.

Shaftesbury, Anthony Ashley Cooper, 1st earl of 1621–83. An unscrupulous politician, yet consistent in his constitutionalist principles, Shaftesbury served first the commonwealth, then Charles II. As leader of the WHIGS after 1673 he backed the TEST ACT, exploited the POPISH PLOT and managed the EXCLUSION CRISIS. Tried and acquitted of treason in 1681, he fled and died abroad.

Shaftesbury, Anthony Ashley Cooper, 7th earl of 1801–85. Combining old-fashioned Toryism as an MP from 1826–61, when he inherited his earldom, with strong Evangelical views, Shaftesbury became a leading advocate of the FACTORY ACTS and other legislation protecting the underprivileged.

Sharp, James 1618–79. A Banffshire man of keen intellect, minister of Crail (1649) and a moderate and royalist during the interregnum, Sharp became archbishop of St Andrews in 1661. As such he was associated with repressive policies for which he had little personal taste and was murdered by fanatical COVENANTERS near St Andrews.

Sheffield Outrages Violence against non-unionized labour tended to be endemic in the Sheffield cutlery trade, and a particularly bad outbreak (1866–7) provoked the government to set up a royal commission on trade unionism.

Shelburne, William Petty, 2nd earl of 1737–1805. President of the board of trade under Bute, Shelburne later served as secretary of state under Chatham (1766–8) and Rockingham (1782). As prime minister (1782) he concluded the American independence war, but resigned when defeated in parliament over the peace treaty. He took no further part in politics.

Sheriff The king's direct representative in each English county, the 'shire-REEVE' rose to prominence with the 11th-century grouping of Anglo-Saxon shires under provincial earls (*see* COUNTY COURT). With the disappearance of these great earldoms at the Norman conquest sheriffs became still more influential, the office generally being held by great feudal magnates. But by the later middle ages their powers had been considerably reduced (though they still controlled the shire-levy and returned members of parliament) and they were chosen annually from the local gentry. In Scotland, where it is known from the 1120s (*see* SHERIFFDOMS), the office soon became hereditary, remaining so until the abolition of HERITABLE JURISDICTIONS (*see* SHERIFF COURTS).

Sheriff courts Originating in the 12th century and held by hereditary right until the abolition of HERITABLE JURISDICTIONS (1747), sheriff courts remain the principal local courts in the Scottish legal system, hearing criminal and certain civil cases. Since 1975 Scotland has been divided into 6 sheriffdoms and 50 sheriff court districts.

Sheriffdoms Scottish administrative divisions generally analogous to SHIRES, sheriffdoms first appeared under David I in the south-east, and by the time of Alexander III covered the lowlands and the north-east. The highlands were not fully brought into the system until the 18th century, when sheriffdoms were rearranged into counties.

Sheriffmuir, battle of 13 November 1715. A battle of the '15' rebellion. Though the fighting was indecisive, Argyll's government troops held the field and prevented Mar's JACOBITES from entering the Scottish lowlands. The subsequent dispersal of the highland army meant the effective end of the rebellion.

Shetlands *see* JAMES III

Shilling Though employed as a unit of account for 12 PENNIES from early medieval times, shillings as such were never minted in Scotland, and in England not until 1544. Thereafter they were issued regularly until decimalization (1971), when they were replaced by a 5 new-pence piece.

Ship money Contributions for the maintenance of ships levied upon maritime counties and ports in times of national emergency and extended to include all England by Charles I in 1635. The legality of the tax was challenged by HAMPDEN (1637) and a massive campaign of tax refusal ensued.

Shire (Old English *scir*, literally 'sphere of office'). By the beginning of the 11th century England south of the Tees had been divided into admistrative shires, a concept apparently originating in 8th-century Wessex. Latinized as 'counties', these survived the Norman conquest and until recent times virtually unchanged, 5 more (Durham, Westmoreland, Cumberland, Lancashire and Rutland) being added in the middle ages and London in 1888. Wales was partially shired in 1284 and fully at the union (1536/42). *See* HUNDRED; KNIGHTS OF THE SHIRE; SHERIFF; SHERIFFDOMS.

Short parliament 1640. A brief parliament summoned to provide money for the BISHOPS' WARS. Many members sympathized with the Scots and PYM used the opportunity to organize concerted opposition to the policies of Charles I's government. Charles promptly dissolved parliament, thereby aggravating the members' sense of grievance.

Shrewsbury, battle of 21 July 1403. HENRY IV attacked HOTSPUR's rebel army of Percy retainers and Cheshiremen before it could be reinforced by Glendower or the earl of Northumberland. After a day's bitter fighting Hotspur was killed by an arrow and the rebels were defeated. The site is marked by Henry IV's Battlefield church.

Shrines Places of particular sanctity, associated with some saint and often housing his relics, which were the objects of pilgrimages, especially during the later middle ages. British pilgrims abroad most frequently visited Rome or St James's tomb at Compostela in Spain. The most popular shrines in England were those of St Thomas BECKET at

The **shrine** of St Candida, in the north transept of the church of Whitchurch Canonicorum, Dorset. Coins and prayer requests are still left inside the 3 openings.

Canterbury and the Virgin's Holy House at Walsingham, Norfolk; in Scotland St Andrew's eponymous shrine and that of St NINIAN at Whithorn, Galloway; and in Wales St DAVID's eponymous shrine and St Winifred's Well in Clwyd. Most were destroyed at the Reformation.

Sicilian business, the HENRY III ill-advisedly promised (1254) to conquer Sicily from the Hohenstaufen enemies of the papacy for his son Edmund, and to pay papal debts already incurred. Violently unpopular in England, the scheme proved impossible to finance, and in 1258 Henry, threatened with excommunication and INTERDICT, was forced to accept the PROVISIONS OF OXFORD in return for baronial co-operation in raising funds and petitioning the pope for release.

Sidmouth, Henry Addington, 1st viscount 1757–1844. Entering parliament in 1783, Addington became Speaker in 1789, succeeded Pitt as prime minister (1801–4) and was responsible for the peace of AMIENS. His later career as home secretary (1812–21) was marked by unimaginative and repressive action against popular radicalism, notably in the SIX ACTS.

Sidney, Sir Philip 1554–86. A courtier, soldier, diplomat and influential poet, Sidney was almost universally loved as a paragon of Elizabethan aristocratic virtues. His stature was confirmed by his heroic death at the battle of Zutphen.

Signet The GREAT SEAL and PRIVY SEAL having successively passed into the public sphere of government, English kings from Edward II endeavoured to retain personal control over the authentication of documents by adopting a (much smaller) personal signet, kept at first by the king's secretary and subsequently (when signets multiplied) by secretaries of state.

Silchester Extensive remains of a deserted Roman town (Calleva Atrebatum) near Basingstoke, Hants. An ATREBATIC OPPIDUM by c. 5, it was later part of the kingdom of COGIDUBNUS, after whose death a Roman town developed as capital of the Atrebatic CIVITAS. It apparently survived until c. 550, when extinguished by Anglo-Saxon expansion.

Silures A warlike tribe, described by Tacitus as swarthy and curly-haired, inhabiting south-east Wales. Persistently hostile to Rome, they continued the struggle after the capture of CARATACUS and in 52 defeated a legion. Finally conquered by Julius Frontinus c. 74, they eventually formed a CIVITAS based on Venta Silurum (Caerwent).

Simnel, Lambert The son of an Oxford joiner, Simnel was coached to impersonate the son of George, duke of CLARENCE, and backed as a Yorkist pretender by the Anglo-Irish magnates (who crowned him at Dublin in May 1487) and Edward IV's sister, Margaret of Burgundy (who sent him 2,000 German mercenaries). Taken at STOKE, he was employed in Henry VII's kitchens.

Simon, Sir John 1816–1904. A great sanitary reformer, Simon was medical officer of health, first to the city of London (1848–55), then to the privy council after the abolition of CHADWICK's general board, and lastly to the LOCAL GOVERNMENT board (1871–6).

Simon, Sir John, viscount 1873–1954. Opposing conscription, Simon resigned as home secretary (1916), but was influential in deploying legal arguments against the General Strike (1926). Having chaired the committee on the Indian constitution (1927–30), he joined the NATIONAL GOVERNMENT, as foreign secretary (1931–5), home secretary (1935–7), and chancellor of the exchequer (1937–40), when he was closely identified with APPEASEMENT.

Simon de Montfort c. 1208–65. An influential French magnate who inherited the earldom of Leicester, Simon de Montfort married HENRY III's sister (1238). A promoter and unbending supporter of the PROVISIONS OF OXFORD, from 1263 he led the movement to enforce them, triumphing at LEWES but dying at EVESHAM. Seen as a liberator, for long afterwards he was a popular hero.

Simony The practice of buying and selling ecclesiastical offices or benefices, generally condemned but widely practised during the middle ages. The name originated with the sorcerer Simon Magus, who attempted to buy spiritual powers from the Apostles (Acts VIII).

Singapore, fall of 15 February 1942. Its fall was due partly to inappropriate defences and partly to sheer loss of nerve by the British when confronted with a fast-moving but badly overstretched Japanese force. The coloured races of the empire saw this as the beginning of the end of British rule. *See* WORLD WAR II.

Sinking fund *see* NATIONAL DEBT

Sinn Fein 'Ourselves'. Founded by GRIFFITH in 1905 to secure the election of an Irish Dail whether HOME RULE were granted or not. It became the focus of Irish discontent with British rule and won an overwhelming victory in 1918. After it split (1921), one section continued to be identified with the Irish Republican Army. In response to the ULSTER EMERGENCY, the party split again (1969), into a Marxist 'official' wing and a nationalist 'Provisional' wing. *See* IRISH CONSTITUTIONAL CRISIS.

Six Acts 1819. Legislation passed after the massacre of PETERLOO, intended to control popular radicalism. The Acts prohibited meetings for military exercises, placed strict limitations on public assemblies, authorized the seizure of arms and seditious literature, extended the Stamp Act to cheap newspapers and pamphlets and modified judicial procedure.

Six Articles *see* REFORMATION

The seal of the Slave Emancipation Society, designed in 1786 by Josiah Wedgwood, who was deeply concerned by the problem of **slavery**: 'Am I not a man and a brother?' is the cry of the negro slave.

Skara Brae near Stromness, ORKNEY. One of the best-preserved prehistoric settlements in Europe, this late neolithic (*c.* 2000 BC) village consists of a huddle of 7 or 8 dry-stone built houses linked by covered alleyways. Each house contained 'box-beds', shelved sideboards, drains and tanks for fresh sea-food, all made of stone slabs.

Slavery British control of the slave trade from west Africa to the Americas was established in the later 17th century by the Royal African Company. During the 18th century trade flourished, contributing greatly to the prosperity of Bristol and Liverpool merchants. The slave trade was made illegal in 1807 (*see* WILBERFORCE, WILLIAM), and slavery itself (*see* MANSFIELD JUDGMENT), following a long campaign by dissenters, radicals and Evangelicals, by the Whigs in 1833. £20 million was paid to West Indian proprietors in compensation.

Slump Large areas of the British ECONOMY were endemically 'depressed' 1922–39 but, following the Wall Street collapse (October 1929), unemployment rose to a peak of 3 million in 1932, this trough affecting all regions of the country.

Sluys, battle of *see* HUNDRED YEARS' WAR

Smertae A northern Scottish tribe which inhabited central Sutherland at the time of Roman Britain.

A **Sinn Fein** postcard of 1918: the 'colours of victory' are the orange, white and green of the republican flag, the shattered parapet that of the Dublin post office.

Smiles, Samuel 1812–1904. A Scots medical man, Smiles gained fame with his *Life of George Stephenson* (1857) and wrote studies of the great engineers of the Industrial Revolution. His gospel of *Self-Help* (1859), which promised like rewards for talent and independence, was translated into 17 languages and was a particular favourite among millionaires.

Smith, Adam 1723–90. Born in Kirkaldy, Smith became professor of logic (1751–5) and of moral philosophy (1755–64) at Glasgow university. He then worked privately on his revolutionary work of economic theory, *The Wealth of Nations* (1776). From 1778 he lived in Edinburgh as commissioner of the Scottish customs. *See* FREE TRADE.

Smuggling Though as old as the practice of charging custom duties itself, smuggling expanded greatly in the 18th century. The smuggling of high-duty commodities from France, conducted as much by bribing officials as by night landings, possibly accounted for a third of Anglo-French trade in this period.

Smuts, Jan Christian 1870–1950. A Boer commando leader (1899–1902), Smuts later played a major role in reconciling Briton and Boer. In Lloyd George's war cabinet (1917–18), he strongly favoured the LEAGUE OF NATIONS and a magnanimous peace with Germany. As South African prime minister (1919–24 and 1939–48) his attitude to the blacks was unenlightened.

Snowden, Philip, viscount 1864–1937. A leading propagandist of the INDEPENDENT LABOUR PARTY, Snowden became Ramsay MacDonald's chancellor of the exchequer (1924 and 1929–31), where his attachment to fiscal orthodoxy worsened the Labour government's problems. Joining the NATIONAL GOVERNMENT (August 1931) he resigned over the OTTAWA CONFERENCE agreements (August 1932), thereafter conducting a venomous campaign against MacDonald.

Social Democratic Federation Founded as the Democratic Federation in 1881 by HYNDMAN, it adopted Marxist aims in 1884. Although it amalgamated with other groups to form the British Socialist Party (1911) which in turn helped to create in 1920 the COMMUNIST PARTY OF GREAT BRITAIN, the SDF resumed its independence, and survived until the 1950s.

Adam **Smith**, 'The Author of *The Wealth of Nations*': etching from John Kay's *Edinburgh Portraits*, 1790.

Society for Constitutional Information Founded by John Horne Tooke in 1770 as an offshoot of WILKES's Society of the Bill of Rights, the society attracted wealthy radicals concerned with parliamentary reform. Suspended in 1784 but revived in 1791, it sponsored editions of radical pamphlets.

Society for the Promoting of Christian Knowledge (SPCK). Established in 1698, the English society encouraged the foundation of CHARITY SCHOOLS supported by voluntary donations and managed by local governors including both Anglicans and dissenters. The Scottish society took direct responsibility for financing and managing schools in parishes previously lacking them. Both were concerned to create a sober, religious, labouring class.

Society of Writers to the Signet *see* LAW

Solemn League and Covenant 1643. The Anglo-Scottish military alliance of the CIVIL WARS. Parliament undertook to pay the Scottish army, to abolish episcopacy and to reform the church of England 'according to the word of God' (a deliberately ambiguous formula). The alliance led to Scottish participation at MARSTON MOOR and to the establishment of the WESTMINSTER ASSEMBLY OF DIVINES.

A playing card published by Carrington Bowles in London from the series 'The **South Sea Bubble**', 10 October 1720. It relates the fate of a wealthy cobbler who invested £500 in 'South Sea' and 'By Aul and End, thus prosper'd till the fall / of cursed South Sea, made an End of all'.

The **Speaker**'s procession prepares for its ceremonial entry into the house of commons. From the left: serjeant-at-arms, carrying the mace; the Speaker, wearing his ceremonial robes used for such occasions as the state opening of parliament; his trainbearer; his secretary and his chaplain. Photograph, 1977.

Solway Moss, battle of 24 November 1542. The rout of an invading Scottish army by the English, which resulted in the capture of 2 earls, 5 barons, 500 lairds and 20 guns. The shock of news of this disaster contributed to the premature death of James V.

Somerset, Edward Seymour, earl of Hertford and duke of 1506–52. As uncle of EDWARD VI, Somerset secured the office of protector in 1547. An able soldier, he proved devoid of political sense and administrative competence and his period of power witnessed growing religious radicalism, economic dislocation and popular rebellion. In 1550 the council deprived him of power and he was subsequently executed.

South Sea Bubble 1720. The wild burst of speculation in the stock of the South Sea Company following the takeover of three-fifths of the NATIONAL DEBT by the directors of the company. The eventual crash in September 1720 ruined many investors.

Spanish civil war *see* NON-INTERVENTION; ORWELL, GEORGE

Spanish succession, war of the *see* MARLBOROUGH'S WARS

Speaker Originally the member chosen to represent the views of the commons to the crown and lords, the first Speaker was Sir Peter de la Mare, appointed during the GOOD PARLIAMENT (1376). The Speaker's importance grew with that of the commons, but declined with the development of CABINET government and, though still presiding over the house, he ceased to take part in debates in 1839.

Speenhamland system A system of subsidizing the wages of agricultural labourers from the poor rates, initiated by the Berkshire JUSTICES OF THE PEACE in 1795 and widely adopted in southern England. Though well-meant, the system was exploited by farmers to keep wages extremely low.

Spence, Thomas 1750–1814. A socialistic radical whose *Meridian Sun of Liberty* (1793) advocated land nationalization through parochial ownership. 'Spencean philanthropists' were associated with the CATO STREET CONSPIRACY (1820).

Spencer, Herbert 1820–1903. An English engineer turned sociologist whose theories, which became known as social Darwinism (*see* DARWIN, CHARLES), supported free competition as a means of eliminating unfit organizations and individuals, and hence opposed state intervention.

Spinning jenny *see* INDUSTRIAL REVOLUTION

Spithead and Nore mutinies 1797. Mutinies of the Channel and North Sea fleets during the NAPOLEONIC WARS. The Spithead men, seeking improved pay and conditions, won both their case and a royal pardon. The Nore mutiny was influenced by radical political ideas and was suppressed, its leader, Richard Parker, being hanged.

Spoils of war According to K. B. McFarlane, in *The Nobility of Later Medieval England* (1973), war in the later middle ages was 'a speculative, but at best hugely profitable trade'. Principal sources of profit were loot, confiscated enemy lands (especially in France under Henry V and Bedford), pay and, above all, ransoms. The English record was the £500,000 asked by Edward III for King Jean II.

Spottiswood, John 1565–1639. As moderator of the general assembly (1610) and archibishop of St Andrews (1615–39), Spottiswood assisted James VI in the revival of episcopal administration in the CHURCH OF SCOTLAND. He later attempted unsuccessfully to moderate Charles I's canons (1635) and prayer book (1637), and on the outbreak of rebellion retired to London.

Spurs, battle of the 16 August 1513. An engagement in HENRY VIII's 1st French campaign. A French attempt to relieve Thérouanne was routed and a number of French noblemen were taken prisoner. The battle's name was derived from the speed of the French retreat.

Stair, Sir James Dalrymple, 1st viscount 1619–95. A distinguished lawyer who served both Oliver Cromwell and Charles II, Stair undertook the systematizing of Scottish LAW in his magisterial *Institutes of the Laws of Scotland* (1681) and other works. Resigning from the privy council in 1681, he lived in exile (1682–8) before returning to high office under William III.

Stair, Sir John Dalrymple, master and 1st earl of 1648–1707. The son of the 1st viscount, Stair served James VII and II as lord-advocate and lord justice clerk, but survived the Glorious Revolution to become joint secretary of state for Scotland under William III. As such he took a leading part in planning the massacre of GLENCOE. He resigned in 1695.

Of the **Spithead and Nore mutinies**, the latter was the more serious. 'Tell him we intend to be masters', says the delegate with his 'Grog can', in this establishment view of the affair. Engraving by George Cruikshank, 9 June 1797.

Stamford Bridge, battle of 25 September 1066. HAROLD GODWINSON, making a forced march from his watch against William the Conqueror in the south, surprised HARALD HARDRADA's invaders as they rested near York after FULFORD. Hardrada and his ally, Godwinson's brother Tostig, were killed and their army routed, but the victory weakened Godwinson's forces.

Stamp Act 1765. An Act attempting to make the defence of the American colonies self-financing by ordering the fixing of revenue stamps to a wide variety of publications and documents. The Act, which provoked violent protests from the colonists under the slogan 'no taxation without representation', was repealed in 1766.

Standard, battle of the 22 August 1138. DAVID I of Scotland, invading England in support of MATILDA and to extend his dominions, was defeated at Cowton, near Northallerton, Yorks., by an army raised by Archbishop Thurstan of York, fighting round a wagon bearing the banners of the northern English saints. To secure peace, however, STEPHEN ceded Northumberland to David in 1139.

Stanhope, James Stanhope, 1st earl of 1673–1721. A Whig politician, Stanhope, after a successful military career, became secretary of state (1714) and was effectively prime minister in 1717–21. His most notable achievements were the negotiation of the QUADRUPLE ALLIANCE and the repeal of the OCCASIONAL CONFORMITY and Schism Acts.

Staple During the middle ages, a monopoly market for goods, especially wool, established by law to facilitate customs collection. English wool was collected at certain 'staple towns' and exported for sale (from 1363 exclusively by the 'merchants of the staple') to a single continental staple, finally fixed at Calais (1392). The Scots staple was generally at Bruges or Middelburg.

Star Chamber A room in Westminster palace where, from the time of Edward IV, elements of the royal COUNCIL met in a judicial capacity, primarily dealing with civil disputes between subjects. By 1540 the court of Star Chamber had developed a distinct identity. Staffed by councillors and the chief justices, it dealt speedily with cases involving riot, the protection of the judicial system and the enforcement of proclamations. Regarded as oppressive, it was abolished by the Long parliament in 1641.

Statute *see* LAW; PARLIAMENT

Stead, William T. 1849–1912. A provincial journalist who first publicized the BULGARIAN ATROCITIES, Stead went on, as editor of the *Pall Mall Gazette*, to assist Josephine BUTLER in her campaign against the Contagious Diseases Acts and against child prostitution.

Brunel's **steamship**, the *Great Western*, engraved 'in commemoration of the establishment of steam navigation between Great Britain and America', 1837.

Steamships The technical breakthroughs were made by 1800, and the 1st commercial steamer, the *Comet*, operated on the Clyde from 1812. Low-pressure engines, using sea water, confined these to coastal use, although high-pressure engines could be used on rivers, and a few operated on long-distance mail routes (*see* BRUNEL, ISAMBARD KINGDOM). The development of the compound engine and the surface condenser meant that they began to take over general freight from the 1860s and they were dominant by the 1890s. *See* NAVY.

Steinkirk, battle of 3 August 1692. A battle of the war of the LEAGUE OF AUGSBURG. Allied troops under William III were defeated while attempting to halt a French advance on Brussels. The British contingent suffered particularly heavy losses.

Stephen king of England (1135–54; b. 1100). The son of Count Stephen of Blois by Adela, daughter of William the Conqueror, on Henry I's death Stephen seized the throne from MATILDA with the support of his brother Henry of Blois, bishop of Winchester, and a majority of the nobility. Personally brave and generous, he was excessively pliable (*see* STANDARD, BATTLE OF THE) and politically imprudent, and from 1139 the nation was in a state of anarchy, a continuous civil war with Matilda and her illegitimate half-brother, Robert of Gloucester, in the west country being accompanied by widespread private feuds and baronial brigandage elsewhere. Defeated and captured at the battle of LINCOLN, Stephen was released after his wife's victory at WINCHESTER (1141), but he was unable either to win the civil war or fully restore order, and in 1153 (after the death of his own son Eustace) he recognized Matilda's son Henry II as his heir. *See* ill. p. 208.

Stephen, Sir Leslie 1832–1904. An agnostic and literary critic, as editor of the *Dictionary of National Biography* (1882–91), Stephen was one of the greatest historical innovators of the 19th century.

Stephenson, George 1781–1848. A Northumbrian colliery engineer, in 1814–17 Stephenson perfected the steam locomotive (1804) of Richard Trevithick (1771–1833) for the haulage of coal. He built the Stockton and Darlington Railway (1822–5) and was appointed engineer to the Liverpool and Manchester Railway. With his son Robert (1803–59), he perfected the *Rocket* for this line, proving that the steam locomotive could become a passenger-hauling machine. *See* SAFETY LAMP.

George **Stephenson** surrounded by his inventions: woven silk picture.

Stone age *see* PREHISTORIC BRITAIN

Stone circles Settings of standing or (occasionally) recumbent stones, occurring mainly in north and west Britain. A few are associated with earlier HENGE MONUMENTS (*see* AVEBURY; STONEHENGE). They were probably local sanctuaries or religious centres. Professor A. Thom, in *Megalithic Sites in Britain* (1967), has shown that many were carefully laid out for astronomical observations during the early bronze age (*c.* 2000–1700 BC).

Stonehenge Wilts. The best-known prehistoric monument in Britain, whose great sanctity is attested by the large number of BARROWS surrounding it. It was apparently begun *c.* 2300 BC as a HENGE MONUMENT. Later, perhaps in the Beaker period (*c.* 2000–1700 BC), 2 concentric circles of bluestones brought from the Prescelly mountains in Dyfed were erected within the henge, and a CURSUS-like avenue built to link it to the nearby River Avon. The final and most spectacular stage, usually attributed to the Wessex culture (*c.* 1700–1400 BC), included the raising of a circle of 30 great sarsen stones joined by carefully worked lintels, with an internal horseshoe-setting of still taller lintelled sarsens and a concentric circle and horseshoe of rearranged bluestones. *See* STONE CIRCLES.

Stonehenge, Wilts.: the north-east sector of the outer stone circle, with some of the larger stones of the inner horseshoe on the right.

Stirling Bridge, battle of 11 September 1297. The vanguard of the English army of occupation, having crossed a narrow bridge over the Forth, was slaughtered by the Scots SCHILTRONS of WALLACE and Andrew Moray, and the remainder fled. Though Moray was mortally wounded, the victory left Wallace supreme in Scotland. *See* SCOTTISH WARS OF INDEPENDENCE.

Stirling castle Commanding the principal crossings of the Forth, and thus the main routeway between northern and southern Scotland, Stirling was perhaps the most fought-over castle in Britain, especially important in the Scottish wars of independence (*see* BANNOCKBURN, BATTLE OF), the civil wars and the Jacobite risings.

Stoke, battle of 16 June 1487. The last battle of the wars of the ROSES. The supporters of SIMNEL, led by the genuine Yorkist claimant John de la POLE, earl of Lincoln, and consisting mainly of Irish levies and German mercenaries, landed from Ireland in Lancashire. They were defeated by Henry VII's army near Newark, Lincoln being killed.

Stonor letters *see* LETTERS, MEDIEVAL COLLECTIONS OF

Stop of the exchequer 1672. The temporary suspension of the repayment of loans advanced by London bankers to Charles II. It provoked the bankruptcy of several bankers, but led also to moves towards the establishment of a funded NATIONAL DEBT when annuities equal to 6% interest were settled on the bankers and their clients.

Strafford, Thomas Wentworth, 1st earl of 1593–1641. A Yorkshire squire and parliamentary critic of the crown, Wentworth became president of the COUNCIL OF THE NORTH (1628) and lord deputy of Ireland (1633), advocating a policy of ruthlessly efficient government. Hated and feared as 'Black Tom Tyrant', he was impeached, attainted and executed by the Long parliament.

Stratford, John d. 1348. The principal counsellor of Edward III's early years and archbishop of Canterbury from 1334, Stratford served as chancellor 1330–4, 1335–7 and 1340, and effective regent 1339–40. Accused in 1340 of withholding supplies for the hundred years' war, he rallied clergy, lords and commons against the king and pressured him into making concessions to all three in return for grants of taxation.

Strathclyde The strongest of the post-Roman British kingdoms of the north, occupying Clydesdale and Galloway and centred on DUMBARTON (*see* DAMNONII). Surviving attacks from the Picts, Scotti, English Northumbria and the Vikings, in the 10th century it annexed Cumbria and briefly even west Yorkshire. It was finally annexed by Scotland (1034), and its southern part was attached to England by William Rufus.

Strawe, Jak *see* PEASANTS' REVOLT

Strict Settlement A legal device safeguarding landed estates, much used from the mid-17th to the 19th centuries. The current owner was invested with a life tenancy which inhibited the sale or mortgaging of parts of the estate reserved for the settlement of dowries, jointures and children's portions.

Strongbow The nickname of Richard de Clare, one of the MARCHER adventurers brought to Ireland (1170) by King Dermot of Leinster. He married Dermot's daughter, inherited his kingdom, de-feated the high king, and seemed likely to found a Norman state in Ireland independent of Henry II, who intervened to establish his own suzerainty (1171–2).

Stuart, Prince Charles Edward ('Bonnie Prince Charlie') 1720–88. The son of the Old Pretender and grandson of James VII and II, Charles Edward trained in the Spanish army before leading the JACOBITE '45' rebellion. Thereafter he lived principally in Italy. On his death without legitimate issue the Stuart claim to the throne passed to his brother, a churchman, and died with him.

Sub-infeudation *see* FEUDALISM

Submission of the clergy *see* REFORMATION

Subsidy The principal English direct tax of the 16th and 17th centuries, granted by parliament. Originally realistically assessed as a proportion of income, the subsidy became fixed at a total sum of about £80,000–100,000 and after 1547 payment was confined to the wealthier groups in society.

Prince Charles Edward **Stuart**, leader of the Jacobite rising of 1745, portrayed here as the romantic hero of legend. Contemporary engraving.

Succession, Acts of 1534 and 1543. Acts regulating the succession to the throne of HENRY VIII. The 1534 Act registered the invalidity of Henry's 1st marriage, excluded Princess Mary and settled the succession on the children of Henry and Anne BOLEYN. The 1543 Act settled the succession upon the future EDWARD VI, MARY I and ELIZABETH I, while reserving to Henry the right to alter the succession by testament.

Sudbury, Simon of archbishop of Canterbury (1375–81) and chancellor (1380–1). *See* PEASANTS' REVOLT.

Suez canal purchase 1875. The Suez canal, largely built by French capital, was opened in 1869. When Khedive Ismail of Egypt, who held many of its shares, faced bankruptcy, Disraeli bought them for Britain, who gained a controlling interest.

Suez crisis 1956. British and French forces invaded Egypt in collusion with the Israelis (November) and took over the Suez canal which Colonel Nasser, the Egyptian leader, had nationalized (July). This resulted in almost total international condemnation and the fall in early 1957 of Eden, the prime minister. It was Britain's last imperial adventure and the prelude both to decolonization and to a period of national self-questioning.

Suffolk, William de la Pole, 1st duke of 1396–1450. Having succeeded Cardinal Beaufort as leader of the peace party, Suffolk's influence increased with Henry VI's marriage to his protegée Margaret of Anjou (1445), and after HUMPHREY's death he virtually ruled England. Disaster in France and corruption at home made him hated, and in 1450 he was impeached and lynched on his way to exile. *See* CADE'S RISING.

Suffragettes A name coined by the *Daily Mail* for militant members of the PANKHURSTS' Women's Social and Political Union (1903–14). *See* WOMEN'S MOVEMENT.

Summer Time An idea for daylight saving advanced in 1907 by William Willett, it did not become law until May 1916, when the government's hand was forced by the necessities of war. It has continued ever since, with Double Summer Time in World War II.

Sunday schools Schools held on Sundays by volunteer teachers to teach reading and religious

Suez crisis: this rally in Trafalgar Square, London, 4 November 1956, with *Daily Herald*, and Labour and Communist party banners prominent, demanded Eden's resignation and 'Law not War'.

A woman struggles with 3 policemen outside Buckingham palace, May 1914, when 200 **suffragettes** attempted to induce the king to receive a deputation.

Sunday schools provided some children with a sort of education. This illustration from Francis Trollope's *Life and Adventures of Michael Armstrong*, 1840, suggests that they were often too worn out to profit from it.

Long after the Factory Acts, **sweated trades** often involved the whole family: toy-making at home, *c.* 1900.

knowledge to poor children. Sunday school foundation was promoted after 1780 by Robert Raikes (1735–1811) and became widespread in all denominations throughout Britain. They played a significant role in popular education before the EDUCATION ACT (1870).

Sunderland, Robert Spencer, 2nd earl of 1641–1702. Suave, urbane and cynical, a skilful administrator and manipulator of patronage, Sunderland was the most pliant of Restoration politicians. He served Charles II, James VII and II and William III in turn, changing his religion and principles with his masters and consistent only in his determination to retain power.

Supremacy, Acts of 1534 and 1559. Acts confirming the supremacy of Henry VIII and Elizabeth I respectively over the CHURCH OF ENGLAND. The 1534 Act was the final enactment of the Henrician REFORMATION. The 1559 Act re-established the church of England after the restoration of obedience to Rome under Mary I.

Supreme court of judicature *see* LAW

Suspending power *see* DISPENSING AND SUSPENDING POWERS

Sussex The comparatively small and primitive kingdom of the South SAXONS which developed gradually from a coastal foothold established by AELLE in the 450s or 470s. It was the last English state to be converted. Apparently divided among several minor dynasties, it became tributary to Mercia *c.* 770 and was annexed by Wessex in 825.

Sutton Hoo *see* RAEDWALD

Sweated trades Industries such as tailoring and dressmaking, which were organized in very small units on the PUTTING-OUT SYSTEM and thus were able to escape the supervision of the FACTORY ACTS. 'Sweating' was brought to an end by Winston Churchill's Trade Boards Act (1909).

Sweyn Forkbeard king of Denmark (d. February 1014). He raided England in 994 and (after the murder of his sister during AETHELRED UNRAED's massacre of Danes in 1002) again in 1003–4. In 1013 he mounted a full-scale invasion, gaining recognition as king of England first in the DANELAW and then (after Aethelred's flight) generally, but died soon afterwards.

The title-page of this account of the **Swing riots**, purporting to be by 'Captain Swing' himself, depicts the rick-burnings from the viewpoint of a poor farm labourer and his family.

Swing riots (or 'last labourers' revolt') 1830. A wave of rick-burnings and destruction of threshing machines – by the rural equivalent of the LUDDITES – in southern and eastern England. Threatening letters to farmers were signed 'Swing'. It was ruthlessly suppressed by the Whig government, and 19 executions and 481 transportations resulted, but wage concessions and a slowing of the mechanization of agriculture were won by the desperate labourers.

Syndicalism A revolutionary form of TRADE UNIONISM originating in France in the 1900s, which advocated the control of industries by their workers, gaining power by a strategic series of strikes. Its ideas were in evidence in British industrial unrest (1911–14) and in GUILD SOCIALISM.

T

Tacksmen Principal tenants (often relatives) of highland chieftains, holding 'tacks' or leases of substantial blocks of land which they sublet to clansmen. Tacksmen acted as viceroys for their chiefs and as officers in war. The system died after 1746 and many former tacksmen subsequently helped organize highland emigration.

Taff Vale judgment 1901. A legal decision making the Amalgamated Society of Railway Servants liable for costs incurred as a result of a dispute with the Taff Vale Railway Company, south Wales. This gave a great impetus to the nascent LABOUR PARTY. In response to union agitation the Liberals passed the 1906 Trades Disputes Act, freeing unions from such liability.

Taiping rebellion 1850–64. As many as 30 million people may have died in this rebellion, which was suppressed by the Chinese government acting though European officers, such as GORDON, who thereafter brought China within the British sphere of influence.

Talavera, battle of 27 July 1809. A battle of the PENINSULAR WAR. British troops under Wellesley defeated a larger French force attempting to halt their advance on Madrid. Nonetheless heavy casualties and the threat of further French armies forced Wellesley to retreat. He was rewarded for the victory with the title Viscount WELLINGTON.

Talbot, John, 1st earl of Shrewsbury c. 1388–1453. The last great English captain of the HUNDRED YEARS' WAR. Though inadequately supported from home, he long delayed Charles VII's reconquest of France, and in October 1452 his expedition expelled the French from Bordeaux and western Aquitaine. But then Charles counterattacked and Talbot was killed at CASTILLON.

Tallage An arbitrary tax levied by a feudal lord on his villeins, or by the crown on the towns and lands of the royal DEMESNE. Such royal tallages (generally for a campaign or other specific purpose) were first levied as such by Henry II (1173–4). Highly unpopular, they were abolished by Edward III (1340).

Tally A medieval device for acknowledging debts, whereby a piece of wood was notched along its length to indicate the amount and then split, the debtor retaining one half and the creditor the other (called the 'stock', hence 'stock exchange'). On payment the halves would be matched to check the sum and retained by the debtor.

Tamworth manifesto 1834. PEEL's election address, which pledged the Tories to accept the REFORM BILL (1832) and to become a party of 'Conservative' reform.

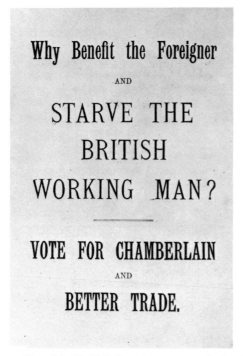

A pamphlet of the **Tariff Reform** League, 1903: despite the deliberate appeal to the working man, the issue helped to ensure the Liberal victory of 1906.

The novelty of the **telephone**: new year's greetings, *Illustrated London News*, 7 January 1882.

Tariff Reform 1903. An attempt by Joseph Chamberlain to revive protectionism (though mainly for industry), which split Balfour's cabinet and allowed the Liberals to defend FREE TRADE in the campaign which gave them the 1906 landslide.

Teheran conference November–December 1943. An inter-allied conference which co-ordinated policy on the second front and agreed to found the UNITED NATIONS.

Teinds *see* TITHES

Telegraph Semaphore systems were used during the Napoleonic wars, and a line from London to Portsmouth survived after them. The 1st electric line was used on the Great Western Railway (1836) and by 1851 lines existed alongside most railways. They were bought over by the post office in 1869.

Telephone Invented in America in 1876 by Alexander Graham Bell, telephones were soon installed in Britain, and by 1891 most belonged to the National Telephone Company. But in that year the post office started its service and by 1912 had taken over the entire service (apart from in Hull), and had 700,000 subscribers. In 1978 there were 13.7 million.

Television *see* BROADCASTING

Telford, Thomas 1757–1834. The son of a Dumfriesshire shepherd, Telford became surveyor of public works for Shropshire in 1787. He subsequently established himself as the leading civil engineer of his age, constructing roads, canals (including the Caledonian canal) and bridges (including the one at Ironbridge and the Menai suspension bridge) throughout Britain.

Temperance The temperance movement rose in response to liberalized licensing laws after 1828, but after 1850 its influence waned, although the United Kingdom Temperance Alliance was set up in 1853. In the 1860s and 1870s the revived movement aimed at state control and more rigid licensing laws. This was partially (but only temporarily) achieved by Acts of 1853 (in Scotland), 1869 and 1904. There was often a close association between temperance and the early Labour movement.

The Temple Church, Lamb Court, London, built by Knights **Templars**: the nave, circular in imitation of the Holy Sepulchre, Jerusalem, with effigies of knights templars including William the Marshal.

Templars, Knights a military order founded in 1118 to defend Jerusalem. From the 1130s they were granted extensive lands in Britain (often recalled by 'Temple' place-names), their 'commanderies' and 'preceptories' being frequently marked by round churches. Their immense wealth caused their suppression on trumped-up charges (1312), much of their property passing to the HOSPITALLERS.

Temple, Rev. William 1881–1944. The son of the archbishop of Canterbury and a religious educator, Temple revived Christian Socialist views and aided working-class education. As archbishop of York (1929–42) he was a respected and conciliatory figure and his translation to Canterbury (1942), for a tragically short time, allied the church firmly with wartime moves towards the welfare state.

Ten Articles *see* REFORMATION

Tenants-in-chief *see* FEUDALISM

Tenchebrai, battle of 28 September 1106. HENRY I defeated ROBERT CURTHOSE's much smaller army, completing his conquest of Normandy and its reunification with England.

Tenures Abolition Act 1746. The abolition of military land tenures in Scotland and their conversion into either 'blench' or 'feu' holdings. The Act was an important contribution to the pacification of the highlands, since it removed the obligation of tenants to follow their landlords to war.

Test Act 1673. An Act requiring civil and military officers to be communicants of the CHURCH OF ENGLAND, to take the oaths of supremacy and allegiance and to subscribe a declaration against transubstantiation. Designed to detect Roman Catholics, the Act also excluded Protestant DISSENTERS. It was repealed in 1828. University tests for undergraduates were abolished in 1854 and 1856, and for dons in 1871. *See* ROMAN CATHOLICISM.

Tettenhall, battle of *see* EDWARD THE ELDER

Tewkesbury, battle of 4 May 1471. Landing at Weymouth too late to assist Warwick the Kingmaker at Barnet, MARGARET OF ANJOU's Lancastrians were heading for Wales when intercepted at the Severn crossing by the swift-marching EDWARD IV. Unwisely leaving their defensive position, they were defeated piecemeal, and the death of Prince Edward, with the subsequent capture of Margaret and murder of Henry VI, extinguished Lancastrian hopes.

Thegn (Old English, 'one who serves'). A term used from the 9th century for the lesser nobleman of Anglo-Saxon England, previously called a gesith (companion) from his membership of a ruler's bodyguard. He generally served a greater lord, who granted him hereditary lands and whose status dictated his own: kings' thegns were thus most important. Since the rank was hereditary to all sons, thegns were numerous.

Theodore of Tarsus, St d. 690. Archbishop of Canterbury from 669. Theodore tactfully unified, regularized and centralized the English church following the synod of WHITBY, establishing several new dioceses and firmly subjecting all to Canterbury. A great ecclesiastical legist, he probably introduced the CHARTER to Britain.

Theodosius, count Sent by the Emperor Valentinian to save Roman Britain from the BARBARIAN CONSPIRACY, Theodosius afterwards (369–70) repaired HADRIAN'S WALL, established the Votadini and Damnonii as FOEDERATI beyond it, built signal stations on the Yorkshire coast and provided many town walls with external artillery turrets, thus laying the foundations of British defence during the heroic age.

Thirty-nine Articles *see* REFORMATION

Thistlewood, Arthur *see* CATO STREET CONSPIRACY

Thomas, James Henry *see* LABOUR PARTY

Thorough The term used by LAUD and STRAFFORD to describe firm and efficient execution of royal policy which would overcome official corruption and local recalcitrance. In fact neither man gained the untrammelled influence over government in England sometimes attributed to them and 'Thorough' remained an aspiration rather than an administrative reality.

Three estates The lords, commons and churchmen in PARLIAMENT. The term is especially used in Scotland.

Throckmorton plot 1583. A plot involving MARY QUEEN OF SCOTS, the Spanish ambassador Mendoza and several Catholic nobles and gentlemen for a rising against ELIZABETH I aided by a Spanish invasion. The arrest, torture and confession of their go-between Francis Throckmorton revealed the plan. Throckmorton was executed and Mendoza was expelled.

The **Titanic** leaving Southampton on her first – and last – trip.

Tillett, Ben 1860–1943. A pioneer of the NEW UNIONISM who founded the Dockers' Union (1887), leading the 1889 DOCK STRIKE, and remaining the union's secretary until it was amalgamated into the Transport and General Workers' Union (1922).

Titanic The 'unsinkable' Atlantic liner which hit an iceberg on its maiden voyage and sank (15 April 1912) causing 1,513 deaths. It has been seen both as a symbol of Britain's coming eclipse and of the divisions in British society.

Tithes The annual levy of one-tenth of all agricultural produce for the maintenance of the church, known in Scotland as 'teinds'. A long process of transition from payment in kind to commutation for cash was completed by the Tithe Commutation Act (1836). 20th-century legislation provides for the full redemption of the tithes by the year 2000.

Tithing An Anglo-Saxon petty policing device originating in the 10th century and regularized under Cnut. Each free man had to belong to a tithing or group of ten, who were collectively responsible for his good behaviour and appearance in court if charged. *See* FRANKPLEDGE.

Titles The highest title in the peerage is that of duke, the 1st creation being the Black Prince as duke of Cornwall (1337). Between 1572 and 1603 there were no dukes in England, and there have never been a great number. Today there are 27, plus 5 royal dukes: Gloucester, Kent, Windsor, Edinburgh, and Cornwall. Next in rank after duke comes marquis (1385) and then EARL. Originally holders of important office, ruling substantial territories such as Northumberland or Mercia, earls became hereditary in the reign of King Stephen. In modern times earl is normally the title taken by a retiring prime minister, if he takes a title at all. Next comes viscount (1440). The lowest grade in the peerage is the baron, orginally applied to the great tenants of the crown. Within each of the 5 grades there are 5 classes, each tied to a stage in the history of the unification of the United Kingdom: those of England, of Scotland, of Great Britain, of Ireland, and of the United Kingdom. All English, British, and United Kingdom peers automatically sit in the house of lords. After 1707 the Scots peers elected 16 of their number to sit in the house of lords; after 1801, 28 of the Irish peers were elected to the lords. By the Peerage Act (1963) all Scots peers are entitled to be members of the lords. All the children of peers are commoners; usually they take a subsidiary title of their fathers, but this is a courtesy title only. Life peerages were created in 1958.

Baronets, dating as an order from 1611 when James I instituted the title to raise money, are hereditary, but not part of the peerage. There were medieval baronets and it is possible that they derived from the knight BANNERETS who led a company of vassals under their own banner, and had precedence over other KNIGHTS. Out of the fighting knights of the middle ages there evolved the knight bachelor. In addition, there evolved 11 orders of chivalry, of which the surviving ones are: the GARTER (1348); the Thistle (reconstituted 1687); the Bath (1399); St Michael and St George (1818) – the Bath and St Michael and St George also have lesser classes of companions; the Royal Victorian order (1896), which also has companions and members, with GCVO denoting a Knight or Dame Grand Cross of the order; the British Empire (1917) – of whose 5 classes, GBE and KBE carry the title of Sir, with women in either of the 2 highest classes being called Dame.

There are 2 further orders of high rank which do not carry a title: the order of merit (OM) and companions of honour (CH). Until the development of modern urban society, Mr was also a title of distinction. Technically, esquire still is, being confined, most significantly, to those created expressly as such, the eldest sons of baronets and knights, noble men of other nations and lairds of Scotland (though in modern times lairds would be styled as, say, John Wemyss of Wemyss), barristers, JUSTICES OF THE PEACE, MAYORS and all officers in the armed forces.

Tizard, Sir Henry 1885–1959. A chemistry don who after World War I became secretary of the DEPARTMENT OF SCIENTIFIC AND INDUSTRIAL RESEARCH and then chief scientific adviser to the government (1935–42). With DOWDING he was responsible for the adoption of RADAR and the perfecting of fighter defence. In so doing he clashed with Winston Churchill's adviser, Lindemann, and when Churchill came to power was edged out of influence, but not before he had arranged vital scientific co-operation with the USA.

Toleration Act 1689. An Act permitting trinitarian Protestant DISSENTERS to hold services in licensed meeting houses and to maintain teachers and preachers in England and Wales, subject to their subscription to certain oaths. Non-trinitarians secured similar rights in 1812. A Scottish Act (1712) granted toleration to dissenters from the CHURCH OF SCOTLAND.

The demonstration in Copenhagen fields, London, 21 April 1834, against the deportation of the **Tolpuddle martyrs**. The procession, suitably attired, is carrying a petition to the king. Engraving by W. Summers, 1836.

Tolpuddle martyrs In February 1834, 6 farm labourers from a village near Dorchester were charged with having administered illegal oaths as part of the great trade union movement of the early 1830s (*see* TRADE UNIONISM). They were sentenced to 7 years' transportation as part of a government offensive against the unions. Almost instantly an energetic working-class agitation got under way. In 1836 the remainder of their sentences was remitted and all 6 later returned to England.

Tories A term originally used to describe Irish Catholic bandits, which was abusively applied during the EXCLUSION CRISIS to the defenders of the principles of hereditary succession and non-resistance to the monarch. The Tories, who lacked the organization of their opponents the WHIGS, were thrown into disarray by the necessity of deposing James VII and II in 1688 (*see* GLORIOUS REVOLUTION). Nevertheless a significant body of consistently Tory members existed in the parliaments of William III and Queen Anne, held together by common devotion to the Anglican church, hostility to DISSENTERS, and continued respect for the ideals of divine right and non-resistance. Outside parliament support came mainly from the Anglican clergy and the provincial squirearchy whose interests the Tories were particularly anxious to defend. With Anne's support the Tories emerged as the ruling party (1710–14), but they were totally discredited in

A 15th-century **tournament**: the earl of Warwick (foreground left) wears a studded brigandine, while the knight on the far right wears full plate armour. Note the blunted tournament swords. Drawing from *Pageant of Birth, Life and Death of Richard Beauchamp, earl of Warwick, c. 1485–90.*

The **Tower of London** in the 15th century, with London bridge in the background. Miniature from *Poems of Charles, Duke of Orleans, 1500.* The duke (in ermine) is shown in 3 different places in the Tower, where he was imprisoned after his capture at Agincourt.

1714 for their alleged Jacobitism (*see* JACOBITES) and passed into the political wilderness for 70 years.

With the fading of issues of principle after 1714, few politicians called themselves Tories, even opponents of the administration preferring the name 'country Whigs'. Revival came only after 1784 when the followers of PITT, most notably CANNING, took up and gave a new respectability to the old party name. In the aftermath of the French revolution, the ruling Tories became increasingly the party of reaction and were defeated in 1830. Thereafter, in the reconstituted party system of the mid-19th century, the name CONSERVATIVE PARTY emerged, though that body remains popularly known as 'the Tories'.

Torres Vedras, lines of Defensive lines constructed across the Lisbon peninsula in 1810 on the orders of WELLINGTON. Natural obstacles were elaborated by engineers to produce 3 lines of fortifications before which Masséna's French army was halted in the winter of 1810–11 and forced to withdraw. *See* PENINSULAR WAR.

Tory Radicals A name given in the 1830s to Tories, largely in Yorkshire, such as Richard Oastler and Michael Sadler, who supported working-class grievances against factory owners and the POOR LAW AMENDMENT ACT. The title was awarded by Disraeli to his YOUNG ENGLAND group, and revived by Randolph Churchill in the 1880s.

Tournament A school of war, an opportunity for gaining fame or wealth, and a favourite participatory and spectator sport from the 12th until the 16th century, tournaments originated as lethal free-for-alls condemned by the church, but became increasingly courtly and stylized.

Tower house A fortified residence containing all its accommodation within a defensible tower, usually surrounded by a lightly defended enclosure for livestock (or 'peel', hence 'peel-tower'). Originating on the borders around 1300, it became the standard type of Scottish CASTLE. Most are rectangular, but some later examples are L- or (in Scotland) Z-shaped in plan.

Tower of London The most famous of English castles, serving as a fortress, royal residence, treasure-house, prison and menagerie, or all at once. Dominated by and named after William the Conqueror's 'White Tower', begun in the 1070s, it was much enlarged and strengthened by Henry III and again by Edward I.

Town walls Urban fortification, general in later Roman Britain (*see* THEODOSIUS, COUNT), was reintroduced in the 10th century (*see* BURHS) and again revived in the early 13th (*see* MURAGE). It was stimulated by Edward I's Welsh wars, the Scottish wars of independence and the hundred years' war. The best extant town walls are at Canterbury, CHESTER, Conwy and YORK.

Townshend, Charles, 2nd viscount 1674–1738. A Norfolk gentleman and leading Whig politician, Townshend served as secretary of state (1721–30) under his brother-in-law WALPOLE. Dismissed in 1730 when his policies threatened war with Spain, he retired to his estates and a new career as an agricultural improver, which earned him the nickname 'Turnip'.

Towton, battle of 29 March 1461. The most decisive battle of the wars of the ROSES, and (with perhaps 50,000 combatants involved) probably the largest ever fought in Britain. EDWARD IV, with a mainly southern army, pursued the Lancastrians northwards after the 2nd battle of St Albans, and attacked them near Tadcaster, west Yorks. After a day-long fight in a snowstorm the Lancastrians were defeated with exceptionally heavy casualties, and the power of the northern magnates (whose retinues formed the mainstay of their force) was broken, leaving Edward effectively master of England.

Toynbee, Arnold 1852–83. Active as a CHARITY ORGANIZATION SOCIETY official, in the CO-OPERATIVE movement and as a historian. Toynbee's lectures (1881) on the Industrial Revolution were the 1st major pessimist statement about its effect on the working classes. After his early death Oxford reformers founded Toynbee Hall in London's east end, which became influential in forming opinion about social reform among the British élite.

Toynbee, Arnold, jnr 1889–1976. The nephew of Arnold TOYNBEE, he became an influential diplomatic consultant at VERSAILLES, and subsequently head of the Royal Institute of International Affairs. His attempt at a great work of historical explanation, *A Study of History* (1934–54), has been more controversial than persuasive.

Trade unionism Organized collective bargaining was a product of the Industrial Revolution. The earliest unions existed in skilled crafts, and in the textile industry among workers such as wool-combers,

'By combination we shall succeed': membership card of a 'new model' skilled **trade union**, the Amalgamated Society of Journeymen and Cloggers, formed *c.* 1873.

croppers and silk-weavers. They bargained for restricted recruitment by APPRENTICESHIP regulations and worked to enforce past protective legislation. Government policy in the 1800s (*see* COMBINATION ACTS) removed such protection and outlawed them but in 1824 they were again made legal.

This was followed by the creation among unskilled and semi-skilled workers, under the leadership of DOHERTY and OWEN, of a 'general union', the GRAND NATIONAL CONSOLIDATED TRADE UNION, which would bring the capitalist system down by a general strike. This was broken by stern government action (1834–5) prohibiting 'illegal oaths' (*see* TOLPUDDLE MARTYRS), and in the later 1830s and 1840s mass working-class activity then assumed the more political form of CHARTISM.

Organization among the skilled artisan trades – woodworkers, printers, bookbinders and so on – which had never really disappeared even when prohibited, increased in the early 1850s, especially among the crafts of the new technology: engineers, shipwrights and pattern-makers. The result was the formation of numbers of 'new model' unions

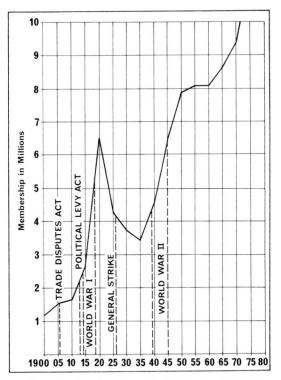

Members of **trade unions** (in millions) affiliated to the TUC.

representing skilled workers, which became the institutional foundation of the LABOUR ARISTOCRACY.

The unions were still disadvantaged at law, and in the 1860s, the JUNTA, in alliance with the POSITIVISTS and advocates of the 2nd REFORM BILL, campaigned for redress. To this end the trades union congress was founded in 1868, and legal inhibitions were finally abolished in 1871–5.

The 1st union MPs, Alexander MACDONALD and Thomas Burt, were elected as Liberals in 1874 and were followed by other 'Lib-Lab' members. But in the 1880s the NEW UNIONISM brought socialist ideas and organizers to the fore. Their influence was magnified both by the success of the DOCK STRIKE (1889) and by setbacks such as the defeat of the engineers' strike (1897). In 1900 the TUC decided to ally with the INDEPENDENT LABOUR PARTY in the Labour Representation Committee. The TAFF VALE JUDGMENT (1901) emphasized the still precarious position of the unions, and as a result the Liberals were prompted to secure them from legal action by the Trades Disputes Act (1906). After a further legal case, the Osborne judgment (1909), which ruled illegal the political levy paid to the LABOUR PARTY,

legislation guaranteeing the unions' rights to support the party in this way was passed in 1913.

After 1906 there was a further expansion in unionization, both of the unskilled and of industries such as the railways, where management had followed a strong anti-union line. This was somewhat influenced by the political ideas of SYNDICALISM; and several fierce strikes (1911–13) and the formation of the TRIPLE ALLIANCE (1914) seemed to have revolutionary overtones.

World War I had 2 main effects: total union membership rose from 4 million (1914) to 8.5 million (1920), thanks to the unions' close links with the government and the war effort; and the political stance of the skilled workers was radicalized by the threat of dilution, which led, especially around Glasgow, to militant revolutionary views being propagated at shop-floor level.

After the war, with the collapse of the Liberal party, the relations of the unions and the Labour party were regularized in the 1918 constitution. But syndicalist attitudes continued, both in the short-lived GUILD SOCIALISM and among the miners, until the collapse of the GENERAL STRIKE (1926). Thereafter, under the leadership of men such as Walter Cirrine and BEVIN, the TUC moved towards a more diplomatic relationship both with business organizations, in the MOND-Turner talks, and with the Labour party. This relationship continued during World War II, exemplified by Bevin's role as minister of labour in Winston Churchill's coalition government. This war had a similar effect on membership as its predecessor but, on the whole, central discipline imposed itself on shopfloor militancy, and continued to do so during the troubled period of post-war austerity, when the unions had to accept a rigid wage policy.

After World War II the TUC responded to the split between the former allies by becoming a sponsor of the 'Western' International Confederation of Free Trade Unions. British trade unionists also played a notable role in re-establishing trade unionism in Germany. The systematic industrial unionism of this reconstruction made no headway in their own movement, and during the 1950s and 1960s British industry was increasingly plagued not simply with confrontations between capital and labour, but with interunion disputes, as new technologies disrupted traditional working patterns. Allied to this came an increased political radicalism, especially on the part of the leadership of the large Transport and General Workers' Union, which ceased to be the main prop of the right wing in the Labour party.

When Harold Wilson came to power (1964) he appointed the Donovan commission on the unions, which reported in 1968 that the main difficulty with them was anomalous organization. In 1969 he and his Labour minister, Barbara Castle, attempted to make the unions subject to a legal code, with the sanction of prosecution and imprisonment for recalcitrant union officials. The unions brought their political strength to bear, and the legislation was dropped. A further attempt, by Edward Heath's government after 1970, passed into law but was not effective and was repealed by Labour (1974).

Although the unions steadily increased in strength in the 1970s (*see* graph), they remained constrained by government wage policies. Although these were virtually condemned as interference with free collective bargaining, a division of opinion was increasingly emerging between those groups of workers in the public sector and ailing or lame-duck industries, who realized that a free-for-all in wages could simply lead to a reduction in government support, and those in the dwindling number of growth sectors, who could still wield some bargaining power.

Trafalgar, battle of 21 October 1805. A decisive naval victory by NELSON over the combined French and Spanish fleets under Villeneuve. Though NELSON was killed in the battle, his victory rendered impossible any revival of the invasion threat to England and established British naval supremacy for the remainder of the NAPOLEONIC WARS.

Horatio Nelson, mortally wounded, is carried below during the battle of **Trafalgar**: contemporary mezzotint after Atkinson.

Electric **tramways** at Finsbury Park, London, 1922. In London the power cables were carried *under* the road.

Trailbaston, commissions of Itinerant judicial commissions first appointed by Edward I in 1304 to deal with the armed robberies, assaults and riots perpetrated by brigands and hired ruffians known as 'trailbastons' (Norman-French, 'club-carriers'). Thereafter they were appointed at intervals until *c.* 1390, dealing more generally with violent crime and minor rebellions.

Train bands Sections of the English militia selected for special training after 1573. With the exception of the London contingents, they never achieved high standards of military efficiency even under Charles I, when particular efforts were made, and they performed badly in the BISHOPS' WARS and the early stages of the CIVIL WARS.

Tramways Horse-drawn lines were first opened in London and Birkenhead (1861), and the Tramways Act (1871) facilitated their spread. Electrification and 'municipalization' came in the 1890s. They contributed greatly to urban expansion and better living conditions but started to be closed down in favour of buses in the 1920s, the last big city system going in the early 1960s. They survive in Blackpool and the Isle of Man.

Transport since 1830. The opening of the Liverpool and Manchester Railway (1830), engineered by STEPHENSON, on which steam locomotives hauled all traffic, inaugurated a period of rapid railway development (encouraged by needs created by the INDUSTRIAL REVOLUTION). In the following decade a network of lines was promoted which connected London with the other main ports and industrial areas. Apart from BRUNEL's Great Western Railway to south-west England, these were all built to the 'Stephenson gauge' of 4 ft 8½ in. (1·43 metres). Ireland ended up with a separate gauge: 5 ft 3 in. (1·60 metres). By the time the 1845 RAILWAY MANIA pushed the system into Scotland and the country districts, it had reached a plateau of technical development which was to remain for almost 50 years. Apart from specifying a maximum 'parliamentary fare' of 1d. per mile (to be available on 1 train per line daily) and safety regulations, the state intervened little, although Gladstone at the board of trade (1844) was prepared to see a state-run system on the model of Belgium. But the most the state could do was to enforce competition, and by the 1850s there was a wide network of lines owned by 150 or so companies, of which the biggest, the London and North Western Railway, was the largest JOINT-STOCK COMPANY in the empire. However, the competitive spirit was qualified by pacts and fare-pooling agreements entered into by the major companies, and by the purchase and effective emasculation of much of the CANAL system by railway companies. Until 1851 the railways got most of their revenue from passengers but in that year (despite the boost to excursion traffic provided by the GREAT EXHIBITION) freight traffic became, and has stayed, the foundation of railway economy.

As the railway expanded, the old trunk coaching network rapidly shrank, and with it went the TURNPIKES. But the numbers of men and horses employed in road transport actually increased as the

Modern **transport** by railway began with the opening of the Liverpool and Manchester line in 1830. There were separate trains for 1st- and 2nd-class 'outside' passengers, and here, 3rd-class carriages are tacked on behind the 2nd-class ones.

pattern of road journeys now became one of cross-country journeys to railway stations. The long-distance wagon vanished but the carrier's cart remained the staple of local transport from market town to village. Travel and carriage by coastal steamer and sailing ship also remained competitive until well into the 20th century and much freight was handled by lighters and barges around estuaries of the Thames, Severn and Humber.

The initial impact of railways in the major cities was destructive. The new terminals were often built, for cheapness, in slum areas, which increased the problems of urban congestion elsewhere. (In London, the growth of the east end was closely related to the promotion of new lines into the old central area by the railways.) Alternatively, the noise and traffic generated by the railways turned hitherto respectable districts into slums or industrial areas. But from quite an early date the well-off were moving out of town to live by the railway and, after the introduction of workers' trains by some companies in the 1860s, working people began to follow their example. The building of suburban railways, and schemes such as the LONDON UNDERGROUND, began at the same time but were soon challenged by the rise of the tramcar, first horse-drawn, then in the 1890s electric and frequently owned by the corporation (*see* TRAMWAYS).

Attempts to mechanize road transport had been made since the early days of the steam engine, and in the 1830s various steam road-vehicles were tried out with reasonable success. But their development was restricted by their lack of robustness, the declining state of the roads under railway competition, the attractiveness as an investment proposition of the railway itself, and the Road Locomotives Act (1860) which restricted their speed to 5 mph. Although the Act did not greatly disadvantage steam traction engines, it did interfere with the exploitation of the internal combustion engine, invented by Gottfried Daimler (1886). It was abolished (1905) as a result of pressure from the growing and very well-to-do MOTORING ORGANIZATIONS. By 1914 an embryonic MOTOR INDUSTRY had grown up whose capabilities were greatly expanded by World War I.

During the war the 120 or so railway companies were put under state control for the duration and when this came to an end (1921) the new ministry of transport (founded 1919) grouped them into 4 large companies, each possessing an effective regional monopoly. This arrangement lasted until national-ization (1948). Although governments gave the companies advantages in competition with road transport and grants for modernization, their technology lagged behind their state-controlled counterparts on the continent. Significantly, the one instance of full-scale nationalization, which created the London passenger transport board (see LONDON UNDERGROUND), was accompanied by a remarkable programme of modernization.

Before World War I personal transport had been restricted to the bicycle and, among the better-off in

Road passenger **transport** expanded rapidly after the waiving of the 5 mph speed limit in 1905: Cornhill traffic scene, 1914, showing buses and the motor car.

country districts, horse-drawn carriages. Between the wars the car (made available in larger quantities by assembly-line manufacture and hire purchase) and the motorcycle became commonplace among the middle classes. Road congestion increased, and the 1st plans were made for large-scale construction of new roads, partly as a means of combating unemployment. Meanwhile the motorbus, which had made a successful début in London before 1914, replaced many local railways and trams, giving a lot of country districts their 1st reliable public transport service. Road freight transport also made its presence felt, as an alternative to the paralysed railways during the General Strike (1926).

World War II saw petrol rationed, private motoring all but disappearing and the railways all but run to death. Rail reconstruction did not really begin until 1955, with an over-ambitious and unrealistic plan which had substantially to be revised by BEECHING and others during the 1960s. From 1952 the number of road vehicles started to grow steadily with encouragement from successive Conservative governments, and in 1955 the MOTORWAY programme was launched, supplemen-ted after the BUCHANAN REPORT (1963) with a programme of urban motorways (1963–73). The Suez crisis (1956) and consequent oil shortage provided a brief check, and the more serious crisis (1973) provoked a relative running down of the road programme and greater funds for public transport, in which British Railways had established a high technological reputation. However, the availability of North Sea oil after 1973 meant that the swing back to public transport was less evident in Britain than elsewhere in Europe, and road haulage still played a disproportionate role in freight transport.

Treason Act 1534. An Act extending the provisions of the statute of Treasons (1352) to defend the royal supremacy in the church and making words treasonable as well as deeds and writings. This provision, repealed in 1549, was re-enacted in 1554, though 2 witnesses were required as proof.

Treasurer In medieval England the head of the EXCHEQUER; his Scots counterpart was the chamber-lain. Known in England as the lord treasurer from Tudor times, he withdrew from the exchequer under Elizabeth I, and in 1714 was finally replaced by the lords commissioners of the treasury.

Treasury *see* EXCHEQUER

Trenchard, Hugh, viscount 1873–1956. 'Father of the RAF', Trenchard was badly wounded in the Boer war and transferred to the royal flying corps (1912), which he built up into an independent force and presided over until 1929, when he became metropolitan police commissioner. He was a firm believer in BOMBING, as possession of this offensive arm was seen as an essential part of an independent air service.

'Trent' case 1861. During the American civil war 2 envoys from the confederate states were captured by a Northern warship while travelling on a British ship, the *Trent*. Britain demanded an apology and the release of the envoys and the situation might have come to war but for the intervention of Prince Albert.

Trevithick, Richard *see* STEPHENSON, GEORGE

Trial by battle A method of establishing guilt or innocence, wherein the accused fought his accuser before a judge. Introduced at the Norman conquest as an alternative to trial by ordeal in criminal cases, it was extended to civil cases (where champions could be employed) in the mid-12th century. Rare after the 15th century, it was not finally abolished until 1819.

Trial by ordeal Ecclesiastically supervised ordeals (by hot iron, water or swallowing a blessed morsel) were widely used in Anglo-Saxon times to determine a suspect's guilt or innocence by submitting him to divine judgment. Partially superseded by trial by battle at the Norman conquest, ordeals were finally abolished in 1215.

Tribune *see* LEGION

Tribune group The successor to the left-wing group of Labour MPs which in the 1950s followed BEVAN, and named after the weekly paper he founded (1936), this acted as a socialist pressure group on the Labour governments (1964–70 and 1974–9). Its bark was worse than its bite.

Triennial Acts 1641, 1664 and 1694. Acts requiring that parliament meet at least once every 3 years. The 1641 Act, a reaction to CHARLES I's 'personal rule', was replaced by the 1664 Act and finally by that of 1694, which also specified that parliaments should not sit longer than 3 years. *See* SEPTENNIAL ACT.

Trinitarians A small religious order devoted especially to ransoming captives of the infidel by collecting money or (in the last resort) by personal substitution. Introduced to England *c.* 1200, and to Scotland *c.* 1248: there they were called Red Friars, though their rule more resembled that of CANONS regular.

Trinovantes A Belgic-influenced British tribe occupying Essex and southern Suffolk. Threatened by the Catuvellauni, it allied with Julius Caesar (54 BC), and thereafter maintained its independence until its conquest by Cunobelinus (*c.* 10). Resenting appropriation of its lands by the COLONIA of COLCHESTER, it subsequently played a leading part in Boudica's revolt.

Triple alliance 1914. A name given to the alliance between the miners', dockers' and railwaymen's unions, which threatened a general strike in autumn 1914. The alliance surfaced again in 1921, when the miners sought its support. The other unions, however, backed down on 15 April, 'Black Friday', and the threat was lifted. It took the failure of the GENERAL STRIKE to dispel it completely.

Trotskyites The original British followers of the expelled Russian Bolshevik Leon Trotsky (1877–1940) left the COMMUNIST PARTY OF GREAT BRITAIN in 1929 to form the Balham group. Later on they affiliated loosely to Trotsky's 4th INTERNATIONAL (1938–) but split in 1950, when the rebels formed the International Socialists (Socialist Workers' Party, 1973). A later split produced the Socialist Labour League (Workers' Revolutionary Party, 1969). The International was revived in Britain in 1969 when the International Marxist Group (1965) affiliated to it. Such tiny bodies have been even more unsuccessful than the Communists in elections, but exert considerable influence in some trade unions and among student organizations.

Troyes, treaty of 21 May 1420. Marking the high point of English success in the HUNDRED YEARS' WAR, this provided that Henry V should become regent of France during Charles VI's lifetime and marry his daughter Katherine of Valois. They and their heirs would inherit the French crown after Charles's death. Charles's son, the dauphin (later Charles VII), was thus disinherited.

Tudor, Owen *see* HENRY VII

Tudor revolution in government A term coined by G. R. Elton, in *The Tudor Revolution in Government* (1953), for the achievements of Thomas CROMWELL. The 'revolution', which has been disputed by some scholars, allegedly involved the establishment of the sovereignty of the king in PARLIAMENT by the jurisdictional REFORMATION and the consolidation of royal authority in England and Wales, together with the reform and bureaucratization of central administration. *See* MONARCHY.

Tull, Jethro 1674–1741. A barrister, farmer and leading publicist of agricultural improvement, Tull was a broadcaster of ideas rather than an innovator. Though he invented an improved horse-drawn seed-drill (1701), he was generally more successful with his writing (notably his *Horse-hoeing Husbandry*, 1733) than with his farming.

Tunnage and poundage Customs duties, granted for life to English kings from the 15th century and the largest item in the crown's ordinary revenue by 1625. In 1625 parliament granted them for 1 year only to CHARLES I and his subsequent collection of this revenue without parliamentary consent became an issue of constitutional conflict.

Turner, Ben *see* MOND, SIR ALFRED

Turnpikes Improved roads built by turnpike trusts licensed by Act of parliament to raise capital by subscription and to levy tolls on road traffic. Piecemeal initiative after the opening of the 1st turnpike at Wadesmill, Herts. (1663), led to a great improvement in road transport in the succeeding century. *See* REBECCA RIOTS.

Tweeddale, John Hay, 2nd marquis of 1645–1713. A prominent figure in the country opposition to the Scottish administration before 1703, Tweeddale became queen's commissioner to the Scottish parliament in 1704. After much hesitation, he led the *Squadrone Volante* or 'new party' in support of the UNION (1707).

'Two-power' Standard The doctrine that the British NAVY should equal the next 2 strongest navies put together.

Tyburn The permanent gallows, 3 miles west of Newgate prison, where condemned London felons were publicly hanged between the early 16th century and 1783. Executions, conducted after a procession from Newgate, attracted large crowds

'The Idle Prentice Executed at **Tyburn**': engraving by William Hogarth, 1747, plate 2 of his 'Industry and Idleness' series. Underneath is a verse from Proverbs: 'Then they shall call upon God, but he will not answer.'

and were frequently accompanied by macabre rituals and preceded by the 'last dying speeches' of notable criminals.

Tyler, Wat *see* PEASANTS' REVOLT

Tyndale, William 1495–1536. A man of great linguistic and literary gifts, Tyndale early conceived the ambition of producing a vernacular BIBLE. Failing to obtain official backing and converted to Lutheranism, he fled abroad where his biblical translations were subsidized by English merchants. Arrested by the Netherlandish authorities, he was strangled and burned.

Tyranni (Lat. for 'tyrants' or 'usurpers'). A name, implying warlords with no legitimate right of succession, applied by GILDAS and others to the rulers of post-Roman British monarchies of the HEROIC AGE.

Tyrconnel, Richard Talbot, earl of 1630–91. A devout Catholic, patriotic Irishman and former royalist soldier, Talbot became attached to the future James VII and II in exile. As military commander in Ireland (1683) and lord deputy (1687) he implemented James's Catholicizing policies. In 1688 he held Ireland for James until defeated at the BOYNE and Aughrim (1691).

Tyrone, Hugh O'Neill, 2nd earl of ?1540–1616. After several years at ELIZABETH I's court, Tyrone spent the years 1568–93 feuding with rival chieftains to establish his supremacy in Ulster as 'the O'Neill'. In 1595 he rebelled against Elizabeth, enjoying considerable success until his defeat by Mountjoy at KINSALE. In 1607 he fled abroad, ultimately dying in Rome.

The army was moved in to contain the terrorism of the **Ulster emergency** in 1969. Here soldiers of the Royal Regiment of Wales patrol the streets.

U-boat campaign *see* CONVOY SYSTEM; NAVY; WORLD WAR I; WORLD WAR II

Ulster emergency In 1968 protests against Protestant domination in Ulster grew, concentrating in particular on inequalities in housing and voting. Marches by Catholic civil-rights activists were answered with police brutality, although Captain Terence O'Neill, the Ulster premier, pledged himself to reform. He lost the confidence of his Unionist party and, after an indecisive election (1969), resigned. Although his successor, Major James Chichester-Clark (*b.* 1923), carried through several of the reforms demanded, unrest worsened and several people died in rioting in Belfast and Londonderry (August 1969). This was accompanied by a split in the Irish Republican Army and the emergence of the militant Provisionals (1969), which may have been aided by ministers of Jack Lynch's Fianna Fail government in Dublin. Unrest got steadily worse (1970–1) after internment without trial, affecting only Catholics, was introduced under Brian Faulkner (1921–77). To polarize the situation further, 13 young Catholics were shot at a demonstration in Londonderry on 'Bloody Sunday' (30 January 1972) and the IRA bombing campaign escalated. Edward Heath instituted direct rule for Ulster (24 March) and a Fine Gael-Labour government markedly less sympathetic to republicanism came to power in Dublin in 1973. Ulster politicians and the British, Irish and Ulster governments came to an agreement at Sunningdale (November–December 1973) in which a power-sharing system, allowing both communities representation in government, was guaranteed for Ulster. The February 1974 election showed, however, that militant unionism had the bit between its teeth, and on 28 May, following a strike of Protestant workers, the executive collapsed. A later attempt to convene a constitutional convention for Ulster was no more successful, and direct rule was still in operation in 1980. By then the violence had claimed over 2,000 victims, although with some diminution in 1977 (112 victims), 1978 (81 victims) and 1979 (113 victims).

Unauthorized Programme 1885. Joseph Chamberlain's schemes for disestablishment, regional government and land reform, which he advertised in his election campaign, and which seemed to promise the breakup of the Liberal alliance.

Uniformity, Acts of 1549, 1552, 1559 and 1662. Acts requiring the use of the BOOK OF COMMON PRAYER in churches throughout England in order to secure religious uniformity, and providing for the punishment of non-conforming clergymen.

Union, Act of (Ireland) 1800. Following the rebellion of the UNITED IRISHMEN, Pitt's government pushed through legislative union against considerable Irish opposition. The Act provided for 100 Irish seats in the commons and 32 in the lords at Westminster, immediate ecclesiastical and gradual fiscal union and the establishment of Free Trade between Great Britain and Ireland.

Union, Act of (Scotland) 1707. The legislative union of England and Scotland, accepted only after fierce controversy in Scotland. Under the Act, Scotland accepted the Hanoverian succession and sent 45 members to the commons and 16 representative peers to the lords at Westminster. A common flag, Free Trade and uniform coinage, weights and measures and fiscal systems were adopted but Scotland's distinctive LAW and church were preserved. In addition a financial 'equivalent' was granted to liquidate the Scottish national debt and compensate shareholders in the Company of Scotland.

Union, Acts of (Wales) *see* WALES

Some signatures and seals of the commissioners who negotiated the treaty of **Union**, 22 July 1706. The Scots signed on the left, the English (headed by the archbishop of Canterbury) on the right. The treaty became law in 1707.

Union of Democratic Control Founded in 1914 by Liberal and socialist critics of the 'secret diplomacy' which they believed had brought about World War I, it played a part both in encouraging the idea of a LEAGUE OF NATIONS and in providing a bridge whereby disillusioned Liberals crossed into the Labour party.

Unitarianism Originally a term for Christians who rejected the doctrine of the trinity, Unitarianism became a separate denomination in the 18th century and absorbed many English Presbyterians. Unitarians were notable for their political and social radicalism during the American and French revolutions. Modern Unitarianism adheres to no set dogma. *See* NONCONFORMITY.

United Irishmen A non-sectarian Irish revolutionary society founded by Wolfe Tone and provided with military organization by James Napper Tandy. On the arrest of their leaders in 1798, the United Irishmen rose, but were defeated at Vinegar Hill and Ballinahinch before supporting French forces could land (*see* NAPOLEONIC WARS). Wolfe Tone committed suicide in prison.

United Nations Originally the self-description of the allies in World War II, the UN was formulated (*see* TEHERAN CONFERENCE) between January 1942 and October 1945, when its charter, drafted by the 'big four' – USA, UK, USSR and China – was ratified at San Francisco, and it succeeded to the responsibilities of the LEAGUE OF NATIONS. Based in New York, it consists of a general assembly of all member nations and a security council of 15. Five of these are permanent members, including the UK. Ineffective in restraining big-power conflicts (because of the veto of individual members of the security council), it has nevertheless been significant in local peacekeeping, economic and educational aid, monetary policy and decolonization.

Universities A university or *studium generale* was originally a scholastic GUILD of masters (e.g. Paris) or students (e.g. Bologna), entitled to confer degrees in several subjects. Oxford, the 1st British university, was the former type, founded in the 1160s by scholars diverted from Paris by HENRY II's quarrel with Becket. Headed by a chancellor from 1214, it finally achieved independence from its diocesan bishop of Lincoln in 1365–7. The division of students into northern and southern 'nations' was abandoned in 1274, but the religious orders, kings, bishops and magnates founded colleges, University college (1249) being the first of 11 secular

The first seal of Cambridge **university**, *c.* 1261, depicting the chancellor seated between the 2 proctors. The River Cam, crossed by a bridge, is below them.

William of Wykeham with doctors (top), masters, bachelors and students (bottom) of Oxford **university**. They are standing before New College, which Wykeham founded in 1379. From the Chandler manuscript, *c.* 1460.

foundations by 1500. Faction fights and disputes with townspeople led to secessions, but only that of 1209 led to a permanent new establishment, at Cambridge. There, Peterhouse (1284) was the first of 10 secular colleges founded by 1500.

Scottish students, albeit hindered by war and SCHISM, journeyed to Paris or England until the foundation of St Andrews university (1411), partly to combat heresy. A 2nd Scottish university, Glasgow, was founded in 1451, and a third, Aberdeen, by JAMES IV in 1495. Everywhere courses were long, a degree in arts being required before proceeding to a higher degree in civil or canon law or theology: students began at about 14, finally graduating at about 34.

The period 1500–1660 saw a major expansion of the universities, with new colleges founded in Oxford and Cambridge and a 4th Scottish university, Edinburgh (1585). The REFORMATION also acted as a stimulus to learning, though the most notable development was less intellectual than social. From *c.* 1550 the traditional students seeking qualifications for clerical and other careers were joined by a growing number of young noblemen and gentlemen who, though rarely taking degrees, sought a general academic education. The dominance of students of gentle birth was consolidated at Oxford and Cambridge after 1660, bringing with it changes in the life styles' of students and dons, though both student numbers and intellectual vitality declined, and entry was still restricted to members of the church of England. In contrast the Scottish universities of the 18th century expanded in size and in curriculum and won renown for the quality of their teaching, particularly in moral philosophy and science.

The 19th century brought reform to the English universities. After the foundation of London university (1836), pressure for change, both of curriculum and government, mounted, and Acts of 1854 and 1856 removed many of the restrictions. The University Tests Act (1871) opened university government to all (*see* TEST ACT), after 1880 fellows of colleges could marry and, by 1900, 5 women's colleges had been established at Oxford and Cambridge. The 1st government grant to universities was in 1889. By 1962 the majority of all university income came from the treasury via the universities grants committee.

Uses *see* ENFEOFFMENT

Ussher, James 1581–1656. A notable patristic scholar and anti-Catholic disputant, Ussher became archibishop of Armagh in 1625. Coming to

England in 1640, he proposed a compromise between Episcopalian and Presbyterian church government and, despite his open royalism, remained highly respected by parliament and the succeeding interregnum regimes.

Uthwatt report *see* ECONOMY, THE

Utilitarianism A philosophical doctrine which assessed the validity of actions in terms of their propensity to result in the greatest good being conferred on the greatest number. It originated with BENTHAM and, in the hands of him, the MILLS and CHADWICK, was an important factor in 19th-century social and legal reform.

Utrecht, treaty of 1713. A unilateral treaty ending MARLBOROUGH'S WARS. Britain gained Hudson bay, Arcadia and Newfoundland from France, and GIBRALTAR, Minorca and colonial trading concessions from Spain. Negotiated by a Tory administration, the treaty was regarded as a betrayal of Britain's allies by the Whigs and passed parliament only with difficulty.

V

Vagabonds A term used to describe 'incorrigible rogues' and vagrants, first legislated against in the 14th century and subject to further enactments as part of the Tudor POOR LAWS. Vagabonds were punished by whipping, branding and incarceration in HOUSES OF CORRECTION prior to the POOR LAW AMENDMENT ACT (1834).

de Valera, Eamon 1882–1973. The leader of SINN FEIN and of resistance to British rule, de Valera was president of Dail Eireann (1918), but split with those who accepted the 1921 Anglo-Irish treaty, and led the republicans in the Irish civil war (1922–3). Prime minister of the Free State (1932–59) – with a few breaks – he kept Ireland neutral in World War II. He was president of the republic of Eire from 1959–73, when the country rapidly rejected his austere Catholic politics. *See* IRISH CONSTITUTIONAL CRISIS.

" BEGOB, EAMON, THERE'S GREAT CHANGES AROUND HERE ! "

The removal of Queen Victoria's statue from outside Leinster house, Dublin, coincided with the replacement of Eamon **de Valera**'s Fianna Fail by the more moderate coalition government. *Dublin Opinion* cartoon, 1948. Ireland finally withdrew from the British commonwealth in April 1949.

Vane, Sir Henry 1613–62. The Puritan son of one of Charles I's councillors, Vane supported PYM in 1640 and played a crucial part in STRAFFORD's trial and later in the negotiation of the SOLEMN LEAGUE AND COVENANT. A central figure in the Rump and a convinced republican, he was tried and executed following the Restoration.

Vereeninging, treaty of *see* BOER WARS

Verneuil, battle of 1424. Known as 'the second Agincourt', this major victory by BEDFORD's English army over a Franco-Scottish force supporting Charles VII marked the high point of English success in the HUNDRED YEARS' WAR, and virtually put an end to Scots intervention in the struggle.

Versailles, treaty of (1783) *see* AMERICAN INDEPENDENCE

Versailles, treaty of 28 July 1919. Actually negotiated in Paris, but signed by Georges Clemenceau, Woodrow Wilson, LLOYD GEORGE and German representatives at Versailles, the treaty brought an end to World War I, and blamed it on Germany who lost territory to France, Poland, Czechoslovakia and Lithuania, and had to submit to partial occupation, REPARATIONS, and naval and military limitations. This severity was condemned in Germany itself (where Hitler was subsequently to campaign on its vindictiveness) and by British liberals, notably Keynes. Such resentments were subsequently to provide a basis for APPEASEMENT policies.

Verulamium Extensive remains (including a unique theatre) of the 3rd largest town in Roman Britain. Founded *c*. 49 at a major CATUVELLAUNIAN settlement, and destroyed by Boudica (60), the rebuilt MUNICIPIUM continued to flourish until the 6th century, but in medieval times was superseded by nearby St Albans (*see* ALBAN, ST).

Vespasian Roman emperor 69–79. Vespasian served as legate of the 2nd LEGION during the invasion of Britain, conquering the Durotriges (43–4). His defeat of Vitellius (69) ended the Roman civil wars that followed Nero's suicide, and as emperor he promoted the expansion of Roman Britain through his governors Cerialis, Julius Frontinus and Agricola.

Vestiarian controversy A controversy within the Elizabethan church over the retention of traditional ecclesiastical vestments. Puritan opponents of the 'rags of Rome' were almost victorious in convocation in 1563, but eventually lost the struggle. A number of ministers were deprived of their livings for refusal to wear the prescribed vestments.

Vicarius From *c*. 300, the name for the overall governor of the 4 provinces of ROMAN BRITAIN.

Vici The lowest grade of towns in ROMAN BRITAIN, not generally inhabited by Roman citizens. They were of 2 types, planned CIVITAS capitals and smaller unplanned vici (enjoying only limited self-government) which developed spontaneously around forts or road junctions, or as market centres.

Victoria queen of Great Britain (1837–1901; b. 1819). The daughter of the duke of Kent (4th son of George III and Princess Victoria of Saxe-Coburg-Gotha), Victoria inherited the throne on the death of William IV (1765–1837). In 1840 she married her mother's nephew, ALBERT, who freed her from the domination of her mother's connections and from a strong political partisanship for Melbourne's Whigs, which she had used to keep Peel from office (1839). From then until his death she was dominated by his progressive and diplomatic views, his relative unpopularity as a foreigner and the 9 children she bore him. Palmerston replaced Peel as her *bête noir* in the 1840s, with his noisy antipathy to European conservative regimes (many of which were run by her relatives). Her displeasure at his encouragement

Queen **Victoria** and her Indian servant, 1891. Noted for her prejudices against Gladstone, Palmerston and political women, Victoria was relatively lacking in racialism.

of Louis Napoleon's *coup d'état* (1851) helped bring him down, although Palmerston's backing of an anti-democratic regime isolated him anyway. The Great Exhibition (1851) and the Crimean war increased the popularity of the monarchy, but were succeeded by Albert's death (1861) and 10 years of self-enforced seclusion. Thereafter she lived at Windsor, Osborne or Balmoral, travelling abroad once a year and seldom visiting or travelling extensively elsewhere in Britain. Her touch in public life reverted to the emotionalism of the days before Albert: she detested Gladstone, who was punctilious, but succumbed to the gross flattery of Disraeli who made her empress of India (1876). However, she always adopted political neutrality in public and her popularity steadily increased from its lowest point in 1870, the nation being entertained to a persistent saga of the marriages, offspring and deaths of her family. Her golden jubilee (1887) disclosed this enthusiasm, which escalated to the 'festival of empire' of her diamond jubilee celebrations 10 years later. She died at Osborne (22 January 1901), having shifted the monarchy from a position of political contention to one of popular veneration.

Victoria cross Instituted in 1856, after the Crimean war, 'for acts of great bravery in the face of the enemy', it is the supreme British decoration and may be awarded posthumously.

Victorines *see* AUGUSTINIAN CANONS

Vienna, congress of 1814–15. A diplomatic congress called by Metternich after the 1st treaty of PARIS, intended to consolidate the peace settlement by restoring the balance of power in Europe and guaranteeing existing frontiers. Britain was represented by CASTLEREAGH. Its decisions were confirmed in the 2nd treaty of Paris.

Vikings A name of uncertain origin (perhaps men of the *viks* or creeks) applied to the seaborne Scandinavian robbers who afflicted Europe, to a greater or lesser extent, *c.* 800–*c.* 1100. Many reasons have been advanced for their irruption, most notably the pressure of population on land and resources, climatic changes and the desire to escape the tyranny of a developing monarchy. Some recent opinion, however, sees Viking raiding and settlement as simply an extension, made possible by remarkable Scandinavian developments in ship-building and navigational techniques, of the war-like activity endemic everywhere during the period. It has been argued that the size of Viking armies, the extent of their devastation and the density of their settlements have all been exaggerated, initially by contemporary ecclesiastical chroniclers whose wealthy and undefended churches (hitherto relatively immune in warfare between Christians) suffered especially from the pagan raiders. But though current research concentrates on the Vikings as colonists, urbanizers and merchants rather than as pirates, there can be no doubt that their principal legacy to Europe was destruction and disruption.

For mainly geographical reasons, their assaults fell most heavily of all upon Britain. The 1st recorded raiders were Norwegians, who attacked Dorset *c.* 789 and Lindisfarne in 793 but thereafter concentrated on the far north. By *c.* 800 they had begun the intensive colonization of the ORKNEYS and Shetlands, subsequently establishing settlements in the Western Isles and mainland Caithness and Sutherland and fortified coastal bases in Ireland. From there, in the early 10th century, 'Norse-Irish' Vikings founded secondary settlements in Cumbria and northern England.

The main threat to England, however, came from the Danes, who sought plunder rather than land and whose raids began in the 830s. In 850 and 854 they wintered in Kent, and thereafter their attack gathered momentum until a great Viking army conquered virtually all England save Wessex (865–75). Then Alfred's resistance turned the tide, and by 899 the invaders were becoming peaceful and increasingly Christian settlers, confined by treaty to the DANELAW. But their lands remained

potential or actual bases for fresh Viking assaults. During the 1st half of the 10th century the West Saxon kings (notably Edward the Elder, Aethelstan and Edmund) re-established English control first over the southern Danelaw and then (with the death of ERIK BLOODAXE and the extinction of the Norse-Irish kingdom of York in 954) over Northumbria.

After a complete respite under Edgar, a 2nd wave of major Viking attacks began in the 990s. Concentrated entirely on England, they were mounted by large and well-organized armies drawn from all over Scandinavia, led by princes such as SWEYN FORKBEARD, and aimed exclusively at the accumulation of loot and DANEGELD (*see* MALDON, BATTLE OF). Unchecked by the incompetent Aethelred Unraed, their ravages continued almost without intermission from 997–1016, culminating in the accession of CNUT and the attachment of England to a Scandinavian empire.

Though English monarchy was restored with Edward the Confessor and HARALD HARDRADA'S

A cross of the **Viking** period from Middleton, north Yorks.: with characteristic ambiguity, the figure beneath the Christian symbol is surrounded by the typical furnishings of a pagan Viking grave.

intervention (1066) was defeated, the Viking threat to England continued until the end of William the Conqueror's reign, while the Norwegian Western Isles and Orkneys were not finally annexed to Scotland until 1266 and 1469 respectively. Scandinavian influence on the English language was still more persistent, and modern standard English derives from the Anglo-Danish dialect of the Danelaw.

Villas Romano-British country houses, almost invariably the centres of agricultural estates. Rectangular, E-shaped or quadrangular, they generally had mosaic floors, heating systems, and bathhouses. Usually exploiting richer soils, they reached a climax of development and prosperity in the 4th century (*see* ROMAN BRITAIN). Best-preserved examples (apart from atypical FISHBOURNE) are Bignor and Lullingstone, Kent; Chedworth, Glos.; and North Leigh, Oxon.

Villein Originally meaning simply 'villager', in the feudal period the term described the large and internally various class of servile tenants who (though not technically SERFS) were bound to labour service and subject to HERIOT, MERCHET and TALLAGE. From the 14th century English villein tenure was increasingly converted to COPYHOLD, and it had disappeared from Scotland by 1364. *See* FEUDALISM.

Vimeiro, battle of 21 August 1808. The 1st battle of the PENINSULAR WAR. A victory over the French by British troops under Wellesley (*see* WELLINGTON, 1ST DUKE OF), sent to aid Spain and Portugal. The gains of victory were squandered by Wellesley's superiors in the convention of Cintra, whereby the defeated French army was repatriated with all arms and equipment.

Virgate A measure of land averaging 30 acres, being 2 BOVATES or a quarter of a CARUCATE. Also called a yardland, it often constituted the holding of the superior class of VILLEIN.

Viscount *see* TITLES

Vitoria, battle of 21 June 1813. The last major battle of the PENINSULAR WAR. WELLINGTON's British and Spanish troops defeated the combined French forces of Joseph Bonaparte and Marshal Jourdan, subsequently driving the French from Spain and advancing into France.

A detail of a late Roman mosaic from a **villa** at Low Ham, Somerset, representing, in vivid colours set against a white background, Dido and Aeneas embracing.

Vortigern ('over-king'). The nickname of a Romano-British aristocrat, traditionally from the Gloucester region and the son-in-law of Magnus Maximus, who dominated HEROIC AGE Britain from *c*. 425. His defence policy (*see* CUNEDDA) was initially successful, but he was unable to control his Anglo-Saxon mercenaries and, after allegedly marrying Hengest's daughter, died disgraced *c*. 460.

Votadini A British tribe inhabiting the eastern side of Scotland from the Tyne to the Forth, with a hillfort capital at Traprain Law, Lothian. It was consistently philo-Roman, and after the BARBARIAN CONSPIRACY became FOEDERATI against the Picts (*see* CUNEDDA). Its kingdom of MANAU GODODDIN was finally overrun by Anglian Northumbria in the mid-7th century.

W

Wade, George 1673–1748. As commander-in-chief, Scotland (1724–38), Wade constructed 250 miles of roads and bridges throughout the highlands and formed a peace-keeping force of highlanders which ultimately became the Black Watch (1739). He was later promoted field-marshal (1743) and commander-in-chief, England (1745).

Wakefield, battle of 30 December 1460. A Lancastrian victory in the wars of the ROSES. Richard of YORK, having marched north to prevent MARGARET OF ANJOU from concentrating an army, ill-advisedly left the safety of Sandal castle and was defeated and killed by a larger Lancastrian force.

Wales Cymru, the land of the 'fellow-countrymen' (CYMRY) or, to the Anglo-Saxons, of the British 'foreigners' (Old English, *wealas*). Its independent history begins in the mid-7th century (*see* HEROIC AGE), when the last British efforts to hold or reconquer lowland England failed (*see* CADWALLAWN; CYNDDYLAN) and the Saxon advance finally separated Wales from the fellow-Britons of Dumnonia and Strathclyde. Long since evangelized by David and a host of other saints, by this time Wales was a chequer-board of small kingdoms – BRYCHEINIOG, DEHEUBARTH, GWYNEDD, MORGANNWG and POWYS – prevented from unification by fierce tribal and dynastic rivalries and from consolidation by the custom of GAVELKIND. These factors helped to ensure that the personal ascendancies established from the 9th century by a succession of princes of Gwynedd or Deheubarth (RHODRI MAWR, HYWEL DDA and GRUFFYDD AP LLYWELYN) would not outlast their deaths. English territorial encroachment effectively ended with the building of OFFA'S DYKE (784–96) and Welsh princes co-operated with Alfred and his successors against Viking attacks, making formal submission to powerful English kings such as Aethelstan and Edgar. But border warfare remained endemic, and English intervention was another important element hindering national unification.

The threat from east of Severn increased catastrophically with the Norman conquest. By *c.* 1100 the Norman MARCHERS, planting castles and fortified trading boroughs and bringing with them feudalism and Latin church organization, had overrun south-east Wales. By the end of Henry I's reign (when the Flemish colony which gave Pembrokeshire its special character was established) they seemed poised to conquer the whole nation, despite fierce resistance in Deheubarth and from GRUFFYDD AP CYNAN in Gwynedd. Then, taking advantage of English and Marcher preoccupation with Stephen's civil wars, OWAIN GWYNEDD led the native princes in a sustained counter-attack, beginning in 1136 and by 1154 driving the invaders from north and west Wales. Henry II halted but could not reverse this process; anxious to distract the Marchers from establishing an independent state in Ireland, he recognized RHYS AP GRUFFYDD as tributary lord of all south Wales (1171–2).

Harlech castle, Gwynedd, one of the 10 royal castles built by Edward I between 1277 and 1294 to secure his conquest of **Wales**. It was originally on the coast but the sea has receded.

On Rhys's death Gwynedd reclaimed national leadership, and LLYWELYN THE GREAT and LLYWELYN AP GRUFFYDD (from 1267 the 1st and only native ruler of all Wales recognized by the English) exploited the weakness of John and Henry III to create the most powerful Welsh state since the Norman conquest. Their expansionism infuriated the Marchers, however, and their policy of feudal centralization reinforced by hitherto alien PRIMOGENITURE antagonized the lesser Welsh princes, and on Edward I's invasion (1277) the nascent state collapsed. An attempt to re-establish it (1282–3) ended in utter defeat, and the last vestiges of Welsh independence were swept away. English rule was consolidated by a system of new CASTLES and fortified towns and, despite the risings of Rhys ap Maredudd (1287) and Madoc ap Llywelyn (1294), and the much more formidable 15th-century revolt of GLENDOWER, it was never again broken.

The new order was established when the statute of Rhuddlan (1284) divided Wales between the Marchers (who now received additional territory but otherwise continued much as before) and the English crown, which held conquered Gwynedd directly. Together with other royal lordships in west Wales, this formed from 1301 (when the future Edward II became the 1st English prince of Wales) an APPANAGE for the monarch's eldest son, the 'principality' being divided into shires and subject to English criminal law, though Welsh custom prevailed in civil matters.

The conquest, indeed, wrought relatively few social changes, and the Welsh gentry generally retained possession of their land, frequently serving as government officials and steadily gaining influence. They suffered a setback from the penal laws (forbidding Welshmen to hold office or town property, to sit on juries or bear arms) enacted during Glendower's rising, but these (though strongly upheld by planted English burgesses) were rarely enforced rigorously after Henry IV's death. Welshmen played a distinguished part in the later HUNDRED YEARS' WAR, and an important one in the wars of the ROSES, especially at BANBURY and MORTIMER'S CROSS, the duchy of Lancaster lands in the south and west generally supporting the Lancastrians and the former Mortimer estates on the border the Yorkists. After the triumph of the Welsh-descended Henry VII many found places in court, government or church.

By now much of the March had fallen to the crown through confiscation or inheritance, but its special status continued as, despite the efforts of the COUNCIL IN THE MARCHES OF WALES, did its notorious lawlessness. Government desire to rectify this situation, and for a uniform administration to implement the REFORMATION, combined with considerable native pressure to produce the Acts of Union with England (1536/42), which have determined the course of Welsh history until the present. These abolished the March, parts of it being attached to existing Welsh and English border counties and the remaining majority forming 5 new shires. Welsh representation in parliament was initiated, Welshmen and Englishmen were accorded full legal equality, tribal law and the already decayed custom of gavelkind were swept away, and a national high court (albeit held in the English language) was created, retaining its independence until 1830.

The Reformation, forging further Anglo-Welsh links, was initially received with comparative indifference, but the Welsh translation of the BOOK OF COMMON PRAYER (1567) and the bible (1588) proved influential in promoting Protestantism and preserving the Welsh language. Both union and Reformation served to increase the power of the native gentry – the latter by granting them monastic lands and (to the subsequent impoverishment of the church) a preponderance of TITHES – and from now until the 19th century they were the dominant element in Welsh history. During the civil wars the great majority sided with Charles I,

making Wales 'the nursery of the King's infantry', though there were pockets of active parliamentarians on the central and northern borders and, under Rowland Laugharne, in Pembrokeshire. Laugharne changed sides in 1648, but after his defeat at St Fagans (8 May) and Oliver Cromwell's reduction of Pembroke castle Wales remained quiet.

Under the commonwealth (1649–53) efforts were made, notably by Vavasor Powell (1617–70) and other itinerant preachers, to introduce Puritanism to Wales, but their success was limited, and after the Restoration (1660) the alliance of gentry and church of England resumed sway. Afflicted by poverty and apathy, by PLURALISM, NON-RESIDENCE and absentee English bishops, the church nevertheless now stood at a low ebb. So did education, until the early 18th-century establishment of CHARITY SCHOOLS by the SOCIETY FOR THE PROMOTING OF CHRISTIAN KNOWLEDGE and of the far more influential Welsh CIRCULATING SCHOOLS, for both adults and children, organized from 1737 by Griffith Jones (1683–1761). These last coincided with a remarkable religious revival and the growth of Calvinistic Methodism, headed by men such as Howell Harris (1714–73) and the great hymn-writer William Williams Pantycelyn (1717–91). Their work was consolidated by Thomas Charles (1755–1814) and in 1811 the now numerous Welsh Methodists became a separate denomination. Politically, Wales remained quiet during the 18th century, local Jacobites failing to rise in 1745 and nascent sympathy for the French revolution evaporating after the ludicrous French 'invasion' of Pembrokeshire in 1797.

The developments which shaped modern Wales began with the somewhat retarded advent of the Industrial Revolution during the decades before the Napoleonic wars, when the iron and coal of the south began to be seriously exploited. A wartime boom was followed by industrial and agricultural depression, which provoked miners' riots at Merthyr (1831), a CHARTIST rising at Llanidloes (1839) and the REBECCA RIOTS. Industrial prosperity returned with the massive expansion of the iron industry during the 1840s and 1850s, prompted by the huge demands of railways (introduced to Wales in 1841) and linked to new processes heralding the changeover to steel. From the 1860s, however, iron was outstripped by the remarkable growth of the coal-export trade: by 1913 annual production exceeded 50 million tons, and CARDIFF was the world's greatest coal-exporting port.

The social changes wrought by industrialization were immense. The population of Wales almost

Port Talbot, south-east of Swansea, south **Wales**: the smoke stacks and cooling towers of the Margam and Abbey steelworks, part of 4½ miles of blast furnaces and rolling mills which form Britain's largest steelworks.

quadrupled from 1815–1914, over 60% of it concentrating in industrial Glamorgan and Gwent while rural areas became depopulated. Methodism continued to spread rapidly, especially in the southern coalfield, and by 1851 roughly 75% of Welshmen were dissenters. An Anglican-biased government report on Welsh education, linking immorality with Nonconformity and the Welsh language ('The Treachery of the BLUE BOOKS', 1847), helped to radicalize Methodist politics, and thus to shake at last the dominance of church and gentry. By 1892 Wales was a Liberal stronghold, and in 1920 the church suffered disestablishment, a third of its endowments going to the university (founded 1893) and national library of Wales (founded 1907).

The peak of Welsh industrial and agricultural prosperity was reached during and immediately following World War I, to be succeeded by a slump of unprecedented proportions, the result of overspecialization in heavy industry. Exacerbated by world factors, this depression continued until 1940. Unemployment rose to over 30% in 1932, fostering the growth of the Labour party and to a lesser extent of political WELSH NATIONALISM, whose cultural antecedents date from the 18th century. World War II greatly improved matters by encouraging and diversifying industry, but rural depopulation continued and continues, along with (despite the efforts of government and cultural organizations) the decline of the Welsh language. Cardiff was proclaimed national capital in 1954, and a further step towards administrative devolution

was taken in 1964, when a secretary of state for Wales with cabinet rank was appointed. In 1979, however, a proposal for a national assembly, with wide but not comprehensive powers, was rejected by the Welsh electorate.

Wallace, William *c.* 1270–1305. The son of a Renfrewshire knight, Wallace began (initially with the encouragement of WISHART and others) the guerilla resistance to Edward I in southern Scotland, attacking Scone in May 1297. Though always held in suspicion by the magnates, he attracted enthusiastic popular support, combining with Andrew Moray's northern forces to rout the English at STIRLING BRIDGE. Thereafter knighted and made sole guardian in the name of John Balliol, he reformed the 'common army' (*see* SCHILTRONS) and ravaged northern England, but resigned after his defeat at FALKIRK (1298). He reappeared in 1303, but was betrayed to the English in August 1305 and brutally executed. *See* SCOTTISH WARS OF INDEPENDENCE.

Walpole, Sir Robert, 1st earl of Orford 1676–1745. The son of a Norfolk gentleman of Whig principles, Walpole entered the commons at 25. Soon known as an orator, he gained office as secretary at war (1708–10) and treasurer of the navy (1710), but was accused of corruption after the 1710 Tory victory. Back in office as paymaster-general in 1714, 1st lord of the treasury and chancellor in 1715, he resigned in 1717 after Townshend's dismissal, returning as paymaster only in 1720.

The turbulent aftermath of the SOUTH SEA BUBBLE made Walpole. His measures to restore public credit and the role in shielding the court which earned him the nickname 'the Screen', coupled with the deaths of STANHOPE and SUNDERLAND, brought him a supremacy which he assiduously consolidated in the succeeding years. Crown patronage was carefully manipulated to build up a reliable court party in parliament. The gratitude of GEORGE I and from 1727 the friendship of GEORGE II's queen Caroline assured him of royal support. His mastery of parliamentary debate and programme of peace, stability and low taxes won the votes of the independent squirearchy in the commons. His years as 1st lord of the treasury (1721–42) transformed the significance of that office, while establishing the commons, from where he presided over the 'Robinocracy' (he was known as Robin to his friends), as the centre of government.

Astonishingly hard-working, undoubtedly corrupt, robust and earthy in character, Walpole was committed to no ideal beyond the maintenance of the 1688 revolutionary settlement, the Hanoverian succession, the interests of the landed class and his own power. Challenged over a stormy issue in the EXCISE CRISIS (1733), he retreated. His fall came only when his conduct of the war against Spain in 1739, which he had resisted, lost the confidence of his cabinet, while the withdrawal of the electoral support of ARGYLL and the prince of Wales in 1741 eroded his parliamentary position. In 1742 he at last accepted a peerage and retired from the management of affairs. 'No saint, no spartan, no reformer', in his own words, he was essentially a peacetime leader, unsuited to the demands of a new age of aggressive national expansion. Unlike Chatham he could not inspire, but by his genius for management he provided a period of stability and consolidation in national affairs without which the achievements of his successors might not have been possible.

Walsingham, Sir Francis ?1530–90. The sternly Puritan organizer of Elizabeth I's intelligence service and secretary of state (1573–90), Walsingham, who often lectured his mistress, was respected rather than liked by her. He consistently advocated a Protestant alliance with the Huguenots and Dutch against Spain and was the implacable enemy of MARY QUEEN OF SCOTS.

Walter, Hubert d. 1205. Perhaps the most notable English administrator of the 12th century, Walter became archbishop of Canterbury in 1193, was Richard I's JUSTICIAR (1193–8) and, having helped John to the throne, served as his chancellor from 1199 until his own death.

Wansdyke 'Woden's Ditch' is a HEROIC AGE earthwork running some 40 miles (64 kilometres) from a point south of Bristol to eastern Wiltshire, with a 15-mile (24-kilometre) gap. Its exact context is uncertain, but it may mark the defensive frontier of British Dumnonia or else relate to struggles within Wessex or between Wessex and Mercia.

Wapentake see HUNDRED

Warbeck, Perkin d. 1499. A Flemish boy trained to impersonate Richard, younger of the PRINCES IN THE TOWER. Appearing at Cork in 1491, he was countenanced in turn by France (1491–2), Burgundy (1492–5) and James IV of Scotland (1495–7), but in each case Henry VII's diplomacy achieved his rejection. He was captured in Cornwall (1497) and executed.

Wardens of the Marches Officers appointed by the English and Scottish crowns for the adminis-

tration and defence of the East, West and Middle Marches of the Anglo-Scottish border. The wardens, generally local magnates, met to settle international disputes and punish malefactors and occasionally led punitive raids. The office lapsed after the union of crowns (1603).

Wardrobe Originally the section of the English ROYAL HOUSEHOLD responsible for the monarch's robes and personal valuables, from the time of Henry III to Edward II it took over household finance from the CHAMBER. Under Edward I and his successors it also came to supervise the payment, victualling, transport and munitioning of armies.

Wards, court of A government department headed by the master of wards and concerned with the administration of the crown's revenues from WARDSHIP, which emerged in the early 16th century and was formally constituted in 1540. It was abolished in 1645.

An aerial view of the **Wansdyke**, looking east from Wiltshire.

Wardships Under feudal law the wardship and (generally) the marriage of minor heirs (under 21 if male, and under 14 if female) of tenants-in-chief pertained to the crown, along with the remarriage of tenants' widows. Their sale constituted a lucrative source of income. *See* ENFEOFFMENT; ESCHEAT; WARDS, COURT OF.

Warwick the Kingmaker 1428–71. As the wealthiest and most powerful supporter of YORK, Richard NEVILLE, earl of Warwick, expected supreme power under Edward IV, but was checked in this and offended by Edward's WOODVILLE marriage (1464). Failing to control Edward by force (1469–70), he defected to the Lancastrians and restored Henry VI, only to be slain by Edward at BARNET. *See* ROSES, WARS OF THE.

Washington conference 1921–2. This attempted to settle the balance of power in the Far East between Britain, the USA and Japan, and to regulate and restrict the size of their fleets.

Water frame *see* ARKWRIGHT, SIR RICHARD; INDUSTRIAL REVOLUTION

Waterloo, battle of 18 June 1815. The final battle of the NAPOLEONIC WARS, ending Napoleon's restoration after his escape from Elba. British, Dutch and Belgian troops under WELLINGTON withstood French attacks until the arrival of Blucher's Prussian army, whereupon a general advance shattered the French army. Napoleon subsequently surrendered and was exiled to St Helena.

Watt, James 1736–1819. Born in Greenock, Watt worked as an instrument-maker in London and Glasgow. His invention of an improved steam engine led to his removal to Birmingham and partnership with James Boulton (1774) to produce engines for the INDUSTRIAL REVOLUTION. Immensely successful, he was greatly honoured in his own lifetime.

Wavell, Archibald, earl 1883–1950. The general who was responsible for defeating the Italians in north Africa (1940–1) in WORLD WAR II. Winston Churchill's demands for extension of operations to the rest of the Middle East (where Wavell was commander-in-chief 1939–41) brought failure against Rommel, and Wavell was sent to India (as commander-in-chief 1941–3) where he had to cope with the Japanese in Burma. He was less successful

as viceroy of India (1943–7), and was replaced by Mountbatten.

Webb, Sidney 1859–1947 **and Beatrice** (*née* Potter) 1858–1943. Social historians, investigators and reformers, the Webbs married in 1889, the year in which their FABIAN SOCIETY published *Fabian Essays*. Among other institutions, they mutually founded the London School of Economics and the *New Statesman*, while Sidney was joint author with HENDERSON of the LABOUR PARTY constitution (1918). Their influence on the highly centralized and authoritarian nature of British social reform was enormous.

James **Watt** in his workshop: engraving by James Scott after James E. Lauder.

Beatrice and Sidney **Webb** with G. B. Shaw (right) during the 1930s.

A **Wedgwood** porcelain vase, with a classical motif, 'The Apotheosis of Homer', designed by John Flaxman, *c.* 1789.

Wedgwood, Josiah 1730–95. The son of a Staffordshire potter, Wedgwood opened his 1st small china factory in 1760. Nine years later he founded the great Etruria works and went on to revolutionize both the production and marketing of china. He was one of the most successful entrepreneurs of the early INDUSTRIAL REVOLUTION.

Wee Frees A name given to those congregations of the Free Church of Scotland who did not join with the United Presbyterians to form the United Free church (1900). It was also applied to those Liberals who continued loyal to Asquith after 1918.

Welfare state The term was coined in the 1930s to indicate a type of social organization, still based on market economics as far as productive industry was concerned, which was subject to government intervention to secure several basic human values: security of employment, adequate housing and health services, and care of those not able to care for themselves – children, the old, and the handicapped in mind and body.

In fact, there had never been a time when the economic system lacked such constraints. DICEY, for many years the leading interpreter of 19th-century social reform, in *Law and Public Opinion. . .* (1905) talked of the dominance of 'a period of Benthamism or Individualism' from *c.* 1830–70. But on closer inspection the two were scarcely the same: Benthamites such as CHADWICK proposed drastic measures of state control in the public health field, while even a measure which accelerated the development of capitalism, such as LIMITED LIABILITY, actually involved a diminution of individual responsibility.

The greatest state interference with market economics was the POOR LAW. Although this was made more rigorous by the POOR LAW AMENDMENT ACT (1834), it still provided a statutory entitlement to assistance virtually unique in Europe. While humanitarians would condemn its lumping together of all classes of pauper – unemployed, ill, old and unfit – in the general, mixed WORKHOUSE, economists saw its non-contributory aspect as a form of income redistribution and realized that humanitarian sentiment (and the physical impossibility of cramming those thrown out of work by trade depression into workhouses) would cause this principle to be extended. In fact, broadly similar Poor Laws also replaced inadequate traditional provisions in Ireland (1838) and in Scotland in 1845. The ban on outdoor relief could not in practice be maintained, and in the 1860s 'workhouse infirmaries' were set up, subsidized by the poor rate, attendance at which did not require a declaration of pauperism.

The ideology of the 1834 reform had been twofold: that the able-bodied poor required to be shocked by a punitive regime into earning their living (once earning, they could then cope with their family's welfare without calling on the state), and that most poverty was actually encouraged by the levels of relief then offered. These were keeping a low-paid labouring class on the land when it could be earning a better income in the new industrial areas. But there was also the problem that these same areas provided death-traps, both at work and in the home, which could easily kill off a breadwinner and throw his family on the parish. Hence the reason for Chadwick's shift to finding a solution in public health reform and the closer regulation of industrial processes.

This, in its turn, required a substantial increase in government activity, both central and local. In a positive way, public health legislation required expenditure on water supply and drainage, and controls over the building and letting of houses – GAS AND WATER SOCIALISM in embryo. Restrictively, it meant that masters and workers, in the mines and textile factories, were no longer in a purely market relationship.

The extension of such types of intervention brought a new factor into play which some historians, notably Professor Oliver MacDonagh, in *A Pattern of Government Growth* (1961), have considered critical: the role of the officials who mediated between central government and the local authorities to secure enforcement of the legislation. Where such legislation had to be modified or extended, he argues, they took the lead, and eventually came to generate legislation themselves. Certainly some factory inspectors, such as Leonard Horner (1785–1864), were very energetic, but the situation seems to have varied according to industry and locality.

In the 1860s and 1870s, as electoral power both centrally and locally came within the grasp of working-class electors, pressure rose for extensions of the FACTORY ACTS, TEMPERANCE legislation, the eight-hour day, WORKMEN'S COMPENSATION, a more liberal interpretation of the Poor Laws and OLD AGE PENSIONS. Locally, there was an increasing amount of more or less collectivist action to provide public utilities at lower cost, and municipal housing, as well as children's services associated with the expansion of state education after 1870.

By the end of the century, with investigations of poverty such as those by BOOTH, a general consensus was emerging that more would have to be spent on social welfare. Even Conservatives could draw on the precedent of Bismarck's social insurance schemes in Germany as means of combating socialism. But what were the targets to be and how was money to be raised? The WEBBS, appealing to the non-party goal of 'national efficiency', aimed at the destruction of the Poor Law and the setting up of a range of specialized welfare agencies. BEVERIDGE and others believed that the key lay in solving what had become recognized as the problem of unemployment, a solution which still paid homage to the liberal ideal of self-help. Other Liberals, such as J. A. Hobson (*see* BRITISH EMPIRE), prompted by the Boer war, saw the plight of the poor as something bound up with Britain's imperial position, with profits being exported to colonial territories instead of going to the workers in the form of increased wages and benefits.

Joseph Chamberlain's solution was to encourage industry and raise revenue by tariffs (*see* TARIFF REFORM), a clean break with Free Trade orthodoxy which cost the Conservatives the 1906 election. The response of the Liberals under Lloyd George was an *ad hoc* combination of various expedients – old age pensions, NATIONAL INSURANCE and EMPLOYMENT EXCHANGES – financed by contributions from employer and employed and by direct taxation increases. Although small compared with present levels, these provoked the controversy over the PEOPLE'S BUDGET (1909), but this did not mask the fact that, fundamentally, the old system remained intact.

The complex social consequences of World War I – the low physical standards of recruits, the experience of welfare work among munitions workers, the social reforms promised by the leadership to the participants and the experience of government controls of food and rents – promised a new departure in the period of reconstruction that followed. Certainly some important reforms took place at the centre. National insurance was extended (1920), and a new ministry of health (1919) took over from the local government board (whose stagnation from 1905–14 under the Liberal minister and former socialist, BURNS, calls into question some of the alleged reforming dynamism of the Liberals). Priority was given to a Housing Act (1919) which required certain uniform standards to be maintained, planned programmes to be implemented, and made the state foot most of the bill. About 214,000 houses were in fact built before the programme, along with many other promised benefits, were cut by the GEDDES AXE (1922), although 2 further Housing Acts, a Conservative one (1923) which subsidized private housebuilding (by £6 a year for 20 years), and a Labour one (1924) which subsidized local authority homes (by £9 a year for 40 years), added a further million houses in the next decade. But Neville Chamberlain as minister of health made no fundamental change in the Poor Law system, save to amalgamate it with county government (1929). The workhouse was no longer used as a means of coercing the able-bodied unemployed, but the MEANS TEST, introduced by the National government (1931), aroused lasting resentment. During the 1930s, BOYD ORR's studies of nutrition and child health and Eleanor Rathbone's campaign for family allowances stressed the connection between ill-health and unemployment and poor living conditions.

Such ideas were activated during World War II when Beveridge was given the task of surveying social security. His report (December 1942) recommended a national health service, family allowances and state benefits as a right, payable without a means test, all this being predicated on the goal of 'full employment in a free society'. Enthusiastically promoted by working-class and radical organizations, and by Beveridge himself, most of its recommendations (including free medical treatment, provided by the NHS) were carried out after the war by the Attlee government, largely through the efforts of BEVAN as minister of health.

The Beveridge blueprint has not subsequently been radically changed, although the ideal of a largely preventive and salaried medical service has continually been deferred. The Conservatives, under Harold Macmillan, increased the housing programme and have generally resisted more doctrinaire attempts to curb state welfare for the benefit of private health insurance schemes. By the 1970s, however, the system was subject to several severe stresses: the ageing of the population creating new demands for geriatric care; the breakup of conventional morality and marriage patterns causing a rise in the number of single-parent families; and the deterioration of inner-city areas provoking new complexes of social problems. At the same time the health service itself had a disproportionate share of low-paid employees, whose protests at their pay and status threatened on several occasions to bring it to a standstill. There was also much consumer disquiet at the undemocratic nature of the control of the system (1973–4), to which regionalization and devolution were seen as solutions.

Wellington, Arthur Wellesley, 1st duke of 1769–1852. Wellesley first made his name as a soldier in India (1797–1805) and subsequently proved a brilliant commander in the PENINSULAR

Arthur Wellesley, duke of **Wellington**: contemporary oil painting by John Lucas.

WAR and at WATERLOO. Thereafter he entered politics and as Tory prime minister (1828–30) pushed through Catholic emancipation (*see* ROMAN CATHOLICISM). He was aloof and authoritarian by nature, but his instinctive opposition to reform was softened by his high sense of public duty.

Wells, Herbert George 1866–1946. A realist novelist, socialist and scientific popularizer, Wells's ideas were a major force in modernizing social attitudes before World War I; and during the war he became the prophet of a new international order. The appearance in World War II of many of the things he foretold, such as atomic and aerial warfare, filled his last years with despair.

Welsh Nationalism A strong political nationalist movement, aimed at securing better status for the Welsh language, religious equality, educational reform and home rule, arose after the 1884 REFORM BILL enfranchised Welsh small farmers and miners. Led by Tom Ellis (1859–99) and Lloyd George, it gained important educational concessions and eventually the disestablishment of the church of Wales (1920). By this time, however, with the decline of Welsh Nonconformity and non-socialist radicalism, its impetus was flagging. The new generation of Welsh politicians, men such as Bevan, had little time for it. The foundation of Plaid Cymru, the Welsh National party (1925), was a reaction against this weakness, and its programme was (probably excessively) literary and cultural. It gained much publicity when some of its leaders burned buildings on an RAF bombing range (1938), but did not elect an MP until its present leader, Gwynfor Evans, was returned at a 1966 by-election. In 1970 he lost his seat, but by October 1974 the Blaid had two MPs besides him and was making inroads into local government. In 1979, following the unsuccessful referendum, its vote fell from 11–9%, but it retained 2 seats.

Wembley exhibition 1924. The Empire exhibition was held in north-west London. A display which was more nostalgic than visionary, it left London its main football stadium.

Wentworth, Peter 1524–97. A Puritan Northamptonshire gentleman, MP (1571–93) and outspoken parliamentary opponent of ELIZABETH I's policies. Wentworth was several times committed to the Tower of London for his views and ultimately died there. One of the fathers of the techniques of parliamentary opposition, he did much to develop the liberty of free speech.

Wergild In Anglo-Saxon England, the compensation payable to the kin of a slain freeman (*wer*) by the slayer or his kin, in order to avoid the otherwise inevitable blood feud. Its amount was fixed by law according to the rank of the slain, a Wessex THEGN's wergild being 6 times that of a CEORL, and a Northumbrian EALDORMAN's 4 times that of a thegn.

Wesley, John *see* METHODISM

Wessex The kingdom of the West SAXONS, traditionally founded by CERDIC *c.* 490. Its early history is obscure, but it may represent the coalescence of Saxons and JUTES landing in Hampshire with earlier settlers along the middle Thames, the Gewisse (confederates), whose name was sometimes applied to the whole kingdom. Under Ceawlin it expanded into Wiltshire and the lower Severn valley, and in the 7th and early 8th centuries into Dorset, Somerset and Devon, but it was frequently pressured by Mercia until the time of Egbert, who annexed Kent, Sussex and the East Saxons. After successfully resisting the Vikings under Alfred, its dynasty (*see* AETHELSTAN; EDGAR; EDWARD THE ELDER) came to rule all Anglo-Saxon England.

Wessex culture *see* PREHISTORIC BRITAIN

Western rebellion 1549. A rising of the commons of Devon and Cornwall, led by Humphrey Arundell, against the religious innovations of SOMERSET. After besieging Exeter, the rebels were crushed by royal troops under Lord Russell at Clyst Heath and Sampford Courtenay.

Westminster, statute of 1931. This regularized precedents and legislation which gave the self-governing dominions autonomy from British politics and law. *See* BRITISH EMPIRE.

Westminster abbey The coronation place of English monarchs since the Norman conquest, the SHRINE of Edward the Confessor, and by the Reformation the wealthiest abbey in Britain. Much of the present church was built by HENRY III in a French style of Gothic, the nave being substantially completed in the late 14th century and Henry VII's splendid PERPENDICULAR chapel being added in the early 16th.

Westminster assembly of divines 1643–9. An assembly of ministers, MPs and Scottish commissioners established to make recommendations for

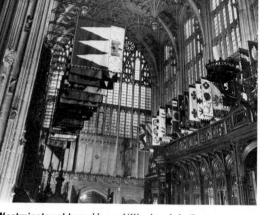

Westminster abbey: Henry VII's chapel, built 1503–*c.* 1512, was intended as a chantry for himself and as a shrine for Henry VI. The marvellous vault unites the theme of the fan vault with that of the pediment.

the religious settlement in England. Though torn by internal dissensions, the assembly prepared the DIRECTORY OF WORSHIP and a catechism and framed the limited form of PRESBYTERIANISM adopted by parliament in 1646.

Whiggamore raid 1648. The rising and capture of Edinburgh by extreme COVENANTERS from south-west Scotland in the aftermath of the defeat of the army of the Scottish ENGAGEMENT at Preston in the CIVIL WARS. Whiggamore was a name given to the cattle-drovers of Galloway.

Whigs A name originally used of cattle-drovers from south-west Scotland, which in the later 17th century was applied first to extremist COVENANTERS and subsequently to the followers of SHAFTESBURY in the EXCLUSION CRISIS. Defeated by Charles II, the Whigs revived quickly after the Glorious Revolution (1688) under the leadership of the JUNTO. In no sense a modern political party with a recognized membership and agreed legislative programme, the Whigs nevertheless possessed a greater degree of party organization than their opponents the TORIES and aspired to a monopoly of political power in the reigns of William III and Anne. In the parliaments of these reigns a substantial block of consistent Whig voters can be discerned, united by attachment to the revolution, defence of religious toleration, support of the wars against France and commitment to the Protestant Hanoverian succession. Though led by aristocrats and having much gentry support, the Whigs were also distinguished by their greater appeal to commercial and professional men and their tendency to support trading interests.

From 1714–60 the Whigs ruled supreme and the elements of principle in party allegiance faded, to be replaced by an organization based more wholly upon patronage and control of political advancement. A distinction could now be made between 'court' Whigs supporting the administration and 'country' Whigs who were scarcely distinguishable from Tories. In the years 1760–1800 the party disintegrated into a variety of personal followings, that of Charles James FOX eventually inheriting the old name when Pitt's disciples revived the Tory party. Eclipsed until 1830, the Whigs returned to power as the proponents of parliamentary reform and put through much reforming legislation in the years 1830–41. Thereafter the old party name was gradually replaced by that of the LIBERAL PARTY.

Whitby, synod of 663. A meeting at which OSWIU decided that the church of Northumbria (and hence of all England) should follow the practices and orders of Rome rather than IONA, specifically in the dating of Easter and the manner of tonsure. Bringing England into the mainstream of Catholic Christianity, its example was followed during the 8th century in Scotland, Ireland and Wales.

White Ship Lost with all hands in the Channel (25 November 1120), this vessel carried a drunken party of some 300 young noblemen including William Audelyn, only legitimate son of Henry I. His death led to the disastrous succession dispute between Matilda and Stephen.

Whitgift, John 1530–1604. As vice-chancellor of Cambridge university, Whitgift came to national prominence by his opposition to the views of CARTWRIGHT. Appointed archbishop of Canterbury (1583) he continued firmly to oppose PURITANISM, despite his own theological Calvinism, and did much to revitalize the CHURCH OF ENGLAND's administration.

Whithorn *see* NINIAN, ST

Whittington, Richard d. 1423. The hero of a legend first recorded in 1605, 'Dick Whittington' was in fact the son of a Gloucestershire gentry family, who became an immensely wealthy clothier. Serving 3 times as lord mayor of London, he made substantial loans to Richard II, Henry IV and Henry V, and became famous for his charitable works and foundations.

Wilberforce, William 1759–1833. The wealthy son of a Hull merchant, an MP (1780–1824) and a leading member of the CLAPHAM SECT, Wilberforce brought great energy and moral conviction to a number of reforming causes. He is chiefly remembered for his contribution to the abolition of the slave trade in 1807 (*see* SLAVERY).

Wilkes, John 1727–97. A notorious rake, Wilkes first emerged as the champion of British liberties in the GENERAL WARRANTS affair (1763). Outlawed and in exile 1764–8, he returned to win the Middlesex election. He eventually took his seat only in 1774 after being expelled from parliament, re-elected and imprisoned amidst tremendous public controversy.

William **Wilberforce**: portrait as a young man, by John Rising.

John **Wilkes** defending himself before the court of king's bench in April 1768, on his return from exile. Satirical engraving from *Gentleman's Magazine*, April 1768.

William the Conqueror king of England (1066–87; b. 1028). One of the most remarkable figures in medieval European history, William was the bastard son of Robert I, duke of Normandy, by Herleve (or Arlette), a tanner's daughter of Falaise. He succeeded his father in 1035, and campaigned almost continuously from 1047–60 against native rebellions exacerbated by French and Angevin intervention, emerging as the victorious ruler of a strong state and the controller of its united aristocracy and reformed church. Both these last proved indispensable to his greatest achievement, the NORMAN CONQUEST of England in pursuit of his rights as chosen heir of his cousin Edward the Confessor.

Landing with about 7,000 men at Pevensey (28 September 1066), he defeated the already weakened Harold Godwinson at HASTINGS, and after a campaign of devastation around London which resulted in the submission of Edgar Atheling and the principal English magnates (*see* FULFORD, BATTLE OF), was crowned on Christmas day. To establish and secure his new conjoint realm, however, William had yet to conduct a series of startlingly energetic campaigns against English rebels and more dangerous external threats from Scandinavia (*see* VIKINGS), Scotland and France. He and his lieutenants FITZ OSBERN and ODO OF BAYEUX subdued southern and midland England (1067–9), and in 1070 northern resistance (stiffened by a Danish fleet led by William's rival claimant King

Swein Estrithson and by the support of Malcolm Canmore) was finally ended by the 'Devastation of the North'. This involved the brutal harrying of much of Yorkshire, Cheshire, Shropshire, Staffordshire and Derbyshire (parts of which were consequently derelict at the time of DOMESDAY BOOK, 1086, and remained impoverished until Stephen's reign). Then, after defeating Hereward the Wake's Danish-backed revolt (1071), William launched a land and sea attack on Scotland (1072), penetrating as far as Perth and forcing Canmore to submit.

With England now relatively secure, William spent much of the period 1073–85 in defending Normandy against French hostility and (after 1078) the intermittent rebellions of his son ROBERT CURTHOSE. A threatened Scandinavian invasion drew him back to England in 1085–6, when his pressing need for war funds prompted the compilation of Domesday Book, but he died on 9 September 1087 while again campaigning in France. The Anglo-Norman state he had created in the midst of incessant warfare nevertheless survived and its permanence is the chief memorial of a great though brutal soldier and a harsh but respected ruler. (D.C. Douglas, *William the Conqueror*, 1964.) *See* ills. pp. 30, 208.

William II Rufus king of England (1087–1100; b. 1057). So-called from his ruddy complexion, this 3rd and favourite son of William the Conqueror was bequeathed England over the head of ROBERT CURTHOSE, thus dividing the loyalty of the Anglo-Norman barons. Many of these rebelled with Odo of Bayeux (1088), but were defeated with English help recruited on false promises. His most notable achievement was the seizure of Cumbria from Malcolm Canmore (1092), but he was hated as a cruel, avaricious and perverted tyrant and, through FLAMBARD, a ruthless despoiler of the church. He was mysteriously killed (probably at the instigation of Henry I) while hunting in the New Forest. *See* ill. p. 208.

William III (of Orange) king of Great Britain (1689–1702; b. 1650). As Stadtholder of Holland William made it his life's work to oppose French hegemony in Europe. This mission underlay his part in the GLORIOUS REVOLUTION and acceptance of the throne jointly with MARY II. Sole monarch from 1694, his French wars necessitated financial reforms which were the principal legacy of his reign.

William IV *see* VICTORIA, QUEEN

William the Lion king of Scotland (1165–1214; b. 1143). The younger brother of Malcolm IV, William joined the alliance against Henry II (1173) to attain his ambition of recovering the English border counties, but his invasion ended with his capture at Alnwick (1174) and a humiliating treaty subjecting Scotland and its church to Henry. Sold revocation by Richard I, he ignominiously failed to wrest the borders from John.

William the Marshal *c.* 1146–1219. Universally respected as 'the pattern of chivalry', William was an impecunious knight who rose by faithful service to Henry II, Richard I (who gave him the heiress and lands of Strongbow) and JOHN (who created him earl of Pembroke). Despite his advanced years, he was appointed regent (1216) by the supporters of Henry III, and his victories at LINCOLN and SANDWICH secured the boy's throne.

Williams, William (Pantycelyn) *see* WALES

Wills An important source of social and economic history, particularly in the medieval period. Before the transfer of jurisdiction to lay courts (1857) they were the responsibility of the church, and therefore occur mainly in ecclesiastical records. The large collection of the prerogative court of Canterbury, now in the public record office, is especially noteworthy.

Winchester The history of Venta Belgarum, the CIVITAS capital of the Belgae (*see* ATREBATES) and the 5th largest town in Roman Britain, resembles that of Silchester, but instead of being abandoned it became (by the 7th century) the capital of Wessex and (after Alfred) of Anglo-Saxon England. Subsequently a medieval wool-town, it was the centre of the wealthiest British bishopric.

Winchester, battle of 14 September 1141. MATILDA, besieging Henry of Blois's palace at Winchester, found herself virtually encircled within the town by a force sent by STEPHEN's wife. Matilda's withdrawal became a rout, her half-brother Robert of Gloucester was taken, and she was forced to release Stephen in exchange for him.

Winchester, statute of *see* HENRY III

Wind of Change A phrase in Harold Macmillan's speech to the South African parliament (3 February 1960), urging it to recognize the reality of African nationalism. It did not, and left the commonwealth in 1961. *See* BRITISH EMPIRE.

Windsor castle, Berks., from the south-east. Etching by Wenceslaus Hollar, 1642.

Windmill Hill culture *see* PREHISTORIC BRITAIN

Windsor castle Centred on the MOTTE raised by William the Conqueror, Windsor was converted by Edward III into a luxurious fortified palace, the headquarters of the order of the garter whose chapel of St George was rebuilt under Edward IV and his successors. Altered by Henry VIII and Charles II, and substantially modernized by George IV, the castle remains a principal royal residence.

Winwaed, battle of *see* OSWIU; PENDA

Wireless It was invented by Guglielmo Marconi (1874–1937) in 1895. By 1901 a transatlantic transmission was possible and by 1914 many of the world's merchant and naval ships were equipped. Its effect on warfare and espionage in World War I was enormous, and thereafter it was quickly adapted to commercial use, the British Broadcasting Company being set up in 1922. *See* BROADCASTING.

Wishart, Robert d. 1316. A guardian after the death of Alexander III, and bishop of Glasgow, Wishart became (with Lamberton) the leading ecclesiastical opponent of English rule during the SCOTTISH WARS OF INDEPENDENCE, encouraging WALLACE to revolt in 1297 and strenuously supporting ROBERT BRUCE's cause in 1306.

Witan (Old English 'men of knowledge'). The COUNCIL of the Anglo-Saxon kings, originally chosen from their war-companions. It later included both lay magnates (always the dominant element) and high ecclesiastics, drawn by Aethelstan's reign from all over England. Its size, frequency of summons and meeting place (generally in the south) varied widely, as did the matters on which it was consulted. It elected kings, not always a mere formality, and though its powers of general veto were limited, its existence prevented the monarchy from ever becoming an autocracy. After the Norman conquest it developed into the medieval 'great council'.

Witchcraft The alleged use of diabolical powers to cause misfortune or death. Originally an ecclesiastical offence, witchcraft was legislated against in the 16th century. Some 1,000 persons were executed for the crime in England and over 4,000 in Scotland before the repeal of the witchcraft statutes (1736).

Wollstonecraft, Mary see WOMEN'S MOVEMENT

Wolseley, Sir Garnet, viscount 1833–1913. An Anglo-Irish soldier who served with distinction in the Crimean war, the Indian mutiny, and China in 1860. As adjutant-general, Wolseley was a strong supporter of Cardwell's reforms and became a leading advocate of modernization in the army. He served in the ASHANTI and Zulu wars, but his attempt to relieve GORDON at Khartoum (1885) failed by 2 days. He was commander-in-chief 1895–9.

Wolsey, Thomas 1471–1530. The brilliant son of an Ipswich butcher, Wolsey rose slowly to eminence. Only in 1507 did he become chaplain to HENRY VII, a post usually held by younger men. However, 2 years later he entered Henry VIII's council and by 1512 he had supplanted all other counsellors in influence with the king. For his successful handling of the French and Scottish wars (1513–14), he was made first bishop of Lincoln, then archbishop of York, and was further rewarded with the lord chancellorship and a cardinalate (1515). Though never to become archbishop of Canterbury, Wolsey became papal legate *a latere* (1518), bearing authority over both provinces of the church in England.

Wolsey dominated both secular and ecclesiastical government from 1518–29. As a churchman he exemplified, in his PLURALISM and financial rapacity, some of the least attractive characteristics of the late medieval church. By his despotic rule he did much

Two witches, their familiars and Matthew Hopkins (d. 1647), the 'witchfinder general'. Hopkins took the lead in some of the most notorious prosecutions for **witchcraft** of the 1640s. Frontispiece woodcut, 1647.

'Had I but served God as diligently as I have served my king', said Thomas **Wolsey**, 'he would not have given me over in my gray hairs.' Anonymous portrait.

to weaken the English church and to focus hostility to the papacy which, however reluctantly, had granted him his ecclesiastical authority. As a statesman he displayed considerable organizational ability and an immense capacity for work. His most positive achievements were in the judicial field, where he did much to develop the courts of chancery and Star Chamber. His attempts to halt the spread of enclosures were less successful. Unlike his protégé and successor Thomas Cromwell, the autocratic Wolsey disliked parliament and was never able to manage it. Unable to obtain adequate parliamentary revenues, he turned to the expedient of forced loans, which aggravated his unpopularity with the POLITICAL NATION. Closer to Wolsey's heart than domestic administration was his diplomacy, aimed at establishing himself as the arbiter of Europe, a position briefly achieved by the treaty of London (1518). His subsequent foreign policy, however, followed the interests of the papacy too closely and left England isolated and ignored by the great powers of Europe after 1525.

Wolsey the man possessed much charm and taste. He was a great builder, commencing Hampton Court and founding Cardinal college, Oxford (later Christ Church). His positive qualities, however, were less noted by contemporaries than his greed, arrogance, ostentatious display of wealth and tactlessness in handling the aristocracy and gentry, who detested him as an upstart. Ultimately his position rested solely on his capacity to retain the king's favour. When, by 1529, it became apparent that Wolsey could not obtain the annulment of the king's 1st marriage, Henry withdrew his support. Wolsey was accused of PRAEMUNIRE, stripped of his offices and attacked in parliament. Restored to the see of York he set out north (1530), but his continued intriguing laid him open to further charges of treason. He died at Leicester while travelling south to face imprisonment in the Tower of London and almost certain execution.

Women's movement The growth of industry, first domestic and then in factories, did much to free women from a state of economic subjection within the 'economic FAMILY' in which they were denied a separate income, any interest in property, and frequently had to undertake hard manual labour. This greater freedom came about partly through their adoption of specialized tasks which, although ill-paid in comparison with men's jobs, increased their responsibility and status; and also because of the advance of liberal political and economic ideas, with their emphasis on equal rights. Such developments, however, benefited working-class rather than middle-class women, who tended to lose the independent sources of income they had enjoyed during the 18th century and become status objects, the wealth of their husbands being measured by the extent to which they were decorative and useless.

Mary Wollstonecraft's *Vindication of the Rights of Woman* (1792), which applied the logic of the French revolution to the status of women, can be taken as the beginning of the women's movement in Britain. Meanwhile, however, the Evangelical revival in the church restated many traditional Christian prejudices against women, although it did encourage an education for them which went beyond the teaching of 'accomplishments', and had its effect in the artistic and propagandist achievement of mid-19th-century women novelists such as Charlotte Bronte, George Eliot and Mrs Gaskell.

Partly due to such increased awareness and partly due to the progress of liberal reform in general, there was a quickening of activity in the 1850s. The Married Woman's Property Act (1857), together with the Divorce Act of the same year, greatly increased women's rights in marriage. At the same time, education for middle-class girls was improved with the foundation of Queen's college, London, under Christian Socialist auspices (1848), Bedford college, London (1849), and several fee-paying day schools for girls, notably the North London Collegiate school (1850), aided by the development of the Oxford local examinations after 1857. In the 1860s agitation to improve women's education was endorsed by the Taunton commission (*see* PUBLIC SCHOOLS) and spread to Cambridge, with the foundation of Hitchin college (1869), which moved to Girton (1873), and of Newnham college. The first 2 women's colleges in Oxford were founded a decade later.

Although women were soon given access to lectures and degrees at Scottish and provincial universities, even in the contentious area of medicine (partly due to the example and efforts of Florence NIGHTINGALE), their progress seemed to slow down in the 1880s. There were several reasons for this. The women's movement had become much more explicitly a political issue after Mill had moved his 1st motion in favour of women's suffrage (1866). This showed a considerable division even among radicals, groups such as the POSITIVISTS being bitterly hostile. It also coincided with growing doubts among the intellectual aristocracy about the principle of democracy, and fear of 'intellectual unemployment' which was always assumed to increase political instability. Further, the move of the middle classes to the suburbs also restricted women's opportunity for political action.

Yet organization within the political parties, through bodies such as the Women's Liberal Federation and the Conservative Primrose League, steadily increased; a ˙ *Woman's Suffrage Journal* existed from 1870, and various local societies formed themselves into the National Union of Women's Suffrage Societies (1896), under the presidency of Millicent FAWCETT. The steady concession of the vote to women in elections to local authorities – town councils (1868), school boards (1870), county councils (1888) and parish councils (1894) – and the granting of the full franchise by several American states from the 1860s, by New Zealand (1893) and Australia (1894–1908), and in most of Scandinavia in the 1900s, made similar action in Britain seem inevitable, especially with the strong support of radical and Labour MPs. But hopes for early action after the Liberal landslide (1906) were confounded by the sheer range of legislative problems confronting the government, and the militant campaign launched by a minority of SUFFRAGETTES under Emmeline and Christabel PANKHURST probably destroyed the prospects of compromise by exacerbating the hostility of Asquith, whose power as prime minister after 1908 was considerable enough to inhibit concessions from his own party.

WORLD WAR I increased the economic involvement of women by about a third, from about 2·5–3·5 million and, by producing new growth areas in munitions, the auxiliary services and clerical work, shifted the orientation of women's work away from textiles and domestic service. Many former suffragettes also adopted a strongly patriotic line. As a result of such developments, the enfranchisement of women became a bipartisan policy, and was carried out in the Reform Bill (February 1918) in which the local authority vote (for women over 30) was extended to parliamentary elections. The age qualification was dropped to 21 by the FLAPPER VOTE Act (1928).

Nevertheless, this advance was not extended by much notable legislation nor, indeed, by substantial female participation in politics. Eleanor Rathbone's campaign for family allowances and Ellen Wilkinson's propaganda for the north-east (*see* JARROW CRUSADE) were exceptions. The number of women MPs never rose above 25 and, following the 'dilution' of the war years, the trade unions wished to return to the pre-war situation, regarding female employment as a cause of male unemployment. It was a reflection of the limited gains women had in fact made that most of them agreed with this. Only in the 1960s and 1970s, due as much to the belated organization of women in the trade unions as to

Christabel Pankhurst, a powerful influence in the **women's movement**, speaking in Trafalgar Square, London, 1907. Despite the male support represented on the platform, votes for women were not in fact achieved until 1918.

The largest demonstration of the **women's movement** since the suffragette campaigns, Trafalgar Square, London, March 1971. Among its demands were equal pay, free contraception and abortion on demand.

liberal pressure, international agreements on women's rights and a reviving feminist movement, was legislation for equal pay and conditions enacted. A liberal Abortion Act was passed (1967), family planning was adopted by the state and extended (1968), grounds for divorce were extended (1968), and the Equal Pay Act was passed (1970). Despite the election of a woman prime minister, Margaret Thatcher (1979), the barriers to an increased women's role in politics (with only 19 women MPs in 1980) still seem formidable.

Woodville, Queen Elizabeth 1437–92. The beautiful widow of a Lancastrian knight, and herself partly of noble stock, Elizabeth had a secret love-match with Edward IV (1464) that was considered a misalliance. The rapid subsequent promotion of her relations (of whom the most notable was her cultivated brother Anthony, Earl Rivers) was also much resented, especially by the king's brother Richard. *See* PRINCES IN THE TOWER; RICHARD III.

Woolton, lord 1883–1964. Fred Marquis, a Liverpool social worker and director of Lewis's Stores was brought into Neville Chamberlain's government (September 1939), and made minister of food (1940) with responsibility for rationing and food conservation (in pursuit of which several intriguing though not necessarily edible recipes appeared). He became minister for reconstruction (1943) and after the war, as a Conservative, modernized the party structure.

'**Worcester** as it stood fortify'd, 3 Sept. 1651.' The battle was fought to the east of the city, though near enough for Charles II to watch it from the cathedral tower. Engraving by Robert Vaughan, 1662.

Dinnertime in St Pancras **workhouse**, London, 1900.

Worcester, battle of 3 September 1651. The last major battle of the CIVIL WARS. Charles II's invading army was intercepted at Worcester, attacked from both sides by commonwealth troops under Oliver Cromwell and utterly defeated. Charles later escaped abroad. Cromwell called the battle 'the crowning mercy'.

Workhouses Institutions for the accommodation and employment of the able-bodied poor. They were originally introduced by particular urban authorities and a Workhouse Act (1723) denied relief to those refusing to enter. They became a central feature of the national poor relief system

Anthony Woodville, Earl Rivers, presenting a book to Edward IV and Elizabeth **Woodville**. Miniature from *Dictes and Sayings of Philosophers*, 15th-century manuscript. At least 12 of the queen's relatives benefited from her marriage.

after the POOR LAW AMENDMENT ACT (1834). Spartan, authoritarian and demoralizing, they were both hated and feared by the poor.

Workmen's Compensation Act 1897. Passed to compel employers to insure their workmen against the risks of their employment, the Act was extended to agriculture in 1900. The result of pressure by Joseph Chamberlain, this implied a major shift away from individualism.

World War I 1914–18. When Germany declared war on Russia (1 August 1914), her Schlieffen plan anticipated a rapid encirclement of Paris while her forces held back a slower Russian mobilization on the eastern front. The Anglo-French MILITARY CONVERSATIONS assumed that Britain would position her troops on the French left, but a full commitment to the war waited on the German invasion of Belgium (3 August) which violated the treaty of London (1839). This *casus belli* quickly gained the status of a crusade after widespread reports of German 'frightfulness' in Belgium, not wholly fabricated but greatly exaggerated by propaganda agencies.

On 3 August Asquith's government appointed KITCHENER as war minister with unrestricted control over the British role in the war. Kitchener mobilized and sent to the front virtually the whole of the professional regular army but relegated its reserve, the Territorials (carefully built up by Haldane), to home defence, preferring instead to appeal for a volunteer 'new army'. (Conscription did not come into force until February 1916.) The British Expeditionary Force under Sir John French fought effectively and managed to slow the German advance through Belgium, but at a considerable cost in highly trained manpower which might have been better employed in training the volunteers. An attempt to hold the port of Antwerp – a brainchild of Winston Churchill – was also abandoned (9 October). After the German advance was halted on the Marne (5–15 September), the BEF was further diminished by having to resist the German drive on the ports, although this too was halted. By 30 October the armies were in confrontation between the small area of Belgium still held by the allies and the Swiss frontier near Mulhouse, and this front line was, until September 1918, never to vary by more than 50 miles (80 kilometres).

Attempts to break out of this deadlock were accompanied by immense losses and gave rise to a variety of responses. Were new technologies to be used to overcome the rigidity of trench warfare, or was there to be a diversion to other fronts? At the

A **World War I** recruiting poster of late 1915, the period when voluntary enlistment was flagging.

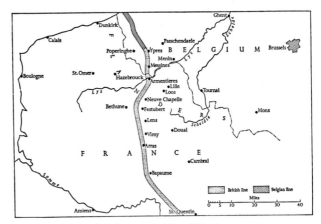

The western front, British sector, in **World War I**.

Discomfort and exhaustion at the front line in **World War I**: Ovillers, during the battle of the Somme, July 1916.

Back at home during **World War I**, the women sign on for munitions work.

2nd battle of YPRES (April–May 1915), the Germans took the technological initiative by using poison gas. Soon the British were experimenting with an armoured track-laying vehicle which could crush barbed wire, bridge trenches and destroy machine guns: such obstacles being the structural components of the western front.

However, the Asquith cabinet, under pressure from Churchill and (less enthusiastically) Kitchener, laid more stress on the opening up of a new front in the Near East, with the aim of knocking out Turkey (*see* MESOPOTAMIAN CAMPAIGN), attacking Austria-Hungary in the Balkans and relieving pressure on Russia, whose expected 'steam-roller' had ground expensively to a halt after the 1914 battles of Tannenberg and the Masurian Lakes. The result was the GALLIPOLI campaign which was aborted by lack of interservice collaboration, military incompetence and Kitchener's failure to provide adequate reserves. Thereafter the western front became dominant, although this also coincided with the end of the politicians' implicit trust in the military (*see* MUNITIONS CRISIS), and the beginning of the contest between 'frocks' and 'brasshats' which was to characterize the rest of the war. Kitchener was shunted out of control, although this was mitigated by the setting up of an all-party coalition (May

1915), whose Conservative members were markedly more sympathetic to the brasshats.

In 1916 – the worst year of the war for Britain – a strategy of full-blown attrition was adopted by the allies, but pre-empted by the German commander-in-chief, Falkenhayn. In his attack on the French fortress of Verdun (February), he intended not to capture it but to 'bleed white' the forces which the French commander-in-chief, Joffre, would – for reasons of national prestige – channel into its fatal salient. The French took up the challenge and by April were gravely weakened. The British commander-in-chief, HAIG, determined on a supportive attack on the Somme, carried out with appalling casualties (1 July–8 November), in the process destroying the morale, as well as the substance, of Kitchener's new army.

At sea the expected clash of battlefleets failed to materialize, the outnumbered German fleet remaining in port. The initiative was taken by strategies of blockade and by new types of vessels, in particular the submarine which rapidly endangered British supplies (1915), and was countered more by the threat of American intervention than by anti-submarine equipment and tactics. A period of virtually unrestricted submarine warfare was succeeded by a virtual truce for 1916. In May the battlefleets at last met at JUTLAND. Although the immediate results were indecisive, the German fleet never put to sea effectively again.

In December 1916 Lloyd George, the energetic munitions minister, together with various Conservative politicians and newspaper magnates, forced the resignation of Asquith. Lloyd George was soon faced with serious developments: the revolution in Russia and the decision (prompted by the resumption of unrestricted U-boat warfare) of the USA to enter the war. In order to strengthen the Russian will to continue the war, the French, under Nivelle, adopted another offensive, whose disastrous results prompted widespread mutinies. In late summer 1917 the British generals gained their desire for a further, fruitless offensive at Ypres (or Passchendaele), while the 1st real tank offensive at Cambrai petered out when reserves were not supplied in adequate numbers.

Despite the promise of American troops, the allies in the west were faced with German troops released by the collapse of Russia after the October revolution. Ludendorff's final offensive (March 1918) pressed the British back on Amiens, but further than that the war-weary Germans were unable to advance. In August Haig's tanks and infantry pushed them on to the retreat, the Americans attacked to the south, and in the Balkans the allied armies at last started to advance from Salonika. Ludendorff decided to accept President Wilson's 'fourteen points' as the basis for armistice negotiations. His desire to get a scapegoat for defeat was aided by the naval revolts in Germany in October, which led to the fall of the Hohenzollern monarchy and the declaration of a republic. On 11 November fighting at last came to an end, and the German armies were allowed, in good order, to retreat. Peace was formally signed the next year at VERSAILLES. The British empire had sent *c.* 9 million men to the war, of whom a tenth did not return.

Politically, the course of the war saw the destruction of the Liberal party and the rise of the trade union movements, later to be reflected in the rise of the Labour party, and the consolidation of the women's movement. *See* ARMY; NAVY; WORLD WARS I AND II, SOCIAL EFFECTS OF.

World War II 1939–45. Britain's *casus belli* was the guarantee Neville Chamberlain had given the Polish government after Hitler's invasion of Prague (March 1939) had shown the failure of the Munich agreements (*see* APPEASEMENT). Accordingly, after Hitler invaded Poland (1 September), Britain, shortly followed by France, declared war on Germany (3 September). There was no attempt to intervene in

support of the Poles, who finally capitulated on 27 September, and until April 1940 a state of PHONEY WAR existed, masking German preparations to invade Scandinavia, the Low Countries and France. Failure to withstand the Germans in Norway led to Chamberlain's fall and his replacement by Winston Churchill at the head of a coalition on the day (10 May) the Germans launched their attack on the western front. This proved rapidly successful. Three weeks later the surviving British (200,000) and French (120,000) troops had to be evacuated from Dunkirk (27 May–4 June).

There was then an interval while Hitler issued overtures (19 July) to Britain, based on a desire to partition the world between the Anglo-Saxon powers. On their contemptuous rejection he made serious preparations to break British morale by air raids and more casual preparations for an invasion by surface forces. Such schemes were halted by the defeat of the Luftwaffe in the battle of Britain (10 July–17 September) after which Hitler switched his attention to the East, while Britain and her Balkan allies enjoyed some success in the Mediterranean against Italy, who had declared war on 10 June.

However, 1941 and early 1942 proved disastrous for Britain. Hitler consolidated his political control of the Balkans, occupied Yugoslavia and Greece (April–May 1941) and defeated the British in Crete, while an armoured division sent to north Africa under Rommel reversed earlier British successes. Although the invasion of Russia (22 June) diverted pressure from Britain, and American aid was building up, reaching its apotheosis with the

Soldiers back from Dunkirk during **World War II**, at a station in Kent, June 1940. Photograph for the *Kent Messenger*.

A **World War II** 'appeal to women' to take up munitions work, issued by the ministry of labour and national service.

World War II: results of the 1940 blitz on Bexley, Kent. Photograph by the celebrated John Topham.

ATLANTIC CHARTER (14 August), Japan's entry into the war was rapidly followed by the destruction of British power in the Far East, culminating with the surrender of SINGAPORE (15 February 1942), an event from which the British empire never recovered. Thereafter America asserted herself as the preponderant power in the alliance. The crisis continued during the year, with U-boats taking a mounting toll of allied shipping in the Atlantic.

By late 1942, however, the tide turned: Rommel was defeated by MONTGOMERY at EL ALAMEIN in October; the following month the Russians won the battle of Stalingrad; combined air-sea operations were coping at last with the threat of the U-boats. The CASABLANCA CONFERENCE (January 1943) saw the allies go on the offensive, deciding on the invasion of Italy. This was carried out in May 1943, with the Italian capitulation coming on 3 September. The TEHERAN CONFERENCE (November-December), which included Stalin, finalized plans for a co-ordinated offensive and a second front, but exposed the strains between Roosevelt and Churchill, the latter becoming increasingly suspicious of Stalin's ambitions in eastern Europe.

Late 1942 and 1943 saw the area-BOMBING campaign against Germany intensified, especially by the British, as a means of 'carrying the war to the enemy'. It proved costly in men and aircraft, and did not halt the growth of German war production after the reorganization of the economy by Albert Speer. This was, however, dissipated by Hitler's concentration on 'wonder weapons', in particular the V1 or DOODLEBUG and the V2 rocket, instead of on anti-aircraft precautions. The flying-bomb assault on London was effectively ended by the NORMANDY LANDINGS on D-day (6 June 1944) but, although France was rapidly liberated, a powerful German counter-attack checked the Anglo-American armies in the Ardennes. By April 1945, however, with a rapid Russian advance in the east, German resistance ended, Hitler committed suicide and Montgomery received the unconditional surrender of the Nazi forces in north Germany at Luneberg. VE day was 7 May.

Japanese resistance continued despite the British recapture of Burma (May) and island-by-island assaults by the Americans in the Pacific. Heavy conventional bombing and the Japanese loss of ascendancy at sea would inevitably have led to capitulation, but this was accelerated by the dropping of atomic bombs on Hiroshima and Nagasaki (6 and 9 August). Surrender came on 14 August.

Precedents existed from World War I for the organization of the war effort; and some com-

Utility furniture, cheap but well designed, was one result of **World War II**: part of a display held by the board of trade at the Building Centre, London, October 1942.

ponents of this, such as AIR-RAID PRECAUTIONS, conscription and RATIONING, were prepared for as the international situation deteriorated after 1936. The rapid collapse of France came as a surprise in May 1940, but so did the maintenance of public morale, which establishment opinion predicted would deteriorate under the stress of bombing. Most historical controversy now tends to concern itself with the extent to which establishment morale itself deteriorated. Dr Paul Addison has argued, in *The Road to 1945* (1975), that the interwar conservative élite never recovered from Chamberlain's defeat and that, on the accession of Churchill to power, it was succeeded by a new 'middle-opinion' élite, personified by KEYNES at the treasury and Beveridge's report on social security (*see* WELFARE STATE). This shift he argues still occurred essentially *within* the establishment. The title of Dr Angus Calder's book *The People's War* (1969), is essentially deeply ironical. He does speak of a devolution of power in 1940–1: 'the people increasingly led itself. Its nameless leaders in the bombed streets, on the factory floor, in the Home Guard drill hall, asserted a new and radical popular spirit.' Yet he too sees the eventual Labour victory (June 1945) as a reassertion (although in considerably more progressive terms than in 1918) of conventional politics. *See* ARMY; NAVY; WORLD WARS I AND II, SOCIAL EFFECTS OF.

World Wars I and II, social effects of How far the wars brought significant social changes to British society has been a matter of debate. Such historians as A.J.P. Taylor (*English History*

1914–1945, 1965) and Arthur Marwick (*The Deluge: British Society and the First World War*, 1965, and *The Home Front: The British and the Second World War*, 1976) have stressed the upheavals in customs and morals, the new organization, status and prosperity brought to the working class, the new freedoms won by women and the progress of social legislation. Angus Calder (*The People's War*, 1969) and Henry Pelling (*Britain and the Second World War*, 1970) have suggested that World War II had an essentially negative effect on British society, while Martin Pugh (*Electoral Reform in War and Peace 1906–18*, 1978) has denied that World War I materially affected votes for women, and Ross McKibbin (*The Evolution of the Labour Party 1910–1924*, 1974) has maintained that it had no significant effect on the evolution of the Labour party. It is perhaps best to see the wars as involving complex interrelationships of many forces creating a general atmosphere favourable to change, rather than to see World War I as having, in any simple way, brought votes for women, or World War II as having brought the welfare state. Clearly, longer-term historical forces are always also involved. The negative effect of World War I in giving an unreal stimulus to Britain's old heavy industries needs to be stressed, as does the spirit of complacency engendered by World War II.

Wrecking The plundering of wrecked ships (sometimes deliberately lured to shore) by coastal dwellers, practised from medieval times but particularly prevalent in the 18th and early 19th centuries. Known on all coasts, though popularly associated with Cornwall, wrecking died out with the advent of steamships, improved navigational aids and better policing.

Writs *see* LAW

Wroxeter A deserted Roman town (Viroconium Cornoviorum), the 4th largest in Britain. Founded as a LEGIONARY FORTRESS *c.* 58, whose site was granted to the Cornovii (*c.* 90) for a CIVITAS capital. This survived in some form into the heroic age (*see* CYNDDYLAN) but in Anglo-Saxon times was abandoned in favour of nearby Shrewsbury.

Wyatt's rebellion 1554. A rising by Sir Thomas Wyatt and a small Kentish force, ostensibly in protest against MARY I's Spanish marriage and religious policies, but secretly intending her deposition and replacement by the future Elizabeth I. Risings planned in support failed and Wyatt was halted outside London and subsequently executed.

Wycliffe, John *c.* 1330–84. A leading Oxford scholar whose belief in predestination, the susceptibility of faith to reason, and the all-sufficiency of scripture, led him eventually to question the whole structure of the church, and most crucially its teaching on the sacraments. His position as an employee of John of Gaunt made his opinions more dangerous by giving them publicity outside the universities, and they were finally condemned as heretical (1382). Though canvassed by the LOLLARDS, the contemporary influence of his views was limited, and he is chiefly important as a precursor of Protestant Nonconformity and the inspiration of the 1st English BIBLE.

Wykeham, William of The son of a serf, William found favour with Edward III as surveyor of building works at Windsor and became bishop of Winchester (1367–1404) and chancellor (1367–71). Blamed for government bankruptcy, he was dismissed by parliament (1371) but became chancellor again in 1389–91. Immensely rich, he founded New college, Oxford, and Winchester college.

York in the 1900s: The Shambles, literally the meat market, still has the appearance of a medieval street.

Y

Yardland *see* VIRGATE

Yeoman A 16th- and 17th-century term for independent farmers of modest wealth. Yeomen are commonly assumed to have been freeholders, though many in fact were COPYHOLD or LEASEHOLD tenants. As a group they prospered from the buoyant agricultural prices of the period 1500–1650, though their position then deteriorated.

York The historic metropolis of northern England was founded by CERIALIS *c.* 71 as a LEGIONARY FORTRESS, and by *c.* 213 had become a COLONIA and provincial capital of Britannia Inferior. Constantius rebuilt the (still partially surviving) fortress wall *c.* 296, and established 'Eboracum' as capital of Britannia Secunda and the headquarters of the DUX BRITANNIARUM. The focus of a powerful British kingdom during the heroic age, it fell to Anglian DEIRA *c.* 580, becoming the effective capital of Northumbria and from 735 an archbishopric. It was the centre of a Viking kingdom (876–954), ruled first by Danes and after 919 intermittently by Norwegians from Ireland (*see* ERIK BLOODAXE). Despite damage after the Norman conquest, York continued to be important through the middle ages, reaching its zenith in the late 14th century, when its population was exceeded only by that of London. The seat of the Tudor COUNCIL OF THE NORTH, it was the scene of a notable siege during the civil wars.

York, house of *see* ROSES, WARS OF THE

York, Richard, duke of 1411–60. The greatest English magnate, and heir-presumptive of Henry VI, York was nevertheless excluded from power by the court party and driven into opposition. His attack on the royalist lords at the 1st battle of ST ALBANS (1455) began the wars of the ROSES and in 1460 he claimed the crown, but was shortly afterwards killed at WAKEFIELD.

York minster The present mother church of northern England covers a Roman headquarters building and earlier Saxon (founded by Edwin *c.* 627) and Norman cathedrals. Built *c.* 1230–*c.* 1472, it displays each successive style of English Gothic architecture, and is particularly famous for its stained glass.

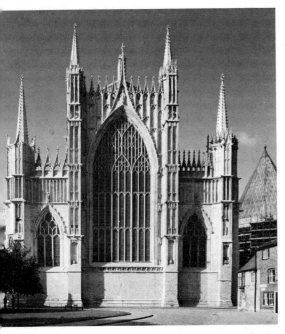

York minster: the east front, with its immense Perpendicular window.

Yorkshire Association 1779–80. An association of country squires inspired by Christopher Wyvill, which began in Yorkshire but later involved 11 other counties. They petitioned parliament for more economical government, lower taxation, more frequent elections and improved county representation. Lack of an acceptable alternative ministry enabled North's government to survive the parliamentary attacks which followed the petitions. *See* REFORM BILLS.

Yorktown, surrender of 19 October 1781. The surrender of 7,000 British troops under Cornwallis, hemmed in by American and French forces and cut off from reinforcement or evacuation by French command of the Atlantic seaboard. Though not militarily decisive, the disaster encouraged the British government to come to terms with the American colonies, ending the AMERICAN INDE-PENDENCE war.

Young, Arthur 1741–1820. The son of a Suffolk clergyman, Young became a prolific writer on agriculture and rural life and an enthusiastic (and somewhat uncritical) advocate of agricultural improvement. As secretary of the board of agriculture (1793) he launched the famous series of county reports on the rural economy of England.

Young England A group of somewhat obscure Tory politicians organized by Disraeli (1837–40) to offer an alliance between the aristocracy and the working classes in opposition to middle-class liberalism and in favour of social reform.

Young Ireland An Irish nationalist and cultural movement, led by young Protestant intellectuals, which attempted to promote revolution along the lines of Giuseppe Mazzini's 'Young Italy'. A rising led by it (1848) was a miserable failure.

Ypres, battles of In the 1st battle (12 October–11 November 1914) the British halted the German attempt to cut them off from the sea. The 2nd battle (22 April–24 May 1915) was a German attack, during which poison gas was first used. The 3rd battle (22 July–20 November 1917) was a British attack to secure the parts of north Belgium which foundered in Flanders mud. There were 300,000–400,000 British casualties plus 50,000 French, as against 250,000 German. *See* WORLD WAR I.

Zeppelin Count Zeppelin perfected his rigid airship in 1900 and in WORLD WAR I it was launched on bombing raids against Britain. Only about 1,913 casualties were inflicted, as the airship was very vulnerable to fighter fire.

Zinoviev letter 1924. Possibly genuine (as the secret service believed) or not (as the left has insisted ever since), this letter, purporting to come from the Soviet president of the Communist International, urged the Communist party to undertake re-volutionary agitation in Britain. Publicized during the general election (August 1924) by the right-wing press, it cost Labour some votes in an election it would have lost anyway.

Zulu war 1879. The rise of a Zulu empire under King Cetewayo menaced the Boers in the Transvaal and the British invaded Zululand. After an initial disaster at Isandhlwana (22 January), Cetewayo was captured (14 July).

Editors' acknowledgments

Christopher Harvie would like to thank Irene Hatt, Peggy MacKay and Pam McLaren for their help in the preparation of his entries.

Charles Kightly would like to thank the following for help and advice with the composition of his entries: Mr Brian Hartley, Miss Pamela King, Mrs Sue Medd, Dr Robert Swanson and Mr Christopher Wilson.

Keith Wrightson would like to thank Mr Bruce Lenman and Dr Geoffrey Seed for their occasional advice during the preparation of his entries.